Microsoft C/C++ 7: The Complete Reference

Microsoft C/C++ 7: The Complete Reference

William H. Murry, III
Chris H. Pappas

Osborne **McGraw-Hill**

Berkeley New York St. Louis San Francisco
Auckland Bogotá Hamburg London Madrid
Mexico City Milan Montreal New Delhi Panama City
Paris São Paulo Singapore Sydney
Tokyo Toronto

Osborne **McGraw-Hill**
2600 Tenth Street
Berkeley, California 94710
U.S.A.

For information on translations or book distributors outside of the U.S.A., please write to Osborne **McGraw-Hill** at the above address.

Microsoft C/C++ 7: The Complete Reference

234567890 DOC 998765432

ISBN 0-07-881664-5

Dedicated to our fathers
William H. Murray, Jr.
Chris Pappas
who have quietly, with their faith, support, and integrity,
committed their lives to our development

Publisher

Kenna S. Wood

Acquisitions Editor

Frances Stack

Associate Editor

Jill Pisoni

Editorial Assistants

Hannah Raiden
Judy Kleppe

Technical Editor

John Ribar

Project Editor

Laura Sackerman

Copy Editor

Dusty Bernard

Proofreading Coordinator

Wendy Rinaldi

Proofreaders

Jeff Barash
Mick Arellano

Indexers

William H. Murray, III
Chris H. Pappas

Illustrator

Marla Shelasky

Computer Designer

Fred Lass

Cover Designer

Bay Graphics Design, Inc.

Contents
at a Glance

Contents

Part I
A Quick Start to C and C++
Programming

1
The Microsoft C and C++
Compiler Package   3

6

Data 139

7

Control 179

8

Writing and Using Functions 217

Part III
Foundations for Object-oriented
Programming in C++

15

**An Introduction to
Object-oriented
Programming** **461**

16

C++ Classes **479**

17

Complete I/O in C++ **513**

Part VI
Appendixes

A
Extended ASCII Table   893

B
DOS 10H, 21H, and 33H Interrupt Parameters   899

C
Windows API Functions and Foundation Class Library Items   913

Acknowledgments

First and foremost, we would like to thank Jeff Pepper, editor-in-chief at Osborne/McGraw-Hill, for his continued help and support during the preparation of this book. Special thanks go to Frances Stack, our acquisitions editor. Frances has done an outstanding job organizing the different phases of this book and guiding us through various technical problems. A project of this size is dependent upon the efforts many good people. Included in this group are Jill Pisoni, Hannah Raiden, Judy Kleppe, Laura Sackerman, Wendy Rinaldi, Dusty Bernard, Allen Wyatt, Barry Bergin, and Fred Lass. Osborne professionals have always been excellent people to work with on a project.

We would like to thank the people at Microsoft Corporation for the outstanding job they have done in developing a top-notch C/C++ compiler. Special recognition must go to the developers of the Foundation Class Library, who have set a new standard for Windows application development.

Microsoft is shipping thousands of pages of documentation with the Microsoft C/C++ compiler. We would like to give credit to those responsible for preparing that documentation; you have done an outstanding job. Your efforts will make learning C, C++, and Windows programming much easier.

Introduction

This book was written with two main goals: to help you become more familiar with the Microsoft C/C++ compiler package and to help people with different programming backgrounds become proficient in C, C++, and Windows programming. This is quite a task, even for a book containing more than 1000 pages, but it was written with you in mind.

Our two major goals encompass a number of specific aims:

1. This book introduces you to the powerful programming tools provided in your Microsoft compiler package. These include the C/C++ compiler, Programmer's WorkBench (PWB), CodeView Debugger, Source Browser, Profiler, and various Windows development tools. This book compliments your Microsoft reference manuals and helps you get a quick start with each of the components of the compiler package.

2. Programmers need a thorough understanding of each programming language they intend to use. You will find that this book covers all the important programming concepts in the C, C++, and Windows languages, including the new Foundation Class Library. If you are a novice programmer, early chapters will help you build the solid foundation you need to write more sophisticated programs. For advanced programmers, early chapters will serve as a reference source and will introduce you to exciting C++ concepts.

3. You will learn how to debug program code and write programs that are free of syntax and logical programming errors.

4. You will gain an understanding of how procedural programming differs from object-oriented programming and how to develop simple OOP programs.

5. You will explore the exciting world of Microsoft Windows programming. Four chapters are devoted to helping you understand Windows concepts and write simple to intermediate programs. Appendix C highlights many important Windows functions and Foundation Class Library items.

We believe in teaching by example. We have made every effort to make each example in this book simple, complete, and bug-free. You can study these examples, alter them, and expand them into programs tailored to fit your needs.

This book will serve as a lasting reference to the Microsoft C/C++ compiler and the tools it supports.

How This Book Is Organized

Chapters 1 through 4 introduce you to the programming tools contained in the Microsoft C/C++ compiler package.

Chapters 5 through 14 teach the foundational programming concepts needed for the C and C++ languages. These are procedure-oriented chapters that teach traditional C and C++ programming concepts.

Chapters 15 through 18 give you a complete introduction to object-oriented programming with C++. Here you will find terminology, definitions, and complete programming examples to help you with your development of object-oriented programs.

Chapters 19 through 21 teach you how to build graphics applications for DOS and how to tap into important library functions. Chapter 19 includes a thorough discussion of Microsoft's graphics and chart libraries. Chapter 20 includes a detailed discussion of C and C++ library functions, and Chapter 21 gives tips for interfacing C, C++, and assembly language code. In Chapter 21 you will learn how to combine C, C++, and assembly language routines, pass arguments, and even interface with external hardware circuits.

Chapters 22 and 23 introduce you to Microsoft Windows concepts and show you how to use the Microsoft C/C++ compiler to develop applications that include GDI primitives, cursors, icons, menus, and dialog boxes. The applications in these chapters are traditional message-based programs.

Chapters 24 and 25 are devoted to programming with the Microsoft Foundation Class Library. By using the power of C++ classes, the Microsoft Foundation Class Library will shorten both your Windows application development cycle and your program length.

How the Book's Material Was Developed

The material in this book was developed on two Dell 450DE computers running at 50 MHz. These 80486 machines contained 8MB of RAM. C, C++, and Windows programs were also tested on two Toshiba T5200 (color) computers running at 20 MHz. These 80386 machines contained 6MB of RAM.

The computers were operated under DOS 5.0 and Windows 3.1. The entire manuscript was prepared with Microsoft Word for Windows. All screen shots were taken with Collage, a Windows and DOS screen capture utility.

A 3 1/2-inch High-density Disk Offer

A 3 1/2-inch high-density floppy disk is available containing all of the program listings in this book. To use the disk, you need a computer capable of using 3 1/2-inch high-density (1.44MB) disks, with the Microsoft C/C++ compiler properly installed and running.

To order the disk, send a bank check, money order, or personal check for $30.00 in U.S. currency to the address below. Please allow three weeks for personal checks to clear. **No purchase orders can be accepted**. For all foreign orders, outside North America, please include a check drawn on a U.S. bank (U.S. currency) for $35.00. Foreign orders will be sent via Air Mail.

Please send me the program listings included in *Microsoft C/C++ 7: The Complete Reference*, by Murray and Pappas. Enclosed is a money order, bank check, or personal check for $30.00 ($35.00 for foreign orders) in U.S. funds, which covers the cost of the disk and all handling and postage. Sorry, no purchase orders can be accepted! This coupon may be copied. Note: Only 3 1/2-inch high-density (1.44MB) disks are available.

Name:_____

Address:_____

City:_____State:_____ZIP:_____

Country:_____

Mail to:
Nineveh National Research
Microsoft C/C++ Disk Offer
P.O. Box 2943
Binghamton, NY 13902

This is solely the offer of the authors. Osborne **McGraw-Hill** takes no responsibility for the fulfillment of this offer.

Part *I*

A Quick Start to C and C++ Programming

Chapter *1*

The Microsoft C and
C++ Compiler Package

The Microsoft C/C++ compiler package provides you with the most comprehensive, up-to-date, production-level development environment for Windows and MS-DOS applications. This latest release from Microsoft incorporates many new and upgraded features. One of the most important enhancements is support for AT&T C++ 2.1, along with other new features like precompiled headers, auto-inlining, an overlay manager, and p-code (packed code).

The Microsoft C/C++ compiler package also provides tools for building Windows programs. The C/C++ compiler includes all the header files, libraries, dialog boxes, and resource editors necessary to create a truly robust Windows application.

You were probably overwhelmed when you opened the Microsoft C/C++ box for the first time. You may even have thought back to the first compiler you ever purchased—the one that came on a single low-density 5 1/4-inch disk and ran in 256K of memory. Now you are staring at ten 3 1/2-inch high-density disks, ten manuals, and support materials.

In this chapter you learn about the various components of the C/C++ compiler, including system requirements and how to set up the development environment. The chapter explains the Microsoft C/C++ system in detail and shows you how to fine-tune it to your particular needs.

Many of the subjects discussed are covered in greater detail throughout the remainder of the book. Entire chapters are dedicated to some of the advanced tools you are introduced to in this chapter.

A Typical Windows Installation

You can configure Microsoft C/C++ to run under the Windows and/or MS-DOS environment. To take full advantage of all the example programs presented in this book, install Microsoft C/C++ to operate in both environments.

If you have enough disk space, choose the default installation. This gives you all the help files, examples, and support information necessary to make your transition to Microsoft C/C++ as effortless as possible. You need approximately 16 megabytes of free hard disk space for a complete installation.

Make certain you have Windows running before you begin the installation. Microsoft C/C++ comes on ten 3 1/2-inch HD disks. Place Disk 1 of 10 in your A drive. Begin the installation by going to the Windows Program Manager, selecting the File | Run menu, and typing **A:SETUP.EXE**. The overall process takes approximately 45 minutes, so make sure you have a fresh cup of coffee before you get started. Following are the steps necessary to select the default system installation:

1. Press ENTER to start installation.

2. Press ENTER to continue the Windows installation.

3. Accept or change the default installation subdirectory:

   C:\c700\

4. Press ENTER to continue with the selected subdirectory.

5. Select the default (small/medium) memory model installation. (Custom installation allows you to add additional libraries, as well as to select different system configurations.)

6. Press ENTER to accept this selection and continue.

7. At this point a prompt tells you that README.TXT is automatically loaded during the install process, and you are urged to read the information during the remainder of the installation.

8. Press ENTER to continue.

9. Select Auto setup of AUTOEXEC.BAT and CONFIG.SYS.

10. Press ENTER to continue.

11. Reboot your system.

A Typical DOS Installation

The Microsoft C/C++ SETUP program automatically detects the presence of Microsoft Windows. If Microsoft Windows is not on your system, SETUP will begin an automatic MS-DOS-only installation. SETUP follows the same procedures outlined for a Windows installation except that it does not load any Windows development tools or libraries.

Recommendations

Following is a list of hardware and software recommendations that will help you get the most out of the Microsoft C/C++ compiler. Many of the suggestions will improve overall system performance, while others will make the product more enjoyable to use.

Minimum Hardware and Software Requirements

Microsoft's C/C++ compiler package operates on a wide range of IBM and IBM-compatible computers. The following is a list of minimum hardware and software requirements for running the Microsoft C/C++ compiler package:

- 80386 or 80486-based PC
- 4MB of RAM
- One high-density floppy disk drive
- 10MB of free hard disk space
- MS-DOS 3.1 or later
- CGA monitor

Recommended Hardware and Software

Minimal hardware and software requirements are not always the optimal choice for ease of use, performance, and overall product enjoyment. The following system profile is recommended by the authors to optimize the development cycle of C/C++ programs:

- 80486 microprocessor, running at 33 MHz
- 6MB of RAM
- 120-MB hard disk
- DOS 5.0
- Windows 3.1
- EGA or higher resolution

You will want a fast microprocessor to handle the size and complexity of advanced Windows applications. Having enough memory maximizes the overall performance of both Microsoft C/C++ and the Windows environment. You obtain the same performance enhancements by having a large amount of free disk space.

MS-DOS 5.0 or later provides many new features that make memory configuration easier. If you have not upgraded to version 5.0 or later, you may want to do so before installing your system files for Microsoft C/C++. Several of the performance recommendations made throughout the book require your system to have these new MS-DOS enhancements.

The improvements made to Windows 3.1 provide you with the features and performance necessary to create state-of-the-art Windows applications. Your eyes will appreciate EGA or higher resolution monitors while you are working in the Windows graphics-based based environments.

Planning a Good Installation

Once you have decided on the various hardware, software, and installation options available to you, you should take a minute to familiarize yourself with some additional information. For example, explore all the subdirectories created by SETUP. Notice the names of the subdirectories and what types of files are stored in each.

If you will be writing C programs, take a minute to locate and print the more commonly used header files, like stdio.h and math.h. Next, locate and print iostream.h for C++ program development and windows.h for Windows programs.

Your AUTOEXEC.BAT and CONFIG.SYS Files

All the performance recommendations made in this section assume you are running MS-DOS 5.0 or later. Your AUTOEXEC.BAT file contains definitions and initial parameters for *environment variables*. These variables must be given specific values for the Microsoft C/C++ tools to work together properly. The following six environment variables are required by Microsoft C/C++ and are automatically inserted and initialized by the SETUP.EXE installation program if you so chose:

- **INCLUDE**   Defines the list of subdirectories where Microsoft C/C++ **#include** header files (.h) are found.

- **INIT**   Defines the subdirectory where CURRENT.STS and TOOLS.INI are found. It is recommended that INIT be set from inside PWB. This variable defines where to find TOOLS.INI and CURRENT.STS. When INIT is undefined, PWB or CodeView creates a CURRENT.STS file in every directory used by the two tools. This usually leads to PWB and CodeView invoking the incorrect status file.

- **LIB**   Defines the list of subdirectories where Microsoft C/C++ library files are found.

- **PATH**   Defines the executable file search path.

- **TMP** Defines where the operating system places temporary files. NMAKE, LINK, and PWB create temporary files. Since Microsoft C/C++ SETUP.EXE uses the LIB utility to build combined libraries, your system should have a minimum of 1MB free on the drive pointed to by TMP. Also, PWB needs a minimum of 1MB free, in the directory defined in TMP, to create its virtual memory file.

- **HELPFILES** Defines the subdirectories where the help files are for PWB, CodeView, and QuickHelp.

You may run into problems if you have not allocated enough environment space for these six environment variables. Your CONFIG.SYS, SYSTEM.INI, and .PIF files define the amount of memory available and the configuration for Windows and MS-DOS. The Microsoft C/C++ SETUP.EXE installation program takes care of updating CONFIG.SYS. To minimize the possibility of allocating too little environment space, set the value for the environment space to at least 1024 bytes (or 1K) by adding the following statement or something similar to your CONFIG.SYS file:

```
SHELL=C:\DOS\COMMAND.COM /e:1024
```

Working Under DOS or Windows

You can run many of the tools provided by Microsoft C/C++ under the integrated PWB Windows environment or by using their stand-alone DOS command-line equivalents. Each application type and development cycle will use different combinations of these.

For example, you may want to use the command-line version of PWB only to develop an MS-DOS application. This would allow you to bypass the overhead associated with running Windows. However, the advantage of running PWB under Windows is that you can create, compile, test, and debug a Windows application. Whether or not you are creating a Windows or an MS-DOS application, you may not be interested in immediately tweaking the program for increased performance. At a later date you could decide to run the Profiler and improve the program's speed characteristics.

Package Components

The following component breakdown contains a high-level overview of the components and tools provided by the Microsoft C/C++ compiler package. As you read the descriptions, make a mental note of those features and tools you will need to use immediately. Unless you are developing an extremely advanced Windows application, you will not need to use all the tools provided by Microsoft C/C++ your first week. You can return to these descriptions as a reference for those utilities you may need as your experience and application requirements grow.

Programmer's WorkBench (PWB)

The Programmer's WorkBench, referred to by Microsoft as PWB, is the center of your project development cycle. This highly sophisticated, easy-to-use development tool is everything you need to create, compile, debug, and upgrade your programs. One of PWB's advanced features is its use of macros. A PWB macro allows you to define a different set of initialization and compiler defaults for each type of application you may be developing. For example, you can predefine one set of paths and include libraries for Windows programs and another set of parameters for DOS C application development.

CL—The DOS Command-line Compiler

The command-line compiler, otherwise known as CL, is Microsoft's C/C++ source compiler and linker. This tool allows you to compile programs from DOS. CL allows you to specify any number of options, filenames, and library names, as long as the command-line length does not exceed the operating system limit.

PWB Integrated Compiler

The Microsoft C/C++ Programmer's WorkBench integrated compiler is a complete and comprehensive application development environment. It combines all of the features of a source code editor, compiler, linker, debugger, and object browser into one easy-to-use package. Many of the integrated PWB utilities have their own stand-alone counterparts. For example, the CodeView debugger and Browser can be activated from within PWB. This duplicity in utilities allows you to select the best development environment for the broadest type of programs.

LINK—The Linker

LINK is Microsoft's segmented executable linker. The purpose of the linker is to combine object and library files into one relocatable executable application or dynamic link library file (DLL). This allows the operating system to load and execute the file in any unused section of memory. LINK can combine files for DOS or Windows. You can also instruct LINK to create a map file listing the segments and symbolic information in the executable file. LINK can be run directly from DOS, automatically when CL is invoked from DOS, or from within PWB.

EXEHDR—The EXE File Header Utility

The EXEHDR utility displays and modifies the contents of an executable file header. You need to be careful when using EXEHDR since MS-DOS header fields often have different meanings in a Windows file. Common uses for EXEHDR include

- Inspecting the number and size of data and code segments
- Inspecting the attributes used by the module-definition file
- Deciding if a file is a DLL (dynamic link library) or an application
- Defining a new stack allocation

Many of the header fields used in these files get their initial values from LINK.

NMAKE—Project Maintenance

Microsoft's NMAKE utility is a sophisticated command processor that saves you time and streamlines project maintenance. Once you tell NMAKE which files are in your project, it takes care of building your project without recompiling files that haven't been modified since the last build. NMAKE is usually run from the DOS command line and requires a special text file to provide it with "build" information.

BUILD—PWB Project Maintenance

Using the BUILD utility is similar to running NMAKE without defining any options or target files, and it uses the project make file and project environment. PWB's BUILD option uses all the files listed in the project make file and runs NMAKE to build the target file. PWB constructs a temporary make file according to the current project template when no project is open.

LIB—The Library Manager

The Microsoft library manager, called LIB, allows you to create, organize, and perform maintenance on libraries. *Libraries* are collections of logically related compiled or assembled object modules that provide a common set of useful routines and data. LIB lets you add modules to a library, delete routines, or simply replace them with updated code. You can even copy or move a module to a separate object file and combine libraries into one library file.

HELPMAKE—Help File Maintenance

The Microsoft help file maintenance utility (HELPMAKE) creates and maintains help databases used by many Microsoft applications to display on-line help. HELPMAKE creates a help database by translating help source files. These files are accessible from within the following environments:

- Microsoft Editor version 1.02
- Microsoft Word version 5.5
- CV/CVW—Microsoft CodeView
- QH—the Microsoft QuickHelp utility
- PWB—the Microsoft Programmer's WorkBench
- Microsoft QuickPascal version 1.0
- Microsoft QuickBASIC version 4.5 or later
- Microsoft QuickC compiler version 2.0 or later
- MS-DOS EDIT version 5.0
- MS-DOS QBasic version 5.0

For complete information about creating a help file, consult the HELPMAKE chapter in the *Microsoft C Environment and Tools* manual.

BSCMAKE and SBRPACK—Browser Database Maintenance

BSCMAKE creates database files that can be read by the Programmer's WorkBench (PWB) Source Browser. SBRPACK packs .SBR files in preparation for use with BSCMAKE.

CVPACK—The Debug Info Compactor

The Microsoft debugging information compactor (CVPACK) prepares an executable file for use with the Microsoft CodeView debugger version 4.00. CVPACK is automatically called by LINK version 5.30 when /CO is specified (or when a debug build is chosen in PWB).

If a file contains debugging information for an earlier version of CodeView or has been linked by another linker, use CVPACK to convert it for use with CodeView 4.00. If the executable file has been packed by an earlier version of CVPACK, you must relink the file.

IMPLIB—The Import Library Manager

IMPLIB creates import libraries that can be used by LINK to link dynamic link libraries (DLLs) with applications.

RM—File Removal

RM moves one or more files to a hidden directory named DELETED. DELETED is a subdirectory of the directory that contains the file being deleted. RM creates a DELETED directory if one does not already exist. Use RM along with UNDEL and EXP to manage backup files.

UNDEL—Undelete

UNDEL restores deleted files by moving them from a hidden DELETED subdirectory to the parent directory. Files are placed in DELETED by RM. Files are also placed in DELETED by PWB when the Backup switch is set to UNDEL. Use UNDEL along with RM and EXP to manage backup files.

EXP—Remove Hidden DELETED Subdirectory

EXP removes the hidden DELETED subdirectory of the current or specified directory and all files contained within it. Files are placed in DELETED by RM. Files are also placed in DELETED by PWB when the Backup switch is set to UNDEL. Use EXP along with RM and UNDEL to manage backup files. After the files are expunged by EXP, they cannot be restored by UNDEL.

CodeView Debugger

The Microsoft CodeView debugger is a diagnostic tool for debugging your programs. There are actually two versions of CodeView—one for DOS applications and another for Microsoft Windows. Both versions allow you to visually inspect constants, variables, pointers, and much more using single-step mode and breakpoints. You can even trace into C++ class constructors and destructors, inline functions, and virtual functions. It is also possible to trace into virtual functions defined in header files.

Since Microsoft C/C++ now includes support for C++ code, CodeView's browse feature lets you view information on a program's objects. With the Browser you can look at class objects, member functions, and friends and determine the private, public, and protected status of each element.

CodeView has been upgraded to include CUA- (common user access) compatible, overlapping windows that can be cascaded, tiled, reduced to an icon, or maximized. The debugger allows you to have a maximum of 16 windows.

If you have an additional VGA monochrome monitor, you can use CodeView for remote debugging. With the help of the RS-232 port, you can debug a C or C++ program from another computer. With remote debugging, you can activate a CodeView session on a local workstation and debug a program running on a remote system. All debugging information appears as if it were being done locally. The location of the remote application is totally invisible to the debugger.

You may be wondering about the usefulness of such a feature. With remote debugging, you can debug the heart of a server-based database program without actually having to sit down at the server itself. Of particular importance is the remote debugger's ability to trace machine-dependent errors. This means that with remote debugging, you can tie into and debug a problem that is specific to one particular PC.

CodeView also allows you to debug Microsoft's p-code (packed) or programs using DPMI- (DOS protected mode interface) compliant MS-DOS extenders.

Profiler

The Microsoft Source Profiler examines the run-time characteristics of your application. The information returned from the Profiler helps you pinpoint time-critical portions of the design. It can even point out those code sections that are never being executed.

The Profiler can usually work with any MS-DOS or Microsoft Windows programs compiled with only CodeView options. This saves you time by not requiring you to recompile the application with an additional set of compiler switches. The Microsoft Source Profiler can be run from within PWB or through the DOS command line.

Source Browser

The PWB Source Browser has 14 commands that let you view your source code from many different perspectives. With the Browser you can select a browser database or go to a specific definition or symbol in a program. You can view complex relationships among program identifiers and display your program as an outline, a class-inheritance tree, or a function-call tree.

Since large projects can involve hundreds of classes and thousands of objects, class hierarchies can be many levels deep, with classes, subclasses, and typdefs nested within other classes. This complex relationship between objects is seen as the biggest stumbling block to achieving productivity with C++.

The Source Browser solves this problem by enabling you to quickly view class hierarchies, data members, objects, and member functions. The class-inheritance tree view shows all of an application's classes in a window. By selecting a class, you can then display its data and function members in another window. This additional information includes those members inherited from the base class.

You can even view all classes sorted by protection and scope levels. For example, if you want to learn how to use a new class object, you can instruct the Source Browser to display only the public, or class interface, members. However, if you are trying to develop a descendant subclass, you can instruct the Source Browser to display only the private and protected members of the parent class.

If you choose to view all the relationships between classes, symbols, objects, and member functions, you can see the descendants of a class, inherited class members, class friends, objects that instantiate a class, and many other combinations.

Windows Development Tools

The Dialog, Image, and Hotspot Editors allow you to customize an application's interface. They allow you to create visually appealing, colorful, and mouse-click-sensitive resources such as dialog boxes, icons, and cursors.

The Dialog Editor

The Dialog Editor is a slick graphical development tool for easily and quickly creating professional-looking dialog boxes. Actually, Microsoft has practically given you, free of charge, another one of their excellent development environments, known as Visual Basic. The Dialog Editor allows you to customize a dialog box's labels; framing, option, and check box selections; text windows; and scroll bars.

If you have used Visual Basic, you already know 90 percent of how the Dialog Editor works. The Toolbox provides 14 controls. A *control* combines a visual graphical representation of some feature with a predefined set of properties you can customize.

For example, many dialog boxes use horizontal or vertical scroll bars. The Dialog Editor allows you to select the scroll bar control from the Toolbox and, with the mouse, visually place the control in a dialog box. You then use the mouse to alter the size and placement of the scroll bar. With another click of the mouse, you can select the scroll bar's style from the following list: Visible, Disabled, Group, and Tab Stop.

The Image Editor

The graphical Image Editor allows you to easily create custom bitmaps, icons, and cursors. A *bitmap* represents a picture of something—for example, an exclamation point used in a warning message. *Icons* are the small color images used to represent an application that has been minimized. Microsoft C/C++ even allows you to use the Image Editor to create custom cursors. For example, you could design a financial package with a cursor that looks like a dollar sign. You can save custom icons, cursors, and bitmaps with an .RC file extension and use them in resource script files.

HotSpot Editor

The Hotspot Editor allows you to create and edit hypergraphics. A *hypergraphic* is a bitmap that includes one or more hotspots. A bitmap can include multiple hotspots that link to help topics or run help macros when selected with the mouse. Hotspots can cover any section of the bitmap, with each hotspot having its own set of attributes:

- Hotspot ID
- Invisible or visible hotspot borders
- Context string
- Link type (pop-up, jump, or macro)

The Hotspot Editor will save the hypergraphics in a special compressed file format with an .SHG file extension.

Resource Compiler

The resource compiler does pretty much what its name suggests. Frequently, a Windows application will use its own resources, such as dialog boxes, menus, and icons. Each of these resources can be predefined in a file called a *resource script file*. This file is then compiled by the resource compiler and the additional information is added to the application's final .EXE file. This allows Windows to load and use the resources from the executable file.

Spy

Spy is one of the most dynamic tools shipped with Microsoft C/C++. This utility allows you to spy on one or all currently loaded Windows applications. The Window option allows you to view each application's name, class, module, parent, display window's screen rectangular coordinates, window style (for example, WS_CHILD), and window ID number.

Spy also lets you view the messages being sent throughout the environment. There are nine check boxes that allow you to predefine the reported message types:

Mouse	Input	System
Window	Init	Clipboard
Other	DDE	Non Client

Generated output can be displayed in synchronous or asynchronous mode and sent to a Spy window, a file, or to COM1 for remote debugging.

WXServer

The WXServer, or WX, will run a Windows application from a DOS prompt within Windows. WX is the command-line version that runs a Windows application from a DOS prompt either in a window or in a full screen. You must be running WXServer under Windows before you can use WX. PWB itself runs WX to run Windows applications and CodeView.

QH Advisor

The stand-alone QuickHelp Advisor provides access to any help file. This utility provides easy access to important topics and utilities supplied with the compiler package, including language, PWB, CodeView, and run-time support libraries.

386MAX

Microsoft is currently shipping a memory manager named 386MAX. 386MAX provides developers with advanced memory-management capabilities, such as advanced memory recovery and optimization tools. 386MAX works with the broadest range of systems: 386, 386SX, 486, and 486SX.

Documentation

Included in your Microsoft C/C++ package is the most extensive documentation for any C/C++ compiler package. There are more than 5000 pages of printed manuals, as well as extensive on-line help utilities. Two of the more useful manuals are the C++ tutorial and a class library cookbook, which quickly bring you up to speed. To help you quickly find the information you need, Microsoft has broken its documentation into ten categories:

- *Getting Started*   This manual explains the installation and setup procedures, along with the features of the professional compiler package.

- *Microsoft C Environment and Tools*   This is the complete documentation on how to use the Programmer's WorkBench, CodeView, NMAKE, the linker, and the Microsoft Advisor on-line help utilities.

- *Programming Techniques*   The information in this manual will teach you how to optimize your C and C++ code for size, speed, and portability. The manual also demonstrates how to link C code with other high-level languages and how to use the inline assembler.

- *C++ Tutorial*   This comprehensive guide takes an experienced C programmer through the transition to C++ object-oriented programming, using Windows programming as the example.

- *Microsoft C Language Reference*   This reference contains a formal description and syntax for all C keywords.

- *Microsoft C++ Language Reference*   This manual is the same as its C counterpart except that it stresses those keywords specific to C++.

- *Microsoft C Run-Time Library Reference*   This user's guide explains all of C's global variables, standard types, and run-time functions.

- *Class Libraries User's Guide*   This is a how-to guide using a tutorial approach to object-oriented Windows programming with class libraries.

- *Microsoft Foundation Class Libraries Reference*   This reference manual describes each class library in detail.

- *Microsoft C Comprehensive Index and Errors Reference*   This manual provides an index to all of the C/C++ printed documentation. The reference also includes a complete error-message reference.

The following list of abbreviations used by the *Microsoft C Comprehensive Index and Errors Reference* will help you locate the correct support materials. The list is ordered for a beginning programmer, with the most frequently used manuals at the top:

ET	Environment and Tools manual
LR	C Language Reference
PT	Programming Techniques
LIB	Run-Time Library Reference
TUT	C++ Tutorial
LR+	C++ Language Reference
XUG	Class Libraries User's Guide
XRF	Class Libraries Reference

C/C++ and Windows Programming Features

Microsoft packs the C/C++ compiler package with many useful enhancements, new features, and options. The following sections introduce you to these improvements and briefly explain their use.

C++ 2.1 Validation Suite

Practically all of the C++ compilers on the market today are an implementation of the ANSI C++ version 2.0 specification. This set of recommendations was published in the middle of 1989. However, the language continues to evolve with new features, corrections, and improvements. Version 2.1 of the ANSI C++ recommendations was published in early 1990.

Microsoft expects the Microsoft C/C++ compiler to be the first correct and comprehensive version of the 2.1 specifications for the PC. This means that you as an applications developer can take advantage of these important new enhancements immediately.

Just one example of the usefulness of these language improvements is the ability to declare true nested types. *Nested types* allow you to declare any data type, including a C++ class, within a class. While this was syntactically legal for version 2.0-compliant C/C++ compilers, version 2.1-compatible compilers allow all symbols declared within a class to remain local to that class instead of being elevated to the scope of the enclosing class. This important feature promotes a more modular class organization by keeping certain identifiers out of the global name space.

Unfortunately, since C++ is a relatively new language, there are many compilers that incorrectly support any ANSI C++ version. To compound the situation, C++ as a language is much more flexible than its C progenitor. This forces the C++ compiler to deal with an immense variety of expressions, which explains why so many C++ compilers simply do not work properly.

The software engineers at Microsoft have focused their attention on producing the most correct version 2.1-compliant compiler. The results of running the PEREN-NIAL C++ conformance test suites indicate that they have succeeded.

Compiler Optimizations

Microsoft C/C++ is a global optimizing compiler that allows you to take advantage of several speed or code size options for every type of program development. The following list of compiler switches is suggested when you are optimizing your code for executable size, speed, or build time or are creating Windows applications. If you do not see an appreciable performance boost, it is possible that your test application does not contain enough code. Note that some switches have certain restrictions to their use.

Optimizing for Smallest .EXE Size

If your code does not use *aliasing*—two pointers that point to the identical memory location—you can use the /Oes switch. In addition, you can select /Gs, which turns off stack checking. The /Oes option optimizes the compiler for smallest .EXE file creation.

Optimizing for Fastest Execution Speed

The /Oax compiler switch also assumes that your code contains no aliasing and optimizes your code for the fastest execution speed. A second switch, /Ob2, activates automatic function inlining that streamlines an application by removing the over-head normally associated with function calls. If you do not select the /Ob2 option, the compiler will generate explicit inlining only as flagged by the **_inline** keyword.

Optimizing for Quickest Build Time

To optimize the compiler for fastest build time, you can use a combination of three switches. The /f switch selects fast compile. Microsoft recommends that you use this option along with /Yu, which signals the presence of precompiled headers. You can use the /Yc switch to create a precompiled header.

Any header file shared across several modules in a large program is a candidate for precompilation. When using CodeView information, you can further enhance rebuild and link times by moving include files from other modules into the pre-compiled file.

Optimizing for Windows Applications

The /GA (optimize entry/exit code) and /GEf (treat all far functions as callbacks) switches are replacements for the older, less efficient Microsoft 6.0 /Gw option. While the compiler does recognize the older switch, the newer switches generate 8 bytes less code per function call.

Optimizing for Large Memory Models

Selecting the /AL option activates the large memory model, while the /Gx switch triggers the data in the DGROUP option. These switches provide the most efficient use of memory when building large programs.

Compiler Memory Models

A memory model allows you to specify the number of code and data segments used in a program. Microsoft C/C++ supports seven memory models: tiny, small, medium, compact, large, huge, and flat. Table 1-1 summarizes the six standard memory models.

You should always select the smallest memory model needed to write an application. Larger memory models require more sophisticated references that slow down an application's overall performance. Memory models are discussed further in Chapter 2.

P-code

One of Microsoft's newest technologies, geared to optimizing code speed and size, is *p-code*, which is short for packed code. P-code can significantly reduce a program's

Memory Model	Max Code Size	Max Data Size	Max Array Size
Tiny	⟶	total 64K	⟵
Small	64K	64K	64K
Medium	no limit	64k	64k
Compact	64k	no limit	64k
Large	no limit	no limit	64k
Huge	no limit	no limit	no limit

Table 1-1.   *Memory Models*

size and execution characteristics by as much as 60 percent. Better yet, you accomplish all of this simply by turning on a specific compiler option. This means that any code written in C or C++ can be compiled normally or with p-code.

This technology compiles an application's source code into *interpreted object code*, which is a higher level and more condensed representation of object code. The process is completed when a small interpreter module is linked into the application.

The most efficient use of this technology does require some expertise, however. Since the interpreter generates object code at run time, p-code runs more slowly than native object code. With a careful use of the **#pragma** directive, an application can generate p-code for space-critical functions and switch back to generating native code for speed-critical functions.

The best candidates for p-code generation are those routines that deal with the user interface, and since many Windows applications spend 50 percent of their time handling the user interface, p-code provides the optimum performance characteristics.

Precompiled Headers and Types

One area that can cause the compiler to slow down has to do with repeatedly compiling portions of code. C++ places generic types, function prototypes, external references, and member function declarations in special files called *header files*. These header files contain many of the critical definitions needed by the multiple source files pulled together to create the executable version of your program. Portions of these header files are typically recompiled for every module that includes the header.

Microsoft C/C++ speeds up this process by allowing you to precompile your header files. While the use of precompiled headers isn't new, the way that Microsoft has implemented the feature is. Precompilation saves the state of compilation up to a given point and represents the relationship that is set up between the source file and the precompiled header. You can also create more than one precompiled header file per source file.

One of the best applications of this technology involves the development life cycle of an application that has frequent code changes, not frequent base class definitions. When you precompile the header file, the compiler can concentrate its time on the changes in the source code. Precompiled headers also provide a compile-time boost for applications with headers that comprise large portions of code for a given module, as often happens with C++ or Windows programs.

The Microsoft C++ compiler assumes that the current state of the compiler environment is the same as when any precompiled headers were compiled. The compiler will issue a warning if it detects any inconsistencies. Sources for this inconsistency include a change in memory models, the state of defined constants, any debugging option changes, and an altered selection of code-generation options.

Unlike many popular C++ compilers, the Microsoft C/C++ compiler does not restrict precompilation to header files. Since the process allows you to precompile a program up to a specified point, you can even precompile source code. This is extremely significant for C++ programs, which contain most of their member functions in header files. In general, precompilation is reserved for those portions of your algorithm considered stable and is designed to minimize the time needed to compile your program.

MOVE—The Microsoft Overlay Virtual Environment

Microsoft designed its C/C++ compiler to meet the needs of a broad range of development environments, including MS-DOS applications. One of the frequent stumbling blocks to designing a C/C++ DOS application is the 640K limit of conventional RAM. Many compilers use a concept called *overlaying* to solve this problem. The basic principle behind overlaying involves a piece of code called the *root* that remains always in memory, while other pieces of the program are swapped in and out of RAM from the disk as needed.

The Microsoft overlay virtual environment, called MOVE, is a new utility for creating overlaid programs. MOVE's technology provides more power, flexibility, and seamless execution than other types of overlay managers. There are five new key features to MOVE that MS-DOS programmers should find useful:

- **Overlaid code and data** The overlay manager doesn't restrict the types of code that can be swapped in and out of RAM. MOVE allows you to overlay both code and data. This can be an especially important option for programs containing large C++ objects or data storage requirements.

- **Multiple RAM-resident overlays** Because more than one overlay can reside in memory at one time, MS-DOS programmers can build programs of almost unlimited size. Applications can use up to 65,535 overlays in a single program.

- **Inter-overlay calls** This feature allows a function in one overlay to call a function in another overlay by using a simple function pointer.

- **Overlay caching** MOVE is capable of caching overlays that are currently not in use. However, should the application need the overlay again, access is much quicker.

- **Function-level and segment-level control** MOVE allows you to decide the contents of the overlay. Your application can place any combination of object files, segments, or functions in an overlay.

Overlay managers work by using a heap located in the portion of available conventional memory not currently occupied by the root. When the program gets to the point where it needs a function or object not currently located in RAM, the overlay containing the requested object is copied into the overlay heap from the executable file. MOVE allows an application to have more than one overlay loaded into memory at the same time. However, if the overlay heap doesn't have enough RAM for the requested overlay, it discards one currently in the heap. It does this by using a least-recently-used algorithm.

The Foundation Class Library

Almost everyone agrees that a properly written Windows application is easy to use. However, these programs are not as easy to develop. Many programmers get waylaid by having to master the more than 500 Windows API (application program interface) functions necessary to write a Windows application.

Microsoft's solution to this steep learning curve is the Foundation class. The more than 60 reusable C++ classes are much easier to master and use. The Microsoft Foundation Class libraries (MFC) take full advantage of the data abstraction offered by C++ and simplify Windows programming. Beginning programmers can use the classes in a "cookbook" fashion, while experienced C++ programmers can extend the classes or integrate them into their own class hierarchy.

MFC features classes for managing Windows objects and offers a number of general-purpose classes that you can use in both MS-DOS and Windows applications. For example, there are classes for creating and managing files, strings, time, persistent storage, and exception handling.

In effect, the Microsoft Foundation Class library represents virtually every Windows API feature and includes sophisticated code that streamlines message processing, diagnostics, and other details that were a normal part of all Windows applications. This logical combination and enhancement of Windows API functions has nine key advantages:

- **Logical and complete encapsulation of the Windows API** The MFC library provides support for all of the frequently used Windows API functions, including windowing functions, messages, controls, menus, dialog boxes, GDI (graphics device interface) objects (fonts, brushes, pens, and bitmaps), object linking, and the multiple document interface, or MDI.

- **Ease of learning** Microsoft has made a concerted effort to keep the names of the MFC functions and associated parameters as similar as possible to their Windows API parent classes. This minimizes the confusion for experienced Windows programmers wanting to take advantage of the simplified MFC platform. It also makes it very easy for beginning Windows programmers to grow into the superset of Windows API functions when they are ready or when the application requires it.

- **More efficient C++ code** An application will consume a mere 39K of RAM when using the 60 classes in the MFC library compiled under the small memory model. Execution speed is almost identical to the application written in C using the standard Windows API. Most MFC applications run a mere five percent more slowly than their Windows API C program counterparts—a very reasonable trade-off, considering the ease of learning and shortened development cycle for MFC designs.

- **Automatic message handling** The Microsoft Foundation Class library eliminates one frequent source of programming errors, the Windows API message loop. The MFC classes are designed to automatically handle every one of the Windows messages. Instead of using the standard switch...case statements, each Window message is mapped directly to a member function, which takes the appropriate action.

- **Self-diagnostic classes** Incorporated into the MFC Library is the ability to perform self-diagnostics. This means you can dump information about various objects to a file and validate an object's member variables, all in an easily understood format.

- **Robust architecture** Anticipating the much-needed ANSI C throw/catch standard, the Microsoft Foundation Class library already incorporates an extensive exception-handling architecture. This allows an MFC object to eloquently recover from standard errors conditions such as "out of memory" errors, invalid option selection, and file- or resource-loading problems. Every component of the architecture is upward compatible with the proposed ANSI C recommendations.

- **Dynamic object typing** This extremely powerful feature delays the typing of a dynamically allocated object until run time. This allows you to manipulate an object without having to worry about its underlying data type. Since information about the object type is returned at run time, you are freed from one additional level of detail.

- **Harmonious coexistence** The most important feature of the Microsoft Foundation Class library is its ability to coexist with C-based Windows applications that use the Windows API. You can use a combination of MFC classes and

Windows API calls within the same program. This allows an MFC application to easily evolve into true C++ object-oriented code as experience or demand requires. This transparent environment is possible because of the common naming conventions between the two architectures. The result is that MFC headers, types, and global definitions do not conflict with Windows API names. Transparent memory management is another key component to this successful relationship.

- **Using MFC with MS-DOS**   The Microsoft Foundation Class library was designed specifically for developing Windows applications. However, many of the classes provide frequently needed objects used for file I/O and string manipulation. For this reason, both Windows and MS-DOS developers can use these general-purpose classes.

Function Inlining

The Microsoft C/C++ compiler supports complete function inlining. This means that functions of any type or combination of instructions can be expanded inline. Many popular C++ compilers restrict inlining to certain types of statements or expressions. For example, the inline option would be ignored by any function containing a **switch**, **while**, or **for** statement. Microsoft's C++ compiler allows you to inline your most speed-critical routines (including seldom-used class member functions or constructors) without restricting their content.

Auto-inlining

Along with complete function inlining, Microsoft C/C++ supports *auto-inlining*. By simply setting a compiler switch, you can instantly achieve up to a ten-percent increase in execution speed. Auto-inlining instructs the compiler to automatically inline functions for you.

To get to this compiler option from within PWB, you click the auto-inlining radio button in PWB's compiler options dialog box. This causes the compiler to scan your source code for functions that represent good candidates for inlining. The compiler will inline only those functions that are small and frequently called, minimizing the impact on a program's overall size.

Inline function expansions eliminate all the clock cycles necessary to push and pop arguments and registers that are a standard part of conventional (non-inline) subroutine calls. Since the overall speed boost from auto-inlining can be quite dramatic, and since the compiler option is so easy to get to, you should try it, especially if your program contains many small functions or code segments that repeatedly call a function.

Chapter 2

Getting Started with the Programmer's WorkBench

The most important tool supplied with your Microsoft C/C++ compiler package is the Programmer's WorkBench. Microsoft typically refers to the Programmer's Work-Bench as the PWB, and this book also adopts that convention. The PWB is an integrated development environment that allows access to

- A full-screen windowed editor for writing new programs and altering old applications

- Options for customized compiling and linking for various environments, such as DOS and Windows

- An on-line help facility, named the Microsoft Advisor, with instant help on C, C++, Windows, and so on

- A "build" facility for building applications. This can make compiling, linking, execution, and debugging almost automatic

- A Source Browser for locating pieces of code

- A Source Profiler for help in optimizing programs

This chapter examines the important features of the PWB and teaches you how to enter and edit application code, compile and link from the integrated environment and from the DOS command line, obtain on-line help, and look at various PWB options. Additional information is available in your *Microsoft Environment and Tools* manual.

Entering the PWB Environment

You can run the PWB from the DOS command line or from within Windows. From the DOS command line, simply type

PWB

From Windows, click the PWB icon within the Microsoft C/C++ group box. In either case, the main PWB window, shown in Figure 2-1, will appear. It is from this level that all other PWB options are chosen.

PWB Main Menu Categories

This section discusses each group in the PWB's main menu and takes a quick look at their various menu items. Later sections in this chapter examine individual menu items as they apply to the tasks being discussed.

If you examine Figure 2-1, you will notice the nine main menu categories. These include File, Edit, Search, Project, Run, Options, Browse, Window, and Help. You

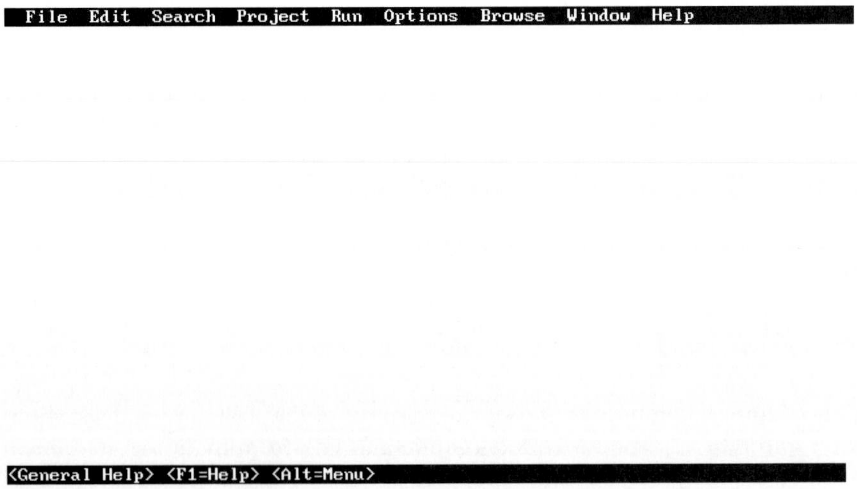

```
File  Edit  Search  Project  Run  Options  Browse  Window  Help
```

```
<General Help>  <F1=Help>  <Alt=Menu>
```

Figure 2-1.   *The main Programmer's WorkBench window*

can examine all pop-up menus by clicking the menu category with the left mouse button or by pressing the ALT key along with the first letter of each menu choice. For example, ALT-F will pop up the File menu items.

File

When you pop up the PWB File menu category, you will see an item list similar to the one in Figure 2-2. The most frequently used File items allow you to

- Start a new program with the New item

- Edit an existing program by opening the File dialog box with the Open item

- Merge two or more files with the Merge item

- Save a file with the Save option or save it under a new name with the Save As item

- Print a copy of the file to the printer with the Print item

- Return to the DOS environment by selecting the DOS Shell item

- Exit the PWB with the Exit option

You can select a menu item by clicking the item with the left mouse button. You can also select items with the ALT key in combination with the boldface letter of the menu item. In certain cases, you can select the menu item without popping up the menu list; for example, you can select Exit with the special ALT-F4 hot-key combination.

Figure 2-2.   *PWB File menu items*

Edit

The PWB Edit menu category has an item list that you will use frequently. The various Edit items are shown in Figure 2-3. The most frequently used Edit items allow you to

- Undo a previous delete operation with the Undo item

- Repeat the previous operation with the Repeat item. If the previous operation was a delete, the Repeat item will continue deleting

- Delete blocks of code with the Cut item. Typically, the code is blocked with the mouse or the ALT-A key combination and then deleted with the Cut item. The Cut information remains in memory until the next block operation

- Copy blocks of code to memory, for later use, with the Copy item. You block the code with the mouse or the ALT-A key combination

- Paste information from memory to the current cursor location by using the Paste item. Information to be pasted is typically placed in memory by a previous Cut or Copy operation

- Delete blocked code with the Delete item. Delete is different from Cut in that the information deleted is not available for Paste operations

Notice that you can select the Cut, Copy, Paste, and Delete items without popping up the Edit menu category, by using several hot-key combinations.

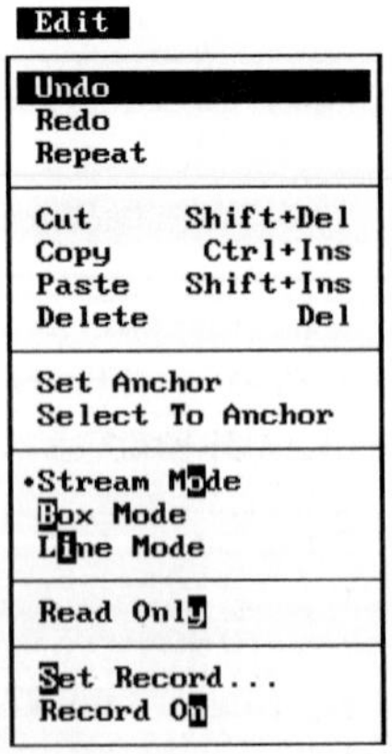

Figure 2-3.   *PWB Edit menu items*

Search

The PWB Search menu category produces an item list such as the one shown in Figure 2-4. Most full-screen editors provide the ability to do search and search/replace operations. The most popular Search items include the ability to

- Find a particular combination of characters and/or numbers with the Find item

- Find a particular combination of characters and/or numbers and replace it with another combination of letters and/or numbers with the Replace item

- Repeat the previous Find and/or Replace operation with the Next Match item. This item continues the operation in the forward direction

- Repeat the previous Find and/or Replace operation with the Previous Match item. This item continues the operation in the reverse direction

Menu items followed by three dots—for example, Find...—produce dialog boxes on the screen for additional user input.

Project

Figure 2-5 shows the items for the PWB Project menu category. Project items allow you to use the integrated environment for compiling and linking C and C++ programs from within the PWB. The most frequently used Project items allow you to

- Compile the current C or C++ program being developed with the Compile item

- Build an executable file with the Build item

- Rebuild all associated files after editing with the Rebuild All option

Figure 2-4.   *PWB Search menu items*

Figure 2-5.   *PWB Project menu items*

- Create a new project file for a customized compilation and link with the New Project item. Project files allow you to save special compilation and link instructions for repeated use

- Open a previously created project file with the Open Project item

- Edit and close project files with the Edit Project and Close Project items

Microsoft uses the .MAK file extension for project make files. Project files are used only from within the PWB environment. If you are building applications from the DOS command line, a different form of make file will be used.

Run

The pop-up menu you see in Figure 2-6 shows the menu items for the PWB Run menu category. When programs have been successfully built—that is, compiled and linked—they can be executed from the Run menu category. Even Windows applications developed while running the PWB under Windows can be executed if the WX

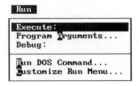

Figure 2-6.   *PWB Run menu items*

Server program icon has been clicked from the Microsoft C/C++ Windows group box. The most popular Run menu items include the ability to

- Execute a successfully compiled and linked application with the Execute item

- Set program arguments with the Program Arguments item

- Execute a debug operation with the executable file with the Debug item

It is usually possible to run and debug after a successful build. A successful build operation presents the user with a dialog box with Run and Debug options.

Options

When you pop up the PWB Options menu category, the item list shown in Figure 2-7 is displayed. The Options category allows you to set options for many different features. For example, the colors for the PWB screen, menu, and so on, can be customized from this level. Other options allow you to alter the environment, change project build features, and so on. The most frequently used Options items allow you to

- Set or change the environment variables with the Environment Variables item. Environment variables include the paths to the INCLUDE subdirectory, LIBRARY subdirectory, HELP subdirectory, and so on

- Change editor key assignments with the Key Assignments item. Typically, you can change hot-key combinations at this level. For example, PWB has already assigned the CTRL-END key combination to go to the end of a file (called *endfile*). You can change this combination from the Key Assignments item

Figure 2-7.   *PWB Options menu items*

- Set editor settings, such as tab characters, tab widths, and so on, with the Editor Settings item

- Set the editor screen colors, including border, text, and background, with the Colors item

- Select a Debug or Release option with the Build Options item. A Debug option includes CodeView information in your executable file. It is the typical option to choose during application development. The Release option allows your final executable file to be as small and fast as possible, without the additional CodeView baggage

- Set specific C and C++ compiler switches with the Language Options item. These switches include a switch for the memory model, microprocessor type, calling convention, and so on

- Generate browse information with the Browse Option item. This is discussed more fully in the next section

- Set various debug and release items with the LINK Options item. Here, additional library information can be included for project build operations. One such case is where you might want to utilize the GRAPHICS.LIB and PGCHART.LIB function calls described in Chapter 19

- Use the PWB Options item when the CodeView debugger is called from within the PWB. The most useful feature of this item is the ability to set the number of display lines for your monitor. A VGA monitor can be set to 25, 43, or 50 lines

For the most part, it is recommended that you do not make any changes in the Options category until you are absolutely sure they are needed. In several sections of this chapter and in subsequent chapters, you will learn when and how to make these changes.

Browse

The PWB Browse menu category produces the menu item list shown in Figure 2-8. As your programs grow in size, you will find the Source Browser to be an important tool for moving about in your code. The Browser can provide information on where symbols are defined and used and also information on various modules. More information on using the Source Browser is included in Chapter 4.

Window

Figure 2-9 shows the menu item list for the PWB Window menu category. The most frequently used Window menu items include the ability to

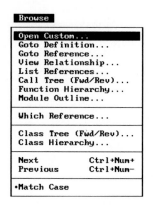

Figure 2-8.   *PWB Browse menu items*

- Create a new PWB editing window with the New item

- Close an existing editing window with the Close item

- Close all editing windows with Close All

- Move and size windows with the Move and Size items

Sometimes you will also find it handy to arrange your various windows in a cascaded or tiled fashion by using the options on this menu.

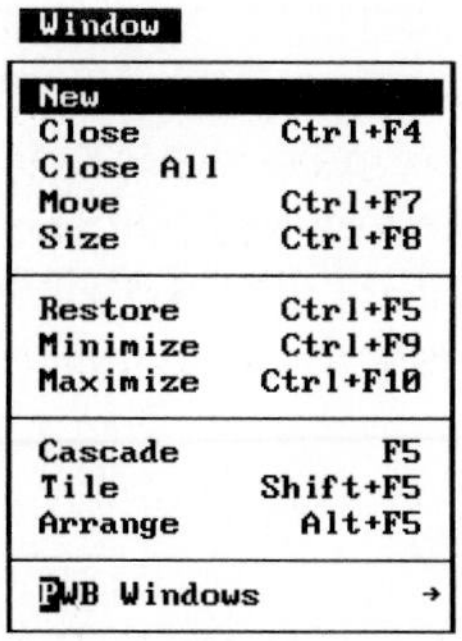

Figure 2-9.   *PWB Window menu items*

Figure 2-10.   *PWB Help menu items*

Help

The last main menu category allows access to the PWB Help items. The item list for this category includes those shown in Figure 2-10. The help facility is very important to new and seasoned progammers alike. From here, a wealth of information is available on compiler tools, C and C++ functions, Foundation Class library objects, and so on. The menu items give you the ability to

- Examine and select items from the extensive help index with the Index item

- Examine categories of items from the Contents item

- Receive help on any line in your program that the cursor is currently placed on with the Topic item

You can also call the help engine directly for a program item by clicking it with the right mouse button.

Writing a New Application

In this section, to help you understand the most essential editing features, an actual C++ program is written, modified, and saved from within the PWB environment.

Enter the PWB environment from either the DOS command line or from within the Microsoft C/C++ group box in Windows. From the PWB's main menu, select the File category. Next, choose the New menu item to open a new editing window.

Type the following C++ code in the PWB window:

```
main()
{
  cout << "Hello Microsoft C++ World\n";
  return(0);
}
```

Your screen should be similar to the one in Figure 2-11.

```
 File  Edit  Search  Project  Run  Options  Browse  Window  Help
■=[  1]══════════════════════ Untitled.001 ═══════════════════════╪↓│↑
│main()                                                                 █
│{
│  cout << "Hello Microsoft C++ World\n";
│  return(0);
│}
                                                                       █
                                                                       █
 ↕                                                                     ↕
<General Help> <F1=Help> <Alt=Menu>                        MP      00005.002
```

Figure 2-11.   *Entering a program in a PWB window*

You can save the program to disk by selecting the Save item from the main menu's File category. When you click the Save item for a new file, the dialog box shown in Figure 2-12 will request a filename.

Name this program 02HELLO.CPP. The 02 in the program name represents the chapter where the program is located, while the remaining characters give a curt indication of what the program is about. The extension for C++ programs is .CPP, while that for C applications is simply .C.

Now, exit the PWB by selecting Exit from the main menu's File category. You can check to see if your program was truly saved by typing the following at the DOS prompt:

Type 02HELLO.CPP

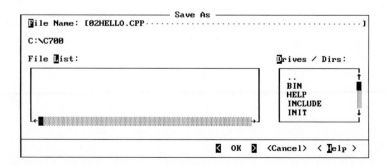

Figure 2-12.   *Saving a new program*

If your program was saved, the program will be listed to the screen. You could also print a copy of the program from the DOS command line by typing

Print 02HELLO.CPP

With this success behind you, return to the PWB environment.

Editing the Application

From within the PWB environment, you can load old applications into a PWB window by selecting the File category and selecting the Open item from the menu. The dialog box shown in Figure 2-13 will request the name of the file to load.

Select the original application by typing the name, 02HELLO.CPP, or by clicking the filename in the list with the left mouse button.

The file should now be in the PWB window. Move the cursor to the top of the screen and add the following comments to the top of the program. (You can move the cursor with the mouse or with the arrow keys.)

```
//
//  02HELLO.CPP
//  A C++ program which says hello to the new
//  Microsoft C++ Programming World.
//
```

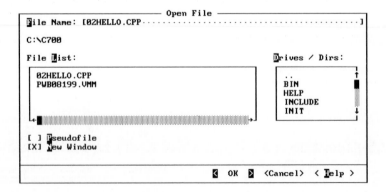

Figure 2-13.   Loading a previously written program in the PWB

Your edited application should now appear similar to the one shown in Figure 2-14.

Select the Save item from the main menu File category. This time, the file is saved without the dialog box requesting additional information. This is because the program had a name when it was loaded into the PWB. It is saved under the same name. By selecting the Save As item, you could assign a new program name.

Copying, Cutting, and Pasting

Return to the previous program if you have left the PWB window. Assume that you wish to print additional lines of text on the screen by copying and pasting the **cout** line. In order to copy, paste, or delete text, you must first block the text. You can block text by moving the cursor to the start of the text to be marked. Then, with the keyboard, block the text by pressing the ALT-A key combination and moving the cursor with the arrow keys. Alternately, place the mouse cursor on the first character and click the left mouse button. Move the mouse to block the required text. You can see the text that is blocked in Figure 2-15.

From the main menu Edit category, select the Copy item to copy the blocked text into memory. Now move the cursor to a position in the window where you wish to place a copy of the text you just copied. From the Edit category, choose the Paste item. If you added the new text immediately under the original text, your screen would appear like the one in Figure 2-16. Since you probably don't want to print the same message twice, block just the message and press the DEL key or select the Delete item from the Edit category.

Type the following text to replace the text just deleted:

```
"From A New C++ Programmer.\n";
```

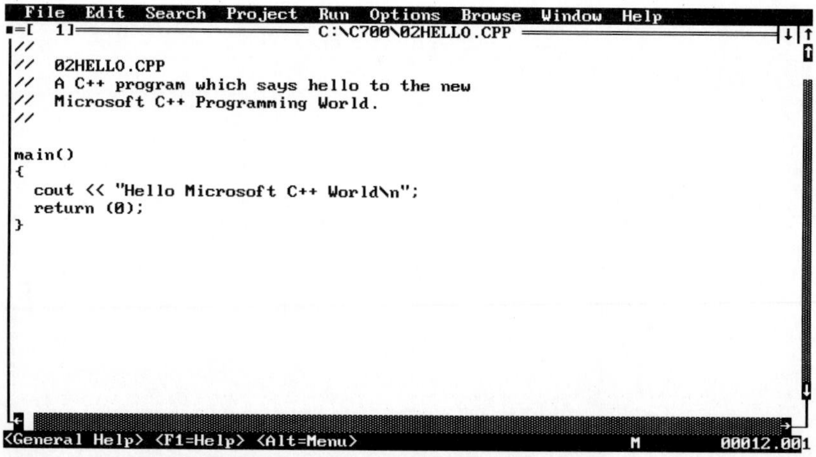

```
 File  Edit  Search  Project  Run  Options  Browse  Window  Help
■=[  1]══════════════════ C:\C700\02HELLO.CPP ═══════════════╗↓↑
//                                                            ▓
//  02HELLO.CPP
//  A C++ program which says hello to the new
//  Microsoft C++ Programming World.
//

main()
{
  cout << "Hello Microsoft C++ World\n";
  return (0);
}




<General Help> <F1=Help> <Alt=Menu>                    M      00012.001
```

Figure 2-14.   *An edited program in a PWB window*

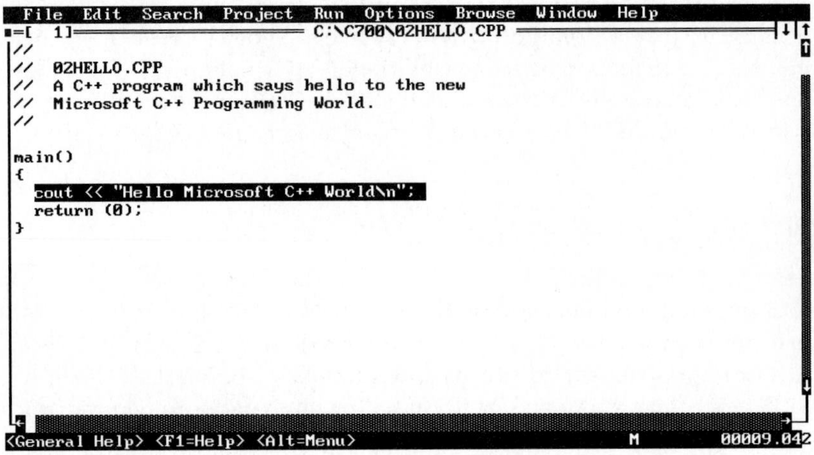

```
 File  Edit  Search  Project  Run  Options  Browse  Window  Help
■=[  1]════════════════ C:\C700\02HELLO.CPP ══════════════════↓|↑
//                                                             ▐
// 02HELLO.CPP
// A C++ program which says hello to the new
// Microsoft C++ Programming World.
//

main()
{
  cout << "Hello Microsoft C++ World\n";
  return (0);
}




<General Help> <F1=Help> <Alt=Menu>                      M      00009.042
```

Figure 2-15.   *Blocking text for copying, cutting, and pasting in the PWB*

Your program should now look like the program shown in Figure 2-17. Save this new version to the disk.

Compiling and Linking

The program 02HELLO.CPP is now ready for compiling and linking. This process can be carried out from within the integrated PWB environment or from the DOS command line.

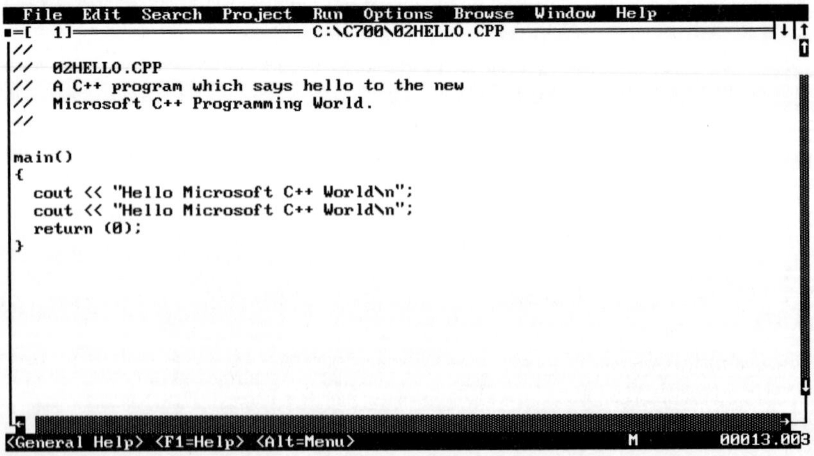

```
 File  Edit  Search  Project  Run  Options  Browse  Window  Help
■=[  1]════════════════ C:\C700\02HELLO.CPP ══════════════════↓|↑
//                                                             ▐
// 02HELLO.CPP
// A C++ program which says hello to the new
// Microsoft C++ Programming World.
//

main()
{
  cout << "Hello Microsoft C++ World\n";
  cout << "Hello Microsoft C++ World\n";
  return (0);
}




<General Help> <F1=Help> <Alt=Menu>                      M      00013.003
```

Figure 2-16.   *Pasting text into a program from within the PWB*

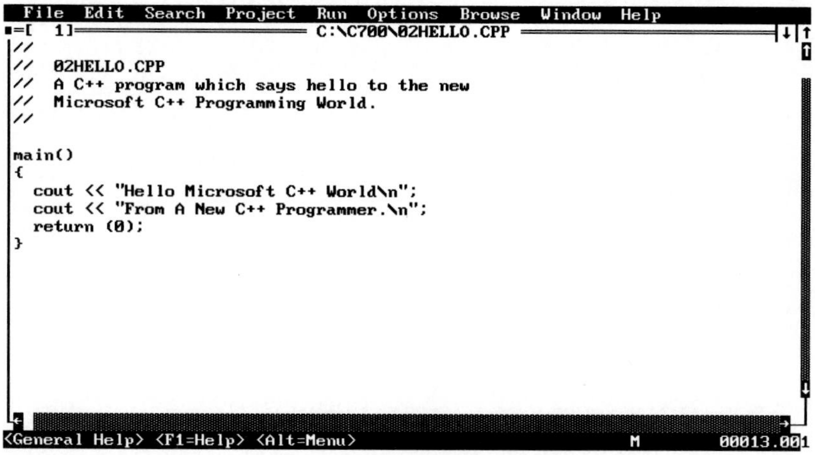

```
 File  Edit  Search  Project  Run  Options  Browse  Window  Help
=[  1]========================= C:\C700\02HELLO.CPP =================↓↑
//                                                                    ◘
//  02HELLO.CPP
//  A C++ program which says hello to the new
//  Microsoft C++ Programming World.
//

main()
{
   cout << "Hello Microsoft C++ World\n";
   cout << "From A New C++ Programmer.\n";
   return (0);
}



<General Help> <F1=Help> <Alt=Menu>                      M       00013.001
```

Figure 2-17. *A modified version of 02HELLO.CPP*

Working from within the PWB integrated environment offers the advantages of point-and-click operations with PWB menu categories and items. The DOS command-line option offers immediate user control over C/C++ and linker switches without the need for the PWB overhead. You'll develop your own preferences as you work through the examples in this book.

Working from the PWB

To compile and link this program using PWB defaults, simply position the mouse on the PWB main menu Project category and select the Build item from the list. The compile and link process should start immediately.

During the build process, an error message similar to the one shown in Figure 2-18 should appear in a PWB window. This was anticipated, at least by the authors, since the program didn't include the **#include** preprocessor statement to the iostream.h header file. The errors reported are a result of this omission.

Close the error message window and add the following line of code immediately under the starting comments for the program:

```
#include <iostream.h>
```

Your complete program should now appear like the code in the following listing:

```
//
//  02HELLO.CPP
//  A C++ program which says hello to the new
//  Microsoft C++ Programming World.
```

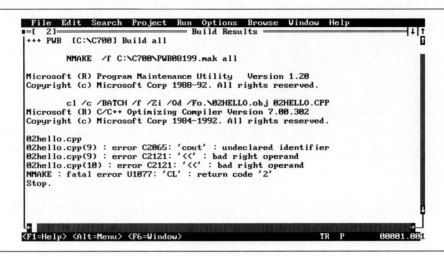

Figure 2-18.   *An error message report from PWB compile and link*

```
//

#include <iostream.h>

main()
{
  cout << "Hello Microsoft C++ World\n";
  cout << "From A New C++ Programmer.\n";
  return (0);
}
```

Save the file in the usual manner, and select the Build item once again. This time the reported news should be better. The screen you see in Figure 2-19 should match the one on your computer.

Now you can choose the Execute option from the Run menu to see the results of your program printed to your screen. The message should be

```
Hello Microsoft C++ World
From A New C++ Programmer.
```

In the next section, you learn how to achieve the same compile and link results from the DOS command line.

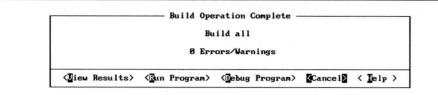

Figure 2-19.   *A PWB window reporting the results of a successful build process*

Working from the DOS Command Line

The syntax for a simple compile and link operation from the DOS command line is

CL [compile options] *filename.extension* [-link options]

For the example program, 02HELLO.CPP, this becomes

CL 02HELLO.CPP

In this case, no additional compile or link options are requested. You can view all of the DOS command-line compile options by typing the following from the command-line prompt:

CL /?

This program's executable file will print the same information to the DOS screen as the PWB's executable file created in the last section.

Using the Microsoft Advisor for Help

If you are not familiar with C and C++ syntax, the commands and statements used in the 02HELLO.CPP simple code can be a puzzle. However, as you develop your own code or work with the code in this book, remember that help is always just a mouse click away. The extensive Microsoft Advisor database is ready to help you with a variety of programming needs.

Help with Program Items

One of the reasons for using the PWB integrated environment is to take advantage of the instant help facility provided by the Microsoft Advisor.

Enter the PWB and load the 02HELLO.CPP program if it is not already present on your computer's screen. Move the mouse cursor over the term <iostream.h>. If you haven't programmed in C++, you might wonder what this statement achieves.

With the cursor over <iostream.h>, click the right mouse button once. Instantly, you are given a detailed description of the topic. Figure 2-20 is the initial information returned on this topic. You will find the Microsoft Advisor an invaluable aid as you venture more deeply into the object-oriented waters of C++.

Help with Other Features

The help that the Microsoft Advisor can provide is not limited to items in the immediate program. For example, you may be entering a program such as 02HELLO.CPP and wonder if you could include the output stream, **cout**, in a **for** loop. Since there is no mention of a **for** loop in your program, you can either type the word **for** on a blank line, place the cusor on it, and click the right mouse button or simply click the Help category and select the Index item. The Microsoft Advisor dialog window will want to know the category you request information for, as shown in Figure 2-21.

For this example, you are obviously working in the C/C++ language, so move the mouse cursor to that position and rapidly click the left mouse button twice. You are now presented with another dialog window, named the Microsoft C/C++ Language and Libraries Index, as shown in Figure 2-22.

Now, move the mouse cursor to the "F" box and rapidly click the left mouse button twice. You are given a list of the C/C++ terms beginning with the letter "F." Scroll down the list with the mouse or arrow keys until you find the keyword **for**. Rapidly click the left mouse button twice to retrieve information on this term. Figure 2-23

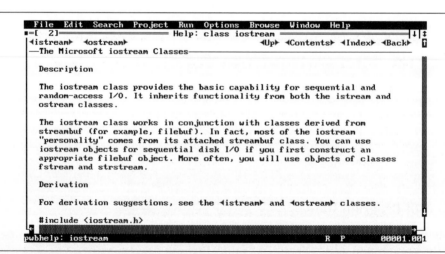

Figure 2-20.   *The Microsoft Advisor provides instant help access for C and C++ programming terms*

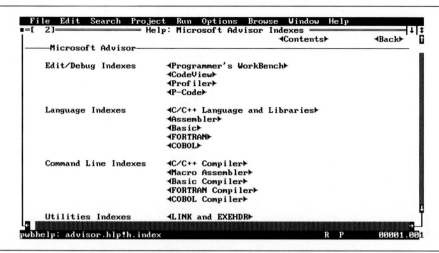

Figure 2-21. *Requesting Microsoft Advisor help by selecting the Index menu item*

shows the initial help screen for this term. It is also possible to use the Help category's Contents item to retrieve the same information.

Printing Help Information

You can print PWB screen information in many ways. Three techniques that are used frequently are

- Printing the whole file by clicking the File category and selecting the Print item. In this case, the whole file will be printed

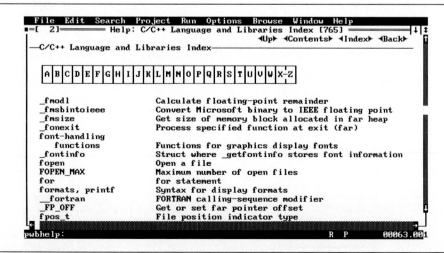

Figure 2-22. *The Microsoft Advisor's C/C++ Language and Libraries Index*

- Printing the screen by using the PRINT SCREEN key on your computer keyboard

- Printing blocked text by blocking text with the mouse or ALT-A keyboard technique and then selecting the File category and Print item. In this case, just the blocked text will be printed

If you want to make a quick copy of a portion of the help information provided on a command, you will most frequently select the third option.

Setting Important PWB Options

If you have been programming for any length of time, you have probably developed your own preferences for editor screen colors, hot-key combinations, and other special features. For the most part, you will find the default PWB environment settings very acceptable. However, there will be those special occasions when you want to change specific features. For example, if you are generating art for a book, screen shots reproduce best if they are shot on black-and-white screens. Also, tab characters within code listings wreak havoc with the typesetting equipment. The solution is to change the default screen color to black and white for screen shots and to turn the tab feature off. You'll learn how to make changes such as these in the following sections.

You can set or change all PWB options from the main menu by selecting the Options category and then clicking the menu item to be changed. You can also alter PWB features by editing the TOOLS.INI file.

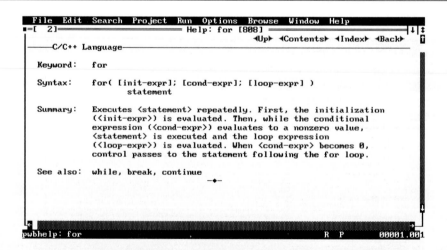

Figure 2-23. *The Microsoft Advisor can provide information on terms not immediately present in a program*

The Key Assignment Menu Item

In earlier sections you probably noticed that certain main menu items featured a keystroke combination that you could use in place of popping up the menu category. For example, you can select the Exit item directly from the keyboard by typing ALT-F4. You hold down the ALT key and press the F4 key; then you release both keys at the same time.

You can alter these hot-key combinations to suit your individual needs. For example, you may wish to exit programs with an ALT-Q combination. Changes such as this can be made for the session or permanently from the main menu Options category.

To make ALT-Q execute the exit function, select the Options category from the main menu, and then choose the Key Assignments item. Scroll down the Key Assignments window, by using the mouse and the scroll bars or the keyboard arrow keys, until you see the word "exit." Click on this term, and it will also appear on the Macro/Function Name line, as shown in Figure 2-24.

Now, simply move the mouse cursor within the brackets of the New Key line and click the left mouse button once. Press ALT-Q for the new key assignment, as shown in Figure 2-25. You can make the change for the current editing session by clicking the Assign button or make it permanent by also clicking the Save button. Permanent changes are saved in the PWB editor's TOOLS.INI file.

The Editor Settings Menu Item

It is from within the Editor Settings window that you can make changes to particular editor features. For example, it is possible to prevent tabs from being entered from the keyboard or to assign a new display character for a particular key.

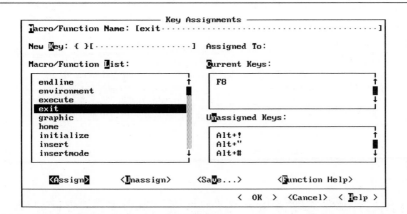

Figure 2-24.   *Using the key assignments item from the Options category to change a hot-key combination*

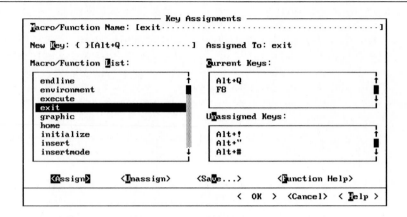

```
┌───────────────────── Key Assignments ────────────────────┐
│ Macro/Function Name: [exit·································]│
│                                                           │
│ New Key: { }[Alt+Q ···········]  Assigned To: exit        │
│                                                           │
│ Macro/Function List:            Current Keys:             │
│ ┌───────────────────────────┐   ┌──────────────────────┐ │
│ │ endline                  ↑│   │ Alt+Q              ↑ │ │
│ │ environment              █│   │ F8                 █ │ │
│ │ execute                   │   │                      │ │
│ │ exit                      │   └──────────────────────┘ │
│ │ graphic                   │   Unassigned Keys:          │
│ │ home                      │   ┌──────────────────────┐ │
│ │ initialize                │   │ Alt+!              ↑ │ │
│ │ insert                    │   │ Alt+"              █ │ │
│ │ insertmode               ↓│   │ Alt+#              ↓ │ │
│ └───────────────────────────┘   └──────────────────────┘ │
│                                                           │
│     <Assign>      <Unassign>     <Save...>    <Function Help> │
│                                                           │
│                        <  OK  >  <Cancel>  < Help >       │
└───────────────────────────────────────────────────────────┘
```

Figure 2-25. *Assigning* ALT-Q *to the exit function in the PWB editor*

Tabs are a particular problem in publishing because of the way typesetting equipment reads program listings. The TAB key can be rendered ineffective with several techniques, but setting the tab stop positions to zero is all that is needed.

From the PWB's main menu, choose the Options category and then select the Editor Settings item. The Editor Settings window shown in Figure 2-26 should appear next.

Now, things get a little tricky. When you are changing options, it is necessary to know, or be able to find, whether the option is a Boolean, numeric, or text switch. The proper category must be set in the Switch Type column. *Boolean switches* are those editor items that are turned either on or off, such as autoload and beep. *Numeric switches* are switch items followed with a numeric value for their parameter, such as cursormode, rmargin, and tabdisp. *Text switches* are switch items that use a text string

```
┌──────────────────── Editor Settings ─────────────────────┐
│ Switch: [·················································]│
│                                                           │
│ ┌──────── Switch Owner: ────────┐  ┌─ Switch Type ─┐      │
│ │[PWB····························]│↓ │ (•) Boolean   │      │
│ └────────────────────────────────┘  │ ( ) Numeric   │      │
│ Switch List:                        │ ( ) Text      │      │
│ ┌───────────────────────────────┐   └───────────────┘     │
│ │ askexit:no                   ↑│                          │
│ │ askrtn:yes                   █│                          │
│ │ autoload:yes                  │                          │
│ │ autosave:no                   │                          │
│ │ beep:yes                      │                          │
│ │ case:no                      ↓│                          │
│ └───────────────────────────────┘                         │
│                                                           │
│     <Set Switch>      <Save...>       <Switch Help>       │
│                                                           │
│                        <  OK  >  <Cancel>  < Help >       │
└───────────────────────────────────────────────────────────┘
```

Figure 2-26. *The Editor Settings window selected from the PWB Options category*

or number to describe their parameter. Text switches include backup, fastfunc, tabstops and readonly.

The switches that are displayed in each category belong to the owner, displayed in the Switch Owner window. The switch owner can be [PWB] or [PWB-modifier]. Switches created and saved under a [PWB-modifier] affect the editor only when you are editing files with the specified extension. For example, the alterations that are made in the following section can be made specific to C and C++ programs by placing the changes under a category named [PWB-.C PWB-.CPP].

To change the PWB tab stops and tab character, select the Options category from the main menu, and then choose the Editor Settings item. The screen you see in Figure 2-27 will appear on your monitor.

The switch owner should display [PWB] as the default that you'll use for both changes. Set the switch type to Numeric by positioning and clicking the mouse or by using the TAB and arrow keyboard keys. Next, scroll down the Switch List until you find tabdisp. That term should also be displayed on the Switch line of the window, along with the current tab display value. The current value is for a blank character. Move the cursor to that line and type a new character value that will be displayed when a cursor is present. For this example, the ASCII character corresponding to a decimal 126 was chosen from Appendix A. You can save this setting for the current session by choosing the Set Switch button or permanently by also selecting the Save button. Now, any time a tab character is present in the text, you'll know by the appearance of the special character.

In order to prevent any tab characters from being entered from the keyboard, the tabstops switch will be set to zero. From the Editor Settings window, set the switch type to Text. Now, scroll the Switch List until you find the Tabstops category. This term should also be displayed on the Switch line of the window. Move the cursor to the Switch line and type **0** for the value. This will disable the TAB key in future programs. You can save this setting for the current session by choosing the Set Switch

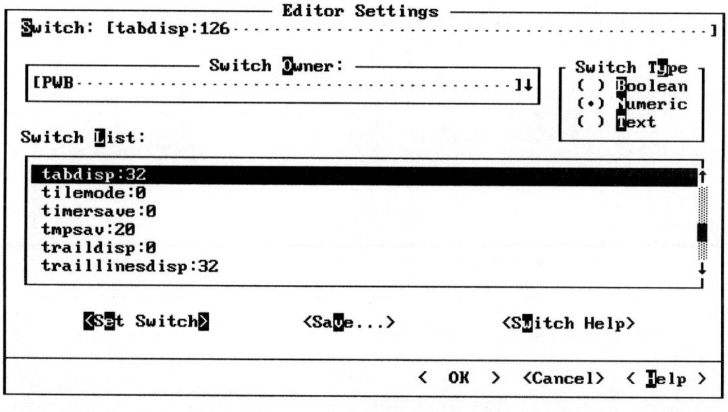

Figure 2-27.   *The Editor Settings window selected from the main menu Options category*

button or permanently by also selecting the Save button. The TAB key will not function in future editing sessions.

The Colors Menu Item

You can assign custom color values to the PWB editor by selecting the main menu Options category and the Colors item. Figure 2-28 shows the Colors window. The PWB items that can be changed, in terms of foreground and background color, are listed in the Color column of this window. These items include background, menu, text and border, and so on. For VGA color monitors, Foreground and Background options include the colors Black, Blue, Green, Cyan, and so on.

Simply select the items you wish to change, and then choose a foreground and background color. An example string shows your current selection. You can save your current color change or group of color changes for the current session by choosing the Set Color Switch button or permanently by also selecting the Save button.

The TOOLS.INI File

Changes to the PWB editor switches are saved in the TOOLS.INI file located by default in the C:\C700\INIT subdirectory. A copy of this file can be created from a template file, TOOLS.C70, supplied with the compiler and also located in the same subdirectory.

Editing the TOOLS.INI file from an editor is another way to make changes to various PWB categories. For example, following is a partial listing of this file showing new values for tabdisp and tabstops that were entered and saved from an editor, rather than changed from within the PWB environment.

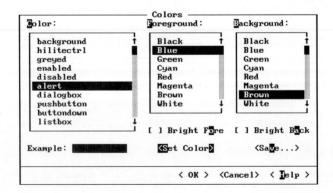

Figure 2-28.   *Setting custom colors in the PWB from the Colors item in the main menu Options category*

```
[pwb pwb-main]

tabdisp: 126
tabstops: 0


;
; To use any of these examples, remove the leading semicolon
; and include the example in your TOOLS.INI file.
;
; Example Programmer's WorkBench macros
;
; undotoggle
; Toggling undo. Repeatedly executing this macro undoes and
;redoes the most recent editing change.
;
;     undotoggle:=meta undo +> undo
;     undotoggle:ctrl+bksp
;
```

.
.
.
.

Editing the TOOLS.INI file directly gives you the ability to quickly change items you are familiar with. Working from within the PWB provides the added advantage of the on-line help facilities for various PWB settings and options.

Altering the Build Process

For most cases, the default setting for building simple programs is sufficient. In Chapters 3 and 4 you will learn how to control various compile and link optimizations for your finished program. You'll also learn how to use the CodeView debugger, Profiler, and Browser tools mentioned in this chapter.

Chapter *3*

Getting Started with
the C/C++ Compiler

This chapter is designed to help you use your Microsoft C/C++ compiler more efficiently. As you learned in the previous chapter, it is possible to compile (and link) programs from within the integrated environment of the Programmer's WorkBench (PWB) or from the DOS command line. This chapter examines default compile operations and also takes a look at additional compiler features. Simple applications illustrate these new concepts for the PWB and the DOS command-line environment.

You will learn how to set compiler switches in order to select special compiler options. Additional topics include definition files (.DEF), project files (.MAK), command-line make files, the resource compiler, P-code generation, and selection of various memory models.

Simple Compiles with Default Compiler Options

You will be able to compile the majority of your programs from either the integrated PWB or DOS command-line environment, using the default compiler options. The various tables of compiler switches contained throughout this chapter list default compiler options in boldface type.

In order to demonstrate compile options, a sample program is needed. Enter the following program, using the PWB, and save it as 03TRIG.CPP:

```
//
//  03TRIG.CPP
//  A C++ program that prints a table of
//  trigonometric values to the screen.
//  Copyright (c) William H. Murray and Chris H. Pappas, 1992
//

#include <iostream.h>
#include <iomanip.h>
#include <math.h>

main()
{
  double ang,rad,s,c,t;

  cout << "Angle" << "\t" << "Sine" << "\t\t"
       << "Cosine" << "\t\t" << "Tangent" << "\n";
  ang=10.0;
  for (int i=0;i<8;i++) {
    rad=3.14159*ang/180.0;
    s=sin(rad); c=cos(rad); t=tan(rad);
    cout << setiosflags(ios::left)
         << setw(8) << ang   //print angle
         << setw(16) << s    //print sine
         << setw(16) << c    //print cosine
         << setw(16) << t    //print tangent
         << "\n";
    ang+=10.0;
  }
  return(0);
}
```

The various C++ functions and streams used in this program are topics in future chapters. Briefly, however, the program will print a table of sine, cosine, and tangent values from 10 to 80 degrees in 10-degree increments. If you experiment with this program, remember that the tangent value approaches infinity at 90 degrees.

Compiling from the PWB

Enter the PWB and load the program 03TRIG.CPP. Before compiling this program, investigate the default compiler options by clicking on the main menu Options category.

If you have changed the default switches in the past, the PWB will retain the change from session to session. Therefore, your defaults might not match those in the following discussion.

From the main menu Options category, pick the Build Options item. This item presents a dialog box with two choices: Use Debug Options and Use Release Options. The Debug option box should be checked as the default. The Debug option includes information in your executable code that can be used by CodeView to help locate logical errors. It also increases the size of your executable file. This switch is useful while you are developing applications. The Release option is usually selected for the final version of a program in order to provide the smallest possible program size.

Next, from the main menu Options category, pick the Language Options item. The initial dialog box asks you to select either the C Compiler option or the C++ Compiler option. For the current example, chose the C++ Compiler option. Another dialog box is opened, similar to the one in Figure 3-1, presenting additional compiler switches.

Note that the default selections include a small memory model targeted for an 8086 processor. Additionally, the C calling convention is used, and the error warning level is set to 1 during compilation. The meanings of these settings are explained later in this chapter. It is also possible to set additional global and debug options from this dialog box.

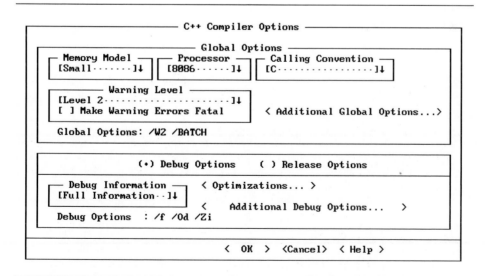

Figure 3-1.   Default C++ compiler options viewed from within the PWB

Return to the main menu and select the Project category. From this category, you achieve a simple compile and link operation by selecting the Build menu item.

If the compile operation isn't successful, you can view the results in the Build Results window. Unsuccessful compilations require that you return to the PWB editor and fix the stated syntax errors.

If the compile operation is successful, a dialog box will allow you to debug the application, in order to eliminate logical errors, or run the application from within the PWB. The CodeView debugger is discussed in Chapter 4. For this program, select the Execute option. You should have the following information printed to your screen:

Angle	Sine	Cosine	Tangent
10	0.173648	0.984808	0.176327
20	0.34202	0.939693	0.36397
30	0.5	0.866026	0.57735
40	0.642787	0.766045	0.839099
50	0.766044	0.642788	1.19175
60	0.866025	0.500001	1.73205
70	0.939692	0.342021	2.74747
80	0.984808	0.173649	5.67124

Working from within the PWB offers an almost seamless environment for developing, compiling, running, and debugging C and C++ programs.

Compiling from the DOS Command Line

Some program developers prefer to work from the DOS command line rather than from the PWB integrated environment. This might be because they prefer to use a different program editor or have clear visible control over compiler options. The Microsoft C/C++ compiler offers compilation from the DOS command line, with a full range of command-line arguments.

To compile the previous program from the DOS command line, simply type

```
CL  03TRIG.CPP
```

With no additional interaction, the C/C++ compiler will generate a release version of the program, using default compiler options.

It is also possible to create a debug version of the same program by using a command-line switch. To place CodeView information in the executable file, type

```
CL -Zi 03TRIG.CPP
```

Again, the program will be built with default options, but with the addition of CodeView debugger information.

Naturally, the screen output from both command-line versions is identical to the listing in the previous section. Just for your own information, you might want to compare the sizes of the release and debug executable files. The size difference is the additional overhead imposed by the debug information.

Placing CodeView information in a program is just one of many compiler options that can be used from either the PWB or the DOS command line. In the next section, you learn about a wide range of compiler options that can be used in place of the standard default values.

Setting Compiler and Linker Switches

As you develop your programming expertise, skills, and needs, additional compiler options will be useful to you. For example, it is possible to use a compiler option to reduce program size to a minimum. Another compiler option allows the generation of the fastest executable code. Windows applications are another type of C or C++ program that requires special compiler options.

Compiler Switches

There are several categories for compiler options provided by Microsoft. Each category, in turn, provides several options. The next sections examine each category of compiler options and discuss frequently used options from that category.

Code-generation Compiler Options

Code-generation options can be set with the command-line switches shown in Table 3-1 or from within the PWB environment.

You use code-generation options to target a particular set of microprocessor instructions or the programming environment for the application.

In Table 3-1, the use of the /G2 switch, for example, would allow the compiler to generate code that might include 80286 instructions. The /G0 option is the default since most applications are designed for the widest possible range of computers.

The 03TRIG.CPP program could be compiled with 80286 instructions by typing either -G2 or /G2:

```
CL -G2 03TRIG.CPP
```

Multiple options are included on the same line, as shown next:

```
CL -G2 -Zi 03Trig.CPP
```

Switch	Function
/G0	**8086 instructions (default)**
/G1	186 instructions included
/G2	286 instructions included
/GA	Entry/exit code for protected-mode Win
/Gc	Pascal calling convention style
/GD	Entry/exit code for protected-mode Win
/Gd	C calling convention style
/Ge	Stack-check calls used
/GE<x>	Entry/exit code for customize Win
/Gn	Deletes p-code native entry points
/Gp<num>	Gives p-code entry tables
/Gq	Backward compatibility with C v. 6
/Gr	_fastcall calling convention style
/Gs	Deletes stack-check calls
/Gt[num]	Sets data size threshold
/GW	Entry/exit code for real-mode Windows
/Gw	Entry/exit code for real-mode Windows
/Gx	Data is near, assumption
/Gy	Functions separated for linker
/Zr	Null pointer check (/f only)

Table 3-1.   *Code Generation Compiler Switches*

Here, debug information is also being included with the executable file. If your target hardware, as is the case for Windows applications, will always be an 80286 or higher microprocessor, choose the /G2 option.

You can also use these options from the PWB by selecting the main menu Options category and selecting the Language Options item. To change the target microprocessor language, select the C++ Compiler option, and then choose Processor in the dialog box.

Output File Compiler Options

Another group of compiler options allows the name of a file to be specified as part of a command-line switch. The following table lists all of the output file switches:

Switch	Function
/Fa[file]	Assembly listing filename
/Fc[file]	Source/object listing filename
/Fe<file>	Executable filename
/Fl[file]	Object listing filename
/Fm[file]	Map filename
/Fo<file>	Object filename
/Fp<file>	.PCH filename
/FR[file]	Extended .SBR filename
/Fr[file]	.SBR filename
/Fs[file]	Source listing filename

For example, you may wish to compile a program where the executable filename differs from the source name. This would be practical where you might want to compile three different executable versions of the same program, but with different optimization options.

To compile the program 03TRIG.CPP into three different executable files, type

```
CL /FeTEST1.EXE 03TRIG.CPP
CL /Zi /FeTEST2.EXE 03TRIG.CPP
CL /Ot /FeTEST3.EXE 03TRIG.CPP
```

Options like those in the previous example are very easy to implement from the DOS command line. This makes testing other options easy, too.

Preprocessor Compiler Options

The use of preprocessing compiler options allows certain preprocessor features to be implemented. The following table lists the command-line compiler switches that implement these options:

Switch	Function
/C	Comments not stripped
/D<name>[=l#text]	Macro definition
/E	Preprocesses to **stdout**
/EP	Similar to /E but no #line
/I<directory>	**#include** path added
/P	Preprocesses to file
/U<name>	Deletes predefined macro
/u	Deletes all defined macros
/X	Disregards "standard places"

The /C switch will preserve comments during preprocessing, if used in conjunction with the /E, /P, or /EP switch. For example:

CL /P /C 03TRIG.CPP

Here, a listing file named 03TRIG.I will be created that contains the original source code from 03TRIG.CPP, including comments and expanded or replaced preprocessor directives.

Language Compiler Options

Additional features can be added to the executable file with the language options shown in the following table:

Switch	Function
/Za	Disables extensions (implies /Op)
/Zd	Adds line number information
/Ze	**Enables extensions (default)**
/Zg	Generates function prototypes
/Zi	CodeView debugging preparation
/Zl	Delete default library name in .OBJ
/Zp[n]	Packs structures on n-byte boundary
/Zs	Checks only syntax

The two options that are used most frequently from this group are the /Ze and /Zi switches. The /Ze switch allows the use of Microsoft language extensions in a program and is the default. The /Zi switch builds the debug executable file.

Floating-point Compiler Options

Several different floating-point options can be included with this group of switches. The following table shows the various options:

Switch	Function
/FPa	Uses altmath
/FPc	Uses emulator
/FPc87	Uses 8087 library
/FPi	**Uses inline with emulator (default)**
/FPi87	Uses inline with 8087

The default option, produced with the /FPi switch, provides inline emulation of the coprocessor (8087 through 80487) if one is not present. If a coprocessor is present, it will be chosen over emulation.

If the /FPi87 switch is used, an executable file will be produced that will require a coprocessor for floating-point math in the computer being used.

Source Listing Compiler Options

The source listing group allows customized formatting of the source code when placed in a listing file. The following table shows the various source listing options:

Switch	Function
/Sl<columns>	Line width set
/Sp<lines>	Page length set
/Ss<string>	Subtitle string set
/St<string>	Title string set

These options are primarily used for generating listing files. Titles, subtitles, line widths, and line lengths are set with these switches.

Miscellaneous Compiler Options

A number of special options fall into the miscellaneous options category. These options and the associated switches are listed in Table 3-2.

The /c switch directs the compiler to compile to an .OBJ file but not link to the final .EXE file. This option is used extensively in compiling Windows applications where a host of files are combined and a wide variety of libraries are used.

The /f switch is useful during the program development process. This switch turns off all optimization defaults for the generated program code. This increases the speed of compiling, but the cost is larger and slower programs.

The /Tc and /Tp switches allow you to identify a file as a C or C++ file without the file extension being present.

Macro Assembler Compiler Options

The small group of macro assembler options, shown in the following table, allows assembly language code to be generated during a compile operation:

Switch	Function
/MA<MASM switch>	Passes switch to MASM
/Ta<file>	Assembles file without the .ASM extension

Switch	Function
/batch	Batch mode compilation
/Bm<num>	Sets compiler's available memory
/c	Compiles without automatically linking
/f	Chooses fast compiler
/f-	Chooses optimizing compiler
/H<num>	Sets external name length
/J	Default character type is **unsigned**
/Mq	QuickWin compile
/ND<name>	Name of data segment
/NM<name>	Name of code segment
/nologo	Copyright message suppressed
/NQ<name>	P-code temp segments combined
/NT<name>	Name of code segment
/NV<name>	Name of far v-table segment
/Tc<file>	Compiles without .C extension
/Tp<file>	Compiles without .CPP extension
/V<string>	Sets version string
/W<num>	Sets warning level (0..4,X)
/Yc	Produces a .PCH file
/Yd	Places debug information in .PCH file
/Yu	Accesses .PCH file
/Zn	Toggles SBRPACK off for .SBR files

Table 3-2.   *Miscellaneous Compiler Switches*

Files with a standard .ASM extension will invoke MASM. All MASM options are supported by the compiler.

Linking Compiler Options

The linker options are passed to the Microsoft linker during the compile and link process. The following table lists the available options:

Switch	Function
/F <hex_num>	Specifies stack size (hexadecimal bytes)
/Ld	Uses dynamic link library
/link [lib]	Specifies library name to linker
/Ln	CRT.LIB not linked
/Lr	Appends "r" to default .OBJ library
/Lw	Uses statically linked library

These are rather specialized switches and are not used too frequently. It's interesting that Microsoft still lists the /Lr switch without its /Lp counterpart. These switches were only needed when both DOS and OS/2 applications were being built by the compiler.

Optimization Compiler Options

Optimization needs vary from program to program. The Microsoft C/C++ compiler provides over 20 optimization options, many of which can be grouped together. Table 3-3 lists compiler optimization switches.

Programs can be compiled for the smallest executable file (.EXE) size by using a combination of several options. For smallest code size, Microsoft recommends the /Oaes (smallest size) and /Gs (no stack checking—see Table 3-1) options. For the sample program, type

```
CL /Oaes /Gs 03TRIG.CPP
```

Programs can be optimized for the fastest executable code with a different combination of switches. Here, Microsoft recommends the /Oax (maximum optimization) and /Ob2 (automatic inlining) options. For the same application, type

```
CL /Oax /Ob2 03TRIG.CPP
```

Usually, optimizations are employed only for release versions of a program.

Memory Model Compiler Options

The final group of compiler options selects the memory model for the compiled program. The following table lists the optional memory model switches:

Switch	Function
/A\<string>	Custom memory model
/AC	Compact memory model
/AH	Huge memory model
/AL	Large memory model
/AM	Medium memory model
/AS	**Small memory model (default)**
/AT	Tiny memory model, produce .COM files

The tiny memory model (/AT) uses one segment for both code and data. .COM files can be produced with this model. The small memory model (/AS) is the default

Switch	Function
/O	Allows optimization (similar to /Ot)
/Oa	Aliasing not assumed
/Ob\<n>	Allows inline expansion
/Oc	Optimizes local common subexpression
/Od	**Disables optimization (default)**
/Oe	Allows registers allocation
/Of[-]	Toggles p-code quoting
/Og	Optimizes global common subexpression
/Oi	Allows intrinsic functions
/Ol	Allows loop optimizations
/On	"unsafe" optimizations not allowed
/Oo[-]	Toggles optimization for post-code generation
/Op	Improves floating-point consistency
/Oq	Allows maximum p-code optimization
/Or	Creates common exit code for CodeView
/Os	Space optimization
/Ot	Speed optimization
/Ov[-]	Toggles p-code frame sorting
/Ow	Assumes cross-function aliasing
/Ox	Maximum optimizations, equivalent to /Ob1cegilnot /Gs
/Oz	"unsafe" optimizations allowed

Table 3-3. *Compiler Optimization Switches*

model size, and it allows one data segment and one code segment. The medium memory model (/AM) allows one data segment and one code segment for each program module. The compact memory model allows multiple data segments but just one code segment. The large code model allows multiple data segments and one code segment per program module. Data items must be smaller than 64K each. The huge memory model is similar to the large memory model, with the exception that data items can be larger than 64K. For applications with large arrays, choose the huge memory model.

Linker Options

The following group of linker options is available when performing separate link operations with .OBJ files. The linker, unlike the compiler, does not accept a dash (-) before the switch value. All linker switches must be preceded with a slash (/).

The syntax for using the linker from the command line is

Link <switches>   *object filename, run filename,*
                   listfile name, libraries,
                   definition filename

Table 3-4 lists the most frequently used linker switches.

You can set these same options within the PWB by selecting the main menu Options category and picking the Link Options item.

The linker is frequently employed when special circumstances warrant. For example, during the building of a Windows application, the following switches are frequently used:

    LINK /NOD /F /PACKC...

Here, the linker is instructed not to use default libraries, to optimize far calls within the same segment, and to pack the code portion of the application.

Controlling Compile Operations with Make Files

As programs and applications grow in size, so does their development time. Large projects usually require many hours of coding, compiling, and debugging. With the large array of compiler and linker options, it's almost natural to anticipate an automatic way of updating executable files.

A crude attempt at this process could be a simple DOS batch file, similar to the one shown in the next listing:

```
/Oax /Ob2 %1
```

Switch	Function
/?	Summary of link options
/A:size	Aligns segments at specified boundary
/B	Suppresses prompt for libraries or object files
/CO	CodeView symbolic data and line numbers
/CPARM:n	Maximum number of 16-byte paragraphs for a program
/DOSS	Forces segment ordering
/DS	Loads data at high end of data segment
/DY	Creates program with overlays
/E	Pack code (null characters, and so on)
/F	Optimizes far calls in same segment
/HE	Calls QuickHelp utility
/HI	Places program as high as possible in memory
/INF	Displays linking information
/LI	Adds line numbers to .MAP file
/M	Adds a .MAP file
/NOD	No default library search
/NOE	No extended dictionaries used
/NOF	No far call translation
/NOG	Ignores group associations
/NOI	Preserves case
/NOL	Deletes the copyright message for linker
/NON	Arranges segments same as /DOSSEG
/NOP	No code segment packing
/NOPACKF	No function packing
/PACKC	Code packing
/PACKD	Data segment packing
/PACKF	Function packing
/PAU	Inserts a pause before .EXE generation
/PM:type	Type of Windows application
/Q	Builds a quick library
/SE:num	Maximum number of program segments
/ST:num	Sets stack size (default=2048)
/T	Tiny option makes .COM file
/W	A fixup for segment executable files

Table 3-4.   *Frequently Used Linker Switches*

This file could be saved as QUICK.BAT and invoked from the DOS command line by typing

QUICK 03TRIG.CPP

While this simple batch file will save you from repeatedly remembering and typing the optimization options, it suffers a major drawback when applied to large programming projects. The drawback is that the entire compile and link operation is performed anew each time.

What is truly needed is a mechanism for taking an intelligent look at an entire project, deciding what must be updated based upon earlier editing, and then invoking only the required tools. A mechanism this intelligent would certainly cut down on overall compile and link time.

Fortunately, Microsoft has provided tools of this quality for both the integrated PWB programming environment and the DOS command-line compiler. The PWB uses a project utility to monitor and update the required pieces of code. Project files are given a .MAK extension. From the DOS command line, you can use a utility named NMAKE for basically the same purpose. The NMAKE utility uses a make file, usually specified without a file extension. The interaction between the PROJECT and NMAKE utilities can be studied in the *Microsoft C/C++ Environment and Tools* manual.

Both types of files can become very complicated in their construction, but both types work on the same premise for updating information. The PROJECT and NMAKE utilities monitor the dates and times of file compilations and links. If an attempt is made to compile and link an application at 8:00 P.M. but the application does not perform as expected, a new build operation can be attempted at a later time. For large projects, the disk may contain one or more source and object files along with a final executable file. Imagine that the following modules are combined in a project:

Source Files

ADDER.CPP	6:00 P.M.
SUBTR.CPP	6:30 P.M.
MUL.CPP	7:00 P.M.
DIV.CPP	7:30 P.M.

Object Files

ADDER.OBJ	8:00 P.M.
SUBTR.OBJ	8:00 P.M.
MUL.OBJ	8:00 P.M.
DIV.OBJ	8:00 P.M.

Executable File

COMPOSIT.EXE   8:01 P.M.

When you return to the PWB editor to fix, say, the MUL.CPP file, the editor will save the new version with a later date and time. This, for example, might occur at 8:10 P.M.

Now, when either the PROJECT or NMAKE utility is invoked, it will be noticed that the MUL.CPP file has a later date than the MUL.OBJ file. At this point, since this is the only exception, the compiler recompiles just the MUL.CPP file into a new .OBJ file.

Next, the PROJECT or NMAKE utility discovers an .OBJ file with a later date than the final executable file. This means all of the files are linked again to produce a new executable file. The new executable file will have the latest date and time of any files in the group.

PWB Project Files

The PWB provides an efficient way to manage the compilation of complex programs from within the integrated environment. The PWB retains information on your programming project in a project make file and a status file.

You develop project files for an application by selecting the main menu item Project Category. Choose the New item to create a new project file. Figure 3-2 shows the dialog box for selecting project file options.

The project name for the example program is 03TRIG. Next, select the Set Project Template... item from the template. This invokes another dialog box, shown in Figure 3-3.

From this dialog box, select the C++ and DOS EXE options. Clicking the OK button will return you to the New Project dialog box. Clicking the OK button in this dialog box will then return you to the Edit Project dialog box, shown in Figure 3-4.

```
────────────────────── New Project ──────────────────────
Project Name: [C:\C700\03TRIG· · · · · · · · · · · · · · · · · · · · · · · · · · · · ]

Current Runtime Support:   C++
Current Project Template:  DOS EXE

<Set Project Template...>

                              <  OK  >  <Cancel>  < Help >
```

Figure 3-2.   *Selecting project file options*

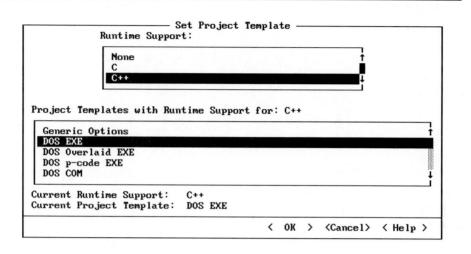

Figure 3-3.   *Setting the run-time and template support for a project*

The Edit Project dialog box allows you to add, delete, and clear items that are part of a programming project. For this simple example, only 03TRIG.CPP is added to the project. Other items could include additional source code modules (.CPP), object files (.OBJ), library files (.LIB), module definition files (.DEF), and resource compiler files (.RC).

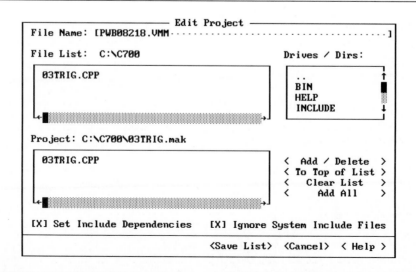

Figure 3-4.   *The Edit Project dialog box*

The PWB generates a project file with an .MAK file extension containing the current set of PWB build options. For example, a project make file for the 03TRIG.CPP example would most likely be named 03TRIG.MAK. You can examine the contents of the generated project file by loading 03TRIG.MAK into the PWB editor. Here is an example of a DOS project file created for the 03TRIG.CPP application:

```
ORIGIN = PWB
ORIGIN_VER = 2.0
PROJ = 03trig
PROJFILE = 03trig.mak
DEBUG = 1

BSCMAKE  = bscmake
SBRPACK  = sbrpack
NMAKEBSC1 = set
NMAKEBSC2 = nmake
CC  = cl
CFLAGS_G  = /W2 /BATCH
CFLAGS_D  = /f /Zi /Od
CFLAGS_R  = /f- /Ot /Oi /Ol /Oe /Og /Gs
CXX  = cl
CXXFLAGS_G  = /W2 /BATCH
CXXFLAGS_D  = /f /Zi /Od
CXXFLAGS_R  = /f- /Ot /Oi /Ol /Oe /Og /Gs
MAPFILE_D  = NUL
MAPFILE_R  = NUL
LFLAGS_G  = /NOI /BATCH /ONERROR:NOEXE
LFLAGS_D  = /CO /FAR /PACKC
LFLAGS_R  = /EXE /FAR /PACKC
LINKER  = link
ILINK  = ilink
LRF  = echo > NUL
ILFLAGS  = /a /e

FILES  = 03TRIG.CPP
OBJS  = 03TRIG.obj
SBRS  = 03TRIG.sbr

all: $(PROJ).exe

.SUFFIXES:
.SUFFIXES:
.SUFFIXES: .obj .sbr .cpp
```

```
03TRIG.obj : 03TRIG.CPP
!IF $(DEBUG)
  $(CXX) /c $(CXXFLAGS_G) $(CXXFLAGS_D) /Fo03TRIG.obj 03TRIG.CPP
!ELSE
  $(CXX) /c $(CXXFLAGS_G) $(CXXFLAGS_R) /Fo03TRIG.obj 03TRIG.CPP
!ENDIF

03TRIG.sbr : 03TRIG.CPP
!IF $(DEBUG)
  $(CXX) /Zs $(CXXFLAGS_G) $(CXXFLAGS_D) /FR03TRIG.sbr 03TRIG.CPP
!ELSE
  $(CXX) /Zs $(CXXFLAGS_G) $(CXXFLAGS_R) /FR03TRIG.sbr 03TRIG.CPP
!ENDIF

$(PROJ).bsc : $(SBRS)
    $(BSCMAKE) @<<
$(BRFLAGS) $(SBRS)
<<

$(PROJ).exe : $(OBJS)
!IF $(DEBUG)
    $(LRF) @<<$(PROJ).lrf
$(RT_OBJS: = +^
) $(OBJS: = +^
)
$@
$(MAPFILE_D)
$(LIBS: = +^
) +
$(LLIBS_G: = +^
) +
$(LLIBS_D: = +^
)
$(DEF_FILE) $(LFLAGS_G) $(LFLAGS_D);
<<
!ELSE
    $(LRF) @<<$(PROJ).lrf
$(RT_OBJS: = +^
) $(OBJS: = +^
)
$@
$(MAPFILE_R)
$(LIBS: = +^
) +
```

```
$(LLIBS_G: = +^
) +
$(LLIBS_R: = +^
)
$(DEF_FILE) $(LFLAGS_G) $(LFLAGS_R);
<<
!ENDIF
    $(LINKER) @$(PROJ).lrf

.cpp.obj :
!IF $(DEBUG)
    $(CXX) /c $(CXXFLAGS_G) $(CXXFLAGS_D) /Fo$@ $<
!ELSE
    $(CXX) /c $(CXXFLAGS_G) $(CXXFLAGS_R) /Fo$@ $<
!ENDIF

.cpp.sbr :
!IF $(DEBUG)
    $(CXX) /Zs $(CXXFLAGS_G) $(CXXFLAGS_D) /FR$@ $<
!ELSE
    $(CXX) /Zs $(CXXFLAGS_G) $(CXXFLAGS_R) /FR$@ $<
!ENDIF

run: $(PROJ).exe
    $(PROJ).exe $(RUNFLAGS)

debug: $(PROJ).exe
    CV $(CVFLAGS) $(PROJ).exe $(RUNFLAGS)
```

The details of a how a project file works are beyond the scope of the current discussion, but if you are interested in the complete details, see the *Microsoft C/C++ Environment and Tools* manual.

The important point is that the PROJECT utility works automatically to maintain your programs, with the least amount of compile and link time.

DOS NMake Utility

You can also build projects from the DOS command line with the NMAKE utility. You invoke the NMAKE utility from the DOS command line by typing

NMAKE 03TRIG

The 03TRIG make file does not usually have an extension, in order to differentiate it from a project make file (.MAK). You write DOS command-line make files as ordinary text files. The following is an example of a simple DOS make file, named 03TRIG:

```
CPPFLAGS= /f /Zi /Od
LINKFLAGS= /CO /FAR /PACKC

all : 03TRIG.exe

03TRIG.exe : 03TRIG.obj
  link $(LINKFLAGS) 03TRIG,,,,;
```

As you can observe from the listing, it is possible to group switch options under a common label called a *macro*. Examine the previous compiler and link options to determine which are being requested in this make file.

The word "all" in the preceding listing is considered a pseudo-target for all build operations referring to 03TRIG.EXE.

The first of the final pair of lines in the listing starts with the target (03TRIG.exe) file followed by any dependent files (03TRIG.obj). The second line contains the commands required to convert the dependent files into the target files. In this case, a link operation is required. The link operation uses standard linker syntax with the exception of the linker switch macro. Macros are preceded with a $ symbol, with the name of the macro in parentheses ().

Even simple make files can become quite complicated as projects grow in size. Examine this example make file from Chapter 25. It is used to compile and link a Windows application named 25BAR:

```
CPPFLAGS= /AS /W3 /GA /GEs /G2
LINKFLAGS=/NOD
CPPFLAGS=$(CPPFLAGS) /Oselg /Gs
LINKFLAGS=$(LINKFLAGS) /FAR /PACKC
LIBS=safxcw libw slibcew

all : 25BAR.exe

25BAR.obj : 25BAR.h 25BARr.h

25BAR.res : 25BARr.h 25BAR.dlg

25BAR.exe : 25BAR.obj 25BAR.def 25BAR.res
  link $(LINKFLAGS) 25BAR,25BAR,NUL,$(LIBS),25BAR.def;
  rc /t 25BAR.res
```

This make file illustrates, in the first five lines of code, that it is possible to use macros within macros. The remainder of the make file is responsible for combining

header (.H), dialog (.DLG), definition (.DEF), and resource code (.RES) file information into a single executable file named 25BAR.EXE.

Usually, when you begin to develop programming projects, you will use a favorite
make file as a template for creating new make files. For example, with minor changes,
this make file could be used to build a similar application named 25PIE. Simply enter
an editor, such as PWB, and do a search/replace operation, substituting 25PIE for
each occurrence of 25BAR.

For additional information on creating custom make files for the NMAKE utility,
refer to the *Microsoft C/C++ Environment and Tools* manual.

Special Compiling Items

Complicated programming projects, such as dynamic link libraries, overlaid DOS
programs, and Windows applications, often require additional files and tools. The
module definition file is typically a component of Windows applications. Windows
programs often use another compiler, too, named the resource compiler. The
resource compiler is used to compile resource script files.

Module Definition Files (.DEF)

The *module definition file* is a text file that describes the name, attributes, exports,
imports, system requirements, and other characteristics of a project. It provides
additional information to the linker during the preparation of the program's executable file. Module definition files are often a component called by the PROJECT
and NMAKE utilities. For example, a typical Windows application will have a module
definition file like the sample code that follows:

```
;25BAR.DEF for Microsoft C/C++


NAME            25BAR
DESCRIPTION     'Microsoft Foundation Class Bar Chart Program'
EXETYPE         WINDOWS
STUB            'WINSTUB.EXE'
CODE            PRELOAD MOVABLE
DATA            PRELOAD MOVEABLE MULTIPLE
HEAPSIZE        4096
STACKSIZE       9216
```

As you can see, a module definition file can contain numerous statements describing an application. Table 3-5 contains a list of module statements.

For the Windows definition file, 25BAR.DEF, the NAME statement is simply the name of the application. The application description, DESCRIPTION, is a short statement placed between single or double quote marks. This is a Windows application, so the EXETYPE type is WINDOWS. Alternative EXETYPEs include DOS and UNKNOWN. The STUB used in this application is the WINSTUB.EXE supplied with the C/C++ compiler. This will print a message to the DOS screen, if the application is executed in DOS, warning the user that the program is a Windows application.

Statement	Description
APPLOADER	Replaces Windows loader with custom loader
CODE	Sets default attributes for code segments
DATA	Sets default attributes for data segments
DESCRIPTION	Embeds text in application or DLL (often used for copyright information)
EXETYPE	Target operating system
EXPORTS	Defines exported functions
FUNCTIONS	Gives function location and order
HEAPSIZE	Sets local heap size in bytes
IMPORTS	Defines imported functions
INCLUDE	Inserts a module statement file
LIBRARY	Name of the DLL library
NAME	Name of the application
OLD	Saves ordinals from a previous DLL
PROTMODE	Protected-mode Windows application
REALMODE	Real-mode Windows application
SEGMENTS	Sets attributes for given segments
STACKSIZE	Sets stack size in bytes
STUB	Adds a DOS executable file to start of application

Table 3-5.   Module Definition File Statements

CODE and DATA can share several parameters, including PRELOAD, MOVABLE, and MULTIPLE. PRELOAD loads a segment when the program starts. MOVABLE indicates that a segment can be moved in memory. MULTIPLE means that DGROUP is copied for each instance of the DLL or application. The size of the application's local heap is given by HEAPSIZE in bytes. In this instance, the heap size is set to 4K (4096 bytes). The stack size is specified for applications with STACKSIZE. Here, the stack size is set to 9K (9216 bytes).

More information on Windows-specific module definition files is given in Chapters 22 through 25. Additional information can also be found in the *Microsoft C/C++ Environment and Tools* manual.

Resource Compiler

The PROJECT and NMAKE utilities often make use of the Microsoft Windows resource compiler. The resource compiler, supplied with the C/C++ compiler package, is responsible for compiling Windows resources such as cursors, icons, bitmaps, and dialog boxes. You can invoke the resource compiler from the DOS command line with the following syntax:

RC [switches] *.RC input file* [.EXE output file]

Table 3-6 lists the resource compiler switch values.

The resource compiler is capable of compiling resource script files (text files with an .RC file extension) into compiled resource files (compiled files with an .RES extension) or into executable files (files with an .EXE extension). You will learn how to use the resource compiler in Chapters 23 and 25, when Windows resources such as icons, cursors, and dialog boxes are added to your applications.

Getting the Bugs Out

As you begin to develop various C and C++ programs, you will no doubt encounter bugs (errors) in your application code. Programming bugs can be divided into two major groups: syntax bugs and logical bugs. Programmers depend upon the error-checking capabilities of the C/C++ compiler to indicate where syntax errors occur

Switch	Description
-30	Marks as a 3.0 application or above (default)[*]
-31	Marks as a 3.1 application or above[*]
-d	Defines a symbol
-e	Creates a driver that uses EMS memory[*]
-fe	Renames an .EXE file
-fo	Renames an .RES file
-i	Adds a path for INCLUDE searches
-k	Segments in .DEF file order[*]
-l	Creates an application using LIM 3.2 EMS[*]
-m	Sets Instance flag (multiple)[*]
-p	Creates a private library[*]
-r	Creates a .RES file only (no .EXE)
-t	Creates protected mode application[*]
-v	Verbose (prints progress messages)
-x	Ignores INCLUDE environment variable
-z	Skips the check for RCINCLUDE statements

[*]Cannot be used when -r is used too.

Table 3-6.   *Resource Compiler Switch Values*

in their programs. The C/C++ compiler, discussed in this chapter, cannot locate logical errors. Logical errors must be detected and eliminated with a group of tools that are discussed in the next chapter. The most important tool in this group is Microsoft's CodeView debugger.

Chapter **4**

Getting Started with Advanced Tools: CodeView, Browser, and Profiler

Microsoft provides several advanced tools with the C/C++ compiler that aid in program development. This chapter examines the important elements of CodeView, Browser, and Profiler.

As you begin developing programs in C, C++, and Windows, you will find that the C/C++ compiler helps locate syntax errors during the compile and link operation. Syntax errors are often the easiest errors to fix because of the detailed help provided by the on-line help facilities. However, just because an application is syntax error free, that doesn't mean it will perform as expected. Perhaps you want to print the time to the screen or a file in a particular format but get another. Maybe the screen was supposed to be blue and the figure drawn in white, but what you got was a white screen and a white figure—kind of difficult to see. It may even be a performance issue—the program was supposed to finish calculations after 15 seconds, but 5 minutes later it is still running. All of these problems fall outside the scope of simple syntax errors. Advanced development tools are needed to correct these problems. Many programming errors fit into a group called logical programming errors. The CodeView debugger is designed to help you find and eliminate logical errors. Inefficient portions of programming code can be detected and corrected with the use of tools such as the Browser and Profiler.

This chapter will serve as an introduction to each tool. You will learn the purpose of each tool and the fundamentals of using the tool and see the tool used in a practical application. As you work through the programming examples in the remainder of the book, you will want to use these tools over and over. Each time you do, you will advance your skill level in using that tool.

CodeView

The CodeView debugger is one of the most powerful tools you have for tracking down logical errors. A CodeView version is provided for both DOS and Windows debugging. The DOS version is intended for debugging DOS version C and C++ applications, while the Windows version is designed only for C and C++ Windows applications. This book describes the Windows application development process in Chapters 22 through 25. All versions use a common user interface, with almost identical menus and menu options.

CodeView is designed to help you track down logical programming errors. Logical errors, as opposed to syntax errors, which are flagged by the compiler, are often the hardest to find. For example, a C or C++ program can be developed to print a simple message to the screen ten times, using a loop. However, when the application is executed, the message is printed only nine times. When this happens, there is something wrong in the design of the program, not in the program's syntax. The CodeView debugger can help you find the problem. Best of all, even though CodeView is an advanced programming tool, you do not have to be an expert to immediately start using the tool.

The CodeView debugger can help you trace through the C, C++, and Windows programs you will develop in this book. Program code can be executed one line at a time, in blocks, to preset break points, or run at full speed. During this execution, you can track variables, microprocessor registers and flags, and even data segments. Actually, CodeView, with its built-in language interpreter, can evaluate any Microsoft high-level language or assembly language program.

CodeView provides windows that allow you to view your source code in one window, commands and responses in another, registers and flags in a third, and the values of variables or expressions in a fourth. Program locations can be accessed through addresses, symbols, or line number references. Debugging can also proceed at the source code level or machine code level.

You can enter CodeView commands from the keyboard or with a mouse. Once you've mastered a group of CodeView commands, you will probably use a combination of both keyboard and mouse entry. The first CodeView example is a simple DOS program. Two additional programs are examined in later sections, one a DOS application and the other a Windows application.

A Simple DOS Example for CodeView

In order for CodeView to be able to reference source code symbols and statements, you must compile and link your program with the correct options. These options direct the compiler and linker to produce an executable file containing line number information and a symbol table, in addition to the executable code. This CodeView information will increase the size of the executable file.

Enter the following DOS program code from within the PWB, and save it with the name 04COUNT.CPP:

```
//
//   04COUNT.CPP
//   A C++ program used to demonstrate several features
//   of the Microsoft CodeView debugger.
//   Copyright (c) William H. Murray and Chris H. Pappas, 1992
//

#include <iostream.h>

main()
{
  cout << "This is the start of a loop\n";
  for (int i=0;i<25;i++) {
    cout << i << "\n";
  }
  cout << "This is the end of a loop\n";
  return(0);
}
```

This program will be compiled with the required CodeView information in the next section.

Compiling and Linking

Compiling and linking can proceed from the DOS command line or from within the PWB integrated environment.

When compiling programs from the DOS command line, use the /Zi compiler option to include CodeView information in the executable file. For example, for the C++ program named 04COUNT, type

    CL /Zi 04COUNT

This line instructs the compiler to include line numbers and symbolic information in the object file. Chapter 3 contains a list of additional C and C++ compiler switches that you might wish to review at this time.

Programs built with the /Zi option will still execute under DOS, like any other executable file, but they are larger because of the extra symbolic information in them.

For example, the program 04COUNT.CPP compiles to a size of 34,460 bytes with the CodeView option selected and 11,867 bytes when it is turned off. Usually, once a program has been thoroughly debugged, a final version is prepared without the CodeView information included. This gives you a release version of your code that occupies the least amount of disk space.

When compiling programs from within the PWB integrated environment, select the main menu Options category and choose the Build Options item. A dialog box will request whether you desire to build a debug or release executable file. To include CodeView information, select the debug option. When your program development is done, you can recompile the program by selecting the release option and produce a smaller executable file.

Starting CodeView

The DOS version of CodeView can be started from the DOS command line or from within Windows.

If you are working from within Windows, select the CodeView icon for DOS from within the C/C++ Windows group. If you wish to start CodeView from the DOS command line, the syntax is simply

CV [*option(s)*] *executable file* [*argument(s)*]

For the application 04COUNT, type

CV 04COUNT

A very useful feature of CodeView for DOS is the /43 and /50 switches, which allow you to view 43 or 50 lines of code per screen, on EGA and VGA monitors. To use these switches, type

CV /43 04COUNT

or

CV /50 04COUNT

The only problem with 43- and 50-line displays is the small character size. (How good are your eyes?)

Table 4-1 shows the CodeView switches you might wish to employ when using the debugger.

Switch	Purpose
@ <response file>	Loads a file containing one or more CodeView options
/B	Starts in black-and-white mode
/C <commands>	Executes commands on startup
/F	Starts with screen flipping (exchanges screen by flipping video pages)
/I [0|1]	Forces handling of nonmaskable interrupts and 8259 interrupt trapping
/L <dll>	Loads DLL or application symbols
/M	Disables the mouse
/N [0|1]	Traps nonmaskable interrupts
/S	Starts with screen swapping (exchanges screen by changing buffers)
/TSF	Reads or ignores State File
/25	Starts in 25-line mode (default)
/43	Starts in 43-line mode
/50	Starts in 50-line mode
/2	Enables use with two monitors
/8	8514 and VGA displays

Table 4-1.   *Optional Command-line CodeView Switches*

The CodeView Display Screen

When the CodeView screen is initially displayed with 04COUNT information, it will appear somewhat like the one in Figure 4-1. CodeView remembers your setup from one debugging session to another, so if the screen is rearranged or if other windows have been opened or closed, the physical appearance may differ from this figure.

The first row of the display screen contains a menu bar that shows the titles of menus that you can activate with the mouse or the keyboard. You can select any of the menu bar commands by pressing the ALT key followed by the letter of the menu command desired. For example, ALT-E would pop up the Edit menu.

CodeView permits you to view various windows containing debugging information. Some of these windows will be present when you start CodeView; others can be opened or closed during the session.

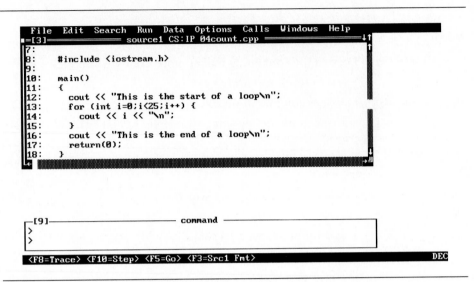

Figure 4-1.   *A typical CodeView screen with two initial windows opened*

The most important window, identified as window [3], is called the Source1 window. This window contains the source code for the program being debugged. When tracing C and C++ code in this window, CodeView will automatically set the cursor on the next instruction to be executed. This line will appear in a different color on color displays. Lines with break points are displayed in high-intensity text. (See the section "Break Points" later in this chapter.)

Your display will also have a flashing cursor indicating the location of the cursor and optionally a small highlighted box representing the mouse cursor. When you use a mouse, the vertical scroll bars on the right side of the screen have an up and a down arrow you can use to scroll through the display.

You can open a Register window to display the contents of the microprocessor registers. For 80386 or newer processors, a 32-bit register set is optional. This window is identified as window [7], and you open it with the ALT-7 key combination. The Register window contains a view of each microprocessor register and the associated flags in the lower portion of the window.

The Command window, window [9], is another important window. From this window, you can enter various commands and arguments at the > prompt.

The Watch window, window [2], allows you to observe the contents of program variables during program execution. Here you can actually study what is being put into or taken out of variables as you step through your code.

Frequently Used CodeView Commands

Getting the source information into CodeView is just the first step in a successful debugging session. Now that you know how to load a program into CodeView, it is time to look at some simple CodeView commands.

Working with the Program Code   If you have loaded the 04COUNT example, you should see a screen similar to the one in Figure 4-1. If you need to open or close additional windows, do so at this time.

Notice that the cursor is blinking next to line 11 in the Source1 window. This indicates, along with the color of the bar, that line 11 is the next program instruction to be executed during a trace. A status bar at the bottom of the screen allows you to select various format and step commands. For example, the F8 key will execute a Trace command. A trace executes program code a single line at a time, stepping over macros and so on. The F10 key permits a single-line step through program code, always executing one line of code at a time. The F5 key executes your program at full speed. If a break point has been set, it will execute to the break point. This allows fast execution through loops and so on. The F3 key allows you to change screen format options. For example, your can view your source as source code or as machine code by pressing this key.

Executing a single trace operation is as easy as pressing F8 or, if you are using a mouse, moving the mouse cursor onto the F8 Trace item in the status bar and clicking the left mouse button once.

Register Display   You activate the Register display window by pressing the ALT-7 key combination. For programs using 32-bit registers, CodeView can be modified to display these extended registers. Select the main menu Option category, and then select the 32-Bit Registers item. If you have the Register window open, you will see the register display change from the 16-bit AX. . .IP to the 32-bit EAX. . .EDI register set.

Flags   Microprocessor flags are displayed whenever the Register window is opened. Flags provide information on microprocessor information, such as *carry, borrow, overflow,* and *zero.* Figure 4-2 shows the Register window with register and flag information.

The following table provides additional details for interpreting flag information:

Flag	Flag Set Symbol	Flag Clear Symbol
overflow	OV	NV
direction	DN	UP
interrupt	EI	DI
sign	NG	PL
zero	ZR	NZ

Flag	Flag Set Symbol	Flag Clear Symbol
auxiliary carry	AC	NA
parity	PE	PO
carry	CY	NC

Examine Figure 4-2 and note that the *overflow* (NV), *direction* (UP), *sign* (PL), *zero* (NZ), *auxiliary carry* (NA), *parity* (PO), and *carry* (NC) flags are initially cleared. Only the *interrupt* flag (EI) is set.

Break Points   Often, when debugging a program, there are portions of the source code that you do not need to see traced. This could be code you have already debugged. There may also be times when you want to concentrate on a single line of code, or several lines together, as in the case of a loop structure.

Break points were designed specifically to manage these conditions. A break point tells CodeView to execute all lines of code up to but not including the break point. Break point lines are shown highlighted.

You can set a break point in one of two ways. You can set a break point with the mouse by positioning the mouse cursor on the line to be used as a break point. Next, quickly click the left mouse button twice. The line will be shaded and the break point set. You can remove break points by repeating the preceding steps. You can also set a break point by selecting the main menu Data category and picking the Set Breakpoint item.

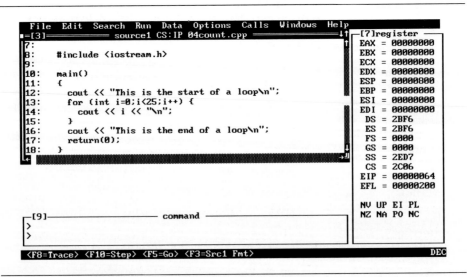

Figure 4-2.   *Viewing CodeView's Register window with microprocessor register and flag information*

The 04COUNT program contains a **for** loop between lines 13 and 15 of the program code:

```
for (int i=0;i<25;i++) {
  cout << i << "\n";
}
```

Instead of single-stepping through each execution of the loop (a time-consuming process), set a break point on line 16, as shown in Figure 4-3.

Once the break point is set, press the F5 key (Go) to execute your program at full speed up to the break point. The cursor will now be on line 16, and the Command window will show the break point.

Once the **for** loop is completed, you can execute the remainder of the program by tracing with the F8 key or executing at full speed with F5.

Restarting Programs   At times you will need to run a program two or three times, possibly to trace different flags, variables, or constants. You can restart a program by selecting the main menu Run category and picking the Restart menu item. When Restart is selected, the cursor moves back to the first line of executable code.

Watches   Watch windows allow you to track the values in various program variables during execution. If you have not already done so at this point, restart the 04COUNT program. Now select the main menu Data category and pick the Add Watch menu

```
 File  Edit  Search  Run  Data  Options  Calls  Windows  Help
=[3]============= source1 CS:IP 04count.cpp ==============
7:
8:    #include <iostream.h>
9:
10:   main()
11:   {
12:     cout << "This is the start of a loop\n";
13:     for (int i=0;i<25;i++) {
14:       cout << i << "\n";
15:     }
16:     cout << "This is the end of a loop\n";
17:     return(0);
18:   }



 [9]================ command ================
 >
 >

 <F8=Trace> <F10=Step> <F5=Go> <F3=Src1 Fmt>                DEC
```

Figure 4-3.   *A break point set in CodeView to allow full-speed program execution up to the break point*

item. The dialog box will request the expression to be watched. If the cursor was resting on an item in the program, that item will be placed in the Expression box. If this is not the item or variable you wish to place in the Watch window, simply type the one desired. For this example, enter the loop variable *i*. Your screen should be similar to the one shown in Figure 4-4.

The message you see concerning the variable in the Watch window occurs because the variable has not been defined at this point in the program's execution.

 If your Watch window is not visible, it may be behind another screen. Resize or close windows and arrange the Source1, Watch, and Command windows so that they are similar to the ones in Figure 4-4.

Now trace the line of code by pressing the F8 key. Once you enter the loop, the variable *i* will increment before your eyes, as F8 is pressed. The screen in Figure 4-5 shows a portion of this trace.

If you wanted an application to print the numbers from zero to 25 and it only printed the numbers from zero to 24, a Watch window would help you determine the cause of the logical error. In this program, the numbers are printed up to, but not including, 25. You can observe this by tracing through each loop, keeping an eye on the Watch window variable.

Quitting   To end a CodeView session, press Q in the Command window or select the main menu File category and select the Quit item.

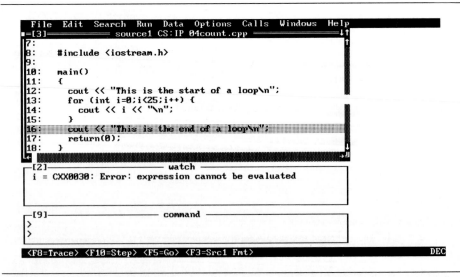

Figure 4-4.   *Placing a variable in CodeView's Watch window*

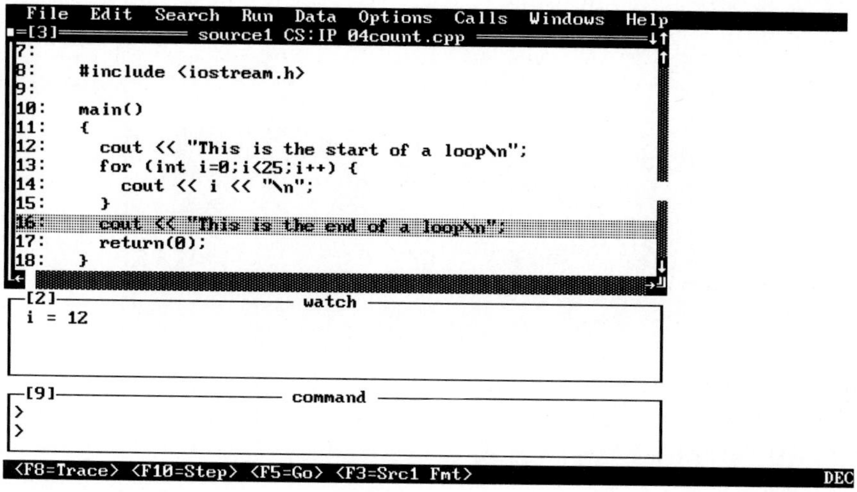

```
 File  Edit  Search  Run  Data  Options  Calls  Windows  Help
=[3]================= source1 CS:IP 04count.cpp =================↓↑
7:
8:      #include <iostream.h>
9:
10:     main()
11:     {
12:       cout << "This is the start of a loop\n";
13:       for (int i=0;i<25;i++) {
14:         cout << i << "\n";
15:       }
16:       cout << "This is the end of a loop\n";
17:       return(0);
18:     }
================================================================
-[2]=========================== watch ===========================
i = 12


-[9]========================== command =========================
>
>
 <F8=Trace> <F10=Step> <F5=Go> <F3=Src1 Fmt>                 DEC
```

Figure 4-5. *Single-stepping a program loop in CodeView to watch the behavior of a variable in the Watch window*

Two Additional CodeView Items

There are two additional items you will find useful during debug sessions. The first is the CTRL-C or CTRL-BREAK key combinations, and the second is the use of the main menu Search category.

CTRL-C and CTRL-BREAK   It is often desirable to terminate a debugging session. For example, your program may have an endless loop that runs forever. To break out of this loop, use either CTRL-C or CTRL-BREAK. These keys terminate an executing or hung program and return control to CodeView.

Search   For large applications, the search feature will help you find specific pieces of program code. This works in the same fashion as the search feature provided in the PWB.

Imagine that you want to set a break point at each **for** loop in a large program. First, select the main menu Search category, and then pick the Find item from the menu. When the dialog box appears, type **for** on the Find What line, as shown in Figure 4-6.

CodeView will now place the cursor on the first occurrence of "for" in your program's code. You could now set a break point by placing the mouse cursor on the line and quickly clicking the left mouse button twice. If your program contained

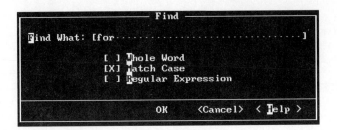

Figure 4-6.   *Doing a search operation while in CodeView*

additional **for** loops, you could continue the search by selecting the Repeat Last Find item from the same category.

Using CodeView with a C++ Program Utilizing Classes

The example for this CodeView session is a program from Chapter 16. This is a simple C++ program used to introduce the use of constructors, destructors, and simple classes. An understanding of how the program works is not important at this time. However, if you are curious, you may wish to study the information in Chapter 16.

Enter the following program code in the integrated PWB environment, and then save the file as 16COINS.CPP:

```
//
//  16COINS.CPP
//  C++ program illustrates the use of constructors and
//  destructors in a simple program.
//  This program converts cents into appropriate coins:
//  (quarters, dimes, nickels, and pennies).
//  Copyright (c) William H. Murray and Chris H. Pappas, 1992
//

#include <iostream.h>
```

```
const int QUARTER=25;
const int DIME=10;
const int NICKEL=5;

class coins {
  int number;

public:
  coins() {cout << "Begin Conversion!\n";}       //constructor
  ~coins() {cout << "\nFinished Conversion!";}  //destructor
  void get_cents(int);
  int quarter_conversion(void);
  int dime_conversion(int);
  int nickel_conversion(int);
};

void coins::get_cents(int cents)
{
  number=cents;
  cout << number <<[{|"|}]cents, converts to:"
       << endl;
}

int coins::quarter_conversion()
{
  cout << number/QUARTER <<[{|"|}]quarter(s), ";
  return(number%QUARTER);
}

int coins::dime_conversion(int d)
{
  cout << d/DIME <<[{|"|}]dime(s), ";
  return(d%DIME);
}

int coins::nickel_conversion(int n)
{
  cout << n/NICKEL <<[{|"|}]nickel(s), and ";
  return(n%NICKEL);
}

main()
{
  int c,d,n,p;
```

```
cout << "Enter the cash, in cents, to convert: ";
cin >> c;

// associate cash_in_cents with coins class.
coins cash_in_cents;

cash_in_cents.get_cents(c);
d=cash_in_cents.quarter_conversion();
n=cash_in_cents.dime_conversion(d);
p=cash_in_cents.nickel_conversion(n);
cout << p <<[{|"|}]penny(ies).";
return (0);
}
```

You can produce an executable file for this program by first selecting the main menu Options category and picking the Build menu item. Next, set the dialog box option to Debug. Now compile and link by selecting the main menu Project category and picking the Build menu item.

Since you are building your program from within the PWB environment, you can select the Debug option from the dialog box presented with a successful compile. Choose the Debug feature with the keyboard or mouse.

This program converts the number of pennies, entered by the user, into proper change in quarters, dimes, nickels, and pennies. For this example, the conversion process will be watched by setting numerous variables in a Watch window, as shown in Figure 4-7.

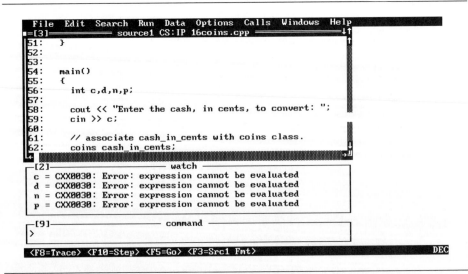

Figure 4-7.   *Setting several variables in a CodeView Watch window for a C++ program utilizing classes*

The variables *c, d, n,* and *p* represent intermediate values in the conversion process. The values in each variable are produced progressively, as the program is single stepped. Figure 4-8 shows the Watch window after several lines of program code have been executed.

Figure 4-9 shows a Watch window after the entire program has been completed. Notice that all variable values are now shown. By single-stepping through code, you can detect logical programming errors.

Using CodeView with a Windows Program

CodeView has the capability to help in the debugging of logical errors found in Windows applications. The CodeView version for Windows is denoted by CVW and must be run in the Windows environment. It can be used only to debug Windows applications.

The example program used in this section is from Chapter 23 and is named 23SINE.C You may wish to turn to Chapter 23 and learn more about the function of this application. For this example, understanding the details of the program is not necessary.

Enter the following code in the PWB if you are going to build this application for the CodeView session:

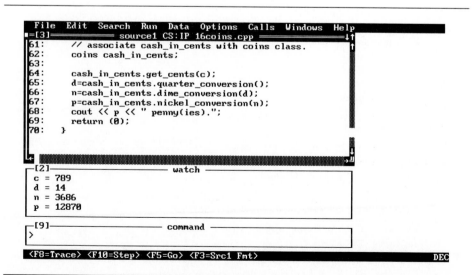

Figure 4-8.   *Single-stepping through program code with CodeView*

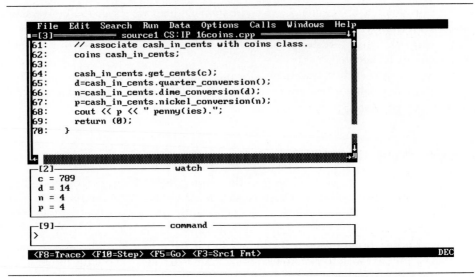

Figure 4-9.   *Examining the same variables after the program has completed operation*

```
/*
 * 23SINE.C
 * An Application Which Draws A Sine Wave In A
 * Window. Developed From The SWA Template.
 * Copyright (c) William H. Murray and Chris H. Pappas, 1992
 */

#include <windows.h>
#include <math.h>

#define pi 3.14159265359

long FAR PASCAL WindowProc(HWND,UINT,UINT,LONG);

char    szProgName[]="ProgName";

int PASCAL WinMain(hInst,hPreInst,lpszCmdLine,nCmdShow)
HANDLE hInst,hPreInst;
LPSTR  lpszCmdLine;
int    nCmdShow;
{
  HWND hwnd;
```

```
MSG   msg;
WNDCLASS wcSwp;
if (!hPreInst) {
  wcSwp.lpszClassName=szProgName;
  wcSwp.hInstance    =hInst;
  wcSwp.lpfnWndProc  =WindowProc;
  wcSwp.hCursor      =LoadCursor(NULL,IDC_ARROW);
  wcSwp.hIcon        =NULL;
  wcSwp.lpszMenuName =NULL;
  wcSwp.hbrBackground=GetStockObject(WHITE_BRUSH);
  wcSwp.style        =CS_HREDRAW|CS_VREDRAW;
  wcSwp.cbClsExtra   =0;
  wcSwp.cbWndExtra   =0;
  if (!RegisterClass (&wcSwp))
    return FALSE;
}
hwnd=CreateWindow(szProgName,"A Sine Wave",
                  WS_OVERLAPPEDWINDOW,CW_USEDEFAULT,
                  CW_USEDEFAULT,CW_USEDEFAULT,
                  CW_USEDEFAULT,NULL,NULL,
                  hInst,NULL);
ShowWindow(hwnd,nCmdShow);
UpdateWindow(hwnd);
while (GetMessage(&msg,NULL,NULL,NULL)) {
  TranslateMessage(&msg);
  DispatchMessage(&msg);
}
return(msg.wParam);
}


long FAR PASCAL WindowProc(hwnd,messg,wParam,lParam)
HWND    hwnd;
UINT    messg;
UINT    wParam;
LONG    lParam;
{
  PAINTSTRUCT ps;
  HDC hdc;
  double y;
  int i;

  switch (messg)
  {
    case WM_PAINT:
      hdc=BeginPaint(hwnd,&ps);
```

```
/*--------- your routines below ---------*/

      /* draw the x & y coordinate axes */
      MoveTo(hdc,100,50);
      LineTo(hdc,100,350);
      MoveTo(hdc,100,200);
      LineTo(hdc,500,200);
      MoveTo(hdc,100,200);

      /* draw the sine wave */
      for (i=0;i<400;i++) {
        y=120.0*sin(pi*i*(360.0/400.0)/180.0);
        LineTo(hdc,i+100,(int) (200.0-y));
      }

/*--------- your routines above ---------*/
      ValidateRect(hwnd,NULL);
      EndPaint(hwnd,&ps);
      break;
    case WM_DESTROY:
      PostQuitMessage(0);
      break;
    default:
      return(DefWindowProc(hwnd,messg,wParam,lParam));
      break;
  }
  return(0L);
}
```

In addition to the program listing, you will also need the 23SINE.RC resource script file and the 23SINE make file from Chapter 23. Make the following modifications to the 23SINE command-line make file; this make file does not have a file extension:

```
all: 23sine.exe

23sine.obj: 23sine.c
    cl -c -AS -FPi -Gsw -Oas -Zpe -Zi 23sine.c

23sine.exe: 23sine.obj 23sine.def
    link /NOD /CO 23sine,,,libw slibcew,23sine.def
```

In this make file, the -Zi option is used for the compiler, while the /CO option is used to install CodeView information from the linker.

With 23SINE, 23SINE.RC, and 23SINE.C present in your directory, you are ready to build the executable file. You can build this file, with CodeView extensions, from the DOS command line by typing

nmake 23SINE

Next, return to the Windows environment and select the CVW icon from within the C/C++ Windows group box. You will now see the 23SINE application within the CVW window, as shown in Figure 4-10.

This application draws a sine wave in the designated window. Imagine that you wish to observe the generation of the value for each sine wave point that is to be plotted. With CodeView, simply place a break point on the **LineTo()** function.

```
/* draw the sine wave */
for (i=0;i<400;i++) {
  y=120.0*sin(pi*i*(360.0/400.0)/180.0);
  LineTo(hdc,i+100,(int) (200.0-y));
}
```

Next, open a Watch window and place the variable *y* in the window. It is now possible to execute an F5 (Go) while watching the value, *y*, change in the Watch window. Figure 4-11 shows the Watch window after several break points have been executed.

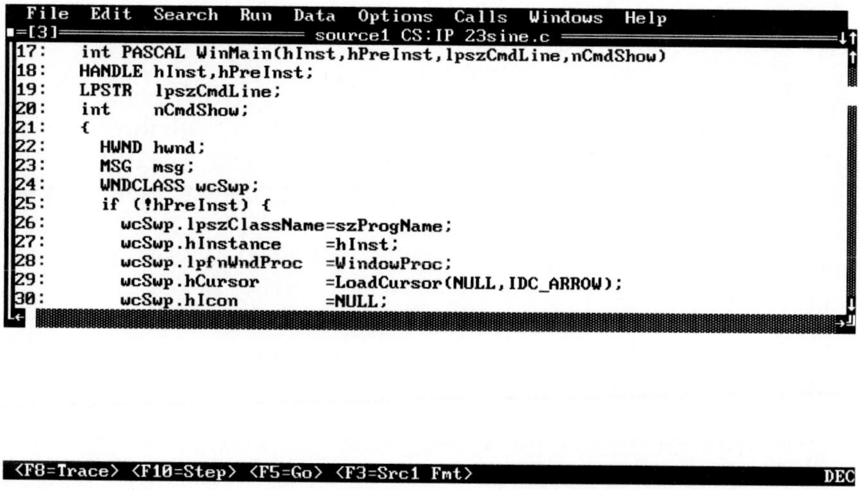

```
 File  Edit  Search  Run  Data  Options  Calls  Windows  Help
=[3]================= source1 CS:IP 23sine.c ================
17:    int PASCAL WinMain(hInst,hPreInst,lpszCmdLine,nCmdShow)
18:    HANDLE hInst,hPreInst;
19:    LPSTR  lpszCmdLine;
20:    int    nCmdShow;
21:    {
22:      HWND hwnd;
23:      MSG  msg;
24:      WNDCLASS wcSwp;
25:      if (!hPreInst) {
26:        wcSwp.lpszClassName=szProgName;
27:        wcSwp.hInstance    =hInst;
28:        wcSwp.lpfnWndProc  =WindowProc;
29:        wcSwp.hCursor      =LoadCursor(NULL,IDC_ARROW);
30:        wcSwp.hIcon        =NULL;

 <F8=Trace> <F10=Step> <F5=Go> <F3=Src1 Fmt>                DEC
```

Figure 4-10. *The 23SINE.C application ready for debugging in CodeView for Windows*

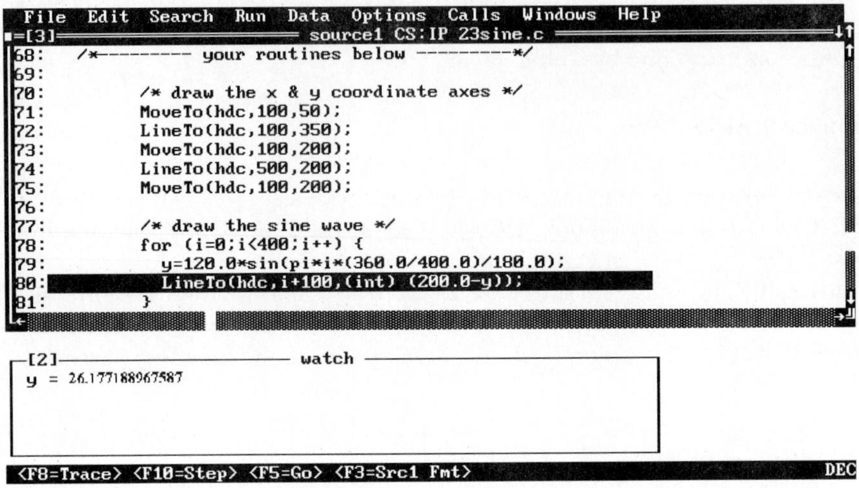

```
 File  Edit  Search  Run  Data  Options  Calls  Windows  Help
=[3]========================= source1 CS:IP 23sine.c =================1↑
68:    /*---------- your routines below ----------*/
69:
70:         /* draw the x & y coordinate axes */
71:         MoveTo(hdc,100,50);
72:         LineTo(hdc,100,350);
73:         MoveTo(hdc,100,200);
74:         LineTo(hdc,500,200);
75:         MoveTo(hdc,100,200);
76:
77:         /* draw the sine wave */
78:         for (i=0;i<400;i++) {
79:            y=120.0*sin(pi*i*(360.0/400.0)/180.0);
80:            LineTo(hdc,i+100,(int) (200.0-y));
81:         }

-[2]-                        watch
 y = 26.177188967587

 <F8=Trace> <F10=Step> <F5=Go> <F3=Src1 Fmt>                    DEC
```

Figure 4-11.   *Studying the generation of sine values while in CodeView for Windows.
(Notice the variable in the Watch window)*

By using CodeView to watch variables change values, such as *y* in the previous example, you can eliminate problems with range errors.

The Source Browser

The Source Browser is an integrated component of the PWB that allows you to find pieces of program code. For example, once a file is compiled with Browser information, it is possible to search the original source code for the location where a variable is defined and the locations where the variable is used in the program. The Browser can also provide a call tree for a program. A *call tree* is a list of the program's function calls and the functions that they, in turn, call. Call trees are useful when you are checking the flow of program code.

Generating Browser Information

The Browser example used in this section is built from the 23SINE.C application discussed in the previous section. This time, the 23SINE.C application will be rebuilt from within the integrated PWB environment. In addition to the 23SINE.C program, you will also need 23SINE.DEF, 23SINE.RC, and 23SINE.MAK from Chapter 23 in your directory. The project make file, 23SINE.MAK, will allow the application to be built with Browser information from within the PWB.

Enter the PWB from the DOS command line or Windows. Next, open the 23SINE.C application. Your screen should appear similar to the one in Figure 4-12.

From the main menu Project category, open the 23SINE.MAK project file. Next, open the main menu Options category and pick the Browse item. From the dialog box, select the option that will generate Browser information. Now, simply rebuild the project. You can rebuild a file by selecting the Project category and the Rebuild All item from the menu.

Browser information is contained in several files, ending with the extensions .BSC and .SBR. For some projects, these files can become quite large. For the 23SINE example, the 23SINE.BSC file is 40K.

Finding Symbol Definitions

Finding the definition for a symbol, such as a variable, within a complex application can be very time consuming. This is especially true for large Windows applications. The Source Browser makes finding this information easy.

With 23SINE.C opened in the PWB window, select the main menu PWB Browse category. From the menu, pick the Goto Definitions item. A dialog box similar to the one in Figure 4-13 will be placed on the screen.

You can find the location of the y variable's definition in your source code by typing **y** at the Name input line. The source code line where y is defined as a double is boldfaced, as shown in Figure 4-14.

The ability to search for an item is similar to the standard string search feature used by most editors, including the PWB. The added feature of a Browser search is that you can specify categories.

Finding Symbol References

Frequently, you will also want to check the location where each variable is used in an application.

With 23SINE.C opened in the PWB window, select the main menu PWB Browse category. From the menu, pick the Goto Reference item. From the Browser dialog box, enter the variable y once again.

The locations of variables used within an application are shown in bold type. Figure 4-15 shows the only source code line where y is used in the 23SINE.C application.

During Browser sessions, it is possible to search for several variables. Each occurrence of the variable will be boldfaced. This application generated values only at the location shown in the figure.

```
  File   Edit   Search   Project   Run   Options   Browse   Window   Help
=[  1]=========================== C:\C700\23sine.c ============================
/*
 *    23SINE.C
 *    An Application Which Draws A Sine Wave In A
 *    Window. Developed From The SWA Template.
 *    Copyright (c) William H. Murray and Chris H. Pappas, 1992
 */

#include <windows.h>
#include <math.h>

#define pi 3.14159265359

long FAR PASCAL WindowProc(HWND,UINT,UINT,LONG);

char    szProgName[]="ProgName";

int PASCAL WinMain(hInst,hPreInst,lpszCmdLine,nCmdShow)
HANDLE hInst,hPreInst;
LPSTR  lpszCmdLine;
int    nCmdShow;
{

<General Help> <F1=Help> <Alt=Menu>                              00001.001
```

Figure 4-12. *Preparing to generate Browser information for a Windows application while in the PWB*

Creating a Call Tree

A call tree provides information on program flow by providing a list of the functions called by the application. This list also includes functions that are called by other functions.

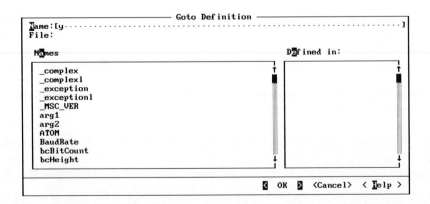

Figure 4-13. *Browser dialog box options*

```
 File  Edit  Search  Project  Run  Options  Browse  Window  Help
=[  1]===================== C:\C700\23sine.c =====================↓↑
{
  PAINTSTRUCT ps;
  HDC hdc;
  double y;
  int i;

  switch (messg)
  {
    case WM_PAINT:
      hdc=BeginPaint(hwnd,&ps);
/*--------- your routines below ---------*/

      /* draw the x & y coordinate axes */
      MoveTo(hdc,100,50);
      LineTo(hdc,100,350);
      MoveTo(hdc,100,200);
      LineTo(hdc,500,200);
      MoveTo(hdc,100,200);

      /* draw the sine wave */
      for (i=0;i<400;i++) {
<General Help> <F1=Help> <Alt=Menu>                        00061.012
```

Figure 4-14.   *Locating the definition of a variable with the help of Browser*

To generate a call tree for the 23SINE.C application, open 23SINE.C in the PWB window. Next, select the main menu PWB Browse category. From the menu, pick the Call Tree item. Select 23SINE.C from the Modules list, as shown in Figure 4-16.

```
 File  Edit  Search  Project  Run  Options  Browse  Window  Help
=[  1]===================== C:\C700\23sine.c =====================↓↑
      /* draw the x & y coordinate axes */
      MoveTo(hdc,100,50);
      LineTo(hdc,100,350);
      MoveTo(hdc,100,200);
      LineTo(hdc,500,200);
      MoveTo(hdc,100,200);

      /* draw the sine wave */
      for (i=0;i<400;i++) {
        y=120.0*sin(pi*i*(360.0/400.0)/180.0);
        LineTo(hdc,i+100,(int) (200.0-y));
      }

/*--------- your routines above ---------*/
      ValidateRect(hwnd,NULL);
      EndPaint(hwnd,&ps);
      break;
    case WM_DESTROY:
      PostQuitMessage(0);
      break;
WindowProc
<General Help> <F1=Help> <Alt=Menu>                        00079.048
```

Figure 4-15.   *Finding the location of a variable in an application with Browser*

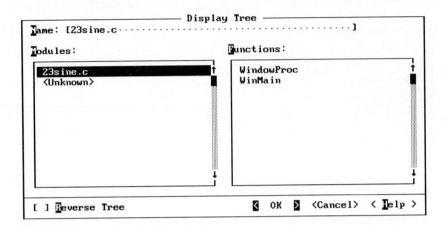

Figure 4-16. *Creating a call tree with the Display Tree option*

Browse also allows the generation of a call tree. The Browser dialog box shows how this feature is selected. A list similar to the one shown here will be generated for 23SINE.C:

```
WindowProc
      BeginPaint?
      MoveTo[3]?
      LineTo[3]?
      sin?
      ValidateRect?
      EndPaint?
      PostQuitMessage?
      DefWindowProc?

WinMain
      WindowProc...
      LoadCursor?
      GetStockObject?
      RegisterClass?
      CreateWindow?
      ShowWindow?
      UpdateWindow?
      GetMessage?
```

```
TranslateMessage?
DispatchMessage?
```

Symbols followed by a ? are functions defined in a library, rather than within your application. Symbols followed by [*n*] are symbols used multiple times within the application—for example, MoveTo[3] and LineTo[3]. Symbols followed by three dots, or an ellipsis (...), indicate that information on that symbol appears elsewhere in the call tree. WindowProc... is one such example.

In **WindowProc()**, the program flow moves in the direction of the listed symbols. **BeginPaint()** is called first, followed by **MoveTo()**, **LineTo()**, **sin()**, and so on.

The Profiler

The Profiler, officially called the Microsoft Source Profiler Performance Analysis Tool, can aid you in finding where an application is spending the majority of its time during execution. This information, in turn, can help you design tighter, more efficient code. Using the Profiler can initially be overwhelming. The Profiler is a complex C/C++ tool, and a complete mastery of its commands and features requires much practice. However, using the Profiler to simply obtain performance information on an application is straightforward. This use is illustrated in the next example.

The Profiler works with all Microsoft languages but is particularly important to C, C++, and Windows programmers. You can execute the Profiler from the DOS command line or from within the PWB integrated environment when installed according to the setup instructions.

In the example that follows, the 23SINE.C application is studied with the help of the Profiler. The Profiler will be run from the DOS command line. The Profiler is installed as a separate C/C++ tool. Make sure you have installed it on your hard disk before proceeding.

Profiler Batch Files

The Profiler provides you with several batch files to aid in the operation. These batch files are discussed in the *Microsoft Source Profiler* manual. The FTIME.BAT batch file is used for C and C++ programs running under DOS. The FTIMEW.BAT batch file is for Windows applications. Both batch files are run from the DOS command line. The FTIMEW batch file will invoke Windows automatically.

In order to use the Profiler, an application must be compiled and linked with CodeView information, as illustrated in previous sections. Before continuing, make sure your version of the 23SINE.C program has been compiled and linked in this fashion. The DOS command-line make file was given in a previous section of this chapter. With all files in place, you can build the application by typing nmake 23SINE

Note that the command-line make file does not have an extension.

To run the Profiler batch file, switch to the Profiler subdirectory containing the FTIMEW batch file. For the authors' installation, that subdirectory was

C:\C700\PROF\BIN

Your subdirectory may be different, so be sure to check for the file's location.

Now type

FTIMEW c:\c700\23sine

The batch file will start Windows and execute and profile the application. A profile on function timing for 23SINE.EXE is returned. It will be similar to the following report:

```
Microsoft PLIST
Profile: Function timing, sorted by time.
Date:    Fri May 29 13:44:28 1992
Program Statistics
------------------
     Total time: 19200.440 milliseconds
     Time outside of functions: 1339.023 milliseconds
     Call depth: 4
     Total functions: 2
     Total hits: 209
     Function coverage: 100.0%
Module Statistics for c:\c700\23sine.exe
----------------------------------------
     Time in module: 17861.417 milliseconds
     Percent of time in module: 100.0%
     Functions in module: 2
     Hits in module: 209
     Module function coverage: 100.0%
     Func                Func+Child          Hit
     Time      %         Time      %         count Function
-----------------------------------------------------------
     16274.061  91.1     17861.417 100.0     1 WinMain
(23sine.c:21)
     1587.356   8.9      1587.356  8.9       208 WindowProc
(23sine.c:58)
```

The Profiler report is returned as a text file with an .OUT file extension. For this example, the filename was 23SINE.OUT.

In a Windows application, **WinMain()** will always occupy a significant portion of time. Note in this example that the application's drawing procedure, **WindowProc()**, uses only 8.9 percent of the execution cycle in drawing the sine wave to the screen.

Writing Code

In this chapter you have learned the fundamentals of using tools that can aid in making your programs work correctly, operate quickly, and run efficiently. As you study the remainder of this book, do not hesitate to call upon the CodeView, Browser, and Profiler tools to examine your program code. As with all tools, skills are developed only through repeated practice and use.

The remaining chapters of this book concentrate on teaching language fundamentals for C, C++, and Windows. Integrate the CodeView, Browser, and Profiler toolkit into your program development as you work through these sections.

Part *II*

C and C++
Programming
Foundations

Chapter 5

C and C++ Foundations

Before you proceed you should be comfortable with the Microsoft C/C++ development environment. By now you should have installed the package, configured it to your personal requirements, and practiced using the compiler and the CodeView debugger.

Beginning with this chapter, you will explore the origins, syntax, and usage of the C and C++ language. A study of C's history is worthwhile because it reveals the language's successful design philosophy and helps you understand why C and C++ may be the language of choice for years to come.

History of C

A history of the C language begins with a discussion of the UNIX operating system since both the system and most of the programs that run on it are written in C. However, this does not mean that C is tied to UNIX or any other operating system or machine. The UNIX/C codevelopment environment has given C a reputation for being a *system programming language* because it is useful for writing compilers and operating systems. C is also very useful for writing major programs in many different domains.

UNIX was originally developed in 1969 on what would now be considered a small DEC PDP-7 at Bell Laboratories in Murray Hill, New Jersey. UNIX was written entirely in PDP-7 assembly language. By design, this operating system was intended to be "programmer friendly," providing useful development tools, lean commands, and a relatively open environment. Soon after the development of UNIX, Ken Thompson implemented a compiler for a new language called B.

At this point it is helpful to examine the origins and history behind Ken Thompson's B language, a direct predecessor to C. Following is a comprehensive C lineage:

Algol 60	Designed by an international committee in early 1960
CPL	(Combined Programming Language) Developed at both Cambridge and the University of London in 1963
BCPL	(Basic Combined Programming Language) Developed at Cambridge, by Martin Richards in 1967
B	Developed by Ken Thompson, Bell Labs, in 1970
C	Developed by Dennis Ritchie, Bell Labs, in 1972

Then, in 1983, the American National Standards Institute (ANSI) committee was formed for the purpose of creating ANSI C—a standardization of the C language.

Algol 60 was a language that appeared only a few years after FORTRAN was introduced. This new language was more sophisticated and had a strong influence on the design of future programming languages. Its authors paid a great deal of attention to the regularity of syntax, modular structure, and other features usually associated with high-level structured languages. Unfortunately, Algol 60 never really caught on in the United States. Many say this was due to the language's abstractness and generality.

The inventors of CPL (Combined Programming Language) intended to bring Algol 60's lofty intent down to the realities of an actual computer. However, just as Algol 60 was hard to learn and difficult to implement, so was CPL. This led to its eventual downfall. Still clinging to the best of what CPL had to offer, the creators of BCPL (Basic Combined Programming Language) wanted to boil CPL down to its basic good features.

When Ken Thompson designed the B language for an early implementation of UNIX, he was trying to further simplify CPL. He succeeded in creating a very sparse language that was well suited for use on the hardware available to him. However, both BCPL and B may have carried their streamlining attempts a bit too far; they became limited languages, useful only for dealing with certain kinds of problems.

For example, no sooner had Ken Thompson implemented the B language than a new machine, called the PDP-11, was introduced. UNIX and the B compiler were immediately transferred to this new machine. While the PDP-11 was a larger machine than its PDP-7 predecessor, it was still quite small by today's standards. It had only 24K of memory, of which the system used 16K, and one 512K fixed disk. Some thought was given to rewriting UNIX in B, but the B language was slow because of its interpretive design. There was another problem as well: B was word oriented, but the PDP-11 was byte oriented. For these reasons work was begun in 1971 on a successor to B, appropriately named C.

Dennis Ritchie is credited with creating C, a language that restored some of the generality lost in BCPL and B. He accomplished this through a shrewd use of data types, while maintaining the simplicity and direct access to the hardware that were the original goal designs of CPL.

Many languages developed by a single individual (C, Pascal, Lisp, and APL) contain a cohesiveness that is missing from languages developed by large programming teams (Ada, PL/I, and Algol 68). It is also typical for a language written by one person to reflect the author's field of expertise. Dennis Ritchie was noted for his work in systems software—computer languages, operating systems, and program generators.

Given Ritchie's areas of expertise, it is easy to understand why C is a language of choice for systems software design. C is a relatively low-level language that allows you to specify every detail in an algorithm's logic to achieve maximum computer efficiency. But C is also a high-level language that can hide the details of the computer's architecture, thereby increasing programming efficiency.

Relationship to Other Languages

You may be wondering what C's relationship is to other languages. A possible continuum is shown in Figure 5-1. If you start at the bottom of the continuum and move upward, you go from the tangible and empirical to the elusive and theoretical. The dots represent major advancements, with many steps left out. Early ancestors of the computer, like the Jacquard loom (1805) and Charles Babbage's "analytical engine" (1834), were programmed in hardware. The day may well come when we will

Direct Neural Path Communication
•
•
•
Artificial Intelligence
Operating System Command Languages
Problem-oriented Languages
Machine-oriented Languages
Assembly Language
•
•
•
Actual Hardware

Figure 5-1.   *A possible continuum of programming languages*

program a machine by plugging a neural path communicator into a socket implanted into the temporal lobe (language memory) or Broca's area (language motor area) of the brain's cortex.

Assembly languages, which go back to the first days of electronic computers, provide a way for working directly with a computer's built-in instruction set, and are fairly easy to learn. Because assembly languages force you to think in terms of hardware, you had to specify every operation in the machine's terms. Therefore, you were always moving bits into or out of registers, adding them, shifting register contents from one register to another, and finally storing the results in memory. This was a tedious and error-prone endeavor.

The first high-level languages, such as FORTRAN, were created as alternatives to assembly languages. High-level languages were much more general and abstract, and they allowed you to think in terms of the problem at hand rather than in terms of the computer's hardware.

Unfortunately, the creators of high-level languages made the fallacious assumption that everyone who had been driving a standard, so to speak, would prefer driving an automatic. Excited about providing ease in programming, they left out some necessary options. Fortran and Algol are too abstract for systems-level work; they are *problem-oriented languages,* the kind used for solving problems in engineering, science, or business. Programmers who wanted to write systems software still had to rely on their machine's assembler.

In reaction to this situation, a few systems software developers took a step backward—or lower, in terms of the continuum—and created the category of *machine-oriented languages.* As you saw in C's genealogy, BCPL and B fit into this class of very low-level software tools. These languages were excellent for a specific machine but not much use for anything else; they were too closely related to a particular architecture. The C language is one step above machine-oriented languages but is still a step below most problem-solving languages. C is close enough to the computer to give you great control over the details of an application's implementation, yet far enough away to ignore the details of the hardware. This is why the C language is considered at once a high- and a low-level language.

Strengths of C

All computer languages have a particular look. APL has its hieroglyphic appearance, assembly language its columns of mnemonics, and Pascal its easily read syntax. And then there's C. Many programmers encountering C for the first time will find its syntax cryptic and perhaps intimidating. C contains very few of the friendly English-like syntax structures found in many other programming languages. Instead, C presents the software engineer with unusual-looking operators and a plethora of pointers. New C programmers will soon discover a variety of language characteristics whose roots go back to C's original hardware/software progenitor. The following sections highlight the strengths of the C language.

Small Size

There are fewer syntax rules in C than in many other languages, and it is possible to write a top-quality C compiler that will operate in only 256K of total memory. There are actually more operators and combinations of operators in C than there are keywords.

The Language Command Set

The original C language, as developed by Dennis Ritchie, contained a mere 27 keywords. The ANSI C standard (discussed later in this chapter in "The ANSI C Standard") has added several reserved words. Microsoft C/C++ further enhances the instruction set with 19 more. This brings the total Microsoft C/C++ keyword count to 66.

Many of the functions commonly defined as part of other programming languages are not included in C. For example, C does not contain any built-in input and output capabilities, nor does it contain any arithmetic operations (beyond those of basic addition and subtraction) or string-handling functions. Since any language missing these capabilities is of little use, C provides a rich set of library functions for input/output, arithmetic operations, and string manipulation. This agreed-upon library set is so commonly used that it can almost be seen as part of the language itself. One of the strengths of C, however, is its loose structure, which enables you to recode these functions easily.

Speed

The C code produced by most compilers tends to be very efficient. The combination of a small language, a small run-time system, and the fact that the language is close to the hardware makes many C programs run at speeds close to their assembly language equivalents.

A Language Not Strongly Typed

Unlike Pascal, which is a strongly typed language, C treats data types somewhat more loosely. (Typing is explained in more detail in "Not Strongly Typed," later in this chapter.) This is a carryover from the B language, which was also a loosely typed language. This looseness allows you to view data in different ways. For example, at one point in a program, the application may need to see a variable as a character and yet, for purposes of uppercasing (by subtracting 32), may want to see the same memory cell as the ASCII equivalent of the character.

A Structured Language

C contains all of the control structures you would expect of a modern-day language. This is impressive when you consider C's 1971 incubation period, which predated formal structured programming. For loops, if and if-else constructs, case (switch) statements, and while loops are all incorporated into the language. C also provides for the compartmentalization of code and data by managing their scope. For example, C provides local variables for this purpose and calls-by-value for subroutine data privacy.

Support of Modular Programming

C supports *modular programming*, which is the concept of separate compilation and linking. This allows you to recompile only the parts of a program that have been changed during development. This feature can be extremely important when you are developing large programs, or even medium-size programs on slow systems. Without support for modular programming, the amount of time required to compile a complete program can make the change, compile, test, and modify cycle prohibitively slow.

Easy Interface to Assembly Language Routines

There is a well-defined method for calling assembly language routines from most C compilers. Combined with the separation of compilation and linking, this makes C a very strong contender in applications that require a mix of high-level and assembler routines. C routines can also be integrated into assembly language programs on most systems.

Bit Manipulation

Often in systems programming it is necessary to manipulate objects at the bit level. Naturally, with C's origins so closely tied to the UNIX operating system, the language provides a rich set of bit-manipulation operators.

Pointer Variables

One of the capabilities of a language required by an operating system is the ability to address specific areas of memory. This capability also enhances the execution speed of a program. The C language meets these design requirements by using pointers (discussed in Chapter 10). While it is true that other languages implement pointers, C is noted for its ability to perform pointer arithmetic. For example, if the variable *index* points to the first element of an array *student_records*, then *index+1* will be the address of the second element of *student_records*.

Flexible Structures

All arrays in C are one-dimensional. Multidimensional arrangements are built from combinations of these one-dimensional arrays. Arrays and structures (records) can be joined in any manner desired, creating database organizations that are limited only by the programmer's ability. Arrays are discussed in Chapter 9.

Memory Efficiency

For many of the same reasons that C programs tend to be fast, they tend to be very memory efficient. The lack of built-in functions saves programs from having to carry around support for functions that are not needed by that application.

Portability

Portability is a measure of the ease of converting a program running on one computer or operating system to another computer or operating system. Programs written in C are among the most portable in the modern computer world. This is especially true in the mini- and microcomputer worlds.

Special Function Libraries

There are many commercial function libraries available for all popular C compilers. Libraries are available for graphics, file handling, database support, screen windowing, data entry, communications, and general support functions. By using these libraries, you can save a great deal of development time.

Weaknesses of C

There are no perfect programming languages. Different programming problems require different solutions. It is the software engineer's task to choose the best language for a project. On any project, this is one of the first decisions you need to make, and it is nearly irrevocable once you start coding. The choice of a programming language can also make the difference between a project's success and failure. The following sections cover some of the weaknesses of the C language to give you a better idea of when to use and when not to use C for a particular application.

Not Strongly Typed

The fact that C is not strongly typed is one of its strengths, but it is also one of its weaknesses. Technically, *typing* is a measure of how closely a language enforces the use of variable types. (For example, integer and floating-point are two different types of numbers). In some languages it is illegal to assign one data type to another without invoking a conversion function. This protects the data from being compromised by unexpected roundoffs.

As discussed earlier, C will allow an integer to be assigned to a character variable, and vice versa. What this means to you is that you are going to have to properly manage your variables. For experienced programmers this will present no problem. However, novice program developers may want to remind themselves that this can be the source of side effects.

A *side effect* in a language is an unexpected change to a variable or other item. Because C is not a strongly typed language, it gives you great flexibility to manipulate data. For example, the assignment operator (=) can appear more than once in the same expression. This flexibility, which you can use to your advantage, means that expressions can be written that have no clear and definite value. To have restricted the use of the assignment and similar operators or to have eliminated all side effects and unpredictable results would have removed from C much of its power and appeal as a high-level assembly language.

Lack of Run-time Checking

C's lack of checking in the run-time system can cause many mysterious and transient problems to go undetected. For example, the run-time system would not warn you if your application exceeded an array's bounds. This is one of the costs of streamlining a compiler for the sake of speed and efficiency.

Programming Discipline

C's tremendous range of features—from bit manipulation to high-level formatted I/O—and its relative consistency from machine to machine have led to its acceptance in science, engineering, and business applications. It has directly contributed to the wide availability of the UNIX operating system on computers of all types and sizes.

Like any other powerful tool, however, C imposes a heavy responsibility on its users. C programmers need to acquire a discipline very quickly, adopting various rules and conventions in order to make their programs understandable both to themselves, long after the programs were written, and to others trying to analyze the code for the first time. In C, programming discipline is essential. The good news is that it comes almost automatically with practice.

The ANSI C Standard

The ANSI (American National Standards Institute) committee has developed standards for the C language. This section describes some of the significant changes suggested and implemented by the committee. Some of these changes are intended to increase the flexibility of the language, while others are attempts to standardize features previously left to the discretion of the compiler implementor.

Previously, the only standard available was the book *The C Programming Language* by B. Kernighan and D. Ritchie (Prentice-Hall, Murray Hill, New Jersey: 1988). This book was not specific on some language details, which led to a divergence among compilers. The ANSI standard strives to remove these ambiguities. Although a few of the proposed changes could cause problems for some previously written programs, they should not affect most existing programs.

The ANSI C standard provides an even better opportunity than before to write portable C code. The standard has not corrected all areas of confusion in the language, however, and because C interfaces efficiently with machine hardware, many programs will always require some revision when they are moved to a different environment. The ANSI committee that developed the standard adopted as guidelines some phrases that collectively have been called the "spirit of C." Some of those phrases are

- Trust the programmer.

- Don't prevent the programmer from doing what needs to be done.

- Keep the language small and simple.

Additionally, the international community was consulted to ensure that ANSI (American) standard C would be identical to the ISO (International Standards Organization) standard version. Because of these efforts, C is the only language that effectively deals with alternate collating sequences, enormous character sets, and multiple user cultures. Table 5-1 highlights just some of the areas the ANSI committee addressed.

The Evolution of C++ and Object-oriented Programming

Simply stated, C++ is a superset of the C language. C++ retains all of C's strengths, including its power and flexibility in dealing with the hardware/software interface;

Feature	Standardization
Data types	Four: character, integer, floating-point, and enumeration
Comments	/* for the opening, */ for the closing; alternatively, //, meaning that anything to the symbol's right is ignored by the compiler
Identifier length	31 characters to distinguish uniqueness
Standard identifiers and header files	An agreed-upon minimum set of identifiers and header files necessary to perform basic operations such as I/O
Preprocessor statements	The # in preprocessor directives can have leading white space (any combination of spaces and tabs), permitting indented preprocessor directives for clarity. Some earlier compilers insisted that all preprocessor directives begin in column 1
New preprocessor directives	Two new preprocessor directives have been added: #if defined *expression* #elif *expression*
Adjacent strings	Adjacent literal strings should be concatenated. This would allow, for example, a **#define** directive to extend beyond a single line
Standard libraries	A basic set of system-level and external routines, such as **read()** and **write()**
Output control	An agreed-upon set of escape codes representing formatting control codes such as newline, new page, and tabs
Keywords	An agreed-upon minimum set of verbs used to construct valid C statements
sizeof()	The **sizeof()** function should return the type **size_t** instead of a system-limiting variable of size integer
Prototyping	All C compilers should handle programs that do and do not employ prototyping
Command-line arguments	In order for the C compiler to properly handle command-line arguments, an agreed-upon syntax was defined
void pointer type	The **void** keyword can be applied to functions that do not return a value. A function that does return a value can have its return value cast to **void** to indicate to the compiler that the value is being deliberately ignored

Table 5-1.   *Features of C Standardized by the ANSI Committee*

Feature	Standardization
Structure handling	Structure handling has been greatly improved. The member names in structure and union definitions need not be unique. Structures can be passed as arguments to functions, returned by functions, and assigned to structures of the same type
Function declarations	Function declarations can include argument-type lists (function prototyping) to notify the compiler of the number and types of arguments
Hexadecimal character constants	Hexadecimal character constants can be expressed by using an introductory \x followed by from one to three hexadecimal digits (0-9, a-f, A-F); for example, 16 decimal = \x10, which can be written as 0x10 using the historic C notation
Trigraphs	Trigraphs define standard symbol sequences that represent those characters that may not readily be available on all keyboards. For example, ??< can be substituted for the more elaborate {} symbol

Table 5-1.   *Features of C Standardized by the ANSI Committee* (continued)

its low-level system programming; and its efficiency, economy, and powerful expressions. However, C++ brings the C language into the dynamic world of object-oriented programming and makes it a platform for high-level problem abstraction, going beyond even Ada in this respect. C++ accomplishes all of this with a simplicity and support for modularity similar to Modula-2, while maintaining the compactness and execution efficiency of C.

This new hybrid language combines the standard procedural language constructs familiar to so many programmers and the object-oriented model, which you can exploit fully to produce a purely object-oriented solution to a problem. In practice, a C++ application can reflect this duality by incorporating both the procedural programming model and the newer object-oriented model. This biformity in C++ presents a special challenge to the beginning C++ programmer; not only is there a new language to learn, but there is also a new way of thinking and problem solving.

History of C++

Not surprisingly, C++ has an origin similar to C's. While C++ is somewhat like BCPL and Algol 68, it also contains components of Simula 67. C++'s ability to overload operators and its flexibility to include declarations close to their first point of application are features found in Algol 68. The concept of subclasses (or derived classes) and virtual functions is taken from Simula 67. Like many other popular programming languages, C++ represents an evolution and refinement of some of the best features of previous languages. Of course, it is closest to C.

Bjarne Stroustrup, of Bell Labs, is credited with developing the C++ language in the early 1980s. (Dr. Stroustrup credits Rick Mascitti with the naming of this new language.) C++ was originally developed to solve some very rigorous event-driven simulations for which considerations of efficiency precluded the use of other languages. C++ was first used outside Dr. Stroustrup's language group in 1983, and by the summer of 1987, the language was still going through a natural refinement and evolution.

One key design goal of C++ was to maintain compatibility with C. The idea was to preserve the integrity of millions of lines of previously written and debugged C code, the integrity of many existing C libraries, and the usefulness of previously developed C tools. Because of the high degree of success in achieving this goal, many programmers find the transition to C++ much simpler than when they first went from some other language, such as FORTRAN, to C.

C++ supports large-scale software development. Because it includes increased type checking, many of the side effects experienced when writing loosely typed C applications are no longer possible.

The most significant enhancement of the C++ language is its support for object-oriented programming (OOP). You will have to modify your approach to problem solving to derive all of the benefits of C++. For example, objects and their associated operations must be identified and all necessary classes and subclasses must be constructed.

Using C++ Objects to Streamline Code Design

What follows is an example of how an abstract data object in C++ can improve upon an older language's limited built-in constructs and features. For example, a FORTRAN software engineer may want to keep records on employees. You could accomplish this with multiple arrays of scalar data that represent each set of data. All of the arrays are necessarily tied together by a common index. Should there be ten fields of information on each employee, ten array accesses would have to be made using the same index location in order to represent the array of records.

In C++, the solution involves the declaration of a simple object, *employee_database*, that can receive messages to *add_employee*, *delete_employee*, *access_employee*, or *display_employee* information contained within the object. The manipulation of the *employee_database* object can then be performed in a natural manner. Inserting a new record into the *employee_database* object becomes as simple as this:

```
employee_database.add_employee(new_recruit)
```

Assuming the *employee_database* object has been appropriately declared, the **add_employee()** function is a method suitably defined in the class that supports *employee_database* objects, and the *new_recruit* parameter is the specific information that is to be added. Note that the class of objects called *employee_database* is not a part of the underlying language itself. Instead, the programmer extends the language to suit the problem. By defining a new class of objects or by modifying existing classes (creating a subclass), a more natural mapping from the problem space to the program space (or solution space) occurs. The biggest challenge comes in truly mastering this powerful enhancement.

Small Enhancements to C

The following sections detail the minor (non-object-oriented) enhancements to the C language.

Comments

C++ introduces the comment to end-of-line delimiter //. However, the comment brackets /* and */ can still be used.

Enumeration Names

The name of an enumeration is a type name. This streamlines the notation by not requiring the qualifier **enum** to be placed in front of the enumeration type name.

Structure or Class Names

The name of a structure or class is a type name. This class construct does not exist in C. In C++ it is not necessary to use the qualifier **struct** or **class** in front of a structure or class name.

Block Declarations

C++ permits declarations within blocks and after code statements. This feature allows you to declare an identifier closer to its first point of application. It even permits the loop control variable to be declared within the formal definition of the control structure, as shown here:

```
// C++ point-of-use variable declaration
   for(int row=0; row<MAX_ROWS; row++)
```

The Scope Qualifier Operator

You use the new scope qualifier operator :: to resolve name conflicts. For example, if a function has a local declaration for a variable *vector_location* and there exists a global variable *vector_location,* the qualifier *::vector_location* allows the global variable to be accessed within the scope of the local function. The reverse is not possible.

The const Specifier

You can use the **const** specifier to lock the value of an entity within its scope. You can also use it to lock the data pointed to by a pointer variable, the value of the pointer address, or the values of both the pointer address and the data pointed to.

Anonymous Unions

Unions without a name can be defined anywhere a variable or field can be defined. You can use this ability for the economy of memory storage by allowing the sharing of memory among two or more fields of a structure.

Explicit Type Conversions

You can use the name of a predefined type or user-defined type as a function to convert data from one type to another. Under certain circumstances, such an explicit type conversion can be used as an alternative to a cast conversion.

Function Declarations

C++ will make many a Pascal, Modula-2, and ADA programmer happy because it permits the specification by name and type for each function parameter inside the parentheses next to the function name. For example:

```
void * dupmem(void *dest,int c,unsigned count)
{
    .
    .
    .
}
```

The equivalent C interface, under the ANSI standard, would look exactly the same. In this case, C++ influenced the ANSI standards committee.

The C++ translator will perform type checking to ensure that the number and type of values sent into a function when it is invoked match the number and type of the formal arguments defined for the function. A check is also made to make certain that the function's return type matches the variable used in the expression invoking the function. This type of parameter checking is missing in most C systems.

Function Overloading

In C++, functions can use the same names if you use the specifier overload, and each of the overloaded functions can be distinguished on the basis of the number and type of its parameters.

Default Function Parameter Values

You can assign default values to trailing sets of C++ function parameters. In this case, the function can be invoked using fewer than the total number of parameters. Any missing trailing parameters assume their default values.

Functions with an Unspecified Number of Parameters

You can define C++ functions with an unknown number and type of parameters by employing the ellipsis (...). When you use this feature, parameter type checking is suppressed to allow flexibility in the interface to the function.

Reference Parameters in a Function

Through the use of the ampersand operator (&), a formal function parameter can be declared as a reference parameter. For example:

```
int i;
increment(i);

  .
  .
  .


void increment(int& variable_reference)
{
  variable_reference++;
}
```

Because &*variable_reference* is defined as a reference parameter, its address is assigned to the address of *i* when **increment()** is invoked. The value of *i* that is sent in is incremented within function **increment()** and returned to variable *i* outside of function **increment()**. It is not necessary for the address of *i* to be explicitly passed into function **increment()**, as it is in C.

The inline Specifier

You can use the **inline** specifier to instruct the compiler to perform inline substitution of a given function at the location where the function is invoked.

The new and delete Operators

The **new** and **delete** operators that are introduced by C++ allow for programmer-controlled allocation and deallocation of heap storage.

void Pointers and Functions that Return void

In C++, the type **void** is used to indicate that a function returns nothing. Pointer variables can be declared to point to **void**. Such pointers can then be assigned to any other pointer that points to an arbitrary base type.

Major Enhancements to C

The most significant major enhancement to C involves the concept of object-oriented programming. The following sections briefly explain all of the C++ enhancements that make object-oriented programming possible.

Class Constructs and Data Encapsulation

The class construct is the fundamental vehicle for object-oriented programming. A class definition can encapsulate all of the data declarations, the initial values, and the set of operations (called *methods*) for data abstraction. Objects can be declared to be of a given class, and messages can be sent to objects. Additionally, each object of a specified class can contain its own private set and public set of data representative of that class.

The struct Class

A *structure* in C++ is a subset of a class definition and has no private or protected sections. This subclass can contain both data (as is expected in ANSI C) and functions.

Constructors and Destructors

Constructor and destructor methods are used to guarantee the initialization of the data defined within an object of a specified class. When an object is declared, the specified initialization constructor is activated. Destructors automatically deallocate storage for the associated object when the scope in which the object is declared is exited.

Messages

As you have seen, the object is the basic fabric of object-oriented programming. You manipulate objects by sending them messages. You send messages to objects (variables declared to be of a given class) by using a mechanism similar to invoking a function. The set of possible messages that can be sent to an object is specified in the class description for the object. Each object responds to a message by determining an appropriate action to take based on the nature of the message. For example, if *Palette_Colors* represents an object, and *SetNumColors_Method* represents a method with a single integer parameter, sending a message to the object would be accomplished by using the following statement:

```
Palette_Colors.SetNumColors_Method(16);
```

Friends

The concept of data hiding and data encapsulation implies a denied access to the inner structures that make up an object. The class's private section is normally totally off-limits to any function outside the class. C++ does allow other functions outside methods or classes to be declared to be a friend to a specified class. Friendship breaks down a normally impenetrable wall and permits access to the class's private data and methods.

Operator Overloading

With C++, the programmer can take the set of predefined operators and functions supplied with the compiler, or user-defined operators and functions, and give them multiple meanings. For example, different functions typically have different names, but for functions performing similar tasks on different types of objects, it is sometimes better to let these functions have the *same* name. When their argument types are different, the compiler can distinguish them and choose the right function to call. What follows is a coded example; you could have one function called **average()** that was overloaded for an array of integers, of floating points, and of double values.

```
int average(int isize, int iarray[]);
float average(int isize, float farray[]);
double average(int isize, double darray[]);
    .
    .
    .
```

Since you have declared the three different functions by the same name, the compiler can look at the invoking statement and automatically decide which function is appropriate for the formal parameter list's arguments:

```
    average(isize,iarray);
    average(isize,farray);
....average(isize,darray);
```

Derived Classes

A *derived class* can be seen as a subclass of a specified class, thereby forming a hierarchy of abstractions. Derived class objects typically inherit all or some of the methods of the parent class. It is also common for a derived class to then incorporate these inherited methods with new methods specific to the subclass. All subclass objects contain the fields of data from the parent class as well as any of their own private data.

Polymorphism Using Virtual Functions

Polymorphism involves a tree structure of parent classes and their subclasses. Each subclass within this tree can receive one or more messages with the same name. When an object of a class within this tree receives a message, the object determines the particular application of the message that is appropriate for an object of the specified subclass.

Stream Libraries

An additional library stream is included with the C++ language. The three classes **cin**, **cout**, and **cerr** are provided for terminal and file input and output. All of the operators within these three classes can be overloaded within a user-defined class. This capability allows the input and output operations to be easily tailored to an application's needs.

The Basic Elements of a C Program

You may have heard that C is a difficult language to master. However, while it is true that a brief encounter with C code may leave you scratching your head, this is only due to C's foreign syntax, structure, and indentation schemes. By the end of this chapter, you should have enough information to have developed a working knowledge of the C language that enables you to write short but meaningful code. In the next section you will learn about the five fundamental components of a "good" program.

The Five Basic Components of a Program

You may be familiar with a problem-solution format called an IPO diagram. *IPO diagrams* were a stylized approach to the age-old programming problem of input/process/output. The following list elaborates on these three fundamentals and encapsulates the entire application development cycle. All programs must address the following five components:

- Programs must obtain information from some input source.

- Programs must decide how this input is to be arranged and stored.

- Programs use a set of instructions to manipulate the input. These instructions can be broken down to four major categories: single statements, conditional statements, loops, and subroutines.

- Programs must report the results of the data manipulation.

- A well-written application incorporates all of the fundamentals just listed, expressed by using good modular design, self-documenting code (meaningful variable names), and a good indentation scheme.

Your First C Program

The following C program illustrates the basic components of a C application. It is suggested that you enter each example as you read about it to help you understand new concepts as you encounter them.

```
/*
 *    05FIRST.C
 *    Your first example C program.
 *    Copyright (c) William H. Murray and Chris H. Pappas, 1992
 */

#include <stdio.h>

main()
{
  printf(" HELLO World! ");

  return(0);
}
```

There is a lot happening in this short piece of code. Let's begin with the comment block:

```
/*
 *    05FIRST.C
 *    Your first example C program.
 *    Copyright (c) William H. Murray and Chris H. Pappas, 1992
 */
```

All well-written source code includes meaningful comments. A meaningful comment is one that neither insults the intelligence of the programmer nor assumes too much. In C, comments begin /* and are terminated with */. Anything between these unique symbol pairs is ignored by the compiler.

The next statement represents one of C's unique features, known as a preprocessor statement:

```
#include <stdio.h>
```

A *preprocessor statement* is like a precompile instruction. In this case the statement instructs the compiler to retrieve the code stored in the predefined stdio.h file into the source code on the line requested. (The stdio.h file is called a header file. *Header files* can include symbolic constants, identifiers, and function prototypes and have these declarations pulled out of the main program for purposes of modularity.)

Following the **#include** statement is the main function declaration:

```
main()
{
    .
    .
    .
    return(0);  /*   or return 0;   */
}
```

All C programs are made up of function calls. Every C program must have one called **main()**. The **main()** function is usually where program execution begins, and it ends with a **return()** from the **main()**. It is also legal to use **return()** statements without the parentheses.

Following the **main()** function header is the body of the function itself. Notice the { and } symbol pairs. These are called *braces.* You use braces to encapsulate multiple statements. These braces may define the body for a function, or they may bundle together statements that are dependent on the same logic control statement, as is the case when several statements are executed based on the validity of an if statement. In this example, the braces define the body of the main program.

The next line is the only statement in the body of the **main()** function and is the simplest example of an output statement:

```
printf(" HELLO World! ");
```

The **printf**() function was previously prototyped in stdio.h. Because no other parameters are specified, the sentence will be printed to the display monitor.

Your First C++ Program

The example that follows performs the same function as the one just discussed, but it takes advantage of those features unique to C++.

```
//
//   05FIRST.CPP
//   Your first C++ example program.
//   Copyright (c) William H. Murray and Chris H. Pappas, 1992
//

#include <iostream.h>

main()
{
  cout << " HELLO World! ";

  return(0);
}
```

There are three major differences between this one and the last. First, the comment designator has been changed from the /* */ pair to //. Second, the **#include** filename has been changed to iostream.h. The third change involves a different output operator call, **cout**. Many of the examples in the book will highlight the sometimes subtle and sometimes dazzling differences between C and C++.

Your Second C Program

The following program is a slightly more meaningful example. It is a little more complete in that it not only outputs information but also prompts the user for input. Many of the components of this program will be elaborated on throughout the remainder of the book.

```
/*
 *   05SECOND.C
 *   This C program prompts the user for a specified length,
 *   in feet, and then outputs the value converted to
 *   meters and centimeters
```

```
*    Copyright (c) William H. Murray and Chris H. Pappas, 1992
*/

#include <stdio.h>

main()
{
  float feet, meters, centimeters;

  printf("Enter the number of feet to be converted: ");
  scanf("%f",&feet);

  while(feet > 0 ) {
    centimeters = feet * 12 * 2.54;
    meters = centimeters/100;
    printf("%8.2f feet equals\n", feet);
    printf("%8.2f meters \n",meters);
    printf("%8.2f centimeters \n",centimeters);
    printf("\nEnter another value to be \n");
    printf("converted (0 ends the program): ");
    scanf("%f",&feet);
  }
  printf(">>> Have a nice day! <<<");

  return(0);
}
```

Data Declarations

The first thing new you will notice in the program is the declaration of three variables:

```
float feet, meters, centimeters;
```

All C variables must be declared before they are used. One of the standard data types supplied by the C language is **float**. The syntax for declaring variables in C requires the definition of the variable's type before the name of the variable. In this example, the **float** type is represented by the keyword **float**, and the three variables *feet, meters,* and *centimeters* are defined.

User Input

The next unconventional-looking statement is used to input information from the keyboard:

```
printf("Enter the number of feet to be converted: ");
scanf("%f",&feet);
```

The **scanf()** function has a requirement that is called a format string. *Format strings* define how the input data is to be interpreted and represented internally. The "%f" function parameter instructs the compiler to interpret the input as float data. In Microsoft C and C++, a **float** occupies 4 bytes. (Chapter 6 contains a detailed explanation of all of the C and C++ language data types.)

Address Operator

In the previous statement you may have noticed that the float variable *feet* was preceded by an ampersand symbol (&). The & is known as an *address operator.* Whenever a variable is preceded by this symbol, the compiler uses the address of the specified variable instead of the value stored in the variable. The **scanf()** function has been written to expect the address of the variable to be filled.

Loop Structure

One of the simplest loop structures to code in C is the **while** loop:

```
while(feet > 0) {
  .
  .
  .
}
```

This pretest loop starts with the reserved word **while** followed by a Boolean expression that returns either a TRUE or a FALSE. The opening brace ({) and closing brace (}) are optional; they are only needed when more than one executable statement is to be associated with the loop repetition. Braced statements are sometimes referred to as a compound statements, compound blocks, or code blocks.

If you are using compound blocks, make certain you use the agreed-upon brace style. While it doesn't matter to the compiler where the braces are placed (in terms of skipped spaces or lines), programmers reading your code will certainly appreciate the style and effort. An opening loop brace is placed at the end of the test condition, and the closing brace is placed in the same column as the first character in the test condition.

Formatted Output

In analyzing the second program, you will notice more complex **printf()** function calls:

```
printf("%8.2f feet equals\n", feet);
printf("%8.2f meters \n",meters);
printf("%8.2f centimeters \n",centimeters);
printf("\nEnter another value to be \n");
printf("converted (0 ends the program): ");
```

If you are familiar with the PL/I language developed by IBM, you will be right at home with the concept of a format or control string. Whenever a **printf()** function is invoked to print not only *literal strings* (any set of characters between double quote marks), but also values, a format string is required. The format string represents two things; a picture of how the output string is to look, combined with the format interpretation for each of the values printed. Format strings are always between double quote marks.

Let's break down the first **printf()** format string ("%8.2f feet equals\n", feet) into its separate components:

Control	Action
%8.2f	Take the value of *feet,* interpret it as a **float**, and print it in a field of 8 spaces with 2 decimal places.
feet equals	After printing the **float** *feet,* skip one space and then print the literal string "feet equals".
\n	Once the line is complete, execute a new line feed.
,	The comma separates the format string from the variable name(s) used to satisfy all format descriptors. (In this case there is only one %8.2f.)

The next two **printf()** statements are similar in execution. Each statement prints a formatted **float** value, followed by a literal string, and ending with a newline feed. If you were to run the program, your output would look similar to this:

```
Enter the number of feet to be converted: 4
   10.00 feet equals
    3.05 meters
  304.80 centimeters

Enter another value to be
converted (0 stops program): 0
```

The C *escape sequences,* or *output control characters,* allow you to use a sequence of characters to represent special characters. Table 5-2 lists all of the output control symbols and a description of how they can be used in format strings. All leading zeros are ignored by the compiler for characters notated in hexadecimal. The compiler

Sequence	Name	Sequence	Name
\a	Alert (bell)	\?	Literal quotation mark
\b	Backspace	\'	Single quotation mark
\f	Form feed	\"	Double quotation mark
\n	Newline	\\	Backslash
\r	Carriage return	\ddd	ASCII character in octal notation
\t	Horizontal tab	\xdd	ASCII character in hex notation
\v	Vertical tab		

Table 5-2.   *C/C++ printf() Escape Sequences*

determines the end of a hex-specified escape character when it encounters either a non-hex character or more than two hex characters, excluding leading zeros.

Also on the subject of format strings, and even though the subject is a bit advanced, are the **scanf()** formatting controls. Table 5-3 describes the **scanf()** formatting controls and their meanings. If you wish to input a string without automatically appending a terminating null character (\0), use %nc, where *n* is a decimal integer. In this case, the **c** type character indicates that the argument is a pointer to a character array. The next *n* characters are read from the input stream into the specified location, and no null character (\0) is appended. If *n* is not specified, the default character array length is 1.

As you learn more about the various C data types, you will be able to refer back to Tables 5-2 and 5-3 for a reminder of how the various controls affect input and output.

Using CodeView

To examine the actual operation of the C code presented in this section, you can use CodeView. When you compile your program, make certain you have turned on debug information. You do this by choosing PWB's Options|Build Options...|Use Debug Options or by pressing ALT-O, D, D, ENTER. This compiler setting specifies that the debug options are to be used when the project is built. Now start CodeView, and single-step (F8) through the program. Use the Watch window to keep an eye on the variables *yard, feet,* and *inch.*

Your Second C++ Program

The following C++ example is identical in function to the previous C example except for some minor variations in the syntax used:

```
//
//  05SECOND.CPP
//  This C++ program prompts the user for a specified length,
//  feet, and then outputs the value converted to
//  meters and centimeters
//  Copyright (c) William H. Murray and Chris H. Pappas, 1992
//

#include <iostream.h>
#include <iomanip.h>

main()
{
   float feet,meters,centimeters;

   cout << "Enter the number of feet to be converted: ";
   cin  >> feet;

   while(feet > 0 ) {
     centimeters = feet * 12 * 2.54;
     meters = centimeters/100;
     cout << setw(8) << setprecision(2) \
          << setiosflags(ios::fixed) << feet << " feet equals \n";
     cout << setw(8) << setprecision(2) \
          << meters << " meters \n";
     cout << setw(8) << setprecision(2) \
          << centimeters << " centimeters \n";
     cout << "\nEnter another value to be \n";
     cout << "converted (0 ends the program): ";
     cin >>  feet;
   }
   cout << ">>> Have a nice day! <<<";

   return(0);
}
```

Character	Input Type Expected	Argument Type
d	Decimal integer	Pointer to **int**
o	Octal integer	Pointer to **int**
x, X	Hexadecimal integer	Pointer to **int**
i	Decimal, hexadecimal, or octal integer	Pointer to **int**
u	Unsigned decimal integer	Pointer to **unsigned int**
e, E	Floating-point value	Pointer to **float**
f, g, G	Consisting of an optional sign (+ or −), a series of one or more decimal digits possibly containing a decimal point, and an optional exponent ("e" or "E") followed by an optionally signed integer value	
c	Character. White space characters that are ordinarily skipped are read when c is specified; to read the next non-white space character, use %1s.	Pointer to **char**
s	String	Pointer to character array auto create null string
n	No input read from stream or buffer	Pointer to **int**, into which is stored the number of characters read from the stream or buffer up to that point in the call to **scanf**
p	In the form *xxxx:yyyy*, where *x* digits and *y* digits are uppercase hexadecimal digits	Pointer to **far**, **void**

Table 5-3. *C Formatting Controls*

There are six major differences between the C++ example and its C counterpart. The first two changes involve the use of **cin** and **cout** for I/O. These statements use the << ("put to," or insertion) and >> ("get from," or extraction) iostream operators. Both operators have been overloaded to handle the output/input of all the pre-defined types. They can also be overloaded to handle user-defined types such as rational numbers.

The last four changes are all related to formatting C++ output. To gain the same output precision easily afforded by C's "%8.2f" format string, the program requires four additional statements. The file IOMANIP.H is included in the program to give access to three specific class member inline functions: **setw()**, **setprecision()**, and **setiosflags()**. As you look at the code, you will notice that the calls to **setw()** and **setprecision()** are repeated. This is because their effect is only for the next output value, unlike **setiosflags()**, which makes a global change to **fixed** output.

C++ programmers who like the power and flexibility of the C output function **printf()** can use **printf()** directly from library stdio.h. The next two statements show the C and C++ equivalents:

```
printf("%8.2f feet equals\n", feet);
cout << setw(8) << setprecision(2) \
     << setiosflags(ios::fixed) << feet << " feet equals \n";
```

Files

Of course there will be times when an application wants either its input or output to deal directly with files rather than the keyboard and display monitor. This brief introduction serves as an example of how to declare and use simple data files:

```
/*
 *    05FILE.CPP
 *    This C++ program demonstrates how to declare and use both
 *    input and output files. The example program
 *    takes the order_price from customer.dat and generates
 *    a billing_price that is printed to billing.dat
 *    Copyright (c) William H. Murray and Chris H. Pappas, 1992
 */

#include <stdio.h>
#define MIN_DISCOUNT .97
#define MAX_DISCOUNT .95

main()
{
  float forder_price, fbilling_price;
```

```
FILE *fin,*fout;

fin=fopen("a:\\customer.dat","r");
fout=fopen("a:\\billing.dat","w");

while (fscanf(fin,"%f",&forder_price) != EOF) {
  fprintf(fout,"Your order of \t\t$%8.2f\n", forder_price);
  if (forder_price < 10000)
     fbilling_price = forder_price * MIN_DISCOUNT;
  else fbilling_price = forder_price * MAX_DISCOUNT;
  fprintf(fout,"is discounted to \t$%8.2f.\n\n", fbilling_price);
}
return(0);
}
```

Each file in a C program must be associated with a file pointer. The *file pointer* is a pointer that points to information that defines various things about a file, including the path to the file, its name, and its status. A file pointer is a pointer variable of type **FILE** and is defined in stdio.h. The following statement from the example program declares two files, *fin and *fout:

```
, FILE *fin,*fout;
```

The next two statements in the program open two separate streams and associate each file with its respective stream:

```
fin=fopen("a:\\customer.dat","r");
fout=fopen("a:\\billing.dat","w");
```

The statements also return the file pointer for each file. Since these are pointers to files, your application should never alter their values.

The second parameter to the **fopen()** function is the file mode. Files may be opened in either text or binary mode. When in text mode, most C compilers translate carriage return/linefeed sequences into newline characters on input. During output, the opposite occurs. However, binary files do not go through such translations. Table 5-4 lists all of the valid file modes.

The r+, w+, and a+ file modes select both reading and writing. (The file is open for update.) When switching between reading and writing, you must remember to reposition the file pointer, using either **fsetpos()**, **fseek()**, or **rewind()**.

C does perform its own file closing automatically whenever the application closes. However, there may be times when you want direct control over when a file is closed. The following listing shows the same program modified to include the necessary closing function calls:

```
/*
 *   05FILE.C
 *   This C program demonstrates how to declare and use both
 *   input and output files. The example program
 *   takes the order_price from customer.dat and generates
 *   a billing_price that is printed to billing.dat
 *   Copyright (c) William H. Murray and Chris H. Pappas, 1992
 */

#include <stdio.h>
#define MIN_DISCOUNT .97
#define MAX_DISCOUNT .95

main()
{
  float forder_price, fbilling_price;
  FILE *fin,*fout;

  fin=fopen("a:\\customer.dat","r");
  fout=fopen("a:\\billing.dat","w");

  while (fscanf(fin,"%f",&forder_price) != EOF) {
    fprintf(fout,"Your order of \t\t$%8.2f\n", forder_price);
```

Access Type	Description
a	Opens in append mode. It creates the file if it does not already exist. All write operations occur at the end of the file. The file pointer can be repositioned using **fseek()** or **rewind()**; it is always moved back to the end of the file before any write operation is carried out
a+	Same as above, but also allows reading
r	Opens for reading. If the file does not exist or cannot be found, the open call will fail
r+	Opens for both reading and writing. If the file does not exist or cannot be found, the open call will fail
w	Opens an empty file for writing. If the file exists, all contents are destroyed
w+	Opens an empty file for both reading and writing. If the file exists, all contents are destroyed

Table 5-4.   *Valid C File Modes*

```
   if (forder_price < 10000)
       fbilling_price = forder_price * MIN_DISCOUNT;
   else fbilling_price = forder_price * MAX_DISCOUNT;
   fprintf(fout,"is discounted to \t$%8.2f.\n\n", fbilling_price);
 }

 fclose(fin);
 fclose(fout);

 return(0);
}
```

The following program performs the same function as the one just examined but is coded in C++:

```
//
//   05FILE.CPP
//   This C++ program demonstrates how to declare and use both
//   input and output files. The example program
//   takes the order_price from customer.dat and generates
//   a billing_price that is printed to billing.dat
//   Copyright (c) William H. Murray and Chris H. Pappas, 1992
//

#include <fstream.h>
#include <iomanip.h>
#define MIN_DISCOUNT .97
#define MAX_DISCOUNT .95

main()
{
  float forder_price, fbilling_price;
  ifstream fin("a:\\customer.dat");
  ofstream fout("a:\\billing.dat");

  fin >> forder_price;
  while (!fin.eof()) {
    fout << setiosflags(ios::fixed);
    fout << "Your order of \t\t$" << setprecision(2) \
         << setw(8) << forder_price << "\n";
    if (forder_price < 10000)
       fbilling_price = forder_price * MIN_DISCOUNT;
    else fbilling_price = forder_price * MAX_DISCOUNT;
```

```
    fout << "is discounted to \t$" << setprecision(2) \
        << setw(8) << fbilling_price << ".\n\n";
  fin >> forder_price;
  }

  fin.close();
  fout.close();

  return(0);
}
```

Disk file input and output are slightly different in C++ than in C. C++ has a two-part design to its stream library; a streambuf object and a stream. This same model performs I/O for keyboard and terminal as well as disk I/O. The same operators and operations perform in precisely the same way. This greatly simplifies a programming task that has always been difficult and confusing. To facilitate disk file I/O, the stream library defines a **filebuf** object, which is a derivative of the standard **streambuf** type. Like its progenitor type, **filebuf** manages a buffer, but in this case, the buffer is attached to a disk file. You will learn more about files in Chapter 11.

Chapter *6*

Data

Fully appreciating all that C and C++ have to offer takes time and practice. Chapter 6 begins your exploration of the underlying structures of the C and C++ languages. The great stability of these languages comes from the standard C and C++ data types and the modifiers and operators that can be used with them.

Identifiers

Identifiers are the names you use to represent variables, constants, types, functions, and labels in your program. You create an identifier by specifying it in the declaration of a variable, type, or function. You can then use the identifier in later program statements to refer to the associated item.

An identifier is a sequence of one or more letters, digits, or underscores that begins with a letter or underscore. Identifiers can contain any number of characters, but only the first 31 characters are significant to the compiler. (However, other programs that read the compiler output, such as the linker, may recognize even fewer characters.)

C and C++ are *case sensitive*. This means that the C compiler considers uppercase and lowercase letters to be distinct characters. For example, the compiler sees the variables *NAME_LENGTH* and *Name_Length* as two unique identifiers representing different memory cells. This feature enables you to create distinct identifiers that have the same spelling but different cases for one or more of the letters.

The selection of case can also help you understand your code. For example, identifiers declared in **#include** header files are often created using only uppercase letters. Because of this, whenever you encounter an uppercase identifier in the source file, you have a visual clue as to where that particular identifier's definition can be found.

While it is syntactically legal, you should not use leading underscores in identifiers you create. Identifiers beginning with an underscore can cause conflicts with the names of system routines or variables and produce errors. As a result, programs containing names beginning with leading underscores are not guaranteed to be portable. Use of two sequential underscore characters (__) in an identifier is reserved for C++ implementations and standard libraries.

One stylistic convention adopted by many C programmers is to precede all identifiers with an abbreviation of the identifier's data type. For example, all integer identifiers would begin with an "i," floats would begin with an "f," null-terminated strings would begin with "sz," pointer variables would begin with a "p," and so on. With this naming convention, you can easily look at a piece of code and not only see which identifiers are being used, but also see their data type. This approach makes it easier to learn how a particular section of code operates and to do line-by-line source debugging. The programs throughout this book use both variable naming conventions since many of the programs you encounter in real life will use one format or another.

The following are examples of identifiers:

```
i
itotal
frange1
szfirst_name
lfrequency
imax
iMax
iMAX
NULL
EOF
```

See if you can determine why the following identifiers are illegal:

```
1st_year
#social_security
Not_Done!
```

The first identifier is illegal because it begins with a decimal number. The second identifier begins with a # symbol, and the last identifier ends with an illegal character.

Take a look at the following identifiers. Are they legal or not?

```
O
OO
OOO
```

_____

Actually, all four identifiers are legal. The first three identifiers use the uppercase letter "O." Since each has a different number of O's, they are all unique. The fourth identifier is composed of five underscore (_) characters. Is it meaningful? Definitely not. Is it legal? Yes. While these identifiers meet the "letter of the law," they greatly miss the "spirit of the law." The point is that all identifiers, functions, constants, and variables should have meaningful names.

Since uppercase and lowercase letters are considered distinct characters, each of the following identifiers is unique:

```
MAX_RATIO
max_ratio
Max_Ratio
```

The C compiler's case sensitivity can create tremendous headaches for the novice C programmer. For example, trying to reference the **printf()** function when it was typed **PRINTF()** will invoke "unknown identifier" complaints from the compiler. In Pascal, however, a writeln is a WRITELN is a WriteLn.

With experience you would probably detect the preceding **printf()** error, but can you see what's wrong with this next statement?

```
printf("%D",integer_value);
```

Assuming that *integer_value* was defined properly, you might think that nothing was wrong. Remember, however, C is case sensitive—the %D print format has never been defined; only %d has.

For more advanced applications, some linkers may further restrict the number and type of characters for globally visible symbols. Also, the linker, unlike the compiler, may not distinguish between uppercase and lowercase letters. By default, the Microsoft C/C++ LINK sees all public and external symbols, such as *MYVARI-ABLE, MyVariable,* and *myvariable,* as the same. You can, however, make LINK case sensitive by using the /NOI option. This would then force LINK to see the preceding three example variables as being unique. Use your PWB Help utility for additional information on how to use this switch.

One last word on identifiers: an identifier cannot have the same spelling and case as a keyword of the language. The next section lists C and C++ keywords.

Keywords

Keywords are predefined identifiers that have special meanings to the C/C++ compiler. You can use them only as defined. Remember, the name of a program identifier cannot have the same spelling and case as a C/C++ keyword. The C language keywords are listed in Table 6-1.

_asm[1,2]	auto	_based[1]	break
case	catch	_cdecl[1]	char
class	const	continue	default
delete	do	double	else
_emit[1,3]	enum	_export[1]	extern
_far[1]	_fastcall[1]	float	for
_fortran[1]	friend	goto	_huge[1]
if	inline	int	_interrupt[1]
long	_loadds[1]	_near[1]	new
operator	_pascal[1]	private	protected
public	register	return	_saveregs[1]
_segment[1]	_segname[1]	_self[1]	short
signed	sizeof	static	_stdcall[1]
struct	_syscall[1]	switch	template[4]
this	throw	try	typedef
union	unsigned	virtual	void
volatile	while		

[1] Microsoft-specific keyword
[2] Replaces standard C++ **asm** syntax
[3] **_emit** is technically not a keyword; it is a pseudo-op for the inline assembler.
[4] The **template** keyword is an experimental instruction reserved for future implementations and is used for defining parameterized types.

Table 6-1.   *Microsoft C/C++ Keywords*

You cannot redefine keywords. However, you can specify text to be substituted for keywords before compilation by using C preprocessor directives.

Standard C and C++ Data Types

All programs deal with some kind of information that you can usually represent by using one of the seven basic C and C++ types: text or **char**, integer values or **int**, floating-point values or **float**, double floating-point values or **double** (**long double**), enumerated or **enum**, valueless or **void**, and pointers. Following is an explanation of the types:

- Text (data type **char**) is made up of single characters, such as a, Z, ?, 3, and strings, such as "There is more to life than increasing its speed". (Usually, 8 bits, or 1 byte per character, with the range of 0 to 255.)

- Integer values are those numbers you learned to count with (1, 2, 7, −45, and 1,345). (Usually, 16 bits wide, 2 bytes, or 1 word, with the range of −32,768 to 32,767.)

- Floating-point values are numbers that have a fractional portion, such as pi (3.14159), and exponents (7.563x1021). These are also known as real numbers. (Usually, 32 bits, 4 bytes, or 2 words, with the range of 3.4E−38 to 3.4E+38.)

- Double floating-point values have an extended range. (Usually, 64 bits, 8 bytes, or 4 words, with the range of 1.7E−308 to 1.7E+308.) Long double floating-point values are even more precise. (Usually, 80 bytes, or 5 words, with the range of 1.18E−4932 to 1.18E+4932.)

- Enumerated data types allow for user-defined types.

- The type **void** is used to signify values that occupy zero bits and have no value. (This type can also be used for the creation of generic pointers, as discussed in Chapter 10.)

- The **pointer** data type doesn't hold information in the normal sense of the other data types; instead, each pointer contains the address of the memory location holding the actual data. (This is also discussed in Chapter 10.)

Characters

Every language uses a set of characters to construct meaningful statements. For instance, all books written in English use combinations of 26 letters of the alphabet, the 10 digits, and the punctuation marks. Similarly, C and C++ programs are written using a set of characters, consisting of the 26 lowercase letters of the alphabet:

abcdefghijklmnopqrstuvwxyz

the 26 uppercase letters of the alphabet:

ABCDEFGHIJKLMNOPQRSTUVWXYZ

the 10 digits:

0 1 2 3 4 5 6 7 8 9

and the following symbols:

```
+ − * / =, . . _ : ; ? \ " ' ~ | ! # % $ & ( ) [ ] { } ^ @
```

C and C++ also use the blank space, sometimes referred to as white space. Combinations of symbols, with no blank space between them, are also valid C and C++ characters. In fact, the following is a mixture of valid C and C++ symbols:

```
++ −− == && || << >> >= <= += −= *= /= ?: :: /* */ //
```

The following C program illustrates how to declare and use **char** data types:

```c
/*
 *    06CHAR.C
 *    A C program demonstrating the char data type and showing
 *    how a char variable can be interpreted as an integer.
 *    Copyright (c) William H. Murray and Chris H. Pappas, 1992
 */

#include <stdio.h>
#include <ctype.h>

main()
{
  char csinglechar, cuppercase, clowercase;

  printf("\nPlease enter a single character: ");
  scanf("%c",&csinglechar);


  cuppercase = toupper(csinglechar);
  clowercase = tolower(csinglechar);

  printf("The UPPERcase character \'%c\' has a decimal ASCII"
          " value of %d\n",cuppercase,cuppercase);
  printf("The ASCII value represented in hexadecimal"
          " is %X\n",cuppercase);

  printf("If you add sixteen you will get \'%c\'\n",
           (cuppercase+16));
  printf("The calculated ASCII value in hexadecimal"
          " is %X\n",(cuppercase+16));
  printf("The LOWERcase character \'%c\' has a decimal ASCII"
          " value of %d\n",clowercase,clowercase);


  return(0);
}
```

The output from the program looks like this:

```
Please enter a single character: z
The UPPERcase character 'Z' has a decimal ASCII value of 90
The ASCII value represented in hexadecimal is 5A
If you add sixteen you will get 'j'
The calculated ASCII value in hexadecimal is 6A
The character 'z' has a decimal ASCII value of 122
```

The %X format control instructs the compiler to interpret the value as an uppercase hexadecimal number.

Three Integers

Microsoft C/C++ supports three types of integers. Along with the standard type **int**, the compiler supports **short int** and **long int**. These are most often abbreviated to just **short** and **long**. Since the C language is so tied to the hardware, the actual sizes of **short**, **int**, and **long** depend upon the implementation. Across all C compilers, the only guarantee is that a variable of type **short** will not be larger than one of type **long**. Microsoft C/C++ allocates 2 bytes for both **short** and **int**. The type **long** occupies 4 bytes of storage.

Unsigned Modifier

All C and C++ compilers allow you to declare certain types to be unsigned. Currently, you can apply the **unsigned** modifier to four types: **char**, **short int, int**, and **long int**. When one of these data types is modified to be unsigned, you can think of the range of values it holds as representing the numbers displayed on a car odometer. An automobile odometer starts at 000..., increases to a maximum of 999..., and then recycles back to 000.... It also displays only positive whole numbers. In a similar way, an unsigned data type can hold only positive values in the range of zero to the maximum number that can be represented.

For example, suppose you are designing a new data type called *my_octal* and have decided that *my_octal* variables can hold only 3 bits. You have also decided that the data type *my_octal* is signed by default. Since a variable of type *my_octal* can only contain the bit patterns 000 through 111 (or zero to 7 decimal) and you want to represent both positive and negative values, you have a problem. You can't have both positive and negative numbers in the range zero to 7 because you need one of the three bits to represent the sign of the number. Therefore, *my_octal*'s range is a subset. When the most significant bit is zero, the value is positive. When the most significant bit is 1, the value is negative. This gives a *my_octal* variable the range of –4 to +3, as represented in Table 6-2.

Unique Combinations of 0's and 1's	Decimal Equivalent
000	+0
001	+1
010	+2
011	+3
100	−4
101	−3
110	−2
111	−1

Table 6-2. *The Hypothetical Signed my_octal Data Type*

However, applying the **unsigned** data type modifier to a *my_octal* variable would yield a range of zero to 7, since the most significant bit can be combined with the lower two bits to represent a broader range of positive values instead of identifying the sign of the number, as you can see in Table 6-3.

This simple analogy holds true for any of the valid C data types defined to be of type **unsigned**. The storage and range for the fundamental C data types are summarized in Table 6-4.

Table 6-5 lists the valid data type modifiers in all of the various legal and abbreviated combinations.

Unique Combinations of 0's and 1's	Decimal Equivalent
000	+0
001	+1
010	+2
011	+3
100	+4
101	+5
110	+6
111	+7

Table 6-3. *The Hypothetical Unsigned my_octal Data Type*

Type	Storage	Range of Values
char	1 byte	−128 to 127
int	2 bytes	−32,768 to 32,767
short	2 bytes	−32,768 to 32,767
long	4 bytes	−2,147,483,648 to 2,147,483,647
unsigned char	1 byte	0 to 255
unsigned int	2 bytes	0 to 65,535
unsigned short	2 bytes	0 to 65,535
unsigned long	4 bytes	0 to 4,294,967,295
float	4 bytes	3.4E−38 to 3.4E+38
double	8 bytes	1.7E−308 to 1.7E + 308
long double	10 bytes	1.1E−4932 to 1.1E+4932
pointer	2 bytes	(near, based)
pointer	4 bytes	(far, huge)

Table 6-4.   *Fundamental Type Storage and Range of Values*

Floating-Point

Microsoft C/C++ uses the three floating-point types **float**, **double**, and **long double**. While the ANSI C standard does not specifically define the values and storage that are to be allocated for each of these types, the standard did require each type to hold a minimum of any value in the range 1E−37 to 1E+37. As you saw in Table 6-4, the Microsoft C/C++ environment has greatly expanded upon this minimum requirement. Historically, most C compilers have always had the types **float** and **double**. The

Type Modifier	Abbreviation
signed char	char
signed int	signed, int
signed short int	short, signed short
signed long int	long, signed long
unsigned char	no abbreviation
unsigned int	unsigned
unsigned short int	unsigned short
unsigned long int	unsigned long

Table 6-5.   *Valid Data Type Modifier Abbreviations*

ANSI C committee added the third type, **long double**. Here are some examples of floating-point numbers:

```
float altitude = 47000;
double joules;
long double budget_deficit;
```

You can use the third type, **long double**, on any computer, even those that have only two types of floating-point numbers. However, if the computer does not have a specific data type of **long double**, then the data item will have the same size and storage capacity as a double.

The following C++ program illustrates how to declare and use floating-point variables:

```
//
//   06FLOAT.CPP
//   A C++ program demonstrating using the float data type.
//   Copyright (c) William H. Murray and Chris H. Pappas, 1992
//

#include <iostream.h>
#include <iomanip.h>

main()
{
  long loriginal_flags=cin.flags();
  float fvalue;

  cout << "Please enter a float value to be formatted: ";
  cin >> fvalue;

  cout << "Standard Formatting:    " << fvalue << "\n";
  cout.setf(ios::scientific);
  cout << "Scientific Formatting: " << fvalue << "\n";

  cout.setf(ios::fixed);
  cout << "Fixed Formatting:       " << setprecision(2) << fvalue;

  cout.flags(loriginal_flags);

  return(0);
}
```

The output looks like this:

```
Please enter a float value to be formatted: 123.45678
Standard Formatting:    123.457
Scientific Formatting:  1.234568e+002
Fixed Formatting:       1.2e+002
```

Notice the different value printed depending on the print format specification default, scientific or fixed.

Enumerated

When an enumerated variable is defined, it is associated with a set of named integer constants called the *enumeration set*. (These are discussed in Chapter 13.) The variable can contain any one of the constants at any time, and the constants can be referred to by name. For example, the following definition creates the enumerated type *air_supply*, the enumerated constants EMPTY, USEABLE, and FULL, and the enumerated variable *instructor_tank*:

```
enum air_supply { EMPTY,
                  USEABLE,
                  FULL=5 } instructor_tank;
```

All the constants and variables are type **int**, and each constant is automatically provided a default initial value unless another value is specified. In the preceding example, the constant name EMPTY has the integer value zero by default since it is the first in the list and was not specifically overridden. The value of USEABLE is 1 since it occurs immediately after a constant with the value of zero. The constant FULL was specifically initialized to the value 5, and if another constant were included in the list after FULL, the new constant would have the integer value of 6.

Having created *air_supply*, you can later define another variable, *student_tank*, as follows:

```
enum air_supply student_tank;
```

After this statement it is legal to say

```
instructor_tank = FULL;
student_tank    = EMPTY;
```

This places the value 5 into the variable *instructor_tank* and the value of zero into the variable *student_tank*.

When defining additional enumerated variables in C++, it is not necessary to repeat the **enum** *keyword. However, both syntaxes are accepted by the C++ compiler.*

One common mistake is to think that *air_supply* is a variable. It is a "type" of data that can be used later to create additional enumerated variables like *instructor_tank* or *student_tank*.

Since the name *instructor_tank* is an enumerated variable of type *air_supply*, *instructor_tank* can be used on the left of an assignment operator and can receive a value. This occurred when the enumerated constant FULL was explicitly assigned to it. The names EMPTY, USEABLE, and FULL are names of constants; they are not variables and their values cannot be changed.

Tests can be performed on the variables in conjunction with the constants. The following is a complete C program that uses the preceding definitions:

```
/*
 *    06ENUM.C
 *    A C program demonstrating the use of enumeration variables
 *    Copyright (c) William H. Murray and Chris H. Pappas, 1992
 */

#include <stdio.h>

main()
{
  enum air_supply { EMPTY,
                    USEABLE,
                    FULL=5 }  instructor_tank;
  enum air_supply student_tank;

  instructor_tank = FULL;
  student_tank = EMPTY;

  printf("The value of instructor_tank is %d\n",instructor_tank);

  if (student_tank < USEABLE) {
    printf("Refill this tank.\n");
    printf("Class is cancelled.\n");
    exit(0);
  }
  if (instructor_tank >= student_tank)
    printf("Proceed with lesson\n");
  else
    printf("Class is cancelled!\n");

  return(0);
}
```

In C, an **enum** type is equivalent to the type **int**. This technically allows a program to assign integer values directly to enumerated variables. C++ enforces a stronger type check and does not allow this mixed-mode operation.

Access Modifiers

The **const** and **volatile** modifiers are new to C and C++. They were added by the ANSI C standard to help identify which variables will never change (**const**) and which variables can change unexpectedly (**volatile**).

const Modifier

At certain times it will be necessary for you to use a value that does not change throughout the program. Such a quantity is called a *constant*. For example, if a program deals with the area and circumference of a circle, the constant value pi=3.14159 would be used frequently. In a financial program, an interest rate might be a constant. In such cases, you can improve the readability of the program by giving the constant a descriptive name.

Using descriptive names can also help prevent errors. Suppose that a constant value (not a constant variable) is used at many points throughout the program. A typographical error might result in the wrong value being typed at one or more of these points. However, if the constant is given a name, a typographical error would then be detected by the compiler because the incorrectly spelled identifier would probably not have been declared.

Suppose you are writing a program that repeatedly uses the value pi. It might seem as though a *variable* called *pi* should be declared with an initial value of 3.14159. However, the program should not be able to change the value of a constant. For instance, if you inadvertently wrote "pi" to the left of an equal sign, the value of pi would be changed, causing all subsequent calculations to be in error. C and C++ provide mechanisms that prevent such an error from occurring: you can establish constants, the values of which cannot be changed.

In C and C++, you declare a constant by writing "const" before the keyword (such as **int**, **float**, or **double**) in the declaration. For example:

```
const int iMIN=1,iSALE_PERCENTAGE=25;
const float fbase_change=32.157;
int irow_index=1,itotal=100,iobject;
double ddistance=0,dvelocity;
```

Because a constant cannot be changed, it must be initialized in its declaration. The integer constants iMIN and iSALE_PERCENTAGE are declared with values 1 and 25, respectively; the constant *fbase_change* is of type **float** and has been initialized to 32.157. In addition, the integer (nonconstant) variables *irow_index, itotal,* and *iobject* have been declared. Initial values of 1 and 100 have been established for *irow_index* and *itotal,* respectively. Finally, *ddistance* and *dvelocity* have been declared to be (nonconstant) variables of type **double**. An initial value of zero has been set up for *ddistance.*

Constants and variables are used in the same way in a program. The only difference is that the initial values assigned to the constants cannot be changed. That is, the constants are not *lvalues;* they cannot appear to the left of an equal sign. (Expressions that refer to memory locations are called *lvalue expressions.* Expressions referring to modifiable locations are modifiable *lvalues.* One example of a modifiable *lvalue* expression is a variable name declared without the **const** specifier.)

Normally, the assignment operation assigns the value of the right-hand operand to the storage location named by the left-hand operand. Therefore, the left-hand operand of an assignment operation (or the single operand of a unary assignment expression) must be an expression that refers to a modifiable memory location.

#define Constants

C and C++ provide another method for establishing constants, the **#define** compiler directive. Let's look at an example. Suppose that at the beginning of a program, you have the statement:

```
#define SALES_TEAM 10
```

The form of this statement is **#define** followed by two strings of characters separated by blanks. When the program is compiled, there are several passes made through the program. The first step is accomplished by the *compiler preprocessor.* The preprocessor does such things as carry out the **#include** and **#define** directives. When the preprocessor encounters the **#define** directive, it replaces every occurrence of SALES_TEAM in the source file(s) with the number 10.

In general, when the preprocessor encounters a **#define** directive, it replaces every occurrence of the first string of characters, "SALES_TEAM", in the program with the second string of characters, "10". Additionally, no value can be assigned to SALES_TEAM because it has never been declared to be a variable. As a result of the syntax, SALES_TEAM has all the attributes of a constant. Note that the **#define** statement is *not* terminated by a semicolon. If a semicolon followed the value 10, then every occurrence of SALES_TEAM would be replaced with "10;". The directive's action is to replace the first string with *everything* in the second string.

All of the programs that have been discussed so far are short and would usually be stored in a single file. If a statement such as the **#define** for SALES_TEAM appeared at the beginning of the file, the substitution of "10" for "SALES_TEAM" would take place throughout the program. (A later chapter of this book discusses breaking a program down into many subprograms, with each subprogram being broken down into separate files.) Under these circumstances, the compiler directive would be effective only for the single file in which it is written.

The preceding discussion explored two methods for defining constants—the keyword **const** and the **#define** compiler directive. In many programs, the action of each of these two methods is essentially the same. On the other hand, the use of the modifier keyword **const** results in a "variable," the value of which cannot be changed. Later in this chapter, in "Storage Classes," you will see how variables can be declared in such a way that they exist only over certain regions of a program. The same can be said for constants declared with the keyword **const**. Thus, the **const** declaration is somewhat more versatile than the **#define** directive. Also, the **#define** directive is found in standard C and is therefore already familiar to C programmers.

volatile Modifier

The **volatile** keyword signifies that a variable can unexpectedly change because of events outside the control of the program. For example, the following definition indicates that the variable *event_time* can have its value changed without the knowledge of the program:

```
volatile int event_time;
```

A definition like this is needed, for example, if *event_time* is updated by hardware that maintains the current clock time. The program that contains the variable *event_time* could be interrupted by the time-keeping hardware and the variable *event_time* changed.

A data object should be declared volatile if it is a memory-mapped device register or a data object shared by separate processes, as would be the case in a multitasking operating environment.

const and volatile Used Together

You can use the **const** and **volatile** modifiers with any other data types (for example, **char** and **float**) and also with each other. The following definition specifies that the program does not intend to change the value in the variable *constant_event_time*:

```
const volatile constant_event_time;
```

However, the compiler is also instructed, because of the **volatile** modifier, to make no assumptions about the variable's value from one moment to the next. Therefore, two things happen. First, an error message will be issued by the compiler for any line of source code that attempts to change the value of the variable *constant_event_time*. Second, the compiler will not remove the variable *constant_event_time* from inside loops since an external process can also be updating the variable while the program is executing.

pascal, cdecl, near, far, and huge Modifiers

The first two modifiers, **pascal** and **cdecl**, are used most frequently in advanced applications. Microsoft C/C++ allows you to write programs that can easily call other routines written in different languages. The opposite of this also holds true. For example, you can write a Pascal program that calls a C++ routine. When you mix languages this way, you have to take two very important issues into consideration: identifier names and the way parameters are passed.

When Microsoft C/C++ compiles your program, it places all of the program's global identifiers (functions and variables) into the resulting object code file for linking purposes. By default, the compiler saves those identifiers using the same case in which they were defined (uppercase, lowercase, or mixed). Additionally, the compiler appends to the front of the identifier an underscore (_). Since Microsoft C/C++'s integrated linking (by default) is case sensitive, any external identifiers you declare in your program are also assumed to be in the same form with a prepended underscore and the same spelling and case as defined.

pascal

The Pascal language uses a different calling sequence than C and C++ do. Pascal (along with FORTRAN) passes function arguments from left to right and does not allow variable-length argument lists. In Pascal, it is also the called function's responsibility to remove the arguments from the stack, rather than having the invoking function do so when control returns from the invoked function.

A C and C++ program can generate this calling sequence in one of two ways. First, it can use the compile-time switch /Gc, which makes the Pascal calling sequence the default for all enclosed calls and function definitions. Second, the C program can override the default C calling sequence explicitly by using the **pascal** keyword in the function definition.

As mentioned earlier, when C generates a function call, by default it prepends an underscore to the function name and declares the function as external. It also preserves the casing of the name. However, when the **pascal** keyword is used, the underscore is not prepended and the identifier (function or variable) is converted to all uppercase.

The following code segment demonstrates how to use the **pascal** keyword on a function. (The same keyword can be used to ensure FORTRAN code compatibility.)

```
float pascal pfcalculate(int iscore, int iweight)
{
    .
    .
    .
}
```

Of course, variables can also be given a Pascal convention, as seen in this next example:

```
#define TABLESIZE 30

float pascal pfcalculate(int iscore, int iweight)
{
    .
    .
    .
}

float pascal pfscore_table[TABLESIZE];

main()
{
    int iscore 95, iweight = 10;

    pfscore_table[0] = pfcalculate(iscore,iweight);

    return(0);
}
```

In this example, *pfscore_table* has been globally defined with the **pascal** modifier. Function **main()** also shows how to make an external reference to a **pascal** function type. Since both functions, **main()** and **pfcalculate()**, are in the same source file, the function **pfcalculate()** is global to **main().**

cdecl

If the /Gc compile-time switch was used to compile your C or C++ program, all function and variable references were generated matching the Pascal calling convention. However, there may be occasions when you want to guarantee that certain identifiers you are using in your program remain case sensitive and keep the underscore at the front. This is most often the case for identifiers being used in another C file.

To maintain this C compatibility (preserving the case and having a leading underscore prepended), you can use the **cdecl** keyword. When the **cdecl** keyword is used in front of a function, it also affects how the parameters are passed.

Note that all C and C++ functions prototyped in the header files of Microsoft C/C++—for example, stdio.h—are of type **cdecl**. This ensures that you can link with the library routines, even when you are compiling using the /Gc option. The following example was compiled using the /Gc option and shows how you would rewrite the previous example to maintain C compatibility:

```
#define TABLESIZE 30

float cdecl cfcalculate(int iscore, int iweight)
{
    .
    .
    .
}

float cdecl cfscore_table[TABLESIZE];

main()
{
    int iscore 95, iweight = 10;

    cfscore_table[0] = cfcalculate(iscore,iweight);

    return(0);
}
```

near, far, and huge

You use the three modifiers **near**, **far**, and **huge** to affect the action of the indirection operator (*); in other words, they modify pointer sizes to data objects. A **near** pointer is only 2 bytes long, a **far** pointer is 4 bytes long, and a **huge** pointer is also 4 bytes long. The difference between the **far** pointer and the **huge** pointer is that the **huge** pointer has to deal with the form of the address. This concept is explored in greater detail in Chapter 10.

Data Type Conversions

In the programs so far, the variables and numbers used in any particular statement were all of the same type—for example, **int** or **float**. You can write statements that perform operations involving variables of different types. These operations are called *mixed-mode operations*. In contrast to some other programming languages, C and C++ perform automatic conversions from one type to another. As you progress through the book, additional types will be introduced, and mixing of those types will be discussed.

Data of different types is stored differently in memory. Suppose that the number 10 is being stored. Its representation will depend upon its type. That is, the pattern of zeros and ones in memory will be different when 10 is stored as an integer than when it is stored as a a floating-point number.

Suppose that the following operation is executed, where both *fresult* and *fvalue* are of type **float**, and the variable *ivalue* is of type **int**:

```
fresult = fvalue * ivalue;
```

The statement is therefore a mixed-mode operation. When the statement is executed, the value of *ivalue* will be converted into a floating-point number before the multiplication takes place. The compiler recognizes that a mixed-mode operation is taking place. Therefore, it generates code to perform the following operations. The integer value assigned to *ivalue* is read from memory. This value is then converted to the corresponding floating-point value, which is then multiplied by the real value assigned to *fvalue,* and the resulting floating-point value is assigned to *fresult.* In other words, the compiler performs the conversion automatically. Note that the value assigned to *ivalue* is unchanged by this process and remains of type **int**.

You have seen that in mixed-mode operations involving a value of type **int** and another value of type **float**, the value of type **int** is converted into a value of type **float** for calculation. This is done without changing the stored integral value during the conversion process. Now let's consider mixed-mode operations between two different types of variables.

Actually, before doing this, you need to know that there is in fact a *hierarchy of conversions,* in that the object of lower priority is temporarily converted to the type of higher priority for the performance of the calculation. The hierarchy of conversions takes the following structure, from highest priority to lowest:

> double
> float
> long
> int
> short

For example, the type **double** has a higher priority than the type **int**. When a type is converted to one that has more significant digits, the value of the number and its accuracy are unchanged.

Look at what happens when a conversion from type **float** to type **int** takes place. Suppose that the variables *ivalue1* and *ivalue2* have been defined to be of type **int**, while *fvalue* and *fresult* have been defined to be of type **float**. Consider the following sequence of statements:

```
ivalue1 = 3;
ivalue2 = 4;
fvalue = 7.0;
fresult = fvalue + ivalue1/ivalue2;
```

The statement *ivalue1/ivalue2* is *not* a mixed-mode operation; instead, it represents the division of two integers, and its result is zero since the fractional part (0.75, in this case) is *discarded* when integer division is performed. Therefore the value stored in *fresult* is 7.0.

What if *ivalue2* had been defined to be of type **float**? In this case *fresult* would have been assigned the floating-point value 7.75 since the statement *ivalue1/ivalue2* would be a mixed-mode operation. Under these circumstances, the value of *ivalue1* is temporarily converted to the floating-point value 3.0, and the result of the division is 0.75. When that is added to *fvalue,* the result is 7.75.

It is important to know that the type of the value to the left of the assignment statement determines the type of the result of the operation. For example, suppose that *fx* and *fy* have been declared to be of type **float** and *iresult* has been declared to be of type **int**. Consider the following statements:

```
fx = 7.0;
fy = 2.0;
iresult = 4.0 + fx/fy
```

The result of executing the statement *fx/fy* is 3.5; when this is added to 4.0, the floating-point value generated is 7.5. However, this value cannot be assigned to *iresult* because *iresult* is of type **int**. The number 7.5 is therefore converted into an integer. When this is done, the fraction part is truncated. The resulting whole number is converted from a floating-point representation to an integer representation, and the value assigned to *iresult* is the integer number 7.

Explicit Type Conversions Using the Cast Operator

You have seen that the C and C++ compiler automatically changes the format of a variable in mixed-mode operations using different data types. However, there are circumstances where, although automatic conversion is *not* performed, type conversion would be desirable. For those occasions, you must specifically designate that a change of type is to be made. These explicit specifications also clarify to other programmers the statements involved. The C language provides several procedures that allow you to designate that type conversion must occur.

One of these procedures is called the *cast operator*. Whenever you want to temporarily change the format of a variable, you simply precede the variable's identifier with the parenthesized type you want it converted to. For example, if *ivalue1* and *ivalue2* were defined to be of type **int** and *fvalue* and *fresult* have been defined to be of type **float**, the following three statements would perform the same operation:

```
fresult = fvalue + (float)ivalue1/ivalue2;
fresult = fvalue + ivalue1/(float)ivalue2;
fresult = fvalue + (float)ivalue1/(float)ivalue2;
```

All three statements perform a floating-point conversion and division of the variables *ivalue1* and *ivalue2*. Because of the usual rules of mixed-mode arithmetic discussed earlier, if either variable is cast to type **float**, a floating-point division occurs. The third statement explicitly highlights the operation to be performed.

Storage Classes

Microsoft C/C++ supports four storage class specifiers. They are

> auto
> register
> static
> extern

The storage class precedes the variable's declaration and instructs the compiler how the variable should be stored. Items declared with the **auto** or **register** specifier have local lifetimes. Items declared with the **static** or **extern** specifier have global lifetimes.

The four storage-class specifiers affect the visibility of a variable or function, as well as its storage class. *Visibility* (sometimes defined as scope) refers to that portion of the source program in which the variable or function can be referenced by name. An item with a global lifetime exists throughout the execution of the source program.

The placement of a variable or a function declaration within a source file also affects storage class and visibility. Declarations outside all function definitions are said to appear at the *external level*, while declarations within function definitions appear at the *internal level*.

The exact meaning of each storage class specifier depends on two factors: whether the declaration appears at the external or internal level and whether the item being declared is a variable or a function.

Variable Declarations at the External Level

Variable declarations at the external level may only use the **static** or **extern** storage class, not **auto** or **register**. They are either definitions of variables or references to variables defined elsewhere. An external variable declaration that also initializes the variable (implicitly or explicitly) is a defining declaration:

```
static int ivalue1;        // implicit 0 by default
static int ivalue1 = 10    // explicit

int ivalue2 = 20;          // explicit
```

Once a variable is defined at the external level, it is visible throughout the rest of the source file in which it appears. The variable is not visible prior to its definition in the same source file. Also, it is not visible in other source files of the program unless a referencing declaration makes it visible, as described shortly.

You can define a variable at the external level only once within a source file. If you give the **static** storage-class specifier, you can define another variable with the same name and the **static** storage-class specifier in a different source file. Since each static definition is visible only within its own source file, no conflict occurs.

The **extern** storage-class specifier declares a reference to a variable defined elsewhere. You can use an external declaration to make a definition in another source file visible or to make a variable visible above its definition in the same source file. The variable is visible throughout the remainder of the source file in which the declared reference occurs.

For an external reference to be valid, the variable it refers to must be defined once, and only once, at the external level. The definition can be in any of the source files that form the program. The following C++ program demonstrates the use of the **extern** keyword:

```
//
//      Source File A
//
#include <iostream.h>

extern int ivalue;                    // makes ivalue visible
                                      // above its declaration

main()
{
  ivalue++;                           // uses the above extern
                                      // reference

  cout << ivalue << "\n";             // prints 11
  function_a();
```

```
   return(0);
}

int ivalue = 10;                    // actual definition of
                                    // ivalue

void function_a(void)
{
  ivalue++;                         // references ivalue
  cout << ivalue << "\n";           // prints 12
  function_b();
}


-----------------------------------------

//
//      Source File B
//

#include <iostream.h>

extern int ivalue;                  // references ivalue
                                    // declared in Source A

void function_b(void)
{
  ivalue++;
  cout <<("%d\n", ivalue);          // prints 13
}
```

Variable Declarations at the Internal Level

You can use any of the four storage-class specifiers for variable declarations at the internal level. (The default is **auto**.) The **auto** storage-class specifier declares a variable with a local lifetime. It is visible only in the block in which it is declared and can include initializers.

The **register** storage-class specifier tells the compiler to give the variable storage in a register, if possible. This specifier speeds access time and reduces code size. It has the same visibility as an **auto** variable. If no registers are available when the compiler encounters a register declaration, the variable is given the **auto** storage class and stored in memory.

ANSI C does not allow for taking the address of a register object. However, this restriction does not apply to C++. Applying the address operator (&) to a C++ register variable forces the compiler to store the object in memory since the compiler must put the object in a location for which an address can be represented.

A variable declared at the internal level with the **static** storage-class specifier has a global lifetime but is visible only within the block in which it is declared. Unlike **auto** variables, **static** variables keep their values when the block is exited. You can initialize a **static** variable with a constant expression. It is initialized to zero by default.

A variable declared with the **extern** storage-class specifier is a reference to a variable with the same name defined at the external level in any of the source files of the program. The internal **extern** declaration is used to make the external-level variable definition visible within the block. The next program demonstrates these concepts:

```
int ivalue1=1;

main()
{ // references the ivalue1 defined above
    extern int ivalue1;

  // default initialization of 0, ivalue2 only visible
  // in main()
    static int ivalue2;

  // stored in a register (if available), initialized
  // to 0
    register int rvalue = 0;

  // default auto storage class, int_value3 initialized
  // to 0
    int int_value3 = 0;

  // values printed are 1, 0, 0, 0:
    cout << ivalue1 << rvalue \
          << ivalue2 << int_value3;
    function_a();
}

void function_a(void)
{
  // stores the address of the global variable ivalue1
    static int *pivalue1= &ivalue1;

  // creates a new local variable ivalue1 making the
```

```
    // global ivalue1 unreachable
       int ivalue1 = 32;

    // new local variable ivalue2
    // only visible within function_a
       static int ivalue2 = 2;

       ivalue2 += 2;

    // the values printed are 32, 4, and 1:
       cout << ivalue1 << ivalue2 \
       << *pivalue1);
    }
```

Since *ivalue1* is redefined in **function_a()**, access to the global *ivalue1* is denied. However, by using the data pointer *pivalue1* (discussed in Chapter 10), the address of the global *ivalue1* was used to print the value stored there.

Variable Scope Review

To review, there are four rules for variable visibility, also called *scope rules*. The four scopes for a variable are the block, function, file, and program. A variable declared within a block or function is known only within the block or function. A variable declared external to a function is known within the file in which it appears, from the point of its appearance to the end of the file. A variable declared as external in one source file and declared as external in other files has program scope.

Function Declarations at the External Level

When declaring a function at the external or internal level, you can use either the **static** or the **extern** storage-class specifier. Functions, unlike variables, always have a global lifetime. The visibility rules for functions vary slightly from the rules for variables.

Functions declared to be static are visible only within the source file in which they are defined. Functions in the same source file can call the static function, but functions in *other* source files cannot. Also, you can declare another static function with the same name in a different source file without conflict.

Functions declared as external are visible throughout *all* source files that make up the program (unless you later redeclare such a function as static). Any function can call an external function. Function declarations that omit the storage-class specifier are external by default.

Operators

C has many operators not found in other languages. These include bitwise operators, increment and decrement operators, conditional operators, the comma operator, and assignment and compound assignment operators.

Bitwise Operators

Bitwise operators treat variables as combinations of bits rather than as numbers. They are useful in accessing the individual bits in memory, such as the screen memory for a graphics display. Bitwise operators can operate only on integral data types, not on floating-point numbers. Three bitwise operators act just like the logical operators, but on each bit in an integer. These are AND (&), OR (|), and XOR (^). An additional operator is the one's complement (~), which simply inverts each bit.

AND

The bitwise AND operation compares two bits; if both bits are a 1, the result is a 1, as shown here:

```
              LOGICAL AND
     BIT 0      BIT 1      RESULT
       0          0          0
       0          1          0
       1          0          0
       1          1          1
```

Note that this is different from binary addition, where the comparison of two 1 bits would result in a sum flag set to zero and the carry flag set to 1. Very often the AND operation is used to select out, or *mask*, certain bit positions.

OR

The bitwise OR operation compares two bits and generates a 1 result if either or both bits are a 1, as shown here:

```
              LOGICAL OR
     BIT 0      BIT 1      RESULT
       0          0          0
       0          1          1
       1          0          1
       1          1          1
```

The OR operation is useful for setting specified bit positions.

XOR

The EXCLUSIVE OR operation compares two bits and returns a result of 1 when and only when the two bits are complementary, as shown here:

```
                    EXCLUSIVE OR
        BIT 0         BIT 1          RESULT
          0             0              0
          0             1              1
          1             0              1
          1             1              0
```

This logical operation can be very useful when it is necessary to complement specified bit positions, as in the case of computer graphics applications.

Following is an example of using these operators with the hexadecimal and octal representation of constants. The bit values are shown for comparison.

```
0xF1       &   0x35              yields 0x31 (hexadecimal)
0361       &   0065              yields 061 (octal)
11110011   &   00110101          yields 00110011 (bitwise)


0xF1       |   0x35              yields 0xF5 (hexadecimal)
0361       |   0065              yields 0365 (octal)
11110011   |   00110101          yields 11110111 (bitwise)


0xF1       ^   0x35              yields 0xC4 (hexadecimal)
0361       ^   0065              yields 0304 (octal)
11110011   ^   00110101          yields 00000000 11000110 (bitwise)


~0xF1                            yields 0xFF0E (hexadecimal)
~0361                            yields 0177416 (octal)
~11110011                        yields 11111111 00001100 (bitwise)
```

Left Shift and Right Shift

C incorporates two shift operators, the left shift (<<) and the right shift (>>). The left shift moves the bits to the left and sets the rightmost (least significant) bit to zero. The leftmost (most significant) bit shifted out is thrown away.

In terms of unsigned integers, shifting the number one position to the left and filling the LSB with a zero doubles the number's value. The following C++ code segment demonstrates how this would be coded:

```
unsigned int value1 = 65;
value1 <<= 1;
cout << value1;
```

If you were to examine *value1*'s lower byte you would see the following bit changes performed:

```
<<   0100 0001 (65  Decimal)
     --------------------------
     1000 0010 (130 Decimal)
```

The right shift operator moves bits to the right. The lower order bits shifted out are thrown away. Halving an unsigned integer is as simple as shifting the bits one position to the right, filling the MSB position with a zero. A C coded example would look very similar to the precding example except for the compound operator assignment statement (discussed later in the chapter) and the output statement:

```
unsigned int value1 = 10;
value1 >>= 1;
printf("%d",value1);
```

Examining just the lower byte of the variable *value1* would reveal the following bit changes:

```
>>   0000 1010 (10 Decimal)
     --------------------------
     0000 0101 ( 5 Decimal)
```

Increment and Decrement

Adding 1 to or subtracting 1 from a number is so common in programs that C has a special set of operators to do this. They are the *increment* (++) and *decrement* (--) *operators*. The two characters must be placed next to each other without any white space. They can be applied only to variables, not to constants. Instead of coding as follows:

```
value1 = value1 + 1;
```

you can write:

```
value1++;
```

or

```
++value1;
```

When these two operators are the sole operators in an expression, you will not have to worry about the difference between the different syntaxes. A **for** loop very often uses this type of increment for the loop control variable:

```
sum = 0;
for(i = 1; i <= 20; i++)
   sum = sum + i;
```

A decrement loop would be coded as

```
sum = 0;
for(i = 20; i >= 1; i--)
   sum = sum + i;
```

If you use these operators in complex expressions, you have to consider *when* the increment or decrement actually takes place.

The postfix increment, for example *i++*, uses the value of the variable in the expression first and then increments its value. However, the prefix increment, for example *++i*, increments the value of the variable first and then uses the value in the expression. Assume the following data declarations:

```
int i=3,j,k=0;
```

See if you can figure out what happens in each of the following statements. For simplicity, for each statement assume the original initialized values of the variables:

```
k = ++i;            // i = 4, k = 4
k = i++;            // i = 4, k = 3
k = --i;            // i = 2, k = 2
k = i--;            // i = 2, k = 3
i = j = k--;        // i = 0, j = 0, k = -1
```

While the subtleties of these two different operations may currently elude you, they are included in the C language because of specific situations that cannot be eloquently handled in any other way. In Chapter 10 you will look at a program that uses array indexes that need to be manipulated by using the initially confusing prefix syntax.

Arithmetic Operators

The C language naturally incorporates the standard set of arithmetic operators for addition (+), subtraction (–), multiplication (*), division (/), and modulus (%). The first four are straightforward and need no amplification. However, an example of the modulus operator will help you understand its usage and syntax:

```
int a=3,b=8,c=0,d;

d = b % a;              // returns 2
d = a % b;              // returns 3

d = b % c;              // returns an error message
```

The modulus operator returns the remainder of integer division. The last assignment statement attempts to divide 8 by zero, resulting in an error message.

Assignment Operator

The assignment operator in C is different than the assignment statement in other languages. Assignment is performed by an assignment operator rather than an assignment statement. Like other C operators, the result of an assignment operator is a value that is assigned. An expression with an assignment operator can be used in a large expression such as this:

```
value1 = 8 * (value2 = 5);
```

Here, *value2* is first assigned the value 5. This is multiplied by the 8, with *value1* receiving a final value of 40.

Overuse of the assignment operator can rapidly lead to unmanageable expressions. There are two places in which this feature is normally applied. First, it can be used to set several variables to a particular value, as in

```
value1 = value2 = value3 = 0;
```

The second use is most often seen in the condition of a **while** loop, such as

```
while ((c = getchar()) != EOF) {
    .
    .
    .
}
```

This assigns the value that **getchar()** returned to *c* and then tests the value against EOF. If it is EOF, the loop is not executed. The parentheses are necessary because the assignment operator has a lower precedence than the nonequality operator. Otherwise, the line would be interpreted as

```
c = (getchar() != EOF)
```

The variable *c* would be assigned a value of 1 (TRUE) each time **getchar()** returned EOF.

Compound Assignment Operators

The C language also incorporates an enhancement to the assignment statement used by other languages. This additional set of assignment operators allows for a more concise way of expressing certain computations. The following code segment shows the standard assignment syntax applicable in many high-level languages:

```
irow_index = irow_index + irow_increment;
ddepth = ddepth - d1_fathom;
fcalculate_tax = fcalculate_tax * 1.07;
fyards = fyards / ifeet_convert;
```

C's compound assignment statements would look like this:

```
irow_index += irow_increment;
ddepth -= d1_fathom;
fcalculate_tax *= 1.07;
fyards /= ifeet_convert;
```

If you look closely at these two code segments, you will quickly see the required syntax. Using a C compound assignment operator requires you to remove the redundant variable reference from the right-hand side of the assignment operator and place the operation to be performed immediately before the =. The bottom of Table 6-6 lists all of the compound assignment operators. Other parts of this table are discussed in the section "Understanding Operator Precedence Levels" later in this chapter.

Meaning	Operator	Associates from
Function call	()	Left to right
Array subscript	[]	
Member selection (struct, union, class)	.	
Member selection (pointer to struct, union, class)	.>	

Table 6-6. *C/C++ Operator Precedence Levels*

Meaning	Operator	Associates from
Pointer to member (objects)	.*	Left to right
Pointer to member (pointers)	.>*	
Postfix increment	+	Right to left
Postfix decrement	– –	
Base operator (not for 32-bit compilation)	:>	Left to right
Scope resolution	::	
Logical NOT	!	Right to left
Bitwise complement	~	
Unary negation	–	
Unary plus	+	
Prefix increment	+	
Prefix decrement	– –	
Address operator	&	
Indirection	*	
Object size in bytes	sizeof	
Type cast	(*type*)	
Dynamic memory allocation	new	
Deallocate memory	delete	
Multiplication	*	Left to right
Division	/	
Remainder	%	
Addition	+	Left to right
Subtraction	–	
Left shift	<<	Left to right
Right shift	>>	
Less than	<	Left to right
Greater than	>	

Table 6-6. *C/C++ Operator Precedence Levels* (continued)

Meaning	Operator	Associates from
Less than or equal	<=	Left to right
Greater than or equal	>=	
Equality	==	Left to right
Inequality	!=	
Bitwise AND	&	Left to right
Bitwise exclusive OR	^	
Bitwise OR	|	
Logical AND	&&	Left to right
Logical OR	||	
Conditional	?:	Right to left
Assignment	=	Right to left
Multiplication assignment	*=	
Division assignment	/=	
Modulus assignment	%=	
Addition assignment	+=	
Subtraction assignment	-=	
Left shift assignment	<<=	
Right shift assignment	>>=	
Bitwise AND assignment	&=	
Bitwise exclusive OR assignment	^=	
Bitwise OR assignment	|=	
Comma	,	Left to right

Table 6-6. *C/C++ Operator Precedence Levels* (continued)

Relational and Logical Operators

All relational operators are used to establish a relationship between the values of the operands. They always produce a value of !0 if the relationship evaluates to TRUE or a 0 value if the relationship evaluates to FALSE. Following is a list of the C and C++ relational operators:

Operator	Meaning
==	Equality (not assignment)
!=	Not equal
>	Greater than
<	Less than
>=	Greater than or equal
<=	Less than or equal

The logical operators AND (&&), OR (||), and NOT (!) produce a TRUE (!0) or FALSE (zero) based on the logical relationship of their arguments. The simplest way to remember how the logical AND && works is to say that an ANDed expression will only return a true (!0) when both arguments are true (!0). The logical OR || operation in turn will only return a FALSE (zero) when both arguments are FALSE (zero). The logical NOT ! simply inverts the value. Following is a list of the C and C++ logical operators:

Operator	Meaning
!	NOT
&&	AND
||	OR

Have some fun with the following C program as you test the various combinations of relational and logical operators. See if you can predict the results ahead of time.

```
/*
 *    06OPRS.C
 *    A C program demonstrating some of the subtleties of
 *    logical and relational operators.
 *    Copyright (c) William H. Murray and Chris H. Pappas, 1992
 */

#include <stdio.h>

main()
{
  float foperand1, foperand2;

  printf("\nEnter foperand1 and foperand2: " );
  scanf("%f%f",&foperand1,&foperand2);
```

```
printf("\n  foperand1  > foperand2 is %d",
          (foperand1 > foperand2));
printf("\n  foperand1  < foperand2 is %d",
          (foperand1 < foperand2));
printf("\n  foperand1 >= foperand2 is %d",
          (foperand1 >= foperand2));
printf("\n  foperand1 <= foperand2 is %d",
          (foperand1 <= foperand2));
printf("\n  foperand1 == foperand2 is %d",
          (foperand1 == foperand2));
printf("\n  foperand1 != foperand2 is %d",
          (foperand1 != foperand2));
printf("\n  foperand1 && foperand1 is %d",
          (foperand1 && foperand2));
printf("\n  foperand1 || foperand2 is %d",
          (foperand1 || foperand2));

  return(0);
}
```

You may be surprised at some of the results obtained for some of the logical comparisons. Remember, there is a very strict comparison that occurs for both data types **float** and **double** when values of these types are compared with zero—a number that is very slightly different from another number is still not equal. Also, a number that is just slightly above or below zero is still TRUE (!0).

The C++ equivalent of the program just examined follows:

```
//
//   06OPRS.CPP
//   A C++ program demonstrating some of the subtleties of
//   logical and relational operators.
//   Copyright (c) William H. Murray and Chris H. Pappas, 1992
//

#include <iostream.h>

main()
{
  float foperand1, foperand2;

  cout << "\nEnter foperand1 and foperand2: ";
  cin >> foperand1 >> foperand2;
  cout << "\n";
```

```
cout << "  foperand1  > foperand2 is "
     <<  (foperand1  > foperand2) << "\n";
cout << "  foperand1  < foperand2 is "
     <<  (foperand1  < foperand2) << "\n";
cout << "  foperand1 >= foperand2 is "
     <<  (foperand1 >= foperand2) << "\n";
cout << "  foperand1 <= foperand2 is "
     <<  (foperand1 <= foperand2) << "\n";
cout << "  foperand1 == foperand2 is "
     <<  (foperand1 == foperand2) << "\n";
cout << "  foperand1 != foperand2 is "
     <<  (foperand1 != foperand2) << "\n";
cout << "  foperand1 && foperand1 is "
     <<  (foperand1 && foperand2) << "\n";
cout << "  foperand1 || foperand2 is "
     <<  (foperand1 || foperand2) << "\n";

return(0);
}
```

Conditional Operator

You can use the conditional operator (?:) in normal coding, but its main use is for creating macros. The operator has the syntax

condition ? *true_expression* : *false-expression*

If the condition is TRUE, the value of the conditional expression is *true-expression*. Otherwise, it is the value of *false-expression*. For example, look at the following statement:

```
if('A' <= c && c <= 'Z')
  printf("%c",'a' + c - 'A');
else
  printf("%c",c);
```

You could rewrite the statement using the conditional operator:

```
printf("%c",('A' <= c && c <= 'Z') ? ('a' + c - 'A') : c );
```

Both statements will make certain that the character printed, "c", is always lowercase.

Comma Operator

The comma operator (,) evaluates two expressions where the syntax allows only one. The value of the comma operator is the value of the right-hand expression. The format for the expression is

left-expression, right-expression

One place where the comma operator commonly appears is in a **for** loop, where more than one variable is being iterated. For example:

```
for(min=0,max=length-1; min < max; min++,max--) {
  .
  .
  .
}
```

Understanding Operator Precedence Levels

The order of evaluation of an expression in C is determined by the compiler. This normally does not alter the value of the expression, unless you have written one with side effects. Side effects are those operations that change the value of a variable while yielding a value that is used in the expression, as seen with the increment and decrement operators. The other operators that have side effects are the assignment and compound assignment operators.

Calls to functions that change values of external variables also are subject to side effects. For example:

```
inum1 = 3;
ianswer = (inum1 = 4) + inum1;
```

This could be evaluated in one of two ways: either *inum1* is assigned 4 and *ianswer* is assigned 8 (4+4); or the value of 3 is retrieved from *inum1* and 4 is then assigned to *inum1*, with the result being assigned a 7.

There are, however, four operators for which the order of evaluation is guaranteed to be left to right: logical AND (&&), logical OR (‖), the comma operator (,), and the conditional operator (?:). Because of this default order of evaluation you can specify a typical test as follows:

```
while((c=getchar()) != EOF) && (C!='\n'))
```

The second part of the logical AND (&&) is performed after the character value is assigned to *c*.

Table 6-6 lists all of the C and C++ operators from highest precedence to lowest and describes how each operator is associated (left to right or right to left). All operators between lines have the same precedence level. Throughout the book you will be introduced to the various operators and how their precedence level affects their performance.

Standard C and C++ Libraries

Certain calculations are routinely performed in many programs and are written by almost all programmers. Taking the square root of a number is an example of such a calculation. Mathematical procedures for calculating square roots make use of combinations of the basic arithmetic operations of addition, subtraction, multiplication, and division.

It would be a waste of effort if every programmer had to design and code a routine to calculate the square root and then to incorporate that routine into the program. C and C++ resolve difficulties like this by providing you with *libraries* of functions that perform particular common calculations. With the libraries, you need only a single statement to invoke such a function.

This section discusses functions that are commonly provided with the C and C++ compiler. These library functions are usually not provided in source form but in compiled form. When linking is performed, the code for the library functions is combined with the compiled programmer's code to form the complete program.

Library functions not only perform mathematical operations, they also deal with many other commonly encountered operations. For example, there are library functions that deal with reading and writing disk files, managing memory, input/output, and a variety of other operations. Library functions are not part of standard C or C++, but virtually every system provides certain library functions.

Most library functions are designed to use information contained in particular files that are supplied with the system. These files, therefore, must be included when the library functions are used and are provided with the Microsoft C/C++ compiler. They usually have the extension .h and are called header files. Table 6-7 lists the header files supplied with Microsoft C/C++.

In general, different header files are required by different library functions. The required header files for a function will be listed in the description for that function. For example, the **sqrt()** function needs the declarations found in the math.h header file. Your *Microsoft C/C++ Run-Time Library Reference* lists all of the library functions and their associated header files.

Header File Name	Description
assert.h	Assert debugging macro
bios.h	BIOS service functions
conio.h	Console and port I/O routines
ctype.h	Character classification
direct.h	Directory control
dos.h	MS-DOS interface functions
errno.h	*errno* variable definitions
fcntl.h	Flags used in **open()** and **sopen()** functions
float.h	Constants needed by math functions
graph.h	Low-level graphics and font routines
io.h	File and low-level I/O handling
limits.h	Ranges of character and integer types
locale.h	Localization functions
malloc.h	Memory allocation functions
math.h	Floating-point routines
memory.h	Buffer manipulation routines
pgchart.h	Presentation graphics
process.h	Process control routines
search.h	Searching and sorting functions
setjmp.h	**setjmp()** and **longjmp()** functions
share.h	Flags used in **sopen()**
signal.h	Constants used by **signal()** function
stdarg.h	Macros for variable-length argument functions
stddef.h	Commonly used values and data types
stdio.h	Standard I/O header file
stdlib.h	Frequently used library functions
string.h	String manipulation functions
time.h	General time functions
varargs.h	Variable length argument-list functions
vmemory.h	Virtual memory functions
sys\locking.h	Locking function flags
sys\stat.h	File status structures and functions
sys\timeb.h	Time function
sys\types.h	Time types and file status
sys\utime.h	**utime()** function

Table 6-7.   *Microsoft C/C++ Header Files*

The following list briefly summarizes the library categories provided by the Microsoft C/C++ compiler:

Classification routines
Conversion routines
Directory control routines
Diagnostic routines
Graphics routines
Input/output routines
Interface routines (DOS, 8086, BIOS)
Manipulation routines
Math routines
Memory allocation routines
Process control routines
Standard routines
Text window display routines
Time and date routines

Check your reference manual for a detailed explanation of the individual functions provided by each library.

After reading this chapter, you should understand C's basic data types and operators, so it's time to move on to the topic of logic control. Chapter 7 introduces you to C's decision, selection, and iteration control statements.

Chapter **7**

Control

In order to begin writing simple C programs, you will need a few more tools. This chapter discusses C's control statements. Many of these control statements are similar to other high-level language controls, such as **if**, **if-else**, and **switch** statements and **for**, **while**, and **do-while** loops. However, there are several new control statements unique to C, such as the **?** (conditional), **break**, and **continue** statements.

Conditional Statements

The C language supports four basic conditional statements: the **if**, the **if-else**, the conditional **?**, and the **switch**. Before a discussion of the individual conditional statements, however, one general rule needs to be highlighted.

You can use most of the conditional statements to selectively execute either a single line of code or multiple lines of related code (called a *block*). Whenever a conditional statement is associated with only one line of executable code, braces ({}) are *not* required around the executable statement. However, if the conditional statement is associated with multiple executable statements, braces are required to relate the block of executable statements with the conditional test. For this reason, **switch** statements are required to have an opening and a closing brace.

if Statements

You use the **if** statement to conditionally execute a segment of code. The simplest form of the **if** statement is

```
if (expression)
    true_action;
```

Notice that the expression must be enclosed in parentheses. To execute an **if** statement, the expression must evaluate to either TRUE or FALSE. If *expression* is TRUE, *true_action* will be performed and execution will continue on to the next statement following the action. However, if *expression* evaluates to FALSE, *true_action* will *not* be executed, and the statement following *action* will be executed. For example, the following code segment will print the message "Have a great day!" whenever the variable *ioutside_temp* is greater than or equal to 72:

```
if(ioutside_temp >= 72)
  printf("Have a great day!");
```

The syntax for an **if** statement associated with a block of executable statements looks like this:

```
if ( expression ) {
    true_action1;
    true_action2;
    true_action3;
    true_action4;
}
```

The syntax requires that all of the associated statements be enclosed by a pair of braces ({}) and that each statement within the block must also end with a semicolon (;). Here is an example of a compound **if** statement:

```
/*
 *   07IF.C
 *   A C program demonstrating an if statement
 *   Copyright (c) William H. Murray and Chris H. Pappas, 1992
 *
 */
#include <stdio.h>
main()
{
    int inum_As, inum_Bs, inum_Cs;
    float fGPA;

    printf("\nEnter number of courses receiving a grade of A: ");
    scanf("%d",&inum_As);
    printf("\nEnter number of courses receiving a grade of B: ");
```

```
    scanf("%d",&inum_Bs);
    printf("\nEnter number of courses receiving a grade of C: ");
    scanf("%d",&inum_Cs);
    fGPA = (inum_As * 4 + inum_Bs * 3 + inum_Cs * 2)/ \
           (float) (inum_As + inum_Bs + inum_Cs);
    printf("\nYour overall GPA is: %5.2f\n",fGPA);

    if(fGPA >= 3.5) {
      printf("\nC O N G R A T U L A T I O N S !\n");
      printf("You are on the President's list.");
    }

    return(0);
}
```

In this example, if *fGPA* is greater than or equal to 3.5, a congratulatory message is added to the calculated *fGPA*. Regardless of whether the **if** block was entered, the calculated *fGPA* is printed.

if-else Statements

The **if-else** statement was invented to allow a program to take two separate actions based on the validity of a particular expression. The simplest syntax for an **if-else** statement looks like this:

> if (*expression*)
>   *true_action*;
>
> else
>   *false_action*;

In this case, if *expression* evaluates to TRUE, *true_action* will be taken; otherwise, when *expression* evaluates to FALSE, *false_action* will be executed. Here is a coded example:

```
if(ckeypressed == UP)
  iy_pixel_coord++;

else
  iy_pixel_coord-;
```

This example takes care of either incrementing or decrementing the current horizontal coordinate location based on the current value stored in the character variable *ckeypressed*.

Of course, either *true_action, false_action,* or both could be compound statements, or blocks, requiring braces. The syntax for these three combinations is straightforward:

```
if (expression) {
    true_action1;
    true_action2;
    true_action3;
}
else
    false_action;


if (expression)
    true_action;
else {
    false_action1;
    false_action2;
    false_action3;
}


if (expression) {
    true_action1;
    true_action2;
    true_action3;
}
else {
    false_action1;
    false_action2;
    false_action3;
}
```

Just remember, whenever a block action is being taken, you do not follow the closing brace (}) with a semicolon.

The following C program uses an **if-else** statement with the **if** part being a compound block:

```
/*
 *   07CMPIF.C
 *   A C program demonstrating the use of a compound
 *   if-else statement.
 *   Copyright (c) William H. Murray and Chris H. Pappas, 1992
 */
```

```
#include <stdio.h>

main()
{
  char c;
  int ihow_many,i,imore;

  imore=1;

  while(imore == 1) {
    printf("Please enter the product name: ");
    if(scanf("%c",&c) != EOF) {
      while(c != '\n') {
        printf("%c",c);
        scanf("%c",&c);
      }
      printf("s purchased? ");
      scanf("%d",&ihow_many);
      scanf("%c",&c);

      for(i = 1;i <= ihow_many; i++)
        printf("*");
      printf("\n");
    }
    else
      imore=0;
  }
  return(0);
}
```

The program prompts the user for a product name, and if the user does not enter a ^Z (EOF), the program inputs the product name character by character, echo printing the information to the next line. The "s purchased" string is appended to the product, requesting the number of items sold. Finally, a **for** loop prints out the appropriate number of asterisks (*). Had the user entered a ^Z, the **if** portion of the **if-else** statement would have been ignored and program execution would have picked up with the **else** setting the *imore* flag to zero, thereby terminating the program.

Nested if-elses

When you are nesting **if** statements, care must be taken to ensure that you know which **else** action will be matched up with which **if**. Look at an example and see if you can figure out what will happen:

```
if(iout_side_temp < 50)
if(iout_side_temp < 30) printf("Wear the down jacket!");
else printf("Parka will do.");
```

The listing was purposely misaligned so as not to give you any visual clues as to which statement went with which **if**. The question becomes, What happens if *iout_side_temp* is 55? Does the "Parka will do." message get printed? The answer is no. In this example, the **else** action is associated with the second **if** expression. This is because C matches each **else** with the first unmatched **if**.

To make debugging as simple as possible under such circumstances, the C compiler has been written to associate each **else** with the closest **if** that does not already have an **else** associated with it.

Of course, proper indentation will always help clarify the situation:

```
if(iout_side_temp < 50)
   if(iout_side_temp < 30) printf("Wear the down jacket!");
   else printf("Parka will do.");
```

The same logic can also be represented by the alternate listing that follows:

```
if(iout_side_temp < 50)
   if(iout_side_temp < 30)
     printf("Wear the down jacket!");
   else
     printf("Parka will do.");
```

Each particular application you write will benefit most by one of the two styles, as long as you are consistent throughout the source code.

See if you can figure out this next example:

```
if(test1_expression)
   if(test2_expression)
     test2_true_action;
else
   test1_false_action;
```

You may be thinking this is just another example of what has already been discussed. That's true, but what if you really did want *test1_ false_action* to be associated with *test1* and not *test2?* The examples so far have all associated the **else** action with the second, or closest, **if**. (By the way, many a programmer has spent needless time debugging programs of this nature. They're indented to work the way you are logically thinking, as was the preceding example, but unfortunately, the compiler doesn't care about your "pretty printing.")

Correcting this situation requires the use of braces:

```
if(test1_expression) {
  if(test2_expression)
    test2_true_action;
  }
else
  test1_false_action;
```

The problem is solved by making *test2_expression* and its associated *test2_true_action* a block associated with a TRUE evaluation of *test1_expression*. This makes it clear that *test1_false_action* will be associated with the **else** clause of *test1_expression*.

if-else-if Statements

The **if-else-if** statement combination is often used to perform multiple successive comparisons. Its general form looks like this:

```
if(expression1)
    test1_true_action;

else if(expression2)
    test2_true_action;

else if(expression3)
    test3_true_action;
```

Of course, each action could be a compound block requiring its own set of braces (with the closing brace *not* followed by a semicolon). This type of logical control flow evaluates each expression until it finds one that is TRUE. When this occurs, all remaining test conditions are bypassed. In the preceding example, if none of the expressions evaluated to TRUE, no action would be taken.

Look at this next example and see if you can guess the result:

```
if(expression1)
    test1_true_action;

else if(expression2)
    test2_true_action;

else if(expression3)
    test3_true_action;
```

```
else
   default_action;
```

Unlike the previous example, this **if-else-if** statement combination will always perform some action. If none of the **if** expressions evaluate to TRUE, the **else** *default_action* will be executed. For example, the following program checks the value assigned to *econvert_to* to decide which type of conversion to perform. If the requested *econvert_to* is not one of the ones provided, the code segment prints an appropriate message.

```
if(econvert_to == YARDS)
   fconverted_value = length / 3;

else if(econvert_to == INCHES)
   fconverted_value = length * 12;

else if(econvert_to == CENTIMETERS)
   fconverted_value = length * 12 * 2.54;

else if(econvert_to == METERS)
   fconverted_value = (length * 12 * 2.54)/100;

else
   printf("No conversion required");
```

The ? Conditional Statement

The conditional statement ? provides a quick way to write a test condition. Associated actions are performed depending on whether *test_expression* evaluates to TRUE or FALSE. The operator can be used to replace an equivalent **if-else** statement. The syntax for a conditional statement is

   test_expression ? *true_action* : *false_action;*

The ? operator is also sometimes referred to as the ternary operator because it requires three operands. Examine this statement:

```
if(fvalue >= 0.0)
   fvalue = fvalue;
else
   fvalue = -fvalue;
```

You can rewrite the statement using the conditional operator:

```
fvalue=(fvalue >= 0.0) ? fvalue : -fvalue;
```

Both statements yield the absolute value of *fvalue*. The precedence of the conditional operator is less than that of any of the other operators used in the expression; therefore, no parentheses are required in the example. Nevertheless, parentheses are frequently used to enhance readability.

The following C++ program uses the ? operator to cleverly format the program's output:

```cpp
//
//  07CONDIT.CPP
//  A C++ program using the CONDITIONAL OPERATOR
//  Copyright (c) William H. Murray and Chris H. Pappas, 1992
//

#include <math.h>                          // for abs macro def.
#include <iostream.h>

main()
{
  float fbalance, fpayment;

  cout << "Enter your loan balance: ";
  cin  >> fbalance;

  cout << "\nEnter your loan payment amount: ";
  cin  >> fpayment;

  cout << "\n\nYou have ";
  cout << ((fpayment > fbalance) ? "overpaid by $" : "paid $");
  cout << ((fpayment > fbalance) ? abs(fbalance - fpayment)) :
                               fpayment);
  cout << " on your loan of $" << fbalance << ".";

  return(0);
}
```

The program uses the first conditional statement inside a **cout** statement to decide which string—"overpaid by $" or "paid $"—is to be printed. The following conditional statement calculates and prints the appropriate dollar value.

switch Statements

You will often want to test a variable or an expression against several values. You could use nested **if-else-if** statements to do this, or you could use a **switch** statement. Be very careful, though; unlike many other high-level language selection statements such as Pascal's case statement, the C **switch** statement has a few peculiarities. The syntax for a **switch** statement is

```
switch (integral_expression) {
    case constant1:
        statements1;
        break;
    case constant2:
        statements2;
        break;
        .
        .
        .
    case constantn:
        statementsn;
        break;
    default: statements;
}
```

The redundant statement you need to pay particular attention to is the **break** statement. If this example had been coded in Pascal and *constant1* equaled *integeral_expression*, *statements1* would have been executed, with program execution picking up with the next statement at the end of the case statement (below the closing brace).

In C the situation is quite different. In the preceding syntax, if the **break** statement had been removed from *constant1*'s section of code, a match similar to the one used in the preceding paragraph would have left *statements2* as the next statement to be executed. It is the **break** statement that causes the remaining portion of the **switch** statements to be skipped. Let's look at a few examples.

Examine the following **if-else-if** code segment:

```
if(emove == SMALL_CHANGE_UP)
    fycoord =    5;

else if(emove == SMALL_CHANGE_DOWN)
    fycoord =   -5;

else if(emove == LARGE_CHANGE_UP)
    fycoord =   10;
```

```
else
  fycoord = -10;
```

You can rewrite this code using a **switch** statement:

```
switch(emove) {
  case  SMALL_CHANGE_UP:
    fycoord =    5;
    break;
  case  SMALL_CHANGE_DOWN:
    fycoord =   -5;
    break;
  case  LARGE_CHANGE_UP:
    fycoord =   10;
    break;
  default:
    fycoord = -10;
}
```

In this example, the value of *emove* is consecutively compared to each **case** value looking for a match. When one is found, *fycoord* is assigned the appropriate value. Then the **break** statement is executed, skipping over the remainder of the **switch** statements. However, if no match is found, the **default** assignment is performed (fycoord = –10). Since this is the last option in the **switch** statement, there is no need to include a **break**. A **switch** default is optional.

Proper placement of the **break** statement within a **switch** statement can be very useful. Look at the following example:

```
/*
 *    07SWITCH.C
 *    A C program demonstrating the
 *    drop-through capabilities of the switch statement.
 *    Copyright (c) William H. Murray and Chris H. Pappas, 1992
 */

main()
{
  char c='a';
  int ivowelct=0, iconstantct=0;

  switch(c) {
    case 'a':
    case 'A':
```

```
        case 'e':
    case 'E':
    case 'i':
    case 'I':
    case 'o':
    case 'O':
    case 'u':
    case 'U': ivowelct++;
                break;
    default : iconstantct++;
  }
  return(0);
}
```

This program actually illustrates two characteristics of the **switch** statement: the enumeration of several test values that all execute the same code section and the drop-through characteristic.

Several other high-level languages have their own form of selection (the case statement in Pascal and the select statement in PL/I), which allows for several test values, all producing the same result, to be included on the same selection line. C, however, requires a separate **case** for each. But notice in this example how the same effect has been created by *not* inserting a **break** statement until all possible vowels have been checked. Should *c* contain a constant, all of the vowel **case** tests will be checked and skipped until the **default** statement is reached.

The next example shows a C program that uses a **switch** statement to invoke the appropriate function:

```
/*
*    07FNSWTH.C
*    A C program demonstrating the switch statement
*    Copyright (c) William H. Murray and Chris H. Pappas, 1992
*/

#include <stdio.h>

#define QUIT 0
#define BLANK ' '

double fadd(float fx,float fy);
double fsub(float fx,float fy);
double fmul(float fx,float fy);
double fdiv(float fx,float fy);

main()
```

```
{
   float fx,fy;
   char cblank, coperator = BLANK;

   while (coperator != QUIT) {
     printf("\nPlease enter an expression (a (operator) b): ");
     scanf("%f%c%c%f", &fx, &cblank, &coperator, &fy);

     switch (coperator) {
       case '+': printf("answer = %8.2f\n", fadd(fx,fy));
                 break;
       case '-': printf("answer = %8.2f\n", fsub(fx,fy));
                 break;
       case '*': printf("answer = %8.2f\n", fmul(fx,fy));
                 break;
       case '/': printf("answer = %8.2f\n", fdiv(fx,fy));
                 break;
       case 'x': coperator = QUIT;
                 break;
       default : printf("\nOperator not implemented");
     }
   }
   return(0);
}

double fadd(float fx,float fy)
   {return(fx + fy);}

double fsub(float fx,float fy)
   {return(fx - fy);}

double fmul(float fx,float fy)
   {return(fx * fy);}

double fdiv(float fx,float fy)
   {return(fx / fy);}
```

While the use of functions in this example is a bit advanced (functions are discussed in Chapter 8), the use of the **switch** statement is very effective. After the user has entered an expression such as 10 + 10 or 23 * 15, the *coperator* is compared in the body of the **switch** statement to determine which function to invoke. Of particular interest is the last set of statements, where the *coperator* equals *x*, and the **default** statement.

If the user enters an expression with an *x* operator, the *coperator* variable is assigned a QUIT value, and the **break** statement is executed, skipping over the **default**

printf() statement. However, if the user enters an unrecognized operator—for example, %—only the **default** statement is executed, printing the message that the *coperator* has not been implemented.

The following C++ program illustrates the similarity in syntax between a C **switch** statement and its C++ counterpart:

```
//
//   07CALNDR.CPP
//   A C++ program using a switch statement
//   to print a yearly calendar.
//   Copyright (c) William H. Murray and Chris H. Pappas, 1992
//

#include <iostream.h>

main()
{
    int jan_1_start_day,num_days_per_month,
        month,date,leap_year_flag;

    cout << "Please enter January 1's starting day;\n";
    cout << "\nA 0 indicates January 1 is on a Monday,";
    cout << "\nA 1 indicates January 1 is on a Tuesday, etc: ";
    cin >> jan_1_start_day;
    cout << "\nEnter the year you want the calendar generated: ";
    cin >> leap_year_flag;
    cout << "\n\n The calendar for the year " << leap_year_flag;

    leap_year_flag=leap_year_flag % 4;
    cout.width(20);

    for (month = 1;month <= 12;month++) {
      switch(month) {
        case 1:
          cout << "\n\n\n" << " January" << "\n";
          num_days_per_month = 31;
          break;
        case 2:
          cout << "\n\n\n" << " February" << "\n";
          num_days_per_month = leap_year_flag ? 28 : 29;
          break;
        case 3:
          cout << "\n\n\n" << "  March " << "\n";
          num_days_per_month = 31;
```

```
      break;
   case 4:
     cout << "\n\n\n" << "   April " << "\n";
     num_days_per_month = 30;
     break;
   case 5:
     cout << "\n\n\n" << "    May  " << "\n";
     num_days_per_month = 31;
     break;
   case 6:
     cout << "\n\n\n" << "   June  " << "\n";
     num_days_per_month = 30;
     break;
   case 7:
     cout << "\n\n\n" << "   July  " << "\n";
     num_days_per_month = 31;
     break;
   case 8:
     cout << "\n\n\n" << " August " << "\n";
     num_days_per_month = 31;
     break;
   case 9:
     cout << "\n\n\n" << "September" << "\n";
     num_days_per_month = 30;
     break;
   case 10:
     cout << "\n\n\n" << " October " << "\n";
     num_days_per_month = 31;
     break;
   case 11:
     cout << "\n\n\n" << "November " << "\n";
     num_days_per_month = 30;
     break;
   case 12:
     cout << "\n\n\n" << "December " << "\n";
     num_days_per_month = 31;
     break;
  }

cout.width(0);
cout << "\nSun  Mon  Tue  Wed  Thu  Fri  Sat\n";
cout << "---  ---  ---  ---  ---  ---  ---\n";

for ( date = 1; date <= 1 + jan_1_start_day * 5; date++ )
  cout << "   ";
```

```
  for ( date = 1; date <= num_days_per_month; date++ ) {
    cout.width(2);
    cout << date;
    if ( ( date + jan_1_start_day ) % 7 > 0 )
      cout <<  "   ";
    else
      cout <<  "\n ";
  }
  jan_1_start_day=(jan_1_start_day + num_days_per_month) % 7;
 }
 return(0);
}
```

The program begins by asking the user to enter an integer code representing the day of the week on which January 1st occurs (zero for Monday, 1 for Tuesday, and so on). The second prompt asks for the year for the calendar. The program can now print the calendar heading, and use the year entered to generate a *leap_year_flag*. Using the modulus operator (%) with a value of 4 generates a remainder of zero whenever it is leap year and a nonzero value whenever it is not leap year.

Next, a 12-iteration loop is entered, printing the current month's name and assigning *num_days_per_month* the correct number of days for that particular month. All of this is accomplished by using a **switch** statement to test the current *month* integer value.

Outside the **switch** statement, after the month's name has been printed, day-of-the-week headings are printed, and an appropriate number of blank columns is skipped, depending on when the first day of the month was.

The last **for** loop actually generates and prints the dates for each month. The last statement in the program prepares the *day_code* for the next month to be printed.

if-else-if and switch Statements Combined

The following example program uses an enumerated type (**enum**) to perform the requested length conversions:

```
/*
 *   07IFELSW.C
 *   A C program demonstrating the if-else-if statement
 *   used in a meaningful way with several switch statements.
 *   Copyright (c) William H. Murray and Chris H. Pappas, 1992
 */

typedef enum conversion_type {YARDS, INCHES, CENTIMETERS, \
                              METERS} C_TYPE;
```

```c
#include <stdio.h>

main()
{
  int iuser_response;
  C_TYPE C_Tconversion;
  int ilength=30;
  float fmeasurement;

  printf("\nPlease enter the measurement to be converted : ");
  scanf("%f",&fmeasurement);

  printf("\nPlease enter :            \
          \n\t\t 0 for YARDS        \
          \n\t\t 1 for INCHES       \
          \n\t\t 2 for CENTIMETERS \
          \n\t\t 3 for METERS       \
          \n\n\t\tYour response -->> ");

  scanf("%d",&iuser_response);

  switch(iuser_response) {
    case 0  :  C_Tconversion = YARDS;
               break;
    case 1  :  C_Tconversion = INCHES;
               break;
    case 2  :  C_Tconversion = CENTIMETERS;
               break;
    default :  C_Tconversion = METERS;
  }


  if(C_Tconversion == YARDS)
    fmeasurement = ilength / 3;

  else if(C_Tconversion == INCHES)
    fmeasurement = ilength * 12;

  else if(C_Tconversion == CENTIMETERS)
    fmeasurement = ilength * 12 * 2.54;

  else if(C_Tconversion == METERS)
    fmeasurement = (ilength * 12 * 2.54)/100;

  else
```

```
    printf("No conversion required");


switch(C_Tconversion) {
  case YARDS       : printf("\n\t\t  %4.2f yards",
                            fmeasurement);
                   break;
  case INCHES      : printf("\n\t\t  %4.2f inches",
                            fmeasurement);
                   break;
  case CENTIMETERS : printf("\n\t\t  %4.2f centimeters",
                            fmeasurement);
                   break;
  default          : printf("\n\t\t  %4.2f meters",
                            fmeasurement);
}

return(0);
}
```

The example program uses an enumerated type to perform the specified length conversion. In standard C, enumerated types exist only within the code itself (for reasons of readability) and cannot be input or output directly. The program uses the first **switch** statement to convert the input code to its appropriate *C_Tconversion* type. The nested **if-else-if** statements perform the proper conversion. The last **switch** statement prints the converted value with its appropriate "literal" type. Of course, the nested **if-else-if** statements could have been implemented by using a **switch** statement. (A further discussion of enumerated types can be found in Chapter 12.)

Loop Statements

The C language includes the standard set of repetition control statements; **for** loops, **while** loops, and **do-while** loops (called repeat-until loops in several other high-level languages). You may be surprised, however, by the ways a program can leave a repetition loop. C provides four methods for altering the repetitions in a loop. All repetition loops can naturally terminate based on the expressed test condition. In C, however, a repetition loop can also terminate because of an anticipated error condition by using either a **break** or **exit** statement. Repetition loops can also have their logic control flow altered by a **break** statement or a **continue** statement.

The basic difference between a **for** loop and a **while** or **do-while** loop has to do with the "known" number of repetitions. Typically, **for** loops are used whenever there is a definite predefined required number of repetitions, and **while** and **do-while** loops are reserved for an "unknown" number of repetitions.

for Loops

The syntax for a **for** loop is

```
for(initialization_exp; test_exp; increment_exp)
    statement;
```

When the **for** loop statement is encountered, the *initialization_exp* is executed first. This is done at the start of the loop, and it is never executed again. Usually this statement involves the initialization of the loop control variable. Following this, *test_exp*, which is called the *loop terminating condition*, is tested. Whenever *test_exp* evaluates to TRUE, the statement or statements within the loop are executed. If the loop was entered, then after all of the statements within the loop are executed, *increment_exp* is executed. However, if *test_exp* evaluates to FALSE, the statement or statements within the loop are ignored, along with *increment_exp*, and execution continues with the statement following the end of the loop. The indentation scheme applied to **for** loops with several statements to be repeated looks like this:

```
for(initialization_exp; test_exp; increment_exp) {
    statement_a;
    statement_b;
    statement_c;
    statement_n;
}
```

When several statements need to be executed, a pair of braces is required to tie their execution to the loop control structure. Let's examine a few examples of **for** loops.

The following example sums up the first five integers. It assumes that *isum* and *ivalue* have been predefined as integers:

```
isum = 0;
for(ivalue=1; ivalue <= 5; ivalue++)
    isum += ivalue;
```

After *isum* has been initialized to zero, the **for** loop is encountered. First, *ivalue* is initialized to 1 (this is done only once); second, *ivalue*'s value is checked against the loop terminating condition, <= 5. Since this is TRUE, a 1 is added to *isum*. Once the statement is executed, the loop control variable (*ivalue*) is incremented by 1. This process continues four more times until *ivalue* is incremented to 6 and the loop terminates.

In C++, the same code segment could be written as follows. See if you can detect the subtle difference:

```
for(int ivalue=1; ivalue <= 5; ivalue++)
   isum += ivalue;
```

C++ allows the loop control variable to be declared and initialized within the **for** loop. This brings up a very sensitive issue among structured programmers, which is the proper placement of variable declarations. In C++, you can declare variables right before the statement that actually uses them. In the preceding example, since *ivalue* is used only to generate an *isum*, with *isum* having a larger scope than *ivalue*, the local declaration for *ivalue* is harmless. However, look at the following code segment:

```
int isum = 0;
for(int ivalue=1; ivalue <= 5; ivalue++)
   isum += ivalue;
```

This would obscure the visual "desk check" of the variable *isum* because it was not declared below the function head. For the sake of structured design and debugging, it is best to localize all variable declarations. It is the rare code segment that can justify the usefulness of moving a variable declaration to a nonstandard place, in sacrifice of easily read, easily checked, and easily modified code.

The value used to increment **for** loop control variables does not always have to be 1 or ++. The following example sums all the odd numbers up to 9:

```
iodd_sum = 0;
for(iodd_value=1; iodd_value <= 9; iodd_value+=2);
   iodd_sum += iodd_value;
```

In this example, the loop control variable *iodd_value* is initialized to 1 and is incremented by 2.

Of course, **for** loops don't always have to go from a smaller value to a larger one. The following example uses a **for** loop to read into an array of characters and then print the character string backward:

```
//
//   07FORLP.CPP
//   A C++ program that uses a for loop to input a character array
//   Copyright (c) William H. Murray and Chris H. Pappas, 1992
//

#include <stdio.h>

#define CARRAY_SIZE 10

main()
{
```

```
   int ioffset;
   char carray[CARRAY_SIZE];

   for(ioffset = 0; ioffset < CARRAY_SIZE; ioffset++)
     carray[ioffset] = getchar();
   for(ioffset = CARRAY_SIZE - 1; ioffset >= 0; ioffset--)
     putchar(carray[ioffset]);

   return(0);
}
```

In this example, the first **for** loop initialized *ioffset* to zero (necessary since all array indexes are offsets from the starting address of the first array element), and while there is room in *carray*, reads characters in one at a time. The second **for** loop initializes the loop control variable *ioffset* to the offset of the last element in the array and, while *ioffset* contains a valid offset, prints the characters in reverse order. This process could be used to parse an infix expression that was being converted to prefix notation.

When you combine **for** loops, as in the next example, take care to include the appropriate braces to make certain the statements execute properly:

```
/*
 *    07NSLOP1.C
 *    A C program demonstrating
 *    the need for caution when nesting for loops.
 *    Copyright (c) William H. Murray and Chris H. Pappas, 1992
 */

#include <stdio.h>

main()
{
  int iouter_val, iinner_val;

  for(iouter_val = 1; iouter_val <= 4; iouter_val++) {
    printf("\n%3d --",iouter_val);
    for(iinner_val = 1; iinner_val <= 5; iinner_val++ )
      printf("%3d",iouter_val * iinner_val);
  }

  return(0);
}
```

The output produced by this program looks like this:

```
1 --   1   2   3   4   5
2 --   2   4   6   8  10
3 --   3   6   9  12  15
4 --   4   8  12  16  20
```

However, suppose the outer **for** loop had been written without the braces, like this:

```
/*
 *    07NSLOP2.C
 *    A C program demonstrating what happens when you nest
 *    for loops without the logically required braces {}.
 *    Copyright (c) William H. Murray and Chris H. Pappas, 1992
 */

#include <stdio.h>

main()
{
  int iouter_val, iinner_val;

  for(iouter_val = 1; iouter_val <= 4; iouter_val++)
    printf("\n%3d --",iouter_val);
    for(iinner_val = 1; iinner_val <= 5; iinner_val++ )
      printf("%3d",iouter_val * iinner_val);

  return(0);
}
```

The output would have looked quite different:

```
1 --
2 --
3 --
4 --   5  10  15  20  25
```

Without the braces surrounding the first **for** loop, only the first **printf()** statement is associated with the loop. Once the **printf()** statement is executed four times, the second **for** loop is entered. The inner loop uses the last value stored in *iouter_val,* or 5, to generate the values printed by its **printf()** statement.

The need to include or not include braces can be a tricky matter at best that needs to be approached with some thought to readability. Look at the next two examples and see if you can figure out if they would produce the same output.

Here is the first example:

```
/*
 *   07LPDMO1.C
 *   Another C program demonstrating the need
 *   for caution when nesting for loops.
 *   Copyright (c) William H. Murray and Chris H. Pappas, 1992
 */

#include <stdio.h>

main()
{
  int iouter_val, iinner_val;

  for(iouter_val = 1; iouter_val <= 4; iouter_val++) {
    for(iinner_val = 1; iinner_val <= 5; iinner_val++ )
      printf("%d ",iouter_val * iinner_val);
  }

  return(0);
}
```

Compare the preceding program with the following example:

```
/*
 *   07LPDMO2.C
 *   A comparison C program demonstrating the need
 *   for caution when nesting for loops.
 *   Copyright (c) William H. Murray and Chris H. Pappas, 1992
 */

#include <stdio.h>

main()
{
  int iouter_val, iinner_val;

  for(iouter_val = 1; iouter_val <= 4; iouter_val++)
    for(iinner_val = 1; iinner_val <= 5; iinner_val++ )
      printf("%d ",iouter_val * iinner_val);

  return(0);
}
```

Both programs produce the identical output:

```
1 2 3 4 5 2 4 6 8 10 3 6 9 12 15 4 8 12 16 20
```

In these last two examples, the only statement associated with the outer **for** loop is the inner **for** loop. The inner **for** loop is considered a single statement. This would still be the case even if the inner **for** loop had multiple statements to execute. Since braces are needed only around code blocks or multiple statements, the outer **for** loop does not need braces to execute the program properly.

while Loops

Just like the **for** loop, the C **while** loop is a *pretest loop*. This means that the program evaluates *test_exp* before entering the statement or statements within the body of the loop. Because of this, pretest loops may be executed from zero to many times. The syntax for a C **while** loop is

```
while(test_exp)
    statement;
```

For **while** loops with several statements, braces are needed:

```
while(test_exp) {
    statement1;
    statement2;
    statement3;
    statementn;
}
```

Usually, **while** loop control structures are used whenever an indefinite number of repetitions is expected. The following C program uses a **while** loop to control the number of times *ivalue* is shifted to the right. The program prints the binary representation of a signed integer.

```
/*
 *   07WHILE.C
 *   A C program using a pretest while loop with flag
 *   Copyright (c) William H. Murray and Chris H. Pappas, 1992
 */

#include <stdio.h>

#define WORD 16
#define ONE_BYTE 8
```

```
main()
{
  int ivalue = 256, ibit_position=1;
  unsigned int umask = 1;

  printf("The following value %d,\n",ivalue);
  printf("in binary form looks like: ");

  while(ibit_position <= WORD) {
    if((ivalue >> (WORD - ibit_position)) & umask) /*shift each*/
      printf("1");                                 /*bit to 0th*/
    else                                           /*position &*/
      printf("0");                                 /*compare to*/
    if(ibit_position == ONE_BYTE)                  /*umask     */
      printf(" ");
    ibit_position++;
  }

  return(0);
}
```

The program begins by defining two constants, *WORD* and *ONE_BYTE*, that can be easily modified for different architectures. *WORD* will be used as a flag to determine when the **while** loop will terminate. Within the **while** loop, *ivalue* is shifted, compared to *umask,* and printed from most significant bit to least. This allows the algorithm to use a simple **printf()** statement to output the results.

The next C program prompts the user for an input filename and an output filename. The program then uses a **while** loop to read in and echo print the input file of unknown size.

```
/*
 *    07DOWHIL.C
 *    A C program using a while loop to echo print a file
 *    The program demonstrates additional file I/O techniques
 *    Copyright (c) William H. Murray and Chris H. Pappas, 1992
 */

#include <stdio.h>
#include <process.h>

#define sz_TERMINATOR 1        /* sz, null-string designator */
#define MAX_CHARS 30

main()
```

```
{
  int c;
  FILE *ifile, *ofile;
  char sziDOS_file_name[MAX_CHARS + sz_TERMINATOR],
       szoDOS_file_name[MAX_CHARS + sz_TERMINATOR];

  fputs("Enter the input file's name: ",stdout);
  gets(sziDOS_file_name);

  if((ifile=fopen(sziDOS_file_name,"r")) == NULL) {
    printf("\nFile: %s cannot be opened",sziDOS_file_name);
    exit(1);
  }

  fputs("Enter the output file's name: ",stdout);
  gets(szoDOS_file_name);

  if((ofile=fopen(szoDOS_file_name,"w")) == NULL) {
    printf("\nFile: %s cannot be opened",szoDOS_file_name);
    exit(2);
  }
  while(!feof(ifile)) {
    c=fgetc(ifile);
    fputc(c,ofile);
  }

  return(0);
}
```

In this example, the **while** loop contains two executable statements, so the brace pair is required. The program also illustrates the use of several file I/O statements like **fgetc()** and **fputc()**, along with **feof()** (discussed in Chapter 11).

do-while Loops

The **do-while** loop differs from both the **for** and **while** loops in that it is a *post-test loop*. In other words, the loop is always entered at least once, with the loop condition being tested at the end of the first iteration. In contrast, **for** loops and **while** loops may execute from zero to many times, depending on the loop control variable. Since **do-while** loops always execute at least one time, they are best used whenever there is no doubt you want the particular loop entered. For example, if your program needs to present a menu to the user, even if all the user wants to do is immediately quit the program, he or she needs to see the menu to know which key terminates the application.

The syntax for a **do-while** loop is

```
do
    action;
while(test_condition);
```

Braces are required for **do-while** statements that have compound actions:

```
do {
    action1;
    action2;
    action3;
    actionn;
} while(test_condition);
```

The following C++ program uses a **do-while** loop to print a menu and obtain a valid user response:

```
//
//   07DOWHIL.CPP
//   A C++ program demonstrating the proper use of a post-test
//   do-while loop to print a menu using text output functions.
//   Copyright (c) William H. Murray and Chris H. Pappas, 1992
//

#include <iostream.h>
#include <conio.h>
#include <graph.h>
#include <stdlib.h>

main()
{
  int iuser_response;
  struct rccoord rcorig_coords;
  struct videoconfig svideo_config;

  if(!_setvideomode(_MAXRESMODE))
    exit(1);

  _getvideoconfig(&svideo_config);
  _settextcolor(9); // Light Blue

  do {
```

```
_clearscreen(_GCLEARSCREEN);
_settextposition(3,23);
_outtext(">>> Welcome to Metro-Teller <<<\n\n");
_settextposition(5,29);
_outtext("Instructions       1\n");
_settextposition(6,29);
_outtext("IRA Balance        2\n");
_settextposition(7,29);
_outtext("Loan Rates         3\n");
_settextposition(8,29);
_outtext("VISA Transaction  4\n");
_settextposition(9,29);
_outtext("Ready-Reserve      5\n");
_settextposition(10,29);
_outtext("Deposit            6\n");
_settextposition(11,29);
_outtext("Withdrawal         7\n");
_settextposition(12,29);
_outtext("Quit               8\n");
_settextposition(14,25);
_outtext("Enter your selection: ");

rcorig_coords = _gettextposition();

cin >> iuser_response;

while(iuser_response < 1 || iuser_response > 8) {
  _settextposition(rcorig_coords.row,rcorig_coords.col);
  _outtext("   ");
  _settextposition(rcorig_coords.row,rcorig_coords.col);
  cin >> iuser_response;
}

} while(iuser_response !=  8);

_setvideomode(_DEFAULTMODE);

return(0);
}
```

To add a little interest to the program, the conio.h and graph.h header files have been included. The header files contain many useful functions for controlling the monitor. The program uses three of these functions: **_gettextposition()**, **_settextposition()**, and **_outtext()**. Before discussing the two **do-while** loops used in the program, let's take a look at these functions. The two functions **_gettextposition()** and

_settextposition() return or set the current screen coordinates of the cursor. The **_outtext**() function outputs text to the graphics screen. (Graphics are discussed in greater detail in Chapter 19.)

The program uses a **do-while** loop to print the menu items and continues to reprint the menu items until the user has selected option 8 to quit.

Notice that the program also has a nested inner **while** loop. It is the responsibility of this loop to make certain the user has entered an acceptable response (a number from 1 to 8, inclusive). Since you don't want the user's incorrect guesses to be "newlined" all the way down the display screen, the inner loop uses the **_settextposition**() statements to keep the cursor on the same line as the first response. The program accomplishes this by obtaining the cursor's original position after the input prompt "Enter your selection:" is printed. The function **_gettextposition**() is designed for this specific purpose.

Once the user has typed a response, however, the cursor's *x* and *y* coordinates change; this requires their original values to be stored in the record fields *rcorig_coords.row* and *rcorig_coords.col* for repeated reference. Once inside the inner **while** loop, the first **_outtext**() statement blanks out any previously entered values and then obtains the next number entered. This process continues until an acceptable *iuser_response* is obtained. When the inner **while** loop is exited, control returns to the outer **do-while** loop, which repeats the menu again until the user enters an 8 to quit. Try to see if you can rewrite the program using **_settextposition**() so that the entire menu doesn't need to be reprinted with each valid *user_response*.

break Statement

The C **break** statement can be used to exit a loop before the test condition becomes FALSE. The **break** statement is similar in many ways to a **goto** statement, only the point jumped to is not known directly. When breaking out of a loop, program execution continues with the next statement following the loop itself. Look at a very simple example:

```
/*
*    07BREAK.C
*    A C program demonstrating the use of the break statement.
*    Copyright (c) William H. Murray and Chris H. Pappas, 1992
*/

main()
{
  int itimes = 1, isum = 0;

  while(itimes < 10){
    isum += isum + itimes;
    if(isum > 20)
```

```
      break;
    itimes++;
  }

  return(0);
}
```

Using CodeView

Use CodeView to trace through the program. Trace the variables *isum* and *itimes*. Pay particular attention to which statements are executed after *isum* reaches the value 21.

What you should have noticed is that when *isum* reached the value 21, the **break** statement was executed. This caused the increment of *itimes* to be jumped over, *itimes++*, with program execution continuing on the line of code below the loop. In this example, the next statement executed was the **return**.

continue Statement

There is a subtle difference between the C **break** statement and the C **continue** statement. As you have already seen from the last example program, **break** causes the loop to terminate execution altogether. In contrast, the **continue** statement causes all of the statements following the **continue** statement to be ignored but does *not* circumvent incrementing the loop control variable or the loop control test condition. In other words, if the loop control variable still satisfies the loop test condition, the loop will continue to iterate.

The following program demonstrates this concept, using a number guessing game:

```
/*
 *    07CONTNU.C
 *    A C program demonstrating the use of the continue statement.
 *    Copyright (c) William H. Murray and Chris H. Pappas, 1992
 */

#include <stdio.h>

#define TRUE 1
#define FALSE 0

main()
{
  int ilucky_number=77,
      iinput_val,
```

```
          inumber_of_tries=0,
          iam_lucky=FALSE;

    while(!iam_lucky){
      printf("Please enter your lucky guess: ");
      scanf("%d",&iinput_val);
      inumber_of_tries++;
      if(iinput_val == ilucky_number)
        iam_lucky=TRUE;
      else
        continue;
      printf("It only took you %d tries to get lucky!",
        inumber_of_tries);
    }

    return(0);
}
```

Using CodeView

Enter the preceding program and trace the variables *iinput_val, inumber_of_tries,* and *iam_lucky.* Pay particular attention to which statements are executed after *iinput_val* is compared to *ilucky_number.*

The program uses a **while** loop to prompt the user for a value, increments the *inumber_of_tries* for each guess entered, and then determines the appropriate action to take based on the success of the match. If no match was found, the **else** statement is executed. This is the **continue** statement. Whenever the **continue** statement is executed, the **printf()** statement is ignored. Note, however, that the loop continues to execute. When *iinput_val* matches *ilucky_number,* the *iam_lucky* flag is set to TRUE and the **continue** statement is ignored, allowing the **printf()** statement to execute.

Using break and continue Together

The **break** and **continue** statements can be combined to solve some interesting program problems. Look at the following C++ example:

```
//
//  07BRACNTG.CPP
//  A C++ program demonstrating the usefulness of combining
//  the break and continue statements.
//  Copyright (c) William H. Murray and Chris H. Pappas, 1992
//

#include <iostream.h>
```

```
#include <ctype.h>

#define NEWLINE '\n'

main()
{
  int c;

  while((c=getchar()) != EOF)
  {
    if(isascii(c) == 0) {
      cout << "Not an ASCII character; ";
      cout << "not going to continue/n";
      break;
    }

    if(ispunct(c) || isspace(c)) {
      putchar(NEWLINE);
      continue;
    }

    if(isprint(c) == 0) {
      c = getchar();
      continue;
    }

    putchar(c);
  }

  return(0);
}
```

Before seeing how the program functions, take a look at the input to the program:

```
word control ^B exclamation! apostrophe' period.
^Z
```

Also examine the output produced:

```
word
control
B
exclamation
```

apostrophe

period

The program continues to read character input until the EOF character ^Z is typed. It then examines the input, removing any nonprintable characters, and places each "word" on its own line. It accomplishes all of this by using some very interesting functions defined in ctype.h, including **isascii()**, **ispunct()**, **isspace()**, and **isprint()**. Each of the functions is passed a character parameter and returns either a zero or some other value indicating the result of the comparison.

The function **isascii()** indicates whether the character passed falls into the acceptable ASCII value range, **ispunct()** indicates whether the character is a punctuation mark, **isspace()** indicates whether the character is a space, and function **isprint()** reports whether the character parameter is a printable character.

Using these functions, the program determines whether to continue the program at all and, if it is to continue, what it should do with each of the characters input.

The first test within the **while** loop evaluates whether the file is even in readable form. For example, the input data could have been saved in binary format, rendering the program useless. If this is the case, the associated **if** statements are executed, printing a warning message and breaking out of the **while** loop permanently.

If all is well, the second **if** statement is encountered; it checks whether the character input is either a punctuation mark or a blank space. If either of these conditions is TRUE, the associated **if** statements are executed. This causes a blank line to be skipped in the output and executes the **continue** statement. The **continue** statement efficiently jumps over the remaining test condition and output statement but does not terminate the loop. It merely indicates that the character's form has been diagnosed properly and that it is time to obtain a new character.

If the file is in an acceptable format and the character input is not punctuation or a blank, the third **if** statement asks whether the character is printable or not. This test takes care of any control codes. Notice that the example input to the program included a control ^B. Since ^B is not printable, this **if** statement immediately obtains a new character and then executes a **continue** statement. In like manner, this **continue** statement indicates that the character in question has been diagnosed, the proper action has been taken, and it is time to get another character. The **continue** statement also causes the **putchar()** statement to be ignored while *not* terminating the **while** loop.

exit() Statement

Under certain circumstances, it is proper for a program to terminate long before all of the statements in the program have been examined and/or executed. For these specific circumstances, C incorporates the **exit()** library function. The function **exit()** expects one integer argument, called a *status value*. The UNIX and MS-DOS operat-

ing systems interpret a status value of zero as signaling a normal program termination, while any nonzero status values signify different kinds of errors.

The particular status value passed to **exit()** can be used by the process that invoked
the program to take some action. For example, if the program were invoked from
the command line and the status value indicated some type of error, the operating
system might display a message. In addition to terminating the program, **exit()** writes
all output waiting to be written and closes all open files.

The following C++ program averages a list of up to 30 grades. The program will
exit if the user requests to average more than *SIZE* number of integers.

```
//
//   07EXIT1.CPP
//   A C++ program demonstrating the use of the exit function
//   Copyright (c) William H. Murray and Chris H. Pappas, 1992
//

#include <iostream.h>
#include <process.h>

#define LIMIT 30

main()
{
  int irow,irequested_qty,iscores[LIMIT];
  float fsum=0,imax_score=0,imin_score=100,faverage;

  cout << "\nEnter the number of scores to be averaged: ";
  cin >>  irequested_qty;
  if(irequested_qty > LIMIT) {
    cout << "\nYou can only enter up to " << LIMIT << \
            " scores" << " to be averaged.\n";
    cout << "\n         >>> Program was exited. <<<\n";
    exit(1);
  }

  for(irow = 0; irow < irequested_qty; irow++) {
    cout << "\nPlease enter a grade " << irow+1 << ":   ";
    cin >> iscores[irow];
  }

  for(irow = 0; irow < irequested_qty; irow++)
    fsum = fsum + iscores[irow];

  faverage = fsum/(float)irequested_qty;
```

```
    for(irow = 0; irow < irequested_qty; irow++) {
      if(iscores[irow] > imax_score)
        imax_score = iscores[irow];
      if(iscores[irow] < imin_score)
        imin_score = iscores[irow];
    }

    cout << "\nThe maximum grade is " << imax_score;
    cout << "\nThe minimum grade is " << imin_score;
    cout << "\nThe average grade is " << faverage;

    return(0);
}
```

The program begins by including the process.h header file. Either process.h or stdlib.h can be included to prototype the function **exit()**. The constant *LIMIT* is declared to be 30 and is used to dimension the array of integers, *iscores*. After the remaining variables are declared, the program prompts the user for the number of *iscores* to be entered. For this program, the user's response is to be typed next to the prompt.

The program inputs the requested value into the variable *irequested_qty* and uses this for the **if** comparison. When the user wants to average more numbers than will fit in *iscores*, the two warning messages are printed and then the **exit()** statement is executed. This terminates the program altogether.

See if you can detect the two subtle differences between the preceding program and the one that follows:

```
//
//   07EXIT2.CPP
//   A C++ program demonstrating the use of the exit function
//   in relation to the difference between the process.h
//   and stdlib.h header files.
//   Copyright (c) William H. Murray and Chris H. Pappas, 1992
//

#include <iostream.h>
#include <stdlib.h>

#define LIMIT 30

main()
{
  int irow,irequested_qty,iscores[LIMIT];
```

```
    float fsum=0,imax_score=0,imin_score=100,faverage;

  cout << "\nEnter the number of scores to be averaged: ";
  cin >>  irequested_qty;
  if(irequested_qty > LIMIT) {
    cout << "\nYou can only enter up to " << LIMIT << \
            " scores" << " to be faveraged.\n";
    cout << "\n         >>> Program was exited. <<<\n";
    exit(EXIT_FAILURE);
  }

  for(irow = 0; irow < irequested_qty; irow++) {
    cout << "\nPlease enter a grade " << irow+1 << ":   ";
    cin >> iscores[irow];
  }

  for(irow = 0; irow < irequested_qty; irow++)
    fsum = fsum + iscores[irow];

  faverage = fsum/(float)irequested_qty;

  for(irow = 0; irow < irequested_qty; irow++) {
    if(iscores[irow] > imax_score)
      imax_score = iscores[irow];
    if(iscores[irow] < imin_score)
      imin_score = iscores[irow];
  }

  cout << "\nThe maximum grade is " << imax_score;
  cout << "\nThe minimum grade is " << imin_score;
  cout << "\nThe average grade is " << faverage;

  return(0);
}
```

By the inclusion of the stdlib.h header file instead of process.h, two additional definitions became visible: **EXIT_SUCCESS** (which returns a value of zero) and **EXIT_FAILURE** (which returns an unsuccessful value). This program used the **EXIT_SUCCESS** definition for a more readable parameter to the function **exit()**.

atexit() Statement

Whenever a program invokes the **exit()** function or performs a normal program termination, it can also call any registered "exit functions" posted with **atexit()**. The following C program demonstrates this capability:

```
/*
 *   07ATEXIT.C
 *   A C program demonstrating the relationship between the
 *   function atexit and the order in which the functions
 *   declared are executed.
 *   Copyright (c) William H. Murray and Chris H. Pappas, 1992
 */

#include <stdio.h>
#include <stdlib.h>

void atexit_fn1(void);
void atexit_fn2(void);
void atexit_fn3(void);

main()
{

  atexit(atexit_fn1);
  atexit(atexit_fn2);
  atexit(atexit_fn3);

  printf("Atexit program entered.\n");
  printf("Atexit program exited.\n\n");
  printf(">>>>>>>>>>> <<<<<<<<<<<\n\n");

  return(0);
}

void atexit_fn1(void)
{
  printf("atexit_fn1 entered.\n");
}

void atexit_fn2(void)
{
  printf("atexit_fn2 entered.\n");
}

void atexit_fn3(void)
{
  printf("atexit_fn3 entered.\n");
}
```

The output from the program looks like this:

```
Atexit program entered.
Atexit program exited.

>>>>>>>>>>> <<<<<<<<<<<

atexit_fn3 entered.
atexit_fn2 entered.
atexit_fn1 entered.
```

The **atexit()** function uses the name of a function as its only parameter and registers the specified function as an exit function. Whenever the program terminates normally, as in the preceding example, or invokes the **exit()** function, all **atexit()** declared functions are executed.

Technically, each time the **atexit()** statement is encountered in the source code, the specified function is added to a list of functions to execute when the program terminates. When the program terminates, any functions that have been passed to **atexit()** are executed, with the *last* function added being the *first* one executed. This explains why the *atexit_fn3* output statement was printed before the similar statement in *atexit_fn1*. **atexit()** functions are normally used as cleanup routines for dynamically allocated objects. Since one object (B) can be built upon another (A), **atexit()** functions execute in reverse order. This would delete object B before deleting object A.

Chapter *8*

Writing and Using Functions

Functions form the cornerstone of C and C++ programming. This chapter introduces you to the concept of a function and how it is prototyped under the latest ANSI C standard. Using many example programs, you will examine the different types of functions and how arguments are passed. You will also learn how to use the standard C/C++ variables *argc* and *argv* to pass command-line arguments to the **main**() function. Additionally, the chapter explores several unique features available in C++.

Functions are the main building blocks of C and C++ programs. By separating and coding parts of your program in separate modules, called *functions,* your program can take on a modular appearance. Modular programming allows a program to be separated into workable parts that contribute to a final program form. For example, one function might be used to capture input data, another to print information, and yet another to write data to the disk. As a matter of fact, all C and C++ programming is done within a function. The one function every C or C++ program has is **main**().

If you have programmed in other languages, you will find that C functions are similar to programming modules in other languages. For example, Pascal uses functions and procedures, while FORTRAN uses just functions. The proper development of C and C++ functions determines, to a great extent, the efficiency, readability, and portability of your program code.

Many programming examples have been included in this chapter with the intent of showing you how to create and implement a wide range of functions. Many of the example programs also use built-in C and C++ library functions that give your program extended power.

Function Prototyping and Style

When the ANSI C standard was implemented for C, it was the C functions that underwent the greatest change. The ANSI C standard for functions is based upon the function prototype that has already been extensively used in C++.

At this point, the world of C programming is in transition. As you read magazine articles and books that use C code, you will see many forms used to describe C functions. These may or may not conform to the new ANSI C standard, as programmers attempt to bring themselves in line with this standard. The Microsoft C/C++ compiler uses the ANSI C standard for functions but will also compile the earlier forms. The C programs in this book conform to the ANSI C standard. An attempt has been made to pattern C++ programs after the ANSI C standard for C since one has not yet been set for C++.

Prototyping

If you are not familiar with writing C functions, you probably have a few questions. What does a function look like? Where do functions go in a program? How are functions declared? What constitutes a function? Where is type checking performed?

Under the ANSI C standard, all functions must be prototyped. The prototyping can take place in the C or C++ program itself or in a header file. For the programs in this book, most function prototyping is contained within the program itself. Function declarations begin with the C and C++ function prototype. The function prototype is simple, and it is usually included at the start of program code to notify the compiler of the type and number of arguments that a function will use. Prototyping enforces stronger type checking than was previously possible when C standards were less strongly enforced.

Although other prototyping style variations are legal, this book recommends the function prototype form that is a replication of the function's declaration line, with the addition of a semicolon at the end, whenever possible. For example:

return_type function_name(argument_type(s)) argument_name(s));

The function can be of type **void**, **int**, **float**, and so on. The *return_type* gives this specification. The *function_name()* is any meaningful name you choose to describe the function. If any information is passed to the function, an *argument_type* followed by an *argument_name* should also be given. Argument types can also be of type **void**, **int**, **float**, and so on. You can pass many values to a function by repeating the argument type and name separated by a comma. It is also correct to list just the argument type, but that prototype form is not used as frequently.

The function itself is actually an encapsulated piece of C or C++ program code that usually follows the **main()** function definition. A function can take the following form:

return_type function_name(argument_types and names)
{

.

.

(*data declarations and body of function*)

.

.

return();
}

Notice that the first line of the actual function is identical to the prototype that is listed at the beginning of a program, with one important exception: it does *not* end with a semicolon. A function prototype and function used in a program are shown in the following C example:

```
/*
 *   08PROTO.C
 *   A C program to illustrate function prototyping.
 *   Function adds two integers
 *   and returns an integer result.
 *   Copyright (c) William H. Murray and Chris H. Pappas, 1992
 */

#include <stdio.h>

int iadder(int ix,int iy);              /* function prototype  */

main()
{
  int ia=23;
  int ib=13;
  int ic;

  ic=iadder(ia,ib);
  printf("The sum is: %d\n", ic);

  return (0);
}

int iadder(int ix,int iy)               /* function declaration */
{
  int iz;

  iz=ix+iy;
```

```
    return(iz);                              /* function return      */
}
```

The function is called **iadder()**. The prototype states that the function will accept two integer arguments and return an integer type. Actually, the ANSI C standard suggests that all functions be prototyped in a separate header file. This, as you might guess, is how header files are associated with their appropriate C libraries. For simple programs, as already mentioned, including the function prototype within the body of the program is acceptable.

The same function written for C++ takes on an almost identical appearance:

```
//   08PROTO.CPP
//   C++ program to illustrate function prototyping.
//   Function adds two integers
//   and returns an integer result.
//   Copyright (c) William H. Murray and Chris H. Pappas, 1992
//

#include <iostream.h>

int iadder(int ix,int iy);              // function prototype

main()
{
  int ia=23;
  int ib=13;
  int ic;

  ic=iadder(ia,ib);
  cout << "The sum is: " << ic << endl;

  return (0);
}

int iadder(int ix,int iy)               // function declaration
{
  int iz;

  iz=ix+iy;
  return(iz);                           // function return
}
```

Call-by-Value and Call-by-Reference

In the previous two examples, arguments have been *passed by value* to the functions. When variables are passed by value, a copy of the variable's actual contents is passed to the function. Since a copy of the variable is passed, the variable in the calling function itself is not altered. Calling a function by value is the most popular means of passing information to a function, and it is the default method in C and C++. The major restriction to the call-by-value method is that the function typically returns only one value.

When you use a *call-by-reference*, the address of the argument, rather than the actual value, is passed to the function. This approach also requires less program memory than a call-by-value. When you use call-by-reference, the variables in the calling function can be altered. Another advantage to a call-by-reference is that more than one value can be returned by the function.

The next example uses the **iadder()** function from the previous section. The arguments are now passed by a call-by-reference. In C, you accomplish a call-by-reference by using a pointer as an argument, as shown here. This same method can be used with C++.

```
/*
 *    08CBREF.C
 *    A C program to illustrate call by reference.
 *    Copyright (c) William H. Murray and Chris H. Pappas, 1992
 */

#include <stdio.h>

int iadder(int *pix,int *piy);

main()
{
  int ia=23;
  int ib=13;
  int ic;

  ic=iadder(&ia,&ib);
  printf("The sum is: %d\n", ic);

  return (0);
}
```

```
int iadder(int *pix,int *piy)
{
  int iz;

  iz=*pix+*piy;
  return(iz);
}
```

As you have learned, in C, you can use variables and pointers as arguments in function declarations. C++ uses variables and pointers as arguments in function declarations and adds a third type. In C++, the third argument type is called a *reference type*. The reference type specifies a location but does not require a dereferencing operator. Many advanced C++ programs use this syntax to simplify the use of pointer variables within called subroutines. Examine the following syntax carefully and compare it with the previous example:

```
//
//   08REFRNC.CPP
//   C++ program to illustrate an equivalent
//   call-by-reference, using the C++ reference type.
//   Copyright (c) William H. Murray and Chris H. Pappas, 1992
//

#include <iostream.h>

int iadder(int &rix,int &riy);

main()
{
  int ia=23;
  int ib=13;
  int ic;

  ic=iadder(ia,ib);
  cout << "The sum is: " << ic << endl;

  return (0);
}

int iadder(int &rix,int &riy)
{
  int iz;
```

```
iz=rix+riy;
return(iz);
}
```

When you examined the listing, did you notice the lack of pointers in the C++ program code? The reference types in this example are **rix** and **riy**. In C++, references to references, references to bit-fields, arrays of references, and pointers to references are not allowed. Regardless of whether you use call-by-reference or a reference type, C++ always uses the address of the argument.

Storage Classes

Storage classes can be affixed to data type declarations, as you saw earlier in Chapter 6. A variable might, for example, be declared as

static float *fyourvariable*;

Functions can also use **extern** and **static** storage class types. A function is declared with an **extern** storage class when it has been defined in another file, external to the present program. A function can be declared static when external access, apart from the present program, is not permitted.

Scope

The *scope* of a variable, when used in a function, refers to the range of effect that the variable has. The scope rules are similar for C and C++ variables used with functions. Variables can have a local, file, or class scope. (Class scope is discussed in Chapter 16.)

You may use a *local variable* completely within a function definition. Its scope is then limited to the function itself. The variable is said to be accessible, or visible, within the function only and has a local scope.

Variables with a *file scope* are declared outside of individual functions or classes. These variables have visibility or accessibility throughout the file in which they are declared and are global in range.

A variable may be used with a file scope and later within a function definition with a *local scope*. When this is done, the local scope takes precedence over the file scope. C++ offers a new programming feature called the scope resolution operator (::). When the C++ resolution operator is used, a variable with local scope is changed to one with file scope. In this situation, the variable would possess the value of the "global" variable. The syntax for referencing the global variable is

::*yourvariable*

Scope rules allow unique programming errors. Various scope rule errors are discussed at the end of this chapter.

Recursion

Recursion occurs in a program when a function calls itself. Initially, this might seem like an endless loop, but it is not. Both C and C++ support recursion. Recursive algorithms allow for creative, readable, and terse problem solutions. For example, the next program uses recursion to generate the factorial of a number. The *factorial* of a number is defined as the number multiplied by all successively lower integers. For example:

8! = 8 * 7 * 6 * 5 * 4 * 3 * 2 * 1
    = 40320

Care must be taken when choosing data types since the product increases very rapidly. The factorial of 15 is 1307674368000.

```c
/*
 *    08FACTR.C
 *    A C program illustrating recursive function calls.
 *    Calculation of the factorial of a number.
 *    Example:  7! = 7 x 6 x 5 x 4 x 3 x 2 x 1 = 5040
 *    Copyright (c) William H. Murray and Chris H. Pappas, 1992
 */

#include <stdio.h>

double dfactorial(double danswer);

main()
{
  double dnumber=15.0;
  double dresult;

  dresult=dfactorial(dnumber);

  printf("The factorial of %15.0lf is: %15.0lf\n",
         dnumber,dresult);

  return (0);
}
```

```
double dfactorial(double danswer)
{
  if (danswer <= 1.0)
    return(1.0);
  else
    return(danswer*dfactorial(danswer-1.0));
}
```

Recursion occurs because the function, **dfactorial()**, has a call to itself within the function. Notice, too, that the **printf()** function uses a new format code for printing a double value: %...lf. Here the "l" is a modifier to the "f" and specifies a double instead of a float.

Function Arguments

In this section you learn about passing function arguments to a function. These arguments go by many different names. Some programmers call them arguments, while others refer to them as parameters or dummy variables.

Function arguments are optional. Some functions you design may receive no arguments, while others may receive many. Function argument types can be mixed; that is, you can use any of the standard data types as a function argument. Many of the following examples illustrate passing various data types to functions. Furthermore, these programs employ functions from the various C and C++ libraries. Additional details on these library functions and their prototypes can be found in the Microsoft C/C++ reference manuals.

Formal and Actual Arguments

Each function definition contains an argument list called the *formal argument list*. Items in the list are optional, so the actual list may be empty or it may contain any combination of data types, such as integer, float, and character.

When the function is called by the program, an argument list is also passed to the function. This list is called the *actual argument list*. In general, there is usually a 1:1 match, when writing ANSI C code, between the formal and actual argument lists, although in reality no strong enforcement is used.

Examine the following coded C example:

```
printf("This is hexadecimal %x and octal %o",ians);
```

In this case, only one argument is being passed to **printf()**, although two are expected. When fewer arguments are supplied, the missing arguments are initialized to meaningless values. C++ overcomes this problem, to a degree, by permitting a default value to be supplied with the formal argument list. When an argument is missing in the actual argument list, the default argument is automatically substituted. For example, in C++, the function prototype might appear as

int *iyourfunction*(int *it*,float *fu*=4.2,int *iv*=10)

Here, if either *fu* or *iv* is not specified in the call to the function **iyourfunction()**, the values shown (4.2 or 10) will be used. C++ requires that all formal arguments using default values be listed at the end of the formal argument list. In other words, **iyourfunction(10)** and **iyourfunction(10,15.2)** are valid. If *fu* is not supplied, *iv* cannot be supplied either.

Type void as an Argument

In ANSI C **void** should be used to explicitly state the absence of function arguments. In C++, the use of **void** is not yet required, but its use is considered wise. The following program has a simple function named **voutput()** that receives no arguments and does not return a value. The **main()** function calls the function **voutput()**. When the **voutput()** function is finished, control is returned to the **main()** function. This is one of the simplest types of functions you can write.

```
/*
 *   08FVOID.C
 *   A C program that will print a message with a function.
 *   Function uses a type void argument and sqrt function
 *   from the standard C library.
 *   Copyright (c) William H. Murray and Chris H. Pappas, 1992
 */

#include <stdio.h>
#include <math.h>

void voutput(void);

main()
{
  printf("This program will find the square root. \n\n");
  voutput();

  return (0);
}
```

```
void voutput(void)
{
  double dt=12345.0;
  double du;

  du=sqrt(dt);
  printf("The square root of %lf is %lf  \n",dt,du);
}
```

If you study the example, you will notice that the **voutput()** function calls a C library function named **sqrt()**. The prototype for the **sqrt()** library function is contained in math.h. It accepts a double as an argument and returns the square root as a double value.

Characters as Arguments

Character information can also be passed to a function. In the next example, a single character is intercepted from the keyboard, in the function **main()**, and passed to the function **voutput()**. The **getch()** function reads the character. There are other functions that are closely related to **getch()** in the standard C library: **getc()**, **getchar()**, and **getche()**. These functions can also be used in C++, but in many cases a better choice will probably be **cin**. Additional details for using **getch()** are contained in your Microsoft C/C++ reference manuals and are available as on-line help. The **getch()** function intercepts a character from the standard input device (keyboard) and returns a character value, without echo to the screen, as shown here:

```
/*
 *    08FCHAR.C
 *    C program will accept a character from keyboard,
 *    pass it to a function and print a message using
 *    the character.
 *    Copyright (c) William H. Murray and Chris H. Pappas, 1992
 */

#include <stdio.h>

void voutput(char c);

main()
{
  char cyourchar;

  printf("Enter one character from the keyboard. \n");
  cyourchar=getch();
```

```
   output(cyourchar);

   return (0);
}

void voutput(char c)
{
   int j;

   for(j=0;j<16;j++)
     printf("The character typed is %c  \n",c);
}
```

From the listing you will notice that a single character is passed to the function. The function then prints a message and the character 16 times. The %c in the **printf()** function specifies that a single character is to be printed.

Integers as Arguments

In the next example, a single integer will be read from the keyboard with C's **scanf()** function. That integer will be passed to the function **vside()**. The **vside()** function uses the supplied length to calculate and print the area of a square, the volume of a cube, and the surface area of a cube.

```
/*
 *    08FINT.C
 *    C program will calculate values given a length.
 *    Function uses a type int argument, accepts length
 *    from keyboard with scanf function.
 *    Copyright (c) William H. Murray and Chris H. Pappas, 1992
 */

#include <stdio.h>

void vside(int is);

main()
{
   int iyourlength;

   printf("Enter the length, as an integer,\n");
   printf("from the keyboard. \n");
   scanf("%d",&iyourlength);
   vside(iyourlength);
```

```
   return (0);
}

void vside(int is)
{
   int iarea,ivolume,isarea;

   iarea=is*is;
   ivolume=is*is*is;
   isarea=6*area;

   printf("The length of a side is %d  \n\n",is);
   printf("A square would have an area of %d \n",iarea);
   printf("A cube would have a volume of %d \n",ivolume);
   printf("The surface area of the cube is %d \n",isarea);
}
```

Notice that *is* and all calculated values are integers. What would happen if *is* represented the radius of a circle and sphere to the calculated types?

Floats as Arguments

Floats are just as easy to pass as arguments to a function as are integer values. In the following C example, two floating-point values are passed to a function called **vhypotenuse()**. **scanf()** is used to intercept both float values from the keyboard.

```
/*
 *    08FFLOAT.C
 *    C program will find hypotenuse of a right triangle.
 *    Function uses a type float argument and accepts
 *    input from the keyboard with the scanf function.
 *    Copyright (c) William H. Murray and Chris H. Pappas, 1992
 */

#include <stdio.h>
#include <math.h>

void vhypotenuse(float fx,float fy);

main()
{
   float fxlen,fylen;
```

```
   printf("Enter the base of the right triangle. \n");
   scanf("%f",&fxlen);
   printf("Enter the height of the right triangle. \n");
   scanf("%f",&fylen);
   vhypotenuse(fxlen,fylen);

   return (0);
}

void vhypotenuse(float ft,float fu)
{
   double dresult;
   dresult=hypot((double) ft,(double) fu);
   printf("The hypotenuse of the right triangle is %g \n",
          dresult);
}
```

Notice that both arguments received by **vhypotenuse()** are cast to doubles when used by the **hypot()** function from math.h. All math.h functions accept and return **double** types. Your programs can use the additional math functions listed in Table 8-1. You can also display the contents of your math.h header file for additional details.

Doubles as Arguments

The **double** type is a very precise float value. All math.h functions accept and return **double** types. The next program accepts two double values from the keyboard. The function named **vpower()** will raise the first number to the power specified by the second number. Since both values are of type **double**, you can calculate $45.7^{5.2}$ and find that it equals 428118741.757.

```
/*
 *    08FDOUBL.C
 *    C program will raise a number to a power.
 *    Function uses a type double argument and the pow function.
 *    Copyright (c) William H. Murray and Chris H. Pappas, 1992
 */

#include <stdio.h>
#include <math.h>

void vpower(double dt,double du);

main()
{
```

Function Name*	Description of Function
abs,labs	Absolute value of an integer
acos,acosl	Arc cosine
asin,asinl	Arc sine
atan,atanl	Arc tangent
atan2,atan2l	Arc tangent of two numbers
atof,_atold	ASCII string to type float
cabs,cabsl	Absolute value of complex number
ceil,ceill	Largest integer in list
cos,cosl	Cosine
cosh,coshl	Hyperbolic cosine
exp,expl	Exponential value
fabs,fabsl	Absolute value of float
floor,floorl	Smallest integer in list
fmod,fmodl	Floating-point mod
frexp,frexpl	Mantissa and exponent of float
hypot,hypotl	Hypotenuse of right triangle
ldexp,ldexpl	Float from mantissa and exponent
log,logl	Natural logarithm
log10,log10l	Common logarithm
modf,modfl	Return mantissa and exponent
pow,powl	Raise x to power y
sin,sinl	Sine
sinh,sinhl	Hyperbolic sine
sqrt,sqrtl	Square root
tan,tanl	Tangent
tanh,tanhl	Hyperbolic tangent

*Functions with the "l" postfix indicate Microsoft's **long double** data type

Table 8-1.   *Microsoft Mathematical Functions Described in math.h*

```
double dtnum,dunum;

printf("Enter the base number. \n");
scanf("%lf",&dtnum);
```

```
    printf("Enter the power. \n");
    scanf("%lf",&dunum);
    vpower(dtnum,dunum);

    return (0);
}


void vpower(double dt,double du)
{
    double danswer;

    danswer=pow(dt,du);
    printf("The result is %lf \n",answer);
}
```

This function uses the library function **pow()** to raise one number to a power, prototyped in math.h.

Arrays as Arguments

In the following example, the contents of an array are passed to a function as a call-by-reference. In this case the address of the first array element is passed via a pointer.

```
/*
 *    08FPNTR.C
 *    C program will call a function with an array.
 *    Function uses a pointer to pass array information.
 *    Copyright (c) William H. Murray and Chris H. Pappas, 1992
 */

#include <stdio.h>

void voutput(int *pinums);

main()
{
    int iyourarray[7]={2,7,15,32,45,3,1};

    printf("Send array information to function. \n");
    voutput(iyourarray);

    return (0);
}
```

```
void voutput(int *pinums)
{
  int t;

  for(t=0;t<7;t++)
    printf("The result is %d \n",pinums[t]);
}
```

Notice that when the function is called, only the name *iyourarray* is specified. In Chapter 9 you will learn more details concerning arrays. In this example, by specifying the name of the array, you are providing the address of the first element in the array. Since *iyourarray* is an array of integers, it is possible to pass the array by specifying a pointer of the element type.

It is also permissible to pass the address information by using an unsized array. The next example shows how you can do this in C++. (The same approach can be used in C.) The information in *iyourarray* is transferred by passing the address of the first element.

```
//
//   08FARRAY.CPP
//   C++ program will call a function with an array.
//   Function passes array information, and calculates
//   the average of the numbers.
//   Copyright (c) William H. Murray and Chris H. Pappas, 1992
//

#include <iostream.h>

void avg(float fnums[]);

main()
{
  float iyourarray[8]={12.3,25.7,82.1,6.0,7.01,
                       0.25,4.2,6.28};

  cout << "Send information to averaging function. \n";
  avg(iyourarray);

  return (0);
}

void avg(float fnums[])
{
```

```
int iv;
float fsum=0.0;
float faverage;

for(iv=0;iv<8;iv++) {
  fsum+=fnums[iv];
  cout << "number " << iv+1 << " is " << fnums[iv] << endl;
}
faverage=fsum/iv;
cout << "\nThe average is " << faverage << endl;
}
```

The average is determined by summing each of the terms together and dividing by the total number of terms. The **cout** stream is used to format the output to the screen.

Function Types

The following sections provide an example for each of the important return types for functions possible in C and C++ programming. Function types specify the type of value returned by the function. None of the examples in the last section returned information from the function and thus were of type **void**.

Function Type void

Since **void** was used in all of the previous examples, the example for this section is a little more involved. As you have learned, C and C++ permit numeric information to be formatted in hexadecimal, decimal, and octal—but not binary. Specifying data in a binary format is useful for doing binary arithmetic or developing bit masks. The function **vbinary()** will convert a decimal number entered from the keyboard to a binary representation on the screen. The binary digits are not packed together as a single binary number but are stored individually in an array. Thus, to examine the binary number, the contents of the array must be printed out.

```
/*
 *    08VOIDF.C
 *    C program illustrates the void function type.
 *    Program will print the binary equivalent of a number.
```

```
*    Copyright (c) William H. Murray and Chris H. Pappas, 1992
*/

#include <stdio.h>

void vbinary(int ivalue);

main()
{
  int ivalue;

  printf("Enter a number (base 10) for conversion to binary.\n");
  scanf("%d",&ivalue);
  vbinary(ivalue);

  return (0);
}

void vbinary(int idata)
{
  int t=0;
  int iyourarray[50];

  while (idata !=0) {
    iyourarray[t]=(idata % 2);
    idata/=2;
    t++;
  }

  t--;
  for(;t>=0;t--)
    printf("%1d",iyourarray[t]);
  printf("\n");
}
```

The conversion process from higher order to lower order bases is a rather simple mathematical algorithm. For example, base 10 numbers can be converted to another base by dividing the number by the new base a successive number of times. If conversion is from base 10 to base 2, a 2 is repeatedly divided into the base 10 number. This produces a quotient and a remainder. The quotient becomes the dividend for each subsequent division. The remainder becomes a digit in the converted number. In the case of binary conversion, the remainder is either a 1 or a zero. For example, this is how 13 is converted to binary:

```
           quotient remainder        1   1   0   1 (binary)
  13/2        6         1    (lsb)  (msb)        (lsb)
   6/2        3         0
   3/2        1         1
   1/2        0         1    (msb)
```

In the function **vbinary()**, a **while** loop is used to perform the arithmetic as long as *idata* has not reached zero. The modulus operator determines the remainder and saves the bit in the array. Division is then performed on *idata*, saving only the integer result. This process is repeated until the quotient (also *data* in this case) is reduced to zero.

The individual array bits, which form the binary result, must be unloaded from the array in reverse order. You can observe this in the program listing. Study the **for** loop used in the function. Can you think of a way to perform this conversion and save the binary representation in a variable instead of an array?

Function Type char

In this section, you will see an example that is a minor variation of an earlier example. The C function **clowercase()** accepts a character argument and returns the same character type. For this example, an uppercase letter received from the keyboard is passed to the function. The function uses the library function **tolower()** (from the standard library and prototyped in ctype.h) to convert the character to a lowercase letter. Related functions to **tolower()** include **toascii()** and **toupper()**.

```c
/*
 *    08CHARF.C
 *    C program illustrates the character function type.
 *    Function receives uppercase character and
 *    converts it to lowercase.
 *    Copyright (c) William H. Murray and Chris H. Pappas, 1992
 */

#include <stdio.h>
#include <ctype.h>

char clowercase(char c);

main()
{
  char clowchar,chichar;

  printf("Enter an uppercase character.\n");
  chichar=getchar();
```

```
  clowchar=clowercase(chichar);
  printf("%c\n",clowchar);

  return (0);
}

char clowercase(char c)
{
  return(tolower(c));
}
```

Function Type int

The following function accepts and returns integers. The function **icube()** accepts a number generated in **main()** (0, 2, 4, 6, 8, 10, and so on), cubes the number, and returns the integer value to **main()**. The original number and its cube are printed to the screen.

```
/*
*    08INTF.C
*    C program illustrates the integer function type.
*    Function receives integers, one at a time, and
*    returns the cube of each, one at a time.
*    Copyright (c) William H. Murray and Chris H. Pappas, 1992
*/

#include <stdio.h>

int icube(int ivalue);

main()
{
  int k,inumbercube;

  for (k=0;k<20;k+=2) {
    inumbercube=icube(k);
    printf("The cube of the number %d is %d \n",
           k,inumbercube);
  }

  return (0);
}

int icube(int ivalue)
{
```

```
    return (ivalue*ivalue*ivalue);
}
```

Function Type long

The following example is a C++ program that accepts an integer value as an argument and returns a type **long**. The **long** type, used by Microsoft C/C++ and other popular compilers, is not recognized as a standard ANSI C type. The function will raise the number 2 to an integer power.

```
//
//   08LONGF.CPP
//   C++ program illustrates the long integer function type.
//   Function receives integers, one at a time, and
//   returns 2 raised to that integer power.
//   Copyright (c) William H. Murray and Chris H. Pappas, 1992
//

#include <iostream.h>

long lpower(int ivalue);

main()
{
  int k;
  long lanswer;

  for (k=0;k<31;k++) {
    lanswer=lpower(k);
    cout << "2 raised to the " << k << " power is "
         << lanswer << endl;
  }

  return (0);
}

long lpower(int ivalue)
{
  int t;
  long lseed=1;

  for (t=0;t<ivalue;t++)
    lseed*=2;
  return (lseed);
}
```

The function simply multiplies the original number by the number of times it is to be raised to the specified power. For example, if you wanted to raise 2 to the 6th power (2^6), the program will perform the following multiplication:

$$2 * 2 * 2 * 2 * 2 * 2 = 64$$

Can you think of a function described in math.h that could achieve the same results? See Table 8-1 for some ideas.

Function Type float

In the next example, a float array argument will be passed to a function and a float will be returned. This C++ example will find the product of all the elements in an array.

```
//
//   08FLOATF.CPP
//   C++ program illustrates the float function type.
//   Function receives an array of floats and returns
//   their product as a float.
//   Copyright (c) William H. Murray and Chris H. Pappas, 1992
//

#include <iostream.h>

float fproduct(float farray[]);

main()
{
  float fmyarray[7]={4.3,1.8,6.12,3.19,0.01234,0.1,9876.2};
  float fmultiplied;

  fmultiplied=fproduct(fmyarray);
  cout << "The product of all array entries is: "
       << fmultiplied << endl;

  return (0);
}

float fproduct(float farray[])
{
  int i;
  float fpartial;
```

```
    fpartial=farray[0];
    for (i=1;i<7;i++)
      fpartial*=farray[i];
    return (fpartial);
}
```

Since the elements are multiplied together, the first element of the array must be loaded into *fpartial* before the **for** loop is entered. Observe that the loop in the function **fproduct()** starts at 1 instead of the normal zero value.

Function Type double

The following C example accepts and returns a **double** type. The function **dtrigcosine()** will convert an angle, expressed in degrees, to its cosine value.

```
/*
 *    08DOUBLE.C
 *    C program illustrates the double function type.
 *    Function receives integers from 0 to 90, one at a
 *    time, and returns the cosine of each, one at a time.
 *    Copyright (c) William H. Murray and Chris H. Pappas, 1992
 */

#include <stdio.h>
#include <math.h>

const double dPi=3.14159265359;

double dtrigcosine(double dangle);

main()
{
  int j;
  double dcosine;

  for (j=0;j<91;j++) {
    dcosine=dtrigcosine((double) j);
    printf("The cosine of %d degrees is %19.181f \n",
           j,dcosine);
  }

  return (0);
}
```

```
double dtrigcosine(double dangle)
{
  double dpartial;
  dpartial=cos((dPi/180.0)*dangle);
  return (dpartial);
}
```

Notice that the **cos()** function described in math.h is used by **dtrigcosine()** for obtaining the answer. Angles must be converted from degrees to radians for all trigonometric functions. Recall that pi radians equals 180 degrees.

Arguments for Function main()

C and C++ share the ability to accept command-line arguments. *Command-line arguments* are those arguments entered along with the program name when called from the operating system's command line. This gives you the ability to pass arguments directly to your program without additional program prompts. For example, a program might pass four arguments from the command line:

```
YOURPROGRAM   Sneakers, Wonderdog, Shadow, Dumbdog
```

In this example, four values are passed from the command line to YOURPROGRAM. Actually, it is **main()** that is given specific information. One argument received by **main()**, *argc,* is an integer giving the number of command-line terms plus 1. The program title is counted as the first term passed from the command line since DOS 3.0. The second argument is a pointer to an array of string pointers called *argv.* All arguments are strings of characters, so *argv* is of type **char** *[*argc*]. Since all programs have a name, *argc* is always one greater than the number of command-line arguments. In the following examples, you will learn different techniques for retrieving various data types from the command line. The argument names *argc* and *argv* are the commonly agreed upon variable names used in all C/C++ programs.

Strings

Arguments are passed from the command line as strings of characters, and thus they are the easiest to work with. In the next example, the C program expects that the user will enter several names on the command line. To ensure that the user enters several names, if *argc* isn't greater than 2, the user will be returned to the command line with a reminder to try again.

```
/*
 *    08SARGV.C
 *    C program illustrates how to read string data
 *    into the program with a command-line argument.
 *    Copyright (c) William H. Murray and Chris H. Pappas, 1992
 */

#include <stdio.h>
#include <process.h>

main(int argc,char *argv[])
{
  int t;

  if(argc<2) {
    printf("Enter several names on the command line\n");
    printf("when executing this program!\n");
    printf("Please try again.\n");
    exit(0);
  }

  for (t=1; t<argc; t++)
    printf("Entry #%d is %s\n",t,argv[t]);

  return (0);
}
```

This program is completely contained in **main()** and does not use additional functions. The names entered on the command line are printed to the screen in the same order. If numeric values are entered on the command line, they will be interpreted as an ASCII string of individual characters and must be printed as such.

Integers

In many programs, it is desirable to be able to enter integer numbers on the command line, perhaps in a program that would find the average of a student's test scores. In such a case, the ASCII character information must be converted to an integer value. The C++ example in this section will accept a single integer number on the command line. Since the number is actually a character string, it will be converted to an integer with the **atoi()** library function. The command-line value *ivalue* is passed to a function used earlier, called **vbinary()**. The function will convert the number in *ivalue* to a string of binary digits and print them to the screen. When control is returned to **main()**, the *ivalue* will be printed in octal and hexadecimal formats.

```
//
//  08IARGV.CPP
//  C++ program illustrates how to read an integer
//  into the program with a command-line argument.
//  Copyright (c) William H. Murray and Chris H. Pappas, 1992
//

#include <iostream.h>
#include <stdlib.h>
#include <process.h>

void vbinary(int idigits);

main(int argc, char *argv[])
{
  int ivalue;

  if(argc!=2) {
    cout << "Enter a decimal number on the command line.\n";
    cout << "It will be converted to binary, octal and\n";
    cout << "hexadecimal.\n";
    exit(1);
  }

  ivalue=atoi(argv[1]);
  vbinary(ivalue);
  cout << "The octal value is: " << oct
       << ivalue << endl;
  cout << "The hexadecimal value is: "
       << hex << ivalue << endl;

  return (0);
}

void vbinary(int idigits)
{
  int t=0;
  int iyourarray[50];

  while (idigits != 0) {
    iyourarray[t]=(idigits % 2);
    idigits/=2;
    t++;
  }
```

```
  t--;
  cout << "The binary value is: ";
  for(;t>=0;t--)
    cout << dec << iyourarray[t];
    cout << endl;
}
```

Of particular interest is the formatting of the various numbers. You learned earlier that the binary number is saved in the array and printed one digit at a time, using decimal formatting, by unloading the array *iyourarray* in reverse order:

```
cout << dec << myarray[i];
```

To print the number in octal format, the statement is

```
cout << "The octal value is: "
     << oct << ivalue << endl;
```

It is also possible to print the hexadecimal equivalent by substituting hex for oct, as shown here:

```
cout << "The hexadecimal value is: "
     << hex << ivalue << endl;
```

Without additional formatting, the hexadecimal values a, b, c, d, e, and f are printed in lowercase. You'll learn many formatting techniques for C++ in Chapters 11 and 12, including how to print those characters in uppercase.

Floats

Once you have learned how to intercept integers from the command line, floats will not present any additional problems. The following C example will allow several angles to be entered on the command line. The cosine of the angles will be extracted and printed to the screen. Since the angles are of type **float**, they can take on values such as 12.0, 45.78, 0.12345, or 15.

```
/*
 *    08FARGV.C
 *    C program illustrates how to read float data types
 *    into the program with a command-line argument.
 *    Copyright (c) William H. Murray and Chris H. Pappas, 1992
 */
```

```
#include <stdio.h>
#include <math.h>
#include <process.h>

const double dPi=3.14159265359;

main(int argc, char *argv[])
{
  int t;
  double ddegree;

  if(argc<2) {
    printf("Type several angles on the command line.\n");
    printf("Program will calculate and print\n");
    printf("the cosine of the angles entered.\n");
    exit(1);
  }

  for (t=1; t<argc; t++) {
    ddegree=(double) atof(argv[t]);
    printf("The cosine of %f is %15.14lf\n",
            ddegree,cos((dPi/180.0)*ddegree));
  }

  return (0);
}
```

The **atof()** function converts the command-line string argument to a **float** type. The program uses the **cos()** function within the **printf()** function to retrieve the cosine information.

Important C++ Features

C++ provides you with the ability to use several special features when writing functions. The ability to write inline functions is one such advantage. The code for an inline function is reproduced at the spot where the function is called in the main program. Since the compiler places the code at the point of the function call, execution time is saved when using short, frequently called functions.

C++ also permits function overloading. *Overloading* permits several function prototypes to be given the same function name. The numerous prototypes are then recognized by their type and argument list, not just by their name. Overloading is very useful when a function is required to work with different data types.

inline

You can think of the **inline** keyword as a directive or, better yet, a suggestion to the C++ compiler to insert the function inline. The compiler may ignore this suggestion for any of several reasons. For example, the function might be too long. Inline functions are used primarily to save time when short functions are called many times within a program.

```
//
//   08INLINE.CPP
//   C++ program illustrates the use of an inline function.
//   Inline functions work best on short functions that are
//   used repeatedly. This example just prints a message
//   several times to the screen.
//   Copyright (c) William H. Murray and Chris H. Pappas, 1992
//

#include <iostream.h>

inline void voutput(void) {cout << "This is an inline function!"
                                << endl;}

main()
{
  int t;

  cout << "Program to print a message several times."
       << endl;

  for (t=0;t<3;t++)
    voutput();

  return (0);
}
```

Overloading

The following example illustrates function overloading. Notice that two functions with the same name are prototyped within the same scope. The correct function will be selected based on the arguments provided. A function call to **adder()** will process integer or float data correctly.

```
//
//   08OVRLOD.CPP
```

```cpp
//   C++ program illustrates function overloading.
//   Overloaded function receives an array of integers or
//   floats and returns either an integer or float product.
//   Copyright (c) William H. Murray and Chris H. Pappas, 1992
//

#include <iostream.h>

int adder(int iarray[]);
float adder(float farray[]);

main()
{
  int iarray[7]={5,1,6,20,15,0,12};
  float farray[7]={3.3,5.2,0.05,1.49,3.12345,31.0,2.007};
  int isum;
  float fsum;

  isum=adder(iarray);
  fsum=adder(farray);
  cout << "The sum of the integer numbers is: "
       << isum << endl;
  cout << "The sum of the float numbers is: "
       << fsum << endl;

  return (0);
}

int adder(int iarray[])
{
  int i;
  int ipartial;

  ipartial=iarray[0];
  for (i=1;i<7;i++)
    ipartial+=iarray[i];
  return (ipartial);
}

float adder(float farray[])
{
  int i;
  float fpartial;

  fpartial=farray[0];
```

```
  for (i=1;i<7;i++)
    fpartial+=farray[i];
  return (fpartial);
}
```

There are a few programming snags to function overloading that must be avoided. For example, if a function differs only in the function type and not in the arguments, the function cannot be overloaded. Also, the following attempt at overloading is not permitted:

int *yourfunction*(int *number*)
int *yourfunction*(int &*value*)   //not allowed

This syntax is not allowed because each prototype would accept the same type of arguments. Despite these limitations, overloading is a very important topic in C++ and is fully exploited starting with Chapter 14.

Ellipsis (...)

You use the ellipsis when the number of arguments is not known. As such, they can be specified within the function's formal argument statement. For example:

void *yourfunction*(int *t*,float *u*,...);

This syntax tells the C compiler that other arguments may or may not follow *t* and *u*, which are required. Naturally, type checking is suspended with the ellipsis.

The following C program demonstrates how to use the ellipsis. You may want to delay an in-depth study of the algorithm, however, until you have a thorough understanding of C string pointer types (see Chapters 9 and 10).

```
/*
 *    08ELIP.C
 *    A C program demonstrating the use of ... and its support
 *    macros va_arg, va_start, and va_end
 *    Copyright (c) William H. Murray and Chris H. Pappas, 1992
 */

#include <stdio.h>
#include <stdarg.h>
#include <string.h>

void vsmallest(char *szmessage, ...);
```

```
main()
{
  vsmallest("Print %d integers, %d %d %d",10,4,1);

  return(0);
}

void vsmallest(char *szmessage, ...)
{
  int inumber_of_percent_ds=0;
  va_list type_for_ellipsis;
  int ipercent_d_format = 'd';
  char *pchar;
  pchar=strchr(szmessage,ipercent_d_format);

  while(*++pchar != '\0') {
    pchar++;
    pchar=strchr(pchar,ipercent_d_format);
    inumber_of_percent_ds++;
  }
  printf("print %d integers,",inumber_of_percent_ds);

  va_start(type_for_ellipsis,szmessage);

  while(inumber_of_percent_ds--)
    printf(" %d",va_arg(type_for_ellipsis,int));

  va_end(type_for_ellipsis);
}
```

The function **vsmallest()** has been prototyped to expect two arguments, a string pointer, and an argument of type ..., or a varying length argument list. Naturally, functions using a varying length argument list are not omniscient. Something within the argument list must give the function enough information to process the varying part. In 08ELIP.C, this information comes from the string argument.

In a very crude approach, **vsmallest()** attempts to mimic the **printf()** function. The subroutine scans the *szmessage* format string to see how many %ds it finds. It then uses this information to make a calculated fetching and printing of the information in the variable argument. While this sounds straightforward, the algorithm requires a sophisticated sequence of events.

The **strchr()** function returns the address of the location containing the "d" in %d. The first %d can be ignored since this is required by the output message. The **while** loop continues processing the remainder of the *szmessage* string looking for the variable number of %ds and counting them (*inumber_of_percent_ds*). With this accomplished, the beginning of the output message is printed.

The **va_start()** macro sets the *type_for_ellipsis* pointer to the beginning of the variable argument list. The **va_arg()** support macro retrieves the next argument in the variable list. The macro uses its second parameter to know what data type to retrieve; for the example program, this is type **int**. The function **vsmallest()** terminates with a call to **va_end()**. The last of the three standard C ellipsis support macros, **va_end()**, resets the pointer to null.

Problems Encountered with Scope Rules

If variables are used with different scope levels, you may run into completely unexpected programming results, called *side effects*. For example, you have learned that it is possible to use a variable of the same name with both file and local scopes. The scope rules state that the variable with a local scope (called a *local variable*) will take precedence over the variable with a file scope (called a *global variable*). That all seems easy enough, but let's now consider some problem areas you might encounter in programming that are not so obvious.

An Undefined Symbol in a C Program

In the following example, four variables are given a local scope within the function **main()**. Copies of the variables *il* and *im* are passed to the function **iproduct()**. This does not violate scope rules. However, when the **iproduct()** function attempts to use the variable *in*, it cannot find the variable. Why? Because the scope of the variable was local to **main()** only.

```
/*
 *    08SCOPEP.C
 *    C program to illustrate problems with scope rules.
 *    Function is supposed to form a product of three numbers.
 *    Compiler signals problems since variable n isn't known
 *    to the function multiplier.
 *    Copyright (c) William H. Murray and Chris H. Pappas, 1992
 */

#include <stdio.h>

int iproduct(int iw,int ix);

main()
{
  int il=3;
```

```
   int im=7;
   int in=10;
   int io;

   io=iproduct(il,im);
   printf("The product of the numbers is: %d\n", io);

   return (0);
}

int iproduct(int iw,int ix)
{
   int iy;

   iy=iw*ix*in;
   return(iy);
}
```

The C compiler issues a warning and an error message. It first reports a warning that the *in* variable is never used within the function and then the error message that *in* has never been declared in the function **iproduct()**. One way around this problem is to give *in* a file scope.

Use a Variable with File Scope

In this example, the variable *in* is given a file scope. Making *in* global to the whole file allows both **main()** and **iproduct()** to use it. Also note that both **main()** and **iproduct()** can change the value of the variable. It is good programming practice not to allow functions to change global program variables if they are created to be truly portable.

```
/*
 *   08FSCOPE.C
 *   C program to illustrate problems with scope rules.
 *   Function is supposed to form a product of three numbers.
 *   Previous problem is solved, c variable is given file scope.
 *   Copyright (c) William H. Murray and Chris H. Pappas, 1992
 */


#include <stdio.h>

int iproduct(int iw,int ix);

int in=10;
```

```
main()
{
  int il=3;
  int im=7;
  int io;

  io=iproduct(il,im);
  printf("The product is: %d\n", io);

  return (0);
}

int iproduct(int iw,int ix)
{
  int iy;

  iy=iw*ix*in;
  return(iy);
}
```

This program will compile correctly and print the product 210 to the screen.

Overriding a Variable with File Scope by a Variable with Local Scope

The scope rules state that a variable with both file and local scope will use the local variable value over the global value. Here is a small program that illustrates this point:

```
/*
 *    08LSCOPE.C
 *    C program to illustrate problems with scope rules.
 *    Function forms a product of three numbers, but which
 *    three?  Two are passed as function arguments. The
 *    variable c has both a file and local scope.
 *    Copyright (c) William H. Murray and Chris H. Pappas, 1992
 */

#include <stdio.h>

int iproduct(int iw,int ix);

int in=10;

main()
```

```
{
  int il=3;
  int im=7;
  int io;

  io=iproduct(il,im);
  printf("The product of the numbers is: %d\n", io);

  return (0);
}

int iproduct(int iw,int ix)
{
  int iy;
  int in=2;

  iy=iw*ix*in;
  return(iy);
}
```

In this example, the variable *in* has both file and local scope. When *in* is used within the function **iproduct()**, the local scope takes precedence and the product of 3 * 7 * 2 = 42 is returned.

A Scope Problem in C++

In the following C++ example, everything works fine up to the point of printing the information to the screen. The **cout** statement prints the values for *il* and *im* correctly. When selecting the *in* value, it chooses the global variable with file scope. The program reports that the product of 3 * 7 * 10 = 42, is clearly a mistake. You know that in this case the **iproduct()** function used the local value of *in*.

```
//
//   08SCOPEP.CPP
//   C++ program to illustrate problems with scope rules.
//   Function forms a product of three numbers. The n
//   variable is of local scope and used by function
//   product. However, main function reports that
//   the n value used is 10. What is wrong here?
//   Copyright (c) William H. Murray and Chris H. Pappas, 1992
//

#include <iostream.h>
```

```
int iproduct(int iw,int ix);

int in=10;

main()
{
  int il=3;
  int im=7;
  int io;

  io=iproduct(il,im);
  cout << "The product of " << il <<" * " << im
       << " * " << in << " is: " << io << endl;

  return (0);
}

int iproduct(int iw,int ix)
{
  int iy;
  int in=2;

  iy=iw*ix*in;
  return(iy);
}
```

If you actually wanted to form the product with the global value of *in*, how could this conflict be resolved? C++ would permit you to use the scope resolution operator mentioned earlier in the chapter, as shown here:

```
iy=iw*ix*::in;
```

The C++ Scope Resolution Operator

In this example, the scope resolution operator (::) is used to avoid conflicts between a variable with both file and local scope. The last program reported an incorrect product since the local value was used in the calculation. Notice in the following listing that the **iproduct()** function uses the scope resolution operator.

```
//
// 08GSCOPE.CPP
// C++ program to illustrate problems with scope rules,
// and how to use the scope resolution operator.
// Function product uses resolution operator to "override"
```

```
//   local scope and utilize variable with file scope.
//   Copyright (c) William H. Murray and Chris H. Pappas, 1992
//

#include <iostream.h>

int iproduct(int iw,int ix);

int in=10;

main()
{
  int il=3;
  int im=7;
  int io;

  io=iproduct(il,im);
  cout << "The product of " << il <<" * " << im
       << " * " << in << " is: " << io;

  return (0);
}

int iproduct(int iw,int ix)
{
  int iy;
  int in=2;

  iy=iw*ix*(::in);
  return(iy);
}
```

The scope resolution operator need not be enclosed in parentheses—they were used for emphasis in this example. Now, the value of the global variable, with file scope, will be used in the calculation. When the results are printed to the screen, you will see that 3 * 7 * 10 = 210.

The scope resolution operator is very important in C++. Additional examples illustrating the resolution operator are given starting with Chapter 16.

Chapter **9**

Arrays

In C, the topics of arrays, pointers, and strings are all related. In this chapter you learn how to define and use arrays. Many C books combine the topics of arrays and pointers into one discussion. This is unfortunate because there are many uses for arrays in C that are not dependent on a detailed understanding of pointers. Also, since there is a great deal of material to cover about arrays in general, it is best not to confuse the topic with a discussion of pointers. Pointers, however, allow you to comprehend fully just how an array is processed. Chapter 10 examines the topic of pointers and completes this chapter's discussion of arrays.

What Is an Array?

You can think of *arrays* as variables containing several homogeneous data types. You access each individual data item by using a subscript, or index, into the variable. In the C language, an array is not a standard data type; instead, it is an aggregate type made up of any other type of data. In C, it is possible to have an array of anything: characters, integers, floats, doubles, arrays, pointers, structures, and so on. Basically, the concept of arrays and their use is the same in both C and C++.

Arrays and C

There are four basic properties to an array:

- The individual data items in the array are called *elements*.

- All elements must be of the same data type.

- All elements are stored contiguously in the computer's memory, and the subscript (or index) of the first element is zero.

- The name of the array is a constant value that represents the address of the first element in the array.

Because all elements are assumed to be the same size, arrays cannot be defined by using mixed data types. Without this assumption, it would be very difficult to determine where any given element was stored. Since the elements are all the same size and since that fact is used to help determine how to locate a given element, it follows that the elements are stored contiguously in the computer's memory (with the lowest address corresponding to the first element, the highest address to the last element). This means that there is no filler space between elements and that they are physically adjacent in the computer.

It is possible to have arrays within arrays, that is, multidimensional arrays. Actually, if an array element is a structure (which will be covered in Chapter 13), then mixed data types can exist in the array by existing inside the structure member.

Finally, the name of an array represents a constant value that cannot change during the execution of the program. For this reason, arrays can never be used as lvalues. *lvalues* represent storage locations that can have their contents altered by the program; they frequently appear to the left of assignment statements. If array names were legal lvalues, your program could change their contents. The effect would be to change the starting address of the array itself. This may seem like a small thing, but some forms of expressions that might appear valid on the surface are not allowed in C. All C programmers eventually learn these subtleties, but it helps if you understand why these differences exist.

Array Declarations

The following are examples of array declarations:

```
int   iarray[12];   /* an array of twelve integers   */
char carray[20];   /* an array of twenty characters  */
```

As is true with all C data declarations, an array's declaration begins with its data type, followed by a valid array name and a pair of matching square brackets enclosing a constant expression. The constant expression defines the size of the array. It is illegal to use a variable name inside the square brackets. For this reason it is not possible to avoid specifying the array size until the program executes. The expression must reduce to a constant value so that the compiler knows exactly how much storage space to reserve for the array.

It is best to use defined constants to specify the size of the array:

```
#define iARRAY_MAX 20
#define fARRAY_MAX 15

int iarray[iARRAY_MAX];
float farray[fARRAY_MAX];
```

Use of defined constants guarantees that subsequent references to the array will not exceed the defined array size. For example, it is very common to use a **for** loop to access array elements:

```
#include <stdio.h>

#define iARRAY_MAX 20

int iarray[iARRAY_MAX];

main()
{
  int i;
  for(i = 0; i < iARRAY_MAX; i++) {
  .
  .
  .
  }
  return(0);
}
```

Array Initialization

There are three techniques for initializing arrays:

- By default when they are created. This applies only to global and static arrays.
- Explicitly when they are created, by supplying constant initializing data.
- During program execution when you assign or copy data into the array.

You can only use constant data to initialize an array when it is created. If the array elements must receive their values from variables, you must initialize the array by writing explicit statements as part of the program code.

Default Initialization

The ANSI C standard specifies that arrays are either global (defined outside of **main()** and any other function) or static automatic (static, but defined after any opening brace) and will always be initialized to binary zero if no other initialization data is supplied. C initializes numeric arrays to zero. (Pointer arrays are initialized to null.) You can run the following program to make certain that any C compiler meets this standard:

```
/*
 *   09INITAR.C
 *   A C program verifying array initialization
 *   Copyright (c) William H. Murray and Chris H. Pappas, 1992
 */

#include <stdio.h>

#define iGLOBAL_ARRAY_SIZE 10
#define iSTATIC_ARRAY_SIZE 20

int iglobal_array[iGLOBAL_ARRAY_SIZE];            /*a global array*/

main()
{
  static int static_iarray[iSTATIC_ARRAY_SIZE]; /*a static array*/
  printf("iglobal_array[0]: %d\n",iglobal_array[0]);
  printf("istatic_array[0]: %d\n",istatic_array[0]);

  return(0);
}
```

When you run the program, you should see zeros printed verifying that both array types are automatically initialized. This program also highlights another very important point: that the first subscript for all arrays in C is zero. Unlike other languages, there is no way to make a C program think that the first subscript is 1. If you are wondering why, remember that one of C's strengths is its close link to assembly language. In assembly language, the first element in a table is always at the zeroth offset.

Explicit Initialization

Just as you can define and initialize variables of type **int**, **char**, **float**, **double**, and so on, you can also initialize arrays. The ANSI C standard lets you supply initialization values for any array, global or otherwise, defined anywhere in a program. The following code segment illustrates how to define and initialize four arrays:

```
int iarray[3] = {-1,0,1};
static float fpercent[4] = {1.141579,0.75,55E0,-.33E1};
static int idecimal[3] = {0,1,2,3,4,5,6,7,8,9};
char cvowels[] = {'A','a','E','e','I','i','O','o','U','u'};
```

The first example declares the *iarray* array to be three integers and provides the values of the elements in curly braces, separated by commas. As usual, a semicolon ends the statement. The effect of this is that after the compiled program loads into the memory of the computer, the reserved space for the *iarray* array will already contain the initial values, so they won't need assignments when the program executes. It is important to realize that this is more than just a convenience—it happens at a different time. If the program goes on to change the values of the *iarray* array, they stay changed. Many compilers permit you to initialize arrays only if they are global or static, as in the second example. This statement initializes the array *fpercent* when the entire program loads.

The third example illustrates putting the wrong count in the array declaration. Many compilers consider this an error, while others reserve enough space to hold whichever is greater—the number of values you ask for or the number of values you provide. This example will draw complaints from the Microsoft C/C++ compiler by way of an error message indicating too many initializers. In the opposite case, when you ask for more space than you provide values for, the values go into the beginning of the array and the extra elements become zeros. This also means that you do not need to count the values when you provide all of them. If the count is empty, as in the fourth example, the number of values determines the size of the array.

Unsized Initialization

Whether you provide the size of the array or the list of actual values doesn't matter for most compilers, as long as you provide at least one of them. For example, a program will frequently want to define its own set of error messages. This can be done two ways. Here is the first method:

```
char szInput_Error[37] = "Please enter a value between 0 - 9:\n";
char szDevice_Error[16] = "Disk not ready\n";
char szMonitor_Error[32] = "Program needs a color monitor.\n";
char szWarning[44]="This operation will erase the active file!\n";
```

This method requires you to count the number of characters in the string, remembering to add 1 to the count for the unseen null-string terminator \0. This can become a very tedious approach at best, straining the eyes as you count the number of characters, and very error prone. The second method allows C to automatically dimension the arrays through the use of unsized arrays, as shown here:

```
char szInput_Error[] = "Please enter a value between 0 - 9:\n";
char szDevice_Error[] = "Disk not ready\n";
char szMonitor_Error[] = "Program needs a color monitor.\n";
char szWarning[] = "This operation will erase the active file!\n";
```

Whenever C encounters an array initialization statement and the array size is not specified, the compiler automatically creates an array big enough to hold all of the specified data.

There are a few major pitfalls that await the inexperienced C programmer when initializing arrays. For example, an array with an empty size declaration and no list of values has a null length. If there are any data declarations after the array, then the name of the null array refers to the same address, and storing values in the null array puts them in addresses allocated to other variables.

Also, unsized array initializations are not restricted to one-dimensional arrays. For multidimensional arrays, you must specify all but the leftmost dimension for C to properly index the array. With this approach you can build tables of varying lengths, with the compiler automatically allocating enough storage.

Accessing Array Elements

A variable declaration usually reserves one or more cells in internal memory and, through a lookup table, associates a name with the cell or cells that you can use to access the cells. For example, the following definition reserves only one integer-sized cell in internal memory and associates the name *ivideo_tapes* with that cell (see the top of Figure 9-1):

```
int ivideo_tapes;
```

On the other hand, the next definition reserves seven contiguous cells in internal memory and associates the name *ivideo_library* with the seven cells (see the bottom of Figure 9-1):

```
int ivideo_library[7];
```

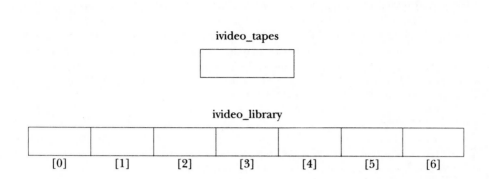

Figure 9-1. *Storing variables and arrays in memory*

Since all array elements must be of the same data type, each of the seven cells in the array *ivideo_library* can hold one integer.

Consider the difference between accessing the single cell associated with the variable *ivideo_tapes* and the seven cells associated with the array *ivideo_library*. To access the cell associated with the variable *ivideo_tapes*, you simply use the name *ivideo_tapes*. For the array *ivideo_library*, you must specify an *index* to indicate exactly which cell among the seven you wish to access. The following statements designate the first cell, the second cell, the third cell, and so on, up to the last cell of the array:

```
ivideo_library[0];
ivideo_library[1];
ivideo_library[2];
ivideo_library[3];
       .
       .
       .
ivideo_library[6];
```

When accessing an array element, the integer enclosed in the square brackets is the index, which indicates the *offset*, or the distance between the cell to be accessed and the first cell.

The principal mistake novice C programmers make has to do with the index value used to reference an array's first element. The first element is not at index position [1]; instead, it is [0] since there is zero distance between the first element and itself. The third cell has an index value of 2 because its distance from the first cell is 2.

When dealing with arrays, you can use the square brackets in two quite different ways. When you are defining an array, the number of cells is specified in square brackets:

```
int ivideo_library[7];
```

But when you are accessing a specific array element, you use the array's name together with an index enclosed in square brackets:

```
ivideo_library[3];
```

Assuming the previous declaration for the array *ivideo_library*, the following statement is logically incorrect:

```
ivideo_library[7] = 53219;
```

It is not a legal reference to a cell under the name *ivideo_library*. The statement attempts to reference a cell that is a distance of 7 from the first cell, that is, the eighth cell. Because there are only seven cells, this is an error. It is up to you to ensure that index expressions remain within the array's bounds.

Examine the following declarations:

```
#define iDAYS_OF_WEEK 7

int ivideo_library[iDAYS_OF_WEEK];
int iweekend = 1;
int iweekday = 2;
```

Take a look at what happens with this set of executable statements:

```
ivideo_library[2];
ivideo_library[iweekday];
ivideo_library[iweekend + iweekday];
ivideo_library[iweekday - iweekend];
ivideo_library[iweekend - iweekday];
```

The first two statements both reference the third element of the array. The first statement accomplishes this with a constant value expression, while the second statement uses a variable. The last three statements demonstrate that you can use expressions as subscripts, as long as they evaluate to a valid integer index. Statement three has an index value of 3 and references the fourth element of the array. The fourth statement, with an index value of 1, accesses the second element of the array. The last statement is illegal because the index value –1 is invalid.

The C programmer can access any element in an array without knowing how big each element is. For example, suppose you want to access the third element in *ivideo_library,* an array of integers. Remember from Chapter 6 that different systems allocate different size cells to the same data type. On one computer system, an integer might occupy 2 bytes of storage, whereas on another system, an integer might occupy 4 bytes of storage. On either system, you can access the third element as *ivideo_library[2].* The index value indicates the number of elements to move, regardless of the number of bits allocated.

This offset addressing holds true for other array types. On one system, integer variables might require twice as many bits of storage as does a **char** type; on another system, integer variables might require four times as many bits as do character variables. Yet to access the fourth element in either an array of integers or an array of characters, you would use an index value of 3.

Calculating Array Dimensions (sizeof())

As you have already learned, the **sizeof()** operator returns the physical size, in bytes, of the data object to which it is applied. You can use it with any type of data object except bit-fields. A frequent use of **sizeof()** is to determine the physical size of a variable when the size of the variable's data type can vary from machine to machine. You have already seen how an integer can be either 2 or 4 bytes, depending on the machine being used. If an additional amount of memory to hold seven integers will be requested from the operating system, some way is needed to determine whether 14 bytes (7 × 2 bytes/integer) or 28 bytes (7 × 4 bytes/integer) are needed. The following program automatically takes this into consideration (and prints a value of 14 for systems allocating 2 bytes per integer cell):

```
/*
 *   09SIZEOF.C
 *   A C program applying sizeof to determine an array's size
 *   Copyright (c) William H. Murray and Chris H. Pappas, 1992
 */

#include <stdio.h>

#define iDAYS_OF_WEEK 7

main()
```

```
{
  int ivideo_library[iDAYS_OF_WEEK]={1,2,3,4,5,6,7};

  printf("There are %d number of bytes in the array"
    " ivideo_library.\n",(int)sizeof(ivideo_library));

  return(0);
}
```

This concept becomes essential when the program must be portable and independent of any particular hardware. If you are wondering why there is an **int** type cast on the result returned by **sizeof()**, in the ANSI C standard **sizeof()** does not return an **int** type. Instead, **sizeof()** returns a data type, **size_t**, that is large enough to hold the return value. The ANSI C standard added this to C because on certain computers an integer is not big enough to represent the size of all data items. In the example, casting the return value to an integer allows it to match the %d conversion character of the **printf()** function. Otherwise, if the returned value had been larger than an integer, the **printf()** function would not have worked properly.

By changing *iarray*'s data type in the following program, you can explore how various data types are stored internally:

```
/*
 *   09ARRAY.C
 *   A C program illustrating contiguous array storage
 *   Copyright (c) William H. Murray and Chris H. Pappas, 1992
 */

#include <stdio.h>

#define iDAYS 7

main()
{
  int index, iarray[iDAYS];

  printf("sizeof(int) is %d\n\n", (int)sizeof(int));

  for(index = 0; index < iDAYS; index++)
    printf("&iarray[%d] = %X\n", index,
            &iarray[index]);

  return(0);
}
```

If the program is run on a machine with a word length of 2 bytes, the output will look similar to the following:

```
sizeof(int) is 2

&iarray[0] = 2F32
&iarray[1] = 2F34
&iarray[2] = 2F36
&iarray[3] = 2F38
&iarray[4] = 2F3A
&iarray[5] = 2F3C
&iarray[6] = 2F3E
```

Notice how the & (address) operator can be applied to any variable, including an array element. An array element can be treated like any other variable; its value can form an expression, it can be assigned a value, and it can be passed as an argument (or parameter) to a function. In this example you can see how the array elements' addresses are exactly 2 bytes apart. You will see the importance of this contiguous storage when you use arrays in conjunction with pointer variables.

The following listing is the C++ equivalent of the program just discussed:

```
//
//  09ARRAY.CPP
//  A C++ program illustrating contiguous array storage
//  Copyright (c) William H. Murray and Chris H. Pappas, 1992
//

#include <iostream.h>

#define iMAX 10

main()
{
  int index, iarray[iMAX];

  cout << "sizeof(int) is %d" << (int)sizeof(int) << "\n\n";

  for(index = 0; index < iMAX; index++)
    cout << "&iarray[" << index << "] = " << index
         << &iarray[index] << endl;

  return(0);
}
```

Array Index Out of Bounds

You've probably heard the saying, "You don't get something for nothing." This holds true with C array types. The "something" you get is faster executing code at the expense of the "nothing," which is zero boundary checking. Remember, since C was designed to replace assembly language code, error checking was left out of the compiler to keep the code lean. Without any compiler error checking, you must be very careful when dealing with array boundaries. For example, the following program elicits no complaints from the compiler, yet it can change the contents of other variables or even crash the program by writing beyond the array's boundary:

```
/*
 *   09NORUN.C
 *   Do NOT run this C program
 *   Copyright (c) William H. Murray and Chris H. Pappas, 1992
 */

#include <stdio.h>

#define iMAX 10
#define iOUT_OF_RANGE 50

main()
{
  int inot_enough_room[iMAX], index;

  for(index=0; index < iOUT_OF_RANGE; index++)
    inot_enough_room[index]=index;

  return(0);
}
```

Output and Input of Strings

While C does supply the data type **char**, it does not have a data type for character strings. Instead, the C programmer must represent a string as an array of characters. The array uses one cell for each character in the string, with the final cell holding the null character \0.

The following program shows how you can represent the three major types of transportation as a character string. The array *szmode1* is initialized character by character by use of the assignment operator, the array *szmode2* is initialized by use of the function **scanf()**, and the array *szmode3* is initialized in the following definition.

```
/*
 *    09STRING.C
 *    This C program demonstrates the use of strings
 *    Copyright (c) William H. Murray and Chris H. Pappas, 1992
 */

#include <stdio.h>

main()
{
  char          szmode1[4],              /* car   */
                szmode2[6];              /* plane */
  static char szmode3[5] = "ship";       /* ship  */

  szmode1[0] = 'c';
  szmode1[1] = 'a';
  szmode1[2] = 'r';
  szmode1[3] = '\0';

  printf("\n\n\tPlease enter the mode --> plane ");
  scanf("%s",szmode2);

  printf("%s\n",szmode1);
  printf("%s\n",szmode2);
  printf("%s\n",szmode3);

  return(0);
}
```

The next definitions show how C treats character strings as arrays of characters:

```
char    szmode1[4],                /* car   */
        szmode2[6];                /* plane */
static char szmode3[5] = "ship";   /* ship  */
```

Even though the *szmode1* "car" has three characters, the array *szmode1* has four cells—one cell for each letter in the mode "car" and one for the null character. Remember, \0 counts as one character. Similarly, the mode "plane" has five characters ("ship" has four) but requires six storage cells (five for *szmode3*), including the null character. Remember, you could also have initialized the *szmode3[5]* array of characters by using braces:

```
static char szmode3[5] = {'s','h','i','p','\0'};
```

When you use double quotes to list the initial values of the character array, the system will automatically add the null terminator \0. Also, remember that the same line could have been written like this:

```
static char szmode3[] = "ship";
```

This uses an unsized array. Of course, you could have chosen the tedious approach to initializing an array of characters that was done with *szmode1*. A more common approach is to use the **scanf()** function to read the string directly into the array as was done with *szmode2*. The **scanf()** function uses a %s conversion specification. This causes the function to skip white space (blanks, tabs, and carriage returns) and then to read into the character array *szmode2* all characters up to the next white space. The system will then automatically add a null terminator. Remember, the array's dimension must be large enough to hold the string along with a null terminator. Look at this statement one more time:

```
scanf("%s",szmode2);
```

Are you bothered by the fact that *szmode2* was not preceded by the address operator **&**? While it is true that **scanf()** was written to expect the address of a variable, as it turns out, an array's name, unlike simple variable names, is an address expression—the address of the first element in the array.

When you use the **printf()** function in conjunction with a %s, the function is expecting the corresponding argument to be the address of some character string. The string is printed up to but not including the null character.

The following listing illustrates these principles by using an equivalent C++ algorithm:

```
//
//   09STRING.CPP
//   This C++ program demonstrates the use of strings
//   Copyright (c) William H. Murray and Chris H. Pappas, 1992
//

#include <iostream.h>

main()
{
   char         szmode1[4],                    // car
                szmode2[6];                    // plane
   static char szmode3[5] = "ship";           // ship

   szmode1[0] = 'c';
   szmode1[1] = 'a';
```

```
    szmode1[2] = 'r';
    szmode1[3] = '\0';

    cout << "\n\n\tPlease enter the mode --> plane ";
    cin >> szmode2;

    cout << szmode1 << "\n";
    cout << szmode2 << "\n";
    cout << szmode3 << "\n";

    return(0);
}
```

The output from the program looks like this:

```
car
plane
ship
```

Multidimensional Arrays

The term *dimension* represents the number of indexes used to reference a particular element in an array. All of the arrays discussed so far have been one-dimensional and require only one index to access an element. By looking at an array's declaration, you can tell how many dimensions it has. If there is only one set of brackets ([]), the array is one-dimensional, two sets of brackets ([][]) indicate a two-dimensional array, and so on. Arrays of more than one dimension are called *multidimensional arrays*. For real-world modeling, the working maximum number of dimensions is usually three.

The following declarations set up a two-dimensional array that is initialized while the program executes:

```
/*
 *   092DARAY.C
 *   A C program demonstrating the use of a two-dimensional array
 *   Copyright (c) William H. Murray and Chris H. Pappas, 1992
 */

#include <stdio.h>

#define iROWS 4
#define iCOLUMNS 5

main()
```

```
{
  int irow;
  int icolumn;
  int istatus[iROWS][iCOLUMNS];
  int iadd;
  int imultiple;

  for(irow=0; irow < iROWS; irow++)
    for(icolumn=0; icolumn < iCOLUMNS; icolumn++) {
      iadd = iCOLUMNS - icolumn;
      imultiple = irow;
      istatus[irow][icolumn] = (irow+1) *
        icolumn + iadd * imultiple;
    }

  for(irow=0; irow<iROWS; irow++) {
    printf("CURRENT ROW: %d\n",irow);
    printf("RELATIVE DISTANCE FROM BASE:\n");
    for(icolumn=0; icolumn<iCOLUMNS; icolumn++)
      printf(" %d ",istatus[irow][icolumn]);
    printf("\n\n");
  }

  return(0);
}
```

The program uses two **for** loops to calculate and initialize each of the array elements to its respective "offset from the first element." The created array has 4 rows (*iROWS*) and 5 columns (*iCOLUMNS*) per row, for a total of 20 integer elements. Multidimensional arrays are stored in linear fashion in the computer's memory. Elements in multidimensional arrays are grouped from the rightmost index inward. In the preceding example, row 1, column 1 would be element three of the storage array. Although the calculation of the offset appears a little tricky, note how easily each array element itself is referenced:

```
istatus[irow][icolumn] = . . .
```

The output from the program looks like this:

```
CURRENT ROW: 0
RELATIVE DISTANCE FROM BASE:
  0  1  2  3  4

CURRENT ROW: 1
```

```
RELATIVE DISTANCE FROM BASE:
  5   6   7   8   9

CURRENT ROW: 2
RELATIVE DISTANCE FROM BASE:
  10  11  12  13  14

CURRENT ROW: 3
RELATIVE DISTANCE FROM BASE:
  15  16  17  18  19
```

Multidimensional arrays can also be initialized in the same way as one-dimensional arrays. For example, the following program defines a two-dimensional array *dpowers* and initializes the array when it is defined. The function **pow()** returns the value of *x* raised to the *y* power:

```c
/*
*    092DADBL.C
*    A C program using a 2-dimensional array of doubles
*    Copyright (c) William H. Murray and Chris H. Pappas, 1992
*/

#include <stdio.h>
#include <math.h>

#define iBASES 6
#define iEXPONENTS 3
#define iBASE 0
#define iRAISED_TO 1
#define iRESULT 2

main()
{
  double dpowers[iBASES][iEXPONENTS]={
    1.1, 1, 0,
    2.2, 2, 0,
    3.3, 3, 0,
    4.4, 4, 0,
    5.5, 5, 0,
    6.6, 6, 0
  };

  int irow_index, icolumn_index;
```

```
for(irow_index=0; irow_index < iBASES; irow_index++)
    dpowers[irow_index][iRESULT] = pow(dpowers[irow_index][iBASE],
dpowers[irow_index][iRAISED_TO]);

for(irow_index=0; irow_index < iBASES; irow_index++) {
    printf("    %d\n",(int)dpowers[irow_index][iRAISED_TO]);
    printf(" %2.1f = %.2f\n\n",dpowers[irow_index][iBASE],
                            dpowers[irow_index][iRESULT]);
}

return(0);
}
```

The array *dpowers* was declared to be of type **double** because the function **pow()** expects two double variables and returns a double. Of course, you must take care when initializing two-dimensional arrays; you must make certain you know which dimension is increasing the fastest. Remember, this is always the rightmost dimension.

The output from the program looks like this:

```
   1
1.1 = 1.10

   2
2.2 = 4.84

   3
3.3 = 35.94

   4
4.4 = 374.81

   5
5.5 = 5032.84

   6
6.6 = 82653.95
```

Arrays as Function Arguments

Just like other C variables, arrays can be passed from one function to another. Because arrays as function arguments can be discussed in full only after an introduction to pointers, this chapter begins the topic and Chapter 10 expands upon this base.

Passing Arrays to C Functions

Consider a function **isum()** that computes the sum of the array elements *inumeric_values[0], inumeric_values[1],..., numeric_values[n]*. Two parameters are required—an array parameter called *iarray_address_received* to hold a copy of the array's address and a parameter called *imax_size* to hold the index of the last item in the array to be summed. Assuming that the array is an array of integers and that the index is also of type **int**, the parameters in **isum()** can be described as

```
int isum(int iarray_address_received[], int imax_size)
```

The parameter declaration for the array includes square brackets to signal the function **isum()** that *iarray_address_received* is an array name and not the name of an ordinary parameter. Note that the number of cells is not enclosed in the square brackets. Of course, the simple parameter *imax_size* is declared as previously described. Invoking the function is as simple as this:

```
itotal = isum(inumeric_values,iactual_index);
```

Passing the array *inumeric_values* is a simple process of entering its name as the argument. When passing an array's name to a function, you are actually passing the *address* of the array's first element. Look at the following expression:

```
inumeric_values
is really shorthand for
&inumeric_values[0]
```

Technically, you can invoke the function **isum()** with either of the following two valid statements:

```
itotal = isum(inumeric_values,iactual_index);
itotal = isum(&inumeric_values[0],iactual_index);
```

In either case, within the function **isum()** you can access every cell in the array.

When a function is going to process an array, the calling function includes the name of the array in the function's argument list. This means that the function receives and carries out its processing on the actual elements of the array, not on a local copy as in single-value variables where functions pass only their values.

By default, C passes all arrays call-by-variable or call-by-reference. This prevents the frequent "stack overruns heap" error message many Pascal programmers encounter if they have forgotten to include the **var** modifier for formal array argument declarations. In contrast, the Pascal language passes all array arguments call-by-value. A call-by-value forces the compiler to duplicate the array's contents. For large arrays, this is time consuming and wastes memory.

When a function is to receive an array name as an argument, there are two ways to declare the argument locally: as an array or as a pointer. Which one you use depends on how the function processes the set of values. If the function steps through the elements with an index, the declaration should be an array with square brackets following the name. The size can be empty since the declaration does not reserve space for the entire array, just for the address where it begins. Having seen the array declaration at the beginning of the function, the compiler then permits brackets with an index to appear after the array name anywhere in the function.

The following program declares an array of five elements, and after printing its values, calls in a function to determine what the smallest value in the array is. To do this, it passes the array name and its size to the function **iminimum**(), which declares them as an array called *iarray[]* and an integer called *isize*. The function then passes through the array, comparing each element against the smallest value it has seen so far, and every time it encounters a smaller value, it stores that new value in the variable *icurrent_minimum*. At the end, it returns the smallest value it has seen for the **main**() to print.

```
/*
 *    09PASARY.C
 *    A C program using arrays as parameters
 *    Copyright (c) William H. Murray and Chris H. Pappas, 1992
 */

#include <stdio.h>

#define iMAX 10
#define iUPPER_LIMIT 100

main()
{
  int iarray[iMAX] = {3,7,2,1,5,6,8,9,0,4};
  int i, ismallest;
  int iminimum(int iarray[],int imax);

  printf("The original list looks like: ");
  for(i = 0; i < iMAX; i++)
    printf("%d ",iarray[i]);
  ismallest = iminimum(iarray,iMAX);
  printf("\nThe smallest value is: %d: \n",ismallest);

  return(0);
}

int iminimum(int iarray[], int imax)
```

```
{
  int i, icurrent_minimum;

  icurrent_minimum = iUPPER_LIMIT;
  for(i = 0; i < imax; i++)
    if (iarray[i] < icurrent_minimum)
      icurrent_minimum = iarray[i];
  return(icurrent_minimum);
}
```

Passing Arrays to C++ Functions

When looking at the following program, you will see a format very similar to the C programs examined so far. The program demonstrates how to declare and pass an array argument.

```
//
//   09FNCARY.CPP
//   A C++ program demonstrating how to use arrays with functions
//   Copyright (c) William H. Murray and Chris H. Pappas, 1992
//

#include <iostream.h>

#define iSIZE 5
void vadd_1(int iarray[]);

main()
{
  int iarray[iSIZE]={0,1,2,3,4};
  int i;

  cout << "iarray before calling add_1:\n\n";
  for(i=0; i < iSIZE; i++)
    cout << "   " << iarray[i];

  vadd_1(iarray);

  cout << "\n\niarray after calling add_1:\n\n";
  for(i=0; i < iSIZE; i++)
    cout << "   " << iarray[i];

  return(0);
}
```

```
void vadd_1(int iarray[])
{
  int i;

  for(i=0; i < iSIZE; i++)
    iarray[i]++;
}
```

The output from the program looks like this:

```
iarray before calling add_1:

 0  1  2  3  4

iarray after calling add_1:

 1  2  3  4  5
```

What do the values in the output tell you about the array argument? Is the array passed call-by-value or call-by-reference? The function **vadd_1()** simply adds 1 to each array element. Since this incremented change is reflected back in **main()** *iarray,* it would appear that the parameter was passed call-by-reference. Previous discussions about what an array name really is indicate that this is true. Remember, array names are addresses to the first array cell.

The following C++ program incorporates many of the array features discussed so far, including multidimensional array initialization, referencing, and arguments:

```
//
//   092DARAY.CPP
//   A C++ program that demonstrates how to define, pass,
//   and walk through the different dimensions of an array
//   Copyright (c) William H. Murray and Chris H. Pappas, 1992
//

#include <iostream.h>

void vdisplay_results(char carray[][3][4]);

char cglobal_cube[5][4][5]= {
                    {
                      {'P','L','A','N','E'},
                      {'Z','E','R','O',' '},
                      {' ',' ',' ',' ',' '},
                      {'R','O','W',' ','3'},
```

```
                    },
                    {
                      {'P','L','A','N','E'},
                      {'O','N','E',' ',' '},
                      {'R','O','W',' ','2'}
                    },
                    {
                      {'P','L','A','N','E'},
                      {'T','W','O',' ',' '}
                    },
                    {
                      {'P','L','A','N','E'},
                      {'T','H','R','E','E'},
                      {'R','O','W',' ','2'},
                      {'R','O','W',' ','3'}
                    },
                    {
                      {'P','L','A','N','E'},
                      {'F','O','U','R',' '},
                      {'r','o','w',' ','2'},
                      {'a','b','c','d','e'}
                    }
            };

int imatrix[4][3]={ {1},{2},{3},{4} };

main()
{
  int iplane_index, irow_index, icolumn_index;
  char clocal_cube[2][3][4];

  cout << "sizeof clocal_cube        = "<< sizeof(clocal_cube)
                                         << "\n";
  cout << "sizeof clocal_cube[0]     = "<< sizeof(clocal_cube[0])
                                         << "\n";
  cout << "sizeof clocal_cube[0][0]   = "<<
            sizeof(clocal_cube[0][0])    << "\n";
  cout << "sizeof clocal_cube[0][0][0]= "<<
            sizeof(clocal_cube[0][0][0]) << "\n";

  vdisplay_results(clocal_cube);

  cout << "cglobal_cube[0][1][2] is    = "
       << cglobal_cube[0][1][2] << "\n";
  cout << "cglobal_cube[1][0][2] is    = "
```

```
                << cglobal_cube[1][0][2] << "\n";

   cout << "\nprint part of the cglobal_cube's plane 0\n";
   for(irow_index=0; irow_index < 4; irow_index++) {
     for(icolumn_index=0; icolumn_index < 5; icolumn_index++)
       cout << cglobal_cube[0][irow_index][icolumn_index];
     cout << "\n";
   }

   cout << "\nprint part of the cglobal_cube's plane 4\n";
   for(irow_index=0; irow_index < 4; irow_index++) {
     for(icolumn_index=0; icolumn_index < 5; icolumn_index++)
       cout << cglobal_cube[4][irow_index][icolumn_index];
     cout << "\n";
   }

   cout << "\nprint all of imatrix\n";
   for(irow_index=0; irow_index < 4; irow_index++) {
     for(icolumn_index=0; icolumn_index < 3; icolumn_index++)
       cout << imatrix[irow_index][icolumn_index];
     cout << "\n";
   }

   return (0);
}

void vdisplay_results(char carray[][3][4])
{
  cout << "sizeof carray          =" << sizeof(carray) << "\n";
  cout << "sizeof carray[0]       =" << sizeof(carray[0]) << "\n";
  cout << "sizeof cglobal_cube    =" << sizeof(cglobal_cube) << "\n";
  cout << "sizeof cglobal_cube[0]=" << sizeof(cglobal_cube[0])
                                    << "\n";
}
```

First, note how *cglobal_cube* is defined and initialized. Braces are used to group the characters together so that they have a form similar to the dimensions of the array. This helps in visualizing the form of the array. The braces are not required in this case since you are not leaving any gaps in the array with the initializing data. If you were initializing only a portion of any dimension, various sets of the inner braces would be required to designate which initializing values should apply to which part of the array. The easiest way to visualize the three-dimensional array is to imagine five layers, each having a two-dimensional, four-row by five-column array (see Figure 9-2).

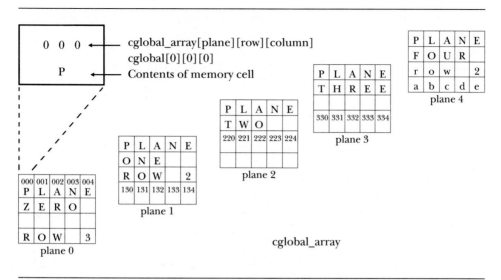

Figure 9-2.   *Conceptual view of the array cglobal_cube*

The first four lines of the program output show the size of the *clocal_cube* array, various dimensions, and an individual element. The output illustrates how the total size of the multidimensional array is the product of all the dimensions times the size of the array data type, that is, 2 * 3 * 4 * *sizeof(char)*, or 24.

Notice how the array element *clocal_cube[0]* is in itself an array that contains a two-dimensional array of [3][4], thereby giving *clocal_cube[0]* the size of 12. The size of *clocal_cube[0][0]* is 4, which is the number of elements in the final dimension since each element has a size of 1, as the *sizeof(clocal_cube[0][0][0])* shows.

In order to fully understand multidimensional arrays, it is very important to realize that *clocal_cube[0]* is both an array name and a pointer constant. Because the program did not subscript the last dimension, the expression does not have the same type as the data type of each fundamental array element. Because *clocal_cube[0]* does not refer to an individual element, but rather to another array, it does not have the type of **char**. Since *clocal_cube[0]* has the type of pointer constant, it is not a legal lvalue and cannot appear to the left of an assignment operator in an assignment expression.

Something very interesting happens when you use an array name in a function argument list, as was done when the function **vdisplay_results()** was invoked with *clocal_cube*. While inside the function, if you perform a **sizeof()** operation against the formal parameter that represents the array name, you do not correctly compute the actual size of *carray*. What the function sees is only a copy of the address of the first element in the array. Therefore, the function **sizeof()** will return the size of the address, not the item to which it refers.

The **sizeof()** *carray[0]* in function **vdisplay_results()** is 12 because it was declared in the function that the formal parameter was an array whose last two dimensions were [3] and [4]. You could not have used any values when you declared the size of these last two dimensions because the function prototype defined them to be [3] and [4]. Without a prototype, the compiler would not be able to detect the difference in the way the array was dimensioned. This would let you redefine the way in which you viewed the array's organization. The function **vdisplay_results()** also outputs the size of the global *cglobal_cube*. This points out that while a function may have access to global data directly, it has access only to the address of an array that is passed to a function as an argument.

In regard to the **main()** function, the next two statements executed demonstrate how to reference specific elements in *cglobal_cube*. *cglobal_cube[0][1][2]* references the zeroth layer, second row, third column, or "R." *cglobal_cube[1][0][2]* references the second layer, row zero, third column, or "A."

The next block of code in **main()** contains two nested **for** loops demonstrating that the arrays are stored in plane-row-column order. As already seen, the rightmost subscript (column) of the array varies the fastest when you view the array in a linear fashion. The first **for** loop pair hardwires the output to the zeroth layer and selects a row, with the inner loop traversing each column in *cglobal_cube*. The program continues by duplicating the same loop structures but printing only the fifth layer (plane [4]), of the *cglobal_cube*.

The last **for** loop pair displays the elements of *imatrix* in the form of a rectangle, similar to the way many people visualize a two-dimensional array.

The output from the program looks like this:

```
sizeof clocal_cube            = 24
sizeof clocal_cube[0]         = 12
sizeof clocal_cube[0][0]      = 4
sizeof clocal_cube[0][0][0]   = 1
sizeof carray                 = 2
sizeof carray[0]              = 12
sizeof cglobal_cube           = 100
sizeof cglobal_cube[0]        = 20
cglobal_cube[0][1][2] is      = R
cglobal_cube[1][0][2] is      = A

print part of the cglobal_cube's plane 0
PLANE
ZERO


ROW 3


print part of the cglobal_cube's plane 4
PLANE
```

```
FOUR
row 2
abcde

print all of imatrix
100
200
300
400
```

Are you bothered by the output? Look at the initialization of *imatrix*. Because each inner set of braces corresponds to one row of the array and enough values were not supplied inside the inner braces, the system padded the remaining elements with zeros. Remember, C automatically initializes all undefined static automatic numeric array elements to zero.

String Functions and Character Arrays

Because of the way C handles string data, many of the functions that use character arrays as function arguments were not discussed. Specifically, these functions are **gets()**, **puts()**, **fgets()**, **fputs()**, **sprintf()**, **stpcpy()**, **strcat()**, **strncmp()**, and **strlen()**. Understanding how these functions operate will be much easier now that you are familiar with the concepts of character arrays and null-terminated strings. One of the easiest ways to explain these functions is to show a few program examples.

gets(), puts(), fgets(), fputs(), and sprintf()

The following example program demonstrates how you can use **gets()**, **puts()**, **fgets()**, **fputs()**, and **sprintf()** to format I/O:

```c
/*
 *   09STRIO.C
 *   A C program using several string I/O functions
 *   Copyright (c) William H. Murray and Chris H. Pappas, 1992
 */

#include <stdio.h>

#define iSIZE 20

main()
```

```
{
  char sztest_array[iSIZE];

  fputs("Please enter the first string  : ",stdout);
  gets(sztest_array);
  fputs("The first string entered is   : ",stdout);
  puts(sztest_array);

  fputs("Please enter the second string : ",stdout);
  fgets(sztest_array,iSIZE,stdin);
  fputs("The second string entered is  : ",stdout);
  fputs(sztest_array,stdout);

  sprintf(sztest_array,"This was %s a test","just");
  fputs("sprintf() created              : ",stdout);
  fputs(sztest_array,stdout);

  return(0);
}
```

Here is the output from the first run of the program:

```
Please enter the first string  : string one
The first string entered is    : string one
Please enter the second string : string two
The second string entered is   : string two
sprintf() created              : This was just a test
```

Because the strings that were entered were less than the size of *sztest_array*, the program works fine. However, when you enter a string longer than *sztest_array*, something like the following can occur when the program is run a second time:

```
Please enter the first string  : one two three four five
The first string entered is    : one two three four five
Please enter the second string : six seven eight nine ten
The second string entered is   : six seven eight ninsprintf() created
   : This was just a testPlease enter the first string  : The first string
entered is    :e ten
The second string entered is   :
```

Take care when running the program. The **gets()** function receives characters from standard input (**stdin**, the keyboard by default for most computers) and places them into the array whose name is passed to the function. When you press the ENTER key to terminate the string, a newline character is transmitted. When the **gets()**

function receives this newline character, it changes it into a null character, thereby ensuring that the character array contains a string. No checking occurs to ensure that the array is big enough to hold all the characters entered.

The **puts()** function echoes to the terminal just what was entered with **gets()**. It also adds a newline character on the end of the string in the place where the null character appeared. The null character, remember, was automatically inserted into the string by the **gets()** function. Therefore, strings that are properly entered with **gets()** can be displayed with **puts()**.

When you use the **fgets()** function, you can guarantee a maximum number of input characters. This function stops reading the designated file stream when *one fewer* character is read than the second argument specifies. Since *sztest_array size* is 20, only 19 characters will be read by **fgets()** from **stdin**. A null character is automatically placed into the string in the last position; and if a newline were entered from the keyboard, it would be retained in the string. (It would appear before the null debug example.) The **fgets()** function does not eliminate the newline character like **gets()** did; it merely adds the null character at the end so that a valid string is stored. In much the same way as **gets()** and **puts()** are symmetrical, so too are **fgets()** and **fputs()**. **fgets()** does not eliminate the newline, nor does **fputs()** add one.

To understand how important the newline character is to these functions, look closely at the second run output given. Notice the phrase "sprintf() created..."; it follows immediately after the numbers six, seven, eight, and nine that had just been entered. The second input string actually had five more characters than the **fgets()** function read in (one fewer than *iSIZE* of 19 characters). The others were left in the input buffer. Also dropped was the newline that terminated the input from the keyboard. (It is left in the input stream because it occurs after the 19th character.) Therefore, no newline character was stored in the string. Since **fputs()** does not add 1 back, the next **fputs()** output begins on the line where the previous output ended. Reliance was on the newline character read by **fgets()** and printed by **fputs()** to help control the display formatting.

The function **sprintf()** stands for "string **printf()**." It uses a control string with conversion characters in exactly the same way as does **printf()**. The additional feature is that **sprintf()** places the resulting formatted data in a string rather than immediately sending the result to standard output. This can be beneficial if the exact same output must be created twice—for example, when the same string must be output to both the display monitor and the printer.

To review:

- **gets()** converts newline to a null.

- **puts()** converts null to a newline.

- **fgets()** retains newline and appends a null.

- **fputs()** drops the null and does not add a newline; instead, it uses the retained newline (if one was entered).

strcpy( ), strcat( ), strncmp( ), and strlen( )

All of the functions discussed in this section are predefined in the string.h header file. Whenever you wish to use one of these functions, make certain you include the header file in your program. Remember, all of the string functions prototyped in string.h expect null-terminated string parameters. The following program demonstrates how to use the **strcpy( )** function:

```
/*
 *   09STRCPY.C
 *   A C program using the strcpy function
 *   Copyright (c) William H. Murray and Chris H. Pappas, 1992
 */

#include <stdio.h>
#include <string.h>

#define iSIZE 20

main()
{
  char szsource_string[iSIZE]="Initialized String!",
       szdestination_string[iSIZE];

  strcpy(szdestination_string,"String Constant");
  printf("%s\n",szdestination_string);

  strcpy(szdestination_string,szsource_string);
  printf("%s\n",szdestination_string);

  return(0);
}
```

The function **strcpy( )** copies the contents of one string, *szsource_string*, into a second string, *szdestination_string*. The preceding program initializes *szsource_string* with the message, "Initialized String!" The first **strcpy( )** function call actually copies "String Constant" into the *szdestination_string*, while the second call to the **strcpy( )** function copies *szsource_string* into *szdestination_string* variable. The program outputs this message:

```
String Constant
Initialized String!
```

The equivalent C++ program is

```
//
//  09STRCPY.CPP
//   A C++ program using the strcpy function
//   Copyright (c) William H. Murray and Chris H. Pappas, 1992
//

#include <iostream.h>
#include <string.h>

#define iSIZE 20

main()
{
  char szsource_string[iSIZE]="Initialized String!",
       szdestination_string[iSIZE];

  strcpy(szdestination_string,"String Constant");
  cout << "\n" << szdestination_string;

  strcpy(szdestination_string,szsource_string);
  cout << "\n" << szdestination_string;

  return(0);
}
```

The strcat() function appends two separate strings. Both strings must be null-terminated and the result itself is null terminated. The following program builds on your understanding of the **strcpy()** function and introduces **strcat()**:

```
/*
 *   09STRCAT.C
 *    A C program demonstrating how to use the strcat function
 *    Copyright (c) William H. Murray and Chris H. Pappas, 1992
 */

#include <stdio.h>
#include <string.h>

#define iSTRING_SIZE 35

main()
{
  char szgreeting[] = "Good morning",
       szname[] =" Carolyn, ",
```

```
        szmessage[iSTRING_SIZE];

  strcpy(szmessage,szgreeting);
  strcat(szmessage,szname);
  strcat(szmessage,"how are you?");
  printf("%s\n",szmessage);

  return(0);
}
```

In this example, both *szgreeting* and *szname* are initialized, while *szmessage* is not. The first thing the program does is to use the function **strcpy()** to copy the *szgreeting* into *szmessage*. Next, the **strcat()** function is used to concatenate *szname* (" Carolyn, ") to "Good morning", which is stored in *szmessage*. The last **strcat()** function call demonstrates how a string constant can be concatenated to a string. Here, "how are you?" is concatenated to the now current contents of *szmessage* ("Good morning Carolyn, "). The program outputs the following:

```
Good morning Carolyn, how are you?
```

The next program demonstrates how to use **strncmp()** to decide if two strings are identical:

```
/*
 *    09SRNCMP.C
 *    A C program that uses strncmp to compare two strings with
 *    the aid of the strlen function
 *    Copyright (c) William H. Murray and Chris H. Pappas, 1992
 */

#include <stdio.h>
#include <string.h>

main()
{
  char szstringA[]="Adam", szstringB[]="Abel";
  int istringA_length,iresult=0;

  istringA_length=strlen(szstringA);
  if (strlen(szstringB) >= strlen(szstringA))
    iresult = strncmp(szstringA,szstringB,istringA_length);
  printf("The string %s found", iresult == 0 ? "was" : "wasn't");
```

```
  return(0);
}
```

The **strlen()** function is very useful; it returns the number of characters, not including the null-terminator, in the string pointed to. In the preceding program it is used in two different forms just to give you additional exposure to its use. The first call to the function assigns the length of *szstringA* to the variable *istringA_length*. The second invocation of the function is actually encountered within the **if** condition. Remember, all test conditions must evaluate to a TRUE (not 0 or !0) or FALSE (0). The **if** test takes the results returned from the two calls to **strlen()** and then asks the relational question >=. If the length of *szstringB* is >= to that of *szstringA*, the **strncmp()** function is invoked.

You are probably wondering why the program used a >= test instead of an = =. To know the answer you need a further explanation of how **strncmp()** works. The function **strncmp()** compares two strings, starting with the first character in each string. If both strings are identical, the function returns a value of zero. However, if the two strings aren't identical, **strncmp()** will return a value less than zero if *szstringA* is less than *szstringB*, or a value greater than zero when *szstringA* is greater than *szstringB*. The relational test >= was used in case you wanted to modify the code to include a report of equality, greater than, or less than for the compared strings.

The program terminates by using the value returned by *iresult*, along with the conditional operator (?:), to determine which string message is printed. For this example, the program output is

```
The string wasn't found
```

Before moving on to the next chapter, remind yourself that two of the most frequent causes for irregular program behavior deal with exceeding array boundaries and forgetting that character arrays, used as strings, must end with \0, a null-string terminator. Both errors can sit dormant for months until that one user enters a response one character too long.

Pointers

In C, the topics of pointers, arrays, and strings are closely related. Consequently, you can consider Chapter 10 to be an extension of Chapter 9. Learning about pointers—what they are and how to use them—can be a challenging experience to the novice programmer. However, by mastering the concept of pointers, you will be able to author extremely efficient, powerful, and flexible C applications.

It is very common practice for most introductory-level programs to use only the class of variables known as static. *Static variables,* in this sense, are variables declared in the variable declaration block of the source code. While the program is executing, the application can neither obtain more of these variables nor deallocate storage for a variable. In addition, you have no way of knowing the address in memory for each variable or constant. Accessing an actual cell is a straightforward process—you simply use the variable's name. For example, in C, if you want to increment the **int** variable *idecade* by 10, you access *idecade* by name:

```
idecade += 10;
```

Defining Pointer Variables

Another, often more convenient and efficient way to access a variable is through a second variable that holds the address of the variable you want to access. Chapter 8 introduced the concept of pointer variables, which are covered in more detail in this chapter. For example, suppose you have an **int** variable called *imemorycell_contents* and another variable called *pimemorycell_address* (admittedly verbose, but highly symbolic) that can hold the *address* of a variable of type **int**. In C, you have already seen that preceding a variable with the & address operator returns the address of the variable instead of its contents. Therefore, the syntax for assigning the address of a variable to another variable of the type that holds addresses should not surprise you:

```
pimemorycell_address = &imemorycell_contents;
```

A variable that holds an address, such as *pimemorycell_address*, is called a *pointer variable*, or simply a *pointer*. Figure 10-1 illustrates this relationship. The variable *imemorycell_contents* has been placed in memory at address 7751. After the preceding statement is executed, the address of *imemorycell_contents* will be assigned to the pointer variable *pimemorycell_address*. This relationship is expressed in English by saying that *pimemorycell_address* points to *imemorycell_contents*. Figure 10-2 illustrates this relationship. The arrow is drawn from the cell that stores the address to the cell whose address is stored.

Accessing the contents of the cell whose address is stored in *pimemorycell_address* is as simple as preceding the pointer variable with an asterisk: **pimemorycell_address*. What you have done is to *dereference* the pointer *pimemorycell_address*. For example, if you execute the following two statements, the value of the cell named *imemorycell_contents* will be 20 (see Figure 10-3).

```
pimemorycell_address = &imemorycell_contents;
*pimemorycell_address = 20;
```

You can think of the * as a directive to follow the arrow (see Figure 10-3) to find the cell referenced. Notice that if *pimemorycell_address* holds the address of *imemorycell_contents*, then both of the following statements will have the same effect; that is, both will store the value of 20 in *imemorycell_contents*:

```
imemorycell_contents = 20;
*pimemorycell_address = 20;
```

Figure 10-1.   *An example pointer variable*

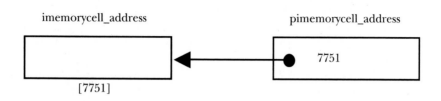

Figure 10-2.   *The pointer variable pimemorycell_address pointing to imemorycell_contents*

Pointer Variable Declarations

C, like any other language, requires a definition for each variable. To define a pointer variable *pimemorycell_address* that can hold the address of an **int** variable, you write

```
int *pimemorycell_address;
```

Actually, there are two separate parts to this declaration. The data type of *pimemorycell_address* is

```
int *
```

and the identifier for the variable is

```
pimemorycell_address
```

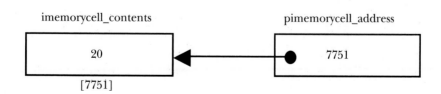

Figure 10-3.   *Using a pointer variable in an assignment statement*

The asterisk following **int** means "pointer to." That is, the following data type is a pointer variable that can hold an address to an **int**:

```
int *
```

This is a very important concept to remember. In C, unlike many other languages, a pointer variable holds the address of a *particular* data type.

Let's look at an example:

```
char *pcaddress;
int *piaddress;
```

The data type of *pcaddress* is distinctly different from the data type of the pointer variable *piaddress*. Run-time errors and compile-time warnings may occur in a program that defines a pointer to one data type and then uses it to point to some other data type. It would be poor programming practice to define a pointer in one way and then use it in some other way. For example, look at the following code segment:

```
int *pi;
float real_value = 98.26;
pi = &real_value;
```

Here *pi* is defined to be of type **int** *, meaning it can hold the address of a memory cell of type **int**. The third statement attempts to assign *pi* the address, *&real_value*, of a declared float variable.

Simple Statements Using Pointer Variables

The following code segment exchanges the contents of the variables *iresult_a* and *iresult_b* but uses the address and dereferencing operators to do so:

```
int iresult_a = 15, iresult_b = 37, itemporary;
int *piresult;

piresult = &iresult_a;
itemporary = *piresult;
*piresult = iresult_b;
iresult_b = itemporary;
```

The first line of the program contains standard definitions and initializations. The statement allocates three cells to hold a single integer, gives each cell a name, and initializes two of them (see Figure 10-4). For discussion purposes, assume that the

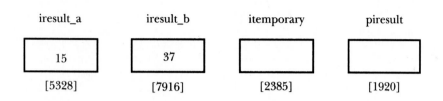

Figure 10-4. *Creation and initialization of memory cells*

cell named *iresult_a* is located at address 5328, the cell named *iresult_b* is located at address 7916, and the cell named *itemporary* is located at address 2385.

The second statement in the program defines *piresult* to be a pointer to an **int** data type. The statement allocates the cell and gives it a name (placed at address 1920). Remember, when the * is combined with the data type (in this case, **int**), the variable contains the *address* of a cell of the same data type. Because *piresult* has not been initialized, it does not point to any particular **int** variable. If your program were to try to use *piresult*, the compiler would not give you any warning and would try to use the variable's garbage contents to point with. The fourth statement assigns *piresult* the address of *iresult_a* (see Figure 10-5).

The next statement in the program uses the expression **piresult* to access the contents of the cell to which *piresult* points—*iresult_a*:

```
itemporary = *piresult;
```

Therefore, the integer value 15 is stored in the variable *itemporary* (see Figure 10-6). If you left off the * in front of *piresult*, the assignment statement would illegally store

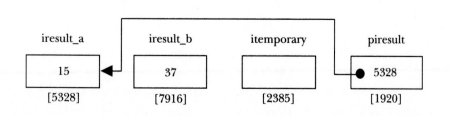

Figure 10-5. *Assigning piresult the address of iresult_a*

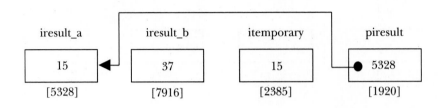

Figure 10-6.   *Using piresult to assign itemporary a value*

the contents of *piresult*—the address 5328—in the cell named *itemporary,* but *itemporary* is supposed to hold an integer, not an address. This can be a very annoying bug to locate since many compilers will not issue any warnings/errors. (The Microsoft C/C++ compiler issues the warning, "different levels of indirection.")

To make matters worse, most pointers are **near**, meaning they occupy 2 bytes, the same data size as a PC-based integer. The fifth statement in the program copies the contents of the variable *iresult_b* into the cell pointed to by the address stored in *piresult* (see Figure 10-7):

```
*piresult = iresult_b;
```

The last statement in the program simply copies the contents of one integer variable, *itemporary,* into another integer variable, *iresult_b* (see Figure 10-8). Make certain you understand the difference between what is being referenced when a pointer variable is preceded (*piresult*) and when it is not preceded (*piresult*) by the dereference operator *. For this example, the first syntax is a pointer to a cell that can contain an integer value. The second syntax references the cell that holds the address to another cell that can hold an integer.

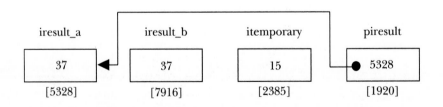

Figure 10-7.   *Another assignment using piresult*

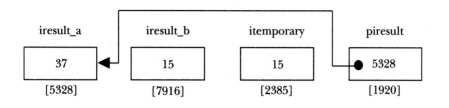

Figure 10-8. *Normal integer assignment*

The following short program illustrates how to manipulate the addresses in pointer variables. Unlike the previous example, which swapped the program's data within the variables, this program swaps the addresses to where the data resides:

```
char cswitch1 = 'S', cswitch2 = 'T';
char *pcswitch1, *pcswitch2, *pctemporary;

pcswitch1   = &cswitch1;
pcswitch2   = &cswitch2;
pctemporary = pcswitch1;
pcswitch1   = pcswitch2;
pcswitch2   = pctemporary;
printf( "%c%c", *pcswitch1, *pcswitch2);
```

Figure 10-9 shows the cell configuration and values after the execution of the first four statements of the program. When the fifth statement is executed, the contents of *pcswitch1* are copied into *pctemporary* so that both *pcswitch1* and *pctemporary* point to *cswitch1* (see Figure 10-10).

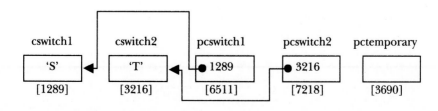

Figure 10-9. *Starting relationship of program variables*

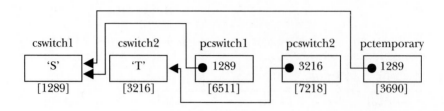

Figure 10-10.   *pctemporary is assigned the address of cswitch1*

Executing the following statement copies the contents of *pcswitch2* into *pcswitch1* so that both pointers point to *cswitch2* (see Figure 10-11):

```
pcswitch1 = pcswitch2;
```

Notice that if the code had not preserved the address to *cswitch1* in a temporary location, *pctemporary,* there would be no pointer access to *cswitch1*. The next to last statement copies the address stored in *pitemporary* into *pcswitch2* (see Figure 10-12). When the **printf** statement is executed, since the value of **pcswitch1* is "T" and the value of **pcswitch2* is "S", you will see

```
TS
```

Notice how the actual values stored in the variables *cswitch1* and *cswitch2* haven't changed from their original initializations. However, since you have swapped the contents of their respective pointers, **pcswitch1* and **pcswitch2*, it *appears* that their order has been reversed. This is an important concept to grasp. Depending on the

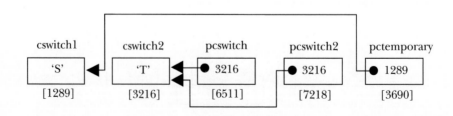

Figure 10-11.   *Assigning pcswitch1 the address in pcswitch2*

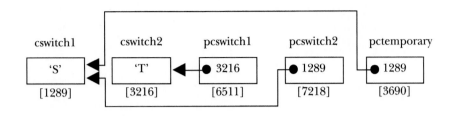

Figure 10-12.   pcswitch2 is assigned the address in pctemporary

size of a data object, moving a pointer to the object can be much more efficient than copying the entire contents of the object.

Pointer Variable Initialization

Pointer variables can be initialized in their definitions, just like many other variables in C. For example, the following two statements allocate storage for the two cells *iresult* and *piresult*:

```
int iresult;
int *piresult = &iresult;
```

The variable *iresult* is an ordinary integer variable and *piresult* is a pointer to an integer. Additionally, the code initializes the pointer variable *piresult* to the address of *iresult*. Be careful: the syntax is somewhat misleading; you are *not* initializing **piresult* (which would have to be an integer value) but *piresult* (which must be an address to an integer). The second statement in the preceding listing can be translated into the following two equivalent statements:

```
int *piresult;
piresult = &iresult;
```

The following code segment shows how to declare a string pointer and then initialize it:

```
/*
 *    10PSZ.C
 *    A C program that initializes a string pointer and
 *    then prints the palindrome backwards then forwards
```

```
*    Copyright (c) William H. Murray and Chris H. Pappas, 1992
*/

#include <stdio.h>
#include <string.h>

void main()
{
  char *pszpalindrome="MADAM I'M ADAM";
  int i;

  for (i=strlen(psz)-1; i >= 0; i--)
    printf("%c",psz[i]);
    printf("%s",psz);
}
```

Technically, the C compiler stores the address of the first character of the string "MADAM I'M ADAM" in the variable *pszpalindrome*. While the program is running, it can use *pszpalindrome* like any other string. This is because all C compilers create a *string table*, which is used internally by the compiler to store the string constants a program is using.

The **strlen()** function prototyped in string.h calculates the length of a string. The function expects a pointer to a null-terminated string and counts all of the characters up to, but not including, the null character itself. The index variable i is initialized to one less than the value returned by **strlen()** since the **for** loop treats the string *psz* like an array of characters. The palindrome has 14 letters. If *psz* is treated as an array of characters, each element is indexed from 0 to 13. This example program highlights the somewhat confusing relationship between pointers to character strings and arrays of characters. However, if you remember that an array's name is actually the address of the first element, you should understand why the compiler issues no complaints.

Improper Use of the Address Operator

You cannot use the address operator on every C expression. The following examples demonstrate those situations where the & address operator cannot be applied:

```
/*
   not with CONSTANTS
*/

pivariable = &48;


/*
```

```
   not with expressions involving operators such as + and /
   given the definition int iresult = 5;
*/

pivariable = &(iresult + 15);



/*
   not preceding register variables
   given the definition register register1;
*/

pivariable = &register1;
```

The first statement tries to illegally obtain the address of a hardwired constant value. Since the 48 has no memory cell associated with it, the statement is meaningless.

The second assignment statement attempts to return the address of the expression iresult + 15. Since the expression itself is actually a stack manipulation process, there is no address associated with the expression.

Normally, the last example honors the programmer's request to define *register1* as a register rather than as a storage cell in internal memory. Therefore, no memory cell address could be returned and stored. Microsoft C/C++ gives the variable memory, not register storage.

Pointers to Arrays

As mentioned, pointers and arrays are closely related topics. Remember from Chapter 9 that an array's name is a constant whose value represents the address of the array's first element. For this reason, the value of an array's name cannot be changed by an assignment statement or by any other statement. Given the following data declarations, the array's name, *ftemperatures,* is a constant whose value is the address of the first element of the array of 20 floats:

```
#define IMAXREADINGS 20

float ftemperatures[IMAXREADINGS];
float *pftemp;
```

The following statement assigns the address of the first element of the array to the pointer variable *pftemp:*

```
pftemp = ftemperatures;
```

An equivalent statement looks like this:

```
pftemp = &ftemperatures[0];
```

However, if *pftemp* holds the address of a float, the following statements are illegal:

```
ftemperatures = pftemp;
&ftemperatures[0] = pftemp;
```

These statements attempt to assign a value to the constant *ftemperatures* or its equivalent *&ftemperatures[0]*, which makes about as much sense as

```
10 = pftemp;
```

Pointers to Pointers

In C, it is possible to define pointer variables that point to other pointer variables, which in turn point to the data, such as an integer. Figure 10-13 illustrates this relationship; *ppi* is a pointer variable that points to another pointer variable whose contents can be used to point to 10.

You may be wondering why this is necessary. The arrival of OS/2 and the Windows programming environment signals the development of multitasking operating environments designed to maximize the use of memory. To compact the use of memory, the operating system has to be able to move objects in memory. If your program points directly to the physical memory cell where the object is stored and the operating system moves it, disaster will strike. Instead of pointing directly to a data object, your application points to a memory cell address that will not change while your program is running (for example, let's call this a *virtual_address*), and the *virtual_address* memory cell holds the *current_physical_address* of the data object. Now, whenever the operating environment wants to move the data object, all the operating system has to do is update the *current_physical_address* pointed to by the *virtual_address*.

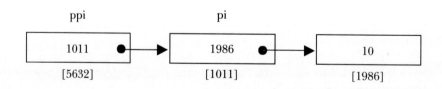

Figure 10-13. *A pointer to a pointer that points to an integer*

As far as your application is concerned, it still uses the unchanged address of the *virtual_address* to point to the updated address of the *current_physical_address*.

To define a pointer to a pointer in C, you simply increase the number of asterisks preceding the identifier:

```
int **ppi;
```

In this example, the variable *ppi* is defined to be a pointer to a pointer that points to an **int** data type. *ppi*'s data type is

```
int **
```

Each asterisk is read "pointer to." The number of pointers that must be followed to access the data item or, equivalently, the number of asterisks that must be attached to the variable to reference the value to which it points is called the *level of indirection* of the pointer variable. A pointer's level of indirection determines how much dereferencing must be done to access the data type given in the definition. Figure 10-14 illustrates several variables with different levels of indirection.

The first four lines of code in Figure 10-14 define four variables: the integer variable *ivalue,* the *pi* pointer variable that points to an integer (one level of indirection), the *ppi* variable that points to a pointer that points to an integer (two levels of indirection), and *pppi,* illustrating that this process can be extended beyond two levels of indirection. The fifth line of code is

```
pi = &ivalue;
```

This is an assignment statement that uses the address operator. The expression assigns the address of *&ivalue* to *pi*. Therefore, *pi*'s contents contain 1111. Notice that there is only one arrow from *pi* to *ivalue*. This indicates that *ivalue,* or 10, can be

---

```
int ivalue = 10;
int *pi;
int **ppi;
int ***pppi;
pi = &ivalue;
ppi = &pi;
pppi = &ppi;
```

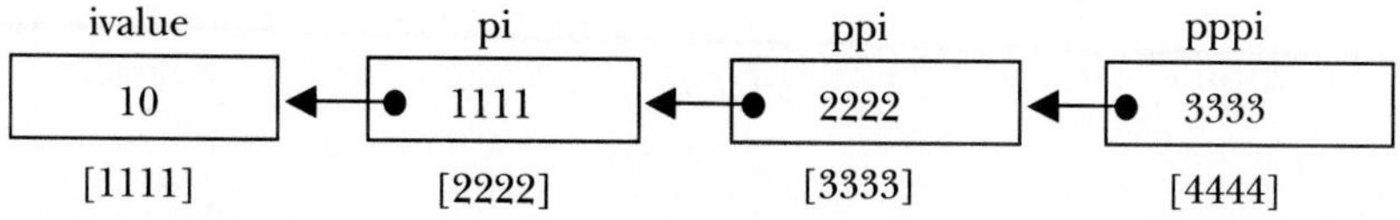

Figure 10-14.   *Using different levels of indirection*

accessed by dereferencing *pi* just once. The next statement, along with its accompanying picture, illustrates double indirection:

```
ppi = &pi;
```

Because *ppi*'s data type is **int ****, to access an integer you need to dereference the variable twice. After the preceding assignment statement, *ppi* holds the address of *pi* (not the contents of *pi*), so *ppi* points to *pi*, which in turn points to *ivalue*. Notice that you must follow two arrows to get from *ppi* to *ivalue*.

The last statement demonstrates three levels of indirection:

```
pppi = &ppi;
```

It also assigns the address of *ppi* to *pppi* (not the contents of *ppi*). Notice that the accompanying illustration shows that three arrows are now necessary to reference *ivalue*.

To review, *pppi* is assigned the address of a pointer variable that indirectly points to an integer, as in the preceding statement. However, ***pppi (the cell pointed to) can only be assigned an integer value, not an address, since ***pppi is an integer:

```
***pppi = 10;
```

C allows pointers to be initialized like any other variable. For example, *pppi* could have been defined and initialized using the following single statement:

```
int ***pppi = &ppi;
```

Pointers to Strings

A string constant such as "File not ready" is actually stored as an array of characters with a null terminator added as the last character (see Figure 10-15). Because a **char** pointer can hold the address of a character, it is possible to define and initialize it. For example:

```
char *psz = "File not ready";
```

This statement defines the **char** pointer *psz* and initializes it to the address of the first character in the string (see Figure 10-16). Additionally, the storage is allocated for the string itself. The same statement could have been written as follows:

```
char *psz;
psz = "File not ready";
```

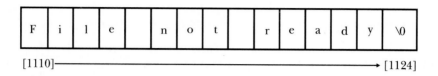

Figure 10-15.   *Null-terminated string in memory*

Again, care must be taken to realize that *psz* was assigned the address, not **psz,* which points to the "F." The second example given helps to clarify this by using two separate statements to define and initialize the pointer variable.

The following example highlights a common misconception when dealing with pointers to strings and pointers to arrays of characters:

```
char *psz = "File not ready";
char pszarray[] = "Drive not ready";
```

The main difference between these two statements is that the value of *psz* can be changed (since it is a pointer variable), but the value of *pszarray* cannot be changed (since it is a pointer constant). Along the same line of thinking, the following assignment statement is illegal:

```
/* NOT LEGAL */
char pszarray[16];
pszarray = "Drive not ready";
```

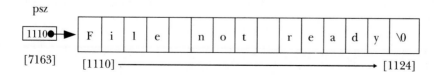

Figure 10-16.   *Initializing a string pointer*

While the syntax looks similar to the correct code in the preceding example, the assignment statement attempts to copy the *address* of the first cell of the storage for the string "Drive not ready" into *pszarray*. Because *pszarray* is a pointer constant, not a pointer variable, an error results.

The following input statement is incorrect because the pointer *psz* has not been initialized:

```
/* NOT LEGAL */
char *psz;
cin >> psz;
```

Correcting the problem is as simple as reserving storage for and initializing the pointer variable *psz*:

```
char sztring[10];
char *psz = sztring;
cin.get(psz,10);
```

Since the value of *sztring* is the address of the first cell of the array, the second statement in the code not only allocates storage for the pointer variable, but it also initializes it to the address of the first cell of the array *sztring*. At this point, the **cin.get** statement is satisfied since it is passed the valid address of the character array storage.

Pointer Arithmetic

If you are familiar with assembly language programming, then you are already comfortable with using actual physical addresses to reference information stored in tables. For those of you who are only used to using subscript indexing into arrays, believe it or not, you have been effectively using the same assembly language equivalent. The only difference is that in the latter case you were allowing the compiler to manipulate the addresses for you.

Remember that one of C's strengths is its closeness to the hardware. In C, you can actually manipulate pointer variables. Many of the example programs seen so far have demonstrated how one pointer variable's address, or address contents, can be assigned to another pointer variable of the same data type. C allows you to perform only two arithmetic operations on a pointer address—namely, addition and subtraction. Let's look at two different pointer variable types and perform some simple pointer arithmetic:

```
//
//  10PTARTH.CPP
//  A C++ program demonstrating pointer arithmetic
//  Copyright (c) William H. Murray and Chris H. Pappas, 1992
```

```
//

#include <iostream.h>

void main()
{
  int *pi;
  float *pf;

  int an_integer;
  float a_real;

  pi = &an_integer;
  pf = &a_real;

  pi++;
  pf++;

}
```

Let's also assume that an integer is 2 bytes and a float is 4 bytes. Also, *an_integer* is stored at memory cell address 2000, and *a_real* is stored at memory cell address 4000. When the last two lines of the program are executed, *pi* will contain the address 2002 and *pf* will contain the address 4004. But wait a minute—didn't you think that the increment operator ++ incremented by 1? This is true for character variables but not always for pointer variables. In Chapter 6, you were introduced to the concept of operator overloading. Increment (++) and decrement (– –) are examples of this C construct. For the immediate example, since *pi* was defined to point to integers (which for the system in this example are 2 bytes), when the increment operation is invoked, it checks the variable's type and then chooses an appropriate increment value. For integers, this value is 2, and for floats, the value is 4 (on the example system). This same principle holds true for whatever data type the pointer is pointing to. Should the pointer variable point to a structure of 20 bytes, the increment or decrement operator would add or subtract 20 from the current pointer's address.

You can also modify a pointer's address by using integer addition and subtraction, not just the ++ and – – operators. For example, moving four float values over from the one currently pointed to can be accomplished with the following statement:

```
pf = pf + 4;
```

Look at the following program carefully and see if you can predict the results. Does the program move the **float** pointer *pf* one number over?

```
//
//   10SIZEPT.CPP
//   A C++ program using sizeof and pointer arithmetic
//   Copyright (c) William H. Murray and Chris H. Pappas, 1992
//

#include <iostream.h>
#include <stddef.h>

void main()
{
   float fvalues[] = {15.38,12.34,91.88,11.11,22.22};
   float *pf;
   size_t fwidth;

   pf = &fvalues[0];

   fwidth = sizeof(float);

   pf = pf + fwidth;

}
```

Try using CodeView to single-step through the program. Use the Trace window to keep an eye on the variables *pf* and *fwidth*.

Assume that the debugger has assigned *pf* the address of *fvalues* and that *pf* contains an FFCA. The variable *fwidth* is assigned the **sizeof(float)** that returns a 4. When you executed the final statement in the program, what happened? The variable *pf* changed to FFDA, not FFDE. Why? You forgot that pointer arithmetic takes into consideration the size of the object pointed to ($4 \times$ (4–byte floats) = 16). The program actually moves the *pf* pointer over four float values to 22.22.

Actually, you were intentionally mislead by the naming of the variable *fwidth*. To make logical sense, the program should have been written as

```
//
//   10PTSIZE.CPP
//   The same C++ program using meaningful variable names
//   Copyright (c) William H. Murray and Chris H. Pappas, 1992
//

#include <iostream.h>

void main()
{
```

```
    float fvalues[] = {15.38,12.34,91.88,11.11,22.22};
    float *pf;
    int inumber_of_elements_to_skip;

    pf = fvalues;

    inumber_of_elements_to_skip = 1;

    pf = pf + inumber_of_elements_to_skip;

}
```

Pointer Arithmetic and Arrays

The following two programs index into a ten-character array. Both programs read in ten characters and then print out the same ten characters in reverse order. The first program uses the more conventional high-level-language approach of indexing with subscripts. The second program is identical except that the array elements are referenced by address, using pointer arithmetic. Here is the first program:

```
/*
 *    10ARYSUB.C
 *    A C program using normal array subscripting
 *    Copyright (c) William H. Murray and Chris H. Pappas, 1992
 */

#include <stdio.h>

#define ISIZE 10

void main()
{
  char string10[ISIZE];
  int i;

  for(i = 0; i < ISIZE; i++)
    string10[i]=getchar();

  for(i = ISIZE-1; i >= 0; i--)
    putchar(string10[i]);
}
```

Here is the second example:

```
/*
*    10ARYPTR.C
*    A C program using pointer arithmetic to access elements
*    Copyright (c) William H. Murray and Chris H. Pappas, 1992
*/

#include <stdio.h>

#define ISIZE 10

void main()
{
  char string10[ISIZE];
  char *pc;
  int icount;

  pc=string10;

  for(icount = 0; icount < ISIZE; icount++) {
    *pc=getchar();
    pc++;
  }

  pc=string10 + (ISIZE - 1);

  for(icount = 0; icount < ISIZE; icount++) {
    putchar(*pc);
    pc--;
  }
}
```

Since the first example is straightforward, the discussion will revolve around the second program, which uses pointer arithmetic. *pc* has been defined to be of type **char ***, which means it is a pointer to a character. Because each cell in the array *string10* holds a character, *pc* is suitable for pointing to each. The following statement stores the address of the first cell of *string10* in the variable *pc*:

```
pc=string10;
```

The **for** loop reads *ISIZE* characters and stores them in the array *string10*. The following statement uses the dereference operator * to ensure that the target, the left-hand side of this assignment (another example of an lvalue), will be the cell to which *pc* points, not *pc* (which itself contains just an address).

```
*pc=getchar();
```

The idea is to store a character in each cell of *string10*, not to store it in *pc*.

To start printing the array backward, the program first initializes the *pc* to the last element in the array:

```
pc = string10 + (ISIZE - 1);
```

By adding 9 (*ISIZE – 1*) to the initial address of *string10*, *pc* points to the *tenth* element. Remember, these are offsets. The first element in the array is at offset zero. Within the **for** loop, *pc* is decremented to move backward through the array elements. Make certain you use CodeView to trace through this example if you are unsure of how *pc* is modified.

Problems with the Operators ++ and – –

Just as a reminder, the following two statements do *not* perform the same cell reference:

```
*pc++ = getchar();
*++pc = getchar();
```

The first statement assigns the character returned by **getchar()** to the *current* cell pointed to by *pc* and then increments *pc*. The second statement increments the address in *pc* first and then assigns the character returned by the function to the cell pointed to by the updated address. Later in this chapter you will use these two different types of pointer assignments to reference the elements of *argv*.

Comparing Pointers

You have already seen examples demonstrating the effect of incrementing and decrementing pointers using the ++ and – – operators and the effect of adding an integer to a pointer. There are other operations that may be performed on pointers. These include

- Subtracting an integer from a pointer
- Subtracting two pointers (usually pointing to the same object)
- Comparing pointers using a relational operator such as <=, =, or >=

Since (pointer – integer) subtraction is so similar to (pointer + integer) addition (these have already been discussed by example), it should be no surprise that the resultant pointer value points to a storage location integer elements before the original pointer.

Subtracting two pointers yields a constant value that is the number of array elements between the two pointers. This assumes that both pointers are of the same type and initially point into the same array. Subtracting pointers that are not of the same type or that initially point to different arrays will yield unpredictable results.

 No matter which pointer arithmetic operation you choose, there is no check to see if the pointer value calculated is outside the defined boundaries of the array.

Pointers of like type (that is, pointers that reference the same kind of data, like **int** and **float**) can also be compared to each other. The resulting TRUE (!0) or FALSE (0) can either be tested or assigned to an integer, just like the result of any logical expression. Comparing two pointers tests whether they are equal, not equal, greater than, or less than each other. One pointer is less than another pointer if the first pointer refers to an array element with a lower number subscript. (Remember that pointers and subscripts are virtually identical.) This operation also assumes that the pointers reference the same array.

Finally, pointers can be compared to zero, the null value. In this case, only the test for equal or not equal is valid since testing for negative pointers makes no sense. The null value in a pointer means that the pointer has no value, or does not point to anything. Null, or zero, is the only numeric value that can be directly assigned into a pointer without a type cast.

It should be noted that pointer conversions are performed on pointer operands. This means that any pointer may be compared to a constant expression evaluating to zero and any pointer may be compared to a pointer of type **void** *. (In this last case, the pointer is first converted to **void** *.)

Pointer Portability

The examples in this section have represented addresses as integers. This may suggest to you that a C pointer is of type **int**. It is not. A pointer holds the address of a particular type of variable, but a pointer itself is not one of the primitive data types **int**, **float**, and the like. A particular C system may allow a pointer to be copied into an **int** variable and an **int** variable to be copied into a pointer; however, C does not guarantee that pointers can be stored in **int** variables. To guarantee code portability, the practice should be avoided.

Also, not all arithmetic operations on pointers are allowed. For example, it is illegal to add two pointers, to multiply two pointers, or to divide one pointer by another.

Using sizeof with Pointers

The actual size of a pointer variable depends on one of two things: the size of the memory model you have chosen for the application or the use of the nonportable, implementation-specific **near**, **far**, and **huge** keywords.

The 80486 to 8088 microprocessors use a *segmented addressing* scheme that breaks an address into two pieces, a segment and an offset. Many local post offices have several walls of post office boxes, with each box having its own unique number. Segment:offset addressing is similar to this design. To get to your post office box, you first need to know which bank of boxes, or wall, yours is on (the *segment*), and then the actual box number (the *offset*).

When you know that all of your application's code and data will fit within one single 64K of memory, you choose the small memory model. Applying this to the post-office box metaphor, this means that all of your code and data will be in the same location, or wall (segment), with the application's code and data having a unique box number (offset) on the wall.

For those applications where this compactness is not feasible, possibly because of the size and the amount of data that must be stored and referenced, you would choose a large memory model. Using the analogy, this could mean that all of your application's code would be located on one wall, while all the data would be on a completely separate wall.

When an application shares the same memory segment for code and data, calculating an object's memory location simply involves finding out the object's offset within the segment. This is a very simple calculation.

When an application has separate segments for code and data, calculating an object's location is a bit more complicated. First, the code or data's segment must be calculated and then its offset within the respective segment. Naturally, this requires more processor time.

C++ also allows you to override the default pointer size for a specific variable by using the keywords **near**, **far**, and **huge**. Note, however, that by including these in your application, you make your code less portable since the keywords produce different results on different compilers. The **near** keyword forces an offset-only pointer when the pointers would normally default to segment:offset. The **far** keyword forces a segment:offset pointer when the pointers would normally default to offset-only. The **huge** keyword also forces a segment:offset pointer that has been normalized. The **near** keyword is generally used to increase execution speed, while the **far** keyword forces a pointer to do the right thing regardless of the memory model chosen.

For many applications, you can simply ignore this problem and allow the compiler to choose a default memory model. But eventually you will run into problems with this approach—for example, when you try to address an absolute location (some piece of hardware, perhaps, or a special area in memory) outside your program's segment area.

On the other hand, you may be wondering why you can't just use the largest memory model available for your application. You can, but there is an efficiency price to pay. If all of your data is in one segment, the pointer is the size of the offset. However, if your data and code range all over memory, your pointer is the size of the segment *and* the offset, and both must be calculated every time you change the pointer. The following program uses the function **sizeof()** to print out the smallest pointer size and largest pointer size available.

This C++ program prints the default pointer sizes, their **far** sizes, and their **near** sizes. The program also uses the *stringize* preprocessor directive (#) with the *A_POINTER* argument, so the name as well as the size of the pointer will be printed.

```
//
//  10STRIZE.CPP
//  A C++ program illustrating the sizeof(pointers)
//  Copyright (c) William H. Murray and Chris H. Pappas, 1992
//

#include <stdio.h>

#define PRINT_SIZEOF(A_POINTER) \
  printf("sizeof\t("#A_POINTER")\t= %d\n", \
  sizeof(A_POINTER))

void main()
{
  char *reg_pc;
  long double *reg_pldbl;
  char far *far_pc;
  long double far *far_pldbl;
  char near *near_pc;
  long double near *near_pldbl;

  PRINT_SIZEOF(reg_pc);
  PRINT_SIZEOF(reg_pldbl);
  PRINT_SIZEOF(far_pc);
  PRINT_SIZEOF(far_pldbl);
  PRINT_SIZEOF(near_pc);
  PRINT_SIZEOF(near_pldbl);
}
```

The output from the program looks like this:

```
sizeof    (reg_pc)      = 2
sizeof    (reg_pldbl)   = 2
```

```
sizeof   (far_pc)      = 4
sizeof   (far_pldbl)   = 4
sizeof   (near_pc)     = 2
sizeof   (near_pldbl)  = 2
```

Pointers to Functions

All the examples so far have shown you how various items of data can be referenced by a pointer. As it turns out, you can also access *portions of code* by using a pointer to a function. Pointers to functions serve the same purpose as do pointers to data; that is, they allow the function to be referenced indirectly, just as a pointer to a data item allows the data item to be referenced indirectly.

A pointer to a function can have a number of important uses. For example, consider the **qsort()** function. The **qsort()** function has as one of its parameters a pointer to a function. The referenced function contains the necessary comparison that is to be performed between the array elements being sorted. The reason **qsort()** has been written to require a function pointer has to do with the fact that the comparison process between two elements can be a complex process beyond the scope of a single control flag. It is not possible to pass a function by value, that is, pass the code itself. C, however, does support passing a pointer to the code, or a pointer to the function.

Many C and C++ books illustrate the concept of function pointers by using the **qsort()** function supplied with the compiler. Unfortunately, these books usually declare the function pointer to be of a type that points to other built-in functions. The following C and C++ programs demonstrate how to define a pointer to a function and how to "roll your own" function to be passed to the stdlib.h function **qsort()**. Here is the C program:

```
/*
 *    10FNCPTR.C
 *    A C program illustrating how to declare your own
 *    function and function pointer to be used with qsort()
 *    Copyright (c) William H. Murray and Chris H. Pappas, 1992
 */

#include <stdio.h>
#include <stdlib.h>

#define IMAXVALUES 10

int icompare_funct(const void *iresult_a, const void *iresult_b);
int (*ifunct_ptr)(const void *, const void *);

void main()
```

```
{
  int i;
  int iarray[IMAXVALUES]={0,5,3,2,8,7,9,1,4,6};

  ifunct_ptr=icompare_funct;
  qsort(iarray,IMAXVALUES,sizeof(int),ifunct_ptr);
  for(i = 0; i < IMAXVALUES; i++)
    printf("%d ",iarray[i]);
}

int icompare_funct(const void *iresult_a, const void *iresult_b)
{
  return((*(int *)iresult_a) - (*(int *) iresult_b));
}
```

The function **icompare_funct()** (which will be called the reference function) was prototyped to match the requirements for the fourth parameter to the function **qsort()** (which will be called the invoking function).

To digress slightly, the fourth parameter to the function **qsort()** must be a function pointer. This reference function must be passed two **const void** * parameters and it must return a type **int**. This is because **qsort()** uses the reference function for the sort comparison algorithm. Now that you understand the prototype of the reference function **icompare_funct()**, take a minute to study the body of the reference function.

If the reference function returns a value < 0, then the reference function's first parameter value is less than the second parameter's value. A return value of zero indicates parameter value equality, with a return value > 0 indicating that the second parameter's value was greater than the first's. All of this is accomplished by the single statement in **icompare_funct()**:

```
return((*(int *)iresult_a) - (*(int *) iresult_b));
```

Since both of the pointers were passed as type **void** *, they were cast to their appropriate pointer type **int** *, and then they were dereferenced (*). The result of the subtraction of the two values pointed to returns an appropriate value to satisfy **qsort()**'s comparison criterion.

While the prototype requirements for **icompare_funct()** are interesting, the meat of the program begins with the pointer function declaration below the **icompare_funct()** function prototype:

```
int icompare_funct(const void *iresult_a, const void *iresult_b);
int (*ifunct_ptr)(const void *, const void *);
```

A function's type is determined by its return value and argument list signature. A pointer to **icompare_funct()** must specify the same signature and return type. You might therefore think the following statement would accomplish this:

```
int *ifunct_ptr(const void *, const void *);
```

That is almost correct. The problem is that the compiler interprets the statement as the definition of a function **ifunct_ptr()** taking two arguments and returning a pointer of type **int ***. The dereference operator unfortunately is associated with the type specifier, not **ifunct_ptr()**. Parentheses are necessary to associate the dereference operator with **ifunct_ptr()**.

The corrected statement declares **ifunct_ptr()** to be a pointer to a function taking two arguments and with a return type **int**—that is, a pointer of the same type required by the fourth parameter to **qsort()**.

In the body of **main()**, the only thing left to do is to initialize **ifunct_ptr()** to the address of the function **icompare_funct()**. The parameters to **qsort()** are the address to the base or zeroth element of the table to be sorted (*iarray*), the number of entries in the table (*IMAXVALUES*), the size of each table element (**sizeof(int)**), and a function pointer to the comparison function (**ifunct_ptr()**).

The C++ equivalent follows:

```
//
//  10QSORT.CPP
//  A C program illustrating how to declare your own
//  function and function pointer to be used with qsort()
//  Copyright (c) William H. Murray and Chris H. Pappas, 1992
//

#include <iostream.h>
#include <stdlib.h>

#define IMAXVALUES 10

int icompare_funct(const void *iresult_a, const void *iresult_b);
int (*ifunct_ptr)(const void *,const void *);

void main()
{
  int i;
  int iarray[IMAXVALUES]={0,5,3,2,8,7,9,1,4,6};
```

```
  ifunct_ptr=icompare_funct;
  qsort(iarray,IMAXVALUES,sizeof(int),ifunct_ptr);
  for(i = 0; i < IMAXVALUES; i++)
    cout <<[{|"|}]" << iarray[i];
}


int icompare_funct(const void *iresult_a, const void *iresult_b)
{
  return((*(int *)iresult_a) - (*(int *)iresult_b));
}
```

Learning to understand the syntax of a function pointer can be challenging. Let's look at just a few examples. Here is the first one:

```
int *(*(*ifunct_ptr)(int))[5];
float (*(*ffunct_ptr)(int,int))(float);
typedef double (*(*(*dfunct_ptr)())[5])();
  dfunct_ptr A_dfunct_ptr;
(*(*function_ary_ptrs())[5])();
```

The first statement defines **ifunct_ptr()** to be a function pointer to a function that is passed an integer argument and returns a pointer to an array of five **int** pointers.

The second statement defines **ffunct_ptr()** to be a function pointer to a function that takes two integer arguments and returns a pointer to a function taking a float argument and returning a float.

By using the **typedef** declaration, you can avoid the unnecessary repetition of complicated declarations. The **typedef** declaration (discussed in greater detail in Chapter 12) is read as follows: **dfunct_ptr()** is defined as a pointer to a function that is passed nothing and returns a pointer to an array of five pointers that point to functions that is passed nothing and returns a double.

The last statement is a function declaration, not a variable declaration. The statement defines **function_ary_ptrs()** to be a function taking no arguments and returning a pointer to an array of five pointers that point to functions taking no arguments and returning integers. The outer functions return the default C and C++ type **int**.

The good news is that you will rarely encounter complicated declarations and definitions like these. However, by making certain you understand these declarations, you will be able to confidently parse the everyday variety.

Dynamic Memory

When a C program is compiled, the computer's memory is broken down into four zones that contain the program's code, all global data, the stack, and the heap. The *heap* is an area of free memory (sometimes referred to as the *free store*) that is manipulated by using the dynamic allocation functions **malloc()** and **free()**.

When **malloc()** is invoked, it allocates a contiguous block of storage for the object specified and then returns a pointer to the start of the block. The function **free()** returns previously allocated memory to the heap, permitting that portion of memory to be reallocated.

The argument passed to **malloc()** is an integer that represents the number of bytes of storage that is needed. If the storage is available, **malloc()** will return a **void ***, which can be cast into whatever type pointer is desired. The concept of *void pointers* was introduced in the ANSI C standard and means a pointer of unknown type, or a generic pointer. A **void** pointer cannot itself be used to reference anything (since it doesn't point to any specific type of data), but it can contain a pointer of any other type. Therefore, any pointer can be converted into a **void** pointer and back without any loss of information.

The following code segment allocates enough storage for 300 float values:

```
float *pf;
int inum_floats = 300;

pf = (float *) malloc(inum_floats * sizeof(float));
```

The **malloc()** function has been instructed to obtain enough storage for 300 * the current size of a float. The cast operator (**float ***) is used to return a **float** pointer type. Each block of storage requested is entirely separate and distinct from all other blocks of storage. Absolutely no assumption can be made about where the blocks are located. Blocks are typically "tagged" with some sort of information that allows the operating system to manage the location and size of the block. When the block is no longer needed, it can be returned to the operating system by using the following statement:

```
free((void *) pf);
```

Just as in C, C++ allocates available memory in two ways. When variables are declared, they are created on the stack by pushing the stack pointer down. When these variables go out of scope (for instance, when a local variable is no longer needed), the space for that variable is freed automatically by moving the stack pointer up. The size of stack-allocated memory must always be known at compilation.

Your application may also have to use variables with an unknown size at compilation. Under these circumstances, you must allocate the memory yourself, on the free store. The free store can be thought of as occupying the bottom of the program's memory space and growing *upward,* while the stack occupies the top and grows *downward.*

Your C and C++ programs can allocate and release free store memory at any point. It is important to realize that free-store-allocated memory variables are not subject to scoping rules, as other variables are. These variables never go out of scope, so once you allocate memory on the heap, you are responsible for freeing it. If you continue to allocate free store space without freeing it, your program could eventually crash.

Most C compilers use the library functions **malloc()** and **free()**, just discussed, to provide dynamic memory allocation, but in C++ these capabilities were considered so important they were made a part of the core language. C++ uses **new** and **delete** to allocate and free free store memory. The argument to **new** is an expression that returns the number of bytes to be allocated; the value returned is a pointer to the beginning of this memory block. The argument to **delete** is the starting address of the memory block to be freed. The following two programs illustrate the similarities and differences between a C and C++ application using dynamic memory allocation. Here is the C example:

```
/*
 *   10MALLOC.C
 *   A simple C program using malloc(), free()
 *   Copyright (c) William H. Murray and Chris H. Pappas, 1992
 */

#include <stdio.h>
#include <stdlib.h>

#define ISIZE 512

void main()
{
  int * pimemory_buffer;
  pimemory_buffer=malloc(ISIZE * sizeof(int));
  if(pimemory_buffer == NULL)
    printf("Insufficient memory\n");
  else
    printf("Memory allocated\n");
  free(pimemory_buffer);
}
```

The first point of interest in the program begins with the second **#include** statement that brings in the stdlib.h header file, containing the definitions for both functions, **malloc()** and **free()**. After the program defines the **int *** pointer variable *pimemory_buffer,* the **malloc()** function is invoked to return the address to a memory block that is ISIZE * sizeof(int) big. A robust algorithm will always check for the success or failure of the memory allocation, and it explains the purpose behind the **if-else** statement. The function **malloc()** returns a null whenever not enough memory is available to allocate the block. This simple program ends by returning the allocated memory to the free store by using the function **free()** and passing it the beginning address of the allocated block.

The C++ program does not look significantly different:

```
//
//   10NEWDEL.CPP
//   A simple C++ program using new and delete
//   Copyright (c) William H. Murray and Chris H. Pappas, 1992
//

#include <iostream.h>
// #include <stdlib.h> not needed for malloc(), free()

#define NULL 0
#define ISIZE 512

void main()
{
  int *pimemory_buffer;

  pimemory_buffer=new int[ISIZE];
  if(pimemory_buffer == NULL)
    cout << "Insufficient memory\n";
  else
    cout << "Memory allocated\n";
  delete(pimemory_buffer);
}
```

The only major difference between the two programs is the syntax used with the function **free()** and the operator **new**. Whereas the function **free()** requires the **sizeof** operator to ensure proper memory allocation, the operator **new** has been written to automatically perform the **sizeof** function on the declared data type it is passed. Both programs will allocate 512 2-byte blocks of consecutive memory (on systems that allocate 2 bytes per integer).

Using void Pointers

Now that you have a detailed understanding of the nature of pointer variables, you can begin to appreciate the need for the pointer type **void**. To review, the concept of a pointer is that it is a variable that contains the address of another variable. If you always knew how big a pointer was, you wouldn't have to determine the pointer type at compile time. You would therefore also be able to pass an address of any type to a function. The function could then cast the address to a pointer of the proper type (based on some other piece of information) and perform operations on the result. This process would enable you to create functions that operate on a number of different data types.

That is precisely the reason C++ introduced the **void** pointer type. When **void** is applied to a pointer, its meaning is different from its use to describe function argument lists and return values (which mean "nothing"). A **void** pointer means a pointer to any type of data. The following C++ program demonstrates this use of **void** pointers:

```
//
//  10VOIDPT.CPP
//  A C++ program using void pointers
//  Copyright (c) William H. Murray and Chris H. Pappas, 1992
//

#include <iostream.h>
#define ISTRING_MAX 50

void voutput(void *pobject, char cflag);

void main()
{
  int *pi;
  char *psz;
  float *pf;
  char cresponse,cnewline;

  cout << "Please enter the dynamic data type\n";
  cout << "    you would like to create.\n\n";
  cout << "Use (s)tring, (i)nt, or (f)loat ";
  cin >> cresponse;
    cin.get(cnewline);
      switch(cresponse) {
        case 's':
          psz=new char[ISTRING_MAX];
          cout << "\nPlease enter a string: ";
          cin.get(psz,ISTRING_MAX);
          voutput(psz,cresponse);
          break;
        case 'i':
          pi=new int;
          cout << "\nPlease enter an integer: ";
```

```
        cin >> *pi;
        voutput(pi,cresponse);
        break;
      case 'f':
        pf=new float;
        cout << "\nPlease enter a float: ";
        cin >> *pf; voutput(pf,cresponse);
        break;
      default:
        cout << "\n\n  Object type not implemented!";
  }
}
void voutput(void *pobject, char cflag)
{
  switch(cflag) {
    case 's':
      cout << "\nThe string read in:  " << *((char *) pobject);
      delete pobject;
      break;
    case 'i':
      cout << "\nThe integer read in: "
           << *((int *) pobject);
      delete pobject;
      break;
    case 'f':
      cout << "\nThe float value read in: "
           << *((float *) pobject);
      delete pobject;
      break;
    }
}
```

The first statement of interest in the program is the **voutput( )** function prototype. Notice that the function's first formal parameter, *pobject*, is of type **void ***, or a generic pointer. Moving down to the data declarations, you will find three pointer variable types: **int ***, **char ***, and **float ***. These will eventually be assigned valid pointer addresses to their respective memory cell types.

The action in the program begins with a prompt asking the user to enter the data type he or she would like to dynamically create. You may be wondering why the two separate input statements are used to handle the user's response. The first **cin** statement reads in the single-character response but leaves the \n linefeed hanging around. The second input statement, **cin.get**(cnewline), remedies this situation.

The **switch** statement takes the user's response and invokes the appropriate prompt and pointer initialization. The pointer initialization takes one of three forms:

```
psz=new char;
pi=new int;
pf=new float;
```

The following statement is used to input the character string, and in this example it limits the length of the string to ISTRING_MAX (50) characters.

```
cin.get(psz,ISTRING_MAX);
```

Since the **cin.get()** input statement expects a string pointer as its first parameter, there is no need to dereference the variable when the **voutput()** function is invoked:

```
voutput(psz,cresponse);
```

Things get a little quieter if the user wants to input an integer or a float. The last two case options are the same except for the prompt and the reference variable's type.

Notice how the three invocations of the function **voutput()** have different pointer types:

```
voutput(psz,cresponse);
voutput(pi,cresponse);
voutput(pf,cresponse);
```

Function **voutput()** accepts these parameters only because the matching formal parameter's type is **void ***. Remember, to use these pointers, you must first cast them to their appropriate pointer type. When using a string pointer with **cout**, you must first cast the pointer to type **char ***.

Just as creating integer and float dynamic variables was similar, printing their values is also similar. The only difference between the last two **case** statements is the string and the cast operator used.

While it is true that all dynamic variables pass into bit oblivion whenever a program terminates, each of the case options takes care of explicitly deleting the pointer variable. When and where your program creates and deletes dynamic storage is application dependent.

Pointers and Arrays

The following sections include many example programs that deal with the topic of arrays and how they relate to pointers.

Strings (Arrays of Type char)

Many string operations in C are generally performed by using pointers and pointer arithmetic to reference character array elements. This is because character arrays or strings tend to be accessed in a strictly sequential manner. Remember, all strings in C are terminated by a null (\0). The following C++ program is a modification of a program used earlier in this chapter to print palindromes and illustrates the use of pointers with character arrays:

```
//
//  10CHRARY.CPP
//  A C++ program that prints a character array backwards
//  using a character pointer and the decrement operator
//  Copyright (c) William H. Murray and Chris H. Pappas, 1992
//

#include <iostream.h>
#include <string.h>

void main()
{
  char pszpalindrome[]="POOR DAN IN A DROOP";
  char *pc;
  int icount;

  pc=pszpalindrome+(strlen(pszpalindrome)-1);
  do {
    cout << *pc ;
    pc--;
  } while (pc >= pszpalindrome);
}
```

After the program declares and initializes the *pszpalindrome* palindrome, it creates a *pc* of type **char ***. Remember that the name of an array is in itself an address variable. The body of the program begins by setting the *pc* to the address of the last character in the array. This requires a call to the function **strlen()**, which calculates the length of the character array.

*The **strlen()** function counts just the number of characters. It does not include in the count the null terminator \0.*

You were probably thinking that was the reason for subtracting the 1 from the function's returned value. This is not exactly true; the program has to take into consideration the fact that the first array character's address is at offset zero.

Therefore, you want to increment the pointer variable's offset address to one less than the number of valid characters.

Once the pointer for the last valid array character has been calculated, the **do-while** loop is entered. The loop simply uses the pointer variable to point to the memory location of the character to be printed and prints it. It next calculates the next character's memory location and compares this value with the starting address of *pszpalindrome*. As long as the calculated value is >=, the loop iterates.

Arrays of Pointers

In C and C++, you are not restricted to making simple arrays and simple pointers. You can combine the two into a very useful construct—arrays of pointers. An *array of pointers* is an array whose elements are pointers to other objects. Those objects can themselves be pointers. This means you can have an array of pointers that point to other pointers.

The concept of an array of pointers to pointers is used extensively in the *argc* and *argv* command-line arguments for **main()** you were introduced to in Chapter 8. The following program finds the largest or smallest value entered on the command line. Command-line arguments can include numbers only, or they may be prefaced by a command selecting a choice for the smallest value entered (-s,-S), or the largest value entered (-l,-L).

```
//
//   10ARGCGV.CPP
//   A C++ program using an array of pointers to process
//   the command-line arguments argc, argv
//   Copyright (c) William H. Murray and Chris H. Pappas, 1992
//

#include <iostream.h>
#include <process.h>      // exit()
#include <stdlib.h>       // atoi()

#define IFIND_LARGEST 1
#define IFIND_SMALLEST 0

int main(int argc,char *argv[])
{
  char *psz;
  int ihow_many;
  int iwhich_extreme=0;
  int irange_boundary=32767;

  if(argc < 2) {
```

```
      cout << "\nYou need to enter an -S,-s,-L,-l"
        " and at least one integer value";
      exit(1);
    }

  while(--argc > 0 && (*++argv)[0] == '-') {
    for(psz=argv[0]+1; *psz != '\0'; psz++) {
      switch(*psz) {
        case 's':
        case 'S':
          iwhich_extreme=IFIND_SMALLEST;
          irange_boundary=32767;
          break;
        case 'l':
        case 'L':
          iwhich_extreme=IFIND_LARGEST;
          irange_boundary=0;
          break;
        default:
          cout << "unknown argument "<< *psz << endl;
          exit(1);
      }
    }
  }

  if(argc==0) {
    cout << "Please enter at least one number\n";
    exit(1);
  }

  ihow_many=argc;

  while(argc--) {
    int present_value;
    present_value=atoi(*(argv++));
    if(iwhich_extreme==IFIND_LARGEST && present_value >
       irange_boundary)
      irange_boundary=present_value;
    if(iwhich_extreme==IFIND_SMALLEST && present_value <
       irange_boundary)
      irange_boundary=present_value;
  }

  cout << "The ";
  cout << ((iwhich_extreme) ? "largest" : "smallest");
```

```
cout << " of the " << ihow_many << " value(s) input is " <<
        irange_boundary << endl;

return(0);
}
```

Before looking at the source code, take a moment to familiarize yourself with the possible command combinations that can be used to invoke the program. The following list illustrates the possible command combinations:

```
10argcgv
10argcgv 98
10argcgv 98 21
10argcgv -s 98
10argcgv -S 98 21
10argcgv -l 14
10argcgv -L 14 67
```

Looking at the **main()** program, you will see the formal parameters *argc* and *argv* that you were introduced to in Chapter 8. To review, *argc* is an integer value containing the number of separate items, or arguments, that appeared on the command line. The variable *argv* refers to an array of pointers to character strings.

 argv *is not a constant. It is a variable whose value can be altered, a key point to remember when viewing how* argv *is used below. The first element of the array,* argv[0], *is a pointer to a string of characters that contains the program name.*

Moving down the code to the first **if** statement, you find a test to determine if the value of *argc* is less than 2. If this test evaluates to TRUE, it means that the user has typed just the name of the program *extremes* without any switches. Since this action would indicate that the user does not know the switch and value options, the program will prompt the user at this point with the valid options and then **exit()**.

The **while** loop test condition evaluates from left to right, beginning with the decrement of *argc*. If *argc* is still greater than zero, the right side of the logical expression will be examined.

The right side of the logical expression first increments the array pointer *argv* past the first pointer entry (++argv), skipping the program's name, so that it now points to the second array entry. Once the pointer has been incremented, it is then used to point (*++argv) to the zeroth offset ((*++argv)[0]) of the first character of the string pointed to. Obtaining this character, if it is a – symbol, the program diagnoses that the second program command was a possible switch—for example, –s or –L.

The **for** loop initialization begins by taking the current pointer address of *argv*, which was just incremented in the line above to point to the second pointer in the array. Since *argv*'s second element is a pointer to a character string, the pointer can be subscripted (argv[0]). The complete expression, argv[0]+1, points to the second character of the second string pointed to by the current address stored in *argv*. This second character is the one past the command switch symbol –. Once the program calculates this character's address, it stores it in the variable *psz*. The **for** loop repeats while the character pointed to by **psz* is not the null terminator \0.

The program continues by analyzing the switch to see if the user wants to obtain the smallest or largest of the values entered. Based on the switch, the appropriate constant is assigned to the *iwhich_extreme*. Each **case** statement also takes care of initializing the variable *irange_boundary* to an appropriate value for the comparisons that follow. Should the user enter an unrecognized switch, for example, –d, the **default** case will take care of printing an appropriate message.

The second **if** statement now checks to see if *argc* has been decremented to zero. An appropriate message is printed if the switches have been examined on the command line and there are no values left to process. If so, the program terminates with an exit code of decimal 1.

A successful skipping of this **if** test means there are now values from the command line that need to be examined. Since the program will now decrement *argc*, the variable *ihow_many* is assigned *argc*'s current value.

The **while** loop continues while there are at least two values to compare. The **while** loop needs to be entered only if there is more than one value to be compared since the **cout** statement following the **while** loop is capable of handling a command line with a single value.

The function **atoi()** converts each of the remaining arguments into an integer and stores the result in the variable *present_value*. Remember, *argv++* needed to be incremented first so that it points to the first value to be compared. Also, the **while** loop test condition had already decremented the pointer to make certain the loop wasn't entered with only a single command value.

The last two **if** statements take care of updating the variable *irange_boundary* based on the user's desire to find either the smallest or largest of all values entered. Finally, the results of the program are printed by using an interesting combination of string literals and the conditional operator.

More on Pointers to Pointers

The next program demonstrates the use of pointer variables that point to other pointers. It is included at this point in the chapter instead of in the section describing pointers to pointers because the program uses dynamic memory allocation. You may want to refer back to the general discussion of pointers to pointers before looking at the program.

```
/*
 *    10DBLPTR.C
 *    A C program using pointer variables with double indirection
 *    Copyright (c) William H. Murray and Chris H. Pappas, 1992
```

```
*/

#include <stdio.h>

#define IMAXELEMENTS 3

void voutput(int **ppiresult_a, int **ppiresult_b,
             int **ppiresult_c);
void vassign(int *pivirtual_array[],int *pinewblock);

void main()
{
  int **ppiresult_a, **ppiresult_b, **ppiresult_c;
  int *pivirtual_array[IMAXELEMENTS];
  int *pinewblock, *pioldblock;

  ppiresult_a=&pivirtual_array[0];
  ppiresult_b=&pivirtual_array[1];
  ppiresult_c=&pivirtual_array[2];

  pinewblock=(int *)malloc(IMAXELEMENTS * sizeof(int));
  pioldblock=pinewblock;

  vassign(pivirtual_array,pinewblock);

  **ppiresult_a=1;
  **ppiresult_b=2;
  **ppiresult_c=3;

  voutput(ppiresult_a,ppiresult_b,ppiresult_c);

  pinewblock=(int *)malloc(IMAXELEMENTS * sizeof(int));

  *pinewblock=**ppiresult_a;
  *(pinewblock+1)=**ppiresult_b;
  *(pinewblock+2)=**ppiresult_c;

  free(pioldblock);

  vassign(pivirtual_array,pinewblock);

  voutput(ppiresult_a,ppiresult_b,ppiresult_c);
}

void vassign(int *pivirtual_array[],int *pinewblock)
```

```
{
  pivirtual_array[0]=pinewblock;
  pivirtual_array[1]=pinewblock+1;
  pivirtual_array[2]=pinewblock+2;
}

void voutput(int **ppiresult_a, int **ppiresult_b, int
**ppiresult_c)
{
  printf("%d\n",**ppiresult_a);
  printf("%d\n",**ppiresult_b);
  printf("%d\n",**ppiresult_c);
}
```

The program is designed so that it highlights the concept of a pointer variable (*ppiresult_a, ppiresult_b,* and *ppiresult_c*), pointing to a constant address (*&pivirtual_array[0], &pivirtual_array[1],* and *&pivirtual_array[2]*), whose pointer address contents can dynamically change.

Look at the data declarations in **main( )**. *ppiresult_a, ppiresult_b,* and *ppiresult_c* have been defined as pointers to pointers that point to integers. Let's take this slowly, looking at the various syntax combinations:

```
ppiresult_a
*ppiresult_a
**ppiresult_a
```

The first syntax references the address stored in the pointer variable *ppiresult_a*. The second syntax references the pointer address pointed to by the address in *ppiresult_a*. The last syntax references the integer that is pointed to by the pointer address pointed to by *ppiresult_a*. Make certain you do not proceed any further until you understand these three different references.

The three variables *ppiresult_a, ppiresult_b,* and *ppiresult_c* have all been defined as pointers to pointers that point to integers **int ****. The variable *pivirtual_array* has been defined to be an array of integer pointers **int ***, of size IMAXELEMENTS. The last two variables, *pinewblock* and *pioldblock,* are similar to the variable *pivitrual_array,* except they are single variables that point to integers **int ***. Figure 10-17 shows what these seven variables look like after their storage has been allocated and, in particular, after *ppiresult_a, ppiresult_b,* and *ppiresult_c* have been assigned the address of their respective elements in the *pivirtual_array.*

It is this array that is going to hold the addresses of the dynamically changing memory cell addresses. Something similar actually happens in a true multitasking environment. Your program thinks it has the actual physical address of a variable stored in memory, when really what it has is a fixed address to an array of pointers that in turn point to the current physical address of the data item in memory. When

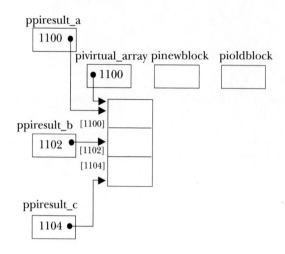

Figure 10-17.   *The variables after ppiresult_a, ppiresult_b, and ppiresult_c get their initial addresses*

the multitasking environment needs to conserve memory by moving your data objects, it simply moves their storage locations and updates the array of pointers. The variables in your program, however, are still pointing to the same physical address, albeit not the physical address of the data but of the array of pointers.

To understand how this operates, pay particular attention to the fact that the physical addresses stored in the pointer variables *ppiresult_a, ppiresult_b,* and *ppiresult_c* never change once they are assigned.

Figure 10-18 illustrates what has happened to the variables after the dynamic array *pinewblock* has been allocated and *pioldblock* has been initialized to the same address of the new array. Most important, notice how the physical addresses of *pinewblock*'s individual elements have been assigned to their respective counterparts in *pivirtual_array.*

The pointer assignments were all accomplished by the **vassign()** function. **vassign()** was passed the *pivirtual_array* (call-by-value) and the address of the recently allocated dynamic memory block in the variable *pinewblock*. The function takes care of assigning the addresses of the dynamically allocated memory cells to each element of the *pivirtual_array.* Since the array was passed call-by-value, the changes are effective in the **main()**.

At this point, if you were to use the debugger to print out *ppiresult_a,* you would see ACC8 (the address of *pivirtual_array*'s first element), and **ppiresult_a* would print

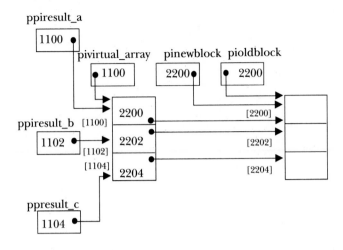

Figure 10-18. *Dynamically creating the block of memory*

1630 (or the contents of the address pointed to). You would encounter a similar dump for the other two pointer variables, *ppiresult_b* and *ppiresult_c.*

Figure 10-19 shows the assignment of three integer values to the physical memory locations. Notice the syntax to accomplish this:

```
**ppiresult_a=7;
**ppiresult_b=10;
**ppiresult_c=15;
```

At this point, the program prints out the values 7, 10, and 15 by calling the function **voutput()**. Notice that the function has been defined as receiving three **int **** variables. Notice that the actual parameter list does *not* need to precede the variables with the double indirection operator ** since that is their type by declaration.

As shown in Figure 10-20, the situation has become very interesting. A new block of dynamic memory has been allocated with the **malloc()** function, with its new physical memory address stored in the pointer variable *pinewblock. pioldblock* still points to the previously allocated block of dynamic memory. Using the incomplete analogy to a multitasking environment, the figure would illustrate the operating system's desire to physically move the data objects' memory locations.

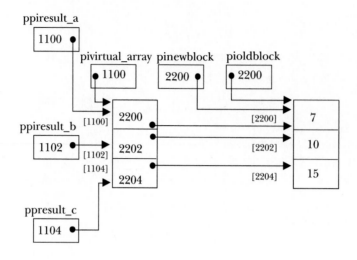

Figure 10-19.   *Filling the memory block with data*

Figure 10-20 also shows that the data objects themselves were copied into the new memory locations. The program accomplished this with the following three lines of code:

```
*pinewblock=**ppiresult_a;
*(pinewblock+1)=**ppiresult_b;
*(pinewblock+2)=**ppiresult_c;
```

Since the pointer variable *pinewblock* holds the address to the first element of the dynamic block, its address is dereferenced (*), pointing to the memory cell itself, and the 7 is stored there. Using a little pointer arithmetic, the other two memory cells are accessed by incrementing the pointer. The parentheses were necessary so that the pointer address was incremented *before* the dereference operator * was applied.

Figure 10-21 shows what happens when the function **free()** is called and the function **vassign()** is called to link the new physical address of the dynamically allocated memory block to the *pivirtual_array* pointer address elements.

The most important fact to notice in this last figure is that the actual physical address of the three pointer variables *ppiresult_a, ppiresult_b,* and *ppiresult_c* has not changed. Therefore, when the program prints the values pointed to **ppiresult_a* and so on, you still see the values 7, 10, and 15, even though their *physical* location in memory has changed.

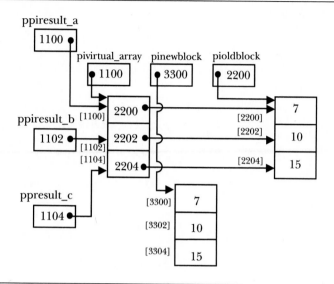

Figure 10-20.   *Dynamically allocating and filling the second block of memory*

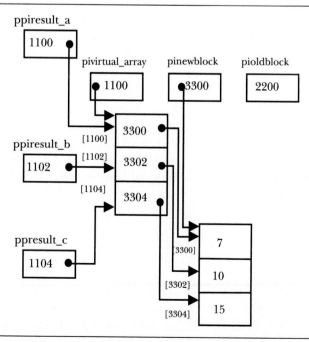

Figure 10-21.   *What happens after updating pivirtual_array with the new physical addresses*

Arrays of String Pointers

One of the easiest ways to keep track of an array of strings is to define an array of pointers to strings. This is much simpler than defining a two-dimensional array of characters. The following program uses an array of string pointers to keep track of three function error messages:

```
/*
 *    10AOFPTR.C
 *    A C program that demonstrates how to define and use
 *    arrays of pointers.
 *    Copyright William H. Murray and Chris H. Pappas, 1992
 */

#include <ctype.h>
#include <stdio.h>

#define INUMBER_OF_ERRORS 3

char *pszarray[INUMBER_OF_ERRORS] =
        {
          "\nFile not available.\n",
          "\nNot an alpha character.\n",
          "\nValue not between 1 and 10.\n"
        };

FILE *fopen_a_file(char *psz);
char cget_a_char(void);
int iget_an_integer(void);

FILE *pfa_file;

void main()
{
  char cvalue;
  int ivalue;

  fopen_a_file("input.dat");
  cvalue = cget_a_char();
  ivalue = iget_an_integer();

}
```

```
FILE *fopen_a_file(char *psz)
{
  const ifopen_a_file_error = 0;

  pfa_file = fopen("psz","r");
  if(!pfa_file)
    printf("%s",pszarray[ifopen_a_file_error]);
  return(pfa_file);
}

char cget_a_char(void)
{
  char cvalue;
  const icget_a_char_error = 1;

  printf("\nEnter a character: ");
  scanf("%c",&cvalue);
  if(!isalpha(cvalue))
    printf("%s",pszarray[icget_a_char_error]);
  return(cvalue);
}

int iget_an_integer(void)
{
  int ivalue;
  const iiget_an_integer = 2;
  printf("\nEnter an integer between 1 and 10: ");
  scanf("%d",&ivalue);
  if( (ivalue < 1) || (ivalue > 10) )
    printf("%s",pszarray[iiget_an_integer]);
  return(ivalue);
}
```

The *pszarray* is initialized outside all function declarations. This gives it a global lifetime. For large programs, an array of this nature could be saved in a separate source file dedicated to maintaining all error message control. Notice that each function, **fopen_a_file()**, **cget_a_char()**, and **iget_an_integer()**, takes care of defining its own constant index into the array. This combination of an error message array and unique function index makes for a very modular solution to error exception handling. If a project requires the creation of a new function, the new piece of code selects a vacant index value and adds one error condition to *pszarray*. The efficiency of this approach allows each code segment to quickly update the entire application to its peculiar I/O requirements without having to worry about an elaborate error detection/alert mechanism.

The C++ Reference Type

C++ provides a form of call-by-reference that is even easier to use than pointers. First, let's examine the use of reference variables in C++. As with C, C++ enables you to declare regular variables or pointer variables. In the first case, memory is actually allocated for the data object; in the second case, a memory location is set aside to hold an address for an object that will be allocated at another time. C++ has a third kind of declaration, the reference type. Like a pointer variable, a *reference variable* refers to another variable location, but like a regular variable, it requires no special dereferencing operators. The syntax for a reference variable is straightforward:

```
int iresult_a=5;
int& riresult_a=iresult_a; // valid
int& riresult_b;           // invalid: uninitialized
```

This example sets up the reference variable *riresult_a* and assigns it to the existing variable *iresult_a*. At this point, the referenced location has two names associated with it—*iresult_a* and *riresult_a*. Because both variables point to the same location in memory, they are, in fact, the same variable. Any assignment made to *riresult_a* is reflected through *iresult_a;* the inverse is also true, and changes to *iresult_a* occur through any access to *riresult_a*. Therefore, with the reference data type, you can create what is sometimes referred to as an *alias* for a variable.

The reference type has a restriction that serves to distinguish it from pointer variables, which, after all, do something very similar. The value of the reference type must be set at declaration, and it cannot be changed during the run of the program. After you initialize this type in the declaration, it always refers to the same memory location. Therefore, any assignments you make to a reference variable change only the data in memory, not the address of the variable itself. In other words, you can think of a reference variable as a pointer to a constant location.

For example, using the preceding declarations, the following statement doubles the contents of *iresult_a* by multiplying 5 * 2:

```
riresult_a *= 2;
```

The next statement assigns *icopy_value* (assuming it is of type **int**) a copy of the value associated with *riresult_a:*

```
icopy_value = riresult_a;
```

The next statement is also legal when using reference types:

```
int *piresult_a = &riresult_a;
```

This statement assigns the address of *riresult_a* to the **int *** variable *piresult_a*.

The primary use of a reference type is as an argument or a return type of a function, especially when applied to user-defined class types (see Chapter 15).

Functions Returning Addresses

When you return an address from a function using either a pointer variable or a reference type, you are giving the user a memory address. The user can read the value at the address, and if you haven't declared the pointer type to be **const**, the user can always write the value. By returning an address, you are giving the user permission to read and, for non-**const** pointer types, write to private data. This is a significant design decision. See if you can anticipate what will happen in this next program:

```
//
//  10REFVAR.CPP
//  A C++ program showing what NOT to do with address variables
//  Copyright (c) William H. Murray and Chris H. Pappas, 1992
//

#include <iostream.h>

int *ifirst_function(void);
int *isecond_function(void);

void main()
{
  int *pi=ifirst_function();
  isecond_function();
  cout << "Correct value? " << *pi;
}

int *ifirst_function(void)
{
  int ilocal_to_first=11;
  return &ilocal_to_first;
}
```

```
int *isecond_function(void)
{
  int ilocal_to_second=44;
  return &ilocal_to_second;
}
```

Using CodeView

To examine the operation of this C++ code under actual operation, you can use the CodeView debugger. Use the Trace window to keep an eye on the variable *pi*.

What has happened? When the **ifirst_function()** is called, local space is allocated on the stack for the variable *ilocal_to_first,* and the value 11 is stored in it. At this point the **ifirst_function()** returns the address of this *local* variable (very bad news). The second statement in the main program invokes the **isecond_function()**. **isecond_function()** in turn allocates local space for *ilocal_to_second* and assigns it a value of 44. So how does the **printf** statement print a value of 44 when it was passed the address of *ilocal_to_first* when **ifirst_function()** was invoked?

Actually, what happened was this. When the address of the *itemporary* local variable *ilocal_to_first* was assigned to *pi* by **ifirst_function()**, the address to the *itemporary* location was retained even after *ilocal_to_first* went out of scope. When **isecond_function()** was invoked, it also needed local storage. Since *ilocal_to_first* was gone, *ilocal_to_second* was given the same storage location as its predecessor. With *pi* hanging onto this same busy memory cell, you can see why printing the value it now points to yields a 44. Extreme care must be taken not to return the addresses of local variables.

When Should You Use Reference Types?

To review, there are four main reasons for using C++ reference types:

- Reference types lend themselves to more readable code by allowing you to ignore details of how a parameter is passed.

- Reference types put the responsibility for argument passing on the programmer who writes the functions, not on the individual who uses them.

- Reference types are a necessary counterpart to operator overloading.

- Reference types are also used with passing classes to functions so constructors and destructors are not called.

These concepts are described in greater detail in Chapter 15.

Chapter 11

Complete I/O in C

Many commonly used high-level languages have restrictive input and output mechanisms. As a result, programmers generate convoluted algorithms to perform sophisticated data retrieval and display. This is not the case with C, which has a very complete I/O function library, although historically I/O was not even part of the C language itself. However, if you have used only simple I/O statements like Pascal's **readln** and **writeln** statements, you're in for a surprise. This chapter discusses the more than 20 different ways to perform I/O in C.

The standard C library I/O routines allow you to read and write data to files and devices. However, the C language itself does not include any predefined file structures. C treats all data as a sequence of bytes. There are three basic types of I/O functions: stream, console and port, and low-level.

All of the stream I/O functions treat a data file or data items as a stream of individual characters. By selecting the appropriate stream function, your application can process data in any size or format required, from single characters to large, complicated data structures.

Technically, when a program opens a file for I/O using the stream functions, the opened file is associated with a structure of type **FILE** (predefined in stdio.h) that contains basic information about the file. Once the stream is opened, a pointer to the file structure is returned. The file pointer, sometimes called the *stream pointer* or the *stream,* is used to refer to the file for all subsequent I/O.

All stream I/O functions provide buffered, formatted, or unformatted input and output. A *buffered stream* provides an intermediate storage location for all information that is input from the stream and output that is being sent to the stream.

Since disk I/O is such a time-consuming operation, stream buffering streamlines the application. Instead of inputting stream data one character at a time or one structure's worth at a time, stream I/O functions access data a block at a time. As the application needs to process the input, it merely accesses the buffer, a much less time-consuming process. When the buffer is empty, another disk block access is made.

The reverse situation holds true for *stream output*. Instead of all data being physically output at the time the output statement is executed, all output data is put into the buffer. When the buffer is full, the data is written to the disk.

Most high-level languages have a problem with buffered I/O that you need to take into consideration. For example, if your program has executed several output statements that do not fill the output buffer, causing it to dump to the disk, that information is lost when your program terminates.

The solution usually involves making a call to an appropriate function to flush the buffer. Unlike other high-level languages, C solves this problem with buffered I/O by automatically flushing the buffer's contents whenever the program terminates. Of course, a well-written application should not rely on these automatic features but should always explicitly detail every action the program is to take. One additional note: when you use stream I/O, if the application terminates abnormally, the output buffers may not be flushed, resulting in loss of data.

Similar in function are the *console and port I/O routines,* which can be seen as an extension of the stream routines. They allow you to read or write to a terminal (console) or an input/output port (such as a printer port). The port I/O functions simply read and write data in bytes. Console I/O functions provide several additional options. For example, you can detect whether a character has been typed at the console and whether or not the characters entered are echoed to the screen as they are read.

The last type of input and output is called *low-level I/O*. None of the low-level I/O functions perform any buffering and formatting; instead, they invoke the operating system's input and output capabilities directly. These routines let you access files and peripheral devices at a more basic level than the stream functions. Files opened in this mode return a *file handle*. This handle is an integer value that is used to refer to the file in subsequent operations.

In general, it is very bad practice to mix stream I/O functions with low-level routines. Since stream functions are buffered and low-level functions are not, attempting to access the same file or device by two different methods leads to confusion and eventual loss of data in the buffers. Therefore, either stream or low-level functions should be used exclusively on a given file. Table 11-1 lists the most commonly used C stream I/O functions.

Stream Functions

To use the stream functions, your application must include the file stdio.h. This file contains definitions for constants, types, and structures used in the stream functions and contains function prototypes and macro definitions for the stream routines.

Function	Definition
clearerr()	Clears the error indicator for a stream and resets the end-of-file indicator to zero
fclose()	Closes a stream
fcloseall()	Closes all open streams
fdopen()	Opens a stream using its handle obtained from **creat, dup, dup2,** or **open**
feof()	Tests for end-of-file on a stream
ferror()	Tests the stream for a read or write error
fflush()	Flushes a stream
fgetc()	This function reads a character from a stream
fgetchar()	This function reads a character from **stdin**
fgetpos()	Gets the current file pointer
fgets()	Gets a string from a stream
filelength()	Gets the stream size in bytes
fileno()	Gets the file handle associated with a stream
flushall()	Flushes all stream buffers
fopen()	Opens a stream
fprintf()	Writes formatted output to a stream
fputc()	The function writes a character to a stream
fputchar()	The function writes a character to **stdout**
fputs()	Outputs a string to a stream
fread()	Reads unformatted data from a stream
freopen()	Reassigns a file pointer
fscanf()	Reads formatted data from a stream
fseek()	Repositions a file pointer to a given location
fsetpos()	Positions the file pointer of a stream
fstat()	Gets open file information
ftell()	Returns the current file pointer position
fwrite()	Writes unformatted data items to a stream
getc()	This macro reads a character from a stream
getchar()	This macro reads a character from **stdin**

Table 11-1.   *C Stream Input and Output Functions*

Function	Definition
gets()	Gets a string from **stdin**
getw()	Reads an integer item from the stream
perror()	Prints a system error to **stderr**
printf()	Writes formatted output to **stdout**
putc()	This macro writes a character to a stream
putchar()	This macro writes a character to **stdout**
puts()	Writes a string to **stdout**
putw()	Writes an integer to a stream
remove()	Removes a file
rename()	Renames a file
rewind()	Repositions the file pointer to the beginning of a stream
scanf()	Scans and inputs formatted data from **stdin**
setbuf()	Overrides automatic buffering, allowing the application to define its own stream buffer
setvbuf()	Same as **setbuf()**, but also allows the size of the buffer to be defined
sprintf()	Writes formatted data to a string
sscanf()	Scans and inputs formatted data from a string
tmpnam()	Generates a unique temporary filename in a given directory
ungetch()	Pushes a character back to the keyboard buffer
vfprintf()	Writes formatted output to a stream using a pointer to the format string
vfscanf()	Scans and formats input from a stream using a pointer to the format string
vprintf()	Writes formatted output to **stdout** using a pointer to the format string
vscanf()	Scans and formats input from **stdin** using a pointer to the format string
vsprintf()	Writes formatted output to a string using a pointer to the format string
vsscanf()	Scans and formats input from a stream using a pointer to the format string

Table 11-1.   *C Stream Input and Output Functions* (continued)

Many of the constants predefined in stdio.h can be useful in your application. For example, *EOF* is defined to be the value returned by input functions at end-of-file, and *NULL* is the null pointer. Also, *FILE* defines the structure used to maintain information about a stream, and *BUFSIZ* defines the default size, in bytes, of the stream buffers.

Opening Streams

You can use one of three functions to open a stream before input and output can be performed on the stream: **fopen()**, **fdopen()**, or **freopen()**. The file mode and form are set at the time the stream is opened. The stream file can be opened for reading, writing, or both and can be opened in either text or binary mode.

All three functions return a file pointer, which is used to refer to the stream. For example, if your program contains the following line, you can use the file pointer variable *pfinfile* to refer to the stream:

```
pfinfile = fopen("input.dat","r");
```

(In Chapter 5, Table 5-4 lists the possible file modes.)

When your application begins execution, five streams are automatically opened. These streams are the standard input (**stdin**), standard output (**stdout**), standard error (**stderr**), standard printer (**stdprn**), and standard auxiliary (**stdaux**).

By default, the standard input, standard output, and standard error refer to the user's console. This means that whenever a program expects input from the standard input, it receives that input from the console. Likewise, a program that writes to the standard output prints its data to the console. Any error messages that are generated by the library routines are sent to the standard error stream, meaning that error messages appear on the user's console. The standard auxiliary and standard print streams usually refer to an auxiliary port and a printer, respectively.

You can use the five file pointers in any function that requires a stream pointer as an argument. Some functions, such as **getchar()** and **putchar()**, are designed to use **stdin** or **stdout** automatically. Since the pointers **stdin**, **stdout**, **stderr**, **stdprn**, and **stdaux** are constants, not variables, do not try to reassign them to a new stream pointer value.

Input and Output Redirection

Modern operating systems consider the keyboard and video display as files. This is reasonable since the system can read from the keyboard just as it can read from a disk or tape file. Similarly, the system can write to the video display just as it can write to a disk or tape file.

Suppose your application reads from the keyboard and outputs to the video display. Now suppose you want the input to come from a file called SAMPLE.DAT. You can use the same application if you tell the system to replace input from the keyboard, considered now as a file, with input from another file, namely the file SAMPLE.DAT. The process of changing the standard input or standard output is called *input redirection* or *output redirection.*

Input and output redirection in MS-DOS are effortless. You use < to redirect the input and > to redirect the output. Suppose the executable version of your application is called REDIRECT. The following system-level command will run the program REDIRECT and use the file SAMPLE.DAT as input instead of the keyboard:

```
redirect < sample.dat
```

The next statement will redirect both the input (SAMPLE.DAT) and the output (SAMPLE.BAK):

```
redirect < sample.dat > sample.bak
```

This last example will redirect the output (SAMPLE.BAK) only:

```
redirect > sample.bak
```

Note, however, that the standard error file STDERR cannot be redirected.

There are two techniques for managing the association between a standard filename and a physical file or device: redirection and piping. *Piping* is the technique of directly connecting the standard output of one program to the standard input of another. The control and invocation of redirection and piping normally occur outside the program, which is exactly the intent since the program itself need not care where the data is really coming from or going to.

The way to connect the standard output from one program to the standard input of another program is to pipe them together by using the vertical bar symbol, |. Therefore, to connect the standard output of the program PROCESS1 to the standard input of the program PROCESS2, you would type

```
process1 | process2
```

The operating system handles all the details of physically getting the output from PROCESS1 to the input of PROCESS2.

Altering the Stream Buffer

All files opened using the stream functions (**stdin()**, **stdout()**, and **stdprn()**) are buffered by default except for the preopened streams **stderr** and **stdaux**. The two streams **stderr** and **stdaux** are unbuffered by default unless they are used in either the **printf()** or **scanf()** family of functions. In this case, they are assigned a temporary buffer. You can buffer **stderr** and **stdaux** with **setbuf()** or **setvbuf()**. The **stdin**, **stdout**, and **stdprn** streams are flushed automatically whenever they are full.

You can use the two functions **setbuf()** and **setvbuf()** to make a buffered stream unbuffered, or you can use them to associate a buffer with an unbuffered stream. Note that buffers allocated by the system are not accessible to the user, but buffers allocated with the functions **setbuf()** and **setvbuf()** are named by the user and can be manipulated as if they were variables. These user-defined stream buffers are very useful for checking input and output before any system-generated error conditions.

You can define a buffer to be of any size; if you use the function **setbuf()**, the size is set by the constant *BUFSIZ* defined in stdio.h. The syntax for **setbuf()** looks like this:

    void setbuf(FILE *stream*, char *buffer*);

The following example program uses setbuf() and BUFSIZ to define and attach a buffer to **stderr**. A buffered **stderr** gives an application greater control over error-exception handling. Using CodeView, single-step the application exactly as you see it.

```
/*
 *    11SETBF.C
 *    A C program demonstrating how to define and attach
 *    a buffer to the unbuffered stderr.
 *    Copyright (c) William H. Murray and Chris H. Pappas, 1992
 */

#include <stdio.h>
char cmyoutputbuffer[BUFSIZ];

void main(void)
{
   /* associate a buffer with the unbuffered output stream */
   setbuf(stderr, cmyoutputbuffer); /* line to comment out */

   /* insert into the output stream buffer */
   fputs("Sample output inserted into the\n",stderr);
   fputs("output stream buffer.\n",stderr);

   /* dump the output stream buffer */
   fflush(stderr);
}
```

Try running the program a second time with the **setbuf()** statement commented out. This will prevent the program from associating a buffer with **stderr**. When you ran the program, did you see the difference? Without a buffered **stderr**, CodeView outputs each **fputs()** statement as soon as the line is executed.

The next application uses the function **setvbuf()**. The syntax for **setvbuf()** looks like this:

int setvbuf(FILE *stream,* char *buffer,* int *buftype,* size_t *bufsize);*

Here, the program determines the size of the buffer instead of using *BUFSIZ* defined in stdio.h:

```
/*
 *    11SETVBUF.C
 *    A C program demonstrating how to use setvbuf()
 *    Copyright (c) William H. Murray and Chris H. Pappas, 1992
 */

#include <stdio.h>
#define MYBUFSIZ 512

void main(void)
{
   char ichar, cmybuffer[MYBUFSIZ];
   FILE *pfinfile, *pfoutfile;

   pfinfile = fopen("sample.in", "r");
   pfoutfile = fopen("sample.out", "w");

   if (setvbuf(pfinfile, cmybuffer, _IOFBF, MYBUFSIZ) != 0)
      printf("pfinfile buffer allocation error\n");
   else
      printf("pfinfile buffer created\n");

   if (setvbuf(pfoutfile, NULL, _IOLBF, 132) != 0)
      printf("pfoutfile buffer allocation error\n");
   else
      printf("pfoutfile buffer created\n");

   while(fscanf(pfinfile,"%c",&ichar) != EOF)
      fprintf(pfoutfile,"%c",ichar);

   fclose(pfinfile);
```

```
    fclose(pfoutfile);
}
```

The program creates a user-accessible buffer pointed to by *pfinfile* and a **malloc()**-allocated buffer pointed to by *pfoutfile*. This last buffer is defined as *buftype*, **_IOLBF**, or line buffered. Other options defined in stdio.h include **_IOFBF**, for fully buffered, and **_IONBF**, for no buffer.

Remember, both **setbuf()** and **setvbuf()** cause the user-defined *buffer* to be used for I/O buffering, instead of an automatically allocated buffer. With **setbuf()**, if the *buffer* argument is set to null, I/O will be unbuffered. Otherwise, it will be fully buffered.

With **setvbuf()**, if the *buffer* argument is null, a buffer will be allocated using **malloc()**. The **setvbuf()** *buffer* will use the *bufsize* argument as the amount allocated and automatically free the memory on close.

Closing Streams

The two functions **fclose()** and **fcloseall()** close a stream or streams, respectively. The **fclose()** function closes a single file, while **fcloseall()** closes all open streams except **stdin**, **stdout**, **stderr**, **stdprn**, and **stdaux**. However, if your program does not explicitly close a stream, the stream is automatically closed when the application terminates. Since the number of streams that can be open at a given time is limited, it is a good practice to close a stream when you are finished with it.

Low-level Input and Output in C

The following table lists the most commonly used low-level input and output functions used by an application:

Function	Definition
close()	Closes a disk file
lseek()	Seeks to the specified byte in a file
open()	Opens a disk file
read()	Reads a buffer of data
unlink()	Removes a file from the directory
write()	Writes a buffer of data

Low-level input and output calls do not buffer or format data. Files opened by low-level calls are referenced by a file handle (an integer value used by the operating system to refer to the file). You use the **open()** function to open files. You can use the **sopen()** macro to open a file with file-sharing attributes.

Low-level functions are different from their stream counterparts because they do not require the inclusion of the stdio.h header file. However, some common constants that are predefined in stdio.h, such as *EOF* and *NULL,* may be useful. Declarations for the low-level functions are given in the io.h header file.

This second disk-file I/O system was originally created under the UNIX operating system. Because the ANSI C standard committee has elected not to standardize this low-level UNIX-like unbuffered I/O system, it cannot be recommended for future use. Instead, the standardized buffered I/O system described throughout this chapter is recommended for all new projects.

Character Input and Output

There are certain character input and output functions defined in the ANSI C standard that are supplied with all C compilers. These functions provide standard input and output and are considered to be high-level routines (as opposed to low-level routines, which access the machine hardware more directly). I/O in C is implemented through vendor-supplied functions rather than keywords defined as part of the language.

Using getc(), putc(), fgetc(), and fputc()

The most basic of all I/O functions are those that input and output one character. The **getc()** function inputs one character from a specified file stream, like this:

```
int ic;
ic = getc(stdin);
```

The input character is passed back in the name of the function **getc()** and then assigns the returned value to *ic*. By the way, if you are wondering why *ic* isn't of type **char**, it is because the function **getc()** has been prototyped to return an **int** type. This is necessary because of the possible system-dependent size of the end-of-file marker, which might not fit in a single **char** byte size.

Function **getc()** converts the integer into an unsigned character. This use of an unsigned character preserved as an integer guarantees that the ASCII values above 127 are not represented as negative values. Therefore, negative values can be used to represent unusual situations like errors and the end of the input file. For example, the end-of-file has traditionally been represented by –1, although the ANSI C standard states only that the constant *EOF* represent some negative value.

Because an integer value is returned by **getc()**, the data item that inputs the value from **getc()** must also be defined as an integer. While it may seem odd to be using an integer in a character function, the C language actually makes very little distinction between characters and integers. If a character is provided when an integer is needed, the character will be converted to an integer.

The complement to the **getc()** function is **putc()**. The **putc()** function outputs one character to the file stream represented by the specified file pointer. To send the same character that was just input to the standard output, use the following statement:

```
putc(ic,stdout);
```

The **getc()** function is normally buffered, which means that when a request for a character is made by the application, control is not returned to the program until a carriage return is entered into the standard input file stream. All the characters entered before the carriage return are held in a buffer and delivered to the program one at a time. The application invokes the **getc()** function repeatedly until the buffer has been exhausted. After the carriage return has been sent to the program by **getc()**, the next request for a character results in more characters accumulating in the buffer until a carriage return is again entered. This means that you cannot use the **getc()** function for one-key input techniques that do not require pressing the carriage return.

One final note: **getc()** and **putc()** are actually implemented as macros rather than as true functions. The functions **fgetc()** and **fputc()** are identical to their macro **getc()** and **putc()** counterparts.

Using getchar(), putchar(), fgetchar(), and fputchar()

The two macros **getchar()** and **putchar()** are actually specific implementations of the **getc()** and **putc()** macros, respectively. They are always associated with standard input (**stdin**) and standard output (**stdout**). The only way to use them on other file streams is to redirect either standard input or standard output from within the program.

The same two coded examples used earlier could be rewritten by using these two functions:

```
int ic;
ic = getchar();
```

and

```
putchar(ic);
```

Like **getc()** and **putc()**, **getchar()** and **putchar()** are implemented as macros. The function **putchar()** has been written to return an *EOF* value whenever an error condition occurs. The following code can be used to check for an *output* error condition. Because of the check for *EOF* on output, it tends to be a bit confusing, although it is technically correct.

```
if(putchar(ic) == EOF)
  printf("An error has occurred writing to stdout");
```

Both **fgetchar()** and **fputchar()** are the function equivalents of their macro **getchar()** and **putchar()** counterparts.

Using getch() and putch()

Both **getch()** and **putch()** are true functions, but they do not fall under the ANSI C standard because they are low-level functions that interface closely with the hardware. For IBM-PC and compatible systems, these functions do not use buffering, which means that they immediately input a character typed at the keyboard. They can be redirected, however, so they are not associated exclusively with the keyboard.

You can use the functions **getch()** and **putch()** exactly like **getchar()** and **putchar()**. Usually, a program running on the IBM-PC will use **getch()** to trap keystrokes ignored by **getchar()**—for example, PGUP, PGDN, HOME, and END. The function **getchar()** sees a character entered from the keyboard as soon as the key is pressed; a carriage return is not needed to send the character to the program. This ability allows the function **getch()** to provide a one-key technique that is not available with **getc()** or **getchar()**.

On an IBM-PC or true compatible, the function **getch()** operates very differently from **getc()** and **getchar()**. This is partly due to the fact that the IBM-PC family can easily determine when an individual key on the keyboard has been pressed. Other systems, such as the DEC and VAX C, do not allow the hardware to trap individual keystrokes. These systems typically echo the input character and require the pressing of a carriage return, with the carriage return character not seen by the program unless no other characters have been entered. Under such circumstances, the carriage return returns a null character or a decimal zero. Additionally, the function keys are not available, and if they are pressed, they produce unreliable results.

String Input and Output

In many applications, it is more natural to handle input and output in larger pieces than characters. For example, a file of boat salesmen may contain one record per line, with each record consisting of four fields: salesman's name, base pay, commission, and number of boats sold, with white space separating the fields. It would be very tedious to use character I/O.

Using gets(), puts(), fgets(), and fputs()

Because of the organization of the file, it would be better to treat each record as a single character string and read or write it as a unit. The function **fgets()**, which reads whole strings rather than single characters, is suited to this task. In addition to the function **fgets()** and its inverse **fputs()**, there are also the macro counterparts **gets()** and **puts()**.

The function **fgets()** expects three arguments: the address of an array in which to store the character string, the maximum number of characters to store, and a pointer to a file to read. The function will read characters into the array until the number of characters read in is one less than the size specified, all of the characters up to and including the next newline character have been read, or the end-of-file is reached, whichever comes first.

If **fgets()** reads in a newline, the newline will be stored in the array. If at least one character was read, the function will automatically append the null string terminator \0. Suppose the file BOATSALE.DAT looks like this:

```
Pat Pharr 32767 0.15 30
Beth Mollen 35000 0.12 23
Gary Kohut 40000 0.15 40
```

Assuming a maximum record length of 40 characters including the newline, the following program will read the records from the file and write them to the standard output:

```
/*
 *    11FGETS.C
 *    A C program that demonstrates how to read
 *    in whole records using fgets and prints
 *    them out to stdout using fputs.
 *    Copyright (c) William H. Murray and Chris H. Pappas, 1992
 */

#include <stdio.h>

#define INULL_CHAR 1
#define IMAX_REC_SIZE 40

main()
{
  FILE *pfinfile;
  char crecord[IMAX_REC_SIZE + INULL_CHAR];

  pfinfile=fopen("a:\\boatsale.dat", "r");
```

```
    while(fgets(crecord,IMAX_REC_SIZE +INULL_CHAR,pfinfile) != NULL)
      fputs(crecord,stdout);
    fclose(pfinfile);

    return(0);
}
```

Because the maximum record size is 40, you must reserve 41 cells in the array; the extra cell is to hold the null terminator \0. The program does not generate its own newline when it prints each record to the terminal but relies instead on the newline read into the character array by **fgets()**. The function **fputs()** writes the contents of the character array, *crecord,* to the file specified by the file pointer, **stdout**.

If your program happens to be accessing a file on a disk drive other than the one where the compiler is residing, it may be necessary to include a path in your filename. Notice this description in the preceding program; the double backslashes (\\) are necessary syntactically to indicate a subdirectory. Remember that a single \ usually signals that a escape or line continuation follows.

While the functions **gets()** and **fgets()** are very similar in usage, the functions **puts()** and **fputs()** operate differently. The function **fputs()** writes to a file and expects two arguments: the address of a null-terminated character string and a pointer to a file; **fputs()** simply copies the string to the specified file. It does not add a newline to the end of the string.

The macro **puts()**, however, does not require a pointer to a file since the output automatically goes to **stdout**, and it automatically adds a newline character to the end of the output string. An excellent example of how these functions differ can be found in Chapter 9 in the section "String Functions and Character Arrays."

Integer Input and Output

For certain types of applications, it may be necessary to read and write stream (or buffered) integer information. The C language incorporates two functions for this purpose: **getw()** and **putw()**.

Using getw() and putw()

The complementary functions **getw()** and **putw()** are very similar to the functions **getc()** and **putc()** except that they input and output integer data instead of character data to a file. You should use both **getw()** and **putw()** only on files that are opened in binary mode. The following program opens a binary file, writes ten integers to it, closes the file, and then reopens the file for input and echo print:

```
/*
 *    11BADFIL.C
 *    A C program that uses the functions getw and putw on
 *    a file created in binary mode.
 *    Copyright (c) William H. Murray and Chris H. Pappas, 1992
 */

#include <stdio.h>

#define ISIZE 10

int main()
{
  FILE *pfi;
  int ivalue,ivalues[ISIZE],i;

  pfi = fopen("a:\\integer.dat", "wb");
  if(pfi == NULL) {
    printf("File could not be opened");
    exit(1);
  }

  for(i = 0; i < ISIZE; i++) {
    ivalues[i]=i+1;
    putw(ivalues[i],pfi);
  }

  fclose(pfi);

  pfi=fopen("a:\\integer.dat", "r+b");
  if(pfi == NULL) {
    printf("File could not be re-opened");
    exit(1);
  }

  while(!feof(pfi)) {
    ivalue = getw(pfi);
    printf("%3d",ivalue);
  }

  return(0);
}
```

Look at the output from this program and see if you can figure out what went wrong:

```
1  2  3  4  5  6  7  8  9 10 -1
```

Because the integer value read in by the last loop may have a value equal to *EOF,* the program uses the function **feof()** to check for the end-of-file marker. However, the function does not perform a look-ahead operation as do some other high-level language end-of-file functions. In C, an actual read of the end-of-file value must be performed in order to flag the condition.

To correct this situation, the program needs to be rewritten using what is called a *priming read statement:*

```c
/*
 *    11GEPUTW.C
 *    A C program that uses the functions getw and putw on
 *    a file created in binary mode.
 *    Copyright (c) William H. Murray and Chris H. Pappas, 1992
 */

#include <stdio.h>

#define ISIZE 10

main()
{
  FILE *pfi;
  int ivalue,ivalues[ISIZE],i;
  pfi = fopen("a:\\integer.dat", "w+b");
  if(pfi == NULL) {
    printf("File could not be opened");
    exit(1);
  }

  for(i = 0; i < ISIZE; i++) {
    ivalues[i]=i+1;
    putw(ivalues[i],pfi);
  }

  fclose(pfi);

  pfi=fopen("a:\\integer.dat", "rb");
  if(pfi == NULL) {
    printf("File could not be re-opened");
```

```
      exit(1);
   }

   ivalue = getw(pfi);
   while(!feof(pfi)) {
     printf("%3d",ivalue);
     ivalue=getw(pfi);
   }

   return(0);
}
```

Before the program enters the final **while** loop, the priming read is performed to check to see if the file is empty. If it is not, a valid integer value is stored in *ivalue*. If the file is empty, however, the function **feof()** will acknowledge this, preventing the **while** loop from executing.

Also notice that the priming read necessitated a rearrangement of the statements within the **while** loop. If the loop is entered, then *ivalue* contains a valid integer. Had the statements within the loop remained the same as the original program, an immediate second **getw()** function call would be performed. This would overwrite the first integer value. Because of the priming read, the first statement within the **while** loop must be an output statement. This is next followed by a call to **getw()** to get another value.

Suppose the **while** loop has been entered nine times. At the end of the ninth iteration, the integer numbers 1 through 8 have been echo printed and *ivalue* has been assigned a 9. The next iteration of the loop prints the 9 and inputs the 10. Since 10 is not *EOF*, the loop iterates, causing the 10 to be echo printed and *EOF* to be read. At this point, the **while** loop terminates because the function **feof()** sees the end-of-file condition.

These two simple example programs should highlight the need to take care when writing code that is based on the function **feof()**. This is a peculiarly frustrating programming task since each high-level language tends to treat the end-of-file condition in a different way. Some languages read a piece of data and at the same time look ahead to see the end-of-file; others, like C, do not.

Formatting Output

C's rich assortment of output formatting controls makes it easy to create a neatly printed graph, report, or table. The two main functions that accomplish this formatted output are **printf()** and the file equivalent form, **fprintf()**.

Using printf() and fprintf()

The following example program defines four variable types: character, array-of-characters, integer, and real, and then demonstrates how to use the appropriate format controls on each variable. The source code has been heavily commented and output line numbering has been included to make associating the output generated with the statement that created it as simple as possible:

```
/*
 *     11PRINTF.C
 *     A C program demonstrating advanced conversions and formatting
 *     Copyright (c) William H. Murray and Chris H. Pappas, 1992
 */

#include <stdio.h>

main()
{
  char    c       =   'A',
          psz1[]  =   "In making a living today many no ",
          psz2[]  =   "longer leave any room for life.";
  int     iln     =   0,
          ivalue  =   1234;
  double dPi       =   3.14159265;


  /*              conversions             */

  /* print the c                    */
  printf("\n[%2d] %c",++iln,c);

  /* print the ASCII code for c     */
  printf("\n[%2d] %d",++iln,c);

  /* print character with ASCII 90  */
  printf("\n[%2d] %c",++iln,90);

  /* print ivalue as octal value    */
  printf("\n[%2d] %o",++iln,ivalue);

  /* print lower-case hexadecimal    */
  printf("\n[%2d] %x",++iln,ivalue);

  /* print upper-case hexadecimal    */
  printf("\n[%2d] %X",++iln,ivalue);
```

```
/* conversions and format options  */

/* minimum width 1                 */
printf("\n[%2d] %c",++iln,c);

/* minimum width 5, right-justify  */
printf("\n[%2d] %5c",++iln,c);

/* minimum width 5, left-justify   */
printf("\n[%2d] %-5c",++iln,c);

/* 33 non-null, automatically       */
printf("\n[%d] %s",++iln,psz1);

/* 31 non-null, automatically       */
printf("\n[%d] %s",++iln,psz2);

/* minimum 5 overridden, auto 33    */
printf("\n[%d] %5s",++iln,psz1);

/* minimum width 38, right-justify */
printf("\n[%d] %38s",++iln,psz1);

/* minimum width 38, left-justify  */
printf("\n[%d] %-38s",++iln,psz2);

/* default ivalue width, 4          */
printf("\n[%d] %d",++iln,ivalue);

/* printf ivalue with + sign        */
printf("\n[%d] %+d",++iln,ivalue);

/* minimum 3 overridden, auto 4     */
printf("\n[%d] %3d",++iln,ivalue);

/* minimum width 10, right-justify */
printf("\n[%d] %10d",++iln,ivalue);

/* minimum width 10, left-justify   */
printf("\n[%d] %-d",++iln,ivalue);

/* right justify with leading 0's   */
printf("\n[%d] %010d",++iln,ivalue);
```

```
/* using default number of digits  */
printf("\n[%d] %f",++iln,dPi);

/* minimum width 20, right-justify */
printf("\n[%d] %20f",++iln,dPi);

/* right-justify with leading 0's  */
printf("\n[%d] %020f",++iln,dPi);

/* minimum width 20, left-justify  */
printf("\n[%d] %-20f",++iln,dPi);

/* no longer available since R1.2  */
/* left-justify with trailing 0's  */



/* additional formatting precision */

/* minimum width 19, print all 17  */
printf("\n[%d] %19.19s",++iln,psz1);

/* prints first 2 chars            */
printf("\n[%d] %.2s",++iln,psz1);

/* prints 2 chars, right-justify   */
printf("\n[%d] %19.2s",++iln,psz1);

/* prints 2 chars, left-justify    */
printf("\n[%d] %-19.2s",++iln,psz1);

/* using printf arguments          */
printf("\n[%d] %*.*s",++iln,19,6,psz1);

/* width 10, 8 to right of '.'     */
printf("\n[%d] %10.8f",++iln,dPi);

/* width 20, 2 to right-justify    */
printf("\n[%d] %20.2f",++iln,dPi);

/* 4 decimal places, left-justify  */
printf("\n[%d] %-20.4f",++iln,dPi);

/* 4 decimal places, right-justify */
```

```
printf("\n[%d] %20.4f",++iln,dPi);

/* width 20, scientific notation    */
printf("\n[%d] %20.2e",++iln,dPi);

return(0);
}
```

The output generated by the program looks like this:

```
[ 1] A
[ 2] 65
[ 3] Z
[ 4] 2322
[ 5] 4d2
[ 6] 4D2
[ 7] A
[ 8]     A
[ 9] A
[10] In making a living today many no
[11] longer leave any room for life.
[12] In making a living today many no
[13]     In making a living today many no
[14] longer leave any room for life.
[15] 1234
[16] +1234
[17] 1234
[18]         1234
[19] 1234
[20] 0000001234
[21] 3.141593
[22]             3.141593
[23] 0000000000003.141593
[24] 3.141593
[25] 3.141593
[26] In making a living
[27] In
[28]                 In
[29] In
[30]             In mak
[31] 3.14159265
[32]                 3.14
[33] 3.1416
```

```
[34]              3.1416
[35]            3.14e+00
```

You can neatly format your application's output by studying the preceding example and selecting those combinations that apply to your program's data types.

Using fseek(), ftell(), and rewind()

You can use the functions **fseek()**, **ftell()**, and **rewind()** to determine or change the location of the file position marker. The function **fseek()** resets the file position marker, in the file pointed to by *pf*, to the number of *ibytes* from the beginning of the file (*ifrom* = 0), from the current location of the file position marker (*ifrom* = 1), or from the end of the file (*ifrom* = 2). C has predefined three constants that can also be used in place of the variable *ifrom*: *SEEK_SET* (offset from beginning-of-file), *SEEK_CUR* (current file marker position), and *SEEK_END* (offset from the end-of-file). The function **fseek()** will return zero if the seek is successful and *EOF* otherwise. The general syntax for the function **fseek()** looks like this:

fseek(*pf, ibytes, ifrom*);

The function **ftell()** returns the current location of the file position marker in the file pointed to by *pf*. This location is indicated by an offset, measured in bytes, from the beginning of the file. The syntax for the function **ftell()** looks like this:

long_variable=ftell(*pf*);

The value returned by **ftell()** can be used in a subsequent call to **fseek()**.

The function **rewind()** simply resets the file position marker in the file pointed to by *pf* to the beginning of the file. The syntax for the function **rewind()** looks like this:

rewind(*pf*);

The following C program illustrates the functions **fseek()**, **ftell()**, and **rewind()**:

```
/*
 *   11FSEEK.C
 *   A C program demonstrating the use of fseek,
 *   ftell, and rewind.
 *   Copyright (c) William H. Murray and Chris H. Pappas, 1992
 */
```

```
#include <stdio.h>

main()
{
  FILE *pf;
  char c;
  long llocation;

  pf=fopen("test.dat","r+t");

  c=fgetc(pf);
  putchar(c);

  c=fgetc(pf);
  putchar(c);

  llocation=ftell(pf);

  c=fgetc(pf);
  putchar(c);

  fseek(pf,llocation,0);

  c=fgetc(pf);
  putchar(c);

  fseek(pf,llocation,0);
  fputc('E',pf);

  fseek(pf,llocation,0);

  c=fgetc(pf);
  putchar(c);

  rewind(pf);

  c=fgetc(pf);
  putchar(c);

  return(0);
}
```

The variable *llocation* has been defined to be of type **long**. This is because C supports files larger than 64K. The input file TEST.DAT contains the string "ABCD". After the program opens the file, the first call to **fgetc()** gets the letter "A" and then prints it to the video display. The next statement pair inputs the letter "B" and prints it.

When the function **ftell()** is invoked, *llocation* is set equal to the file position marker's current location. This is measured as an offset, in bytes, from the beginning of the file. Since the letter "B" has already been processed, *llocation* contains a 2. This means that the file position marker is pointing to the third character, which is 2 bytes over from the first letter, "A".

Another I/O pair of statements now reads the letter "C" and prints it to the video display. After the program executes this last statement pair, the file position marker is 3 offset bytes from the beginning of the file, pointing to the fourth character, "D".

At this point in the program, the function **fseek()** is invoked. It is instructed to move *location* offset bytes (or 2 offset bytes) from the beginning of the file (since the third parameter to the function **fseek()** is a zero, as defined earlier). This repositions the file position marker to the third character in the file. The variable *c* is again assigned the letter "C", and it is printed a second time.

The second time the function **fseek()** is invoked, it uses parameters identical to the first invocation. The function **fseek()** moves the pointer to the third character, "C" (2 offset bytes into the file). However, the statement that follows doesn't input the "C" a third time, but it instead writes over it with a new letter, "E". Since the file position marker has now moved past this new "E", to verify that the letter was indeed placed in the file, the function **fseek()** is invoked still another time.

The nest statement pair inputs the new "E" and prints it to the video display. With this accomplished, the program invokes the function **rewind()**, which moves the *pf* back to the beginning of the file. When the function **fgetc()** is then invoked, it returns the letter "A" and prints it to the file. The output from the program looks like this:

```
ABCCEA
```

You can use the same principles illustrated in this simple character example to create a random-access file of records. Suppose you have the following information recorded for a file of individuals: social security number, name, and address. Suppose also that you are allowing 11 characters for the social security number, in the form ddd-dd-dddd, with the name and address being given an additional 60 characters (or bytes). So far, each record would be 11 + 60 bytes long, or 71 bytes.

All of the possible contiguous record locations on a random-access disk file may not be full; the personnel record needs to contain a flag indicating whether or not that disk record location has been used or not. This requires adding one more byte to the personnel record, bringing the total for one person's record to 72 bytes, plus 2 additional bytes to represent the record number, for a grand total record byte count of 74 bytes. One record could look like the following:

```
1 U111-22-3333Linda Lossannie, 521 Alan Street, Anywhere, USA
```

Record 1 in the file would occupy bytes zero through 73; record 2 would occupy bytes 74 through 147; record 3, 148 through 221; and so on. If you use the record number in conjunction with the **fseek()** function, any record location can be located on the disk. For example, to find the beginning of record 2, use the following statements:

```
loffset=(iwhich_record - 1) * sizeof(stA_PERSON);
fseek(pfi,loffset,0);
```

Once the file position marker has been moved to the beginning of the selected record, the information at that location can either be read or written by using various I/O functions such as **fread()** and **fwrite()**.

With the exception of the comment block delimiter symbols /* and */ and the header stdio.h, the program just discussed would work the same in C++. Just substitute the symbol // for both /* and */ and change stdio.h to iostream.h.

Using CodeView

Try entering this next program and printing out the value stored in the variable *stcurrent_person.irecordnum* after you have asked to search for the 25th record:

```
/*
 *    11RNDACS.C
 *    A C random access file program using fseek, fread,
 *    and fwrite.
 *    Copyright (c) William H. Murray and Chris H. Pappas, 1992
 */

#include <stdio.h>
#include <string.h>

#define iFIRST 1
#define iLAST 50
#define iSS_SIZE 11
#define iDATA_SIZE 60
#define cVACANT 'V'
#define cUSED 'U'

typedef struct strecord {
  int   irecordnum;
  char cavailable;                 /* V free, U used */
```

```
        char csoc_sec_num[iSS_SIZE];
        char cdata[iDATA_SIZE];
} stA_PERSON;

main()
{
  FILE *pfi;
  stA_PERSON stcurrent_person;
  int i,iwhich_record;
  long int loffset;

  pfi=fopen("A:\\sample.fil","r+");

  for(i = iFIRST; i <= iLAST; i++) {
    stcurrent_person.cavailable=cVACANT;
    stcurrent_person.irecordnum=i;
    fwrite(&stcurrent_person,sizeof(stA_PERSON),1,pfi);
  }

  printf("Please enter the record you would like to find.");
  printf("\nYour response must be between 1 and 50: ");
  scanf("%d",&iwhich_record);

  loffset=(iwhich_record - 1) * sizeof(stA_PERSON);
  fseek(pfi,loffset,0);
  fread(&stcurrent_person,sizeof(stA_PERSON),1,pfi);

  fclose(pfi);

  return(0);
}
```

The **typedef** has defined *stA_PERSON* as a structure that has a 2-byte *irecordnum*, a 1-byte *cavailable* character code, an 11-byte character array to hold a *csoc_sec_num* number, and a 60-byte *cdata* field. This brings the total structure's size to 2 + 1 + 11 + 60, or 74 bytes.

Once the program has opened the file in read-and-update text mode, it creates and stores 50 records, each with its own unique *irecordnum* and all initialized to *cVACANT*. The **fwrite()** statement wants the address of the structure to output, the size in bytes of what it is outputting, how many to output, and which file to send it to. With this accomplished, the program next asks the user which record he or she would like to search for.

Finding the record is accomplished in two steps. First, an offset address from the beginning of the file must be calculated. For example, record 1 is stored in bytes zero to 73, record 2 is stored in bytes 74 to 148, and so on. By subtracting 1 from the record number entered by the user, the program multiplies this value by the number of bytes occupied by each structure and calculates the *loffset*. For example, finding the 2 record is accomplished with the following calculation: (2-1) × 74. This gives the second record a starting byte offset of 74. Using this calculated value, the **fseek()** function is then invoked and moves the file position marker *loffset* bytes into the file.

As you are tracing through the program asking to view records 1 through 10, all seems fine. However, when you ask to view the 11th record, what happens? You get garbage. The reason for this is that the program opened the file in text mode. Records 1 through 9 are all exactly 74 bytes, but records 10 and up take 75 bytes. Therefore, the 10th record starts at the appropriate *loffset* calculation but it goes 1 byte further into the file. Therefore, the 11th record is at the address arrived at by using the following modified calculation:

```
loffset=((iwhich_record - 1) * sizeof(stA_PERSON)) + 1;
```

However, this calculation won't work with the first nine records. The solution is to open the file in binary mode:

```
pfi=fopen("A:\\sample.fil","r+b");
```

In character mode, the program tries to interpret any two-digit number as two single characters, increasing records with two-digit *record_number*s by 1 byte. In binary mode, the integer *record_number* is interpreted properly. Exercise care when deciding how to open a file for I/O.

Formatting Input

Formatted input can be obtained for a C program by using the very versatile functions **scanf()** and **fscanf()**. The main difference between the two functions is that the latter requires that you specifically designate the input file from which the data is to be obtained. Table 11-2 lists all of the possible control string codes that can be used with the functions **scanf()**, **fscanf()**, and **sscanf()**.

Using scanf(), fscanf(), and sscanf()

You can use all three input functions, **scanf()**, **fscanf()**, and **sscanf()**, for extremely sophisticated data input. For example, look at the following statement:

```
scanf("%2d%5s%4f",&ivalue,psz,&fvalue);
```

Code	Interpretation	Example Input	Receiving Address Parameter Type
c	A character	W	char
s	A string	William	char
d	int	23	int
hd	short	−99	short
ld	long	123456	long
o	octal	1727	int
ho	short octal	1727	short
lo	long octal	1727	long
x	hexadecimal	2b5	int
hx	short hexadecimal	2b5	short
lx	long hexadecimal	2b5	long
e	float as float	3.14159e+03	float
f	Same as e		
le	float as double	3.14159e+03	double
lf	Same as le		
[A-Za-z]	String with only chars	Test string	char
[0-9]	String with only digits	098231345	char

Table 11-2.   *Control Codes for scanf(), fscanf(), and sscanf()*

The statement inputs only a two-digit integer, a five-character string, and a real number that occupies a maximum of four spaces (2.97, 12.5, and so on). See if you can even begin to imagine what this next statement does:

```
scanf("%*[ \t\n]\"%[^A-Za-z]%[^\"]\"",ps1,ps2);
```

The statement begins by reading and *not* storing any white space. This is accomplished with the following format specification: "%*[\t\n]". The * symbol instructs the function to obtain the specified data but not to save it in any variable. As long as only a space, tab, or newline is on the input line, **scanf()** will keep reading until it encounters a double quote ("). This is accomplished by the \" format specification, which says the input must match the designated symbol. However, the double quote is not input.

Once **scanf()** has found the double quote, it is instructed to input all characters that are digits into *ps1*. The %[^A-Za-z] format specification accomplishes this with the caret (^) modifier, which says to input anything not an uppercase letter "A" through "Z" or lowercase letter "a" through "z". Had the caret been omitted, the string would have contained only alphabetic characters. It is the hyphen between the two symbols "A" and "Z" and "a" and "z" that indicates the entire range is to be considered.

The next format specification, %[^\"], instructs the input function to read all remaining characters up to but not including a double quote into *ps2*. The last format specification, \", indicates that the string must match and end with a double quote. You can use the same types of input conversion control with the functions **fscanf()** and **sscanf()**. The only difference between the two functions **scanf()** and **fscanf()** is that the latter requires that an input file be specified. The function **sscanf()** is identical to **scanf()** except that the data is read from an array rather than a file.

The next example shows how you can use **sscanf()** to convert a string (of digits) to an integer. If *ivalue* is of type **int** and *psz* is an array of type **char** that holds a string of digits, then the following statement will convert the string *psz* into type **int** and store it in the variable *ivalue*:

```
sscanf(psz,"%d",&ivalue);
```

Very often, the functions **gets()** and **sscanf()** are used in combination since the function **gets()** reads in an entire line of input and the function **sscanf()** goes into a string and interprets it according to the format specifications.

One problem often encountered with **scanf()** occurs when programmers try to use it in conjunction with various other character input functions such as **getc()**, **getch()**, **getchar()**, **gets()**, an so on. The typical scenario goes like this: **scanf()** is used to input various data types that would otherwise require conversion from characters to something else. Then the programmer tries to use a character input function such as **getch()** and finds that **getch()** does not work as expected. The problem occurs because **scanf()** sometimes does not read all the data that is waiting to be read, and the waiting data can fool other functions (including **scanf()**) into thinking that input has already been entered. To be safe, if you use **scanf()** in a program, don't also use other input functions in the same program.

Chapter 12 introduces you to the basics of C++ I/O. Chapters 13 through 16 explain the concepts necessary to do advanced C++ I/O, and Chapter 17 completes the subject of I/O in C++.

Chapter *12*

An Introduction to I/O
in C++

In many cases, the C++ equivalent of a C program streamlines the way your program inputs and outputs data. However, this is not always true. Chapter 12 introduces you to C++ I/O.

The topic of advanced C++ input and output is continued in Chapter 17. The division of the topic is necessary because of the diverse I/O capabilities available to C++ programmers. Chapters 15 and 16 teach the fundamentals of object-oriented programming. Once you understand how objects are created, it will be much easier to understand advanced object-oriented C++ I/O. Chapter 17 picks up with C++'s ability to effortlessly manipulate objects.

Streamlining I/O with C++

The software supplied with the C++ compiler includes a standard library that contains functions commonly used by the C++ community. The standard I/O library for C, described by the header file stdio.h, is still available in C++. However, C++ introduces its own header file, called iostream.h, which implements its own collection of I/O functions.

The C++ stream I/O is described as a set of classes in iostream.h. These classes overload the "put to" and "get from" operators, << and >>. To better understand why the stream library in C++ is more convenient than its C counterpart, let's first review how C handles input and output.

First, recall that C has no built-in input or output statements; functions such as **printf()** are part of the standard library but not part of the language itself. Similarly, C++ has no built-in I/O facilities. The absence of built-in I/O gives you greater flexibility to produce the most efficient user interface for the data pattern of the application at hand.

The problem with the C solution to input and output lies with its implementation of these I/O functions. There is little consistency among them in terms of return values and parameter sequences. Because of this, programmers tend to rely on the formatted I/O functions **printf()**, **scanf()**, and so on—especially when the objects being manipulated are numbers or other noncharacter values. These formatted I/O functions are convenient and, for the most part, share a consistent interface, but they are also big and unwieldy because they must manipulate many kinds of values.

In C++, the class provides modular solutions to your data manipulation needs. The standard C++ library provides three I/O classes as an alternative to C's general-purpose I/O functions. These classes contain definitions for the same pair of operators—>> and <<—that are optimized for all kinds of data. (See Chapter 16 for a discussion of classes.)

cin, cout, and cerr

The C++ stream counterparts to **stdin**, **stdout**, and **stderr**, prototyped in stdio.h, are **cin**, **cout**, and **cerr**, which are prototyped in iostream.h. These three streams are opened automatically when your program begins execution and become the interface between the program and the user. The **cin** stream is associated with the terminal keyboard. The **cout** and **cerr** streams are associated with the video display.

The >> Extraction and << Insertion Operators

Input and output in C++ have been significantly enhanced and streamlined by the stream library operators >> ("get from" or *extraction*) and << ("put to" or *insertion*). One of the major enhancements that C++ added to C was operator overloading. Operator overloading allows the compiler to determine which like-named function or operator is to be executed based on the associated variables' data types. The extraction and insertion operators are good examples of this new C++ capability. Each operator has been overloaded so it can handle all of the standard C++ data types, including classes. The following two code segments illustrate the greater ease of use for basic I/O operations in C++. First, take a quick look at a C output statement using **printf()**:

```
printf("Integer value: %d, Float value: %f",ivalue,fvalue);
```

Here is the C++ equivalent:

```
cout << "Integer value: " << ivalue << ", Float value: "
    << fvalue;
```

A careful examination of the C++ equivalent will reveal how the insertion operator has been overloaded to handle the three separate data types: string, integer, and float. If you are like many C programmers, you are not going to miss having to hunt down the % symbol needed for your **printf()** and **scanf()** format specifications. As a result of operator overloading, the insertion operator will examine the data type you have passed to it and determine an appropriate format.

An identical situation exists with the extraction operator, which performs data input. Look at the following C example and its equivalent C++ counterpart:

```
/* C code */
scanf("%d%f%c",&ivalue,&fvalue,&c);

// C++ code
cin >> ivalue >> fvalue >> c;
```

No longer is it necessary to precede your input variables with the & address operator. In C++, the extraction operator takes care of calculating the storage variable's address, storage requirements, and formatting.

Having looked at two examples of the C++ operators << and >>, you might be slightly confused as to why they are named the way they are. The simplest way to remember which operator performs output and which performs input is to think of these two operators as they relate to the stream I/O files. When you want to input information, you extract it (>>) from the input stream, **cin**, and put the information into a variable—for example, *ivalue*. To output information, you take a copy of the information from the variable *fvalue* and insert it (<<) into the output stream, **cout**.

As a direct result of operator overloading, C++ will allow a program to expand upon the insertion and extraction operators. The following code segment illustrates how the insertion operator can be overloaded to print the new type **stclient**:

```
ostream& operator << (ostream& osout, stclient staclient)
{
  osout << " " << staclient.pszname;
  osout << " " << staclient.pszaddress;
  osout << " " << staclient.pszphone;
}
```

Assuming the structure variable *staclient* has been initialized, printing the information becomes a simple one-line statement:

```
cout << staclient;
```

Last but not least, the insertion and extraction operators have an additional advantage—their final code size. The general-purpose I/O functions **printf()** and **scanf()** carry along code segments into the final executable version of a program that are often unused. In C, even if you are dealing only with integer data, you still pull along all of the conversion code for the additional standard data types. In contrast, the C++ compiler incorporates only those routines actually needed.

The following program demonstrates how to use the input, or extraction, operator >> to read different types of data:

```
//
//  12INSRT1.CPP
//  A C++ program demonstrating how to use the
//  extraction >> operator to input a char,
//  integer, float, double, and string.
//  Copyright (c) William H. Murray and Chris H. Pappas, 1992
//

#include <iostream.h>

#define INUMCHARS 45
#define INULL_CHAR 1

void main(void)
{
  char canswer;
  int ivalue;
  float fvalue;
  double dvalue;
  char pszname[INUMCHARS + INULL_CHAR];

  cout << "This program allows you to enter various data types.";
  cout << "Would you like to try it? << "\n\n";
  cout << "Please type a Y for yes and an N for no: ";

  cin  >> canswer;

  if(canswer == 'Y') {

    cout << "\n" << "Enter an integer value: ";
    cin >> ivalue;
    cout << "\n\n";

    cout << "Enter a float value: ";
    cin >> fvalue;
```

```
    cout << "\n\n";

    cout << "Enter a double value: ";
    cin >> dvalue;
    cout << "\n\n";

    cout << "Enter your first name: ";
    cin >> pszname;
    cout << "\n\n";
  }


}
```

In this example, the insertion operator << is used in its simplest form to output literal string prompts. Notice that the program uses four different data types and yet each input statement, **cin >>**, looks identical except for the variable's name. For those of you who are fast typists but are tired of trying to find the infrequently used %, ", and & symbols (required by **scanf()**), you can give your fingers and eyes a rest. The C++ extraction operator makes code entry much simpler and less error prone.

Because of the rapid evolutionary development of C++, you have to be careful when using C or C++ code found in older manuscripts. For example, if you had run the previous program under a C++ compiler, Release 1.2, the program execution would look like the following example:

```
This program allows you to enter various data types
Would you like to try it?

Please type a Y for yes and an N for no: Y

Enter an integer value:
                          10
```

This is because the C++ Release 1.2 input stream is processing the newline character you entered after typing the letter "Y". The extraction operator >> reads up to but does not get rid of the newline. The following program solves this problem by adding an additional input statement:

```
//
//  12INSRT2.CPP
//  A C++ program demonstrating how to use the
//  extraction >> operator to input a char,
//  integer, float, double, and string.
//  Copyright (c) William H. Murray and Chris H. Pappas, 1992
//
```

```
#include <iostream.h>

#define INUMCHARS 45
#define INULL_CHAR 1

void main(void)
{
  char canswer,c0x0Anewline;
  int ivalue;
  float fvalue;
  double dvalue;
  char pszname[INUMCHARS + INULL_CHAR];

  cout << "This program allows you to enter various data types.";
  cout << "Would you like to try it? << "\n\n";
  cout << "Please type a Y for yes and an N for no: ";

  cin  >> canswer;
  cin.get(c0x0Anewline);

  if(canswer == 'Y') {

    cout << "\n" << "Enter an integer value: ";
    cin >> ivalue;
    cout << "\n\n";

    cout << "Enter a float value: ";
    cin >> fvalue;
    cout << "\n\n";

    cout << "Enter a double value: ";
    cin >> dvalue;
    cout << "\n\n";

    cout << "Enter your first name: ";
    cin >> pszname;
    cout << "\n\n";
  }

}
```

Did you notice the change? After *canswer* is read in, the program executes

```
cin.get(c0x0Anewline);
```

This processes the newline character so that when the program runs it now looks like this:

```
This program allows you to enter various data types
Would you like to try it?

Please type a Y for yes and an N for no:

Enter an integer value: 10
```

Both algorithms work properly since the introduction of C++ Release 2.0. However, it is worth mentioning that you must take care when modeling your code from older texts. Mixing what is known as historic C and C++ with current compilers can cause you to spend many hours trying to figure out why your I/O doesn't perform as expected.

This next example demonstrates how to use the output, or insertion, operator <<
in its various forms:

```
//
//   12EXTRCT.CPP
//   A C++ program demonstrating how to use the
//   insertion << operator to input a char,
//   integer, float, double, and string.
//   Copyright (c) William H. Murray and Chris H. Pappas, 1992
//

#include <iostream.h>

void main(void)
{
  char c='A';
  int ivalue=10;
  float fvalue=45.67;
  double dvalue=2.3e32;
  char fact[]="For all have...";

  cout << "Once upon a time there were ";
  cout << ivalue << " people. endl";
  cout << "Some of them earned " << fvalue;
  cout << " dollars per hour." << "\n";
  cout << "While others earned " << dvalue << " per year!";
  cout << "\n\n" << "But you know what they say: ";
```

```
cout << fact << "\n\n";
cout << "So, none of them get an ";
cout << c;
cout << "!";

}
```

The output from the program looks like this:

```
Once upon a time there were 10 people.
Some of them earned 45.67 dollars per hour.
While others earned 2.3e+32 per year!

But you know what they say: "For all have..."

So, none of them get an A!
```

When comparing the C++ source code with the output from the program, one thing you should immediately notice is that the insertion operator << does not automatically generate a newline. You still have complete control over when this occurs by including the newline symbol \n or **endl** when necessary.

endl is very useful for outputting data in an interactive program because it not only inserts a newline into the stream but also flushes the output buffer. You can also use **flush**; however, this does not insert a newline. Notice too that the placement of the newline symbol can be included after its own << insertion operator or as part of a literal string, as is contrasted in the second and fourth << statements in the program.

Also notice that while the insertion operator very nicely handles the formatting of integers and floats, it isn't very helpful with doubles. Another interesting facet of the insertion operator has to do with C++ Release 1.2 character information. Look at the following line of code:

```
cout << c;
```

This would have given you the following output in Release 1.2:

```
So, none of them get an 65!
```

This is because the character is translated into its ASCII equivalent. The Release 1.2 solution is to use the **put()** function for outputting character data. This would require you to rewrite the statement in the following form:

```
cout.put(c);
```

Try running this next example:

```
//
//   12STRING.CPP
//   A C++ program demonstrating what happens when you use
//   the extraction operator >> with string data.
//   Copyright (c) William H. Murray and Chris H. Pappas, 1992
//

#include <iostream.h>

#define INUMCHARS 45
#define INULL_CHARACTER 1

void main(void)
{
  char pszname[INUMCHARS + INULL_CHARACTER];

  cout << "Please enter your first and last name: ";
  cin >> pszname;
  cout << "\n\nThank you, " << pszname;

}
```

A sample execution of the program looks like this:

```
Please enter your first and last name: Kirsten Tuttle

Thank you, Kirsten
```

There is one more fact you need to know when inputting string information. The extraction operator >> is written to stop reading in information as soon as it encounters white space. *White space* can be a blank, tab, or newline. Therefore, when *pszname* is printed, only the first name entered is output. You can solve this problem by rewriting the program and using the **cin.get()** function:

```
//
//   12CINGET.CPP
//   A C++ program demonstrating what happens when you use
//   the extraction operator >> with cin.get() to process an
//   entire string.
//   Copyright (c) William H. Murray and Chris H. Pappas, 1992
//
```

```
#include <iostream.h>

#define INUMCHARS 45
#define INULL_CHARACTER 1

void main(void)
{
  char pszname[INUMCHARS + INULL_CHARACTER];

  cout << "Please enter your first and last name: ";
  cin.get(pszname,INUMCHARS);
  cout << "\n\nThank you, " << pszname;
}
```

The output from the program now looks like this:

```
Please enter your first and last name: Kirsten Tuttle

Thank you, Kirsten Tuttle
```

The **cin.get()** function has two additional parameters. Only one of these, the number of characters to input, was used in the previous example. The function **cin.get()** will read everything, including white space, until the maximum number of characters specified has been read in, or up to the next newline, whichever comes first. The optional third parameter, not shown, identifies a terminating symbol. For example, the following line would read into *pszname INUMCHARS* characters, all of the characters up to but not including a * symbol, or a newline, whichever comes first:

```
cin.get(pszname,INUMCHARS,'*');
```

From stream.h to iostream.h

One of the most exciting enhancements to the compiler is the new C++ I/O library, referred to as the iostream library. By not including input/output facilities within the C++ language itself, but rather implementing them in C++ and providing them as a component of a C++ standard library, I/O can evolve as needed. This new iostream library replaces the earlier version of the I/O library referred to as the Release 1.2 stream library (described in Stroustrup's *The C++ Programming Language* [Addison-Wesley, Reading, Massachusetts: 1990]).

At its lowest level, C++ interprets a file as a sequence, or *stream,* of bytes. At this level, the concept of a data type is missing. One component of the I/O library is involved in the transfer of these bytes. From the user's perspective, however, a file is composed of a series of intermixed alphanumerics, numeric values, or possibly, class objects. A second component of the I/O library takes care of the interface between these two viewpoints. The iostream library predefines a set of operations for handling reading and writing of the built-in data types. The library also provides for user-definable extensions to handle class types.

Basic input operations are supported by the **istream** class and basic output via the **ostream** class. Bidirectional I/O is supported via the **iostream** class, which is derived from both **istream** and **ostream**. There are four stream objects predefined for the user:

cin	An **istream** class object linked to standard input
cout	An **ostream** class object linked to standard output
cerr	An unbuffered output **ostream** class object linked to standard error
clog	A buffered output **ostream** class object linked to standard error

Any program using the iostream library must include the header file iostream.h. Since iostream.h treats stream.h as an alias, programs written using stream.h may or may not need alterations, depending on the particular structures used.

You can also use the new I/O library to perform input and output operations on files. You can tie a file to your program by defining an instance of one of the following three class types:

fstream	Derived from **iostream** and links a file to your application for both input and output
ifstream	Derived from **istream** and links a file to your application for input only
ofstream	Derived from **ostream** and links a file to your application for output only

Operators and Member Functions

The extraction operator and the << insertion operator have been modified to accept arguments of any of the built-in data types, including **char** *. They can also be extended to accept class argument types.

Probably the first upgrade incompatibility you will experience when converting a C++ program using the older I/O library will be the demised **cout << form** extension. Under the new release, each iostream library class object maintains a *format state* that controls the details of formatting operations, such as the conversion base for integral numeric notation or the precision of a floating-point value.

You can manipulate the format state flags by using the **setf()** and **unsetf()** functions. The **setf()** member function sets a specified format state flag. There are two overloaded instances:

```
setf(long);
setf(long,long);
```

The first argument can be either a format bit *flag* or a format bit *field*. Table 12-1 lists the format flags you can use with the **setf(long)** instance (using just the format flag).

Flag	Meaning
ios::showbase	Displays numeric constants in a format that can be read by the C++ compiler
ios::showpoint	Shows floating-point values with a decimal point and trailing zeros
ios::dec	Formats numeric values using base 10 (decimal) (default radix)
ios::oct	Formats numeric values using base 8 (octal)
ios::hex	Formats numeric values using base 16 (hexadecimal)
ios::fixed	Shows floating-point numbers with fixed format
ios::scientific	Shows floating-point numbers with scientific format
ios::showpos	Displays plus signs (+) in front of positive values
ios::skipws	Skips white space on input
ios::left	Left-aligns values (pad on the right with the specified fill character)
ios::right	Right-aligns all values (pad on the left with the specified fill character—default alignment)
ios::internal	Adds fill characters after any leading sign or base indication, but before the value
ios::uppercase	Displays uppercase "A" through "F" for hexadecimal values and "E" for scientific values
ios::unitbuf	Causes **ostream::osfx** to flush the stream after each insertion (default, **cerr** is buffered)
ios::stdio	Causes **ostream::osfx** to flush **stdout** and **stderr** after each insertion

Table 12-1. *Format Flags*

The following table lists some of the format bit fields you can use with the **setf(long,long)** instance (using a format flag and format bit field):

Bit Field	Meaning	Flags
ios::basefield	Integral base	ios::hex, ios::oct, ios::dec
ios::floatfield	Floating-point	ios::fixed, ios::scientific

There are certain predefined defaults. For example, integers are written and read in decimal notation. You can change the base to octal, hexadecimal, or back to decimal. By default, a floating-point value is output with six digits of precision. You can modify this by using the precision member function. The following C++ program uses these new member functions:

```
//
//   12ADVIO.CPP
//   A C++ program demonstrating advanced conversions and
//   formatting member functions since Release 2.0. The program
//   will also demonstrate how to convert each of the older
//   Release 1.2 form statements.
//   Copyright (c) Chris H. Pappas and William H. Murray, 1990
//

#include <string.h>
#include <strstream.h>

#define INULL_TERMINATOR 1

void row (void);

main()
{
  char    c         =   'A',
          psz1[]    =   "In making a living today many no ",
          psz2[]    =   "longer leave any room for life.";
  int     iln       =   0,
          ivalue    =   1234;
  double dPi        =   3.14159265;

  // new declarations needed for Release 2.0
  char psz_padstring5[5+INULL_TERMINATOR],
```

```
    psz_padstring38[38+INULL_TERMINATOR];

// conversions

// print the c
// R1.2 cout << form("\n[%2d] %c",++ln,c);
// Notice that << has been overloaded to output char
row(); // [ 1]
cout << c;

// print the ASCII code for c
// R1.2  form("\n[%2d] %d",++ln,c);
row(); // [ 2]
cout << (int)c;

// print character with ASCII 90
// R1.2  form("\n[%2d] %c",++ln,90);
row(); // [ 3]
cout << (char)90;

// print ivalue as octal value
// R1.2  form("\n[%2d] %o",++ln,ivalue);
row(); // [ 4]
cout << oct << ivalue;

// print lower-case hexadecimal
// R1.2  form("\n[%2d] %x",++ln,ivalue);
row(); // [ 5]
cout << hex << ivalue;

// print upper-case hexadecimal
// R1.2  form("\n[%2d] %X",++ln,ivalue);
row(); // [ 6] cout.setf(ios::uppercase);
cout << hex << ivalue;
cout.unsetf(ios::uppercase);    // turn uppercase off
cout << dec;                     // return to decimal base

// conversions and format options

// minimum width 1
// R1.2  form("\n[%2d] %c",++ln,c);
row(); // [ 7]
cout << c;

// minimum width 5, right-justify
```

```
// R1.2  form("\n[%2d] %5c",++ln,c);
row(); // [ 8]
// ostrstream(psz_padstring5,sizeof(psz_padstring5))
  << "     " << c << ends;
cout << psz_padstring5;

// minimum width 5, left-justify
// R1.2  form("\n[%2d] %-5c",++ln,c);
row(); // [ 9]
// ostrstream(psz_padstring5,sizeof(psz_padstring5))
  << c << "     " << ends;
cout << psz_padstring5;

// 33 automatically
// R1.2  form("\n[%d] %s",++ln,psz1);
row(); // [10]
cout << psz1;

// 31 automatically
// R1.2  form("\n[%d] %s",++ln,psz2);
row(); // [11]
cout << psz2;

// minimum 5 overriden, auto
// R1.2  form("\n[%d] %5s",++ln,psz1);
// notice that the width of 5 cannot be overriden!
row(); // [12]
cout.write(psz1,5);

// minimum width 38, right-justify
// R1.2  form("\n[%d] %38s",++ln,psz1);
// notice how the width of 38 ends with garbage data
row(); // [13]
cout.write(psz1,38);

// the following is the correct approach
cout << "\n\nCorrected approach:\n";
ostrstream(psz_padstring38,sizeof(psz_padstring38)) << "      "
  << psz1 << ends;
row(); // [14]
cout << psz_padstring38;

// minimum width 38, left-justify
// R1.2  form("\n[%d] %-38s",++ln,psz2);
ostrstream(psz_padstring38,sizeof(psz_padstring38))
```

```
      << psz2 << "          " << ends;
row(); // [15]
cout << psz_padstring38;

// default ivalue width
// R1.2  form("\n[%d] %d",++ln,ivalue);
row(); // [16]
cout << ivalue;

// printf ivalue with + sign
// R1.2  form("\n[%d] %+d",++ln,ivalue);
row(); // [17]
cout.setf(ios::showpos);     // don't want row number with +
cout << ivalue;
cout.unsetf(ios::showpos);

// minimum 3 overridden, auto
// R1.2  form("\n[%d] %3d",++ln,ivalue);
row(); // [18]
cout.width(3); // don't want row number padded to width of 3
cout << ivalue;

// minimum width 10, right-justify
// R1.2  form("\n[%d] %10d",++ln,ivalue);
row(); // [19]
cout.width(10);    // only in effect for first value printed
cout << ivalue;

// minimum width 10, left-justify
// R1.2  form("\n[%d] %-d",++ln,ivalue);
row(); // [20]
cout.width(10);
cout.setf(ios::left);
cout << ivalue;
cout.unsetf(ios::left);

// right-justify with leading 0's
// R1.2  form("\n[%d] %010d",++ln,ivalue);
row(); // [21]
cout.width(10);
cout.fill('0');
cout << ivalue;
cout.fill(' ');

// using default number of digits
```

```
// R1.2  form("\n[%d] %f",++ln,dPi);
row(); // [22]
cout << dPi;

// minimum width 20, right-justify
// R1.2  form("\n[%d] %20f",++ln,dPi);
row(); // [23]
cout.width(20);
cout << dPi;

// right-justify with leading 0's
// R1.2  form("\n[%d] %020f",++ln,dPi);
row(); // [24]
cout.width(20);
cout.fill('0');
cout << dPi;
cout.fill(' ');

// minimum width 20, left-justify
// R1.2  form("\n[%d] %-20f",++ln,dPi);
row(); // [25]
cout.width(20);
cout.setf(ios::left);
cout << dPi;

// left-justify with trailing 0's
// R1.2  form("\n[%d] %-020f",++ln,dPi);
row(); // [26]
cout.width(20);
cout.fill('0');
cout << dPi;
cout.unsetf(ios::left);
cout.fill(' ');

// additional formatting precision

// minimum width 19, print all 17
// R1.2  form("\n[%d] %19.19s",++ln,psz1);
row(); // [27]
cout << psz1;

// prints first 2 chars
// R1.2  form("\n[%d] %.2s",++ln,psz1);
row(); // [28]
cout.write(psz1,2);
```

```
// prints 2 chars, right-justify
// R1.2  form("\n[%d] %19.2s",++ln,psz1);
row(); // [29]
cout << "                   "; cout.write(psz1,2);

// prints 2 chars, left-justify
// R1.2  form("\n[%d] %-19.2s",++ln,psz1);
row(); // [30]
cout.write(psz1,2);

// using printf arguments
// R1.2  form("\n[%d] %*.*s",++ln,19,6,psz1);
row(); // [31]
cout << "               "; cout.write(psz1,6);

// width 10, 8 to right of '.'
// R1.2  form("\n[%d] %10.8f",++ln,dPi);
row(); // [32]
cout.precision(9);
cout << dPi;

// width 20, 2 to right-justify
// R1.2  form("\n[%d] %20.2f",++ln,dPi);
row(); // [33]
cout.width(20);
cout.precision(2);
cout << dPi;

// 4 decimal places, left-justify
// R1.2  form("\n[%d] %-20.4f",++ln,dPi);
row(); // [34]
cout.precision(4);
cout << dPi;

// 4 decimal places, right-justify
// R1.2  form("\n[%d] %20.4f",++ln,dPi);
row(); // [35]
cout.width(20);
cout << dPi;

// width 20, scientific notation
// R1.2  form("\n[%d] %20.2e",++ln,dPi);
row(); // [36] cout.setf(ios::scientific); cout.width(20);
cout << dPi; cout.unsetf(ios::scientific);
```

```
    return(0);
}

void row (void)
{
    static int ln=0;
    cout << "\n[";
    cout.width(2);
    cout << ++ln << "] ";
}
```

You can use the output from the program to help write advanced output statements of your own:

```
[ 1] A
[ 2] 65
[ 3] Z
[ 4] 2322
[ 5] 4d2
[ 6] 4D2
[ 7] A
[ 8]      A
[ 9] A
[10] In making a living today many no
[11] longer leave any room for life.
[12] In ma
[13] In making a living today many no A
Corrected approach:

[14]       In making a living today many no
[15] longer leave any room for life.
[16] 1234
[17] +1234
[18] 1234
[19]         1234
[20] 1234
[21] 0000001234
[22] 3.14159
[23]                 3.14159
[24] 00000000000003.14159
[25] 3.14159
[26] 3.141590000000000000
[27] In making a living today many no
```

```
[28]  In
[29]                         In
[30]  In
[31]                  In mak
[32]  3.14159265
[33]                    3.1
[34]  3.142
[35]                  3.142
[36]            3.1416e+000
```

The following section highlights those output statements used in the preceding program that need special clarification. One point needs to be made: iostream.h is automatically included by strstream.h. The latter file is needed to perform string output formatting. If your application needs to output numeric data or simple character and string output. you will need to include only iostream.h.

C++ Character Output

In the new I/O library (since Release 2.0), the insertion operator << has been overloaded to handle character data. With the earlier release, the following statement would have output the ASCII value of *c*:

```
cout << c;
```

In the current I/O library, the letter itself is output. For those programs needing the ASCII value, a case is required:

```
cout << (int)C;
```

C++ Base Conversions

There are two approaches to outputting a value using a different base:

```
cout << hex << ivalue;
```

and

```
cout.setf(ios::hex,ios::basefield);
cout << ivalue;
```

Both approaches cause the base to be permanently changed from the statement forward (not always the effect you want). Each value output will now be formatted

as a hexadecimal value. Returning to some other base is accomplished with the
unsetf() function:

```
cout.unsetf(ios::hex,ios::basefield);
```

If you are interested in uppercase hexadecimal output, use the following statement:

```
cout.setf(ios::uppercase);
```

When it is no longer needed, you will have to turn this option off:

```
cout.unsetf(ios::uppercase);
```

C++ String Formatting

Printing an entire string is easy in C++. However, string formatting has changed
because the Release 1.2 cout << form is no longer available. One approach to string
formatting is to declare an array of characters and then select the desired output
format, printing the string buffer:

```
pszpadstring38[38+INULL_TERMINATOR];
.
.
.
ostrstream(pszpadstring38,sizeof(pszpadstring38))
    << "      "    << psz1;
```

The **ostrstream()** member function is part of strstream.h and has three parameters: a pointer to an array of characters, the size of the array, and the information to
be inserted. This statement appends leading blanks to right justify *psz1*. Portions of
the string can be output using the **write** form of **cout**:

```
cout.write(psz1,5);
```

This statement will output the first five characters of *psz1*.

C++ Numeric Formatting

You can easily format numeric data with right or left justification, varying precisions,
varying formats (floating-point or scientific), leading or trailing fill patterns, and
signs. There are certain defaults. For example, the default for justification is right
and for floating-point precision is six. The following code segment outputs *dPi* left
justified in a field width of 20, with trailing zeros:

```
cout.width(20);
cout.setf(ios::left);
cout.fill('0');
cout << dPi;
```

Had the following statement been included, *dPi* would have been printed with a precision of two:

```
cout.precision(2);
```

With many of the output flags such as left justification, selecting uppercase hexadecimal output, base changes, and many others, it is necessary to unset these flags when they are no longer needed. The following statement turns left justification off:

```
cout.unsetf(ios::left);
```

Selecting scientific format is a matter of flipping the correct bit flag:

```
cout.setf(ios::scientific);
```

You can print values with a leading + sign by setting the *showpos* flag:

```
cout.setf(ios::showpos);
```

There are many minor details of the current I/O library functions that will initially cause some confusion. This has to do with the fact that certain operations, once executed, make a permanent change until turned off, while others take effect only for the next output statement. For example, an output width change, as in **cout.width(20);**, affects only the next value printed. That is why the function **row()** has to repeatedly change the width to get the output row numbers formatted within two spaces, as in [1]. However, other formatting operations like base changes, uppercase, precision, and floating-point/scientific remain active until specifically turned off.

C++ File Input and Output

All of the examples so far have used the predefined streams **cin** and **cout**. It is possible that your program will need to create its own streams for I/O. If an application needs to create a file for input or output, it must include the fstream.h header file (fstream.h includes iostream.h). The classes **ifstream** and **ofstream** are derived from **istream** and **ostream** and inherit the extraction and insertion operations, respectively. The following C++ program demonstrates how to declare a file for reading and writing using **ifstream** and **ofstream**, respectively:

```
//
//  12FSTRM.CPP
//  A C++ program demonstrating how to declare an
//  ifstream and ofstream for file input and output.
//  Copyright (c) William H. Murray and Chris H. Pappas, 1992
//

#include <fstream.h>

int main(void)
{
  char c;

  ifstream ifsin("a:\\text.in",ios::in);
  if( !ifsin )
    cerr << "\nUnable to open 'text.in' for input.";

  ofstream ofsout("a:\\text.out",ios::out);
  if( !ofsout )
    cerr << "\nUnable to open 'text.out' for output.";

  while( ofsout && ifsin.get(c) )
    ofsout.put(c);

  ifsin.close();
  ofsout.close();

  return(0);
}
```

The program declares *ifsin* to be of class **ifstream** and is associated with the file TEXT.IN stored in the A drive. It is always a good idea for any program dealing with files to verify the existence or creation of the specified file in the designated mode. By using the handle to the file *ifsin*, a simple **if** test can be generated to check the condition of the file. A similar process is applied to *ofsout*, with the exception that the file is derived from the **ostream** class.

The **while** loop continues inputting and outputting single characters while the *ifsin* exists and the character read in is not *EOF*. The program terminates by closing the two files. Closing an output file can be essential to dumping all internally buffered data.

There may be circumstances when a program will want to delay a file specification or when an application may want to associate several file streams with the same file descriptor. The following code segment demonstrates this concept:

```
ifstream ifsin;
.

.

.

ifsin.open("week1.in");
.

.

.

ifsin.close();
ifsin.open("week2.in");
.

.

.

ifsin.close();
```

Whenever an application wishes to modify the way in which a file is opened or used, it can apply a second argument to the file stream constructors. For example:

```
ofstream ofsout("week1.out",ios::app|ios::noreplace);
```

This statement declares *ofsout* and attempts to append it to the file named WEEK1.OUT. Because **ios::noreplace** is specified, the file will not be created if WEEK1.OUT doesn't already exist. The **ios::app** parameter appends all writes to an existing file. The following table lists the second argument flags to the file stream constructors that can be logically ORed together:

Mode Bit	Action
ios::in	Opens for reading
ios::out	Opens for writing
ios::ate	Seeks to *EOF* after file is created
ios::app	All writes added to end of file
ios::trunc	If file already exists, truncates
ios::nocreate	Unsuccessful open if file does not exist
ios::noreplace	Unsuccessful open if file does exist
ios::binary	Opens file in binary mode(default text)

An **fstream** class object can also be used to open a file for both input and output. For example, the following definition opens the file UPDATE.DAT in both input and append mode:

```
fstream io("update.dat",ios::in|ios::app);
```

You can reposition all **iostream** class types by using either the **seekg()** or **seekp()** member function, which can move to an absolute address within the file or move a byte offset from a particular position. Both **seekg()** (sets or reads the get pointer's position) and **seekp()** (sets or reads the put pointer's position) can take one or two arguments. When used with one parameter, the **iostream** is repositioned to the specified pointer position. When it is used with two parameters, a relative position is calculated. The following listing highlights these differences, assuming the preceding declaration for *io*.

```
streampos current_position = io.tellp();
io << obj1 << obj2 << obj3;
io.seekp(current_position);
io.seekp(sizeof(MY_OBJ),ios::cur);
io << objnewobj2;
```

The pointer *current_position* is first derived from **streampos** and initialized to the current position of the put-file pointer by the function **tellp()**. With this information stored, three objects are written to *io*. Using **seekp()**, the put-file pointer is repositioned to the beginning of the file. The second **seekp()** statement uses the **sizeof()** operator to calculate the number of bytes necessary to move one object's width into the file. This effectively skips over *obj1*'s position, permitting an *objnewobj2* to be written.

If a second argument is passed to **seekg()** or **seekp()**, it defines the direction to move: **ios::beg** (from the beginning), **ios::cur** (from the current position), and **ios::end** (from the end of the file). For example, this line will move into the get_file pointer file 5 bytes from the current position:

```
io.seekg(5,ios::cur);
```

The next line will move the get_file pointer 7 bytes backward from the end of the file:

```
io.seekg(-7,ios::end);
```

C++ File Condition States

Associated with every stream is an error state. When an error occurs, bits are set in the state according to the general category of the error. By convention, inserters ignore attempts to insert things into an ostream with error bits set, and such attempts do not change the stream's state. The iostream library object contains a set of predefined condition flags, which monitor the ongoing state of the stream. The following table lists the seven member functions that can be invoked:

Member Function	Action
eof()	Returns a nonzero value on end-of-file
fail()	Returns a nonzero value if an operation failed
bad()	Returns a nonzero value if an error occurred
good()	Returns a nonzero value if no state bits are set
rdstate()	Returns the current stream state
clear()	Sets the stream state (int=0)

You can use these member functions in various algorithms to solve unique I/O conditions and to make the code more readable:

```
ifstream pfsinfile("sample.dat",ios::in);
if(pfsinfile.eof())
  pfsinfile.clear(); // sets the state of pfsinfile to 0

if(pfsinfile.fail())
  cerr << ">>> sample.dat creation error <<<";

if(pfsinfile.good())
  cin >> my_object;

if(!pfsinfile) // shortcut
  cout << ">>> sample.dat creation error <<<";
```

Chapters 13 through 16 cover C++ fundamentals that are necessary to understand and use advanced C++ I/O. You will learn about advanced C++ I/O in Chapter 17.

Chapter *13*

Structures, Unions, and Miscellaneous Items

In this chapter you will investigate several advanced C and C++ types, such as structures, unions, and bit-fields, along with other miscellaneous topics. You will learn how to create and use structures in programs. The chapter also covers how to pass structure information to functions, use pointers with structures, create and use unions in programs, and use other important features, such as **typedef** and enumerated types (**enum**).

The main portion of the chapter concentrates on two important features common to C and C++, the structure and the union. The C or C++ structure is conceptually an array or vector of closely related items. Unlike an array or vector, however, a structure permits the contained items to be of assorted data types.

The structure is very important to C and C++. Structures serve as the flagship of a more advanced C++ type, called the class. If you become comfortable with structures, it will be much easier for you to understand C++ classes. This is because C++ classes share, and expand upon, many of the features of a structure. Chapters 16 and 18 are devoted to the C++ class.

Unions, another advanced type, allow you to store different data types at the same place in your system's memory. These advanced data types serve as the foundation of most spreadsheet and database programs.

In the section that follows, you learn how to build simple structures, create arrays of structures, pass structures and arrays of structures to functions, and access structure elements with pointers.

C and C++ Structures

The notion of a data structure is a very familiar idea in everyday life. A card file containing friends' addresses, telephone numbers, and so on, is a structure of related items. A file of favorite CDs or LP records is a structure. A computer's directory listing is a structure. These are examples that use a structure, but what is a structure? Literally, a *structure* can be thought of as a group of variables, which can be of different types, held together in a single unit. The single unit is the structure.

C and C++ Structures: Syntax and Rules

In C or C++, you form a structure by using the keyword **struct**, followed by an optional tag field, and then a list of members within the structure. The optional tag field is used to create other variables of the particular structure's type. The syntax for a structure with the optional tag field looks like this:

```
struct tag_field {
    member_type member1
    member_type member2
    member_type member3

          .
          .
          .

    member_type membern
};
```

A semicolon terminates the structure definition because it is actually a C and C++ statement. Several of the example programs in this chapter use a structure similar to the following:

```
struct stboat {
  char sztype [iSTRING15 + iNULL_CHAR];
  char szmodel[iSTRING15 + iNULL_CHAR];
  char sztitle[iSTRING20 + iNULL_CHAR];
  int iyear;
  long int lmotor_hours;
  float fsaleprice;
};
```

The structure is created with the keyword **struct** followed by the tag field or type for the structure. In this example, *stboat* is the tag field for the structure.

This structure declaration contains several members; *sztype, szmodel,* and *sztitle* are null-terminated strings of the specified length. These strings are followed by an integer, *iyear,* a long integer, *lmotor_hours,* and a float, *fsaleprice.* The structure will be used to save sales information for a boat.

So far, all that has been defined is a new hypothetical structure type called **stboat**. However, no variable has been associated with the structure at this point. In a program, you can associate a variable with a structure by using a statement similar to the following:

```
struct stboat stused_boat;
```

The statement defines *stused_boat* to be of the type **struct stboat.** Notice that the declaration required the use of the structure's tag field. If this statement is contained within a function, then the structure, named *stused_boat,* is local in scope to that function. If the statement is contained outside of all program functions, the structure will be global in scope. It is also possible to declare a structure variable using this syntax:

```
struct stboat {
  char sztype [iSTRING15 + iNULL_CHAR];
  char szmodel[iSTRING15 + iNULL_CHAR];
  char sztitle[iSTRING20 + iNULL_CHAR];
  int iyear;
  long int lmotor_hours;
  float fsaleprice;
} stused_boat;
```

Here, the variable declaration is sandwiched between the structure's closing brace (}) and the required semicolon (;). In both examples, *stused_boat* is declared as structure type **stboat**. Actually, when only one variable is associated with a structure type, the tag field can be eliminated, so it would also be possible to write

```
struct {
  char sztype [iSTRING15 + iNULL_CHAR];
  char szmodel[iSTRING15 + iNULL_CHAR];
  char sztitle[iSTRING20 + iNULL_CHAR];
  int iyear;
  long int lmotor_hours;
  float fsaleprice;
} stused_boat;
```

Notice that this structure declaration does not include a tag field and creates what is called an *anonymous structure type.* While the statement does define a single variable, *stused_boat,* there is no way the application can create another variable of the same type somewhere else in the application. Without the structure's tag field, there is no syntactically legal way to refer to the new type. However, it is possible to associate several variables with the same structure type, without specifying a tag field, as shown in the following listing:

```
struct {
  char sztype [iSTRING15 + iNULL_CHAR];
  char szmodel[iSTRING15 + iNULL_CHAR];
  char sztitle[iSTRING20 + iNULL_CHAR];
  int iyear;
  long int lmotor_hours;
  float fsaleprice;
} stboat1,stboat2,stboat3;
```

The C and C++ compiler allocates all necessary memory for the structure members, as it does for any other variable. To decide if your structure declarations need a tag field, ask yourself the following questions: "Will I need to create other variables of this structure type somewhere else in the program?" and "Will I be passing the structure type to functions?" If the answer to either of these questions is yes, you need a tag field.

C++ Structures: Syntax and Rule Extensions

In many cases, C++ can be described as a superset of C. In general, this means that what works in C should work in C++.

Using C design philosophies in a C++ program often ignores C++'s streamlining enhancements.

The structure declaration syntax styles just described all work with both the C and C++ compilers. However, C++ has one additional method for declaring variables of a particular structure type. This exclusive C++ shorthand notation eliminates the need to repeat the keyword **struct**. The following example highlights this subtle difference:

```
/* legal C and C++ structure declaration syntax */
struct stboat stused_boat;

// exclusive C++ structure declaration syntax
stboat stused_boat;
```

Accessing Structure Members

It is possible to reference the individual members within a structure by using the *dot* or *member operator* (.). The syntax is

stname.*mname*

Here, *stname* is the variable associated with the structure type and *mname* is the name of any member variable in the structure.

In C, for example, information can be placed in the *szmodel* member with a statement such as

```
gets(stused_boat.szmodel);
```

Here, *stused_boat* is the name associated with the structure and *szmodel* is a member variable of the structure. In a similar manner, you can use a **printf()** function to print information for a structure member:

```
printf("%ld",stused_boat.lmotor_hours);
```

The syntax for accessing structure members is basically the same in C++:

```
cin >> stused_boat.sztype;
```

This statement will read the make of the *stused_boat* into the character array, while the next statement will print the *stused_boat* selling price to the screen:

```
cout << stused_boat.fsaleprice;
```

Structure members are handled like any other C or C++ variable with the exception that the dot operator must always be used with them.

Constructing a Simple Structure

The example program for this section will use a structure similar to the *stboat* structure given earlier in this chapter. Examine the listing that follows to see if you understand how the various structure elements are accessed by the program:

```
/*
 *    13STRUCT.C
 *    C program illustrates how to construct a structure.
 *    Program stores data about your boat in a C structure.
 *    Copyright (c) William H. Murray and Chris H. Pappas, 1992
 */

#include <stdio.h>

#define iSTRING15 15
#define iSTRING20 20
#define iNULL_CHAR 1

struct stboat {
  char sztype [iSTRING15 + iNULL_CHAR];
  char szmodel[iSTRING15 + iNULL_CHAR];
  char sztitle[iSTRING20 + iNULL_CHAR];
  int iyear;
  long int lmotor_hours;
  float fsaleprice;
} stused_boat;

int main(void)
{
  printf("\nPlease enter the make of the boat: ");
  gets(stused_boat.sztype);

  printf("\nPlease enter the model of the boat: ");
  gets(stused_boat.szmodel);

  printf("\nPlease enter the title number for the boat: ");
  gets(stused_boat.sztitle);

  printf("\nPlease enter the model year for the boat: ");
  scanf("%d",&stused_boat.iyear);

  printf("\nPlease enter the current hours on ");
  printf("the motor for the boat: ");
  scanf("%ld",&stused_boat.lmotor_hours);

  printf("\nPlease enter the purchase price of the boat: ");
  scanf("%f",&stused_boat.fsaleprice);

  printf("\n\n\n");
  printf("A %d %s %s with title number #%s\n",
```

```
      stused_boat.iyear,stused_boat.sztype,
      stused_boat.szmodel,stused_boat.sztitle);
  printf("currently has %ld motor hours",
      stused_boat.lmotor_hours);
  printf(" and was purchased for $%8.2f\n",
      stused_boat.fsaleprice);

  return (0);
}
```

The output from the preceding example shows how information can be manipulated with a structure:

```
A 1952 Chris Craft with title number #CC1011771018C
currently has 34187 motor hours and was purchased for $68132.98
```

You might notice, at this point, that *stused_boat* has a global file scope since it was declared outside of any function.

Passing Structures to Functions

There will be many occasions where it is necessary to pass structure information to functions. When a structure is passed to a function, the information is passed call-by-value. Since only a copy of the information is being passed in, it is impossible for the function to alter the contents of the original structure. You can pass a structure to a function by using the following syntax:

```
fname(stvariable);
```

If *stused_boat* was made local in scope to **main( )**, if you move its declaration inside the function, it could be passed to a function named **vprint_data( )** with the statement

```
vprint_data(stused_boat);
```

The **vprint_data( )** prototype must declare the structure type it is about to receive, as you might suspect:

```
/* legal C and C++ structure declaration syntax */
void vprint_data(struct stboat stany_boat);

// exclusive C++ structure declaration syntax
void vprint_data(stboat stany_boat);
```

Passing entire copies of structures to functions is not always the most efficient way of programming. Where time is a factor, the use of pointers might be a better choice. If saving memory is a consideration, the **malloc()** function for dynamically allocating structure memory in C when using linked lists is often used instead of statically allocated memory. You'll see how this is done in the next chapter.

The next example shows how to pass a complete structure to a function. Notice that it is a simple modification of the last example. The next four example programs use the same basic approach. Each program modifies only that portion of the algorithm necessary to explain the current subject. This approach will allow you to easily view the code and syntax changes necessary to implement a particular language feature. Study the listing and see how the structure, *stused_boat*, is passed to the function, **vprint_data()**.

```c
/*
 *   13PASSST.C
 *   C program shows how to pass a structure to a function.
 *   Copyright (c) William H. Murray and Chris H. Pappas, 1992
 */

#include <stdio.h>

#define iSTRING15 15
#define iSTRING20 20
#define iNULL_CHAR 1

struct stboat {
  char sztype [iSTRING15 + iNULL_CHAR];
  char szmodel[iSTRING15 + iNULL_CHAR];
  char sztitle[iSTRING20 + iNULL_CHAR];
  int iyear;
  long int lmotor_hours;
  float fsaleprice;
};

void vprint_data(struct stboat stany_boat);

int main(void)
{
  struct stboat stused_boat;

  printf("\nPlease enter the make of the boat: ");
  gets(stused_boat.sztype);

  printf("\nPlease enter the model of the boat: ");
```

```
  gets(stused_boat.szmodel);

  printf("\nPlease enter the title number for the boat: ");
  gets(stused_boat.sztitle);

  printf("\nPlease enter the model year for the boat: ");
  scanf("%d",&stused_boat.iyear);

  printf("\nPlease enter the current hours on ");
  printf("the motor for the boat: ");
  scanf("%ld",&stused_boat.lmotor_hours);

  printf("\nPlease enter the purchase price of the boat: ");
  scanf("%f",&stused_boat.fsaleprice);

  vprint_data(stused_boat);

  return (0);
}

void vprint_data(struct stboat stany_boat)
{
  printf("\n\n");
  printf("A %d %s %s with title number #%s\n",stany_boat.iyear,
      stany_boat.sztype,stany_boat.szmodel,stany_boat.sztitle);
  printf("currently has %ld motor hours",stany_boat.lmotor_hours);
  printf(" and was purchased for $%8.2f",
         stany_boat.fsaleprice);
}
```

In this example, an entire structure was passed by value to the function. The calling procedure simply invokes the function by passing the structure variable, *stused_boat*. Notice that the structure's tag field, *stboat*, was needed in the **vprint_data()** function prototype and declaration. As you will see later in this chapter, it is also possible to pass individual structure members by value to a function. The output from this program is similar to the previous example.

Constructing an Array of Structures

A structure can be considered as being similar to a single card from a card file. The real power in using structures comes about when a collection of structures, called an *array of structures,* is used. An array of structures is similar to the whole card file containing a great number of individual cards. If you maintain an array of structures, a database of information can be manipulated for a wide range of items.

This array of structures might include information on all of the boats at a local marina. It would be practical for a boat dealer to maintain such a file and be able to pull out of a database all boats on the lot selling for less than $45,000 or all boats with a minimum of one stateroom. Study the following example and note how the code has been changed from earlier examples:

```c
/*
 *   13STCARY.C
 *   C program uses an array of structures.
 *   This example creates a "used boat inventory" for
 *   Nineveh Boat Sales.
 *   Copyright (c) William H. Murray and Chris H. Pappas, 1992
 */

#include <stdio.h>

#define iSTRING15 15
#define iSTRING20 20
#define iNULL_CHAR 1
#define iMAX_BOATS 50

struct stboat {
  char sztype [iSTRING15 + iNULL_CHAR];
  char szmodel[iSTRING15 + iNULL_CHAR];
  char sztitle[iSTRING20 + iNULL_CHAR];
  char szcomment[80];
  int iyear;
  long int lmotor_hours;
  float fretail;
  float fwholesale;
};

int main(void)
{
  int i,iinstock;
  struct stboat astNineveh[iMAX_BOATS];

  printf("How many boats in inventory? ");
  scanf("%d",&iinstock);

  for (i=0; i<iinstock; i++) {

    flushall();      /* flush keyboard buffer */
    printf("\nPlease enter the make of the boat: ");
```

```
        gets(astNineveh[i].sztype);

        printf("\nPlease enter the model of the boat: ");
        gets(astNineveh[i].szmodel);

        printf("\nPlease enter the title number for the boat: ");
        gets(astNineveh[i].sztitle);

        printf("\nPlease enter a one line comment about the boat: ");
        gets(astNineveh[i].szcomment);

        printf("\nPlease enter the model year for the boat: ");
        scanf("%d",&astNineveh[i].iyear);

        printf("\nPlease enter the current hours on ");
        printf("the motor for the boat: ");
        scanf("%ld",&astNineveh[i].lmotor_hours);

        printf("\nPlease enter the retail price of the boat :");
        scanf("%f",&astNineveh[i].fretail);

        printf("\nPlease enter the wholesale price of the boat :");
        scanf("%f",&astNineveh[i].fwholesale);
    }

    printf("\n\n\n");

    for (i=0; i<iinstock; i++) {
        printf("A %d %s %s beauty with %ld low hours.\n",
                astNineveh[i].iyear,astNineveh[i].sztype,
                astNineveh[i].szmodel,astNineveh[i].lmotor_hours);
        printf("%s\n",astNineveh[i].szcomment);
        printf(
            "Grab the deal by asking your Nineveh salesperson for");
        printf(" #%s ONLY! $%8.2f.\n",astNineveh[i].sztitle,
                astNineveh[i].fretail);
        printf("\n\n");
    }

    return (0);
}
```

Here, Nineveh Boat Sales has an array of structures set up to hold information about the boats in the marina.

The variable *astNineveh[iMAX_BOATS]* associated with the structure, **struct stboat**, is actually an array. In this case, *iMAX_BOATS* sets the maximum array size to 50. This simply means that data on 50 boats can be maintained in the array of structures. It will be necessary to know which of the boats in the file you wish to view. The first array element is zero. Therefore, information on the first boat in the array of structures can be accessed with a statement such as

```
gets(astNineveh[0].sztitle);
```

As you study the program, notice that the array elements are accessed with the help of a loop. In this manner, element members are obtained with code, such as

```
gets(astNineveh[i].sztitle);
```

The **flushall()** statement inside the **for** loop is necessary to remove the newline left in the input stream from the previous **scanf()** statements (the one before the loop is entered and the last **scanf()** statement within the loop). Without the call to **flushall()**, the **gets()** statement would be skipped over. Remember, **gets()** reads everything up to and including the newline. Both **scanf()** statements leave the newline in the input stream. Without the call to **flushall()**, the **gets()** statement would simply grab the newline from the input stream and move on to the next executable statement.

The previous program's output serves to illustrate the small stock of boats on hand at Nineveh Boat Sales. It also shows how structure information can be rearranged in output statements:

```
A 1957 Chris Craft Dayliner 124876 low hours.
A great riding boat owned by a salesperson.
Grab the deal by asking your Nineveh salesperson for
#BS12345BFD ONLY! $36234.00.

A 1988 Starcraft Weekender a beauty with 27657 low hours.
Runs and looks great. Owned by successful painter.
Grab the deal by asking your Nineveh salesperson for
#BG7774545AFD ONLY! $18533.99.

A 1991 Scarab a wower with 1000 low hours.
A cheap means of transportation. Owned by grandfather.
Grab the deal by asking your Nineveh salesperson for
#156AFG4476 ONLY! $56999.99.
```

When you are working with arrays of structures, be aware of the memory limitations of the system you are programming on—statically allocated memory for arrays of structures can require large amounts of system memory.

Using Pointers to Structures

In the next program, an array of structures is created in a similar manner to the last program. The *arrow operator* is used in this example to access individual structure members. The arrow operator can be used *only* when a pointer to a structure has been created.

```
/*
 *   13PTRSTC.C
 *   C program uses pointers to an array of structures.
 *   The Nineveh boat inventory example is used again.
 *   Copyright (c) William H. Murray and Chris H. Pappas, 1992
 */

#include <stdio.h>

#define iSTRING15 15
#define iSTRING20 20
#define iNULL_CHAR 1
#define iMAX_BOATS 50

struct stboat {
  char sztype [iSTRING15 + iNULL_CHAR];
  char szmodel[iSTRING15 + iNULL_CHAR];
  char sztitle[iSTRING20 + iNULL_CHAR];
  char szcomment[80];
  int iyear;
  long int lmotor_hours;
  float fretail;
  float fwholesale;
};

int main(void)
{
  int i,iinstock;
  struct stboat astNineveh[iMAX_BOATS],*pastNineveh;
  pastNineveh=&astNineveh[0];

  printf("How many boats in inventory? ");
  scanf("%d",&iinstock);


    for (i=0; i<iinstock; i++) {
       flushall();      /*  flush keyboard buffer */
       printf("\nPlease enter the make of the boat: ");
```

```
        gets(pastNineveh->sztype);

        printf("\nPlease enter the model of the boat: ");
        gets(pastNineveh->szmodel);

        printf("\nPlease enter the title number for the boat: ");
        gets(pastNineveh->sztitle);

        printf(
           "\nPlease enter a one line comment about the boat: ");
        gets(pastNineveh->szcomment);

        printf("\nPlease enter the model year for the boat: ");
        scanf("%d",&pastNineveh->iyear);

        printf("\nPlease enter the current hours on ");
        printf("the motor for the boat: ");
        scanf("%ld",&pastNineveh->lmotor_hours);

        printf("\nPlease enter the retail price of the boat: ");
        scanf("%f",&pastNineveh->fretail);

        printf(
           "\nPlease enter the wholesale price of the boat: ");
        scanf("%f",&pastNineveh->fwholesale);

        pastNineveh++;
      }

    pastNineveh=&astNineveh[0];
    printf("\n\n\n");

    for (i=0; i<iinstock; i++) {
      printf("A %d %s %s beauty with %ld low hours.\n",
                pastNineveh->iyear,pastNineveh->sztype,
                pastNineveh->szmodel,pastNineveh->lmotor_hours);
      printf("%s\n",pastNineveh->szcomment);
      printf(
         "Grab the deal by asking your Nineveh salesperson for:");
      printf("\n#%s ONLY! $%8.2f.\n",pastNineveh->sztitle,
            pastNineveh->fretail);
            printf("\n\n");
            pastNineveh++;
      }
```

```
    return (0);
}
```

The array variable, *astNineveh[iMAX_BOATS]*, and the pointer, **pastNineveh*, are associated with the structure by using the following statement:

```
struct stboat astNineveh[iMAX_BOATS],*pastNineveh;
```

The address of the array, *astNineveh*, is copied into the pointer variable, *pastNineveh*, with the following code:

```
pastNineveh=&astNineveh[0];
```

While it is syntactically legal to reference array elements with the syntax that follows, it is not the preferred method:

```
gets((*pastNineveh).sztype);
```

Because of operator precedence, the extra parentheses are necessary to prevent the dot (.) member operator from binding before the pointer, **pastNineveh*, is dereferenced. It is better to use the arrow operator, which makes the overall operation much cleaner:

```
gets(pastNineveh->sztype);
```

While this is not a complex example, it does illustrate the use of the arrow operator. The example also prepares you for the real advantage in using pointers— passing an array of structures to a function.

Passing an Array of Structures to a Function

Earlier in the chapter it was mentioned that passing a pointer to a structure could have a speed advantage over simply passing a copy of a structure to a function. This fact becomes more evident when a program makes heavy use of structures. The next program shows how an array of structures can be accessed by a function with the use of a pointer:

```
/*
 *   13PSASTC.C
 *   C program shows how a function can access an array
 *   of structures with the use of a pointer.
 *   The Nineveh stboat inventory is used again!
```

```
*    Copyright (c) William H. Murray and Chris H. Pappas, 1992
*/

#include <stdio.h>

#define iSTRING15 15
#define iSTRING20 20
#define iNULL_CHAR 1
#define iMAX_BOATS 50

int iinstock;

struct stboat {
  char sztype [iSTRING15 + iNULL_CHAR];
  char szmodel[iSTRING15 + iNULL_CHAR];
  char sztitle[iSTRING20 + iNULL_CHAR];
  char szcomment[80];
  int iyear;
  long int lmotor_hours;
  float fretail;
  float fwholesale;
};

void vprint_data(struct stboat *stany_boatptr);

int main(void)
{
  int i;
  struct stboat  astNineveh[iMAX_BOATS],*pastNineveh;
  pastNineveh=&astNineveh[0];

  printf("How many boats in inventory?\n");
  scanf("%d",&iinstock);

  for (i=0; i<iinstock; i++) {

    flushall();      /*  flush keyboard buffer */
    printf("\nPlease enter the make of the boat: ");
    gets(pastNineveh->sztype);

    printf("\nPlease enter the model of the boat: ");
    gets(pastNineveh->szmodel);

    printf("\nPlease enter the title number for the boat: ");
    gets(pastNineveh->sztitle);
```

```
      printf("\nPlease enter a one line comment about the boat: ");
      gets(pastNineveh->szcomment);

      printf("\nPlease enter the model year for the boat: ");
      scanf("%d",&pastNineveh->iyear);

      printf("\nPlease enter the current hours on ");
      printf("the motor for the boat: ");
      scanf("%ld",&pastNineveh->lmotor_hours);

      printf("\nPlease enter the retail price of the boat: ");
      scanf("%f",&pastNineveh->fretail);

      printf("\nPlease enter the wholesale price of the boat: ");
      scanf("%f",&pastNineveh->fwholesale);

      pastNineveh++;
   }

   pastNineveh=&astNineveh[0];

   vprint_data(pastNineveh);

   return (0);
}

void vprint_data(struct stboat *stany_boatptr)
{
   int i;
   printf("\n\n\n");
   for (i=0; i<iinstock; i++) {
      printf("A %d %s %s beauty with %ld low hours.\n",
             stany_boatptr->iyear,stany_boatptr->sztype,
             stany_boatptr->szmodel,stany_boatptr->lmotor_hours);
      printf("%s\n",stany_boatptr->szcomment);
      printf(
         "Grab the deal by asking your Nineveh salesperson for");
      printf(" #%s ONLY! $%8.2f.\n",stany_boatptr->sztitle,
             stany_boatptr->fretail);
      printf("\n\n");
      stany_boatptr++;
   }
}
```

The first indication that this program will operate differently from the last program comes from the **vprint_data()** function prototype:

```
void vprint_data(struct stboat *stany_boatptr);
```

This function expects to receive a pointer to the structure mentioned. In the function, **main()**, the array *astNineveh[iMAX_BOATS]*, and the pointer **pastNineveh* are associated with the structure with the following code:

```
struct stboat astNineveh[iMAX_BOATS],*pastNineveh;
```

Once the information has been collected for Nineveh Stboat Sales, it is passed to the **vprint_data()** function by passing the pointer:

```
vprint_data(pastNineveh);
```

One major advantage of passing an array of structures to a function using pointers is that the array is now passed call-by-variable, or call-by-reference. This means that the function can now access the original array structure, not just a copy. With this calling convention, any change made to the array of structures within the function is global in scope. The output from this program is the same as for the previous examples.

Structure Use in C++

Next is a C++ program that is similar to the last C program. In terms of syntax, both languages can handle structures in an identical manner. However, the example program takes advantage of C++'s shorthand structure syntax:

```
//
//  13STRUCT.CPP
//  C++ program shows the use of pointers when
//  accessing structure information from a function.
//  Note:  Comment line terminates with a period (.)
//  Copyright (c) William H. Murray and Chris H. Pappas, 1992
//

#include <iostream.h>

#define iSTRING15 15
#define iSTRING20 20
#define iNULL_CHAR 1
#define iMAX_BOATS 50
```

```
int iinstock;

struct stboat {
  char sztype [iSTRING15 + iNULL_CHAR];
  char szmodel[iSTRING15 + iNULL_CHAR];
  char sztitle[iSTRING20 + iNULL_CHAR];
  char szcomment[80];
  int iyear;
  long int lmotor_hours;
  float fretail;
  float fwholesale;
};

void vprint_data(stboat *stany_boatptr);

int main(void)
{
  int i;
  char newline;
  stboat astNineveh[iMAX_BOATS],*pastNineveh;
  pastNineveh=&astNineveh[0];

  cout << "How many boats in inventory? ";
  cin >> iinstock;

  for (i=0; i<iinstock; i++) {
    cout << "\nPlease enter the make of the boat: ";
    cin >> pastNineveh->sztype;

    cout << "\nPlease enter the model of the boat: ";
    cin >> pastNineveh->szmodel;

    cout << "\nPlease enter the title number for the boat: ";
    cin >> pastNineveh->sztitle;

    cout << "\nPlease enter the model year for the boat: ";
    cin >> pastNineveh->iyear;

    cout << "\nPlease enter the current hours on "
         << "the motor for the boat: ";
    cin >> pastNineveh->lmotor_hours;

    cout << "\nPlease enter the retail price of the boat: ";
    cin >> pastNineveh->fretail;
```

```
    cout << "\nPlease enter the wholesale price of the boat: ";
    cin >> pastNineveh->fwholesale;

    cout << "\nPlease enter a one line comment about the boat: ";
    cin.get(newline);    // process carriage return
    cin.get(pastNineveh->szcomment,80,'.');
    cin.get(newline);    // process carriage return

    pastNineveh++;
  }

  pastNineveh=&astNineveh[0];
  vprint_data(pastNineveh);

  return (0);
}

void vprint_data(stboat *stany_boatptr)
{
  int i;
  cout << "\n\n\n";
  for (i=0; i<iinstock; i++) {
    cout << "A[{|"|}]<< stany_boatptr->iyear <<[{|"|}]"
         << stany_boatptr->sztype <<[{|"|}]"
         << stany_boatptr->szmodel <<[{|"|}]beauty with "
         << stany_boatptr->lmotor_hours <<[{|"|}]low hours.\n";
    cout << stany_boatptr->szcomment << endl;
    cout << "Grab the deal by asking your Nineveh "
         << "salesperson for #";
    cout << stany_boatptr->sztitle << "ONLY! $"
         << stany_boatptr->fretail << "\n\n";
    stany_boatptr++;
  }
}
```

One of the real differences between the C++ and C programs is how stream I/O is handled. Usually, simple C++ **cout** and **cin** streams can be used to replace the standard C **printf()** and **gets()** functions. For example:

```
cout << "\nPlease enter the wholesale price of the boat: ";
cin >> pastNineveh->fwholesale;
```

One of the program statements requests that the user enter a comment about each boat. The C++ input statement needed to read in the comment line uses a different approach for I/O. Recall that **cin** will read character information until the first white space. In this case, a space between words in a comment serves as white space. If **cin** were used, only the first word from the comment line would be saved in the *szcomment* member of the structure. Instead, a variation of **cin** is used so that a whole line of text can be entered:

```
cout << "\nPlease enter a one line comment about the boat: ";
cin.get(newline);    // process carriage return
cin.get(pastNineveh->szcomment,80,'.');
cin.get(newline);    // process carriage return
```

First, **cin.get**(*newline*) is used in a manner similar to the **flushall**() function of earlier C programs. In a buffered keyboard system, it is often necessary to strip the newline character from the input buffer. There are, of course, other ways to accomplish this, but they are not more eloquent. The statement **cin.get**(*newline*) receives the newline character and saves it in *newline*. The variable *newline* is just a collector for the information and is not actually used by the program. The comment line is accepted with the following code:

```
cin.get(pastNineveh->szcomment,80,'.');
```

Here, **cin.get**() uses a pointer to the structure member, followed by the maximum length of the *szcomment*, 80, followed by a termination character (.). In this case, the comment line will be terminated when (n–1) or 80–1 characters are entered or a period is typed (the nth space is reserved for the null string terminator, \0). The period is not saved as part of the comment, so the period is added back when the comment is printed. Locate the code that performs this action.

Additional Manipulations with Structures

There are a few things with regard to structures that the past several examples have not illustrated. For example, it is also possible to pass individual structure members to a function. Another property allows the nesting of structures.

Passing Structure Members to a Function

Passing individual structure members is an easy and efficient means of limiting access to structure information within a function. For example, a function might be used to print a list of wholesale boat prices available on the lot. In that case, just the *fwholesale* price, which is a member of the structure, would be passed to the function. If this is the case, the call to the function would take the form

```
vprint_price(astNineveh.fwholesale);
```

In this case, **vprint_price()** is the function name and *astNineveh.fwholesale* is the structure name and member.

Nesting Structures Within Structures

It is also feasible to nest structure declarations. That is, one structure contains a member or members that are structure types. Consider that the following structure could be included in yet another structure:

```
struct strepair {
   int ioilchange;
   int iplugs;
   int iairfilter;
   int ibarnacle_cleaning;
};
```

In the main structure, the **strepair** structure could be included as follows:

```
struct stboat {
   char sztype [iSTRING15 + iNULL_CHAR];
   char szmodel[iSTRING15 + iNULL_CHAR];
   char sztitle[iSTRING20 + iNULL_CHAR];
   char szcomment[80];
   struct strepair strepair_record;
   int iyear;
   long int lmotor_hours;
   float fretail;
   float fwholesale;
} astNineveh[iMAX_BOATS];
```

If a particular member from **strepair_record** is desired, it can be reached by using the following code:

```
printf("%d\n",astNineveh[0].strepair_record.ibarnacle_cleaning);
```

Structures and Bit-fields

C and C++ give you the ability to access individual bits within a larger data type, such as a byte. This is useful, for example, in altering data masks used for system information and graphics. The capability to access bits is built around the C and C++ structure.

Consider, for example, that it might be desirable to alter the keyboard status register in a computer. The keyboard status register on an IBM computer contains the following information:

	register bits
Keyboard Status:	7 6 5 4 3 2 1 0
Port (417h)	

where

bit 0 = RIGHT SHIFT depressed (1)
bit 1 = LEFT SHIFT depressed (1)
bit 2 = CTRL depressed (1)
bit 3 = ALT depressed (1)
bit 4 = SCROLL LOCK active (1)
bit 5 = NUM LOCK active (1)
bit 6 = CAPS LOCK active (1)
bit 7 = INS active (1)

In order to access and control this data, a structure could be constructed that uses the following form:

```
struct stkeybits {
  unsigned char
              ucrshift  : 1,        /* lsb */
              uclshift  : 1,
              ucctrl    : 1,
              ucalt     : 1,
              ucscroll  : 1,
              ucnumlock : 1,
              uccaplock : 1,
              ucinsert  : 1;        /* msb */
} stkey_register;
```

The bits are specified in the structure starting with the least significant bit (lsb) and progressing toward the most significant bit (msb). It is feasible to specify more than one bit by just typing the quantity (in place of the 1). Only integer data types can be used for bit-fields.

The members of the bit-field structure are accessed in the normal fashion.

Unions

A *union* is another data type that can be used in many distinctive ways. A specific union, for example, could be construed as an integer in one operation and a float or double in another operation. Unions have an appearance similar to structures. However, they are very dissimilar. A union can contain a group of many data types, as does a structure. In a union, however, those data types all share the same location in memory! Thus, a union can contain information on only one data type at a time. Many other high-level languages refer to this capability as a "variant record."

Unions: Syntax and Rules

A union is constructed by using the keyword **union** and the syntax that follows:

```
union tag_field {
    type field1
    type field2
    type field3
        .
        .
        .
    type fieldn
};
```

A semicolon is used for termination because the structure definition is actually a C and C++ statement.

Notice the declaration syntax similarities between structures and unions in the following example declaration:

```
union unmany_types {
    char c;
    int ivalue;
    float fvalue;
    double dvalue;
} unmy_union
```

The union is defined with the keyword **union** followed by the optional tag field, *unmany_types*. The union's optional tag field operates exactly the way its structure counterpart does. This union contains several members: a character, integer, float, and double. The union will allow *unmany_types* to save information on any one data type at a time.

The variable associated with the union is *unmy_union*. If this statement is contained in a function, the union is local in scope to that function. If the statement is contained outside of all functions, the union will be global in scope.

As with structures, it is also possible to associate several variables with the same union. Also, like a structure, members of a union are referenced by using the dot (.) operator. The syntax is simply

unname.*mname*

In this case, *unname* is the variable associated with the union type and *mname* is the name of any member of the union.

Constructing a Simple Union

To illustrate some concepts about unions, the following C++ program creates a union of the type just discussed. The purpose of this example is to show that a union can contain the definitions for many types but can hold the value for only one data type at a time.

```
//
//   13UNIONS.CPP
//   C++ program demonstrates the use of a union.
//   A union is created with several data types.
//   Copyright (c) William H. Murray and Chris H. Pappas, 1992
//

#include <iostream.h>

union unmany_types {
  char c;
  int ivalue;
  float fvalue;
  double dvalue;
} unmy_union;

int main(void)
{
  // valid I/O

  unmy_union.c='b';
  cout << unmy_union.c << "\n";
```

```
unmy_union.ivalue=1990;
cout << unmy_union.ivalue << "\n";

unmy_union.fvalue=19.90;
cout << unmy_union.fvalue << "\n";

unmy_union.dvalue=987654.32E+13;
cout << unmy_union.dvalue << "\n";

// invalid I/O

cout << unmy_union.c << "\n";
cout << unmy_union.ivalue << "\n";
cout << unmy_union.fvalue << "\n";
cout << unmy_union.dvalue << "\n";

// union size
cout << "The size of this union is: "
     << sizeof(unmany_types) <<[{|"|}]bytes." << "\n";

return (0);
}
```

The first part of this program simply loads and unloads information from the union. The program works because the union is called upon to store only one data type at a time. In the second part of the program, however, an attempt is made to output each data type from the union. The only valid value is the double since it was the last value loaded in the previous portion of code.

```
b
1990
19.9
9.876543e+18

—
-26216
-2.054608e+33
9.876543e+18
The size of this union is: 8 bytes.
```

Unions set aside storage room for the largest data type contained in the union. All other data types in the union share part, or all, of this memory location.

By using CodeView, you can get an idea of what is happening with storage within a union.

Miscellaneous Items

There are two further topics worth mentioning at this point: **typedef** declarations and enumerated types, **enum**. Both **typedef** and **enum** have the capability to clarify program code when used appropriately.

Using typedef

You can associate new data types with existing data types by using **typedef**. In a mathematically intense program, for example, it might be necessary to use the data types **fixed**, **whole**, **real**, or **complex**. These new types can be associated with standard C types with **typedef**. In the next program, two novel data types are created:

```
/*
 *    13TYPEDF.C
 *    C program shows the use of typedef.
 *    Two new types are created, "whole" and "real",
 *    which can be used in place of "int" and "float".
 *    Copyright (c) William H. Murray and Chris H. Pappas, 1992
 */

#include <stdio.h>

typedef int whole;
typedef float real;

int main(void)
{
  whole wvalue=123;
  real  rvalue=5.6789;

  printf("The whole number is %d.\n",wvalue);
  printf("The real number is %f.\n",rvalue);
  return (0);
}
```

Be aware that using too many newly created types can have a reverse effect on program readability and clarity. Use **typedef** carefully.

You can use a **typedef** declaration to simplify declarations. Look at the next two coded examples and see if you can detect the subtle code difference introduced by the **typedef** keyword:

```
struct stboat {
  char sztype [iSTRING15 + iNULL_CHAR];
  char szmodel[iSTRING15 + iNULL_CHAR];
  char sztitle[iSTRING20 + iNULL_CHAR];
  int iyear;
  long int lmotor_hours;
  float fsaleprice;
} stused_boat;
typedef struct {
  char sztype [iSTRING15 + iNULL_CHAR];
  char szmodel[iSTRING15 + iNULL_CHAR];
  char sztitle[iSTRING20 + iNULL_CHAR];
  int iyear;
  long int lmotor_hours;
  float fsaleprice;
} STBOAT;
```

Three major changes have taken place:

- The optional tag field has been deleted. (However, when using **typedef** you can still use a tag field, although it is redundant in meaning.)

- The tag field, *stboat,* has now become the new type **STBOAT** and is placed where structure variables have been defined traditionally.

- There now is no variable declaration for *stused_boat.*

The advantage of **typedef**s lies in their usage. For the remainder of the application, the program can now define variables of the type **STBOAT** using the simpler syntax

```
STBOAT STused_boat;
```

The use of the uppercase letters is not syntactically required by the C/C++ compiler; however, it does illustrate an important coding convention. With all of the possible sources for an identifier's declaration, C programmers have settled on using uppercase to indicate the definition of a new type, constant, enumerated value, and macro, usually defined in a header file. The visual contrast between lowercase keywords and uppercase user-defined identifiers makes for more easily understood code since all uppercase usually means, "Look for this declaration in another file."

Using enum

The enumerated data type, **enum**, exists for one reason only, to make your code more readable. In other computer languages, this data type is referred to as a user-defined type. The general syntax for enumerated declarations looks like this:

enum *op_tag_field* { *val1,. . .valn* } *op_var_dec* ;

As you may have already guessed, the optional tag field operates exactly as it does in structure declarations. If you leave the tag field off, you must list the variable or variables after the closing brace. Including the tag field allows your application to declare other variables of the tag type. When declaring additional variables of the tag type in C++, it is not necessary to repeat the keyword **enum**.

Enumerated data types allow you to associate a set of easily understood human symbols—for example, Monday, Tuesday, Wednesday, and so on—with an integral data type. They also help you create self-documenting code. For example, instead of having a loop that goes from 0 to 4, it can now read from Monday to Friday:

```
enum eweekdays { Monday, Tuesday, Wednesday, Thursday, Friday };

/* C enum variable declaration    */
enum eweekdays ewToday;

/* Same declaration in C++        */
eweekdays ewToday;

/* Not using the enumerated type */
for(i = 0; i <= 4; i++)
    .

    .

    .

/* Using the enumerated type    */
for(ewToday = Monday; ewToday <= Friday; ewToday++)
```

Historically speaking, C compilers have seen no difference between the data type **int** and **enum**. This meant that a program could assign an integer value to an enumerated type. In C++ the two types generate a warning message from the compiler without an explicit type cast:

```
/* legal in C not C++ */
ewToday = 1;

/* correcting the problem in C++ */
ewToday = (eweekdays)1;
```

The use of **enum** is popular in programming when information can be represented by a list of integer values such as the number of months in a year or the number of days in a week. This type of list lends itself to enumeration.

The following example contains a list of the number of months in a year. These are in an enumeration list with a tag name *emonths*. The variable associated with the list is *emcompleted*. Enumerated lists will always start with zero unless forced to a different integer value. In this case, January is the first month of the year.

```
/*
*    13ENUM.C
*    C program shows the use of enum types.
*    Program calculates elapsed months in year, and
*    remaining months using enum type.
*    Copyright (c) William H. Murray and Chris H. Pappas, 1992
*/

#include <stdio.h>

enum emonths {
  January=1,
  February,
  March,
  April,
  May,
  June,
  July,
  August,
  September,
  October,
  November,
  December
} emcompleted;

int main(void)
{
  int ipresent_month;
  int isum,idiff;
```

```
    printf("\nPlease enter the present month (1 to 12): ");
    scanf("%d",&ipresent_month);

    emcompleted = December;
    isum = ipresent_month;
    idiff = (int)emcompleted - ipresent_month;

    printf("\n%d month(s) past, %d months to go.\n",isum,idiff);

    return (0);
}
```

The enumerated list is actually a list of integer values, from 1 to 12, in this program. Since the names are equivalent to consecutive integer values, integer arithmetic can be performed with them. The enumerated variable *emcompleted*, when set equal to December, is actually set to 12.

This short program will simply perform some simple arithmetic and report the result to the screen:

```
Please enter the current month (1 to 12): 4
4 month(s) past, 8 months to go.
```

Chapter 14 completes the coverage of standard C and C++ programming features. After completing Chapter 14, you will be ready to launch into the fundamentals of object-oriented programming, which are presented in Chapter 15.

Chapter *14*

Advanced C and C++ Programming Topics

Chapter 14 deals with advanced programming concepts common to both C and C++. Many of the topics discussed, such as type compatibility and macros, will point out those areas of the language where you must use caution when designing your algorithm. Other topics discussed, like compiler-supplied macros and conditional preprocessor statements, will help you create more streamlined applications. The chapter ends by explaining the concepts and syntax necessary to create dynamic linked lists. Once you have completed Chapters 5 through 14, you will have a detailed-enough background in C/C++ to make a knowledgeable jump to the idea of object-oriented programming discussed in the remainder of the book.

Type Compatibility

As you now well know, C is not a strongly typed language, while C++ is only slightly more strongly typed (for example, enumerated types). You have also seen how C can perform automatic type conversions and explicit type conversions using the cast operator. The following section highlights the sometimes confusing way the C/C++ compiler interprets compatible types.

ANSI C Definition for Type Compatibility

The whole idea for the issue of compatible types came from the ANSI C committee. Many of the committee's recommendations added features to C, such as function prototyping, that made the language more readily maintained. The committee tried to define a set of rules or coded syntax that nailed down the language's automatic behind-the-scenes behavior.

The ANSI C committee decided that for two types to be compatible, they must either be the same type or be pointers, functions, or arrays with certain properties, as described in the following sections.

What Is an Identical Type?

The term *composite type* is associated with the subject of compatibility. The composite type is the common type that is produced by two compatible types. Any two types that are the same are compatible and their composite type is the same type.

Two arithmetic types are identical if they are the same type. Abbreviated declarations for the same type are also identical. In the following example, both *shivalue1* and *shivalue2* are identical types:

```
short shivalue1;
short int shivalue2;
```

And the type **int** is the same as **signed int** in this next example:

```
int sivalue1;
signed int sivalue2;
```

However, the types **int**, **short**, and **unsigned** are all different. When dealing with character data, the types **char**, **signed char**, and **unsigned char** are always different.

The ANSI C committee stated that any type preceded by an access modifier generates incompatible types. For example, the next two declarations are not compatible types:

```
int ivalue1;
const int ivalue2;
```

In this next set of declarations, see if you can guess which types are compatible:

```
char *pc1, * pc2;
struct {int ix, iy;} stanonymous_coord1, stanonymous_coord2;
struct stxy {int ix, iy;} stanycoords;
typedef struct stxy STXY;
STXY stmorecoords;
```

Both *pc1* and *pc2* are compatible character pointers since the additional space between the *** symbol and *pc2* in the declaration is superfluous.

You are probably not surprised that the compiler sees *stanonymous_coord1* and *stanonymous_coord2* as the same type. However, the compiler does not see *stanycoords* as being the identical type to the previous pair of variables. Even though all three variables seem to have the same two integer fields, *stanonymous_coord1* and *stanonymous_coord2* are of an anonymous structure type, while *stanycoords* is of tag type, *stxy*.

Because of the **typedef** declaration, the compiler does see *struct stxy* as being the identical type to *STXY*. For this reason *stanycoords* is identical to *stmorecoords*.

It is important to remember that the compiler sees **typedef** declarations as being synonymous for types, not totally new types. The following code segment defines a new type called *MYFLOAT* that is the same type as **float**:

```
typedef float MYFLOAT;
```

Enumerated Types

The ANSI C committee initially stated that each enumerated type be compatible with the implementation-specific integral type; this is not the case with C++. In C++, enumeration types are not compatible with integral types. In both C and C++, no two enumerated type definitions in the same source file are compatible. This rule is analogous to the tagged and untagged (anonymous) structures. This explains why *ebflag1* and *ebflag2* are compatible types, while *eflag1* is not a compatible type:

```
enum boolean {0,1} ebflag1;
enum {0,1} eflag1;
enum boolean ebflag2;
```

Array Types

If two arrays have compatible array elements, the arrays are considered compatible. If only one array specifies a size, or neither does, the types are still compatible. However, if both arrays specify a size, both sizes must be identical for the arrays to be compatible. See if you can find all of the compatible arrays in the following declarations:

```
int imax20[20];
const int cimax20[20];
int imax10[10];
int iundefined[];
```

The undimensioned integer array *iundefined* is compatible with both *imax20* and *imax10*. However, this last pair is incompatible because they use different array bounds. The arrays *imax20* (element type **int**) and *cimax20* (element type **const int**) are incompatible because their elements are not compatible. If either array specifies an array bound, the composite type of the compatible arrays has that size also. Using the preceding code segment, the composite type of *iundefined* and *imax20* is *int[20]*.

Function Types

There are three conditions that must be met in order for two prototyped functions to be considered compatible. The two functions must have the same return types and the same number of parameters, and the corresponding parameters must be compatible types. However, parameter names do not have to agree.

Structure and Union Types

Each new structure or union type a program declares introduces a new type that is not the same as, nor compatible with, any other type in the same source file. For this reason, the variables *stanonymous1*, *stanonymous2*, and *stfloat1* in the following code segment are all different.

However, a reference to a type specifier that is a structure, a union, or an enumerated type is the same type. You use the tag field to associate the reference with the type declaration. For this reason, the tag field can be thought of as the name of the type. This rule explains why *stfloat1* and *stfloat2* are compatible types.

```
struct {float fvalue1, fvalue2;} stanonymous1;
struct {float fvalue1, fvalue2;} stanonymous2;
struct sttwofloats {float fvalue1, fvalue2} stfloat1;
struct sttwofloats stfloat2;
```

Pointer Types

Two pointer types are considered compatible if they both point to compatible types. The composite type of the two compatible pointers is the same as the pointed-to composite type.

Multiple Source File Compatibility

Since the compiler views each declaration of a structure, a union, or an enumerated type as being a new noncompatible type, you might be wondering what happens when you want to reference these types across files within the same program.

Multiple structure, union, and enumerated declarations are compatible across source files if they declare the same members, in the same order, with compatible member types. However, with enumerated types, the enumeration constants do not have to be declared in the same order, although each constant must have the same enumeration value.

Macros

In Chapter 6, you learned how to use the **#define** preprocessor to declare symbolic constants. You can use the same preprocessor to define macros. A *macro* is a piece of code that can look and act just like a function.

The advantage of a properly written macro is in its execution speed. A macro is expanded (replaced by its **#define** definition) during preprocessing, creating what is called *inline code*. For this reason, macros do not have the overhead normally associated with function calls. However, each substitution lengthens the overall code size.

Conversely, function definitions expand only once no matter how many times they are called. The trade-off between execution speed and overall code size can help you decide which way to write a particular routine.

There are other subtle differences between macros and functions that have their roots based on when the code is expanded. These differences fall into three categories.

In C, a function name evaluates to the address of where to find the subroutine. Because macros sit inline and can be expanded many times, there is no one address associated with a macro. For this reason, a macro cannot be used in a context requiring a function pointer. Also, you can declare pointers to functions, but you cannot declare a pointer to a macro.

The C compiler sees a function declaration differently from a **#define** macro. Because of this, the compiler does not do any type checking on macros. The result is that the compiler will not flag you if you pass the wrong number or wrong type of arguments to a macro.

Because macros are expanded before the program is actually compiled, some macros treat arguments incorrectly when the macro evaluates an argument more than once.

Defining Macros

You define macros the same way you define symbolic constants. The only difference is that the *substitution_string* usually contains more than a single value:

#define *search_string substitution_string*

The following example uses the preprocessor statement to define both a symbolic constant and a macro to highlight the similarities:

```
/* #define symbolic constant */
#define iMAX_ROWS 100
```

```
/* #define macro               */
#define NL putchar('\n')
```

The NL macro causes the preprocessor to search through the source code looking for every occurrence of NL and replace it with putchar('\n'). Notice that the macro did not end with a semicolon. The reason for this has to do with how you invoke a macro in your source code:

```
int main(void)
{
    .
    .
    .
  NL;
```

The compiler requires that the macro call end with a semicolon. Suppose the *substitution_string* of the macro had ended with a semicolon:

```
#define NL putchar('\n');
```

Then, after the macro expansion had taken place, the compiler would see the following code:

```
int main(void)
{
    .
    .
    .
  putchar('\n');;
```

Macros and Parameters

C supports macros that take arguments. These macros must be defined with parameters, which serve a purpose similar to that of a function's parameters. The parameters act as placeholders for the actual arguments. The following example demonstrates how to define and use a paramaterized macro:

```
/* macro definition */
#define READ_RESPONSE(c)  scanf("%c",(&c))
#define MULTIPLY(x,y)  ((x)*(y))

int main(void)
{
  char cresponse;
```

```
int a = 10, b = 20;
   .
   .
   .
READ_RESPONSE(cresponse); /* macro expansions */
printf("%d",MULTIPLY(a,b));
```

In this example *x*, *y*, and *c* serve as placeholders for *a*, *b*, and *cresponse*, respectively. The two macros, READ_RESPONSE and MULTIPLY, demonstrate the different ways you can invoke macros in your program. For example, MULTIPLY is substituted within a **printf()** statement, while READ_RESPONSE is stand-alone.

Problems with Macro Expansions

Macros operate purely by substituting one set of characters, or tokens, with another. The actual parsing of the declaration, expression, or statement invoking the macro occurs after the macro expansion process. This can lead to some surprising results if care is not taken. For example, the following macro definition looks perfectly legal:

```
#define SQUAREIT(x) x * x
```

Suppose the statement is invoked with a value of 5, as in:

```
iresult = SQUAREIT(5);
```

The compiler sees the following statement:

```
iresult = 5 * 5;
```

On the surface everything looks OK. However, suppose the same macro is invoked with this next statement:

```
iresult = SQUAREIT(x + 1);
```

It is seen by the compiler as

```
iresult = x + (1 * x) + 1;
```

instead of

```
iresult = (x + 1) * (x + 1);
```

As a general rule, it is safest to always parenthesize each parameter appearing in the body of the macro, as seen in the previous READ_RESPONSE and MULTIPLY macro definitions. And under those circumstances where the macro expansion may appear in a cast expression, for example

```
dresult = (double)SQUAREIT(x + 1);
```

it is best to paramaterize the entire body of the macro:

```
#define SQUAREIT(x) ((x) * (x))
```

Most of the time the C compiler is insensitive to additional spacing within standard C statements. This is not the case with macro definitions. Look closely at this next example and see if you can detect the error:

```
/* incorrect macro definition */
#define BAD_MACRO (ans) scanf("%d",(&ans))
```

Remember that the **#define** preprocessor searches for the *search_string* and replaces it with the *substitution_string*. These two strings are delineated by one or more blanks. The preceding definition, when expanded, looks to the compiler like

```
(ans) scanf("%d",(&ans));
```

This creates an illegal statement. The problem has to do with the space between the macro name BAD_MACRO and (*ans*). That extra space made the parameter list part of the *substitution_string* instead of putting it in its proper place as part of the *search_string*. To fix the BAD_MACRO definition, you need to remove the extra space:

```
#define BAD_MACRO(ans) scanf("%d",(&ans))
```

To see if you really do understand the hidden problems that you can encounter when using macros, see if you can figure out what this statement would evaluate to:

```
int x = 5;
iresult = SQUAREIT(x++);
```

The situation gets worse when you use certain C operators like increment (++) and decrement (--). The result of this expression may be 30, instead of the expected 25, because the implementations of C compilers are free to evaluate the expression in several different ways. For example, the macro could be expanded syntactically to read

```
/* iresult = x * x; */
iresult = 5 * 5;
```

or

```
/* iresult = x * (x+1); */
iresult = 5 * 6;
```

Creating and Using Your Own Macros

Macros can include other macros in their definitions. You can use this feature to streamline your source code. For example, look at the following progressive macro definitions:

```
#define NL putchar('\n')
#define TAB putchar('\t')
#define FORMAT1 NL, NL, TAB
#define FORMAT2 NL, TAB, TAB
#define BEGIN_PROMPT FORMAT1, printf("Want to begin?"); \
                              printf("\nType 1 for yes, 0 for no")
#define READ_RESPONSE FORMAT2,scanf("%d",(&c))
#define FORMAT_PRINT(ccontrol,ivalue,fvalue) \
        printf("\n%c\t%d\t%8.2f",(ccontrol),(ivalue),(fvalue))
```

Now, instead of your main program including all of the code defined in the macro, your program looks like this:

```
int main(void)
{
  char cresponse;
  int ivalue = 23;
  float fvalue = 56.78;
     .
     .
     .

  BEGIN_PROMPT;
  READ_RESPONSE(cresponse);
  FORMAT_PRINT(cresponse,ivalue,fvalue);
```

However, remember that you are trading off automatic compiler type checking for source code readability, along with possible side effects generated by the invoking statement's syntax.

Macros Shipped with the Compiler

The ANSI C committee has recommended that all C compilers define five special, predefined macros that take no arguments. Each macro name begins and ends with two underscore characters, as listed in the following table:

Macro Name	Meaning
_ _LINE_ _	A decimal integer constant representing the line number of the current source program line
_ _FILE_ _	A string constant representing the name of the current source file
_ _DATE_ _	A string constant representing the calendar date of the translation in the form *Mmm dd yyyy*
_ _TIMESTAMP_ _	A string constant representing the date and time of the last modification of the source file, in the form *Ddd Mmm hh:mm:ss yyyy*
_ _STDC_ _	Represents a decimal 1 if the compiler is ANSI C compatible

You invoke a predefined macro the same way you would a user-defined macro. For example, to print your program's name, date, and current line number to the screen, you would use the following statement:

```
printf(
    "%s | %s | Line number: %d",_ _FILE_ _,_ _DATE_ _,_ _LINE_ _);
```

Advanced Preprocessor Statements

There are actually 12 standard preprocessor statements, sometimes referred to as *directives*. They are listed in the following table. You are already familiar with two of the 12—**#include** and **#define**.

#include	#define	#ifdef	#endif
#undef	#ifndef	#if	#else
#elif	#line	#error	#pragma

Remember that the C preprocessor processes a C source file before the compiler translates the program into object code. By carefully selecting the correct directives, you can create more efficient header files, solve unique programming problems, and prevent combined files from crashing in on your declarations.

The following section explains the unique function of each of the ten new preprocessor directives not previously discussed. Some of the examples will use the code found in stdio.h in order to illustrate the construction of header files.

#ifdef and #endif Directives

The **#ifdef** and **#endif** directives are two of several conditional preprocessor statements. You can use them to selectively include certain statements in your program. The **#endif** directive is used with all of the conditional preprocessor statements to signify the end of the conditional block. For example, if the name *LARGE_CLASSES* has been previously defined, the following code segment will define a new name called *MAX_SEATS*:

```
#ifdef LARGE_CLASSES
#define MAX_SEATS 100
#endif
```

Whenever a C++ program uses standard C functions, you can use the **#ifdef** directive to modify the function declarations so that they have the required **extern "C"** linkage, which inhibits the encoding of the function name. This usually calls for the following pair of directive code segments to encapsulate the translated code:

```
/*  used in graph.h  */
#ifdef __cplusplus
extern "C" {          /* allow use with C++ */
#endif

/* translation units */

#ifdef __cplusplus
}
#endif
```

#undef Directive

The **#undef** directive tells the preprocessor to cancel any previous definition of the specified identifier. This next example combines your understanding of **#ifdef** with the use of **#undef** to change the dimension of *MAX_SEATS*:

```
#ifdef LARGE_CLASSES
#undef MAX_SEATS 30
#define MAX_SEATS 100
#endif
```

In case you were wondering, the compiler will not complain if you try to undefine a name not previously defined. Notice that once a name has been undefined, it may be given a completely new definition with another **#define** directive.

#ifndef Directive

Undoubtedly you are beginning to understand how the conditional directives operate. The **#ifndef** preprocessor checks to see if the specified identifier does not exist and then performs some action. The code segment that follows is taken directly from stdio.h:

```
#ifndef _SIZE_T_DEFINED
typedef unsigned int size_t;
#define _SIZE_T_DEFINED
#endif
```

In this case, the conditionally executed statements include both a **typedef** and **#define** preprocessor. This code takes care of defining the type **size_t**, specified by the ANSI C committee as the return type for the operator **sizeof()**. Make sure you read the section "Proper Use of Header Files" later in this chapter so you will understand what types of statements can go into header files.

#if Directive

The **#if** preprocessor also recognizes the term **defined**. The code

```
#if defined(LARGE_CLASSES) && !defined (PRIVATE_LESSONS)
#define MAX_SEATS 30
#endif
```

shows how the **#if** directive, together with the **defined** construct, accomplishes what would otherwise require an **#ifndef** nested in an **#ifdef**:

```
#ifdef LARGE_CLASSES
#ifndef PRIVATE_LESSONS
#define MAX_SEATS 30
#endif
```

The two examples produce the same result, but the first is more immediately discerned. Both **#ifdef** and **#ifndef** directives are restricted to a single test expression. However, the **#if** combined with **defined** allows compound expressions.

#else Directive

The **#else** directive has the expected use. Suppose you know that a program is going to be run on a VAX computer and a PC. The VAX allocates 4 bytes, or 32 bits, to the type integer, while the PC allocates only 2 bytes, or 16 bits. The following code segment uses the **#else** directive to make certain that an integer is seen the same on both systems:

```
#ifdef VAX_SYSTEM
#define INTEGER short int
#else
#define INTEGER int
#endif
```

Of course, the program will have to take care of defining the identifier *VAX_SYSTEM* when you run it on the VAX. As you can readily see, combinations of preprocessor directives make for interesting solutions.

#elif Directive

The **#elif** directive is an abbreviation for "else if" and provides an alternate approach to nested **#if** statements. The following code segment checks to see which class size is defined and uniquely defines the BILL macro:

```
#if defined (LARGE_CLASSES)
     #define BILL printf("\nCost per student $100.00.\n")
  #elif defined (PRIVATE_LESSONS)
     #define BILL printf("\nYour tuition is $1000.00.\n")
   #else
     #define BILL printf("\nCost per student $150.00.\n")
#endif
```

Notice that the preprocessors don't have to start in column 1. The ability to indent preprocessor statements for readability is only one of the many useful recommendations made by the ANSI C committee and adopted by Microsoft C/C++.

#line Directive

The **#line** directive overrides the compiler's automatic line numbering. You can use it to help in debugging your program. Suppose you have just merged a 50-line routine into a file of over 400 statements. All you care about are any errors that could be generated within the merged code.

Normally, the compiler starts line numbering from the beginning of the file. If your routine had an error, the compiler would print a message with a line number of, say, 289. From your merged file's point of view, where is that?

However, if you include a **#line** directive in the beginning of your freshly merged subroutine, the compiler would give you a line error number relative to the beginning of the function:

```
#line 1
int imy_mergefunction(void)
{
        .
        .
        .
}
```

#error Directive

The **#error** directive instructs the compiler to generate a user-defined error message. It can be used to extend the compiler's own error-detection and message capabilities. After the compiler encounters an **#error** directive, it scans the rest of the program for syntax errors but does not produce an object file. For example, the following code prints a warning message if _CHAR_UNSIGNED is undefined:

```
#if !defined( _CHAR_UNSIGNED )
#error /J option required.
#endif
```

#pragma Directive

The **#pragma** directive gives the compiler implementation-specific instructions. The Microsoft C/C++ compiler supports the following pragmas:

alloc_text	auto_inline	check_pointer
check_stack	code_seg	comment
data_seg	function	hdrstop
inline_depth	inline_recursion	init_seg
intrinsic	linesize	loop_opt
message	native_caller	optimize
pack	page	pagesize
skip	subtitle	title
warning		

Conditional Compilation

You won't always find preprocessor statements in header files. You can use preprocessor directives in your source code to generate efficient compilations. Look at this next code segment and see if you can detect the subtle difference (hint: executable code size):

```
/* compiled if statement */
if(DEBUG_ON) {
  printf("Entering Example Function");
  printf("First argument passed has a value of %d",ifirst_arg);
}


/* comparison statement   */
#if defined(DEBUG_ON)
  printf("Entering Example Function");
  printf("First argument passed has a value of %d",ifirst_arg);
#endif
```

The first **if** statement is always compiled. This means that the debugging informa-tion is perpetually reflected in the executable size of your program. But what if you don't want to ship a product with your intermediate, development-cycle code? The solution is to conditionally compile these types of statements.

The second portion of the code demonstrates how to selectively compile code with the **#if defined** directive. To debug your program, you simply define *DEBUG_ON*. This makes the nested **#if...#endif** statements visible to the compiler. However, when you are ready to ship the final product, you remove the *DEBUG_ON* definition. This makes the statements invisible to the compiler, reducing the size of the executable file.

Try the following simple test to prove to yourself how invisible the **#if...#endif** directives make the **printf()** statement pair. Copy the previous code segment into a simple C program that does nothing else. Include all necessary overhead (**#include**, **main()**, {, and so on). Do not define *DEBUG_ON*. Make certain that when you compile the program, there are no error messages. Now, remove the **#include <stdio.h>** statement from the program and recompile.

At this point, the compiler stops at the first **printf()** statement nested within the **if...printf()** block statement. The message printed is "Function 'printf' should have a prototype." You would expect this since the **printf()** statement within the **if** is always visible to the compiler. Now, simply remove or comment out the **if...printf()** block statement and recompile.

The compiler does not complain about the **printf()** statements nested within the **#if...#endif** preprocessors. It never saw them. They would only become visible to the compilation phase of the compiler if *DEBUG_ON* is defined. You can use this selective visibility for more than executable statements. Look at this next code-streamlining option:

```
#if defined(DEBUG_ON)
  /******************************************/
  /* The following code segment performs    */
  /* a sophisticated enough solution step   */
  /* to require a comment and debug output  */
```

```
/*********************************/
    printf("    debug code goes here        ");
#endif
```

This example not only has a conditional output debug statement, but it also provides room for an explanatory comment. The little extra time it takes to write conditionally compiled code has its trade-off in easily debugged code and small executable code size.

Advanced Preprocessor Operators

There are three operators that are available only to preprocessor directives. These are the stringize (#), concatenation (##), and charizing (#@) operators.

Stringize Operator

Placing a single # in front of a macro parameter causes the compiler to insert the name of the argument instead of its value. This has the overall effect of converting the argument name into a string. The operator is necessary because parameters are not replaced if they occur inside string literals that are explicitly coded in a macro. The following example demonstrates the syntax for the stringize operator:

```
#define STRINGIZE(ivalue) printf(#ivalue " is: %d",ivalue)
      .
      .
      .

int ivalue = 2;
   STRINGIZE(ivalue);
```

The output from the macro looks like this:

```
ivalue is: 2
```

Concatenation Operator

One use for the concatenation operator is for building variable and macro names dynamically. The operator concatenates the items, removing any white space on either side, forming a new token. When ## is used in a macro, it is processed after the macro parameters are substituted and before the macro is examined for any additional macro processing. For example, the following code shows how to create preprocessed variable names:

```
#define IVALUE_NAMES(icurrent_number) ivalue ## icurrent_number;
    .
    .
    .
int IVALUE_NAMES(1);
```

This is seen by the compiler as the following declaration:

```
int ivalue1;
```

Notice that the preprocessor removed the blanks so that the compiler didn't see *ivalue1* as *ivalue 1*. The operator can be combined with other preprocessor directives to form complex definitions. The following example uses the concatenation operator to generate a macro name, which causes the preprocessor to invoke the appropriate macro:

```
#define MACRO1 printf("MACRO1 invoked.")
#define MACRO2 printf("MACRO2 invoked.")

#define MAKE_MACRO(n) MACRO ## n
    .
    .
    .
MAKE_MACRO(1);
```

The output from the example looks like this:

```
MACRO1 invoked.
```

#@ Charizing Operator

The charizing preprocessor precedes formal parameters in a macro definition. This causes the actual argument to be treated as a single character with single quotation marks around it. For example:

```
#define CHARIZEIT(cvalue) #@cvalue
    .
    .
    .
cletter = CHARIZEIT(z);
```

This is seen by the compiler as

```
cletter = 'z';
```

Proper Use of Header Files

Because header files are made up of syntactically correct C/C++ ASCII text and are included in other files at the point of the **#include** directive, many beginning programmers misuse them. Sometimes they are incorrectly used to define entire functions or collections of functions. While this approach does not invoke any complaints from the compiler, it is a logical misuse of the structure.

Header files are used to define and share common declarations with several source files. They provide a centralized location for the declaration of all external variables, function prototypes, class definitions, structures, unions, enums, and inline functions. Files that must declare a variable, function, or class **#include** header files.

This provides two safeguards. First, all files are guaranteed to contain the same declarations. Second, should a declaration require updating, only one change to the header file need be made. The possibility of failing to update the declaration in a particular file is removed. Header files are frequently made up of

       Preprocessor directives
       Const declarations
       Function prototypes
       Typedefs
       Structure definitions
       Enumerated types
       References to externs

Some care should be taken in designing header files. The declarations provided should logically belong together. A header file takes time to compile. If it is too large or filled with too many disparate elements, programmers will be reluctant to incur the compile-time cost of including them.

A second consideration is that a header file should never contain a nonstatic definition. If two files in the same program include a header file with an external definition, most link editors will reject the program because of multiply defined symbols. Because constant values are often required in header files, the default linkage of a **const** identifier is static. For this reason, constants can be defined inside header files.

Making Header Files More Efficient

You make the compiling of header files more efficient by using combinations of preprocessor directives. The best way to learn how to construct an efficient header file is to look at an example:

```
#ifndef _INC_IOSTREAM
#define _INC_IOSTREAM

#if !defined(_INC_DEFS )
#include <_defs.h>
#endif

#if !defined(_INC_MEM )
#include <mem.h>    // to get memcpy and NULL
#endif

#endif  /* !_INC_IOSTREAM */
```

Before looking at the individual statements in the example, you need to know that pass one of the compiler builds a symbol table. One of the entry types in a symbol table is the *mangled* names of header files. Mangling is something that the compiler does to distinguish one symbol from another. The C compiler prepends an underscore to these symbols.

The easiest way to control the compiled visibility of a header file is to surround the code within the header file with a tri-statement combination in the form

```
#ifndef _INC_myheader
#define _INC_myheader   /* begin _INC_MYHEADER visibility */
       .
       .
       .
#endif /* end of conditional _INC_MYHEADER visibility */
```

This is exactly what was done with the previous coded example, where *_INC_IOSTREAM* was substituted for *_INC_MYHEADER*. The first time the compiler includes this header file, *_INC_IOSTREAM* is undefined. The code segment is included, making all of the nested statements visible. From this point forward, any additional **#include <iostream.h>** statements, found in any of the other files used to create the executable file, bypass the nested code.

Precompiled Header Files

You can not only speed up the compiling of a program by writing efficient header files, but you can also precompile header files. Precompilation is most useful for compiling a stable body of code for use with another body of code that is under development.

Creating Precompiled Headers

The /Yc option instructs the compiler to create a precompiled header (.PCH) file. The syntax looks like this:

/Yc*yourfile*

No space is allowed between /Yc and *yourfile*. The /Yc switch causes the compiler to compile the entire source file, including any and all included header files. The precompiled file is saved with the *yourfile* name of the source file and a .PCH extension.

Using Precompiled Headers with PWB

You must follow a certain procedure to create a PWB project that uses precompiled headers. The use of precompiled headers in a PWB project make file has certain restrictions. First, there can be only one precompiled header *yourfile*.pch file for each source language in the project (C and/or C++).

Second, all files for a given language must use the identical precompiled header. Additionally, each source file must include the same set of include files, in the same order, up to the include file that you specify in the Include File box in the Additional Global Options dialog box. The same path must be specified with the include file in each source file.

Following are the four steps necessary to create a PWB project that uses precompiled headers:

1. Start by creating a normal PWB project, making sure you add at least one source file to the project file list. You can specify the source file from which the .pch file will be generated by selecting this file in the file list of the Edit Project dialog box and choosing the To Top of List command.

2. Choose the appropriate Compiler Options command from the Language Options menu (C or C++).

3. Select the Additional Global Options button and turn on the Use Precompiled Header option. The cursor immediately moves to the Include File text box.

4. Type the name of the last include file to be contained in the .pch file. At this point, the .pch file will take the *yourfile* name of the specified include file and be created in the same directory as the project make file.

limits.h and float.h

To help you write portable code, the ANSI C committee requires that all C compilers document the system-dependent ranges of integer and floating-point types. Table 14-1 contains a listing of the ANSI C-required integral definitions found in limits.h.

#define CHAR_BIT	8	Number of bits in a char
#define SCHAR_MIN	(–127)	Minimum signed char value
#define SCHAR_MAX	127	Maximum signed char value
#define UCHAR_MAX	0xff	Maximum unsigned char value
#define SHRT_MIN	(–32767)	Minimum (signed) short value
#define SHRT_MAX	32767	Maximum (signed) short value
#define USHRT_MAX	0xffff	Maximum unsigned short value
#define INT_MIN	(–32767)	Minimum (signed) int value
#define INT_MAX	32767	Maximum (signed) int value
#define UINT_MAX	0xffff	Maximum unsigned int value
#define LONG_MIN	(–2147483647)	Minimum (signed) long value
#define LONG_MAX	2147483647	Maximum (signed) long value
#define ULONG_MAX	0xffffffff	Maximum unsigned long value
#define CHAR_MIN	SCHAR_MIN	Mimimum char value
#define CHAR_MAX	SCHAR_MAX	Maximum char value

Table 14-1. *Values Defined in limits.h (ANSI C)*

Your code can use these ranges to make certain your data will fit in the specified data type. For example, a VAX integer is 4 bytes, while a PC-based integer is only 2. One solution to this storage-size problem looks like this:

```
if (PROGRAM_NEEDED_MAX > INT_MAX)
  pvoid = new llong_storage;
else
  pvoid = new iinteger_storage;
```

Table 14-2 shows the ANSI C required floating-point definitions.

Handling Errors: perror()

One of the many interesting functions prototyped in stdio.h is a function called **perror()**. The function prints to the **stderr** stream the system error message for the last library routine called that generated an error. It does this by using **errno** and

#define FLT_RADIX	2	Exponent radix
#define FLT_ROUNDS	1	Addition rounding: near

```
/* smallest such that 1.0+FLT_EPSILON != 1.0 */
#define FLT_EPSILON 1.192092896e-07F
```

```
/* smallest such that 1.0+DBL_EPSILON != 1.0 */
#define DBL_EPSILON 2.2204460492503131e-016
```

```
/* smallest such that 1.0+LDBL_EPSILON != 1.0 */
#define LDBL_EPSILON 1.084202172485504434e-019L
```

#define FLT_DIG	6	# of decimal digits of precision
#define DBL_DIG	15	# of decimal digits of precision
#define LDBL_DIG	18	# of decimal digits of precision
#define FLT_MIN	1.175494351e-38F	Min positive val
#define DBL_MIN	2.2250738585072014e-308	Min positive val
#define LDBL_MIN	3.3621031431120935063e-4932L	Min pos val
#define FLT_MIN_EXP	(-125)	Min binary exponent
#define DBL_MIN_EXP	(-1021)	Min binary exponent
#define LDBL_MIN_EXP	(-16381)	Min binary exponent
#define FLT_MIN_10_EXP	(-37)	Min decimal exponent
#define DBL_MIN_10_EXP	(-307)	Min decimal exponent
#define LDBL_MIN_10_EXP	(-4931)	Min decimal exponent
#define FLT_MAX	3.402823466e+38F	Max value
#define DBL_MAX	1.7976931348623158e+308	Max value
#define LDBL_MAX	1.189731495357231765e+4932L	Max value
#define FLT_MAX_EXP	128	Max binary exponent
#define DBL_MAX_EXP	1024	Max binary exponent
#define LDBL_MAX_EXP	16384	Max binary exponent
#define FLT_MAX_10_EXP	38	Max decimal exponent
#define DBL_MAX_10_EXP	308	Max decimal exponent
#define LDBL_MAX_10_EXP	4932	Max decimal exponent

Table 14-2. *Values defined in float.h (ANSI C)*

_sys_errlist, prototyped in stdlib.h. **_sys_errlist** is an array of error message strings. **errno** is an index into the message string array and is automatically set to the index for the error generated. The number of entries in the array is determined by another constant, **_sys_nerr**, also defined in stdlib.h.

The function **perror()** has only one parameter, a character string. Normally, the argument passed is a string representing the file or function that generated the error condition. The following example demonstrates the simplicity of the function:

```
/*
 *  14PERROR.C
 *  A C program demonstrating the function perror()
 *  prototyped in STDIO.H
 *  Copyright (c) William H. Murray and Chris H. Pappas, 1992
 */

#include <stdio.h>

void main(void)
{
   FILE *fpinfile;
   fpinfile = fopen("input.dat", "r");

   if (!fpinfile)
     perror("Could not open input.dat in file main() :");
}
```

The output from the program looks like this:

```
Could not open input.dat in file main() : No such file or directory
```

Memory Models

The Microsoft C/C++ compiler supports six standard memory models—tiny, small, medium, compact, large, and huge—as well as a customized model. The customized model is used for those applications requiring special data and code storage requirements. By carefully choosing the precise memory model needed by your application, you can maximize the use of your system's resources and program execution characteristics. The following brief descriptions summarize the distinguishing attributes of each of the six standard memory models.

Tiny

Programs using the tiny-model option create a program with a .COM file extension. Tiny programs contain a single 64K segment for both code and data. All code and data items are accessed with near addresses. Tiny programs cannot use libraries that contain far functions, such as the graphics libraries. You can only load .COM files under DOS. Also, the Microsoft C/C++ compiler does not support p-code for the tiny model. Programs using the tiny model use memory in the same way as the small-model programs described in the next section. However, tiny-model applications link CRTCOM.LIB with the object file. The resulting executable file is a .COM file instead of an .EXE file.

Small

With the small-model option, a program can contain two segments: one for data and one for code. Small-model programs compile to files with an .EXE extension. The small model is the default when no other memory model is specified. Each data and code segment is limited to 64K. A program using the small model cannot exceed 128K. Near code addressing and near data addressing are the defaults in small-model programs.

Medium

Choosing the medium model allows your program to have a single segment for data but multiple segments for code. For this reason, a medium-model program can have more than 64K of code but never more than 64K of data. While the program's code can occupy as much space as needed, the program's total data size cannot be greater than 64K. Medium-memory model programs default to far code addressing and near data addressing. You can override the defaults with the _ _**near** keyword.

Compact

Compact-memory models allow your program to have multiple segments for data but only one segment for code. This memory model can be the best choice for C applications that have a large amount of data but only a small amount of code. Compact-model applications allow the data to occupy as much space as needed and as many segments as required. Near code addressing and far data addressing are the defaults when using the compact-memory model. The application can override these defaults by using the _ _**near** or _ _**huge** keyword for data and the _ _**far** keyword for code.

Large

As you might guess, large-memory-model applications can occupy multiple data and code segments. However, no single data object can exceed 64K. Large-model applications are useful for major programs that require sizable amounts of data storage. Far code addressing and far data addressing are the defaults in large-model programs. The application can override these defaults by using the _ _**near** or _ _**huge** keyword for data and the _ _**far** keyword for code.

Huge

The huge and large memory models are similar. The major difference is that the huge model removes the size restriction for individual data objects. However, there are size limitations to elements of a huge array when the array is larger than 64K. Array elements are not permitted to cross segment boundaries. This permits the efficient addressing of each element. For this reason, no single array element can be larger than 64K. Additionally, for arrays larger than 128K, each element must have a byte size equal to some power of 2. However, for arrays 128K or smaller, each element can be any size up to a maximum of 64K.

You can select the memory model you want to use directly from within PWB. You simply choose Option | Language Options from the main menu and then select C or C++ Compiler options.... The next dialog box you see will have a Memory Model entry. Simply click on the down arrow to make your selection.

Dynamic Memory Allocation: Linked Lists

Linked lists are often the best choice when you are trying to create memory-efficient algorithms. Previous example programs, involving arrays of structures, have all included definitions for the total number of structures used. For example, *MAX_BOATS* has been set to 50. This means that the program can accept data for a maximum of 50 boats. If 70 or 100 boats are brought onto the marina, the program itself will have to be altered to accommodate the increased number. This is because the structure allocation is static (not to be confused with the storage class modifier **static**). *Static* used in this sense means a variable that is created by the compiler at compile time. These types of variables exist for their normal scope, and you cannot create more of them, or destroy any of them, while the program is executing. You can immediately see the disadvantage of static allocation.

One way around the problem is to set the number of structures higher than needed. If *MAX_BOATS* is set to 5000, not even Nineveh Boat Sales could have a marina that large. However, 5000 means you are requiring the computer to set aside more than 100 times more memory than before. This is not an efficient way to program.

A better approach is to set aside memory *dynamically* as it is needed. With this approach, memory allocation for structures is requested as the inventory grows. Linked lists allow the use of dynamic memory allocation.

A *linked list* is a collection of structures. Each structure in the list contains an element or pointer that points to another structure in the list. This pointer serves as the link between structures. The concept is similar to an array but enables the list to grow dynamically. Figure 14-1 shows a simple linked list for the Nineveh Boat Sales Program.

The linked list for this example includes a pointer to the next boat in the inventory:

```c
struct stboat {
    char sztype[15];
    char szmodel[15];
    char sztitle[20];
    char szcomment[80];
    int iyear;
    long int lmotor_hours;
    float fretail;
    float fwholesale;
    struct stboat *nextboat;
} Nineveh, *firstboat,*currentboat;
```

The user-defined structure type **stboat** is technically known as a *self-referential structure* because it contains a field that holds an address to another structure just like itself. The pointer *nextboat* contains the address of the next related structure. This allows the pointer **nextboat* in the first structure to point to the second structure, and so on. This is the concept of a linked list of structures.

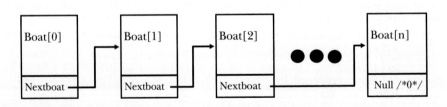

Figure 14-1.   *Implementation of a standard linked list*

Considerations When Using Linked Lists

To allow your program to dynamically reflect the size of your data, you need a means for allocating memory as each new item is added to the list. In C, memory allocation is accomplished with the **malloc()** function; in C++, **new()** is used. In the next section, "A Simple Linked List," the complete program allocates memory for the first structure with the code:

```
firstboat=(struct stboat *) new (struct stboat);
```

The following code segment demonstrates how you can use a similar statement to achieve subsequent memory allocation for each additional structure. The **while** loop continues the entire process while there is valid data to be processed:

```
while (datain(&Nineveh) == 0) {
  currentboat->nextboat = (struct stboat *) new (struct stboat);
  if (currentboat->nextboat == NULL) return(1);
  currentboat=currentboat->nextboat;
  *currentboat=Nineveh;
}
```

To give you some experience with passing structures, the **while** loop begins by sending **datain()** the address of the **stboat** structure, &Nineveh. The function **datain()** takes care of filling the structure with valid data or returns a value of 1 if the user has entered the letter "Q" indicating that he or she wants to quit. If **datain()** does not return a 1, the pointer *currentboat->nextboat* is assigned the address of a dynamically allocated *stboat* structure. Notice that the address returned by **new()** was cast (**struct stboat ***) so that it matched the data type of the receiving variable. The **if** statement checks to see if the function call to **new()** was successful or not. (**new()** returns a null if unsuccessful.)

Since the logical use for *currentboat* is to keep track of the address of the last valid **stboat** structure in the list, the statement after the **if** updates *currentboat* to the address of the new end of the list, namely *currentboat*'s new *nextboat* address.

The last statement in the loop takes care of copying the contents of the **stboat** structure Nineveh into the new dynamically allocated structure pointed to by **currentboat.* The last structure in the list will have its pointer set to null. Using null marks the end of a linked list. See if you can tell where this is done in the complete program that follows.

A Simple Linked List

The following program shows how to implement the Nineveh Boat Sales example using linked lists. Compare this program with the one in Chapter 13 in the section "Constructing an Array of Structures." The C example in Chapter 13 is similar except that it uses a static array implementation. Study the two listings and see which items are similar and which items have changed.

```
//
//    C++ program is an example of a simple linked list.
//    Nineveh used boat inventory example is used again
//    Copyright (c) William H. Murray and Chris H. Pappas, 1992
//

#include <stdlib.h>
#include <iostream.h>

struct stboat {
    char sztype[15];
    char szmodel[15];
    char sztitle[20];
    char szcomment[80];
    int iyear;
    long int lmotor_hours;
    float fretail;
    float fwholesale;
    struct stboat *nextboat;
} Nineveh, *firstboat,*currentboat;

void boatlocation(struct stboat *node);
void output_data(struct stboat *boatptr);
int datain(struct stboat *Ninevehptr);

main()
{
  firstboat=(struct stboat *) new (struct stboat);

  if (firstboat==NULL) exit(1);

  if (datain(&Nineveh) != 0) exit(1);

  *firstboat=Nineveh;
  currentboat=firstboat;

  while (datain(&Nineveh)==0) {
    currentboat->nextboat=
    (struct stboat *) new (struct stboat);
    if (currentboat->nextboat==NULL) return(1);
    currentboat=currentboat->nextboat;
```

```
      *currentboat=Nineveh;
  }

  currentboat->nextboat=NULL; // signal end of list

  boatlocation(firstboat);

  return (0);
}



void boatlocation(struct stboat *node)
{
  do {
    output_data(node);
  } while ((node=node->nextboat) != NULL);
}

void output_data(struct stboat *boatptr)
{
  cout << "\n\n\n";
  cout << "A[{|"|}]<< boatptr->iyear <<[{|"|}]"
   << boatptr->sztype << boatptr->szmodel <<[{|"|}]"
   << "beauty with[{|"|}]<< boatptr->lmotor_hours <<[{|"|}]"
   << "low miles.\n";
  cout << boatptr->szcomment << ".\n";
  cout << "Grab the deal by asking your Nineveh salesperson for";
  cout <<[{|"|}]#" << boatptr->sztitle <<[{|"|}]ONLY! $"
   << boatptr->fretail << ".\n";
}

int datain(struct stboat *Ninevehptr)
{
  char newline;

  cout << "\n[Enter new boat information - a Q quits]\n\n";
  cout << "Enter the make of the boat.\n";
  cin >> Ninevehptr->sztype;

  if (*(Ninevehptr->sztype) == 'Q') return(1);

  cout << "Enter the model of the boat.\n";
  cin >> Ninevehptr->szmodel;

  cout << "Enter the title number for the boat.\n";
```

```
    cin >> Ninevehptr->sztitle;

    cout << "Enter the model year for the boat.\n";
    cin >> Ninevehptr->iyear;

    cout << "Enter the number of hours on the boat motor.\n";
    cin >> Ninevehptr->lmotor_hours;

    cout << "Enter the retail price of the boat.\n";
    cin >> Ninevehptr->fretail;

    cout << "Enter the wholesale price of the boat.\n";
    cin >> Ninevehptr->fwholesale;

    cout << "Enter a one line comment about the boat.\n";
    cin.get(newline);     // process carriage return
    cin.get(Ninevehptr->szcomment,80,'.');

    cin.get(newline);     // process carriage return
    return(0);
}
```

Notice that the three functions are all passed pointers to an **stboat** structure:

```
int datain(struct stboat *Ninevehptr)
void boatlocation(struct stboat *node)
void output_data(struct stboat *boatptr)
```

The function **boatlocation()** checks the linked list for entries before calling the function **output_data()**. It does this with a **do...while** loop that is terminated whenever *node* pointer is assigned a null address. This is true only when you have tried to go beyond the last **stboat** structure in the list. The **output_data()** function formats the output from each linked-list structure.

In most high-level languages, linked-lists provide program solutions that are very memory efficient and often the most difficult to debug. However, as you will learn throughout the remainder of the book, object-oriented C++ classes are even more efficient.

Beginning with Chapter 15, you will be introduced to the concept of object-oriented programming; you will learn about C++ classes in Chapter 16. In Chapter 18, you will combine the two concepts.

Part *III*

Foundations for Object-oriented Programming in C++

An Introduction to Object-oriented Programming

This chapter discusses various object-oriented programming (OOP) concepts. You'll discover the differences between the traditional procedure-oriented programming approach to a problem, used up to this point in the book, and the object-oriented approach. The chapter also discusses terms associated with C++ and object-oriented programming. These terms include, among others, "objects," "encapsulation," "hierarchy," "inheritance," and "polymorphism."

Later in the chapter, simple examples show you how the C++ **class** type is an outgrowth of the C **struct** type. In the next chapter you will learn the details of how the C++ **class** type forms the foundation for object-oriented programming.

There Is Nothing New Under the Sun

Advertisers know that a product will sell better if the word "new" appears somewhere on the product's label. If, however, the saying "There is nothing new under the sun" is applied to programming, the conclusion would have to be that object-oriented programming is not a new programming concept at all. Scott Guthery states that "object-oriented programming has been around since subroutines were invented in the 1940s" ("Are the Emperor's New Clothes Object Oriented?", *Dr. Dobb's Journal*, December 1989). The article continues by suggesting that objects, the foundation of object-oriented programming, have appeared in earlier languages, such as FOR-TRAN II.

Considering these statements, why are we only hearing about object-oriented programming in the closing decade of the 1900s? Why is object-oriented programming being touted as the newest programming technique of the century? It seems that the bottom line is packaging. OOP concepts may have been available in 1940, but we certainly didn't have them packaged in a usable container.

Early programmers, growing up with the BASIC language, often wrote large programs without the use of structured programming concepts. Pages and pages of programming code were tied together with one- or two-letter variables that had a global scope. **goto** statements abounded. The code was a nightmare to read, understand, and debug. Adding new features to such a program was like unlocking Pandora's box. The code, to say the least, was very difficult to maintain.

In the 1960s, structured programming concepts were introduced suggesting the use of meaningful variable names, global and local variable scope, and a procedure-oriented top-down programming approach. Applying these concepts made code easier to read, understand, and debug. Program maintenance was improved because the program could now be studied and altered one procedure at a time. Programming languages such as Ada, C, and Pascal encourage a structured approach to programming problems.

Bjarne Stroustrup is considered the father of C++ and developed the language at Bell Labs in the early 1980s. He may well be the father of object-oriented programming as we know it in the C++ language. Jeff Duntemann pronounced that "Object-oriented programming is structured structured programming. It's the second derivative of software development, the Grand Unifying Theory of program structure" ("Dodging Steamships," *Dr. Dobb's Journal,* July 1989). Indeed, what you'll see is that object-oriented programming, using C++, builds upon foundations established earlier in the C language. Even though C++ is the foundational language for object-oriented programming, it is still possible to write unstructured code or procedure-oriented code. The choice is yours.

There might not be anything new under the sun if Scott Guthery's statements are taken to mean "programming concepts," but this chapter introduces you to the most elegant packaging method for a programming concept you have ever seen. At last, we truly have the tools, with languages such as C++, to enter the age of object-oriented programming.

Traditional Structured Programming

The earlier chapters of this book were devoted to teaching traditional procedure-oriented structured programming techniques for solving C and C++ problems. These chapters introduced you to fundamental C and C++ syntax in a familiar programming environment. (If you have been programming in a language such as Pascal for any length of time, you have probably been using a structured procedure approach in solving programming problems. A procedural approach is common among all structured languages including C, C++, Pascal and PL/I.) You have seen that a procedure-oriented C or C++ program is structured in such a way that there is typically a main function and possibly one or more functions (subroutines) that are called from the main function. This is a top-down approach. The main function is typically short, shifting the work to the remaining functions in the program. Program execution flows from the top of the main function and terminates at the bottom of the same function.

In this approach, code and data are separate. Procedures define what is to happen to data, but the two never become one. You'll see that this changes in object-oriented programming. The procedural approach suffers from several disadvantages, the chief of which is program maintenance. When additions or deletions must be made to the program code, such as in a database program, often the entire program must be reworked to include the new routines. This approach takes enormous amounts of time in both development and debugging. A better approach toward program maintenance is needed.

Object-oriented Programming

Object-oriented programs (OOPs) function differently from the traditional procedural approach. They require a new programming strategy that is often difficult for traditional procedure-oriented programmers to grasp. In the next four chapters you will be introduced to the concepts that make up object-oriented programming in C++. If you have already written or examined program code for Microsoft Windows or the OS/2 Presentation Manager, you have had a taste of one of the concepts used in object-oriented programming—that a program consists of a group of objects that are often related. With C++, you form objects by using the new **class** data type. A class provides a set of values (data) and the operations (methods or member functions) that act on those values. You can then manipulate the resulting objects by using messages.

It is the message component of object-oriented languages that is also common to Windows and Presentation Manager programs. In object-oriented programming, objects hold not only the data (member data) but the methods (member functions) for working on that data. The two items have been combined into one working concept. Simply put, objects contain data and the methods for working on that data.

There are three distinct advantages offered to the programmer by object-oriented programming. The first is program maintenance. Programs are easier to read and understand, and object-oriented programming controls program complexity by allowing only the necessary details to be viewed by the programmer. The second advantage is program alteration (adding or deleting features). You can often make additions and deletions to programs, such as in a database program, by simply adding or deleting objects. New objects can inherit everything from a parent object, and they only need to add or delete items that differ. The third advantage is that you can use objects numerous times. You can save well-designed objects in a toolkit of useful routines that you can easily insert into new code, with few or no changes to that code.

In the earlier chapters of this book, you discovered that you could convert many C programs to C++, and vice versa, by making simple program alterations. For example, **printf** is switched to **cout** for I/O streams. This is an easy switch because the conversion is from and to a procedural programming structure. However, object-oriented programming is exclusively in the C++ realm because C does not provide the vital link—the abstract data type **class**. It is therefore more difficult to convert a procedure-oriented program to object-oriented form. Programs have to be reworked, with traditional functions being replaced with objects. In some cases, it turns out to be easier to discard the old program and create an object-oriented program from the ground up. This can be considered a distinct disadvantage.

C++ and Object-oriented Programming

Object-oriented programming concepts cross language boundaries. Microsoft Quick Pascal, for example, was one of the first languages to allow the use of objects. What does C++ have that makes it a suitable language for developing object-oriented programs? The answer is, as previously mentioned, the **class** data type. It is C++'s **class** type, built upon C's **struct** type, that gives the language the ability to build objects. Also, C++ brings several additional features to object-oriented programming not inlcuded in other languages that simply make use of objects. C++'s advantages include strong typing, operator overloading, and less emphasis on the preprocessor. It is true that you can do object-oriented programming with other products and in other languages, but with C++ the benefits are outstanding. This is a language that was designed, not retrofitted, for object-oriented programming.

In the next section of this chapter you learn some object-oriented terminology. These terms and definitions will help you form a solid understanding of this programming technique. Be prepared; the new terminology will be your biggest hurdle as you enter the world of object-oriented programming.

Object-oriented Terminology

Much of the terminology of object-oriented programming is language independent; that is, it is not associated with a specific language such as Pascal or C++. Therefore, many of the following definitions apply to the various implementations of object-oriented languages. Chapter 16 discusses terms that are more C++ specific.

Object-oriented programming is a programming technique that allows you to view concepts as a variety of objects. By using objects, you can represent the tasks that are to be performed, their interaction, and any given conditions that must be observed. A data structure often forms the basis of an object; thus, in C or C++, the **struct** type can form an elementary object. Communicating with objects can be done through the use of messages, as mentioned earlier. Using messages is similar to calling a function in a procedure-oriented program. When an object receives a message, methods contained within the object respond. *Methods* are similar to the functions of procedure-oriented programming. However, methods are part of an object.

The C++ class is an extension of the C and C++ **struct** type and forms the required abstract data type for object-oriented programming. The class can contain closely related items that share attributes. Stated more formally, an object is simply an instance of a class. In Figure 15-1, the Lincoln automobile class is illustrated.

Assume that the Lincoln automobile class is described in the program's code. This class might include a description of items that are common to all Lincolns and data concerning maintenance intervals. At run time, three additional objects of the Lincoln class can be created. They could include the Lincoln Town Car, the Lincoln Mark VII, and the Lincoln Continental. The additional objects might include details of features and data common to each individual model. For example, a Mark VII is an object that describes a particular type of Lincoln automobile. It is an instance of the Lincoln class.

If a message is sent to the instance of the Lincoln class (similar to a call to a function) with instructions to dynamically adjust the air suspension on all four wheels

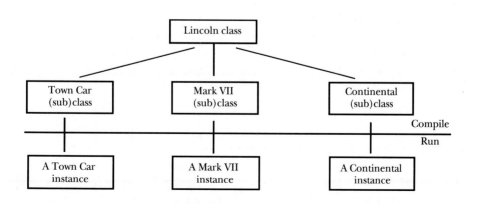

Figure 15-1. *A diagram of the Lincoln class*

during a sharp turn, that message could be utilized only by the Continental (at least in 1992 models) object of the class. Only the Lincoln Continental had an active air suspension in the 1992 model.

Ultimately, there should emerge class libraries containing many object types. You could use instances of those object types to piece together program code. You will see interesting examples of this when Windows class libraries are described in Chapters 24 and 25.

Before you examine these terms in closer detail, it is a good idea to become familiar with several additional concepts that relate to C++ and object-oriented programming, as described in the next few sections.

Encapsulation

Encapsulation refers to the way each object combines its member data and member functions (methods) into a single structure. Figure 15-2 illustrates how you can combine data fields and methods to build an object.

Typically, an object's description is part of a C++ class and includes a description of the object's internal structure, how the object relates with other objects, and some form of protection that isolates the functional details of the object from outside the class. The C++ **class** structure does all of this.

In a C++ class, you control functional details of the object by using private, public, and/or protected descriptors. In object-oriented programming, the *public* section is typically used for the interface information (methods) that makes the class reusable

Data Fields	Methods
Data	Member function
	Member function
Data	Member function
Data	Member function
	Member function
Data	Member function

Figure 15-2. *Data fields and methods combined to build an object*

across applications. If data or methods are contained in the public section, they are available outside the class. The *private* section of a class limits the availability of data or methods to the class itself. A *protected* section containing data or methods is limited to the class and any derived subclasses.

Class Hierarchy

The C++ class actually serves as a template or pattern for creating objects. The objects formed from the class description are *instances* of the class. It is possible to develop a *class hierarchy* where there is a parent class and several child classes. In C++, the basis for doing this revolves around *derived classes.* Parent classes represent more general-ized tasks, while derived child classes are given specific tasks to perform. For example, the Lincoln class discussed earlier might contain data and methods common to the entire Lincoln line, such as engines, instrumentation, batteries, braking ability, and handling. Child classes derived from the parent, such as Town Car, Mark VII, and Continental, could contain items specific to the class. For example, the 1992 Conti-nental was the only car in the line with an active suspension system.

Inheritance

Inheritance in object-oriented programming allows a class to inherit properties from a class of objects. The parent class serves as a pattern for the derived class and can be altered in several ways. (In the next chapter you will learn that member functions can be overloaded, new member functions can be added, and member access privileges can be changed.) If an object inherits its attributes from a single parent, it is called *single inheritance.* If an object inherits its attributes from multiple parents, it is called *multiple inheritance.* Inheritance is an important concept since it allows reuse of a class definition without requiring major code changes. Inheritance encourages the reuse of code since child classes are extensions of parent classes.

Polymorphism

Another important object-oriented concept that relates to the class hierarchy is that common messages can be sent to the parent class objects and all derived subclass objects. In formal terms, this is called *polymorphism.*

Polymorphism allows each subclass object to respond to the message format in a manner appropriate to its definition. Imagine a class hierarchy for gathering data. The parent class might be responsible for gathering the name, social security number, occupation, and number of years of employment for an individual. You could then use child classes to decide what additional information would be added based on occupation. In one case a supervisory position might include yearly salary, while in another case a sales position might include an hourly rate and commission informa-tion. Thus, the parent class gathers general information common to all child classes while the child classes gather additional information relating to specific job descriptions. Polymorphism allows a common data-gathering message to be sent to each class. Both the parent and child classes respond in an appropriate manner to the message. Polymorphism encourages extendability of existing code.

Virtual Functions

Polymorphism gives objects the ability to respond to messages from routines when the object's exact type is not known. In C++ this ability is a result of *late binding*. With late binding, the addresses are determined dynamically at run time, rather than statically at compile time, as in traditional compiled languages. This static (fixed) method is often called *early binding*. Function names are replaced with memory addresses. You accomplish late binding by using *virtual functions*. Virtual functions are defined in the parent class when subsequent derived classes will overload the function by redefining the function's implementation. When you use virtual functions, messages are passed as a pointer that points to the object instead of directly to the object.

Virtual functions utilize a table for address information. The table is initialized at run time by using a constructor. A constructor is invoked whenever an object of its class is created. The job of the constructor here is to link the virtual function with the table of address information. During the compile operation, the address of the virtual function is not known; rather, it is given the position in the table (determined at run time) of addresses that will contain the address for the function.

A First Look at the C++ Class

It has already been stated that the C++ **class** type is an extension of C's **struct** type. In this section, you learn how you can use the **struct** type in C++ to form a primitive class, complete with data and members. Next, you examine the formal syntax for defining a class and see several simple examples of its implementation. The section discusses the differences between a primitive **struct** class type and an actual C++ class and presents several simple examples to illustrate class concepts. (Chapter 16 is devoted to a detailed analysis of the C++ class as it applies to object-oriented programming.)

A Structure as a Primitive Class

Chapter 13 discussed structures for C and C++. In many respects, the structure in C++ is an elementary form of a class. You use the keyword **struct** to define a structure. Examine the following code:

```
//
//   15SQROOT.CPP
//   C++ program using the keyword "struct" to illustrate a
//   primitive form of class. Here several member functions
//   are defined within the structure.
//   Copyright (c) William H. Murray and Chris H. Pappas, 1992
//

#include <iostream.h>
#include <math.h>

struct math_operations {
  double data_value;

  void set_value(double ang) {data_value=ang;}
  double get_square(void) {double answer;
                           answer=data_value*data_value;
                           return (answer);}
  double get_square_root(void) {double answer;
                                answer=sqrt(data_value);
                                return (answer);}
} math;

main()
{
  // set numeric value to 35.63
  math.set_value(35.63);

  cout << "The square of the number is: "
       << math.get_square() << endl;
  cout << "The square root of the number is: "
       << math.get_square_root() << endl;
  return (0);
}
```

The first thing to notice in this code is that the structure definition contains member data and functions. While you are used to seeing data declarations as part of a structure, this is probably the first time you have seen member functions defined within the structure definition. There was no mention of member functions in the discussion of the **struct** type in Chapter 13 because they are exclusive to C++. These member functions can act upon the data contained in the structure (or class) itself.

Recall that a class can contain member data and functions. By default, in a **struct** declaration in C++, member data and functions are public. (A public section is one in which the data and functions are available outside the structure.) Here is the output sent to the screen when the program is executed:

```
C:\C700>15sqroot
The square of the number is: 1269.5
The square root of the number is: 5.96909
```

In this example, the structure definition contains a single data value:

```
double data_value;
```

Next, three member functions are defined. Actually, the code for each function is contained within the structure:

```
void set_value(double ang) {data_value=ang;}
double get_square(void) {double answer;
                         answer=data_value*data_value;
                         return (answer);}
double get_square_root(void) {double answer;
                              answer=sqrt(data_value);
                              return (answer);}
```

The first member function is responsible for initializing the variable, *data_value*. The remaining two member functions return the square and square root of *data_value*. Notice that the member functions are not passed a value; *data_value* is available to them as members of the structure. Both member functions return a **double**.

The program's **main()** function sets the value of *data_value* to 35.63 with a call to the member function, **set_value()**:

```
math.set_value(35.63);
```

Notice that the name *math* has been associated with the structure **math_operations**.

The remaining two member functions return values to the **cout** stream:

```
cout << "The square of the number is: "
     << math.get_square() << endl;
cout << "The square root of the number is: "
     << math.get_square_root() << endl;
```

This example contains a structure with member data and functions. The functions are contained within the structure definition. You won't find an example simpler than this one.

In the next program, the **struct** keyword is still used to develop a primitive class, but this time the member functions are written outside the structure. This is the way you will most commonly see structures and classes defined.

This example contains a structure definition with one data member, *data_value*, and seven member functions. The member functions return information for various trigonometric values.

```cpp
//
//   15TSTRUC.CPP
//   C++ program using the keyword "struct" to illustrate a
//   primitive form of class. This program uses a structure
//   to obtain trigonometric values for an angle.
//   Copyright (c) William H. Murray and Chris H. Pappas, 1992
//

#include <iostream.h>
#include <math.h>

const double DEG_TO_RAD=0.0174532925;

struct degree {
  double data_value;

  void set_value(double);
  double get_sine(void);
  double get_cosine(void);
  double get_tangent(void);
  double get_secant(void);
  double get_cosecant(void);
  double get_cotangent(void);
} deg;

void degree::set_value(double ang)
{
  data_value=ang;
}

double degree::get_sine(void)
{
  double answer;

  answer=sin(DEG_TO_RAD*data_value);
  return (answer);
}
```

```
double degree::get_cosine(void)
{
  double answer;

  answer=cos(DEG_TO_RAD*data_value);
  return (answer);
}

double degree::get_tangent(void)
{
  double answer;

  answer=tan(DEG_TO_RAD*data_value);
  return (answer);
}

double degree::get_secant(void)
{
  double answer;

  answer=1.0/sin(DEG_TO_RAD*data_value);
  return (answer);
}

double degree::get_cosecant(void)
{
  double answer;

  answer=1.0/cos(DEG_TO_RAD*data_value);
  return (answer);
}

double degree::get_cotangent(void)
{
  double answer;

  answer=1.0/tan(DEG_TO_RAD*data_value);
  return (answer);
}

main()
{
  // set angle to 25.0 degrees
```

```
   deg.set_value(25.0);

   cout << "The sine of the angle is: "
        << deg.get_sine() << endl;
   cout << "The cosine of the angle is: "
        << deg.get_cosine() << endl;
   cout << "The tangent of the angle is: "
        << deg.get_tangent() << endl;
   cout << "The secant of the angle is: "
        << deg.get_secant() << endl;
   cout << "The cosecant of the angle is: "
        << deg.get_cosecant() << endl;
   cout << "The cotangent of the angle is: "
        << deg.get_cotangent() << endl;
   return (0);
}
```

Notice that the structure definition contains the prototypes for the member functions. The variable, *deg*, is associated with the **degree** structure type.

```
struct degree {
  double data_value;

  void set_value(double);
  double get_sine(void);
  double get_cosine(void);
  double get_tangent(void);
  double get_secant(void);
  double get_cosecant(void);
  double get_cotangent(void);
} deg;
```

Immediately after the structure is defined, the various member functions are developed and listed. The member functions are associated with the structure or class by means of the scope operator (::). Other than the use of the scope operator, the member functions take on the appearance of normal functions.

Examine the first part of the **main()** function:

```
// set angle to 25.0 degrees
deg.set_data(25.0);
```

Here the value 25.0 is being passed as an argument to the **set_value()** function. Observe the syntax for this operation. The **set_value()** function itself is very simple:

```
void degree::set_value(double ang)
{
  data_value=ang;
}
```

The function accepts the argument and assigns the value to the class variable, *data_value*. This is one way of initializing class variables. From this point forward, in the class, *data_value* is accessible by each of the six member functions. The job of the member functions is to calculate the sine, cosine, tangent, secant, cosecant, and cotangent of the given angle. The respective values are printed to the screen from the **main()** function with statements similar to the following:

```
cout << "The sine of the angle is: "
     << deg.get_sine() << endl;
```

You can use the dot notation commonly used for structures to access the member functions. Pointer variables can also be assigned to a structure or class, in which case, the arrow operator is used. You will see examples of this in Chapter 16.

The Syntax and Rules for C++ Classes

The definition of a C++ class begins with the keyword class. The class name (tag type) immediately follows the keyword. The framework of the class is very similar to the **struct** type definition you have already seen.

```
class type {
  type var1
  type var2
  type var3
     .
     .
     .
public:
  member function 1
  member function 2
  member function 3
  member function 4
     .
     .
     .
} name associated with class type;
```

Member variables immediately follow the class declaration. These variables are, by default, private to the class and can be accessed only by the member functions that follow. Member functions typically follow a public declaration. This allows access to the member functions from calling routines external to the class. All class member functions have access to public, private, and protected parts of a class.

The following is an example of a class that is used in the next programming example:

```
class degree {
  double data_value;

public:
  void set_value(double);
  double get_sine(void);
  double get_cosine(void);
  double get_tangent(void);
  double get_secant(void);
  double get_cosecant(void);
  double get_cotangent(void);
} deg;
```

This class has a type (tag name) **degree**. A private variable, *data_value*, will share degree values among the various member functions. Seven functions make up the function members of the class. They are **set_value()**, **get_sine()**, **get_cosine()**, **get_tangent()**, **get_secant()**, **get_cosecant()**, and **get_cotangent()**. The name that is associated with this class type is *deg*. Unlike this example, the association of a variable name with the class name is most frequently made in the **main()** function.

Does this class definition look familiar? It is basically the structure definition from the previous example converted to a true class.

A Simple C++ Class

In a C++ class, the visibility of class members is by default private. That is, member variables are accessible only to member functions of the class. If the member functions are to have visibility beyond the class, you must explicitly specify that visibility.

The conversion of the last program's structure to a true C++ class is simple and straightforward. First, the **struct** keyword is replaced by the **class** keyword. Second, the member functions that are to have public visibility are separated from the private variable of the class with the use of a public declaration. Examine the complete program:

```
//
//   15TCLASS.CPP
//   C++ program illustrates a simple but true class and
//   introduces the concept of private and public.
//   This program uses a class to obtain the trigonometric
//   value for given angle.
//   Copyright (c) William H. Murray and Chris H. Pappas, 1992
//

#include <iostream.h>
#include <math.h>

const double DEG_TO_RAD=0.0174532925;

class degree {
  double data_value;

public:
  void set_value(double);
  double get_sine(void);
  double get_cosine(void);
  double get_tangent(void);
  double get_secant(void);
  double get_cosecant(void);
  double get_cotangent(void);
} deg;

void degree::set_value(double ang)
{
  data_value=ang;
}

double degree::get_sine(void)
{
  double answer;

  answer=sin(DEG_TO_RAD*data_value);
  return (answer);
}

double degree::get_cosine(void)
{
  double answer;

  answer=cos(DEG_TO_RAD*data_value);
```

```
    return (answer);
}

double degree::get_tangent(void)
{
  double answer;

  answer=tan(DEG_TO_RAD*data_value);
  return (answer);
}

double degree::get_secant(void)
{
  double answer;

  answer=1.0/sin(DEG_TO_RAD*data_value);
  return (answer);
}

double degree::get_cosecant(void)
{
  double answer;

  answer=1.0/cos(DEG_TO_RAD*data_value);
  return (answer);
}

double degree::get_cotangent(void)
{
  double answer;

  answer=1.0/tan(DEG_TO_RAD*data_value);
  return (answer);
}

main()
{
  // set angle to 25.0 degrees
  deg.set_value(25.0);

  cout << "The sine of the angle is: "
       << deg.get_sine() << endl;
  cout << "The cosine of the angle is: "
       << deg.get_cosine() << endl;
  cout << "The tangent of the angle is: "
```

```
            << deg.get_tangent() << endl;
    cout << "The secant of the angle is: "
            << deg.get_secant() << endl;
    cout << "The cosecant of the angle is: "
            << deg.get_cosecant() << endl;
    cout << "The cotangent of the angle is: "
            << deg.get_cotangent() << endl;
    return (0);
}
```

In this example, the body of the program remains the same. The structure definition has been converted to a true, but elementary, class definition with private and public parts.

Note that the variable, *data_value*, is private to the class (by default) and as a result is accessible only by the member functions of the class. The member functions themselves have been declared public in visibility and are accessible from outside the class. Each class member, however, whether public or private, has access to all other class members, public or private.

Here is the output from the program:

```
C:\C700>15tclass
The sine of the angle is: 0.422618
The cosine of the angle is: 0.906308
The tangent of the angle is: 0.466308
The secant of the angle is: 2.3662
The cosecant of the angle is: 1.10338
The cotangent of the angle is: 2.14451
```

Again, class member functions are usually defined immediately after the class has been defined and before the **main()** function of the program. Nonmember class functions are still defined after the function **main()** and are prototyped in the normal fashion.

The next chapter looks at the details of C++ classes more closely.

Chapter *16*

C++ Classes

In Chapter 15 you learned that you could create a primitive C++ class by using the **struct** keyword. Next, several elementary C++ classes were created by using the **class** keyword. Both types of examples illustrated the simple fact that classes can contain member data and member functions that act on that data. In this chapter, you learn more details about C++ classes. This chapter discusses nesting of classes and structures, the use of constructors and destructors, overloading member functions, friend functions, operator overloading, derived classes, virtual functions, and other miscellaneous topics. These class structures create objects that form the foundation of object-oriented programs.

Much of the programming flexibility offered to the C++ programmer is a result of the various data types discussed in earlier chapters. The C++ class gives you another advantage: the benefits of a structure along with the ability to limit access to specific data to functions that are also members of the class. As a result, classes are one of the greatest contributions made by C++ to programming. The added features of the class, over earlier structures, include the ability to initialize and protect sensitive functions and data.

In studying C and C++ programming, consider the increase in programming power you have gained with each new data type. Vectors or one-dimensional arrays allow a group of like data types to be held together. Next, structures allow related items of different data types to be combined in a group. Finally, the C++ class concept takes you one step further with abstract data types. A class allows you to implement a member data type and associate member functions with the data. Using classes gives you the storage concept associated with a structure along with the member functions to operate on the member variables.

Additional Class Features

In the last chapter you learned the syntax for creating an elementary C++ class. Classes have extended capabilities that go far beyond this simple syntax. This section is devoted to exploring these capabilities with an eye toward object-oriented programming. In Chapter 18, class objects will be woven into more complicated object-oriented programs.

A Simple Class

The following is a short review of a simple class based on the definitions from Chapter 15. Remember that a class starts with the keyword **class** followed by a class name (tag). In the following example, the class tag name is **car**. If the class contains member variables, they are defined at the start of the class. Their declaration type is private, by default. This example defines three member variables: *mileage, tire_pressure*, and *speed*. Class member functions follow the member variable list. Typically, the member functions are declared public. A private declaration limits the member variables to member functions within the class. This is often referred to as *data hiding*. A public declaration makes the member functions available outside of the class:

```
class car {
   int    mileage;
   int    tire_pressure;
   float  speed;

public:
   int maintenance(int);
   int wear_record(int);
   int air_resistance(float);
} mycar;
```

Here, three member functions are prototyped within the class definition. They are **maintenance()**, **wear_record()**, and **air_resistance()**. All three return an **int** type. Typically, however, the contents of the member functions are defined outside the class definition—usually, immediately after the class itself.

Let's continue the study of classes with a look at additional class features.

Nesting Classes

Recall from Chapter 13 that structures can be nested. This also turns out to be true for C++ classes. When using nested classes, you must take care not to make the resulting declaration more complicated than necessary. The following examples illustrate the nesting concept.

Nesting Structures Within a Class

The following is a simple example of how two structures can be nested within a class definition. Using nesting in this fashion is both common and practical. You can also use the **class** keyword in this manner.

```
//
//   16WAGES.CPP
//   C++ program illustrates the use of nesting concepts
//   in classes. This program calculates the wages for
//   the named employee.
//   Copyright (c) William H. Murray and Chris H. Pappas, 1992
//

#include <iostream.h>

char newline;

class employee {
  struct emp_name {
    char firstname[20];
    char middlename[20];
    char lastname[20];
  } name;
  struct emp_hours {
    double hours;
    double base_sal;
    double overtime_sal;
  } hours;

public:
  void emp_input(void);
  void emp_output(void);
};

void employee::emp_input()
{
  cout << "Enter first name of employee: ";
  cin >> name.firstname;
```

```
    cin.get(newline);      // flush carriage return
    cout << "Enter middle name of employee: ";
    cin >> name.middlename;
    cin.get(newline);
    cout << "Enter last name of employee:  ";
    cin >> name.lastname;
    cin.get(newline);

    cout << "Enter total hours worked:  ";
    cin >> hours.hours;
    cout << "Enter hourly wage (base rate):   ";
    cin >> hours.base_sal;
    cout << "Enter overtime wage (overtime rate): ";
    cin >> hours.overtime_sal;
    cout << "\n\n";
}

void employee::emp_output()
{
  cout << name.firstname << " " << name.middlename
       << " " << name.lastname << endl;
  if (hours.hours <= 40)
    cout << "Base Pay:  $"
         << hours.hours * hours.base_sal << endl;
    else {
      cout << "Base Pay:  $"
           << 40 * hours.base_sal << endl;
      cout << "Overtime Pay: $"
           << (hours.hours-40) * hours.overtime_sal
           << endl;
    }
}

main()
{
  employee acme_corp;    // associate acme_corp with class

  acme_corp.emp_input();
  acme_corp.emp_output();
  return (0);
}
```

In the next example, two classes are nested within the **employee** class definition. As you can see, the use of nesting can be quite straightforward.

```
class employee {
  class emp_name {
    char firstname[20];
    char middlename[20];
    char lastname[20];
  } name;
  class emp_hours {
    double hours;
    double base_salary;
    double overtime_sal;
  } hours;

public:
  void emp_input(void);
  void emp_output(void);
};
```

The **employee** class includes two nested classes, **emp_name** and **emp_hours**. The nested classes, while part of the private section of the **employee** class, are actually available outside the class. In other words, the visibility of the nested classes is the same as if they were defined outside the **employee** class. The individual member variables, for this example, are accessed through the member functions (public, by default) **emp_input()** and **emp_output()**.

Both member functions, **emp_input()** and **emp_output()**, are of type **void** and do not accept arguments. The **emp_input()** function prompts the user for employee data that will be passed to the nested structures (classes). The data collected includes the employee's full name, the total hours worked, the regular pay rate, and the overtime pay rate. Output is generated when the **emp_output()** function is called. The employee's name, base pay, and overtime pay will be printed to the screen:

```
Enter first name of employee: George
Enter middle name of employee: Harry
Enter last name of employee: Smith
Enter total hours worked: 52
Enter hourly wage (base rate): 7.50
Enter overtime wage (overtime rate): 10.00

John James Jones
Base Pay:  $300.00
Overtime Pay: $120.00
```

The **main()** function in this program is fairly short. This is because most of the work is being done by the member functions of the class:

```
employee acme_corp;      // associate acme_corp with class

acme_corp.emp_input();
acme_corp.emp_output();
```

First, the variable *acme_corp*, representing the Acme Computer Corporation, is associated with the **employee** class. To request a member function, the dot operator is used. Next, **acme_corp.emp_input()** is called to collect the employee information, and then **acme_corp.emp_output()** is used to calculate and print the payroll results.

An Alternate Nesting Form

The following form of nesting is also considered acceptable syntax:

```
class cars {
  int mileage;
public:
  void trip(int t);
  int speed(float s);
};

class contents {
  int count;
public:
  cars mileage;
  void rating(void);
{
```

Here, **cars** becomes nested within the **contents** class. Nested classes, whether inside or outside, have the same scope.

Constructors and Destructors

A *constructor* is a class member function. Constructors are useful for initializing class variables or allocating memory storage. The constructor always has the same name as the class it is defined within. Constructors have additional versatility: they can accept arguments and be overloaded. A constructor is executed automatically when an object of the **class** type is created. *Free store objects* are objects created with the **new** operator and serve to allocate memory for the objects created. Constructors are generated by Microsoft's C/C++ compiler if they are not explicitly defined.

A *destructor* is a class member function typically used to return memory allocated from free store memory. The destructor, like the constructor, has the same name as the class it is defined in, preceded by the tilde character (~). Destructors are the complement to their constructor counterparts. A destructor is automatically called when the **delete** operator is applied to a class pointer or when a program passes beyond the scope of a class object. Destructors, unlike their constructor counterparts, cannot accept an argument and may not be overloaded. Destructors are also generated by Microsoft's C/C++ compiler if they are not explicitly defined.

Creating a Simple Constructor and Destructor

In the first example involving the use of constructors and destructors, a constructor and destructor are used to signal the start and end of a coin conversion example. This program illustrates that constructors and destructors are called automatically:

```
//
//   16COINS.CPP
//   C++ program illustrates the use of constructors and
//   destructors in a simple program.
//   This program converts cents into appropriate coins:
//   (quarters, dimes, nickels, and pennies).
//   Copyright (c) William H. Murray and Chris H. Pappas, 1992
//

#include <iostream.h>

const int QUARTER=25;
const int DIME=10;
const int NICKEL=5;

class coins {
  int number;

public:
  coins() {cout << "Begin Conversion!\n";}       // constructor
  ~coins() {cout << "\nFinished Conversion!";}  // destructor
  void get_cents(int);
  int quarter_conversion(void);
  int dime_conversion(int);
  int nickel_conversion(int);
};

void coins::get_cents(int cents)
{
  number=cents;
  cout << number << " cents, converts to:"
       << endl;
```

```
}

int coins::quarter_conversion()
{
  cout << number/QUARTER << " quarter(s), ";
  return(number%QUARTER);
}

int coins::dime_conversion(int d)
{
  cout << d/DIME << " dime(s), ";
  return(d%DIME);
}

int coins::nickel_conversion(int n)
{
  cout << n/NICKEL << " nickel(s), and ";
  return(n%NICKEL);
}

main()
{
  int c,d,n,p;

  cout << "Enter the cash, in cents, to convert: ";
  cin >> c;

  // associate cash_in_cents with coins class.
  coins cash_in_cents;

  cash_in_cents.get_cents(c);
  d=cash_in_cents.quarter_conversion();
  n=cash_in_cents.dime_conversion(d);
  p=cash_in_cents.nickel_conversion(n);
  cout << p << " penny(ies).";
  return (0);
}
```

This program uses four member functions. The first function passes the number of pennies to the private class variable *number*. The remaining three functions convert cash, given in cents, to the equivalent cash in quarters, dimes, nickels, and pennies. Notice in particular the placement of the constructor and destructor in the class definition. The constructor and destructor function descriptions contain nothing more than a message that will be printed to the screen. Constructors are not specifically called by a program. Their appearance on the screen is your key that the constructor and destructor were automatically called when the object was created and destroyed.

```
class coins {
   int number;

public:
   coins() {cout << "Begin Conversion!\n";}       // constructor
   ~coins() {cout << "\nFinished Conversion!";}  // destructor
   void get_cents(int);
   int quarter_conversion(void);
   int dime_conversion(int);
   int nickel_conversion(int);
};
```

Here is an example of the output from this program:

```
Enter the cash, in cents, to convert: 157
Begin Conversion!
157 cents, converts to:
6 quarter(s), 0 dime(s), 1 nickel(s), and 2 penny(ies).
Finished Conversion!
```

In this example, the function definition is actually included within the constructor and destructor. When the function definition is included with member functions, it is said to be *implicitly defined*. Member functions can be defined in the typical manner or declared explicitly as inline functions.

You can expand this example to include dollars and half-dollars.

Using Constructors to Initialize Member Variables

Another practical use for constructors is for initialization of private class variables. In the previous examples, class variables were set by utilizing separate member functions. In the next example, the original class of the previous program is modified slightly to eliminate the need for user input. In this case, the variable *number* will be initialized to 431 pennies.

```
class coins {
   int number;

public:
   coins() {number=431;}                         // constructor
   ~coins() {cout << "\nFinished Conversion!";}  // destructor
```

```
   int quarter_conversion(void);
   int dime_conversion(int);
   int nickel_conversion(int);
};
```

The route to class variables is always through class member functions. Remember that the constructor is considered a member function.

Creating a Pointer Class

The next example illustrates another use for constructors and destructors while also teaching you how to incorporate the features of the Microsoft mouse in your programs. Study the complete program listing that follows and pay attention to the definition of the **pointer** class. Note in particular that the constructor and destructor are defined, like member functions, outside the class definition.

```
//
//  16MOUSE.CPP
//  C++ program creates a pointer class that will allow
//  the use of the Microsoft mouse for DOS mode programs.
//  A constructor initializes the mouse, while a
//  destructor hides the mouse pointer.
//  Copyright (c) William H. Murray and Chris H. Pappas, 1992
//

#include <iostream.h>
#include <dos.h>         // for mouse
#include <process.h>     // for exit

class pointer {
   int l_button;
   int r_button;

public:
   pointer();
   ~pointer();
   void p_latent(void);
   void p_visible(void);
   int p_lbinfo(void);
   int p_rbinfo(void);
   int p_xinfo(void);
   int p_yinfo(void);
} ms_mouse;
```

```
pointer::pointer()
{
  union REGS regs;

  regs.x.ax=0;
  int86(0x33,&regs,&regs);
}

pointer::~pointer()
{
  union REGS regs;

  regs.x.ax=2;
  int86(0x33,&regs,&regs);
}

void pointer::p_latent(void)
{
  union REGS regs;

  regs.x.ax=2;
  int86(0x33,&regs,&regs);
}

void pointer::p_visible(void)
{
  union REGS regs;

  regs.x.ax=1;
  int86(0x33,&regs,&regs);
}

int pointer::p_lbinfo(void)
{
  union REGS regs;

  l_button=0;
  regs.x.ax=3;
  int86(0x33,&regs,&regs);
  if(regs.x.bx & 1)
    l_button=1;
  return(l_button);
}

int pointer::p_rbinfo(void)
```

```
{
  union REGS regs;

  r_button=0;
  regs.x.ax=3;
  int86(0x33,&regs,&regs);
  if(regs.x.bx & 2)
    r_button=1;
  return(r_button);
}

int pointer::p_xinfo(void)
{
  union REGS regs;

  regs.x.ax=3;
  int86(0x33,&regs,&regs);
  return(regs.x.cx);
}

int pointer::p_yinfo(void)
{
  union REGS regs;

  regs.x.ax=3;
  int86(0x33,&regs,&regs);
  return(regs.x.dx);
}

main()
{
  ms_mouse.p_visible();   // start with mouse visible

  for(;;) {
    if(ms_mouse.p_lbinfo()==1)
      ms_mouse.p_visible();
      cout << ms_mouse.p_xinfo() << "\t"
           << ms_mouse.p_yinfo() << endl;
    if(ms_mouse.p_rbinfo()==1)
      ms_mouse.p_latent();
      cout << ms_mouse.p_xinfo() << "\t"
           << ms_mouse.p_yinfo() << endl;
    if(ms_mouse.p_lbinfo()==1 && ms_mouse.p_rbinfo()==1)
      exit(0);
  }
```

```
  return (0);
}
```

The **pointer** class uses a constructor, **pointer()**, and a destructor, **~pointer()**. In order to utilize the Microsoft mouse, under DOS, an interrupt 33h is used in conjunction with the **int86()** function. By programming specific values in specified registers, you can make the mouse do many tasks. Appendix B lists all of the special register values you can use with the mouse and the various functions they perform. The incorporation of the mouse under Windows is handled differently and is discussed in Chapters 23 and 24. Under DOS, the mouse can be initialized by passing a zero in the **ax** register, as shown in the constructor's definition:

```
pointer::pointer()
{
  union REGS regs;

  regs.x.ax=0;
  int86(0x33,&regs,&regs);
}
```

Here, a union is used to allow communication with the system's registers.

A unique application available with destructors can be seen, during execution, when the mouse pointer is automatically erased when the destructor is called. The destructor passes a 2 to the **ax** register and then calls the mouse interrupt. Again, refer to Appendix B for details.

```
pointer::~pointer()
{
  union REGS regs;

  regs.x.ax=2;
  int86(0x33,&regs,&regs);
}
```

The remaining class member functions return information on mouse buttons and x,y screen coordinate positions for the mouse. The structure of these remaining member functions is fairly consistent and makes good use of unions. More details regarding hardware control involving mice, keyboards, and so on, are presented in Chapters 20 and 21.

If you execute this program, the x and y screen coordinates will be continuously printed to the screen. If you press the right mouse button, the mouse pointer will disappear from the screen. You will still be able to track the mouse's position; you just won't be able to see the mouse pointer on the screen. You can make the mouse pointer visible again by pressing the left mouse button. Pressing both buttons at the same time will terminate the execution of the program and also erase the mouse pointer. Can you think of any applications that you might want to write that might make good use of the mouse?

Using Constructors and Destructors for Creating and Deleting Free Store Memory

Perhaps the most significant reason for using a constructor is in utilizing free store memory. In the next example, a constructor is used to allocate memory for the *string1* pointer with the **new** operator. A destructor is also used to release the allocated memory back to the system, when the object is destroyed. This is accomplished with the use of the **delete** operator.

```
class string_operation {
  char *string1;
  int  string_len;

public:
  string_operation(char *) {string1=new char[string_len];}
  ~string_operation() {delete string1;}
  void input_data(char *);
  void output_data(char *);
};
```

The memory allocated by **new** to the pointer *string1* can only be deallocated with a subsequent call to **delete**. For this reason, you will usually see memory allocated to pointers in constructors and deallocated in destructors. This also ensures that if the variable assigned to the class passes out of its scope, the allocated memory will be returned to the system. These operations make memory allocation dynamic and are most useful in programs that utilize linked lists.

The memory used by data types, such as **int** and **float**, is automatically restored to the system.

Overloading Class Member Functions

Class member functions, like ordinary C++ functions, can be overloaded. *Overloading* functions means that more than one function can have the same function name in the current scope. It becomes the compiler's responsibility to select the correct function based upon the number and type of arguments used during the function call. The first example in this section illustrates the overloading of a class function named **number()**. This overloaded function will return the absolute value of an integer or double with the use of the math functions **abs()**, which accepts and returns integer values, and **fabs()**, which accepts and returns double values. With an overloaded function, the argument types determine which member function will actually be used.

```
//
//  16ABSOL.CPP
//  C++ program illustrates member function overloading.
//  Program determines the absolute value of an integer
//  and a double.
//  Copyright (c) William H. Murray and Chris H. Pappas, 1992
//

#include <iostream.h>
#include <math.h>
#include <stdlib.h>

class absolute_value {
public:
  int number(int);
  double number(double);
};

int absolute_value::number(int test_data)
{
  int answer;

  answer=abs(test_data);
  return (answer);
}

double absolute_value::number(double test_data)
{
  double answer;

  answer=fabs(test_data);
  return (answer);
}

main()
{
  absolute_value neg_number;

  cout << "The absolute value is "
       << neg_number.number(-583) << endl;
  cout << "The absolute value is "
```

```
              << neg_number.number(-583.1749) << endl;
   return (0);
}
```

Notice that the dot operator is used in conjunction with the member function name to pass a negative integer and negative double values. The program selects the proper member function based upon the type (integer or double) of argument passed along with the function name. The positive value returned by each function is printed to the screen:

```
the absolute value is 583
the absolute value is 583.1749
```

In another example, angle information is passed to member functions in one of two formats—a double or a string. With member function overloading, it is possible to process both types.

```
//
// 16OVERLD.CPP
// C++ program illustrates overloading two class member
// functions. The program allows an angle to be entered
// in decimal or deg/min/sec format. One member function
// accepts data as a double, the other as a string. The
// program returns the sine, cosine, and tangent.
// Copyright (c) William H. Murray and Chris H. Pappas, 1992
//

#include <iostream.h>
#include <math.h>
#include <string.h>

const double DEG_TO_RAD=0.0174532925;

class trigonometric {
  double angle;
  double answer_sine;
  double answer_cosine;
  double answer_tangent;

public:
  void trig_calc(double);
  void trig_calc(char *);
};
```

```
void trigonometric::trig_calc(double degrees)
{
  angle=degrees;
  answer_sine=sin(angle * DEG_TO_RAD);
  answer_cosine=cos(angle * DEG_TO_RAD);
  answer_tangent=tan(angle * DEG_TO_RAD);
  cout << "\nFor an angle of " << angle
       << " degrees." << endl;
  cout << "The sine is " << answer_sine << endl;
  cout << "The cosine is " << answer_cosine << endl;
  cout << "The tangent is " << answer_tangent << endl;
}

void trigonometric::trig_calc(char *dat)
{
  char *deg,*min,*sec;

  deg=strtok(dat,"° ");   //make ° with alt-248
  min=strtok(0,"' ");
  sec=strtok(0,"\"");
  angle=atof(deg)+((atof(min))/60.0)+((atof(sec))/360.0);
  answer_sine=sin(angle * DEG_TO_RAD);
  answer_cosine=cos(angle * DEG_TO_RAD);
  answer_tangent=tan(angle * DEG_TO_RAD);
  cout << "\nFor an angle of " << angle
       << " degrees." << endl;
  cout << "The sine is " << answer_sine << endl;
  cout << "The cosine is " << answer_cosine << endl;
  cout << "The tangent is " << answer_tangent << endl;
}

main()
{
  trigonometric data;

  data.trig_calc(75.0);
  data.trig_calc("35° 75' 20\"");
  data.trig_calc(145.72);
  data.trig_calc("65° 45' 30\"");
  return (0);
}
```

This program makes use of a very powerful built-in function, **strtok()**, prototyped in string.h. The syntax for using **strtok()** is straightforward:

```
char *strtok(string1,string2);      //locates token in string1
char *string1;                      //string that has token(s)
const char *string2;                //string with delimiter chars
```

The **strtok()** function will scan the first string, *string1,* looking for a series of character tokens. For this example, the tokens representing degrees, minutes, and seconds are used. The actual length of the tokens can vary. The second string, *string2,* contains a set of delimiters. Spaces, commas, or other special characters can be used for delimiters. The tokens in *string1* are separated by the delimiters in *string2.* Because of this all of the tokens in *string1* can be retrieved with a series of calls to the **strtok()** function. **strtok()** alters *string1* by inserting a null character after each token is retrieved. The function returns a pointer to the first token the first time it is called. Subsequent calls return a pointer to the next token, and so on. When there are no more tokens in the string, a null pointer is returned.

This example permits angle readings formatted as decimal values, or in degrees, minutes, and seconds of arc. For the latter case, **strtok()**, uses the degree symbol (°) to find the first token. For minutes, a minute symbol (') will pull out the token containing the number of minutes. Finally, a \" symbol is used to retrieve seconds. The last delimiter uses two symbols because the double quote by itself is used for terminating strings.

This program produces the following formatted output:

```
For an angle of 75 degrees.
The sine is 0.965926
The cosine is 0.258819
The tangent is 3.732051

For an angle of 36.305556 degrees.
The sine is 0.592091
The cosine is 0.805871
The tangent is 0.734722

For an angle of 145.72 degrees.
The sine is 0.563238
The cosine is -0.826295
The tangent is -0.681642

For an angle of 65.833333 degrees.
The sine is 0.912358
The cosine is 0.409392
The tangent is 2.228568
```

Class member function overloading gives programs and programmers flexibility when dealing with different data formats. If you are not into math or engineering programs, can you think of any applications that interest you where this feature might be helpful? Consider this possibility: if you are the cook in your household, you could develop an application that modifies recipes. You could write a program that would accept data as a decimal value or in mixed units. For example, the program might allow you to enter "3.75 cups, 1 pint 1.75 cups" or "1 pint 1 cup 12 tbs".

Using Friend Functions to Access Private Class Variables

One important feature of classes is their ability to hide data. Recall that member data is private by default in classes—that is, sharable only with member functions of the class. It is almost ironic, then, that there exists a category of functions specifically designed to override this feature. Functions of this type are called *friend functions*. Friend functions allow the sharing of private class information with nonmember functions. Friend functions, not defined in the class itself, can share the same class resources as member functions.

Friend functions offer the advantage that they are external to the class definition, as shown here:

```
//
//  16SECS.CPP
//  C++ program illustrates the use of friend functions.
//  Program will collect a string of date and time
//  information from system. Time information will
//  be processed and converted into seconds.
//  Copyright (c) William H. Murray and Chris H. Pappas, 1992
//

#include <iostream.h>
#include <time.h>     // for tm & time_t structure
#include <string.h>   // for strtok function prototype
#include <stdlib.h>   // for atol function prototype

class time_class {
  long secs;
  friend char * present_time(time_class);  //friend
public:
  time_class(char *);
};

time_class::time_class(char *tm)
{
  char *hours,*minutes,*seconds;

  // data returned in the following string format:
```

```
  // (day month date hours:minutes:seconds year)
  // Thus, need to skip over three tokens, ie.
  // skip day, month and date
  hours=strtok(tm," ");
  hours=strtok(0," ");
  hours=strtok(0," ");

  // collect time information from string
  hours=strtok(0,":");
  minutes=strtok(0,":");
  seconds=strtok(0," ");

  // convert data to long type and accumulate seconds.
  secs=atol(hours)*3600;
  secs+=atol(minutes)*60;
  secs+=atol(seconds);
}

char * present_time(time_class);  // prototype

main()
{
  // get the string of time & date information
  struct tm *ptr;
  time_t ltime;
  ltime=time(NULL);
  ptr=localtime(&ltime);

  time_class tz(asctime(ptr));

  cout << "The date/time string information: "
       << asctime(ptr) << endl;
  cout << "The time converted to seconds: "
       << present_time(tz) << endl;
  return (0);
}

char * present_time(time_class tz)
{
  char *ctbuf;
  ctbuf=new char[40];
  long int seconds_total;

  seconds_total=tz.secs;
  ltoa(seconds_total,ctbuf,10);
```

```
    return (ctbuf);
}
```

Notice in the class definition the use of the keyword **friend** along with the description of the **present_time()** function. When you examine the program listing you will notice that this function, external to the class, appears after the **main()** function description. In other words, it is written as a traditional C++ function, external to member functions of the defined class.

This program has a number of additional interesting features. In the function **main()**, the system's time is obtained with the use of *time_t* and its associated structure *tm*. In this program, *ltime* is the name of the variable associated with *time_t*. Local time is initialized and retrieved into the pointer, *ptr*, with the next two lines of code. By using **asctime(ptr)**, the pointer will point to an ASCII string of date and time information.

```
struct tm *ptr;
time_t ltime;
ltime=time(NULL);
ptr=localtime(&ltime);

time_class tz(asctime(ptr));
```

The date and time string is formatted in this manner:

day month date hours:minutes:seconds year\n\0

For example:

```
Mon Sep 17  13:12:21 1992
```

There is a more detailed discussion of built-in functions, including those prototyped in time.h, in Chapter 20.

The string information that is retrieved is sent to the class by associating *tz* with the class **time_class**:

```
time_class tz(asctime(ptr));
```

A constructor, **time_class(char *)**, is used to define the code required to convert the string information into integer data. This is accomplished by using the **strtok()** function.

The date/time information is returned in a rather strange format. To process this information, **strtok()** must use a space as the delimiter in order to skip over the day, month, and date information in the string. In this program the variable *hours* initially serves as a junk collector for unwanted tokens. The next delimiter is a colon (:), which is used in collecting both hour and minute tokens from the string. Finally, the number of seconds can be retrieved by reading the string until another space is encountered. The string information is then converted to a **long** type and converted to the appropriate number of seconds. The variable *secs* is private to the class but accessible to the friend function.

The friend function takes the number of accumulated seconds, *tz.seconds,* and converts it back to a character string. The memory for storing the string is allocated with the **new** operator. This newly created string is a result of using the friend function.

The program prints two pieces of information:

```
The date/time string information: Mon May 25 16:01:55 1992

The time converted to seconds: 57715
```

First, **cout** sends the string produced by **asctime()** to the screen. This information is obtainable from the **time_t()** function and is available to the **main()** function. Second, the system time is printed by passing *present_time* to the **cout** stream.

While friend functions offer some interesting programming possibilities when programming with C++ classes, they should be used with caution.

Using the this Pointer

The keyword **this** is used to identify a self-referential pointer that is implicitly declared in C++, as follows:

```
class_name *this;    //class_name is class type.
```

The **this** pointer is used to point to the object for which the member function is invoked. Here is an example, used in a class definition:

```
class class_name {
  char chr;

public:
  void begin_conv(char k) {chr=k;}
  char conv_chr(void) {return (this -> chr);}
};
```

In this case, the pointer **this** is used to access the private class variable member *chr.*

There are additional uses for the **this** pointer. You can use it to include a link on a doubly linked list or when writing constructors and destructors involving memory allocations. Examine the following example:

```
class class_name {
  int x,y,z;
  char chr;

public:
  class_name(size) {this=new(size);}
  ~class_name(void) {delete(this);}
};
```

Using Operator Overloading

Earlier in this chapter you learned that it is possible to overload member functions in a class. In this section, you will learn that it is also possible to overload C++ operators. In C++, new definitions can be applied to such familiar operators as +, –, *, and / in a given class.

The idea of operator overloading is common in numerous programming languages, even if it is not specifically implemented. For example, all compiled languages make it possible to add two integers, two floats, or two doubles (or their equivalent types) with the + operator. This is the essence of operator overloading—using the same operator on different data types. In C++ it is possible to extend this simple concept even further. In most compiled languages it is not possible, for example, to take a complex number, matrix, or character string and add them together with the + operator.

These operations are valid in all programming languages:

```
3 + 8
3.3 + 7.2
```

These operations are typically not valid operations:

```
(4 – j4) + (5 + j10)
(15° 20' 45") + (53° 57' 40")
"combine " + "strings"
```

If the last three operations were possible with the + operator, the workload of the programmer would be greatly reduced when designing new applications. The good news is that in C++, the + operator can be overloaded and the previous three operations can be made valid. Many additional operators can also be overloaded. Operator overloading is used extensively in C++. You will find examples throughout the various Microsoft C++ libraries.

Overloading Operators and Function Calls

In C++, the following operators can be overloaded.

+	−	*	/	=	<	>	+=	−=
*=	/=	<<	>>	>>=	<<=	==	!=	<=
>=	+	− −	%	&	^	!	|	~
&=	^=	|=	&&	||	%=	[]	()	new
delete								

The main restrictions are that the syntax and precedence of the operator must remain unchanged from its originally defined meaning. Another important point is that operator overloading is valid only within the scope of the class in which overloading occurs.

The Syntax of Overloading

In order to overload an operator, the **operator** keyword is followed by the operator itself:

type operator *opr*(*param list*)

For example:

```
angle_value operator +(angle_argument);
```

Here, **angle_value** is the name of the class type, followed by the **operator** keyword, then the operator itself (+) and a parameter to be passed to the overloaded operator.

Within the scope of a properly defined class, several angles specified in degrees/minutes/seconds could be directly added together:

```
angle_value angle1("37° 15′ 56\"");
angle_value angle2("10° 44′ 44\"");
angle_value angle3("75° 17′ 59\"");
angle_value angle4("130° 32′ 54\"");
angle_value sum_of_angles;
```

```
sum_of_angles=angle1+angle2+angle3+angle4;
```

As you know from earlier examples, the symbol for seconds is the double quote mark ("). This symbol is also used to signal the beginning and ending of a character string. The quote symbol can be printed to the screen if it is preceded with a backslash. This book uses this format for data input.

There is another problem that must be taken into account in programs such as this: the carry information from seconds-to-minutes and from minutes-to-hours must be handled properly. A carry occurs in both cases when the total number of seconds or minutes exceeds 59. This doesn't have anything to do with operator overloading directly, but the program must take this fact into account if a correct total is to be produced, as shown here:

```cpp
//
//   16OPOVER.CPP
//   C++ program illustrates operator overloading.
//   Program will overload the "+" operator so that
//   several angles, in the format degrees minutes seconds,
//   can be added directly.
//   Copyright (c) William H. Murray and Chris H. Pappas, 1992
//

#include <strstrea.h>
#include <stdlib.h>
#include <string.h>

class angle_value {
  int degrees,minutes,seconds;

  public:
  angle_value() {degrees=0,
                 minutes=0,
                 seconds=0;}   // constructor
  angle_value(char *);
  angle_value operator +(angle_value);
  char * info_display(void);
};

angle_value::angle_value(char *angle_sum)
{
  degrees=atoi(strtok(angle_sum,"°"));
  minutes=atoi(strtok(0,"' "));
  seconds=atoi(strtok(0,"\""));
```

```
}

angle_value angle_value::operator+(angle_value angle_sum)
{
  angle_value ang;
  ang.seconds=(seconds+angle_sum.seconds)%60;
  ang.minutes=((seconds+angle_sum.seconds)/60+
             minutes+angle_sum.minutes)%60;
  ang.degrees=((seconds+angle_sum.seconds)/60+
             minutes+angle_sum.minutes)/60;
  ang.degrees+=degrees+angle_sum.degrees;
  return ang;
}

char * angle_value::info_display()
{
  char *ang[15];
  // strstream.h required for incore formatting
  ostrstream(*ang,sizeof(ang)) << degrees << "°"
                               << minutes << "' "
                               << seconds << "\""
                               << ends;
  return *ang;
}

main()
{
  angle_value angle1("37° 15' 56\"");    //make with alt-248
  angle_value angle2("10° 44' 44\"");
  angle_value angle3("75° 17' 59\"");
  angle_value angle4("130° 32' 54\"");
  angle_value sum_of_angles;

  sum_of_angles=angle1+angle2+angle3+angle4;
  cout << "the sum of the angles is "
       << sum_of_angles.info_display() << endl;
  return (0);
}
```

The details of how the mixed units are added together are included in the small piece of code that declares that the + operator is to be overloaded:

```
angle_value angle_value::operator+(angle_value angle_sum)
{
```

```
angle_value ang;
ang.seconds=(seconds+angle_sum.seconds)%60;
ang.minutes=((seconds+angle_sum.seconds)/60+
              minutes+angle_sum.minutes)%60;
ang.degrees=((seconds+angle_sum.seconds)/60+
              minutes+angle_sum.minutes)/60;
ang.degrees+=degrees+angle_sum.degrees;
return ang;
}
```

Here, divide and modulus operations are performed on the sums to ensure correct carry information.

Further details of the program's operation are omitted since you have seen most of the functions and modules in earlier examples. However, it is important to remember that when you overload operators, proper operator syntax and precedence must be maintained.

The output from this program shows the sum of the four angles to be as follows:

```
the sum of the angles is 253° 51′ 33"
```

Is this answer correct?

Derived Classes

A derived class can be considered an extension or inheritance of an existing class. The original class is known as a *base* or *parent class* and the derived class as a *subclass* or *child class*. As such, a derived class provides a simple means for expanding or customizing the capabilities of a parent class, without the need for re-creating the parent class itself. With a parent class in place, a common interface is possible to one or more of the derived classes.

Any C++ class can serve as a parent class, and any derived class will reflect its description. The derived class can add additional features to those of the parent class. For example, the derived class can modify access privileges, add new members, or overload existing ones. When a derived class overloads a function declared in the parent class, it is said to be a *virtual member function*. You will see that virtual member functions are very important to the concept of object-oriented programming.

The Syntax of a Derived Class

You describe a derived class by using the following syntax:

class *derived-class-type* :(public/private/protected) . . .
    parent-class-type { . . . .};

For example, in creating a derived class, you might write

```
class retirement:public consumer { . . . .};
```

In this case, the derived class tag is **retirement**. The parent class has public visibility, and its tag is **consumer**.

A third visibility specifier is often used with derived classes—protected. A protected specifier is the same as a private specifier with the added feature that class member functions and friends of derived classes are given access to the class.

Creating Derived Classes

The next program depicts the concept of a derived class. The parent class collects and reports information on a consumer's name, address, city, state, and ZIP code. Two similar child classes are derived. One child class maintains information on a consumer's accumulated airline mileage, while the second derived child class reports information on a consumer's accumulated rental car mileage. Both derived child classes inherit information from the parent class. Study the listing and see what you can discern about these derived classes.

```
//
//  16DERCLS.CPP
//  C++ program illustrates derived classes.
//  The parent class contains name, street, city,
//  state, and zip information. Derived classes add
//  either airline or rental car mileage information
//  to parent class information.
//  Copyright (c) William H. Murray and Chris H. Pappas, 1992
//

#include <iostream.h>
#include <string.h>

char newline;

class consumer {
  char name[60],
       street[60],
       city[20],
       state[15],
```

```
        zip[10];
public:
  void data_output(void);
  void data_input(void);
};

void consumer::data_output()
{
  cout << "Name: " << name << endl;
  cout << "Street: " << street << endl;
  cout << "City: " << city << endl;
  cout << "State: " << state << endl;
  cout << "Zip: " << zip << endl;
}

void consumer::data_input()
{
  cout << "Enter The Consumer's Full Name: ";
  cin.get(name,59,'\n');
  cin.get(newline);       //flush carriage return
  cout << "Enter The Street Address: ";
  cin.get(street,59,'\n');
  cin.get(newline);
  cout << "Enter The City: ";
  cin.get(city,19,'\n');
  cin.get(newline);
  cout << "Enter The State: ";
  cin.get(state,14,'\n');
  cin.get(newline);
  cout << "Enter The Five Digit Zip Code: ";
  cin.get(zip,9,'\n');
  cin.get(newline);
}

class airline:public consumer {
  char airline_type[20];
  float acc_air_miles;
public:
  void airline_consumer();
  void disp_air_mileage();
};

void airline::airline_consumer()
{
  data_input();
```

```
    cout << "Enter Airline Type: ";
    cin.get(airline_type,19,'\n');
    cin.get(newline);
    cout << "Enter Accumulated Air Mileage: ";
    cin >> acc_air_miles;
    cin.get(newline);        //flush carriage return
}

void airline::disp_air_mileage()
{
    data_output();

    cout << "Airline Type: " << airline_type
         << endl;
    cout << "Accumulated Air Mileage: "
         << acc_air_miles << endl;
}

class rental_car:public consumer {
    char rental_car_type[20];
    float acc_road_miles;
public:
    void rental_car_consumer();
    void disp_road_mileage();
};

void rental_car::rental_car_consumer()
{
    data_input();
    cout << "Enter Rental_car Type: ";
    cin.get(rental_car_type,19,'\n');
    cin.get(newline);        //flush carriage return
    cout << "Enter Accumulated Road Mileage: ";
    cin >> acc_road_miles;
    cin.get(newline);
}

void rental_car::disp_road_mileage()
{
    data_output();

    cout << "Rental Car Type: "
         << rental_car_type << endl;
    cout << "Accumulated Mileage: "
         << acc_road_miles << endl;
```

```
}

main()
{
  //associate variable names with classes
  airline jetaway;
  rental_car varooom;

  //get airline information
  cout << "\n--Airline Consumer--\n";
  jetaway.airline_consumer();


  //get rental_car information
  cout << "\n--Rental Car Consumer--\n";
  varooom.rental_car_consumer();

  //now display all consumer information
  cout << "\n--Airline Consumer--\n";
  jetaway.disp_air_mileage();
  cout << "\n--Rental Car Consumer--\n";
  varooom.disp_road_mileage();

  return (0);
}
```

In the example, the parent class is type **consumer**. The private part of this class accepts consumer information for name, address, city, state, and ZIP code. The public part describes two functions, **data_output()** and **data_input()**. You have seen functions similar to these to gather class information in earlier programs. The first derived child class is **airline**.

```
class airline:public consumer {
  char airline_type[20];
  float acc_air_miles;
public:
  void airline_consumer(void);
  void disp_air_mileage(void);
};
```

This derived child class contains two functions, **airline_consumer()** and **disp_air_mileage()**. The first function, **airline_consumer()**, uses the parent class to obtain name, address, city, state, and ZIP code, and *attaches* the airline type and accumulated mileage.

```
void airline::airline_consumer()
{
  data_input();
  cout << "Enter Airline Type: ";
  cin.get(airline_type,19,'\n');
  cin.get(newline);
  cout << "Enter Accumulated Air Mileage: ";
  cin >> acc_air_miles;
  cin.get(newline);        //flush carriage return
}
```

Do you understand how the derived class is being used? A call to the function **data_input()** is a call to a member function that is part of the parent class. The remainder of the derived class is involved with obtaining the additional airline type and accumulated mileage.

The information on accumulated air mileage can be displayed for a consumer in a similar manner. The parent class function, **data_output()**, prints the information gathered by the parent class (name, address, and so on), while **disp_air_mileage()** attaches the derived child class's information (airline type and mileage) to the output. The process is repeated for the rental car consumer.

Thus, one parent class serves as the data-gathering base for two derived child classes, each obtaining its own specific information.

The following is a sample output from the program:

```
--Airline Consumer--
Name: George X. McDade
Street: 401 West Summit Avenue
City: Dover
State: Delaware
Zip: 19804
Airline Type: US AIR
Accumulated Air Mileage: 45321.0

--Rental Car Consumer--
Name: Harry Z. Ballbat
Street: 407 East Wedgemire Road
City: Pinkerton
State: New Mexico
Zip: 25697
Rental Car Type: Lincoln
Accumulated Road Mileage: 23456.2
```

Experiment with this program by entering your own database of information. You might also consider adding additional member functions to the **consumer** class.

Now that you have learned about the **class** structure, you'll look at complete I/O in C++ in the next chapter.

Chapter *17*

Complete I/O in C++

Chapter 12 introduced you to the **iostream** objects **cin** and **cout**, along with the "put to" (insertion) operator, <<, and the "get from" (extraction) operator, >>. This chapter explains the classes behind C++ I/O streams. First, however, the chapter introduces several additional topics of concern when writing C++ code, such as how to use C library functions in a C++ program.

enum Types

User-defined enumerated types behave differently in C++ than their C counterparts. In particular, C **enum** types are compatible with the type **int**. This means they can be cross-assigned with no complaints from the compiler. However, in C++ the two types are incompatible.

The second difference between C and C++ enumerated types involves the syntax shorthand when you define C++ **enum** variables. The following example program highlights the enumerated type differences between the two languages:

```
//
//  17ENUM.CPP
//  C++ program demonstrates how to use enumerated types and
//  how C++ enumerated types differ from C enumerated types
//  Copyright (c) William H. Murray and Chris H. Pappas, 1992
//
```

```
#include <iostream.h>

typedef enum boolean { FALSE, TRUE };

void main(void)
{
// enum boolean bflag = 0; legal C, but illegal C++ statement
   boolean bcontinue, bflag = FALSE;

   bcontinue = (boolean)1;

   bflag = bcontinue;
}
```

The example starts off by defining the enumerated type *boolean,* which is a standard type in several other high-level languages. Because of the ordering of the definition—FALSE, then TRUE—the compiler assigns a zero to FALSE and a 1 to TRUE. This is perfect for their logical use in a program.

The commented-out statement in the **main()** program represents a legal C statement. Remember, when you define enumerated variables in C, such as *bflag,* you must use the **enum** keyword with the enumerated type's tag field—in this case, *boolean.* Since C **enum** types are compatible with **int** types, it is also legal to initialize a variable with an integer value. This statement would not get past the C++ compiler. The second statement in **main()** shows the legal C++ counterpart.

The last two statements in the program show how to use enumerated types. Notice that in C++, an explicit cast *(boolean),* is needed to convert the 1 to a *boolean* compatible type.

Remember that user-defined types cannot be directly input from a file or output to a file. Either they must go through a conversion routine or you can custom overload the >> and << operators, as discussed in Chapter 12.

Reference Variables

A feature of C++ you will grow to appreciate more and more is the reference variable. This is because it simplifies the syntax and readability of the more confusing pointer notation. Remember that by using pointer parameters, a program could pass something to a function either call-by-reference or call-by-variable, which enabled the function to change the item passed. In contrast, call-by-value sends a copy of the variable's contents to the function. Any change to the variable in this case is a local change not reflected in the calling routine.

The following program passes an *stStudent* structure to a function, using the three possible calling methods: call-by-value, call-by-reference with pointer notation, and call-by-reference using the simpler C++ reference type. If the program were sending the entire array to the subroutine, by default, the array parameter would be passed call-by-reference. However, single structures within the array, by default, are passed call-by-value.

```cpp
//
//  17REFVAR.CPP
//  C++ program demonstrating how the C++ reference type
//  eliminates the more confusing pointer notation.
//  The program also demonstrates how to pass a single
//  array element, call by value, variable, and reference.
//  Copyright (c) William H. Murray and Chris H. Pappas, 1992
//

#include <iostream.h>

struct stStudent {
  char    pszName[66],
          pszAddress[66],
          pszCity[26],
          pszState[3],
          pszPhone[13];
  int     icourses;
  float   GPA;
};

void vByValueCall     (stStudent    stAStudent);
void vByVariableCall  (stStudent *pstAStudent);
void vByReferenceCall (stStudent &rstAStudent);

void main(void)
{
  stStudent astLargeClass[100];

  astLargeClass[0].icourses = 10;

  vByValueCall    ( astLargeClass[0]);
  cout << astLargeClass[0].icourses << "\n"; // icourses still 10

  vByVariableCall (&astLargeClass[0]);
  cout << astLargeClass[0].icourses << "\n"; // icourses = 20

  vByReferenceCall ( astLargeClass[0]);
```

```
    cout << astLargeClass[0].icourses << "\n"; // icourses = 30
}

void vByValueCall(stStudent   staStudent)
{
  staStudent.icourses += 10;    // normal structure syntax
}

void vByVariableCall(stStudent *pstAStudent)
{
  pstAStudent->icourses += 10;  // pointer syntax
}

void vByReferenceCall(stStudent &rstAStudent)
{
  rstAStudent.icourses += 10;   // simplified reference syntax
}
```

The following code section has spliced together each function's prototype, along with its matching invoking statement:

```
void vByValueCall      (stStudent   staStudent);
     vByValueCall      ( astLargeClass[0]     );

void vByVariableCall   (stStudent *pstAStudent);
     vByVariableCall   (&astLargeClass[0]     );

void vByReferenceCall  (stStudent &rstAStudent);
     vByReferenceCall  ( astLargeClass[0]     );
```

The first thing you should notice is the simpler syntax needed to send a reference variable, *astLargeClass[0]* (the last statement), over the equivalent pointer syntax, *&astLargeClass[0]*. At this point the difference may appear small. However, as your algorithms become more complicated, this simpler syntax can avoid unnecessary precedence-level conflicts with other operators such as the pointer dereference operator (*) and the period member operator (.), which qualifies structure fields.

The following three statements were pulled out of the program's respective functions to show the syntax for using the structure within each function:

```
staStudent.icourses    += 10;  // normal structure syntax
pstAStudent->icourses  += 10;  // pointer syntax
rstAStudent.icourses   += 10;  // simplified reference syntax
```

The last two statements make a permanent change to the passed *stStudent* structure because the structure was passed call-by-reference (variable). Notice that the last statement did not require the pointer operator.

The difference between the first and third statements is dramatic. Although they look identical, the first statement references only a copy of the stStudent structure. In this case, when *stAstudent.icourses* is incremented, it is done only to the function's local copy. Exiting the function returns the structure to bit-oblivion, along with the incremented value. This explains why the program outputs 10, 20, 30, instead of 20, 30, 40.

Default Arguments

C++ allows you to prototype a function by using default arguments. This means that if the invoking statement omits certain fields, predefined default values will be supplied by the function. Default argument definitions cannot be spread throughout a function's prototype; they must be the last formal parameters defined. The following example program demonstrates how to define and use such a function:

```
//
//  17DEFARG.CPP
//  C++ program demonstrates how to prototype functions
//  with default arguments. Default arguments must always
//  be the last formal parameters defined.
//  Copyright (c) William H. Murray and Chris H. Pappas, 1992
//

#include <iostream.h>

void fdefault_argument(char ccode='Q', int ivalue=0,
                       float fvalue=0);

void main(void)
{
  fdefault_argument('A',2,12.34);
  fdefault_argument();

}

void fdefault_argument(char ccode, int ivalue, float fvalue)
{
  if(ccode == 'Q')
    cout << "\n\nUsing default values only.";
```

```
   cout << "\nivalue = " << ivalue;
   cout << "\nfvalue = " << fvalue;
}
```

In this program, all three formal parameter types have been given default values. The function **fdefault()** checks the *ccode* value to switch on or off an appropriate message. The output from the program is straightforward:

```
ivalue = 2
fvalue = 12.34

Using default values only.
ivalue = 0
fvalue = 0
```

Careful function prototyping, using default argument assignment, can be an important approach to avoiding unwanted side effects. This is one means of guaranteeing that dynamically allocated variables will not have garbage values if the user did not supply any. Another way to initialize dynamically allocated memory is with the function **memset()**.

memset()

You can use **memset()** to initialize a dynamically allocated byte, or bytes, to a specific character. The prototype for **memset()** looks like this:

> void *memset(void *dest, int *cchar,* size_t *count*);

After a call to **memset()**, *dest* points to *count* bytes of memory initialized to the character *cchar.* The following example program demonstrates the difference between a static and a dynamic structure declaration:

```
//
//   17MEMSET.CPP
//   C++ program demonstrating the function memset(),
//   which can initialize dynamically allocated memory.
//   Copyright (c) William H. Murray and Chris H. Pappas, 1992
//

#include <iostream.h>
```

```
struct keybits {
  unsigned char rshift, lshift,  ctrl,    alt,
                scroll, numlock, caplock, insert;
};

void main(void)
{
  keybits stkgarbage, *pstkinitialized;

  pstkinitialized = new keybits;
  memset(pstkinitialized, 0, sizeof(keybits));
}
```

Thanks to **memset()**, the dynamically allocated structure pointed to by *pstkinitialized* contains all zeros, while the compiler left the statically created *stkgarbage* full of random data. The call to the function **memset()** also used the **sizeof()** operator instead of hardwiring the statement to a "magic number." The use of **sizeof()** allows the algorithm to automatically adjust to the size of any object passed to it. Also, remember that C++ does not require the **struct** keyword to precede a structure tag field (*keybits*) when defining structure variables, as is the case with *stkgarbage* and *pstkinitialized*.

Formatting Output

The following example programs continue the discussion of C++-formatted output introduced in Chapter 12. The first program demonstrates how to print a table of factorials using long doubles with the default right justification:

```
//
//  17FACT1.CPP
//  A C++ program that prints a table of
//  factorials for the numbers from 1 to 25.
//  Program uses the long double type.
//  Formatting includes precision, width and fixed
//  with default of right justification when printing.
//  Copyright (c) William H. Murray and Chris H. Pappas, 1992
//

#include <iostream.h>
#include <iomanip.h>

main()
```

```
{
  long double number,factorial;

  number=1.0;
  factorial=1.0;

  cout.precision(0);              // no decimal place
  cout.setf(ios::fixed);          // use fixed format

  for(int i=0;i<25;i++) {
    factorial*=number;
    number=number+1.0;
    cout.width(30);               // width of 30 characters
    cout << factorial << endl;
  }

  return (0);
}
```

The **precision()**, **width()**, and **setf()** class members were repeated in the loop. The output from the program looks like this:

```
                             1
                             2
                             6
                            24
                           120
                           720
                          5040
                         40320
                        362880
                       3628800
                      39916800
                     479001600
                    6227020800
                   87178291200
                 1307674368000
                20922789888000
               355687428096000
              6402373705728000
            121645100408832000
           2432902008176640000
          51090942171709440000
        1124000727777607680000
```

```
    2585201673888497664000
   62044840173323943936000
1551121004333098598400000
```

The next program/output pair demonstrates how to vary output column width and override the default right justification:

```cpp
//
//  17FACT2.CPP
//  A C++ program that prints a table of
//  factorials for the numbers from 1 to 15.
//  Program uses the long double type.
//  Formatting includes precision, width, alignment,
//  and format of large numbers.
//  Copyright (c) William H. Murray and Chris H. Pappas, 1992
//

#include <iostream.h>
#include <iomanip.h>

main()
{
  long double number,factorial;

  number=1.0;
  factorial=1.0;

  cout.precision(0);              // no decimal point
  cout.setf(ios::left);           // left justify numbers
  cout.setf(ios::fixed);          // use fixed format

  for(int i=0;i<25;i++) {
    factorial*=number;
    number=number+1.0;
    cout.width(30);               // width of 30 characters
    cout << factorial << endl;
  }

  return (0);
}
```

The left-justified output looks like this:

```
1
2
6
24
120
720
5040
40320
362880
3628800
39916800
479001600
6227020800
87178291200
1307674368000
20922789888000
355687428096000
6402373705728000
121645100408832000
2432902008176640000
51090942171709440000
1124000727777607680000
25852016738884976640000
620448401733239439360000
15511210043330985984000000
```

The third format example prints out a table of numbers, their squares, and their square roots. The program demonstrates how easy it is to align columns, pad with blanks, fill spaces with zeros, and control precision in C++.

```
//
//   17SQRT.CPP
//   A C++ program that prints a table of
//   numbers, squares, and square roots for the
//   numbers from 1 to 15. Program uses the type
//   double. Formatting aligns columns, pads blank
//   spaces with '0' character, and controls
//   precision of answer.
//   Copyright (c) William H. Murray and Chris H. Pappas, 1992
//

#include <iostream.h>
```

```
#include <iomanip.h>
#include <math.h>

main()
{
  double number,square,sqroot;

  cout << "num\t" << "square\t\t" << "square root\n";
  cout << "_____\n";

  number=1.0;
  cout.setf(ios::fixed);            // use fixed format

  for(int i=1;i<16;i++) {
    square=number*number;           // find square
    sqroot=sqrt(number);            // find square root

    cout.fill('0');                 // fill blanks with zeros
    cout.width(2);                  // column 2 characters wide
    cout.precision(0);              // no decimal place
    cout << number << "\t";

    cout.width(6);                  // column 6 characters wide
    cout.precision(1);              // print 1 decimal place
    cout << square << "\t\t";

    cout.width(8);                  // column 8 characters wide
    cout.precision(6);              // print 6 decimal places
    cout << sqroot << endl;

    number+=1.0;
  }
  return (0);
}
```

The formatted table looks like this:

num	square	square root
01	0001.0	1.000000
02	0004.0	1.414214
03	0009.0	1.732051
04	0016.0	2.000000
05	0025.0	2.236068

```
06        0036.0              2.449490
07        0049.0              2.645751
08        0064.0              2.828427
09        0081.0              3.000000
10        0100.0              3.162278
11        0121.0              3.316625
12        0144.0              3.464102
13        0169.0              3.605551
14        0196.0              3.741657
15        0225.0              3.872983
```

C/C++ I/O Options

Chapter 16 introduced you to the concepts and syntax for object-oriented classes, constructors, destructors, member functions, and operators. Now you are ready for a deeper understanding of C++ I/O.

Just like C, C++ does not have any built-in I/O routines. Instead, all C++ compilers come bundled with object-oriented **iostream** classes. These standard I/O class objects have a cross-compiler syntax consistency because they were developed by the authors of the C++ language. If you are trying to write a C++ application that is portable to other C++ compilers, you will want to use these **iostream** classes. The Microsoft C/C++ compiler provides the following five ways to perform C/C++ I/O:

- **Unbuffered C library I/O** The C compiler provides unbuffered I/O through functions such as **_read()** and **_write()**. These functions are very popular with C programmers because of their efficiency and the ease with which they can be customized.

- **ANSI C buffered I/O** C also supports buffered functions such as **fread()** and **fwrite()**. These stdio.h library functions perform their own buffering before calling the direct I/O base routines.

- **C console and port I/O** C provides additional I/O routines that have no C++ equivalent, such as **_getch()**, **_ungetch()**, and **_kbhit()**. All non-Windows applications can use these functions, which give you direct access to the hardware.

- **Microsoft iostream class library** The **iostream** class library provides C++ programs with object-oriented I/O. You can use them in place of functions such as **scanf()**, **printf()**, **fscanf()**, and **fprintf()**. However, while these **iostream** classes are not required by C++ programs, many of the character-mode objects, such as **cin**, **cout**, **cerr**, and **clog**, are incompatible with the Windows graphical user interface.

- **Microsoft Foundation Class library** The Microsoft **CFile** class found in the Foundation Class library provides C++ and especially Windows applications with objects for disk I/O. Using this library of routines guarantees that your application will be portable and easy to maintain.

iostream Class List

With the exception of the stream buffer classes, all of the I/O objects defined in the **iostream** class library share the same abstract stream base class, called **ios**. These derived classes fall into four categories, as listed in Table 17-1.

Input Stream Classes

istream	Used for general-purpose input or as a parent class for other derived input streams
ifstream	Used for file input
istream_withassign	Used for cin input
istrstream	Used for string input

Output Stream Classes

ostream	Used for general-purpose output or as a parent class for other derived output streams
ofstream	Used for file output
ofstream_withassign	Used for **cout**, **cerr**, and **clog**
ostrstream	Used for string output

Input/Output Stream Classes

iostream	Used for general-purpose input and output, or as a parent class for other derived I/O streams
fstream	File I/O stream class
strstream	String I/O stream class
stdiostream	Standard I/O stream class

Stream Buffer Classes

streambuf	Used as a parent class for derived objects
filebuf	Disk file stream buffer class
strstreambuf	Stream buffer class for strings
stdiobuf	Stream buffer class for standard file I/O

Table 17-1.   *The Four ios Class Categories*

Figure 17-1 illustrates the interrelationship between these **ios** stream classes. All **ios**-derived **iostream** classes use a **streambuf** class object for the actual I/O processing. The **iostream** class library uses the following three derived buffer classes with streams:

filebuf	Provides buffered disk file I/O
strstreambuf	Provides an in-memory array of bytes to hold the stream data
stdiobuf	Provides buffered disk I/O with all buffering done by the standard I/O system

Remember that all derived classes usually expand upon their inherited parent class definitions. This explains why you will often use an operator or member function for a derived class that doesn't directly appear to be in the derived class's definition.

This means that if you are going to fully understand how any derived class operates, you will have to research back to the root or parent class definition. Since C++ derives so many of its classes from the **ios** class, a portion of ios.h follows. You will be able to use this as an easy reference for understanding any class derived from **ios**.

```
#ifndef EOF
#define EOF (-1)
#endif

class streambuf;
class ostream;

class ios {

public:
```

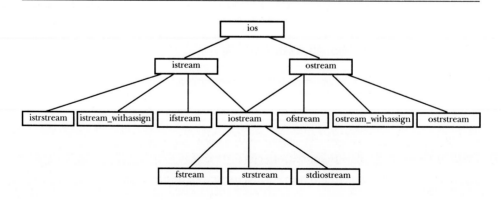

Figure 17-1.   *C++ ios stream class hierarchy*

```
enum io_state {  goodbit   = 0x00,
                 eofbit    = 0x01,
                 failbit   = 0x02,
                 badbit    = 0x04 };

enum open_mode { in        = 0x01,
                 out       = 0x02,
                 ate       = 0x04,
                 app       = 0x08,
                 trunc     = 0x10,
                 nocreate  = 0x20,
                 noreplace = 0x40,
                 binary    = 0x80 }; // not in latest spec.

enum seek_dir { beg=0, cur=1, end=2 };

enum {  skipws     = 0x0001,
        left       = 0x0002,
        right      = 0x0004,
        internal   = 0x0008,
        dec        = 0x0010,
        oct        = 0x0020,
        hex        = 0x0040,
        showbase   = 0x0080,
        showpoint  = 0x0100,
        uppercase  = 0x0200,
        showpos    = 0x0400,
        scientific = 0x0800,
        fixed      = 0x1000,
        unitbuf    = 0x2000,
        stdio      = 0x4000
                               };

static const long basefield;   // dec | oct | hex
static const long adjustfield; // left | right | internal
static const long floatfield;  // scientific | fixed

ios(streambuf*);                  // differs from ANSI
virtual ~ios();

inline long flags() const;
inline long flags(long _l);

inline long setf(long _f,long _m);
inline long setf(long _l);
```

```
    inline long unsetf(long _l);

    inline int width() const;
    inline int width(int _i);

    inline ostream* tie(ostream* _os);
    inline ostream* tie() const;

    inline char fill() const;
    inline char fill(char _c);

    inline int precision(int _i);
    inline int precision() const;

    inline int rdstate() const;
    inline void clear(int _i = 0);

//  NOTE: inline operator void*() const;
    operator void *() const { if(state&(badbit|failbit) ) \
                                  return 0; return (void *)this; }
    inline int operator!() const;

    inline int  good() const;
    inline int  eof() const;
    inline int  fail() const;
    inline int  bad() const;
```

All of the example programs that follow use a derived class based on some parent class. Some of the example program code uses derived class member functions, while other statements use inherited characteristics. These examples will help you understand the many advantages of derived classes and of inherited characteristics. While these concepts may appear difficult or frustrating at first, you'll quickly appreciate how you can inherit functionality from a predefined class simply by defining a derived class based on the predefined one.

Input Stream Classes

The **ifstream** class used in the next example program is derived from **fstreambase** and **istream**. It provides input operations on a **filebuf**. The program concentrates on text stream input.

```
//
//  17IFSTRM.CPP
//  C++ program demonstrating how to use ifstream class,
```

```
//   derived from the istream class.
//   Copyright (c) William H. Murray and Chris H. Pappas, 1992
//
//   Valid member functions for ifstream include:
//          ifstream::open        ifstream::rdbuf
//
//   Valid member functions for istream include:
//          istream::gcount       istream::get
//          istream::getline      istream::ignore
//          istream::istream      istream::peek
//          istream::putback      istream::read
//          istream::seekg        istream::tellg


#include <fstream.h>
#define iCOLUMNS 80

void main(void)
{
  char cOneLine[iCOLUMNS];

  ifstream ifMyInputStream("17IFSTRM.CPP",ios::in);
  while(ifMyInputStream) {
    ifMyInputStream.getline(cOneLine,iCOLUMNS);
    cout << '\n' << cOneLine;
  }
  ifMyInputStream.close();
}
```

The first statement in the program uses the **ifstream** constructor to create an **ifstream** object and connect it to an open file descriptor, *ifMyInputStream*. The syntax uses the name of a file, including a path if necessary ("17IFSTRM.CPP"), along with one or more open modes (for example, **ios::in** | **ios::nocreate** | **ios::binary**). The default is text input. The optional **ios::nocreate** parameter tests for the file's existence. The *ifMyInputStream* file descriptor's integer value can be used in logical tests such as **if** and **while** statements and the value is automatically set to zero on *EOF.*

The **getline()** member function inherited from the **iostream** class allows a program to read whole lines of text up to a terminating null character. Function **getline()** has three formal parameters: a *char **, the number of characters to input—including the null character—and an optional delimiter (default = '\n').

Since **char** array names are technically pointers to characters, *cOneLine* meets the first parameter requirement. The number of characters to be input matches the array's definition, or *iCOLUMNS*. No optional delimiter was defined. However, if you knew your input lines were delimited by a special character—for example, '*'—you could have written the **getline()** statement like this:

```
ifMyInputStream.getline(cOneLine,iCOLUMNS,'*');
```

The example program continues by printing the string and then manually closes the file ifMyInputStream.close().

Output Stream Classes

All **ofstream** classes are derived from **fstreambase** and **ostream** and allow a program to perform formatted and unformatted output to a **streambuf**. The output from this program is used later in this chapter in the section entitled "Binary Files" to contrast text output with binary output.

The program uses the **ofstream** constructor, which is very similar to its **ifstream** counterpart, described earlier. It expects the name of the output file, "MYOSTRM.OUT", and the open mode, **ios::out**.

```
//
// 17OSTRM.CPP
// C++ program demonstrating how to use the ofstream class
// derived from the ostream class.
// Copyright (c) William H. Murray and Chris H. Pappas, 1992

// Valid ofstream member functions include:
//          ofstream::open     ofstream::rdbuf

// Valid ostream member functions include:
//          ostream::flush     ostream::ostream
//          ostream::put       ostream::seekp
//          ostream::tellp     ostream::write

#include <fstream.h>
#include <string.h>
#define iSTRING_MAX 40

void main(void)
{
  int i=0;
  long ltellp;
  char pszString[iSTRING_MAX] = "Sample test string\n";

  // file opened in the default text mode
  ofstream ofMyOutputStream("MYOSTRM.OUT",ios::out);


  // write string out character by character
```

```
// notice that '\n' IS translated into 2 characters

while(pszString[i] != '\0') {
  ofMyOutputStream.put(pszString[i]);
  ltellp = ofMyOutputStream.tellp();
  cout << "\ntellp value: " << ltellp;
  i++;
}


// write entire string out with write member function

ltellp = ofMyOutputStream.tellp();
cout << "\ntellp's value before writing 2nd string: "
     << ltellp;
ofMyOutputStream.write(pszString,strlen(pszString));
ltellp = ofMyOutputStream.tellp();
cout << "\ntellp's updated value: " << ltellp;

ofMyOutputStream.close();

}
```

The first **while** loop prints out the *pszString* character by character with the **put()** member function. After each character is output, the variable *ltellp* is assigned the current put pointer's position as returned by the call to the **tellp()** member function. It is important that you stop at this point to take a look at the output generated by the program, shown at the end of this section.

The string variable *pszString* is initialized with 19 characters plus a '\0' null terminator, bringing the count to a total of 20. However, although the program output generates a *tellp* count of 1..20, the 20th character isn't the '\0' null terminator. This is because in text mode, the *pszString*'s '\n' is translated into a 2-byte output, one for the carriage return (19th character) and the second for the linefeed (20th character). The null terminator is not output.

The last portion of the program calculates the output pointer's position before and after using the **write()** member function to print *pszString* as a whole string. Notice that the *tellp* values printed show that the function **write()** also translates the single null terminator into a two-character output. If the character translation had not occurred, *tellp*'s last value would be 39 (assuming **put()** left the first count at 20, not 19). The abbreviated output from the program looks like this:

```
tellp value: 1
tellp value: 2
tellp value: 3
```

.
.
.

```
tellp value: 17
tellp value: 18
tellp value: 20
tellp's value before writing 2nd string: 20
tellp's updated value: 40
```

Fortunately, **istream**-derived class member functions such as **get()** and **read()** automatically convert the 2-byte output back to a single '\n'. The program highlights the need for caution when dealing with file I/O. Were the file created by this program used later on as an input file, opened in binary mode, a disaster would occur because binary files do not use such translation; file positions and contents would be incorrect.

Buffered Stream Classes

The **streambuf** class is the foundation for C++ stream I/O. This general class defines all of the basic operations that can be performed with character-oriented buffers. The **streambuf** class is also used to derive file buffers (**filebuf** class) and the **istream** and **ostream** classes that contain pointers to **streambuf** objects.

Any derived classes based on the **ios** class inherit a pointer to a **streambuf**. The **filebuf** class, as seen in Figure 17-2, is derived from **streambuf** and specializes the parent class to handle files.

The following program begins by defining two **filebuf** handles, *fbMyInputBuf* and *fbMyOutputBuf*, using the **open()** member function to create each text file. Assuming there were no file-creation errors, each handle is then associated with an appropriate **istream** (input) and **ostream** (output) object. With both files opened, the **while** loop performs a simple echo print from the input stream **is.get()** to the output stream **os.put()**, counting the number of linefeeds, '\n'. The overloaded **close()** member function manually closes each file.

```
//
//   17FILBUF.CPP
//   C++ program demonstrating how to use filebuf class.
```

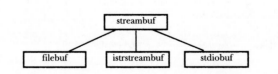

Figure 17-2.   *The streambuf and derived classes*

```
//   Copyright (c) William H. Murray and Chris H. Pappas, 1992
//
//   Valid member functions include:
//          filebuf::attach       filebuf::close
//          filebuf::fd           filebuf::~filebuf
//          filebuf::filebuf      filebuf::is_open
//          filebuf::open         filebuf::overflow
//          filebuf::seekoff      filebuf::setbuf
//          filebuf::sync         filebuf::underflow
//

#include <fstream.h>
#include <fcntl.h>
#include <process.h> // exit prototype

void main(void)
{
  char ch;
  int iLineCount=0;
  filebuf fbMyInputBuf, fbMyOutputBuf;

  fbMyInputBuf.open("17FILBUF.CPP",_O_RDONLY | _O_TEXT);
  if(fbMyInputBuf.is_open() == 0) {
    cerr << "Can't open input file";
    exit (1);
  }

  istream is(&fbMyInputBuf);

  fbMyOutputBuf.open("output.dat",_O_WRONLY | _O_TEXT);
  if(fbMyOutputBuf.is_open() == 0) {
    cerr << "Can't open output file";
    exit (2);
  }

  ostream os(&fbMyOutputBuf);

  while(is) {
    is.get(ch);
    os.put(ch);
    iLineCount += (ch == '\n');
  }

  fbMyInputBuf.close();
  fbMyOutputBuf.close();
```

```
    cout << "You had " << iLineCount << " lines in your file";
}
```

String Stream Class

You can use the **streambuf** class to extend the capabilities of the **iostream** class. Figure 17-1 illustrated the relationship between the **ios** and derived classes. It is the **ios** class that provides the derived classes with the programming interface and formatting features. However, it is the **streambuf** public members and virtual functions that do all the work. All derived **ios** classes make calls to these routines.

All buffered **streambuf** objects manage a fixed memory buffer called a *reserve area*. This reserve area can be divided into a get area for input and a put area for output. If your application requires, the get and put areas may overlap. Your program can use protected member functions to access and manipulate the two separate get and put pointers for character I/O. Each application determines the behavior of the buffers and pointers based on the program's implementation of the derived class.

There are two constructors for **streambuf** objects. Their syntax looks like this:

```
streambuf::streambuf();
streambuf::streambuf(char* pr, int nLength);
```

The first constructor is used indirectly by all **streambuf** derived classes. It sets all the internal pointers of the **streambuf** object to null. The second constructor creates a **streambuf** object that is attached to an existing character array. The following program demonstrates how to declare a string **strstreambuf** object derived from the **streambuf** base class. Once the *stbMyStreamBuf* object is created, the program outputs a single character using the **sputc()** member function and then reads the character back in with the **sgetc()** member function.

```
//
//  17STRBUF.CPP
//  C++ program demonstrating how to use the streambuf class.
//  Copyright (c) William H. Murray and Chris H. Pappas, 1992
//

#include <strstrea.h>
#define iMYBUFFSIZE 1024

void main(void)
{
  char c;

  strstreambuf stbMyStreamBuf(iMYBUFFSIZE);
```

```
    stbMyStreamBuf.sputc('A');  // output single character to buffer
    c = stbMyStreamBuf.sgetc();
    cout << c;
}
```

Just remember that there are two separate pointers for **streambuf**-based objects, a put to and a get from. Each is manipulated independently of the other. The reason the **sgetc()** member function retrieves the 'A' is to return the contents of the buffer at the location to which the get pointer points. **sputc()** moves the put pointer but does not move the get pointer and does not return a character from the buffer.

The following list gives the names and explanations for all **streambuf** public members and highlights which functions manipulate the put and get pointers:

Public Member	Meaning
sgetc	Returns the character pointed to by the get pointer. However, sgetc does not move the pointer
sgetn	Gets a series of characters from the streambuf buffer
sputc	Puts a character in the put area and moves the put pointer
sputn	Puts a sequence of characters into the streambuf buffer and then moves the put pointer
snextc	Moves the get pointer and returns the next character
sbumpc	Returns the current character and then moves the get pointer
stossc	Advances the get pointer one position. However, stossc does not return a character
sputbackc	Attempts to move the get pointer back one position. Character put back must match one from previous get
out_waiting	Reports the number of characters in the put area
in_avail	Reports the number of characters in the get area
dbp	Outputs streambuf buffer statistics and pointer values

The following list gives the names and explanations for all **streambuf** virtual functions:

Virtual Function	Meaning
seekoff	Seeks to the specified offset
seekpos	Seeks to the specified position
overflow	Clears out the put area
underflow	Fills the get area if necessary
pbackfail	Extends the sputbackc() function

Virtual Function	Meaning
setbuf	Tries to attach a reserve area to the streambuf
sync	Clears out the put and get area

The following list gives the names and explanations for all **streambuf** protected members:

allocate	Allocates a buffer by calling doalloc
doallocate	Allocates a reserve area (virtual function)
base	Returns a pointer to the beginning of the reserve area
ebuf	Returns a pointer to the end of the reserve area
blen	Returns the size of the reserve area
pbase	Returns a pointer to the beginning of the put area
pptr	Returns the put pointer
gptr	Returns the get pointer
eback	Returns the lower bound of the get area
epptr	Returns a pointer to the end of the put area
egptr	Returns a pointer to the end of the get area
setp	Sets all the put area pointers
setg	Sets all the get area pointers
pbump	Increments/decrements the put pointer
gbump	Increments/decrements the get pointer
setb	Sets up the reserve area
unbuffered	Sets or tests the streambuf buffer state variable

As you can readily see, the **streambuf** class comes equipped with every function a program could possibly need for manipulating a stream buffer. Since the **streambuf** class is used to derive file buffers (**filebuf** class) and **istream** and **ostream** classes, they all inherit **streambuf** characteristics.

Binary Files

Most of the example programs presented so far have used standard text files, or streams, as they are more appropriately called. This is not surprising since streams were originally designed for text, and text, therefore, is their default I/O mode.

Standard text files, or streams, contain a sequence of characters including carriage returns and linefeeds. In text mode, there is no requirement that individual characters remain unaltered as they are written to or read from a file. This can cause problems for certain types of applications. For example, the ASCII value for the newline character is a decimal 10. However, it could also be written as an 8-bit, hexadecimal 0A. In a C/C++ program, it is considered to be the single character constant '\n'.

As it turns out, under MS-DOS the newline is physically represented as a character pair—carriage return (decimal 13)/linefeed (decimal 10). Normally, this isn't a problem since the program automatically maps the two-character sequence into the single newline character on input, reversing the sequence on output. The problem is that a newline character occupies 1 byte, while the CR/LF pair occupies 2 bytes of storage.

Binary files, or streams, contain a sequence of bytes with a one-to-one correspondence to the sequence found in the external device (disk, tape, or terminal). In a binary file, no character translations will occur. For this reason, the number of bytes read or written will be the same as that found in the external device.

If you are writing a program that needs to read an executable file, the file should be read as a binary file. You should also use binary files when reading or writing pure data files, like databases. This guarantees that no alteration of the data occurs except those changes performed explicitly by the application.

The following program is identical to 17OSTRM.CPP, described earlier in the section entitled "Output Stream Classes," except that the output file mode has been changed from text to **ios::binary**:

```
//
// 17BINARY.CPP
// This program is a modification of 17OSTRM.CPP and
// demonstrates binary file output.
// Copyright (c) William H. Murray and Chris H. Pappas, 1992
// Valid ofstream member functions include:
//         ofstream::open     ofstream::rdbuf
// Valid ostream member functions include:
//         ostream::flush     ostream::ostream
//         ostream::put       ostream::seekp
//         ostream::tellp     ostream::write

#include <fstream.h>
#include <string.h>
#define iSTRING_MAX 40

void main(void)
{
  int i=0;
  long ltellp;
  char pszString[iSTRING_MAX] = "Sample test string\n";
```

```
// file opened in binary mode!
ofstream ofMyOutputStream("MYOSTRM.OUT",ios::out | ios::binary);

// write string out character by character
// notice that '\n' is NOT translated into 2 characters!
while(pszString[i] != '\0') {
  ofMyOutputStream.put(pszString[i]);
  ltellp = ofMyOutputStream.tellp();
  cout << "\ntellp value: " << ltellp;
  i++;
}

// write entire string out with write member function
ltellp = ofMyOutputStream.tellp();
cout << "\ntellp's value before writing 2nd string: " << ltellp;
ofMyOutputStream.write(pszString,strlen(pszString));
ltellp = ofMyOutputStream.tellp();
cout << "\ntellp's updated value: " << ltellp;

ofMyOutputStream.close();

}
```

The abbreviated output, seen in the following listing, illustrates the one-to-one relationship between a file and the data's internal representation:

```
tellp value: 1
tellp value: 2
tellp value: 3
     .
     .
     .
tellp value: 17
tellp value: 18
tellp value: 19
tellp's value before writing 2nd string: 19
tellp's updated value: 38
```

The string *pszString*, which has 19 characters plus a '\0' null string terminator, is output exactly as stored, without the appended '\0' null terminator. This explains why **tellp()** reports a multiple of 19 at the completion of each string's output.

Combining C and C++ Code Using extern "C"

In previous discussions (in Chapter 7), you have seen how the **extern** keyword specifies that a variable or function has external linkage. This means that the variable or function referenced is defined in some other source file or later on in the same file.

However, in C/C++, you can use the **extern** keyword with a string. The string indicates that another language's linkage conventions are being used for the identifier(s) being defined. For C++ programs, the default string is "C++".

In C++, functions are overloaded by default. This causes the C++ compiler to assign a new name to each function. You can prevent the compiler from assigning a new name to each function by preceding the function definition with **extern "C"**. This is necessary so that C functions and data can be accessed by C++ code. Naturally, this is only done for one of a set of functions with the same name. Without this override, the linker would find more than one global function with the same name. Currently, "C" is the only other language specifier supported by Microsoft C/C++. The syntax for using **extern "C"** looks like this:

extern "C" *freturn_type fname(param_type(s) param(s))*

The following listing demonstrates how **extern "C"** is used with a single-function prototype:

```
extern "C" int fprintf(FILE *stream, char *format, ...);
```

To modify a group of function prototypes, a set of braces, {}, is needed:

```
extern "C"
  {
     .
     .
     .
  }
```

The next code segment modifies the **getc()** and **putc()** function prototypes:

```
extern "C"
  {
     int getc(FILE *stream);
     int putc(int c, FILE *stream);
  }
```

The following example program demonstrates how to use **extern "C"**:

```
//
//  17CLINK.CPP
//  C++ program demonstrating how to link C++ code
//  to C library functions
//  Copyright (c) William H. Murray and Chris H. Pappas, 1992
//

#include <iostream.h>
#include <string.h>
#include <stdlib.h>

#define iMAX 9

extern "C" int imycompare(const void *pi1, const void *pi2);

void main(void)
{
  int iarray[iMAX] = { 1, 9, 2, 8, 3, 7, 4, 6, 5};

  for(int i = 0; i < iMAX; i++)
    cout << iarray[i] << " ";

  qsort(iarray,iMAX,sizeof(int),imycompare);

  for(i = 0; i < iMAX; i++)
    cout << iarray[i] << " ";
}

extern "C" int imycompare(const void *pi1, const void *pi2)
{
  return( *(int *)pi1 - *(int *)pi2);
}
```

All the Microsoft C include files use **extern "C"**. This makes it possible for a C++ program to use the C run-time library functions. Rather than repeat **extern "C"** for every definition in these header files, the following conditional statement pair surrounds all C header file definitions:

```
// 3-statements found at the beginning of header file.

#ifdef __cplusplus
extern "C" {
```

```
#endif


// 3-statements found at the end of the header file.

#ifdef __cplusplus
}
#endif
```

When compiling a C++ program, the compiler automatically defines the **__cplusplus** name. This in turn makes the **extern "C" {** statement and the closing brace, }, visible only when needed.

Writing Your Own Manipulators

Chapter 12 introduced you to the concept of stream manipulators. You use manipulators with the insertion, <<, and extraction, >>, operators, exactly as if they represented data for output or variables to receive input. As the name implies, however, manipulators can carry out arbitrary operations on the input and output streams.

Several of the example programs used the built-in manipulators **dec**, **hex**, **oct**, **setw**, and **setprecision**. Now you will learn how to write your own custom manipulators. To gradually build your understanding of the syntax necessary to create your own manipulators, the example programs begin with the simplest type of manipulator, one with no parameters, and then move on to ones with parameters.

Manipulators Without Parameters

You can create a custom manipulator any time you need to repeatedly insert the same character sequence into the output stream. For example, maybe your particular application needs to flag the user to an important piece of data. You even want to beep the speaker to get the user's attention just in case he or she isn't looking directly at the monitor. Without custom manipulators, your output statements would look like this:

```
cout << '\a' << "\n\n\t\tImportant data: "
     << fcritical_mass << endl;
```

Every time you wanted to grab the user's attention, you would repeat the bell prompt, '\a', and the "...Important data: " string. An easier approach is to define a manipulator, called *beep*, that automatically substitutes the desired sequence. The *beep* manipulator also makes the statement easier to read:

```
cout << beep << fcritical_mass << endl;
```

The following program demonstrates how to define and use the **beep()** function:

```
//
//  17BEEP.CPP
//  C++ program demonstrates how to create your own
//  non-parameterized manipulator
//  Copyright (c) William H. Murray and Chris H. Pappas, 1992
//

#include <iostream.h>

ostream& beep(ostream& os) {
  return os << '\a' << "\n\n\t\t\tImportant data: ";
}

void main(void)
{
 double fcritical_mass = 12459876.12;

 cout << beep << fcritical_mass;
}
```

The globally defined **beep()** function uses an **ostream&** formal parameter and returns the same **ostream&**. *Beep* works because it is automatically connected to the stream's << operator. The stream's insertion operator, <<, is overloaded to accept this kind of function with the following inline function:

```
Inline ostream& ostream::operator<<(ostream& (*f)(ostream&)) {
  (*f)(*this);
  return *this;
}
```

The inline function associates the << operator with the custom manipulator by accepting a pointer to a function passed an **ostream&** type and that returns the same. This is exactly how **beep()** is prototyped. Now when << is used with **beep()**, the compiler dereferences the overloaded operator, finding where function **beep()** sits, and then executes it. The overloaded operator returns a reference to the original **ostream**. Because of this, you can combine manipulators, strings, and other data with the << operators.

Manipulators with One Parameter

The Microsoft **iostream** Class library, prototyped in iomanip.h, defines a special set of macros for creating parameterized macros. The simplest parameterized macro you can write accepts either one **int** or **long** parameter.

The following listing shows a prototype for such a manipulator, *fc*. The example program demonstrates the syntax necessary to create a single-parameter custom manipulator:

```
//
//  171MANIP.CPP
//  C++ program demonstrating how to create and use
//  one-parameter custom manipulators.
//  Copyright (c) William H. Murray and Chris H. Pappas, 1992 //

#include <iostream.h>
#include <iomanip.h>
#include <string.h>
#define iSCREEN_WIDTH 80

ostream& fc(ostream& os, int istring_width)
{
  os << '\n';
  for(int i=0; i < ((iSCREEN_WIDTH - istring_width)/2); i++)
    os << ' ';
  return(os);
}


OMANIP(int) center(int istring_width)
{
  return OMANIP(int) (fc, istring_width);
}

void main(void)
{
  char *psz = "This is auto-centered text!";
  cout << center(strlen(psz)) << psz;
}
```

The *center* custom-parameterized manipulator accepts a single value, *strlen(psz)*, representing the length of a string. iomanip.h defines a macro, OMANIP(int), and expands into the class, **__OMANIP_int**. The definition for this class includes a constructor and an overloaded **ostream** insertion operator. When function **center()** is inserted into the stream, it calls the constructor that creates and returns an **__OMANIP_int** object. The object's constructor then calls the **fc()** function.

Manipulators with Multiple Parameters

You may think the next example looks somewhat familiar. Actually, it is the same code (17SQRT.CPP) seen earlier in the chapter to demonstrate how to format numeric output. However, the program has been rewritten using a two-parameter custom manipulator to format the data.

The first modification to the program involves a simple structure definition to hold the format manipulator's actual parameter values:

```
struct stwidth_precision {
  int iwidth;
  int iprecision;
};
```

When you create manipulators that take arguments other than **int** or **long**, you must use the IOMANIPdeclare macro. This macro declares the classes for your new data type. The definition for the *format* manipulator begins with the OMANIP macro:

```
OMANIP(stwidth_precision) format(int iwidth, int iprecision)
{
  stwidth_precision stWidth_Precision;
  stWidth_Precision.iwidth = iwidth;
  stWidth_Precision.iprecision = iprecision;
  return OMANIP (stwidth_precision)(ff, stWidth_Precision);
}
```

In this example, the custom manipulator is passed two integer arguments, *iwidth* and *iprecision*. The first value defines the number of spaces to be used by *format,* and the second value specifies the number of decimal places. Once *format* has initialized the stWidth_Precision structure, it calls the constructor, which creates and returns an __**OMANIP** object. The object's constructor then calls the **ff()** function, which sets the specified parameters:

```
static ostream& ff(ostream& os, stwidth_precision
                   stWidth_Precision)
{
  os.width(stWidth_Precision.iwidth);
  os.precision(stWidth_Precision.iprecision);
  os.setf(ios::fixed);
  return os;
}
```

The complete program follows. All of the code replaced by the call to *format* has been left in the listing for comparison. Notice how the *format* custom manipulator streamlines each output statement.

```
//
//   172MANIP.CPP
//   This C++ program is the same as 17SQRT.CPP, except
//   for the fact that it uses custom parameterized
//   manipulators to format the output.
//   A C++ program that prints a table of
//   numbers, squares, and square roots for the
//   numbers from 1 to 15. Program uses the type
//   double. Formatting aligns columns, pads blank
//   spaces with '0' character, and controls
//   precision of answer.
//   Copyright (c) William H. Murray and Chris H. Pappas, 1992
//

#include <iostream.h>
#include <iomanip.h>
#include <math.h>

struct stwidth_precision {
  int iwidth;
  int iprecision;
};

IOMANIPdeclare(stwidth_precision);

static ostream& ff(ostream& os, stwidth_precision
                   stWidth_Precision)
{
  os.width(stWidth_Precision.iwidth);
  os.precision(stWidth_Precision.iprecision);
  os.setf(ios::fixed);
  return os;
}

OMANIP(stwidth_precision) format(int iwidth, int iprecision)
{
  stwidth_precision stWidth_Precision;
  stWidth_Precision.iwidth = iwidth;
  stWidth_Precision.iprecision = iprecision;
  return OMANIP (stwidth_precision)(ff, stWidth_Precision);
```

```
}

main()
{
  double number,square,sqroot;

  cout << "num\t" << "square\t\t" << "square root\n";
  cout << "_____\n";

  number=1.0;

//cout.setf(ios::fixed);          // use fixed format
  for(int i=1;i<16;i++) {
    square=number*number;         // find square
    sqroot=sqrt(number);          // find square root

    cout.fill('0');               // fill blanks with zeros
//  cout.width(2);                // column 2 characters wide
//  cout.precision(0);            // no decimal place
    cout << format(2,0) << number << "\t";

//  cout.width(6);                // column 6 characters wide
//  cout.precision(1);            // print 1 decimal place
    cout << format(6,1) << square << "\t\t";

//  cout.width(8);                // column 8 characters wide
//  cout.precision(6);            // print 6 decimal places
    cout << format(8,6) << sqroot << endl;

    number+=1.0;
  }
  return (0);
}
```

Now that you are more comfortable with advanced C++ object-oriented I/O, you are ready to move on to object-oriented design philosophies. Chapter 18 explains how important good class design is to a sucessful object-oriented problem solution.

Chapter *18*

Working in an Object-oriented Environment

There are several object-oriented languages available to programmers in addition to C++. However, each language produces object-oriented code that shares several common features. In his book *Object-oriented Software Construction* (Prentice Hall), Bertrand Meyer suggests that there are seven features standard to true object-oriented programs as a whole:

- Object-based modularization
- Abstract data types
- Memory management (automatic)
- Classes
- Inheritance
- Polymorphism
- Inheritance (multiple)

From your study of C++ classes in Chapter 16, you have learned that Microsoft C/C++ provides these features to the object-oriented programmer. In fact, you might conclude that to do true object-oriented programming you must work in a language, such as C++, that is itself object oriented. There are valid arguments against this notion, as you will see later in this book. For example, programs written for

Microsoft's Windows contain many of the seven previously mentioned features, even though they can be written in C.

An Object-oriented Stack in C++

In Chapter 16, you were exposed to many object-oriented concepts. For example, you learned that the C++ class, an abstract data type, provides the encapsulation of data structures and the operations on those structures (member functions). As such, the C++ class serves as the mechanism for forming objects. The following simple example of object creation with a C++ class demonstrates the implementation of an object-oriented stack.

Stack operations in this example are carried out in the traditional FILO (first-in, last-out) manner. The **stack** class provides six member functions: **clear()**, **top()**, **empty()**, **full()**, **push()**, and **pop()**. Examine the following listing and observe how these member functions are implemented:

```
//
//                      Top points to last value pushed : not usual
//   18STACK.CPP        Usual : top points to next available space
//   C++ program illustrates object-oriented programming
//   with a classical stack operation using a string of
//   characters.
//   Copyright (c) William H. Murray and Chris H. Pappas, 1992
//

#include <iostream.h>
#include <string.h>

#define maxlen 80

class stack {
   char str1[maxlen];
   int *first;        // char

public:
   void clear(void);
   char top(void);
   int  empty(void);
   int  full(void);
   void push(char chr);
   char pop(void);
};
```

As pointers:

```
void stack::clear(void)
{
  first=0;
}
```

first = str1

```
char stack::top(void)
{
  return (str1[first]);
}
```

return *first

```
int stack::empty(void)
{
  return (first==0);
}
```

First == str1

```
int stack::full(void)
{
  return (first==maxlen-1);
}
```

f first == first + maxlen -

```
void stack::push(char chr)
{
  str1[++first]=chr;
}
```

*++first = chr

```
char stack::pop(void)
{
  return (str1[first—]);
}
```

return (* first --)

```
main()
{
  stack mystack;
  char str[11]="0123456789";

  // clear the stack
  mystack.clear();

  // load the string, char-by-char, on the stack
  cout << "\nLoad character data on stack" << endl;
  for(int i=0;i<strlen(str);i++) {
    if (!mystack.full())
      mystack.push(str[i]);
      cout << str[i] << endl;
  }
```

```
  // unload the stack, char-by-char
  cout << "\nUnload character data from stack" << endl;
  while (!mystack.empty())
    cout << mystack.pop() << endl;

  return (0);
}
```

In this program, characters from a string are pushed, one character at a time, onto the stack. Next, the stack is unloaded one character at a time. Loading and unloading are done from the stack top, so the first character information loaded on the stack is pushed down most deeply in the stack.

Observe in the following listing that the character for the number zero was pushed onto the stack first. It should be no surprise that it is the last character popped off the stack.

```
Load character data on stack
0
1
2
3
4
5
6
7
8
9


Unload character data from stack
9
8
7
6
5
4
3
2
1
0
```

While this example lacks many of the more advanced object-oriented concepts such as memory management, inheritance, and polymorphism, it is nevertheless a simple object-oriented program. However, the power of object-oriented thinking is more apparent as more and more of Meyer's seven points are actually implemented.

An Object-oriented Linked List in C++

In Chapter 14, a linked-list program was developed in C++ using a traditional procedural programming approach. When using the traditional approach, you learned that the linked-list program is difficult to alter and maintain. In this chapter, a linked-list program using objects is developed that will allow you to create a list of employee information. It will also be possible to add and delete employees from the list. To limit the size of the linked-list program, no user interface will be used for gathering employee data. Data for the linked list has been hardwired in the **main**() function. Examples of how to make this program interactive and able to accept information from the keyboard have been shown in earlier chapters.

This program is slightly more difficult than the example in Chapter 14. You will find that it includes, in addition to linked-list concepts, all seven of the object-oriented concepts listed earlier.

Creating a Parent Class

This program uses several child classes derived from a common parent class. The parent class for this linked-list example is named **NNR**. "NNR" represents the Nineveh National Research Company, developers of computer-related books and software. The linked-list program is a database that will keep pertinent information and payroll data on company employees. The purpose of the parent class **NNR** is to gather information common to all subsequent derived child classes. For this example, that common information includes an employee's last name, first name, occupation title, social security number, and year hired at the company. The parent class **NNR** has three levels of isolation: public, protected, and private. The protected section of this class shows the structure for gathering data common to each derived child class. The public section (member functions) show how that information will be intercepted from the function **main**().

```
// PARENT CLASS
class NNR {

friend class payroll_list;

protected:
  char lstname[20];
  char fstname[15];
```

```
      char job_title[30];
      char social_sec[12];
      int year_hired;
      NNR *pointer;
      NNR *next_link;

   public:
     NNR(char *lname,char *fname,char *ss,
         char *job,int y_hired)
     {
       strcpy(lstname,lname);
       strcpy(fstname,fname);
       strcpy(social_sec,ss);
       strcpy(job_title,job);
       year_hired=y_hired;
       next_link=0;
     }
             .
             .
             .
             .
```

The parent class and all derived child classes will use a friend class named
payroll_list. When you study the full program listing in the section entitled "Examining the Complete Program" later in this chapter, notice that all derived child classes
share this common variable, too. (Remember how the terms "private" and "public"
relate to encapsulation concepts used by object-oriented programmers.)

A Derived Child Class

This program uses four derived child classes. Each of these is derived from the parent
class **NNR** shown in the last section. This segment presents one child class, **salespersons**, which represents the points common to all four derived classes. A portion of
this derived class is shown next. The derived child class satisfies the object-oriented
concept of inheritance.

```
//SUB OR DERIVED CHILD CLASS
class salespersons:public NNR {

friend class payroll_list;

private:
  float disk_sales;
  int comm_rate;
```

```
public:
  salespersons(char *lname,char *fname,char *ss,
              char *job,int y_hired,
              float d_sales,int c_rate):
              NNR(lname,fname,ss,
              job,y_hired)
  {
    disk_sales=d_sales;
    comm_rate=c_rate;
  }
          .
          .
          .
          .
```

In this case, the **salespersons** child class gathers information and adds it to the information already gathered by the parent class. This in turn forms a data structure composed of last name, first name, social security number, year hired, the total sales, and the appropriate commission rate.

Now take a look at the remainder of the child class description:

```
          .
          .
          .
          .

  void fill_sales(float d_sales)
  {
    disk_sales=d_sales;
  }

  void fill_comm_rate(int c_rate)
  {
    comm_rate=c_rate;
  }

  void add_info()
  {
    pointer=this;
  }

  void send_info()
  {
```

```
  NNR::send_info();
  cout << "\n Sales (disks): " << disk_sales;
  cout << "\n Commission Rate: " << comm_rate;
}

};
```

Instead of **add_info()** setting aside memory for each additional linked-list node by using the **new** free store operator, the program uses each object's **this** pointer. The *pointer* is being assigned the address of an **NNR** node.

Output information on a particular employee is constructed in a unique manner. In the case of the **salespersons** class, notice that **send_info()** makes a request to **NNR**'s **send_info()** function. **NNR**'s function prints the information common to each derived class; then the **salespersons**' **send_info()** function prints the information unique to the particular child class. For this example, this information includes the sales and the commission rate.

It would also have been possible to print the information about the salesperson completely from within the child class, but the method used allows another advantage of object-oriented programming to be illustrated—the use of virtual functions.

Using a Friend Class

The friend class, **payroll_list**, contains the means for printing the linked list and for the insertion and deletion of employees from the list. Here is a small portion of this class:

```
//FRIEND CLASS
class payroll_list {

private:
  NNR *location;

public:
  payroll_list()
  {
    location=0;
  }

  void print_payroll_list();

  void insert_employee(NNR *node);

  void remove_employee_id(char *social_sec);
```

```
};
```

    .

    .

    .

    .

Notice that messages that are sent to the member functions **print_payroll_list()**, **insert_employee()**, and **remove_employee_id()** form the functional part of the linked-list program.

    Consider the function **print_payroll_list()**, which begins by assigning the pointer to the list to the pointer variable *present*. While the pointer *present* is not zero, it will continue to point to employees in the linked list, direct them to *send_info*, and update the pointer until all employees have been printed. The next section of code shows how this is achieved:

    .

    .

    .

    .

```
void payroll_list::print_payroll_list()
{
  NNR *present=location;

  while(present!=0) {
    present->send_info();
    present=present->next_link;
  }
}
```

    .

    .

    .

    You might recall from an earlier discussion that the variable *pointer* contains the memory address of nodes inserted via **add_info()**. This value is used by **insert_employee()** to form the link with the linked list. The insertion technique inserts data alphabetically by an employee's last name. Thus, the linked list is always ordered alphabetically by last name.

    The program accomplishes a correct insertion by comparing the last name of a new employee with those already in the list. When a name (*node->lstname*) already in the list is found that is greater than the *current_node->lstname*, the first **while** loop ends. This is a standard linked-list insert procedure that leaves the pointer variable, *previous_node*, pointing to the node behind where the new node is to be inserted and leaves *current_node* pointing to the node that will follow the insertion point for the new node.

When the insertion point is determined, the program creates a new link or node by calling **node->add_info()**. The *current_node* is linked to the new node's *next_link*. The last decision that must be made is whether or not the new node is to be placed as the front node in the list or between existing nodes. The program establishes this by examining the contents of the pointer variable *previous_node*. If the pointer variable is zero, it cannot be pointing to a valid previous node, so *location* is updated to the address of the new node. If *previous_node* contains a nonzero value, it is assumed to be pointing to a valid previous node. In this case, *previous_node->next_link* is assigned the address of the new node's address, or *node->pointer.*

```
                .
                .
                .
                .
void payroll_list::insert_employee(NNR *node)
{
  NNR *current_node=location;
  NNR *previous_node=0;

  while (current_node != 0 &&
         strcmp(current_node->lstname,node->lstname) < 0) {
    previous_node=current_node;
    current_node=current_node->next_link;
  }
  node->add_info();
  node->pointer->next_link=current_node;
  if (previous_node==0)
    location=node->pointer;
  else
    previous_node->next_link=node->pointer;
}
                .
                .
                .
                .
```

The program can remove items from the linked list only by knowing the employee's social security number. This technique adds a level of protection against accidentally deleting an employee.

As you examine **remove_employee_id()**, shown in the next listing, note that the structure used for examining the nodes in the linked list is almost identical to that of **insert_employee()**. However, the first **while** loop leaves the *current_node* pointing to the node to be deleted, not the node after the one to be deleted.

```
          .
          .
          .
          .
void payroll_list::remove_employee_id(char *social_sec)
{
  NNR *current_node=location;
  NNR *previous_node=0;

  while(current_node != 0 &&
        strcmp(current_node->social_sec,
        social_sec) != 0) {
    previous_node=current_node;
    current_node=current_node->next_link;
  }

  if(current_node != 0 && previous_node == 0) {
    location=current_node->next_link;
    delete current_node;
  }
  else if(current_node != 0 && previous_node != 0) {
    previous_node->next_link=current_node->next_link;
    delete current_node;
  }
}
```

The first compound **if** statement takes care of deleting a node in the front of the list. The program accomplishes this by examining the contents of *previous_node* to see if it contains a zero. If it does, then the front of the list, *location,* needs to be updated to the node following the one to be deleted. This is achieved with the following line:

```
current_node->next_link
```

The second **if** statement takes care of deleting a node between two existing nodes. This requires the node behind to be assigned the address of the node after the one being deleted.

```
previous_node->next_link=current_node->next_link.
```

Now that the important pieces of the program have been examined, the next section puts them together to form a complete program.

Examining the Complete Program

The following listing is the complete operational C++ object-oriented linked-list
program. The only thing it lacks is an interactive user interface. When the program
is executed, it will add nine employees, with their different job titles, to the linked
list and then print the list. Next, the program will delete two employees from the list.
This is accomplished by supplying their social security numbers. The altered list is
then printed. The **main()** function contains information on which employees are
added and deleted.

```cpp
//
//   18NNR.CPP
//   C++ program illustrates object-oriented programming
//   with a linked list. This program keeps track of
//   employee data at Nineveh National Research (NNR).
//   Copyright (c) William H. Murray and Chris H. Pappas, 1992
//

#include <iostream.h>
#include <string.h>

// PARENT CLASS
class NNR {

friend class payroll_list;

protected:
  char lstname[20];
  char fstname[15];
  char job_title[30];
  char social_sec[12];
  int year_hired;
  NNR *pointer;
  NNR *next_link;

public:
  NNR(char *lname,char *fname,char *ss,
      char *job,int y_hired)
  {
    strcpy(lstname,lname);
    strcpy(fstname,fname);
    strcpy(social_sec,ss);
    strcpy(job_title,job);
    year_hired=y_hired;
```

```
  next_link=0;
}

NNR()
{
  lstname[0]=NULL;
  fstname[0]=NULL;
  social_sec[0]=NULL;
  job_title[0]=NULL;
  year_hired=0;
  next_link=0;
}

void fill_lstname(char *l_name)
{
  strcpy(lstname,l_name);
}

void fill_fstname(char *f_name)
{
  strcpy(fstname,f_name);
}

void fill_social_sec(char *soc_sec)
{
  strcpy(social_sec,soc_sec);
}

void fill_job_title(char *o_name)
{
  strcpy(job_title,o_name);
}

void fill_year_hired(int y_hired)
{
  year_hired=y_hired;
}

virtual void add_info() {
}

virtual void send_info()
{
  cout << "\n\n" << lstname << ", " << fstname
     << "\n Social Security: #" << social_sec;
```

```
    cout << "\n Job Title: " << job_title;
    cout << "\n Year Hired: " << year_hired;
  }

};


//SUB OR DERIVED CHILD CLASS
class administration:public NNR {

friend class payroll_list;

private:
  float yearly_salary;

public:
  administration(char *lname,char *fname,char *ss,
                 char *job,int y_hired,
                 float y_salary):
                 NNR(lname,fname,ss,
                 job,y_hired)
  {
    yearly_salary=y_salary;
  }

  administration():NNR()
  {
    yearly_salary=0.0;
  }

  void fill_yearly_salary(float salary)
  {
    yearly_salary=salary;
  }

  void add_info()
  {
    pointer=this;
  }

  void send_info()
  {
    NNR::send_info();
    cout << "\n Yearly Salary: $" << yearly_salary;
  }
```

```
};


//SUB OR DERIVED CHILD CLASS
class salespersons:public NNR {

friend class payroll_list;

private:
  float disk_sales;
  int comm_rate;

public:
  salespersons(char *lname,char *fname,char *ss,
               char *job,int y_hired,
               float d_sales,int c_rate):
               NNR(lname,fname,ss,
               job,y_hired)
  {
    disk_sales=d_sales;
    comm_rate=c_rate;
  }

  salespersons():NNR()
  {
    disk_sales=0.0;
    comm_rate=0;
  }

  void fill_sales(float d_sales)
  {
    disk_sales=d_sales;
  }

  void fill_comm_rate(int c_rate)
  {
    comm_rate=c_rate;
  }

  void add_info()
  {
    pointer=this;
  }
```

```
  void send_info()
  {
    NNR::send_info();
    cout << "\n Sales (disks): " << disk_sales;
    cout << "\n Commission Rate: " << comm_rate;
  }

};


//SUB OR DERIVED CHILD CLASS
class technicians:public NNR {

friend class payroll_list;

private:
  float hourly_salary;

public:
  technicians(char *lname,char *fname,char *ss,char *job,
              int y_hired,float h_salary):
              NNR(lname,fname,ss,job,y_hired)
  {
    hourly_salary=h_salary;
  }

  technicians():NNR()
  {
    hourly_salary=0.0;
  }

  void fill_hourly_salary(float h_salary)
  {
    hourly_salary=h_salary;
  }

  void add_info()
  {
    pointer=this;
  }

  void send_info()
  {
    NNR::send_info();
    cout << "\n Hourly Salary: $" << hourly_salary;
```

```
    }

};


//SUB OR DERIVED CHILD CLASS
class supplies:public NNR {

friend class payroll_list;

private:
  float hourly_salary;

public:
  supplies(char *lname,char *fname,char *ss,char *job,
           int y_hired,float h_salary):
           NNR(lname,fname,ss,
           job,y_hired)
  {
    hourly_salary=h_salary;
  }

  supplies():NNR()
  {
    hourly_salary=0.0;
  }

  void fill_hourly_salary(float h_salary)
  {
    hourly_salary=h_salary;
  }

  void add_info()
  {
    pointer=this;
  }

  void send_info()
  {
    NNR::send_info();
    cout << "\n Hourly Salary: $" << hourly_salary;
  }

};
```

```
//FRIEND CLASS
class payroll_list {

private:
  NNR *location;

public:
  payroll_list()
  {
    location=0;
  }

  void print_payroll_list();

  void insert_employee(NNR *node);

  void remove_employee_id(char *social_sec);

};

void payroll_list::print_payroll_list()
{
  NNR *present=location;

  while(present!=0) {
    present->send_info();
    present=present->next_link;
  }
}

void payroll_list::insert_employee(NNR *node)
{
  NNR *current_node=location;
  NNR *previous_node=0;

  while (current_node != 0 &&
         strcmp(current_node->lstname,node->lstname) < 0) {
    previous_node=current_node;
    current_node=current_node->next_link;
  }
  node->add_info();
  node->pointer->next_link=current_node;
  if (previous_node==0)
    location=node->pointer;
```

```
    else
      previous_node->next_link=node->pointer;
}

void payroll_list::remove_employee_id(char *social_sec)
{
  NNR *current_node=location;
  NNR *previous_node=0;

  while(current_node != 0 &&
      strcmp(current_node->social_sec,social_sec) != 0) {
    previous_node=current_node;
    current_node=current_node->next_link;
  }

  if(current_node != 0 && previous_node == 0) {
    location=current_node->next_link;
    // delete current_node; needed if new() used in add_info()
  }
  else if(current_node != 0 && previous_node != 0) {
    previous_node->next_link=current_node->next_link;
    // delete current_node; needed if new() used in add_info()
  }
}


main()
{
  payroll_list workers;

  // static data to add to linked list
  salespersons salesperson1("Harddrive","Harriet","313-56-7884",
                        "Salesperson",1985,6.5,7.5);
  salespersons salesperson2("Flex","Frank","663-65-2312",
                        "Salesperson",1985,3.0,3.2);
  salespersons salesperson3("Ripoff","Randle","512-34-7612",
                        "Salesperson",1987,9.6,6.8);
  technicians techperson1("Align","Alice","174-43-6781",
                        "Technician",1989,12.55);
  technicians techperson2("Tightscrew","Tom","682-67-5312",
                        "Technician",1992,10.34);
  administration vice_president1("Stuckup","Stewart",
                        "238-18-1119","Vice President",
                        1980,40000.00);
  administration vice_president2("Learnedmore","Lawrence",
                        "987-99-9653","Vice President",
```

```
                                1984,45000.00);
       supplies supplyperson1("Allpart","Albert","443-89-3772",
                              "Supplies",1983,8.55);
       supplies supplyperson2("Ordermore","Ozel","111-44-5399",
                              "Supplies",1988,7.58);


       // add the nine workers to the linked list
       workers.insert_employee(&techperson1);
       workers.insert_employee(&vice_president1);
       workers.insert_employee(&salesperson1);
       workers.insert_employee(&supplyperson1);
       workers.insert_employee(&supplyperson2);
       workers.insert_employee(&salesperson2);
       workers.insert_employee(&techperson2);
       workers.insert_employee(&vice_president2);
       workers.insert_employee(&salesperson3);


       // print the linked list
       workers.print_payroll_list();


       // remove two workers from the linked list
       workers.remove_employee_id("238-18-1119");
       workers.remove_employee_id("512-34-7612");


       cout << "\n\n**********************************";


       // print the revised linked list
       workers.print_payroll_list();


       return (0);
   }
```

Study the complete listing and see if you understand how employees are inserted and deleted from the list. If it is still a little confusing, go back and study each major section of code discussed earlier.

Linked-list Output

The linked-list program sends output to the monitor. The first section of the list contains the nine employee names that were used to create the original list. The last part of the list shows the list after two employees are deleted. Here is a sample output sent to the screen:

Align, Alice
 Social Security: #174-43-6781
 Job Title: Technician
 Year Hired: 1989
 Hourly Salary: $12.55

Allpart, Albert
 Social Security: #443-89-3772
 Job Title: Supplies
 Year Hired: 1983
 Hourly Salary: $8.55

Flex, Frank
 Social Security: #663-65-2312
 Job Title: Salesperson
 Year Hired: 1985
 Sales (disks): 3
 Commission Rate: 3

Harddrive, Harriet
 Social Security: #313-56-7884
 Job Title: Salesperson
 Year Hired: 1985
 Sales (disks): 6.5
 Commission Rate: 7

Learnedmore, Lawrence
 Social Security: #987-99-9653
 Job Title: Vice President
 Year Hired: 1984
 Yearly Salary: $45000

Ordermore, Ozel
 Social Security: #111-44-5399
 Job Title: Supplies
 Year Hired: 1988
 Hourly Salary: $7.58

Ripoff, Randle
 Social Security: #512-34-7612
 Job Title: Salesperson
 Year Hired: 1987
 Sales (disks): 9.6
 Commission Rate: 6

```
Stuckup, Stewart
 Social Security: #238-18-1119
 Job Title: Vice President
 Year Hired: 1980
 Yearly Salary: $40000

Tightscrew, Tom
 Social Security: #682-67-5312
 Job Title: Technician
 Year Hired: 1992
 Hourly Salary: $10.34


*************************************

Align, Alice
 Social Security: #174-43-6781
 Job Title: Technician
 Year Hired: 1989
 Hourly Salary: $12.55

Allpart, Albert
 Social Security: #443-89-3772
 Job Title: Supplies
 Year Hired: 1983
 Hourly Salary: $8.55

Flex, Frank
 Social Security: #663-65-2312
 Job Title: Salesperson
 Year Hired: 1985
 Sales (disks): 3
 Commission Rate: 3

Harddrive, Harriet
 Social Security: #313-56-7884
 Job Title: Salesperson
 Year Hired: 1985
 Sales (disks): 6.5
 Commission Rate: 7

Learnedmore, Lawrence
 Social Security: #987-99-9653
 Job Title: Vice President
 Year Hired: 1984
 Yearly Salary: $45000
```

```
Ordermore, Ozel
  Social Security: #111-44-5399
  Job Title: Supplies
  Year Hired: 1988
  Hourly Salary: $7.58

Tightscrew, Tom
  Social Security: #682-67-5312
  Job Title: Technician
  Year Hired: 1992
  Hourly Salary: $10.34
```

More Object-oriented C++

If in the course of this chapter you have developed an interest in object-oriented programming, you will really be interested in the Windows applications developed in Chapters 24 and 25. These particular Windows applications make use of Microsoft's new Foundation Class library. This library contains the reusable classes that make programming under Windows much easier.

Part ***IV***

DOS Graphics, System Access, Libraries, and Mixed Language Interface

Chapter *19*

Graphics Under DOS

This chapter takes a detailed look at the traditional Microsoft C graphics and presentation graphics libraries used for DOS mode programming. The details and function prototypes for the examples in this chapter can be found in the graph.h and pgchart.h header files. Programs developed in this chapter will work under most versions of DOS and in the DOS box under Windows. Most of the programs developed in this chapter can be switched from the C environment to the C++ environment with only minor changes. If you write in C++, you will have the added advantage of incorporating your own object libraries for powerful graphics programs.

The graphics functions in this chapter are unique to the Microsoft C/C++ environment and are not part of the ANSI C standard. Since special graphics libraries are needed, be certain that during installation of your Microsoft C/C++ compiler, these libraries were installed. If you did install them, graph.h and pgchart.h will be in your include directory and graphics.lib and pgchart.lib in your library directory. It will be necessary to specify the libraries during compile/link. From the Programmer's WorkBench (PWB), choose the Option and then the Link selection from the command bar; this allows you to then add the appropriate library names/extensions to the list of global libraries.

These functions are very hardware dependent. The programs you develop can work on a wide range of computers, from 8088 PCs to powerful 80486 machines. However, because these functions use special graphics libraries, they are less portable.

This chapter also teaches you how to use Microsoft graphics function calls to set video modes, check installed hardware, set environment parameters, and even return to the original screen mode when the graphics program is completed. From there, you will learn how to utilize many basic graphics primitives. These are functions capable of drawing simple shapes such as lines, rectangles, ellipses, and so on. By using these simple graphics primitives as the foundation for more complicated shapes, you can develop intricate graphics programs. Font functions will allow you to add text to the graphics screen. You'll see how to select different fonts and place them on the screen and also how to scale and rotate them until they suit your needs.

Developing presentation pie, line, bar, and scatter charts has been made very easy with Microsoft's presentation graphics library. With just a few simple function calls, you will be able to create graphs and charts that have a professional touch.

Text and Graphics Modes

There are two fundamental video display modes—text and graphics. In text mode, alphanumeric characters are placed on the screen as a composite block of pixels. That block might measure as few as 8x8 or as many as 8x20 pixels. Each block that describes an ASCII or extended ASCII character is contained in ROM hardware or system software that can be accessed by the video adapter. Text modes can be set to several configurations, but 80 characters across and 25 lines on a screen are considered standard. High-resolution monitors are capable of extending this range to 80x43 or 80x50; however, the print gets a little hard to read.

DOS and the DOS compatibility box of Windows offer the text mode screen you are most familiar with. However, a revolution is upon us. With the introduction of Microsoft Windows, the default screen mode is quickly changing from text to graphics.

In graphics mode, each pixel is addressable by the programmer. A pixel represents the finest dot that can be drawn on the screen. This gives you the capability of programming in resolutions from 320x200 to 640x480 pixels on the most common video adapters. Additionally, many color combinations are available. This book emphasizes programming for the EGA and VGA video adapters because they are currently the most common graphics adapters. The VGA mode is exciting because the number of pixels for a given distance is equal in both vertical and horizontal directions. This means you can draw perfect circles without the need to scale x and y coordinates. The VGA mode also offers a maximum resolution of 640x480 in 16 colors or 320x200 in 256 colors. This is quite a departure from the original CGA adapter, which allowed 4 colors on a 320x200-pixel screen. New video modes such as Super-VGA and XGA have recently been introduced and offer even higher screen resolutions. Microsoft C/C++ allows you to take advantage of these new modes.

In developing graphics programs, the first job is to get the computer to switch from the default text mode to a graphics mode. A special function allows you to determine video hardware configurations: **_getvideoconfig()**. The function prototype for **_getvideoconfig()** is

```
struct videoconfig _far *_getvideoconfig(
                        struct videoconfig _far *config);
```

The structure for videoconfig is

```
struct videoconfig {
                short numxpixels;       /*x axis pixels*/
                short numypixels;       /*y axis pixels*/
                short numtextcols;      /*text columns*/
                short numtextrows;      /*text rows*/
                short numcolors;        /*available colors*/
                short bitsperpixel;     /*bits/pixel*/
                short numvideopages;    /*available video
pages*/
                short mode;             /*current video mode*/
                short adapter;          /*active display
adapter*/
                short monitor;          /*active display monitor*/
                short memory;           /*video adapter memory
                                         (k bytes)*/};
```

This graphics function returns the parameters on the graphics environment in the videoconfig structure just shown. Information from this structure should be utilized when an attempt is made to switch to a different video mode.

Once **_getvideoconfig()** has been called, a particular video mode can be requested with the **_setvideomode()** function. Here is the current list of video mode functions:

```
short _setvideomode(short mode);
short _setvideomoderows(short mode,short rows);
short _setactivepage(short page);
short _setvisualpage(short page);
short _getactivepage(void);
short _getvisualpage(void);
```

The following table contains a short description of the mode's resolution and available colors:

Mode	Value	Description
_MAXRESMODE	(−3)	Highest resolution mode
_MAXCOLORMODE	(−2)	Greatest available colors
_DEFAULTMODE	(−1)	Restore original screen mode

Mode	Value	Description
_TEXTBW40	0	Text, 40-column, 16 gray
_TEXTC40	1	Text, 40-column, 16/8 color
_TEXTBW80	2	Text, 80-column text, 16 gray
_TEXTC80	3	Text, 80-column text, 16/8 color
_MRES4COLOR	4	Graphics, 320x200, 4 color
_MRESNOCOLOR	5	Graphics, 320x200, 4 gray
_HRESBW	6	Graphics, 640x200, BW
_TEXTMONO	7	Text, 80-column text, BW
_HERCMONO	8	Graphics, 720x348, BW for HGC
_MRES16COLOR	13	Graphics, 320x200, 16 color
_HRES16COLOR	14	Graphics, 640x200, 16 color
_ERESNOCOLOR	15	Graphics, 640x350, BW
_ERESCOLOR	16	Graphics, 640x350, 4 or 16 color
_VRES2COLOR	17	Graphics, 640x480, BW
_VRES16COLOR	18	Graphics, 640x480, 16 color
_MRES256COLOR	19	Graphics, 320x200, 256 color
_ORESCOLOR	64	Graphics, 640x400, 1 of 16 colors

Do not set the mode values that require VESA SuperVGA BIOS extensions without the proper monitor and video card. There is a real risk of damaging the monitor if it is not suited for the resolution. For safety, MAXRESMODE and MAXCOLORMODE never select the SRES, XRES, or ZRES mode.

_ORES256COLOR	0x0100	Graphics, 640x400, 256 color
_VRES256COLOR	0x0101	Graphics, 640x480, 256 color
_SRES16COLOR	0x0102	Graphics, 800x600, 16 color
_SRES256COLOR	0x0103	Graphics, 800x600, 256 color
_XRES16COLOR	0x0104	Graphics, 1024x768, 16 color
_XRES256COLOR	0x0105	Graphics, 1024x768, 256 color
_ZRES16COLOR	0x0106	Graphics, 1280x1024, 16 color
_ZRES256COLOR	0x0107	Graphics, 1280x1024, 256 color

The following table contains video configuration adapter values:

Adapter	Value	Description
_MDPA	0x0001	Monochrome display adapter (MDPA)
_CGA	0x0002	Color graphics adapter (CGA)
_EGA	0x0004	Enhanced graphics adapter (EGA)
_VGA	0x0008	Video graphics array (VGA)
_MCGA	0x0010	Multicolor graphics array (MCGA)
_HGC	0x0020	Hercules graphics card (HGC)
_OCGA	0x0042	Olivetti color graphics adapter (OCGA)
_OEGA	0x0044	Olivetti enhanced graphics adapter (OEGA)
_OVGA	0x0048	Olivetti video graphics array (OVGA)
_SVGA	0x0088	Super VGA with VESA BIOS support (SVGA)

This table shows video configuration monitor values:

Monitor Type	Value	Description
_MONO	0x0001	Monochrome
_COLOR	0x0002	Color
_ENHCOLOR	0x0004	Enhanced color
_ANALOGMONO	0x0008	Monochrome, analog
_ANALOGCOLOR	0x0010	Color, analog
_ANALOG	0x0018	Monochrome/color, analog

Naturally, your equipment must be capable of the video mode that is requested or an error message will be returned via the **grstatus()** function. The prototype for the **grstatus()** function is shown here:

```
short _grstatus(void);
```

The following table lists the error and warning messages that may most frequently be returned:

Message	Value
_GROK	0
_GRERROR	−1
_GRMODENOTSUPPORTED	−2
_GRNOTINPROPERMODE	−3
_GRINVALIDPARAMETER	−4

_GRFONTFILENOTFOUND	–5
_GRINVALIDFONTFILE	–6
_GRCORRUPTEDFONTFILE	–7
_GRINSUFFICIENTMEMORY	–8
_GRINVALIDIMAGEBUFFER	–9
_GRNOOUTPUT	1
_GRCLIPPED	2
_GRPARAMETERALTERED	3

All video modes are selectable under DOS or the DOS compatibility box under Windows. The function **_setvideomode()** can be called to set the video mode, without an earlier call to **_getvideoconfig()** if you are sure of the programming environment. However, to make programs as portable as possible between hardware configurations, **_getvideoconfig()** is an indispensable tool.

To promote compatibility across a wide range of hardware configurations and to make programming as easy as possible, two special **_setvideomode()** arguments are also available: _MAXRESMODE and _MAXCOLORMODE. _MAXRESMODE will select the highest resolution that the current video adapter supports, while _MAX-COLORMODE will select the mode with the greatest number of colors. The following table shows various combinations of modes for different video adapters:

Adapter	_MAXRESMODE	_MAXCOLORMODE
CGA (color)	_HRESBW	_MRES4COLOR
CGA (BW)	_HRESBW	_MRESNOCOLOR
EGA (256K color)	_HRES16COLOR	_HRES16COLOR
EGA (64K color)	_HRES16COLOR	_HRES16COLOR
EGA (256K ecd)	_ERESCOLOR	_ERESCOLOR
EGA (64K ecd)	_ERESCOLOR	_HRES16COLOR
EGA (BW)	_ERESNOCOLOR	_ERESNOCOLOR
VGA	_VRES16COLOR	_MRES256COLOR

Once the proper video mode has been selected by the application, your program is ready to enter the graphical environment and utilize a wide range of powerful Microsoft graphics functions.

Utilizing Simple Graphics Functions

The first graphics example teaches you how to write a very simple program that draws a white rectangle on a green graphics screen. From there, you learn how to determine the graphics screen resolution or any other information contained in the video configuration structure. Finally, you see how to utilize calls to various graphics drawing primitives and learn to draw lines, rectangles, ellipses, and pie shapes. Interwoven with the graphics drawing primitives are functions that will allow you to control the drawing color and background color.

Various tables in this section list the function prototypes and parameters used with them. These prototypes are listed for your reference and are not explained in detail. (That would require another book of this size.) Additional details of how a particular function operates or how an argument is passed can be found in the help utility available under the Programmer's WorkBench (PWB) or in your Microsoft manuals. It is also recommended that you print a copy of graph.h and pgchart.h. These files are found in your Microsoft C/C++ include directory.

Drawing a Rectangle

The sample program in this section demonstrates how simple graphics programming can be. However, be warned that this program does not check equipment and handles no error messages. In short, this programming style is a "quick and dirty" way of checking the operation of various graphic functions, but it is not a style for finished products.

Examine the program listing and determine where the graphics function calls are made:

```
/*
 *    19RECT.C
 *    A C program that demonstrates how to draw a simple shape
 *    on a CGA screen. This is as easy as it gets.
 *    Copyright (c) William H. Murray and Chris H. Pappas, 1992
 */

#include <conio.h>
#include <graph.h>

main()
{
  _setvideomode(_MRES4COLOR);
  _clearscreen(_GCLEARSCREEN);
  _setbkcolor(_GREEN);

  _rectangle(_GFILLINTERIOR,75,50,245,150);

  getch();
  _setvideomode(_TEXTC80);
```

```
    return (0);
}
```

As you can see, five functions are used to place the rectangle on the screen; actually, only two are necessary. **_setvideomode()** is the first required function. Here, the video mode is set to 320x200 four-color graphics mode—a safe bet for CGA, EGA, and VGA monitors. The **_clearscreen()** and **_setbkcolor()** functions are optional. As you can guess, the first clears the graphics screen, and the second sets the background color to green. The **_setbkcolor()** function prototype is

```
long  _setbkcolor(long color);
long  _getbkcolor(void);
long  _remappalette(short index,long color);
short _remapallpalette(const long _far * colors);
short _selectpalette(short number);
```

Here is a list of the long color values that can be used:

Color	Value
BLACK	0x000000L
BLUE	0x2a0000L
GREEN	0x002a00L
CYAN	0x2a2a00L
RED	0x00002aL
MAGENTA	0x2a002aL
BROWN	0x00152aL
WHITE	0x2a2a2aL
GRAY	0x151515L
LIGHTBLUE	0x3F1515L
LIGHTGREEN	0x153f15L
LIGHTCYAN	0x3f3f15L
LIGHTRED	0x15153fL
LIGHTMAGENTA	0x3f153fL
YELLOW	0x153f3fL
BRIGHTWHITE	0x3f3f3fL

The **_rectangle()** function is the second necessary function in this example. The details of the **_rectangle()** function arguments will be explained later in this section, but the call to the **_rectangle()** function requests that a filled rectangle be drawn with the following screen dimensions: *x1*=75, *y1*=50, *x2*=245, and *y2*=150. These values represent the upper left and lower right coordinates of the rectangle.

Once the rectangle is drawn, the program pauses at the **getch()** function until a key is pressed. Then, **_setvideomode()** is called a second time to return the user to the 80-column color text mode. Without this function call, the program would leave you in graphics mode. It is also possible to simply request the default video mode. In this case, the program returns you to the mode you left before making the switch. Figure 19-1 shows the output for this program.

Determining the Screen's Resolution

The following example serves two main purposes. First, it shows you how to use the **_getvideoconfig()** function to determine the characteristics of the installed video adapter and make a switch (using a **case** statement) to the desired mode. Second, you learn how to retrieve the horizontal and vertical resolution of the mode selected. Examine the listing and see which graphics functions are used:

```
/*
 *    19RESOL.C
 *    A C program that demonstrates how to select the highest
 *    resolution mode on either a CGA, EGA, or VGA screen.
 *    Copyright (c) William H. Murray and Chris H. Pappas, 1992
 */
```

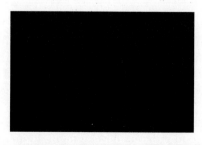

Figure 19-1. The screen for the first graphics program

```
#include <stdio.h>
#include <conio.h>
#include <graph.h>
main()
{
  struct videoconfig vc;

  /* check for CGA, EGA or VGA adapter */
  /* and make switch for highest resolution mode */
  _getvideoconfig(&vc);
  switch(vc.adapter) {
    case _CGA:
      _setvideomode(_HRESBW);
      break;
    case _EGA:
      _setvideomode(_HRES16COLOR);
      break;
    case _VGA:
      _setvideomode(_VRES16COLOR);
      break;
  }

  /* get coordinate values and set window */
    printf("The selected mode has %d horizontal pixels\n",
        vc.numxpixels);
  printf("and %d vertical pixels.\n",vc.numypixels);

  getch();
  _setvideomode(_TEXTC80);
  return (0);
}
```

The case statement values, _CGA, _EGA, and _VGA, are selected from the list shown earlier. Additional case statements can be added for additional video configurations if needed. Note that the variable *vc* is associated with the structure type videoconfig. The horizontal and vertical resolutions are obtained from *vc.numxpixels* and *vc.numypixels*.

This is certainly an easy program to understand, but the information returned is very, very important to good program development. Remember in the first example that a rectangle was drawn on the screen by specifying *exact* coordinate positions. This is not always a good practice when programs are being designed for several video configurations. For example, 640 horizontal pixels are available on CGA, EGA, and VGA monitors. However, the vertical resolutions are 200, 350, and 480. The rectangle from the first example would have different vertical sizes on each of these monitors.

The better graphics technique involves working with ratios of object sizes rather than exact coordinates. If you can obtain the maximum number of pixels—and you can from videoconfig—you can specify coordinate positions with ratios. For example, the following function call will produce the same size rectangle on the CGA, EGA, and VGA screen since *midx* and *midy* are variable values derived from the screen resolutions:

```
_rectangle_w(_GBORDER,-midx/4,-midy/8,+midx/4,+midy/8);
```

The horizontal and vertical screen resolutions are parameters that will be utilized in many future programs. Figure 19-2 shows the screen output for a system equipped with a VGA adapter and color monitor.

Information on the Graphical Environment

It is a simple step from the previous example of obtaining horizontal and vertical screen resolutions to printing all of the information in the videoconfig structure, as the next example shows:

```
/*
 *    19COMODE.C
 *    A C program that demonstrates how to select the highest
 *    color mode on a given adapter.
 *    Copyright (c) William H. Murray and Chris H. Pappas, 1992
```

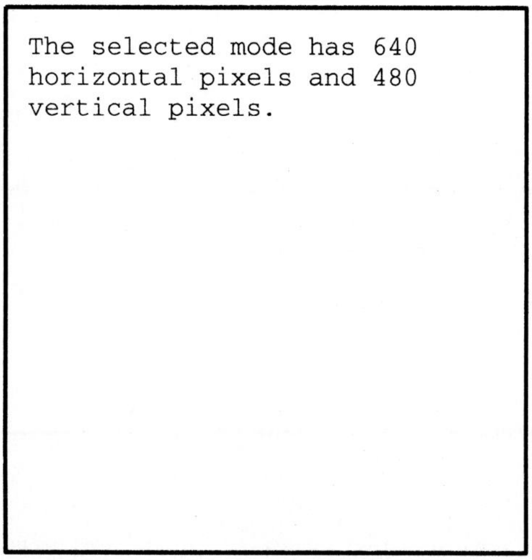

```
The selected mode has 640
horizontal pixels and 480
vertical pixels.
```

Figure 19-2.   *Screen coordinates reported for a VGA screen*

```
*/

#include <stdio.h>
#include <conio.h>
#include <graph.h>

main()
{
  struct videoconfig vc;

  _setvideomode(_MAXCOLORMODE);

  /* printing configuration data */
  _getvideoconfig(&vc);
  printf("Active display adapter: %d\n",vc.adapter);
  printf("Bits per pixel: %d\n",vc.bitsperpixel);
  printf("Adapter video memory: %d\n",vc.memory);
  printf("Video mode: %d\n",vc.mode);
  printf("Display monitor: %d\n",vc.monitor);
  printf("Colors indexes available: %d\n",vc.numcolors);
  printf("Number of text columns: %d\n",vc.numtextcols);
  printf("Number of text rows: %d\n",vc.numtextrows);
  printf("Number of video pages: %d\n",vc.numvideopages);
  printf("Number of horizontal pixels: %d\n",vc.numxpixels);
  printf("Number of vertical pixels: %d\n",vc.numypixels);

  getch();
  _setvideomode(_TEXTC80);
  return (0);
}
```

Note in particular that this program requests _MAXCOLORMODE. For a VGA graphics adapter, the maximum number of color indexes is 256. Why not try this example and see what it reports for your system? Examine Figure 19-3 and see the values returned for a VGA adapter and monitor.

Graphics Details

This section teaches you how to program with a wide variety of graphics functions, including the graphics primitives mentioned earlier in this chapter. *Graphics primitives* are those functions that draw simple shapes like lines, boxes, circles, ellipses, and pie wedges. From these simple shapes, you can create more complicated shapes. For example, you can use rectangles to create bar charts. You can couple together short

```
Active display adapter: 8
Bits per pixel: 8
Adapter video memory: 256
Video mode: 19
Display monitor: 24
Colors indexes available: 256
Number of text columns: 40
Number of text rows: 25
Number of video pages: 1
Number of horizontal pixels: 320
Number of vertical pixels: 200
```

Figure 19-3. *Complete video adapter parameters for a VGA adapter*

line segments to draw smooth curves, such as sine waves. You can section pie wedges together to draw a complete presentation-quality pie chart.

Here is a list of the function prototypes for the Microsoft graphics primitives:

```
void _clearscreen(short area);
struct xycoord _moveto(short x,short y);
struct _wxycoord _moveto_w(double wx,double wy);
struct xycoord _getcurrentposition(void);
struct _wxycoord _getcurrentposition_w(void);
short _lineto(short x,short y);
short _lineto_w(double wx,double wy);
short _rectangle(short control,short x1,short y1,
                 short x2,short y2);
short _rectangle_w(short control,double wx1,double wy1,
                   double wx2,double wy2);
short _rectangle_wxy(short control,
                     struct _wxycoord _far *pwxy1,
                     struct _wxycoord _far *pwxy2);
short _polygon(short control,
               struct xycoord _far *points,
               short numpoints);
short _polygon_w(short control,double_far *points,
```

```
                            short numpoints);
short _polygon_wxy(short control,
                   struct _wxycoord _far *points,
                   short numpoints);
short _arc(short x1,short y1,short x2,short y2,
           short x3,short y3,short x4,short y4);
short _arc_wxy(struct _wxycoord _far *pwxy1,
               struct _wxycoord _far *pwxy2,
               struct _wxycoord _far *pwxy3,
               struct _wxycoord _far *pwxy4);
short _ellipse(short control,short x1,short y1,
               short x2,short y2);
short _ellipse_w(short control,double wx1,double wy1,
                 double wx2,double wy2);
short _ellipse_wxy(short control,
                   struct _wxycoord _far *pwxy1,
                   struct _wxycoord _far *pwxy2);
short _pie(short control,
           short x1,short y1,short x2,short y2,
           short x3,short y3,short x4,short y4);
short _pie_wxy(short control,
               struct _wxycoord _far *pwxy1,
               struct _wxycoord _far *pwxy2,
               struct _wxycoord _far *pwxy3,
               struct _wxycoord _far *pwxy4);
short _getarcinfo(struct xycoord _far *start,
                  struct xycoord _far *end,
                  struct xycoord _far *fillpoint);
short _setpixel(short x,short y);
short _setpixel_w(double wx,double wy);
short _getpixel(short x,short y);
short _getpixel_w(double wx,double wy);
short _floodfill(short x,short y,short boundary);
short _floodfill_w(double wx,double wy,short boundary);
```

The control values for the Microsoft graphics primitives are listed next. The control values for **_ellipse()**, **_rectangle()**, **_pie()**, and **_polygon()** are

_GBORDER	2	outline shape
_GFILLINTERIOR	3	fill shape, use present fill mask

The area values for **_clearscreen()** are

_GCLEARSCREEN	0
_GVIEWPORT	1
_GWINDOW	2

Take a minute to examine the preceding list of function prototypes for the Microsoft graphics primitives and observe the various shapes that come packaged with the graphics library. Many of these functions are discussed in this chapter as they are encountered in programs.

In addition to drawing basic shapes, it is sometimes necessary to change screen coordinates, viewports, and origins. Figures 19-4, 19-5, and 19-6 show three *physical screen coordinate* systems for the high-resolution modes of the CGA, EGA, and VGA adapters. Physical screen coordinates reflect the actual capabilities of a video mode.

The origin for all three modes is in the upper-left corner of the physical display. Sometimes it is beneficial, if not necessary, to change the location of the origin. You cannot change the *physical origin*, but you can change the *viewport origin*. Examine the **_setvieworg()** function prototype shown here:

```
struct xycoord _setvieworg(short x,short y);
struct xycoord _getviewcoord(short x,short y);
struct xycoord _getviewcoord_w( double wx, double wy);
struct xycoord _getviewcoord_wxy(struct _wxycoord _far *pwxy1);
struct xycoord _getphyscoord(short x,short y);
```

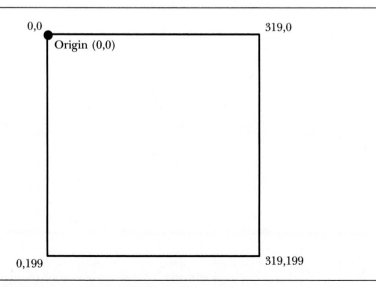

Figure 19-4.   *CGA physical coordinates for the four-color mode*

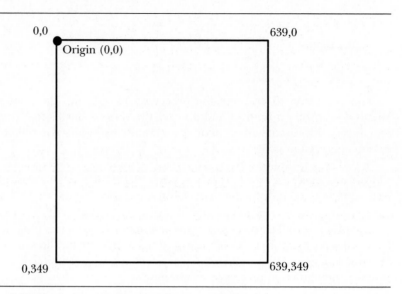

Figure 19-5. *EGA physical coordinates for the high-resolution mode*

```
void _setcliprgn(short x1,short y1,short x2,short y2);
void _setviewport(short x1,short y1,
                  short x2,short y2);
short _setwindow(short finvert,double wx1,double wy1,
                  double wx2,double wy2);
```

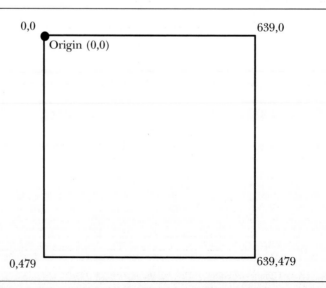

Figure 19-6. *VGA physical coordinates for the high-resolution mode*

When entering a graphics mode, the physical origin and viewport origin are by default in the upper-left corner of the display. The **_setvieworg()** function allows you to change the viewport origin by specifying a displacement in physical origin coordinates. For example, if you wished to place the viewport origin in the center of a VGA screen, you could write

```
_setvieworg(320,240);
```

This would then change the viewport coordinates, as shown in Figure 19-7.

Recall that the physical screen coordinates do not change for a given mode. When entering a graphical mode, a viewport is present, as previously mentioned. The coordinates of the viewport match the coordinates of the physical screen. However, unlike the physical coordinates, the viewport coordinates can be changed. Again, examine the **_setviewport()** function prototype just listed.

The structures for the **_setviewport()** function are

```
struct _xycoord {short xcoord;
                 short ycoord;};
struct _wxycoord {double wx;
                  double wy;};
```

The values passed to this function are physical screen coordinates. With the **_setviewport()** function, it is possible to create a new, and even smaller, viewport within the physical screen coordinates. For example:

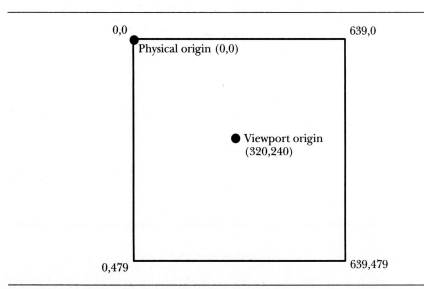

Figure 19-7.   *Setting a new origin on the physical screen*

```
_setviewport(100,100,200,200);
```

This function call produces the viewport (window) shown in Figure 19-8.

This new viewport has an origin located in the upper-left corner of the viewport itself. Clipping occurs at the boundaries of the viewport. The same results could be had with two separate function calls to **_setcliprgn()** and **_setvieworg()**.

You can achieve another alteration to the physical screen coordinates with the **_setwindow()** function. Take a minute to examine the function prototype shown earlier. With this function, the screen coordinates can be scaled to any size within the current viewport. Additionally, the screen coordinate values can be expressed as floating-point numbers. Any of the primitive graphics functions shown previously that end with a _w respond to window coordinates. For example, this function call produces the window coordinate system and graphics figure shown in Figure 19-9:

```
_setwindow(1,0.0,0.0,100.0,200.0);
_rectangle_w(_GBORDER,10,20,30,40);
```

Note the use of the invert flag as the first argument to the **_setwindow()** function. If the value is TRUE (where TRUE is defined as 1 and FALSE as zero), the coordinates will be reversed. If you consider the physical screen coordinates reversed already, then this function with the invert flag set to TRUE will straighten them out.

As you examined the graphics primitives shown earlier, you probably observed that some functions end with _wxy. Others utilized structure references, such as xycoord or wxycoord, as arguments.

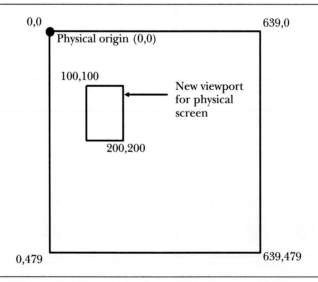

Figure 19-8.   *Setting a new viewport*

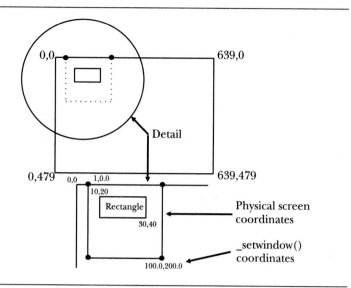

Figure 19-9.   *Using the _setwindow() function*

These structures allow two values to be assigned to a single variable name. Thus, the coordinate values of a point, or pixel, can be referenced with a single variable name. The xycoord structure (using shorts) is for use by viewport coordinate functions, while the _wxycoord structure (using doubles) is used by window coordinate functions. For example, the rectangle function could be called in three ways:

```
          .
          .
          .


struct _wxycoord pt1,pt2;

pt1.wx=30.7;
pt1.wy=51.5;
pt2.wx=150.0;
pt2.wy=200.0;

_rectangle(_GBORDER,10,20,30,40);
_rectangle_w(_GBORDER,35.0,60.25,71.3,120.7);
_rectangle_wxy(_GBORDER,&pt1,&pt2);

          .
          .
          .
```

Several graphics primitives use a *bounding rectangle* for enclosing such figures as an arc, an ellipse, or a pie section. The bounding rectangle, as illustrated in Figure 19-10, specifies a rectangle that encloses a figure. The center of the figure is the center of the bounding rectangle. To draw a portion of a pie (a pie wedge), use additional points to indicate the starting and ending points. In Figure 19-10, these points are (and can be) specified outside the bounding rectangle.

Here are some additional graphics function prototypes:

```
short  _setcolor(short);
short  _getcolor(void);
void   _setlinestyle(unsigned short mask);
unsigned short _getlinestyle(void);
short  _setwritemode(short action);
short  _getwritemode(void);
void   _setfillmask(const unsigned char _far *mask);
unsigned char _far * _getfillmask(unsigned char _far *mask);
```

The action arguments for **_setwritemode()** are listed here:

• _GAND transfers the image over an existing image on the screen. The result is the logical AND of the two images. Points that had the same color in the

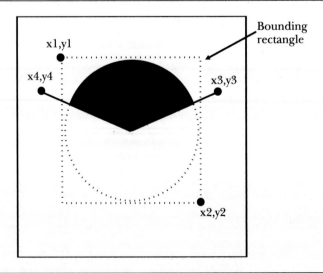

Figure 19-10.   *A bounding rectangle used to describe a graphics primitive*

existing image and the new one will remain the same; only points having different colors are logically ANDed.

- _GOR transfers the image over an existing image. The transferred image does not erase the previous screen contents. All points are logically ORed together.

- _GPRESET moves data point by point to the screen. Here, each point has the inverse of the color attribute it previously had when retrieved by the **_getimage()** function. This action produces a negative of the image.

- _GPSET moves the data point by point to the screen. Here, each point has the same color attribute it had when previously retrieved by the **_getimage()** function.

- _GXOR causes any point on the screen to be inverted where that point exists in the image buffer. This is a useful parameter because when an image is drawn against a background twice, the background is restored without being changed. This allows an object to be moved about without erasing the background.

Functions starting with **_set** have the ability to change the parameter involved, while functions starting with **_get** return the current parameter value. For example, the **_setcolor()** function allows the user to select a drawing color from the current palette by specifying a short value. The value passed to this function is a short and cannot be chosen from the long color values shown earlier.

The **_setlinestyle()** function accepts a mask used for line drawing. The mask is a 16–bit array, with each bit representing a pixel on the line being drawn. When a bit is 1, the corresponding pixel is set to the color of the line. When a bit is zero, the corresponding pixel is not changed. This pattern is repeated for the whole length of the line. The default mask is a solid line created with a 0xFFFF mask.

The **_setfillmask()** function sets the current fill mask, which determines the fill pattern. This mask is created by an 8x8 array of bits, where each bit represents a pixel. A 1 sets the corresponding pixel to the current color, while a zero does not change the pixel. The pattern is repeated for the whole fill area. If no mask is specified, the mask is null, and only the color is used for the area fill operation.

The **_setwritemode()** function sets the logical write mode, used when drawing lines with **_lineto()** and **_rectangle** functions. The argument, _GAND, _GOR, _GPRESET, _GPSET, or _GXOR, defines the mode.

Working with Graphics Primitives

This section uses many of the graphics primitives just discussed. Examine the following listing and see if you can anticipate what graphics results will be produced on the screen:

```
//
//  19PRIMIT.CPP
//  A C++ program that demonstrates how to draw a number of
//  primitive graphics shapes on the screen.
//  Copyright (c) William H. Murray and Chris H. Pappas, 1992
//

#include <graph.h>
#include <conio.h>

main()
{
  double midx,midy;
  struct videoconfig vc;

  // check adapter and make switch
  _getvideoconfig(&vc);
  switch(vc.adapter) {
    case _EGA:
      _setvideomode(_HRES16COLOR);
      break;
    case _VGA:
      _setvideomode(_VRES16COLOR);
      break;
  }

  // get coordinate values and set viewport origin
  _getvideoconfig(&vc);
  midx=vc.numxpixels/2;
  midy=vc.numypixels/2;
  _setvieworg(midx,midy);

  _setbkcolor(_WHITE);

  _setcolor(2);
  _rectangle_w(_GBORDER,-midx/4,-midy/8,+midx/4,+midy/8);
  _outtext("An outlined rectangle");

  getch();
  _clearscreen(_GWINDOW);

  _setcolor(3);
  _rectangle_w(_GFILLINTERIOR,-midx/4,-midy/4,+midx/4,+midy/4);
  _outtext("A filled rectangle");
```

```
    getch();
    _clearscreen(_GWINDOW);

    _setcolor(4);
    _ellipse_w(_GBORDER,-midx/4,-midy/4,+midx/4,+midy/4);
    _outtext("An outlined ellipse");

    getch();
    _clearscreen(_GWINDOW);

    _setcolor(5);
    _ellipse_w(_GFILLINTERIOR,-midx/8,-midy/4,+midx/8,+midy/4);
    _outtext("A filled ellipse");

    getch();
    _clearscreen(_GWINDOW);

    _setcolor(6);
    _moveto_w(-midx/4,-midy/4);
    _lineto_w(+midx/4,+midy/4);
    _outtext("A diagonal line");

    getch();
    _clearscreen(_GWINDOW);

    _setcolor(9);
    _pie_w(_GBORDER,-midx/4,-midy/4,+midx/4,+midy/4,
           -midx/8,-midy/8,+midx/8,+midy/8);
    _outtext("An outlined pie wedge");

    getch();
    _clearscreen(_GWINDOW);

    _setcolor(10);
    _pie_w(_GFILLINTERIOR,-midx/4,-midy/4,+midx/4,+midy/4,
           -midx/32,-midy/8,+midx/32,+midy/8);
    _outtext("A filled pie wedge");

    getch();
    _setvideomode(_TEXTC80);
    return (0);
}
```

This program draws several outlined and filled primitive shapes to the center of the physical screen. The shapes are drawn over (on top of) each other. You can select subsequent shapes during execution simply by pressing any key on the keyboard.

The following is an interesting portion of program code that should be examined:

```
// get coordinate values and set viewport origin
_getvideoconfig(&vc);
midx=vc.numxpixels/2;
midy=vc.numypixels/2;
_setvieworg(vc.numxpixels/2,vc.numypixels/2);

_setbkcolor(_WHITE);
```

Recall the discussion from the previous section regarding coordinate values. If the program is to be as portable as possible among many video adapter types, you should not use specific screen coordinate values, but rather screen ratios. This is one such example. The variables *midx* and *midy* are doubles that will be used by the graphics drawing primitives. Both values represent one-half of the screen width and height for any given adapter.

 This program was written for EGA and VGA adapters only.

Next, the **_setvieworg()** function changes the viewport origin to the center of the physical screen. This means that the center of the screen will have the coordinates 0,0.

Finally, the **_setbkcolor()** function sets the viewport background color to _WHITE.

The first shape is the outline of a rectangle. The rectangle is drawn with window coordinates by calling **_rectangle_w()**:

```
_setcolor(2);
_rectangle_w(_GBORDER,-midx/4,-midy/8,+midx/4,+midy/8);
_outtext("An outlined rectangle");

getch();
_clearscreen(_GWINDOW);
```

The upper-left corner of the rectangle is given by −*midx*/4 and −*midy*/8. The lower-right corner is given by +*midx*/4 and +*midy*/8.

If a VGA adapter is used in high-resolution mode, *midx* will be equal to 640/2, or 320. The value for *midy* will be 480/2, or 240. However, if an EGA adapter is used, the *midy* variable will take on the value 350/2, or 175. Regardless of the adapter, the rectangle will be drawn the same size on the screen. Also note that this figure is centered on the screen. The center has the coordinates 0,0; thus, the upper-left corner of the rectangle uses negative coordinate values.

The **_clearscreen()** function uses the argument _GWINDOW to clear the window between images. This function can also accept a _GCLEARSCREEN argument to clear the whole physical screen or _GVIEWPORT to clear a specified viewport.

The **_outtext()** function prints the string at the current cursor position. Its prototype is shown here:

```
short _settextrows(short rows);
void _settextwindow(short r1,short c1,
                    short r2,short c2);
void _gettextwindow(short _far *r1,short _far *c1,
                    short _far *r2,short _far *c2);
void _scrolltextwindow(short lines);
void _outmem(const unsigned char _far *text,
             short length);
void _outtext(const unsigned char _far *text);
short _wrapon(short option);
short _displaycursor(short toggle);
short _settextcursor(short attr);
short _gettextcursor(void);
struct rccoord _settextposition(short row,short column);
struct rccoord _gettextposition(void);
short _settextcolor(short index);
short _gettextcolor(void);
```

The toggle values for the **_outtext()** function are

_GCURSOROFF	0
_GCURSORON	1

The option values for the **_outtext()** function are

_GWRAPOFF	0
_GWRAPON	1

The line values for the **_outtext()** function are

_GSCROLLUP	1
_GSCROLLDOWN	–1

The row value for the **_outtext()** function is

_MAXTEXTROWS   −1

The prototype for text position is

```
struct rccoord {
                short row;
                short col;
};
```

An ellipse can also be drawn and filled. The parameters that are passed are similar to those given for a rectangle:

```
_setcolor(5);
_ellipse_w(_GFILLINTERIOR,-midx/8,-midy/4,+midx/8,+midy/4);
_outtext("A filled ellipse");

getch();
_clearscreen(_GWINDOW);
```

In terms of window coordinates, specifying the values for a pie slice is a little more involved. If a VGA adapter is used, the bounding rectangle for the ellipse from which the pie slice is selected is −320/4, −240/4, +320/4, and +240/4. This translates to an upper-left window coordinate point given by −80,−60 and a lower-right point given by +80,+60. Again, the center of the screen has the coordinates 0,0. Here is the code required to draw a small pie wedge:

```
_setcolor(9);
_pie_w(_GBORDER,-midx/4,-midy/4,+midx/4,+midy/4,
       -midx/8,-midy/8,+midx/8,+midy/8);
_outtext("An outlined pie wedge");

getch();
_clearscreen(_GWINDOW);
```

The starting point for the pie slice is a line that runs from the center of the ellipse to a point −320/8,−240/8 or −40,−30. The end point is found in a similar manner and runs from the center of the ellipse to a point with coordinate values 40,30.

All other primitive graphics shapes are self explanatory. Figures 19-11, 19-12, and 19-13 show several sample screen displays from this program.

Figure 19-11.   An outlined rectangle with the origin set to the center of the screen

Using Fonts in Graphics Mode

The graphics library provides a means of writing text to the screen in graphics mode with several functions and graphics fonts. The important function prototypes are shown here:

```
short _registerfonts(unsigned char _far *pathname);
void  _unregisterfonts(void);
short _setfont(unsigned char _far *options);
short _getfontinfo(struct _fontinfo _far *fontbuffer);
void _outgtext(unsigned char _far *text);
short _getgtextextent(unsigned char _far *text);
struct xycoord _setgtextvector(short x,short y);
struct xycoord _getgtextvector(void);
```

Here is the structure used in the next two example programs:

```
Used by _getfontinfo():
 struct _fontinfo {
                 int type;        /*set=vector,clear=bit map*/
                 int ascent;      /*top to baseline pixel dist*/
                 int pixwidth;    /*character width (pixels)*/
                 int pixheight;   /*character height (pixels)*/
```

Figure 19-12.   *An outlined ellipse with the origin set to the center of the screen*

```
        int avgwidth;    /*avg char width (pixels)*/
        char filename[81]; /*font file name with path*/
        char facename[32]; /*font face name*/
};
```

Figure 19-13.   *A filled pie wedge*

Additional details on these functions can be obtained from the on-line help facility provided with your C/C++ compiler.

Six of the most popular typefaces supplied with Microsoft C/C++ are Courier, Helvetica, Times Roman, Modern, Script, and Roman. Courier, Helvetica, and Times Roman are bitmapped fonts. Bitmapped fonts are supplied in a number of type sizes. They cannot be scaled to sizes beyond those supplied. Table 19-1 gives additional information on the various fonts and the typeface sizes.

Modern, Script, and Roman typefaces are vector-mapped fonts and can be scaled to any desirable size. Each of these typefaces is contained in its own file, ending with an .FON extension. Starting with Windows 3.1, TrueType fonts are supplied with the Windows product. You might also want to experiment with these.

A *font* is a complete set of characters of the same typeface and size. Fonts include letters, punctuation marks, and additional symbols. The size of a font is usually measured in points. For example, 12-point Times Roman is a different font from 12-point Times Roman Italic, 14-point Times Roman, or 12-point Helvetica. A *point*

Typeface	Spacing	Sizes	Type
Courier	Fixed	10x8	Bitmapped
		12x9	
		15x12	
Helvetica	Proportional	10x5	Bitmapped
		12x7	
		15x8	
		18x9	
		22x12	
		28x16	
Times Roman	Proportional	10x5	Bitmapped
		12x6	
		15x8	
		16x9	
		20x12	
		26x16	
Modern	Proportional	Any size	Vector-mapped
Script	Proportional	Any size	Vector-mapped
Roman	Proportional	Any size	Vector-mapped

Table 19-1. *Font Typeface, Spacing, Size, and Type*

is the smallest unit of measure used in typography. There are 12 points in a pica and 72 points in an inch. The next section examines font characteristics.

Basic Font Attributes

All fonts are made up of a basic set of characteristics. Table 19-2 describes the basic elements that make up a character in a font. The relationship of these terms to a font character is shown in Figure 19-14.

Each font character is more complex than just the symbol drawn on the screen or output device. The symbol itself is placed within a rectangular region called a *character cell*. Each cell consists of a predefined number of rows and columns and is described by the six measurement points, given in Table 19-2: ascent, baseline, descent, height, origin, and width. While some of these terms are obvious in meaning, others are specific to the field of typography.

A *typeface* is a basic character design that is defined by a stroke width and a serif (a smaller line used to finish off a main stroke of a letter, as at the top and bottom of the uppercase letter "M" in certain fonts). As already mentioned, a font represents a complete set of characters from one specific typeface, all with a certain size and style, such as italics or bold. Usually, the system owns all of the font resources and shares them with the application program. Fonts are not usually compiled into the final executable version of a program and therefore the font files (.FON) must be present on the system. Also, a path to their location is needed.

Fonts that display all characters using the same width are called *fixed fonts*. Fixed fonts make for easier alignment because ten i's, for example, occupy the same space as ten uppercase W's. The Courier font is an example of a fixed font.

Attribute	Description
Ascent	Defines the distance in character-cell rows from the character-cell baseline to the top of the character cell
Baseline	Identifies the base on which all of the characters stand. Lowercase letters like "p" and "a" have descenders that descend below the baseline
Descent	Defines the distance in character-cell rows from the character-cell baseline to the bottom of the character cell
Height	Identifies the height of a character-cell row
Origin	The upper-left corner of the character cell, used as a point of reference as a character is output to a particular device or display
Width	Identifies the width of a character-cell column

Table 19-2.   *Font Attributes*

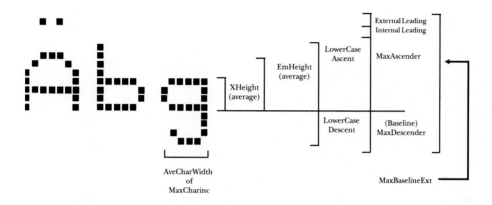

Figure 19-14. *Using various fields to define a font*

Proportional fonts, on the other hand, allocate differing amounts of line spacing to different characters, in much the same way as you would script them. With a proportionally spaced font, ten i's would not occupy the same line space as ten uppercase W's. All the remaining fonts included with Microsoft C/C++ are proportional fonts. Many individuals feel that proportional fonts are easier to read than fixed fonts. Microsoft Windows (starting with version 3.0) uses proportional fonts.

Displaying Different Fonts in Different Sizes

The next example shows you how to register and select a font. This application also illustrates the shape and characteristics of all six font types on the screen. Examine the following program:

```
/*
*    19FONT1.C
*    A C program that demonstrates how to print a string in a
*    variety of fonts & font sizes on a VGA screen.
*    Copyright (c) William H. Murray and Chris H. Pappas, 1992
*/

#include <stdlib.h>
#include <string.h>
#include <conio.h>
```

```c
#include <graph.h>

#define NOINVERT 0

main()
{
  static char stringtitle[16]="Graphics is fun";
  char fontname[20];
  int  a,b;
  struct videoconfig vc;

  /* fixed for VGA screen only */
  _setvideomode(_VRES16COLOR);

  /* get coordinate values */
  _getvideoconfig(&vc);
  _setwindow(NOINVERT,0,0,vc.numxpixels,vc.numypixels);

  _clearscreen(_GCLEARSCREEN);
  _setbkcolor(_GREEN);

  _registerfonts("courb.fon");
  strcpy(fontname,"t'courier'");
  strcat(fontname,"h10w5b");
  _setfont(fontname);
  a=10;
  b=15;
  _moveto(a,b);
  _outgtext(stringtitle);

  _registerfonts("helvb.fon");
  strcpy(fontname,"t'helv'");
  strcat(fontname,"h20w10b");
  _setfont(fontname);
  a=10;
  b+=30;
  _moveto(a,b);
  _outgtext(stringtitle);

  _registerfonts("tmsrb.fon");
  strcpy(fontname,"t'tms rmn'");
  strcat(fontname,"h30w15b");
  _setfont(fontname);
  a=10;
  b+=45;
```

```
_moveto(a,b);
_outgtext(stringtitle);

_registerfonts("modern.fon");
strcpy(fontname,"t'modern'");
strcat(fontname,"h40w20b");
_setfont(fontname);
a=10;
b+=60;
_moveto(a,b);
_outgtext(stringtitle);

_registerfonts("script.fon");
strcpy(fontname,"t'script'");
strcat(fontname,"h50w25b");
_setfont(fontname);
a=10;
b+=75;
_moveto(a,b);
_outgtext(stringtitle);

_registerfonts("roman.fon");
strcpy(fontname,"t'roman'");
strcat(fontname,"h60w30b");
_setfont(fontname);
a=10;
b+=90;
_moveto(a,b);
_outgtext(stringtitle);

getch();
_setvideomode(_TEXTC80);
return (0);
}
```

In this example, designed for the VGA screen, there are eight lines of program code repeated six times for each typeface used. Here is one such block used to print a fixed font:

```
_registerfonts("courb.fon");
strcpy(fontname,"t'courier'");
strcat(fontname,"h10w5b");
_setfont(fontname);
a=10;
```

```
b=15;
_moveto(a,b);
_outgtext(stringtitle);
```

The **_registerfonts()** function is used to register the Courier font. The name used must be the actual filename containing the font. Path information should also be used here if the file resides in a subdirectory. This example assumes that the font file resides in the current directory. When this function is called, header information on the specific file is read and a list of file information is collected.

In order to select a font from the registered font file, the **_setfont()** function must be called. Information passed to this function is in the form of a string containing several parameters, as shown in Table 19-3.

Since the Courier font is a bitmapped font and is available only in fixed font sizes (see Table 19-1), the request for a font height of 10 and a font width of 5 will go unheeded. Instead, the font size closest to that requested will be selected. In this case, a 10x8 bitmapped font will be used.

Next, a **_moveto()** function call places the cursor at the desired position on the graphics screen. Finally, the **_outgstring()** function prints the desired text, in the size nearest the specified font, to the screen.

While the request for a Script font looks very similar to the request for a Courier font, the overall action is quite different. Remember, the Courier font is a bitmapped font, while the Script font is vector mapped. Here is how a script vector font can be used in your program.

Option	Description
f	Fixed-space font
p	Proportionally spaced font
hy	Font height in pixels
wx	Font width in pixels
r	Bitmapped font
v	Vector-mapped font
nx	Registered font number (first registered font is 1, then 2, and so on). Select the best fit (the font closest to what you request)
t'name'	Typeface name: courier helv tms rmn modern script roman

Table 19-3. *_setfont() String Options*

```
_registerfonts("script.fon");
strcpy(fontname,"t'script'");
strcat(fontname,"h50w25b");
_setfont(fontname);
a=10;
b+=75;
_moveto(a,b);
_outgtext(stringtitle);
```

In the case of a vector-mapped font, such as the script font, the font can be sized to any desired pixel height. Here, the request for a font 50 pixels high and 25 pixels wide will be met exactly. Before you get too excited about vector-mapped fonts, though, remember this: the larger they are scaled, the larger the font blemishes become.

Figure 19-15 shows the screen containing each of the six fonts in the previous program.

Rotating Fonts

The next application is a simple adaptation of the previous program. Fonts can be rotated. This is particularly important where charts and graphs require vertical and horizontal axis labels.

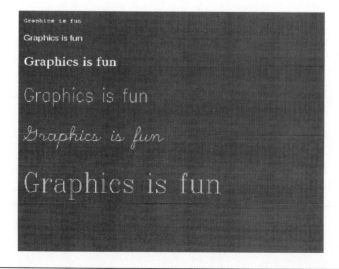

Figure 19-15.   *Six basic fonts shown in different sizes*

This program prints the same text string at a variety of angles:

```
/*
 *   19FONT2.C
 *   A C program that demonstrates how to print a string at a
 *   variety of angles on an EGA or VGA screen.
 *   Copyright (c) William H. Murray and Chris H. Pappas, 1992
 */

#include <stdlib.h>
#include <string.h>
#include <conio.h>
#include <graph.h>

#define INVERT 1
#define YELLOW 14

main()
{
  static char stringtitle[24]="  A picture is worth...";
  char fontname[20];
  int  a,b,midx,midy;
  struct videoconfig vc;

  /* check adapter and make switch */
  _getvideoconfig(&vc);
  switch(vc.adapter) {
    case _EGA:
      _setvideomode(_HRES16COLOR);
      break;
    case _VGA:
      _setvideomode(_VRES16COLOR);
      break;
  }

  /* get coordinate values */
  _getvideoconfig(&vc);
  midx=vc.numxpixels/2;
  midy=vc.numypixels/2;

  _setwindow(INVERT,-vc.numxpixels/2,-vc.numypixels/2,
            vc.numxpixels/2,vc.numypixels/2);

  _setbkcolor(_BLUE);
```

```
      _setcolor(YELLOW);
      _registerfonts("modern.fon");
      strcpy(fontname,"t'modern'");
      strcat(fontname,"h15w10b");
      _setfont(fontname);

      _moveto(midx,midy);
      _setgtextvector(1,0);          /* 0 degrees */
      _outgtext(stringtitle);
      _moveto(midx,midy);
      _setgtextvector(1,1);          /* 45 degrees */
      _outgtext(stringtitle);
      _moveto(midx,midy);
      _setgtextvector(0,1);          /* 90 degrees */
      _outgtext(stringtitle);
      _moveto(midx,midy);
      _setgtextvector(-1,1);         /* 135 degrees */
      _outgtext(stringtitle);
      _moveto(midx,midy);
      _setgtextvector(-1,0);         /* 180 degrees */
      _outgtext(stringtitle);
      _moveto(midx,midy);
      _setgtextvector(-1,-1);        /* 225 degrees */
      _outgtext(stringtitle);
      _moveto(midx,midy);
      _setgtextvector(0,-1);         /* 270 degrees */
      _outgtext(stringtitle);
      _moveto(midx,midy);
      _setgtextvector(1,-1);         /* 315 degrees */
      _outgtext(stringtitle);

      getch();
      _setvideomode(_TEXTC80);
      return (0);
}
```

Figure 19-16 shows the window selected with the **_setwindow()** function call.

The strings will be rotated about the center of the screen. The coordinates for the center of the screen have been set to 0,0. A Modern font is requested with a pixel height of 15 and a width of 10.

Font angles are set with a call to the **_setgtextvector()** function. The function accepts two short arguments. Figure 19-17 shows how these values are used to represent the sides of a right triangle (*x,y*) for specifying the angle.

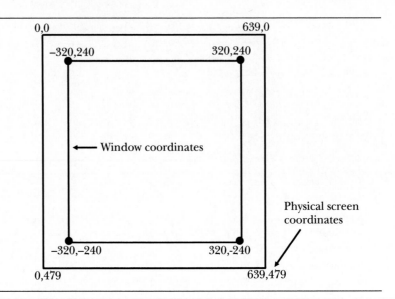

Figure 19-16. *Changing the screen coordinates*

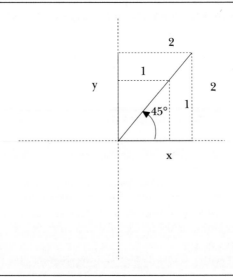

Figure 19-17. *Using a triangle to determine font angles*

The following table shows some additional combinations for selecting angles for the **_setgtextvector()** function (with 0,0 at the center of the window):

short x	short y	angle (degrees)
1	0	0
1	1	45
0	1	90
−1	1	135
−1	0	180
−1	−1	225
0	−1	270
1	−1	315

Here is an example:

$$\tan A = y/x$$
$$= 3/4$$
$$= .75, \text{ then}$$

$$A = 36.87 \text{ degrees}$$

You can determine other values with this equation.

Figure 19-18 shows the screen output and the pinwheel effect generated by the rotated string. What can you observe from this figure with regard to font sizes?

Figure 19-18. *Rotating fonts with the _settestvector() function*

Scientific and Business Applications with Graphics Primitives

Graphics are a way of communicating ideas and concepts in a pictorial format. Depending on your area of interest, you may want to express information in the form of bar, pie, or line chart. If you have an engineering, scientific, or mathematical background, you may be more interested in plotting a mathematical equation. The first two examples in this section do just that. The first example plots a simple sine wave. To do this, the program uses the trigonometric sine function multiplied by a constant. The second example shows you how to build a triangular waveform by adding terms in a Fourier series. This is a mathematically intense application and can be used as a benchmark program when testing a computer's speed and graphics capabilities. The third program allows you to create a presentation-quality pie chart. This program allows you to enter data on the various pie slices, automatically scale them to size, and plot them correctly on an EGA or a VGA screen.

Drawing a Sine Wave

This program uses the **sin()** function, which is prototyped in the math.h header file. As you study the listing, you will also notice that the program is embellished with labels and special coloring. This program uses many of the features that have already been discussed concerning graphics programming.

```
/*
 *    19SINE.C
 *    A C program that demonstrates how to draw a
 *    sine wave on an EGA or VGA screen.
 *    Copyright (c) William H. Murray and Chris H. Pappas, 1992
 */

#include <stdlib.h>
#include <conio.h>
#include <string.h>
#include <math.h>
#include <graph.h>

#define AMPLITUDE 150.0
#define ANG_TO_RAD 1.745329252E-2
#define XOFFSET 100
#define WHITE 15

main()
{
```

```
static char labeltitle[12]="A Sine Wave";
static char labelx[21]="The X axis (degrees)";
static char labely[23]="The Y axis (amplitude)";
char fontname[20];
int i,a,b;
double midx,midy,x,y;
struct videoconfig vc;

/* check adapter and make switch */
_getvideoconfig(&vc);
switch(vc.adapter) {
  case _EGA:
    _setvideomode(_HRES16COLOR);
    break;
  case _VGA:
    _setvideomode(_VRES16COLOR);
    break;
}

/* get coordinate values and set window */
_getvideoconfig(&vc);
midx=vc.numxpixels/2;
midy=vc.numypixels/2;
_setvieworg(XOFFSET,vc.numypixels/2);

_clearscreen(_GCLEARSCREEN);
_setbkcolor(_RED);
_setcolor(WHITE);

/* draw horizontal axis */
_moveto_w(0,0);
_lineto_w(vc.numxpixels,0);

/* draw vertical axis */
_moveto_w(0,-midy*7/8);
_lineto_w(0,+midy*7/8);
_moveto_w(0,0);

x=0.0;
for(i=0;i<vc.numxpixels;i++) {
  y=AMPLITUDE*sin(ANG_TO_RAD*0.6679*i);
  _lineto_w(x,-y);
  x++;
}
```

```
_floodfill_w(midx/2,-30,WHITE);
_floodfill_w(midx*4/3,+30,WHITE);

/* register a font for chart use */
if(_registerfonts("roman.fon")<0)
{
  _outtext("Error: cannot register this font\n");
  exit(0);
}

/* scale font for graph name */
strcpy(fontname,"t'roman'");
strcat(fontname,"h40w30pb");
_setfont(fontname);

/* print graph title label */
a=midx-XOFFSET/2-(_getgtextextent(labeltitle)/2);
b=midy*15/16;
_moveto_w(a,-b);
_outgtext(labeltitle);

/* scale font for title labels */
strcpy(fontname,"t'roman'");
strcat(fontname,"h25w20pb");
_setfont(fontname);

/* print X axis label */
a=midx-XOFFSET/2-(_getgtextextent(labelx)/2);
b=midy*7/8;
_moveto_w(a,b);
_outgtext(labelx);

/* print Y axis label */
a=XOFFSET*3/8;
b=(_getgtextextent(labely)/2);
_moveto_w(-a,b);
_setgtextvector(0,1);
_outgtext(labely);

getch();
_setvideomode(_TEXTC80);
return (0);
}
```

Figure 19-19 shows the window and the viewport origin for this figure. This is set by calling the **_setvieworg()** function:

```
_setvieworg(XOFFSET,vc.numypixels/2);
```

Next, the screen is cleared, and the background color set to RED and the drawing color to WHITE. Note that WHITE was defined earlier in the program listing.

```
_clearscreen(_GCLEARSCREEN);
_setbkcolor(_RED);
_setcolor(WHITE);
```

The next several lines of code are responsible for drawing the *x* and *y* coordinate axes for the graph. These are done in window coordinates for the viewport origin set earlier. Study this code and make sure you understand how these values were derived:

```
/* draw horizontal axis */
_moveto_w(0,0);
_lineto_w(vc.numxpixels,0);

/* draw vertical axis */
_moveto_w(0,-midy*7/8);
_lineto_w(0,+midy*7/8);
_moveto_w(0,0);
```

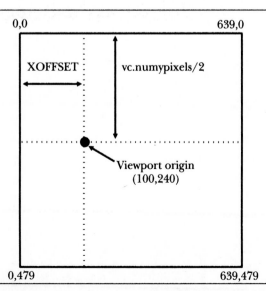

Figure 19-19. *Setting a new origin for the sine wave program*

The mathematical equation is scaled to fit the current screen. AMPLITUDE sets the vertical extent to 150 pixels above and below the x axis. Since an offset of 100 pixels was used when setting the origin for the plot, there are 639-100=539 pixels left to plot 360 degrees in. That's a ratio of 360/539, or 0.6679.

```
x=0.0;
for(i=0;i<vc.numxpixels;i++) {
  y=AMPLITUDE*sin(ANG_TO_RAD*0.6679*i);
  _lineto_w(x,-y);
  x++;
}
```

Notice that the **_lineto()** function is used to draw a line between successive points on the plot. Also notice that the *y* value is inverted. This is because the screen coordinates still go from *y*=0 at the top of the screen to *y*=*vc.numypixels* at the bottom.

Next, a new function named **_floodfill_w()** is used to fill the sine wave with the current drawing color:

```
_floodfill_w(midx/2,-30,WHITE);
_floodfill_w(midx*4/3,+30,WHITE);
```

This function fills an area bound with the specified color (white). The coordinate points passed to this function must be in the area to be bound. For this example, both areas to be shaded are bound by the mathematical curve and the x axis. If the x axis had not been drawn, **_floodfill_w()** would have filled the whole screen with color.

This program prints a main heading and the x and y axis labels using a Roman font. The font is registered in the usual manner:

```
/* register a font for use chart use */
if(_registerfonts("roman.fon")<0)
{
  _outtext("Error: cannot register this font\n");
  exit(0);
}
```

The labels are scaled to different font heights and centered. You can accomplish centering with a call to the **_getgtextextent()** function. The following is a portion of code that correctly centers the main graph title:

```
/* print graph title label */
a=midx-XOFFSET/2-(_getgtextextent(labeltitle)/2);
b=midy*15/16;
```

```
_moveto_w(a,-b);
_outgtext(labeltitle);
```

The x axis label is scaled, centered, and printed in a similar manner. The y axis is handled a little differently. Since the y axis is a vertical axis, the label must be printed vertically. This is not a major problem, as you know from previous work, since you can use the **_setgtextvector()** function. Here is a portion of code used to print this label:

```
/* print Y axis label */
a=XOFFSET*3/8;
b=(_getgtextextent(labely)/2);
_moveto_w(-a,b);
_setgtextvector(0,1);
_outgtext(labely);
```

Figure 19-20 shows the screen output from this program.

A Fourier Series

The following example is similar to the previous sine wave example, but with a new twist. First, here is a little information on a Fourier series.

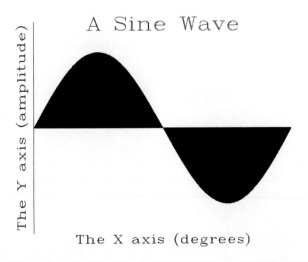

Figure 19-20.   *Drawing a sine wave with labels*

A mathematician named Fourier (1768-1830) observed that almost any periodic waveform can be constructed by simply adding the correct combinations of sinewave harmonics together. (A more detailed treatment of this subject can be found in college-level physics or electrical engineering text books.) Fourier's formal equation can be expressed as

$$y = A + A1(SIN\ wt) + A2(SIN\ 2wt) + A3(SIN\ 3wt) + A4(SIN\ 4wt)...$$

To generate some waveforms, only odd or even harmonics are included, while for others, all terms in the series are included. For some waveforms, the signs alternate + or − between adjacent terms of the series. This example constructs a triangular-type wave by adding together all the harmonic terms in a Fourier series. The more terms used in the series, the more the final result will approach a precise triangular-type wave. For this waveform, the general Fourier series equation becomes this exact equation:

$$y = (SIN\ wt) + (1/2)(SIN\ 2wt) + (1/3)(SIN\ 3wt) + (1/4)(SIN\ 4wt)$$

Thus, all harmonics will contribute to the final result. Notice from the equation that if only one harmonic is plotted, the results will be a sine wave. Also notice that each successive term uses a fractional multiplier; in other words, each successively higher harmonic affects the final waveform less and less.

To fully appreciate what this program accomplishes, remember that each term in a Fourier series will be calculated separately by the program, with the sum of these individual terms being continuously updated. Therefore, if you ask for 500 harmonics, 500 separate sine values will be scaled, calculated, and added together to form a single point on the screen. But this must be repeated for each point that is to be plotted on the screen. Therefore, 500 calculations × 360 points = 180,000 calculations. How long would it take you to do that with a calculator? It took this author 5 minutes to do 50 terms on a calculator, so for 500 terms that would be 50 minutes. Fifty minutes × 360 points = 18,000 minutes, or 12.5 (nonstop) days. (Fourier didn't even have a calculator!) Study this listing and see the additional programming features this program has that weren't contained in the previous example:

```
/*
 *    19FOUR.C
 *    A C program that demonstrates how to draw a mathematically
 *    intense Fourier series on an EGA or VGA screen.
 *    Copyright (c) William H. Murray and Chris H. Pappas, 1992
 */

#include <stdio.h>
#include <stdlib.h>
#include <conio.h>
```

```
#include <string.h>
#include <math.h>
#include <graph.h>

#define AMPLITUDE 125.0
#define ANG_TO_RAD 1.745329252E-2
#define XOFFSET 100

main()
{
  static char labeltitle[26]="A Fourier Series Waveform";
  static char labelx[16]="angle (radians)";
  static char labely[10]="Amplitude";
  char fourier[10],fontname[20];
  int terms,i,j;
  double a,b,midx,midy,x,y;
  struct videoconfig vc;

  printf("THIS PROGRAM WILL DRAW A FOURIER SERIES
          WAVEFORM.\n\n");
  printf("Enter the number of harmonics to compute
          (1-9999):\n");
  gets(fourier);
  terms=atoi(fourier);

  /* check adapter and make switch */
  _getvideoconfig(&vc);
  switch(vc.adapter) {
    case _EGA:
      _setvideomode(_HRES16COLOR);
      break;
    case _VGA:
      _setvideomode(_VRES16COLOR);
      break;
  }

  /* get coordinate values and set window */
  _getvideoconfig(&vc);
  midx=vc.numxpixels/2;
  midy=vc.numypixels/2;
  _setvieworg(XOFFSET,vc.numypixels/2);

  _clearscreen(_GCLEARSCREEN);
  _setbkcolor(_BLUE);
```

```
_moveto_w(0,0);
x=0.0;
for(i=0;i<vc.numxpixels;i++) {
  for(j=1;j<terms+1;j++) {
    y+=(AMPLITUDE/j)*sin(ANG_TO_RAD*1.3358*i*j);
  }
  _lineto_w(x,-y);
  x++;
  y=0.0;
}

/* draw horizontal axis */
_moveto_w(0,0);
_lineto_w(vc.numxpixels,0);

/* draw vertical axis */
_moveto_w(0,-midy*7/8);
_lineto_w(0,+midy*7/8);

/* register a font for use chart use */
if(_registerfonts("modern.fon")<0)
{
  _outtext("Error: cannot register this font\n");
  exit(0);
}

/* scale font for graph name */
strcpy(fontname,"t'modern'");
strcat(fontname,"h20w10pb");
_setfont(fontname);

/* print graph title label */
a=midx-XOFFSET/2-(_getgtextextent(labeltitle)/2);
b=midy*15/16;
_moveto_w(a,-b);
_outgtext(labeltitle);

/* scale font for title labels */
strcpy(fontname,"t'modern'");
strcat(fontname,"h15w10pb");
_setfont(fontname);

/* print X axis label */
a=midx-XOFFSET/2-(_getgtextextent(labelx)/2);
b=midy*7/8;
```

```
_moveto_w(a,b);
_outgtext(labelx);

/* print Y axis label */
a=XOFFSET*3/8;
b=(_getgtextextent(labely)/2);
_moveto_w(-a,b);
_setgtextvector(0,1);
_outgtext(labely);

getch();
_setvideomode(_TEXTC80);
return (0);
}
```

Even though the mathematics are much more complicated in this program compared with the last example, the program itself is very similar. The only major difference lies in the mathematical equation itself and the fact that the program allows the user to enter the number of harmonics to plot. Examine just this portion of code:

```
_moveto_w(0,0);
x=0.0;
for(i=0;i<vc.numxpixels;i++) {
  for(j=1;j<terms+1;j++) {
    y+=(AMPLITUDE/j)*sin(ANG_TO_RAD*1.3358*i*j);
  }
  _lineto_w(x,-y);
  x++;
  y=0.0;
}
```

Notice that the **sin()** function is again used, but this time it is contained within two loops. The inner loop controls how many Fourier terms to calculate for each point on the screen, and the outer loop sequences through the number of horizontal screen pixels. If you examine the constants within the **sin()** function call, you will notice that the 0.6679 value from the previous example has been doubled and is now 1.3358. With this value doubled, the program will now draw two complete waveform cycles on the screen. Obviously, if the original value were cut in half, only one-half of a cycle would be shown. Also recall from the original discussion that each successive term is reduced by a fractional amount. This is what happens each time j is incremented. The value AMPLITUDE/j decreases with each successive term.

Figures 19-21 and 19-22 show two different harmonic values for the Fourier series. This program will be a little sluggish if you don't have a coprocessor installed on your

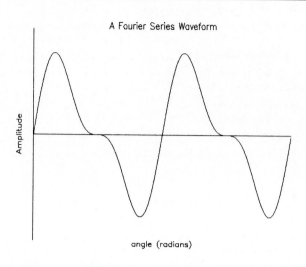

Figure 19-21. *A triangular waveform created with two harmonics in a Fourier series*

system, but look out if you do; the speed of the optimized C program approaches that of an equivalent assembly language program.

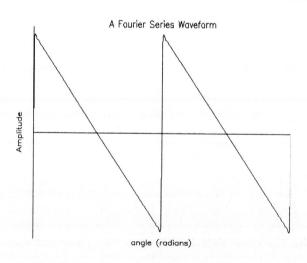

Figure 19-22. *A triangular waveform created with 500 harmonics in a Fourier series*

A Pie Chart from Graphics Primitives

The example in this section is a program that allows you to draw a pie chart on the screen. It is a presentation-quality chart programmed with the graphics primitives discussed to this point. In the next section, you learn techniques for producing presentation-quality graphs with the addition of Microsoft's chart-plotting library.

In this example, the user may specify between one and ten pie slice sizes to plot on the EGA or VGA screen. From this information, a complete pie chart will automatically be scaled and plotted. The colors of adjacent pie slices will be chosen from the default palette and selected in a sequential manner. A legend relating colors and pie slice labels will also be drawn.

```c
/*
 *    19PIE1.C
 *    A C program that demonstrates how to produce a
 *    presentation quality pie chart for EGA or VGA screens,
 *    using graphics primitives in graph.h.
 *    Copyright (c) William H. Murray and Chris H. Pappas, 1992
 */

#include <stdio.h>
#include <stdlib.h>
#include <conio.h>
#include <string.h>
#include <math.h>
#include <graph.h>

#define INVERT 1
#define MAXWEDGE 10
#define PI 3.14159265359
#define RADIUS 100.0

main()
{
  char pie[10];
  char leg[10][20],fontname[20];
  char label1[30],label2[30];
  int nwedges,i,x,y,midx,midy;
  double totalwedge[MAXWEDGE+1],wedgesize[MAXWEDGE+1];
  struct videoconfig vc;

  printf("THIS PROGRAM WILL DRAW A PIE CHART.\n\n");
  printf("Chart titles are optional.\n");
  printf("Enter top of chart label.\n");
  gets(label1);
```

```
printf("Enter bottom of chart label.\n");
gets(label2);
printf("\n\n");

printf("Enter up to 10 values for the pie wedges.\n");
printf("Follow each value with a carriage return.\n");
printf("(no value and carriage return ends input)\n");

nwedges=0;
for (i=0;i<MAXWEDGE;i++) {
  printf("pie wedge value #%d ",i+1);
  gets(pie);
  if (strlen(pie) == 0) break;
  wedgesize[i]=atof(pie);
  nwedges++;
  printf("pie legend label: ");
  gets(leg[i]);
}

totalwedge[0]=0;
for (i=0;i<nwedges;i++)
  totalwedge[i+1]=totalwedge[i]+wedgesize[i];

/* check adapter and make switch */
_getvideoconfig(&vc);
switch(vc.adapter) {
  case _EGA:
    _setvideomode(_HRES16COLOR);
    break;
  case _VGA:
    _setvideomode(_VRES16COLOR);
    break;
}

/* get coordinate values and set window */
_getvideoconfig(&vc);
midx=vc.numxpixels/2;
midy=vc.numypixels/2;
_setwindow(INVERT,-midx,-midy,+midx,+midy);

 /* draw and fill pie chart wedges */
 for (i=0;i<nwedges;i++) {
  _setcolor(i+1);
  _pie_w(_GFILLINTERIOR,-RADIUS*1.42,RADIUS*1.42,
         RADIUS*1.42,-RADIUS*1.42,
```

```
                RADIUS*cos(2*PI*totalwedge[i]/
                        totalwedge[nwedges]),
                RADIUS*sin(2*PI*totalwedge[i]/
                        totalwedge[nwedges]),
                RADIUS*cos(2*PI*totalwedge[i+1]/
                        totalwedge[nwedges]),
                RADIUS*sin(2*PI*totalwedge[i+1]/
                        totalwedge[nwedges]));
     }
     /* register a font for chart use */
     if(_registerfonts("modern.fon")<0)
     {
       _outtext("Error: cannot register this font\n");
       exit(0);
     }

     /* scale font for legend labels */
     strcpy(fontname,"t'modern'");
     strcat(fontname,"h10w6pb");
     _setfont(fontname);

     /* print legend names and colors */
     _setcolor(15);
     _moveto(midx+150,midy-80);
     _outgtext("Legend");
     for (i=0;i<nwedges;i++) {
       _setcolor(i+1);
       _rectangle(_GFILLINTERIOR,midx+150,(midy-50)+10*i,
                  midx+160,(midy-40)+10*i);
       _moveto(midx+170,(midy-50)+10*i);
       _outgtext(leg[i]);
     }

     /* scale font for title labels */
     strcpy(fontname,"t'modern'");
     strcat(fontname,"h20w15pb");
     _setfont(fontname);

     /* print main pie chart label */
     _setcolor(14);  /* yellow */
     x=midx-_getgtextextent(label1)/2;
     y=(vc.numypixels)*1/8;
     _moveto(x,y);
     _outgtext(label1);
```

```
/* print secondary pie chart label */
_setcolor(7);    /* white */
x=midx-_getgtextextent(label2)/2;
y=(vc.numypixels)*7/8;
_moveto(x,y);
_outgtext(label2);

getch();
_setvideomode(_TEXTC80);
return (0);
}
```

First, notice that the physical center of the screen will contain the origin for this graph. This is set by calling the **_setwindow()** function:

```
/* get coordinate values and set window */
_getvideoconfig(&vc);
midx=vc.numxpixels/2;
midy=vc.numypixels/2;
_setwindow(INVERT,-midx,-midy,+midx,+midy);
```

The program allows the user to enter values for a number of pie slices. These values are saved in an array named *wedgesize*. For example, if the pie chart is to have four slices, the numbers 10, 40, 20, and 30 might be entered. Data is retrieved with the following portion of code:

```
nwedges=0;
for (i=0;i<MAXWEDGE;i++) {
  printf("pie wedge value #%d ",i+1);
  gets(pie);
  if (strlen(pie) == 0) break;
  wedgesize[i]=atof(pie);
  nwedges++;
  printf("pie legend label: ");
  gets(leg[i]);
}
```

Input is terminated when a carriage return, without data, is entered as input. The number of pie slices is determined by the number of loops that are made in the previous portion of code. Thus, *nwedges* will hold the correct number of pie slices. For the suggested example, a 4 would be stored in *nwedges*. Regardless of the number of pie slices or their values, the total number of pie slices must always fill a 360-degree pie. Thus, pie slice sizes must be scaled.

To aid in this scaling, a progressive total of wedge values will be returned to the *totalwedge* array:

```
totalwedge[0]=0;
for (i=0;i<nwedges;i++)
  totalwedge[i+1]=totalwedge[i]+wedgesize[i];
```

These values will also be used to calculate where one pie slice ends on the screen and the next starts. For example, with the values 10, 40, 20, and 30 for wedge sizes, *totalwedge* will contain the values 10, 50, 70 and 100.

The values contained in *totalwedge* are needed in order to calculate the beginning and ending points for each pie wedge. The **_pie_w()** function accepts nine parameters. The first parameter determines if the pie slice is to be filled or outlined, and the next four values specify the coordinates of the bounding rectangle. In this case, the radius of the pie chart will be set to 125 pixels, so the diagonal length is approximately RADIUS*1.42. The bounding rectangle is thus –RADIUS*1.42, RADIUS*1.42, RADIUS*1.42, and –RADIUS*1.42. The remaining four parameters designate the starting *x,y* pair and the ending *x,y* pair for each pie wedge. To calculate *x* values, the cosine function is used; to calculate *y* values, the sine function is used. For example, the first *x* position is determined by multiplying the radius of the pie by the cosine of 2*pi*totalwedge[0]. The 2*pi value is needed for the conversion from degrees to radians. The *y* value is found with the sine function in an identical way. Those two points serve as the starting coordinates for the first slice. The ending coordinates are found with the same equations, but using the next value contained in *totalwedge*. In order to scale each of these points to make all slices proportional and to fit a 360-degree pie, each coordinate point is divided by the grand total of all individual slices. This grand total is the last number contained in *totalwedge*. Observe how this calculation is achieved in the next piece of code:

```
/* draw and fill pie chart wedges */
for (i=0;i<nwedges;i++) {
  _setcolor(i+1);
  _pie_w(_GFILLINTERIOR,-RADIUS*1.42,RADIUS*1.42,
         RADIUS*1.42,-RADIUS*1.42,
         RADIUS*cos(2*PI*totalwedge[i]/
                   totalwedge[nwedges]),
         RADIUS*sin(2*PI*totalwedge[i]/
                   totalwedge[nwedges]),
         RADIUS*cos(2*PI*totalwedge[i+1]/
                   totalwedge[nwedges]),
         RADIUS*sin(2*PI*totalwedge[i+1]/
                   totalwedge[nwedges]));
}
```

The loop is used to draw and fill all pie slices. This loop will index through all *nwedge* values. Since you are using trigonometric functions, the math.h header file is included at the start of this program.

A legend is drawn to the right of the pie figure. The legend prints a small rectangle, in a color corresponding to a pie slice, and then the legend label. This is achieved with the following portion of code:

```
/* print legend names and colors */
_setcolor(15);
_moveto(midx+150,midy-80);
_outgtext("Legend");
for (i=0;i<nwedges;i++) {
  _setcolor(i+1);
  _rectangle(_GFILLINTERIOR,midx+150,(midy-50)+10*i,
            midx+160,(midy-40)+10*i);
  _moveto(midx+170,(midy-50)+10*i);
  _outgtext(leg[i]);
}
```

Figures 19-23 and 19-24 show several pie chart examples.

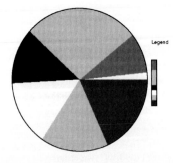

Figure 19-23.   *A simple pie chart, with each wedge drawn in a different color; legend values match pie wedge colors*

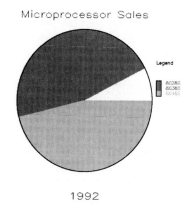

Figure 19-24.   *Adding a touch of class to the pie chart program*

Presentation Graphics

Microsoft has included an additional graphics library devoted exclusively to plotting high-quality presentation charts. Remember that you must select the graphics library option when installing your compiler in order to install the graphics header and library files.

The following pages list the structures and type definitions used by the PGCHART library and the parameters used by the chart functions. The prototypes of the chart functions included in this library can be found in the pgchart.h header file and are also listed in the next few pages for your convenience. Here are the PGCHART structures and type definitions:

```
struct {
    char title[_PG_TITLELEN];    /*chart title*/
    short titlecolor;            /*chart title text color*/
    short justify;               /*_PG_LEFT,_PG_CENTER,_PG_RIGHT*/
} titletype;
struct {
    short grid;                  /*TRUE=grid;FALSE=no grid*/
    short gridstyle;             /*style number for grid lines*/
    titletype axistitle;         /*axis title*/
    short axiscolor;             /*axis color*/
    short labeled;               /*TRUE=tic marks and titles*/
    short rangetype;             /*_PG_LINEARAXIS,_PG_LOGAXIS*/
```

```
        float logbase;                 /*Base for log axis */
        short autoscale;             /*TRUE=following values automatic*/
        float scalemin;                /*scale minimum*/
        float scalemax;                /*scale maximum*/
        float scalefactor;             /*scale factor for axis*/
        titletype scaletitle;          /*scale factor title*/
        float ticinterval;       /*tic mark separation in world coord*/
        short ticformat;               /*_PG_EXPFORMAT, _PG_DECFORMAT*/
        short ticdecimals;          /*tic label decimal places (max=9)*/
    } axistype;
    struct {
        short x1;                      /*left window coord. (pixels)*/
        short y1;                      /*top window coord.*/
        short x2;                      /*right window coord.*/
        short y2;                      /*bottom window coord.*/
        short border;                  /*TRUE=border,FALSE=no border*/
        short background;              /*palette color for background*/
        short borderstyle;             /*border style*/
        short bordercolor;             /*border color*/
    } windowtype;
    struct {
        short legend;                  /*TRUE=legend;FALSE=no legend*/
        short place;                /*_PG_RIGHT,_PG_BOTTOM,_PG_OVERLAY*/
        short textcolor;               /*palette color for text*/
        short autosize;                /*TRUE=auto calculation*/
        windowtype legendwindow;       /*window definition for legend*/
    } legendtype;
    struct {
        short charttype;               /*_PG_BAR,_PG_COLUMN,_PG_LINE,*/
                                       /*_PG_SCATTER,_PG_PIE*/
        short chartstyle;              /*chart style type*/
        windowtype chartwindow;        /*chart window*/
windowtype datawindow;                 /*data window*/
        titletype maintitle;           /*chart title (main)*/
        titletype subtitle;            /*chart sub-title*/
        axistype xaxis;                /*x-axis type*/
        axistype yaxis;                /*y-axis type*/
        legendtype legend;             /*legend type*/
    } chartenv;
    unsigned char charmap[8];
    unsigned char fillmap[8];
    struct {
        unsigned short color;
```

```
        unsigned short style;
        fillmap fill;
        char plotchar;
}   paletteentry;
paletteentry palettetype[_PG_PALETTELEN];
unsigned short styleset[_PG_PALETTELEN];
```

Here is a list of presentation graphics parameters:

Parameter	Value	Description
_PG_PALETTELEN	16	Number of palette entries
_PG_MAXCHARTTYPE	5	Maximum chart type
_PG_MAXCHARTSTYLE	2	Maximum chart style
_PG_TITLELEN	70	Maximum title length
_PG_LEFT	1	Positions for titles and legends
_PG_CENTER	2	
_PG_RIGHT	3	
_PG_BOTTOM	4	
_PG_OVERLAY	5	
_PG_LINEARAXIS	1	Axis types
_PG_LOGAXIS	2	
_PG_DECFORMAT	1	Tic mark label format
_PG_EXPFORMAT	2	
_PG_BARCHART	1	Bar chart
_PG_COLUMNCHART	2	Column chart
_PG_PLAINBARS	1	Styles for above
_PG_STACKEDBARS	2	
_PG_LINECHART	3	Line chart
_PG_SCATTERCHART	4	Scatter chart
_PG_POINTANDLINE	1	Styles for above
_PG_POINTONLY	2	
_PG_PIECHART	5	Pie chart
_PG_PERCENT	1	Styles for pie
_PG_NOPERCENT	2	
_PG_MISSINGVALUE	(-FLT_MAX)	Missing data values

Parameter	Value	Description
_PG_NOTINITIALIZED	102	Library not initialized
_PG_BADSCREENMODE	103	Graphics mode not set
_PG_BADCHARTSTYLE	04	Style invalid
_PG_BADCHARTTYPE	104	Type invalid
_PG_BADLEGENDWINDOW	105	Invalid legend window
_PG_BADCHARTWINDOW	07	x1=x2 or y1=y2 in chart
_PG_BADDATAWINDOW	107	Chart window too small
_PG_NOMEMORY	108	Short on memory for arrays
_PG_BADLOGBASE	05	Log base <= 0
_PG_BADSCALEFACTOR	06	Scale factor=0
_PG_TOOSMALLN	109	Number of data points<=0
_PG_TOOFEWSERIES	110	Number of series<=0

Here are popular presentation graphics function prototypes:

```
short _pg_initchart(void);
short _pg_defaultchart(chartenv _far *env,short charttype,
                    short chartstyle);
short _pg_chart(chartenv _far *env,
              char _far *_far *categories,
              float _far *values,short n);
short _pg_chartms(chartenv _far *env,
              char _far *_far *categories,
              float _far *values,short nseries,
              short n,short arraydim,
              char _far *_far *serieslabels);
short _pg_chartscatter(chartenv _far *env,
                  float _far *xvalues,
                  float _far *yvalues,short n);
short _pg_chartscatterms(chartenv _far *env,
                    float _far *xvalues,
                    float _far *yvalues,
                    short nseries,short n,
                    short rowdim,
                    char _far *_far *serieslabels);
short _pg_chartpie(chartenv _far *env,
              char _far *_far *categories,
              float _far *values,
              short _far *explode,short n);
short _pg_hlabelchart(chartenv _far *env,short x,
```

```
                          short y,short color,
                          char _far *label);
short _pg_vlabelchart(chartenv _far *env,
                          short x,short y,short color,
                          char _far *label);
short _pg_analyzechart(chartenv _far *env,
                          char _far *_far *categories,
                          float _far *values,short n);
short _pg_analyzechartms(chartenv _far *env,
                          char _far *_far *categories,
                          float _far *values,
                          short nseries,short n,
                          short arraydim,
                          char _far *_far *serieslabels);
short _pg_analyzescatter(chartenv _far *env,
                          float _far *xvalues,
                          float _far *yvalues,short n);
short _pg_analyzescatterms(chartenv _far *env,
                          float _far *xvalues,
                          float _far *yvalues,
                          short nseries,short n,
                          short rowdim,
                          char _far *_far *serieslabels);
short _pg_analyzepie(chartenv _far *env,
                          char _far *_far *categories,
                          float _far *values,
                          short _far *explode,short n);
short _pg_getpalette(paletteentry _far *palette);
short _pg_setpalette(paletteentry _far *palette);
short _pg_resetpalette(void);
void _pg_getstyleset(unsigned short _far *styleset);
void _pg_setstyleset(unsigned short _far *styleset);
void  _pg_resetstyleset(void);
short _pg_getchardef(short charnum,
                          unsigned char _far *chardef);
short _pg_setchardef(short charnum,
                          unsigned char _far *chardef);
```

These functions are used in conjunction with those prototyped in the graph.h header file.

In the following applications, you will see examples of interactive pie, bar, and line charts. A scatter chart example shows you how to plot two sets of data on the same chart. The greatest advantage of using this library of functions is the similarity between programs. Whether you are doing a pie, bar, or line chart, only minor programming differences are required to switch chart styles.

An Interactive Pie Chart

A presentation-quality pie chart was developed as an earlier application using graphics primitives. With the functions prototyped in pgchart.h, it will be even easier.

Compare the following listing with the earlier pie chart example:

```c
/*
 *   19PIE2.C
 *   A C program that demonstrates how to produce a
 *   presentation quality pie chart for EGA or VGA screens.
 *   Copyright (c) William H. Murray and Chris H. Pappas, 1992
 */

#include <stdio.h>
#include <stdlib.h>
#include <conio.h>
#include <string.h>
#include <graph.h>
#include <pgchart.h>

#define MAXSLICES 10
#define P "              "

typedef enum {FALSE,TRUE} boolean;

main()
{
  chartenv env;
  char pie[10],label1[20],
       label2[20],*legend;
  int nwedges;
  short explode[MAXSLICES]={0};
  float value[MAXSLICES];
  char far *category[MAXSLICES]={P,P,P,P,P,
                                 P,P,P,P,P};
  struct videoconfig vc;

  printf("THIS PROGRAM WILL DRAW A PIE CHART.\n\n");
  printf("Chart titles are optional.\n");
  printf("Enter pie chart title:\n");
  gets(label1);
  printf("Enter secondary title:\n");
  gets(label2);
  printf("\n\n");
```

```
printf("Enter up to 10 values for the pie wedges.\n");
printf("Values are followed by a carriage return.\n");
printf("No value and carriage return ends input.\n");

for (nwedges=0;nwedges<MAXSLICES;nwedges++) {
  printf("pie wedge value #%d ",nwedges+1);
  gets(pie);
  if (strlen(pie) == 0) break;
  value[nwedges]=(float) atof(pie);
  printf("legend label: ");
  gets(legend);
  _fstrcpy(category[nwedges],legend);
}

/* check adapter and make switch */
_getvideoconfig(&vc);
switch(vc.adapter) {
  case _EGA:
    _setvideomode(_HRES16COLOR);
    break;
  case _VGA:
    _setvideomode(_VRES16COLOR);
    break;
}

_pg_initchart();
_pg_defaultchart(&env,_PG_PIECHART,_PG_NOPERCENT);

/* set optional environment parameters */
env.maintitle.titlecolor=15;        /* yellow */
env.maintitle.justify=_PG_RIGHT;    /* right justify */
env.subtitle.titlecolor=6;          /* magenta */
env.subtitle.justify=_PG_RIGHT;     /* right justify */
env.chartwindow.border=FALSE;       /* no border */

strcpy(env.maintitle.title,label1);
strcpy(env.subtitle.title,label2);

if(_pg_chartpie(&env,category,value,explode,nwedges)) {
  _setvideomode(_TEXTC80);
  _outtext("not possible to draw pie chart");
}
  else {
    getch();
    _setvideomode(_TEXTC80);
```

```
    }
  return (0);
}
```

No doubt by this time you have become an experienced programmer with respect to entering data into programs. This program is similar to earlier examples. First, it allows the user to enter a main and secondary title from the keyboard. The program then polls the reader for pie slice information. Up to ten pie slice values can be entered at this time. It should also be noted that pie slices can be *exploded* (that is, separated from the main pie) if the slice value is specified in the *explode* array. The sizes of the various pie slices for this example are entered and saved in an array called *value*.

```
for (nwedges=0;nwedges<MAXSLICES;nwedges++) {
  printf("pie wedge value #%d ",nwedges+1);
  gets(pie);
  if (strlen(pie) == 0) break;
  value[nwedges]=atof(pie);
  printf("legend label: ");
  gets(legend);
  _fstrcpy(category[nwedges],legend);
 }
```

Look at the following segment:

```
_pg_initchart();
 _pg_defaultchart(&env,_PG_PIECHART,_PG_NOPERCENT);
```

The first chart function encountered is **_pg_initchart()**. This function initializes the graphics package and sets the plotting defaults, such as color and line style. All programs using the Microsoft pgchart.h file must use this function call. The second function typically used is **_pg_defaultchart()**. This function initializes all variables utilized by the chart environment specified. The chart types include _PG_BARCHART, _PG_COLUMNCHART, _PG_LINECHART, _PG_SCATTERCHART and _PG_PIECHART. (Additional information on chart parameters can be found near the beginning of the "Presentation Graphics" section in this chapter.)

You can use environment parameters to produce custom charts suited to your needs. The variable *env* was associated with the chart structure chartenv at the start of the program. This structure (shown near the beginning of the "Presentation Graphics" section) allows you to set title colors and justifications and chart borders. Notice that this structure is used in conjunction with yet another structure. For this example, title colors and justifications are set with the following nugget of program code:

```
/* set optional environment parameters */
 env.maintitle.titlecolor=15;          /* yellow */
 env.maintitle.justify=_PG_RIGHT;      /* right justify */
 env.subtitle.titlecolor=6;            /* magenta */
 env.subtitle.justify=_PG_RIGHT;       /* right justify */
 env.chartwindow.border=FALSE;         /* no border */
```

Title and subtitle information is copied to the correct chart locations using the **strcpy()** function:

```
strcpy(env.maintitle.title,label1);
 strcpy(env.subtitle.title,label2);
```

Finally, with all values in place, the pie chart can be plotted with a call to the **_pg_chartpie()** function:

```
if(_pg_chartpie(&env,category,value,explode,nwedges)) {
   _setvideomode(_TEXTC80);
   _outtext("not possible to draw pie chart");
 }
```

Study the function prototype shown earlier and the values passed in this example to make sure you understand how this function is utilized. Figure 19-25 shows a sample pie chart and legend produced with this program.

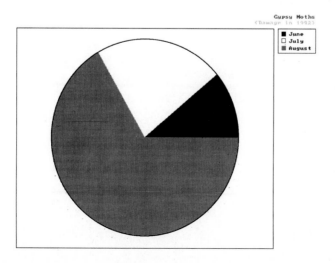

Figure 19-25. *A presentation-quality pie chart using pgchart.h functions*

An Interactive Bar Chart

The next example produces a vertical bar chart, which Microsoft calls a column chart. Microsoft's bar chart produces horizontal bars.

The pie chart example in the last program produced a rather generic pie chart that didn't utilize many customizing features available in the charting library. This example, in addition to plotting a new type of chart, alters several items. First, examine the total program and note how similar this program is to the pie chart program in the last section:

```c
/*
 *   19BAR.C
 *   A C program that demonstrates how to produce a
 *   presentation quality bar chart for EGA or VGA screens.
 *   Copyright (c) William H. Murray and Chris H. Pappas, 1992
 */

#include <stdio.h>
#include <stdlib.h>
#include <conio.h>
#include <string.h>
#include <graph.h>
#include <pgchart.h>

#define MAXBARS 20

typedef enum {FALSE,TRUE} boolean;

main()
{
  chartenv env;
  int nbars;
  float value[MAXBARS];
  char bar[10],label1[20],label2[20],label3[20];
  char far *category[MAXBARS]={"1","2","3","4","5",
                               "6","7","8","9","10",
                               "11","12","13","14","15",
                               "16","17","18","19","20"};
  struct videoconfig vc;

  printf("THIS PROGRAM WILL DRAW A BAR CHART.\n\n");
  printf("All chart titles are optional.\n");
  printf("Enter chart title.\n");
  gets(label1);
  printf("Enter vertical axis label.\n");
```

```
gets(label2);
printf("Enter horizontal axis label.\n");
gets(label3);
printf("\n\n");

printf("Up to 20 bars can be plotted.\n");
printf("Follow each entered value with a carriage
        return.\n");
printf("(no value and carriage return ends input)\n");

for (nbars=0;nbars<MAXBARS;nbars++) {
  printf("bar value #%d ",nbars+1);
  gets(bar);
  if (strlen(bar) == 0) break;
  value[nbars]=(float) atof(bar);
}

/* check adapter and make switch */
_getvideoconfig(&vc);
switch(vc.adapter) {
  case _EGA:
    _setvideomode(_HRES16COLOR);
    break;
  case _VGA:
    _setvideomode(_VRES16COLOR);
    break;
}

_pg_initchart();
_pg_defaultchart(&env,_PG_COLUMNCHART,_PG_PLAINBARS);

/* set optional environment parameters */
env.maintitle.titlecolor=15;          /* yellow */
env.maintitle.justify=_PG_CENTER;     /* center title */
env.chartwindow.border=TRUE;          /* draw border */
env.chartwindow.bordercolor=16;       /* bright white */
env.yaxis.axiscolor=8;                /* white */
env.xaxis.axiscolor=8;                /* white */
env.datawindow.background=10;         /* light blue */
env.chartwindow.background=2;         /* blue */
strcpy(env.maintitle.title,label1);
strcpy(env.yaxis.axistitle.title,label2);
strcpy(env.xaxis.axistitle.title,label3);

if(_pg_chart(&env,category,value,nbars)) {
```

```
   _setvideomode(_TEXTC80);
   _outtext("not possible to draw bar chart");
 }
   else {
     getch();
     _setvideomode(_TEXTC80);
   }
 return (0);
}
```

The labels that will identify individual bars are drawn from an array named *category*. These can be numbers representing weeks, months, or years, or even strings of letters such as Jan, Feb, Mar, and so on. Remember, however, that they must fit within a rather narrow column for each bar.

```
char far *category[MAXBARS]={"1","2","3","4","5",
                             "6","7","8","9","10",
                             "11","12","13","14","15",
                             "16","17","18","19","20"};
```

The two functions **_pg_initchart()** and **_pg_defaultchart()** are called. This time, a column chart is requested with plain bars:

```
_pg_initchart();
 _pg_defaultchart(&env,_PG_COLUMNCHART,_PG_PLAINBARS);
```

From the following listing you can see that a title will be centered and printed in yellow. A border will be drawn about the chart in bright white. An x and y axis will be drawn in white. The data window (the area in which points are plotted) will be light blue, while the chart window (the area for labels and so on) will be blue. This combination of features produces a stunning bar chart.

```
/* set optional environment parameters */
 env.maintitle.titlecolor=15;              /* yellow */
 env.maintitle.justify=_PG_CENTER;         /* center title */
 env.chartwindow.border=TRUE;              /* draw border */
 env.chartwindow.bordercolor=16;           /* bright white */
 env.yaxis.axiscolor=8;                    /* white */
 env.xaxis.axiscolor=8;                    /* white */
 env.datawindow.background=10;             /* light blue */
 env.chartwindow.background=2;             /* blue */
```

The various titles and labels are copied in the usual manner:

```
strcpy(env.maintitle.title,label1);
strcpy(env.yaxis.axistitle.title,label2);
strcpy(env.xaxis.axistitle.title,label3);
```

You use the **_pg_chart()** function when plotting bar, column, and line charts:

```
if(_pg_chart(&env,category,value,nbars)) {
  _setvideomode(_TEXTC80);
  _outtext("not possible to draw bar chart");
 }
```

Figure 19-26 shows an example of a chart produced with this program.

An Interactive Line Chart

A line chart is the next chart type to investigate. This chart plots a series of points on a graph interconnected with lines. You'll also learn how to use some additional features for customizing your line chart. Here is a complete program listing:

```
/*
 *   19LINE.C
 *   A C program that demonstrates how to produce a
 *   presentation quality line chart for EGA or VGA screens.
```

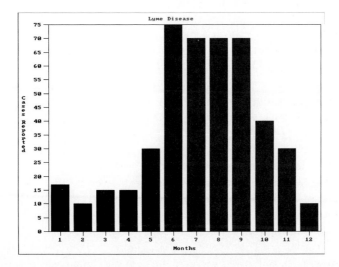

Figure 19-26. *A presentation-quality bar chart using pgchart.h functions*

```
*    Copyright (c) William H. Murray and Chris H. Pappas, 1992
*/

#include <stdio.h>
#include <stdlib.h>
#include <conio.h>
#include <string.h>
#include <graph.h>
#include <pgchart.h>

#define MAXPOINTS 20

typedef enum {FALSE,TRUE} boolean;

main()
{
  chartenv env;
  int npoints;
  float value[MAXPOINTS];
  char fontname[20];
  char pts[10],label1[20],label2[20],label3[20];
  char far *category[MAXPOINTS]={"1","2","3","4","5",
                                 "6","7","8","9","10",
                                 "11","12","13","14","15",
                                 "16","17","18","19","20"};
  struct videoconfig vc;

  printf("THIS PROGRAM WILL DRAW A LINE CHART.\n\n");
  printf("Chart titles are optional.\n");
  printf("Enter the name of this line chart:\n");
  gets(label1);
  printf("Enter the vertical axis label:\n");
  gets(label2);
  printf("Enter the horizontal axis label:\n");
  gets(label3);
  printf("\n\n");

  printf("Up to 20 points can be plotted.\n");
  printf("Follow each entered value with a carriage return.\n");
  printf("(no value and carriage return ends input)\n");

  for (npoints=0;npoints<MAXPOINTS;npoints++) {
    printf("point value #%d ",npoints+1);
    gets(pts);
    if (strlen(pts) == 0) break;
```

```
    value[npoints]=(float) atof(pts);
}

/* check adapter and make switch */
_getvideoconfig(&vc);
switch(vc.adapter) {
  case _EGA:
    _setvideomode(_HRES16COLOR);
    break;
  case _VGA:
    _setvideomode(_VRES16COLOR);
 }

_pg_initchart();
_pg_defaultchart(&env,_PG_LINECHART,_PG_POINTANDLINE);

/* register a new font for use */
if(_registerfonts("modern.fon") < 0)
{
  _outtext("Error: cannot register this font");
  exit(0);
}

/* set optional environment parameters */
env.maintitle.titlecolor=15;           /* bright white */
env.maintitle.justify=_PG_CENTER;      /* center title */
env.chartwindow.border=FALSE;          /* no border */
env.xaxis.grid=TRUE;                   /* draw x grid */
env.yaxis.grid=TRUE;                   /* draw y grid */
env.xaxis.axiscolor=4;                 /* x grid is cyan */
env.yaxis.axiscolor=4;                 /* y grid is cyan */

/* scale new font for all labels */
strcpy(fontname,"t'modern'");
strcat(fontname,"h20w15pb");
_setfont(fontname);

strcpy(env.maintitle.title,label1);
strcpy(env.yaxis.axistitle.title,label2);
strcpy(env.xaxis.axistitle.title,label3);

if(_pg_chart(&env,category,value,npoints)) {
  _setvideomode(_TEXTC80);
  _outtext("not possible to draw line chart");
}
```

```
    else {
      getch();
      _setvideomode(_TEXTC80);
    }
  return (0);
}
```

As you examine the program, notice that a new font will be used rather than the chart's default font. This font is registered and scaled in the usual manner.

The interesting part of this program involves a new feature, grids. Grids allow you to more easily determine values plotted on a chart. It is possible to plot both x and y axis grids, as this program does. You can also specify the grid colors:

```
/* set optional environment parameters */
 env.maintitle.titlecolor=15;            /* bright white */
 env.maintitle.justify=_PG_CENTER;       /* center title */
 env.chartwindow.border=FALSE;           /* no border */
 env.xaxis.grid=TRUE;                    /* draw x grid */
 env.yaxis.grid=TRUE;                    /* draw y grid */
 env.xaxis.axiscolor=4;                  /* x grid is cyan */
 env.yaxis.axiscolor=4;                  /* y grid is cyan */
```

The line chart is plotted with a call to **_pg_chart()**. All other parameters are similar to previous examples:

```
if(_pg_chart(&env,category,value,npoints)) {
   _setvideomode(_TEXTC80);
   _outtext("not possible to draw line chart");
 }
```

Figure 19-27 shows an example of this program in action.

A Scatter Chart

The previous examples utilized only one set of data. This example plots two sets of data on a scatter chart. A scatter chart allows the user to enter points for both x and y values. This program has not been made interactive with the hope that the resulting code may be easier to understand.

```
/*
 *    19SCATER.CPP
 *    A C program that demonstrates how to produce a
 *    presentation quality scatter chart for EGA or VGA screens.
```

```
*    Program also illustrates how to plot two series of data.
*    Copyright (c) William H. Murray and Chris H. Pappas, 1992
*/

#include <conio.h>
#include <string.h>
#include <graph.h>
#include <pgchart.h>

#define PTS 6
#define ITEM 2

typedef enum {FALSE,TRUE} boolean;
char far *semiconductor[ITEM]={"Semiconductor #1",
                               "Semiconductor #2"};

main()
{
  chartenv env;
  int i;
  float xpts[ITEM][PTS]={{10,20,30,40,50,60},
                         {5,10,30,45,63,70}};
  float ypts[ITEM][PTS]={{80,20,30,10,50,60},
                         {14,17,5,20,57,85}};
  struct videoconfig vc;
```

Figure 19-27.   *A presentation-quality line chart using pgchart.h functions*

```
/* check adapter and make switch */
_getvideoconfig(&vc);
switch(vc.adapter) {
  case _EGA:
    _setvideomode(_HRES16COLOR);
    break;
  case _VGA:
    _setvideomode(_VRES16COLOR);
  }

_pg_initchart();
_pg_defaultchart(&env,_PG_SCATTERCHART,_PG_POINTANDLINE);
/* set optional environment parameters */
env.maintitle.titlecolor=2;        /* blue */
env.maintitle.justify=_PG_LEFT;    /* left justify title */
env.chartwindow.border=TRUE;       /* border */
env.xaxis.grid=TRUE;               /* draw x grid */
env.yaxis.grid=TRUE;               /* draw y grid */
env.xaxis.axiscolor=10;            /* x grid light blue */
env.yaxis.axiscolor=10;            /* y grid light blue */
env.datawindow.background=8;       /* white */
env.chartwindow.background=8;      /* white */

strcpy(env.maintitle.title,"Semiconductor Performance");
strcpy(env.yaxis.axistitle.title,"Voltage (millivolts)");
strcpy(env.xaxis.axistitle.title,"Current (milliamps)");

_pg_chartscatterms(&env,(float far *)xpts,(float far *)ypts,
                ITEM,PTS,PTS,semiconductor);

getch();
_setvideomode(_TEXTC80);

return (0);
}
```

Notice that the program will allow individual labels for each series of data that is being plotted:

```
char far *semiconductor[ITEM]={"Semiconductor #1",
                               "Semiconductor #2"};
```

Next, two separate variables are used for storing x and y data values. For this example, *xpts* and *ypts* are 2x6 arrays. For the first series of points, the x values are 10, 20, 30, 40, 50, and 60 and the corresponding y values are 80, 20, 30, 10, 50, and 60. The second series of points has x values equal to 5, 10, 30, 45, 63, and 70 and y values equal to 14, 17, 5, 20, 57, and 85.

```
float xpts[ITEM][PTS]={{10,20,30,40,50,60},
                       {5,10,30,45,63,70}};
float ypts[ITEM][PTS]={{80,20,30,10,50,60},
                       {14,17,5,20,57,85}};
```

Everything in this program is similar to previous examples, down to the **_pg_chartscatterms**() function call:

```
_pg_chartscatterms(&env,(float far *)xpts,(float far *)ypts,
                   ITEM,PTS,PTS,semiconductor);
```

Any function call ending with the letters "ms" is capable of plotting multiple series of data.

Study the function prototype and the example used here and identify how the various data arrays and labels are used. Figure 19-28 is a screen output for this program.

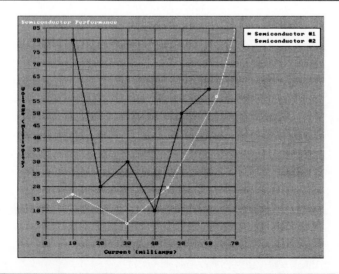

Figure 19-28. *A presentation-quality scatter chart using pgchart.h functions*

Special Graphical Effects

The most frequently used graphics functions in the graph.h and pgchart.h header files were illustrated in earlier programs. Microsoft's graphics libraries also contain functions that can be used to create special effects. For example, multiple viewports can be placed on the screen, each with its own origin and coordinate system. A viewport can be sized, with a small time delay inserted between each size. This technique allows you to size a figure without changing the dimensions of the figure itself. You can apply simple animation techniques with calls to functions such as **_getimage()**, **_imagesize()** and **_putimage()**. In the following sections, you learn how to use many of these functions.

Using Four Viewports

The first example in this section divides the screen into four equal viewports. The origin of each viewport is then set to be the center of each individual viewport. The background color of each viewport will be different. A call to **getch()** has been inserted between viewport figures to more clearly illustrate the effect. Examine the following listing and see if you understand how the four viewports are sized from the physical screen dimensions. Remember, this program will work with EGA or VGA systems.

```
/*
 *   19VIEWS.C
 *   A C program that demonstrates how to draw graphics
 *   primitives in four separate viewports.
 *   Copyright (c) William H. Murray and Chris H. Pappas, 1992
 */

#include <graph.h>
#include <conio.h>

main()
{
  int midx,midy;
  struct videoconfig vc;

  /* check adapter and make switch */
  _getvideoconfig(&vc);
  switch(vc.adapter) {
    case _EGA:
      _setvideomode(_HRES16COLOR);
      break;
```

```
  case _VGA:
    _setvideomode(_VRES16COLOR);
    break;
}

/* get coordinate values and set viewport origin */
_getvideoconfig(&vc);
midx=vc.numxpixels/2;
midy=vc.numypixels/2;

_setviewport(0,0,midx,midy);
_setvieworg(midx/2,midy/2);
_setcolor(14);                          /* yellow */
_floodfill_w(0,0,14);
_setcolor(0);                           /* black */
_rectangle_w(_GBORDER,-80,-60,+80,+60);
getch();

_setviewport(midx,midy,vc.numxpixels,vc.numypixels);
_setvieworg(vc.numypixels,midy*3/2);
_setcolor(5);                           /* magenta */
_floodfill_w(0,0,5);
_setcolor(14);                          /* yellow */
_pie(_GFILLINTERIOR,-60,-60,+60,+60,
    -30,-30,+20,+20);
getch();

_setviewport(midx,0,vc.numxpixels,midy);
_setvieworg(vc.numypixels,midy/2);
_setcolor(1);                           /* blue */
_floodfill_w(0,0,1);
_setcolor(15);                          /* bright white */
_ellipse_w(_GFILLINTERIOR,-60,-60,+60,+60);
getch();

_setviewport(0,midy,midx,vc.numypixels);
_setvieworg(midx/2,midy*3/2);
_setcolor(4);                           /* red */
_floodfill_w(0,0,4);
_setcolor(10);                          /* light green */
_moveto_w(-60,-60);
_lineto_w(60,60);

getch();
_setvideomode(_TEXTC80);
```

```
    return (0);
}
```

Most of the code that you see in this program uses traditional graphics programming with the graphics primitives from graph.h.

There are four similar blocks of code used to establish each of the four viewports. Examine the following; it is the code for creating the viewport in the upper-left corner of the screen:

```
_setviewport(0,0,midx,midy);
 _setvieworg(midx/2,midy/2);
 _setcolor(14);                              /* yellow */
 _floodfill_w(0,0,14);
 _setcolor(0);                               /* black */
 _rectangle_w(_GBORDER,-80,-60,+80,+60);
 getch();
```

The viewport dimensions are set with the **_setviewport()** function, using physical screen coordinates. For a VGA screen, for example, the upper-left coordinate would be 0,0, and the lower-right coordinate would be 320,240. In order to set the viewport origin to the center of this viewport, the **_setvieworg()** function uses physical screen coordinates. For a VGA screen, these values are 160,120. The background color is set with a little trick. First, the drawing color is set to yellow, and then the **_floodfill()** function is used to fill the viewport. This viewport has a rectangle drawn in it. The drawing color is changed to black, and the **_rectangle_w()** function is used to draw an outlined rectangle. The **getch()** function allows a pause between viewport figures.

All of the remaining viewports are established in a similar manner. Figures 19-29 and 19-30 show the screen at various stages in the execution of this program. Try the program; the effects are very interesting.

Sizing the Viewport

The next program illustrates an interesting effect. If you change the size of a viewport with the **_setwindow()** function, the size of a figure with fixed dimensions can be made to shrink on the screen. Naturally, the reverse effect is also true. Examine the program:

```
/*
*    19SIZING.C
*    A C program that demonstrates that expanding a graphics
*    window actually shrinks a given figure.
*    Copyright (c) William H. Murray and Chris H. Pappas, 1992
*/
```

```
#include <graph.h>
#include <conio.h>

main()
{
  int y,midx,midy;
  struct videoconfig vc;

  /* check adapter and make switch */
  _getvideoconfig(&vc);
  switch(vc.adapter) {
    case _EGA:
      _setvideomode(_HRES16COLOR);
      break;
    case _VGA:
      _setvideomode(_VRES16COLOR);
      break;
  }

  /* get coordinate values and set viewport origin */
  _getvideoconfig(&vc);
  midx=vc.numxpixels/2;
  midy=vc.numypixels/2;

  _setbkcolor(_BLUE);
  _setcolor(15);     /* bright white */

  /* note that figure size is fixed */
  /* only the window changes */
  for(y=4;y<vc.numypixels;y+=20) {
    _setwindow(1,-y,-y,+y,+y);
    _clearscreen(_GWINDOW);
    _ellipse_w(_GBORDER,-10,-10,10,10);
    getch();
  }

  getch();
  _setvideomode(_TEXTC80);
  return (0);
}
```

Figure 19-29.   *A figure drawn in a viewport on the screen*

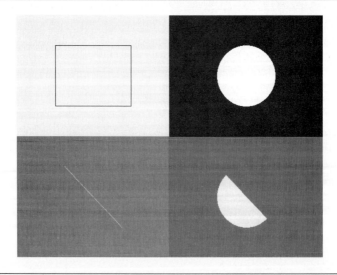

Figure 19-30.   *Three figures, each in a viewport, drawn on the screen; each figure is drawn with a different background color*

Most of the program code in this example is similar to earlier applications. The real action takes place in the following nugget of code:

```
/* note that figure size is fixed */
/* only the window changes */
for(y=4;y<vc.numypixels;y+=20) {
  _setwindow(1,-y,-y,+y,+y);
  _clearscreen(_GWINDOW);
  _ellipse_w(_GBORDER,-10,-10,10,10);
  getch();
}
```

A loop is repeated several times, with an ellipse being drawn with the **_ellipse_w()** function. It is significant that the dimensions of the ellipse are fixed at –10,–10,10,10. This means that under normal circumstances, the size of the figure will not change. However, also in the same loop is the **_setwindow()** function. This function has traditionally been used with fixed dimensions, but for this example, it contains the variable *y*, which will change the dimensions of the window.

The first window that is established has the dimensions –20,–20 and 20,20. This means that 40 units in both the x and y directions will fill the physical screen. The figure is drawn in a rectangle with coordinates –10,–10 and 10,10—in other words, 20 units in both directions. Initially, the figure's bounding rectangle will occupy one-half of the total screen area. However, as the window's dimensions increase, the portion of screen specified with the bounding rectangle shrinks proportionally. Overall, this gives the effect of a shrinking figure. Figures 19-31 and 19-32 show the program during several stages of execution.

Simple Animation

If a picture is worth a thousand words, an animated scene must be worth ten thousand. You can use many animation techniques in C and C++ programming. In this section, a simple animation technique is used to move a train engine image back and forth across the screen. This method uses the draw, delay, erase, move, and draw technique over and over again. Examine the complete listing and locate the functions responsible for this action. They are **_getimage()**, **_imagesize()**, and **_putimage()**. Here are the prototypes for these functions:

```
void _getimage(short x1,short y1,
               short x2,short y2,
               char _huge *image);
void _getimage_w(double wx1,double wy1,
                 double wx2,double wy2,
                 char _huge *image);
```

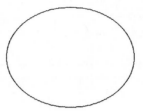

Figure 19-31.   *A figure with fixed values that can still be sized by changing the viewport*

```
void _getimage_wxy(struct _wxycoord _far *pwxy1,
                   struct _wxycoord _far *pwxy2,
                   char _huge *image);
void _putimage(short x,short y,char _huge *image,
               short action);
```

Figure 19-32.   *The figure in Figure 19-31 with a different viewport*

```
void _putimage_w(double wx,double wy,
                 char _huge *image,short action);
long _imagesize(short x1,short y1,short x2,short y2);
long _imagesize_w(double wx1,double wy1,
                  double wx2,double wy2);
long _imagesize_wxy(struct _wxycoord _far *pwxy1,
                    struct _wxycoord _far *pwxy2);
```

These are the action values that apply to the function prototypes:

Parameter	Value
_GPSET	3
_GPRESET	2
_GAND	1
_GOR	0
_GXOR	4

Here is the complete program:

```
/*
 *   19ANIMAT.C
 *   A C program that demonstrates a simple animation
 *   technique—draw,delay,erase,move,draw.
 *   Copyright (c) William H. Murray and Chris H. Pappas, 1992
 */

#include <conio.h>
#include <stddef.h>
#include <stdlib.h>
#include <malloc.h>
#include <graph.h>
#include <sys\timeb.h>

void time_delay(unsigned short);

main()
{
  char _huge *image_buffer;
  long image_size;
  int i,y,t;
  int x=0;
  int midx,midy;
  int step_size=2;
  struct videoconfig vc;
```

```
/* check adapter and make switch */
_getvideoconfig(&vc);
switch(vc.adapter) {
  case _EGA:
    _setvideomode(_HRES16COLOR);
    break;
  case _VGA:
    _setvideomode(_VRES16COLOR);
    break;
}

/* get coordinate values and set viewport origin */
_getvideoconfig(&vc);
midx=vc.numxpixels/2;
midy=vc.numypixels/2;

/* reserve memory to hold train image */
image_size=_imagesize(0,0,40,40);
image_buffer=halloc(image_size,1);

_setvieworg(0,midy);

/* draw original image of train */
_setcolor(2);
_ellipse(_GFILLINTERIOR,5,29,15,39);
_ellipse(_GFILLINTERIOR,25,29,35,39);
_setcolor(3);
_rectangle(_GFILLINTERIOR,2,19,37,29);
_setcolor(4);
_rectangle(_GFILLINTERIOR,17,0,23,19);

/* capture original train image then erase */
_getimage(0,0,40,40,image_buffer);
_putimage(0,0,image_buffer,_GXOR);

/* prepare to replicate train images */
for(t=0;t<2;) {
  if((x+40>=vc.numxpixels)||(x<0)) {
    step_size=-step_size;
    t++;
  }
  _putimage(x,0,image_buffer,_GXOR);
  time_delay(100);
  _putimage(x,0,image_buffer,_GXOR);
```

```
    x+=step_size;
  }

  hfree(image_buffer);
  _setvideomode(_TEXTC80);
  return (0);
}

void time_delay(unsigned short t)
{
  struct timeb initial,final;

  ftime(&initial);
  ftime(&final);
  while((final.millitm-initial.millitm) < t)
    ftime(&final);
  return;
}
```

This program draws the simple figure of a train engine, saves it to allocated memory, and then replicates it a number of times across the screen. This gives the effect of a train engine in motion.

Before the figure is drawn, memory is allocated to hold the train engine image in memory:

```
/* reserve memory to hold train image */
image_size=_imagesize(0,0,40,40);
image_buffer=halloc(image_size,1);
```

The viewport is set so that the train will travel across the middle of the screen on an imaginary track.

The train engine itself is constructed of two ellipses (circles) and two rectangles. Observe the construction in the following code:

```
_setvieworg(0,midy);

/* draw original image of train */
_setcolor(2);
_ellipse(_GFILLINTERIOR,5,29,15,39);
_ellipse(_GFILLINTERIOR,25,29,35,39);
_setcolor(3);
_rectangle(_GFILLINTERIOR,2,19,37,29);
_setcolor(4);
_rectangle(_GFILLINTERIOR,17,0,23,19);
```

```
/* capture original train image then erase */
_getimage(0,0,40,40,image_buffer);
_putimage(0,0,image_buffer,_GXOR);
```

Once the train is drawn for the first time, its image is captured with a call to the **_getimage()** function. Notice that the dimensions for **_getimage()** are identical to those of **_imagesize()**, which was used earlier when memory was allocated for storage. In the case of the **_getimage()** function, these values represent the location on the screen of the image to be captured. The image is then drawn to the same screen position with **_putimage()**. With this function, only the coordinates of the first point (0,0) need to be specified. However, note that the *action* value in this function is set to _GXOR. This means that the image will be exclusively ORed with the current image on the screen. The exclusive OR action is a quick way to erase a figure that has just been drawn. Remember, however, that it will only erase a copy of itself.

The technique is now to draw the train engine with one call to **_putimage()**, wait a small amount of time, and erase that image with another call to **_putimage()**. The cursor will then be moved and the action repeated.

```
/* prepare to replicate train images */
for(t=0;t<2;) {
  if((x+40>=vc.numxpixels)||(x<0)) {
    step_size=-step_size;
    t++;
  }
```

Figure 19-33.   *The train engine figure used in the simple animation program*

```
   }
   _putimage(x,0,image_buffer,_GXOR);
   time_delay(100);
   _putimage(x,0,image_buffer,_GXOR);
   x+=step_size;
}
```

The variable *step_size* determines how many screen pixels are moved between replicated images. Smaller step sizes produce smoother movements but also require more time for drawing the increased number of images. The **time_delay()** function used in this program allows the time delay to be entered in milliseconds. Thus, 100 milliseconds (0.1 second) are inserted between images. The *y* coordinate never changes, but *x* is a summation of the number of steps taken. When a border is encountered (the edge of the window), the *step_size* variable has its sign changed. Thus, *x* is always a point within the window.

Before the program ends, the memory allocated for the train engine image is deallocated:

```
   hfree(image_buffer);
   _setvideomode(_TEXTC80);
   return (0);
}
```

Figure 19-33 shows a quick glimpse of the moving train engine.

Windows graphics applications will be discussed in Chapters 22 through 25.

Chapter *20*

Power Programming: Tapping Important C and C++ Libraries

Programmers rely heavily on functions built into C and C++ compiler libraries. These built-in functions save you from "reinventing the wheel" when you need a special routine. Both C and C++ offer extensive support for character, string, math, and special functions that allow you to address the hardware features of the computer. Most library functions are portable from one computer to another and from one operating system to another. There are some functions, however, that are system or compiler dependent. Using these functions efficiently requires you to know where to locate the library functions and how to call them properly.

Many C and C++ functions have already been heavily used in earlier chapters. These include, for example, functions prototyped in the stdio.h and iostream.h header files. It is difficult to do any serious programming without taking advantage of their power. This chapter does not repeat a study of their use; it concentrates on new functions that will enhance character, string, and math work.

Microsoft C and C++ Header Files

If you do a directory listing of your Microsoft C/C++ INCLUDE subdirectory, the frequently used header files shown in the following table should be present:

Header File	Description
bios.h[*]	BIOS interrupts
conio.h	Console and port I/O
ctype.h	Character functions
dos.h[*]	DOS interrupts
io.h	File handling and low-level I/O
math.h[*]	Math functions
stdio.h	Stream routines for C
stdlib.h[*]	Standard library routines
iostream.h	Stream routines for C++
string.h[*]	String functions
time.h[*]	Date and time utilities

There will be others, too, but these are the header files you will use repeatedly. Since these files are in ASCII format, you may want to print a copy of their contents for a reference. You will find that some header files are short while others are quite long. All contain function prototypes and many contain built-in macros.

This chapter will illustrate a use for many popular functions prototyped in the header files marked with an asterisk in the preceding table. These include the system-independent functions prototyped in stdlib.h, ctype.h, math.h, string.h, and time.h and the system-dependent functions prototyped in bios.h and dos.h. Other functions contained in stdio.h, iostream.h, and so on, have been already been used throughout the book.

The Standard Library Functions (stdlib.h)

The standard library macros and functions comprise a powerful group of items for data conversion, memory allocation, and other miscellaneous operations. The most frequently encountered macros and functions are shown in Table 20-1. The prototypes are found in stdlib.h.

As you examine Table 20-1, notice that almost half of the functions shown perform a data conversion from one format to another.

Performing Data Conversions

The first important group of functions described in stdlib.h is the data converting functions. The principal job of these functions is to convert data from one data type to another. For example, the **atol()** function converts string information to a long.

Macro or Function	Description
_exit()	Terminates program
_lrotl()	Rotates an unsigned long to the left
_lrotr()	Rotates an unsigned long to the right
_rotl()	Rotates an unsigned integer to the left
_rotr()	Rotates an unsigned integer to the right
abort()	Aborts program; terminates abnormally
abs()	Absolute value of an integer
atexit()	Registers termination function
atof()	Converts a string to a float
atoi()	Converts a string to an integer
atol()	Converts a string to a long
bsearch()	Binary search of an array
calloc()	Allocates main memory
div()	Divides integers
_ecvt()	Converts a float to a string
exit()	Terminates program
_fcvt()	Converts a float to a string
free()	Frees memory
_gcvt()	Converts a float to a string
getenv()	Gets a string from the environment
_itoa()	Converts an integer to a string
labs()	Absolute value of a long
ldiv()	Divides two long integers
_ltoa()	Converts a long to a string
malloc()	Allocates memory
_putenv()	Puts a string in the environment
qsort()	Performs a quick sort
rand()	Random number generator
realloc()	Reallocates main memory
srand()	Initializes random number generator
strtod()	Converts a string to a double

Table 20-1.   *The Most Frequently Encountered Macros and Functions*

Macro or Function	Description
strtol()	Converts a string to a long
strtoul()	Converts a string to an unsigned long
_swab()	Swaps bytes from s1 to s2
system()	Invokes DOS COMMAND.COM file
_ultoa()	Converts an unsigned long to a string

Table 20-1.   *The Most Frequently Encountered Macros and Functions* (continued)

The syntax of each function is shown in the following prototypes:

```
double atof(const char *s)
int atoi(const char *s)
long atol(const char *s)
char *ecvt(double value,int n,int *dec,int *sign)
char *fcvt(double value,int n,int *dec,int *sign)
char *gcvt(double value,int n,char *buf)
char *itoa(int value,char *s,int radix)
char *ltoa(long value,char *s,int radix)
double strtod(const char *s,char **endptr)
long strtol(const char *s,char **endptr,int radix)
unsigned long strtoul(const char *s,char **endptr,int radix)
char *ultoa(unsigned long value,char *s,int radix)
```

In these functions, *s* points to a string. *value* is the number to be converted. *n* represents the number of digits in the string. *dec* locates the decimal point relative to the start of the string. *sign* represents the sign of the number. *buf* is a character buffer. *radix* represents the number base for the converted value. *endptr* is usually null. If not, the function sets it to the character that stops the scan.

The use of several of these functions is illustrated in the following programs.

Changing a Float to a String

The **fcvt()** function converts a float to a string. It is also possible to obtain information regarding the sign and location of the decimal point.

```
/*
 *    20FCVT.C
 *    Demonstrating the use of the fcvt function.
 *    Copyright (c) William H. Murray and Chris H. Pappas, 1992
 */

#include <stdlib.h>

main()
{
  int dec_pt,sign;
  char *ch_buffer;
  int num_char=7;

  ch_buffer = fcvt(-234.5678,num_char,&dec_pt,&sign);
  printf("The buffer holds: %s\n",ch_buffer);
  printf("The sign (+=0, -=1) is stored as a: %d\n",sign);
  printf("The decimal place is %d characters from right\n",
         dec_pt);
  return (0);
}
```

The output from this program is shown here:

```
The buffer holds: 2345678000
The sign (+=0, -=1) is stored as a: 1
The decimal place is 3 characters from right
```

Changing a String to a Long Integer

The **strtol()** function converts the specified string, in the given base, to its decimal equivalent. The following example shows a string of binary characters that will be converted to a decimal number:

```
/*
 *    20STRTO.C
 *    Demonstrating the use of the strtol function.
 *    Copyright (c) William H. Murray and Chris H. Pappas, 1992
 */

#include <stdlib.h>
#include <stdio.h>

main()
```

```
{
  char *s="101101",*endptr;
  long long_number;

  long_number=strtol(s,&endptr,2);
  printf("The binary value %s is equal to %ld decimal.\n",
         s,long_number);
  return (0);
}
```

In this example, "101101" is a string that represents several binary digits. The program produces the following results:

```
The binary value 101101 is equal to 45 decimal.
```

This is an interesting function since it allows a string of digits to be specified in one base and converted to another. This function would be a good place to start if you wanted to develop a general base change program.

Performing Searches and Sorts

You can use the **bsearch()** function to perform a binary search of an array. The **qsort()** function performs a quick sort. The **lfind()** function performs a linear search for a key in an array of sequential records, and the **lsearch**() function performs a linear search on a sorted or unsorted table.

```
void *bsearch(const void *key,const void *base,
    size_t nelem,size_t width,int(*fcmp)(const void *,
    const void *))

void qsort(void *base,size_t nelem,size_t width,
    int(*fcmp)(const void *,const void *))

void *lfind(const void *key,const void *base,
    size_t *,size_t width,int(*fcmp)
    (const void *,const void *))

void *lsearch(const void *key, void *base,
    size_t *,size_t width,int(*fcmp)
    (const void *,const void *))
```

Here, *key* represents the search key. *base* is the array to search. *nelem* contains the number of elements in the array. *width* is the number of bytes for each table entry. *fcmp* is the comparison routine used. *num* reports the number of records.

The next applications shows the use of two of the search and sort functions just described.

Using qsort() to Sort a Group of Integers

In C and C++, as in any language, sorting data is very important. Microsoft C/C++ provides the **qsort()** function for sorting data. The following example is one application in which **qsort()** can be used.

```c
/*
 *    20QSORT.C
 *    Demonstrating the use of the qsort function.
 *    Copyright (c) William H. Murray and Chris H. Pappas, 1992
 */

#include <stdlib.h>

int int_comp(const void *i,const void *j);

int list[12]={95,53,71,86,11,28,34,53,10,11,74,-44};

main()
{
  int i;

  qsort(list,12,sizeof(int),int_comp);

  printf("The array after qsort:\n");
  for(i=0;i<12;i++)
    printf("%d ",list[i]);
  return (0);
}

int int_comp(const void *i,const void *j)
{
  return ((*(int *)i)-(*(int *)j));
}
```

The original numbers, in *list*, are signed integers. The **qsort()** function will arrange the original numbers in ascending order, leaving them in the variable *list*. Here, the original numbers are sorted in ascending order:

```
The array after qsort:
-44 10 11 11 28 34 53 53 71 74 86 95
```

Can **qsort()** be used with floats? Why not alter the preceding program and see.

Finding an Integer in an Array of Integers

You use the **bsearch()** function to perform a search in an integer array. The search value for this example is contained in *search_number*.

```c
/*
 *    20BSEARH.C
 *    Demonstrating the use of the bsearch function.
 *    Copyright (c) William H. Murray and Chris H. Pappas, 1992
 */

#include <stdlib.h>
#include <stdio.h>

int int_comp(const void *i,const void *j);

int data_array[]={100,200,300,400,500,
                  600,700,800,900};

main()
{
   int *search_result;
   int search_number=400;

   printf("Is 400 in the data_array? ");
   search_result=bsearch(&search_number,data_array,9,
                         sizeof(int),int_comp);
   if (search_result) printf("Yes!\n");
     else printf("No!\n");
   return (0);
}

int int_comp(const void *i,const void *j)
{
   return ((*(int *)i)-(*(int *)j));
}
```

This application sends a simple message to the screen regarding the outcome of the search, as shown here:

```
Is 400 in the data_array? Yes!
```

You can also use this function to search for a string of characters in an array.

Miscellaneous Operations

There are several miscellaneous functions, listed in Table 20-2 and described in this section, that perform a variety of diverse operations. These operations include calculating the absolute value of an integer and bit rotations. Bit rotation functions give you the ability to perform operations that were once just in the realm of assembly language programmers.

Using the Random Number Generator

Microsoft C/C++ provides a random number function. The random number generator can be initialized or seeded with a call to **srand()**. The seed function accepts an integer argument and starts the random number generator.

```
/*
 *   20RAND.C
 *   Demonstrating the use of the srand and rand,
 *   random number functions.
 *   Copyright (c) William H. Murray and Chris H. Pappas, 1992
 */

#include <stdlib.h>
#include <stdio.h>

main()
{
  int x;

  srand(3);

  for (x=0;x<8;x++)
    printf("Trial #%d, random number=%d\n",
           x,rand());
  return (0);
}
```

Function	Description
Abort or End:	
void abort(void)	Returns an exit code of 3
int atexit(atexit_t func)	Calls function prior to exit
void exit(int status)	Returns zero for normal exit
int system(const char *command)	Command is a DOS command
void _exit(int status)	Terminates with no action
Math:	
div_t div(int numer,int denom)	Divides and returns quotient and remainder in *div_t*
int abs(int x)D	Determines absolute value of *x*
long labs(long x)	Determines absolute value of *x*
ldiv_t ldiv(long numer,long denom)	Similar to **div()** with longs
int rand(void)	Calls random number generator
void srand(unsigned seed)	Seeds random number generator
Rotate:	
unsigned long _lrotl (unsigned long val,int count)	Rotates the long *val* to the left
unsigned long _lrotr (unsigned long val,int count)	Rotates the long *val* to the right
unsigned _rotl (unsigned val, int count)	Rotates the integer *val* to the left
unsigned _rotr (unsigned val, int count)	Rotates the integer *val* to the right
Miscellaneous:	
char *getenv(const char *name)	Gets environment string
int putenv(const char *name)	Puts environment string
void _swap (char *from,char *to, int nbytes)	Swaps the number of characters specified

Table 20-2.   Miscellaneous Functions

An example of random numbers generated by **rand()** is shown here:

```
Trial #0, random number=48
Trial #1, random number=7196
Trial #2, random number=9294
Trial #3, random number=9091
Trial #4, random number=7031
Trial #5, random number=23577
Trial #6, random number=17702
Trial #7, random number=23503
```

Random number generators are important in programming for statistical work and for applications that rely on the generation of random patterns. It is important that the numbers produced be unbiased, that is, that all numbers have an equal probability of appearing.

Rotating Data Bits

C and C++ provide a means of rotating the individual bits of integers and longs to the right and to the left. In the next example, two rotations in each direction are performed:

```
/*
 *   20ROTATE.C
 *   Demonstrating the use of the _rotl and _rotr
 *   bit rotate functions.
 *   Copyright (c) William H. Murray and Chris H. Pappas, 1992
 */

#include <stdlib.h>

main()
{
 unsigned int val = 0x2345;

 printf("rotate bits of %X to the left 2 bits and get %X\n",
        val,_rotl(val,2));
 printf("rotate bits of %X to the right 2 bits and get %X\n",
        val,_rotr(val,2));
}
```

Here are the results:

```
rotate bits of 2345 to the left 2 bits and get 8D14
rotate bits of 2345 to the right 2 bits and get 48D1
```

Note that the original numbers are in hexadecimal format.

The use of the bit rotation functions and the use of logical operators such as **and**, **or**, **xor**, and so on, give C and C++ the ability to manipulate data bit by bit.

The Character Functions (ctype.h)

Characters are defined in most languages as single-byte values. Chinese is one case where 2 bytes are needed. The character macros and functions in C and C++, prototyped or contained in ctype.h, take integer arguments but utilize only the lower byte of the integer value. Automatic type conversion usually permits character arguments to also be passed to the macros or functions. The macros and functions shown in Table 20-3 are available. These macros and functions allow characters to be tested for various conditions or to be converted between lowercase and uppercase characters.

Macro	Description
isalnum()	Checks for alphanumeric character
isalpha()	Checks for alpha character
isascii()	Checks for ASCII character
iscntrl()	Checks for control character
isdigit()	Checks for decimal digit (0-9)
isgraph()	Checks for printable character (no space)
islower()	Checks for lowercase character
isprint()	Checks for printable character
ispunct()	Checks for punctuation character
isspace()	Checks for white–space character
isupper()	Checks for uppercase character
isxdigit()	Checks for hexadecimal digit
toascii()	Translates character to ASCII equivalent
tolower()	Translates character to lowercase if uppercase
toupper()	Translates character to uppercase if lowercase

Table 20-3. *Character Macros Available in C and C++*

Checking for Alphanumeric, Alpha, and ASCII Values

The following three macros allow ASCII-coded integer values to be checked with the use of a lookup table:

Macro	Description
int isalnum(ch)	Checks for alphanumeric values A-Z, a-z, and 0-9. *ch* is integer
int isalpha(ch)	Checks for alpha values A-Z and a–z. *ch* is integer
int isascii(ch)	Checks for ASCII values 0–127 (0-7Fh). *ch* is integer

The following program checks the ASCII integer values from zero to 127 and reports which of the preceding three functions produce a TRUE condition for each case:

```
/*
 *   20ALPHA.C
 *   Demonstrating the use of the isalnum, isalpha, and isascii
 *   library functions.
 *   Copyright (c) William H. Murray and Chris H. Pappas, 1992
 */

#include <ctype.h>

main()
{
  int ch;
  for (ch=0;ch<=127;ch++) {
    printf("The ASCII digit %d is an:\n",ch);
    printf("%s",isalnum(ch) ? "  alpha-numeric char\n" : "");
    printf("%s",isalpha(ch) ? "  alpha char\n" : "");
    printf("%s",isascii(ch) ? "  ascii char\n" : "");
    printf("\n");
  }
  return (0);
}
```

A portion of the information sent to the screen is shown here:

```
The ASCII digit 0 is an:
  ascii char

The ASCII digit 1 is an:
```

```
    ascii char
            .
            .
            .
The ASCII digit 48 is an:
  alpha-numeric char
  ascii char

The ASCII digit 49 is an:
  alpha-numeric char
  ascii char
            .
            .
            .
The ASCII digit 65 is an:
  alpha-numeric char
  alpha char
  ascii char

The ASCII digit 66 is an:
  alpha-numeric char
  alpha char
  ascii char
```

These functions are very useful in checking the contents of string characters.

Checking for Control, White Space, and Punctuation

The following routines are implemented as both macros and functions:

Routine	Description
int iscntrl(ch)	Checks for control character
int isdigit(ch)	Checks for digit 0–9
int isgraph(ch)	Checks for printable characters (no space)
int islower(ch)	Checks for lowercase a–z
int isprint(ch)	Checks for printable character
int ispunct(ch)	Checks for punctuation
int isspace(ch)	Checks for white space
int isupper(ch)	Checks for uppercase A–Z
int isxdigit(ch)	Checks for hexadecimal value 0-9, a-f, or A-F

These routines allow ASCII-coded integer values to be checked via a lookup table. A zero is returned for FALSE and a nonzero for TRUE. A valid ASCII character set is assumed. The value *ch* is an integer.

The next application checks the ASCII integer values from zero to 127 and reports which of the preceding nine functions give a TRUE condition for each value:

```c
/*
 *   20CONTRL.C
 *   Demonstrating several character functions such as
 *   isprint, isupper, iscntrl, etc.
 *   Copyright (c) William H. Murray and Chris H. Pappas, 1992
 */

#include <ctype.h>

main()
{
  int ch;
  for (ch=0;ch<=127;ch++) {
    printf("The ASCII digit %d is a(n):\n",ch);
    printf("%s",isprint(ch)  ? "  printable char\n" : "");
    printf("%s",islower(ch)  ? "  lowercase char\n" : "");
    printf("%s",isupper(ch)  ? "  uppercase char\n" : "");
    printf("%s",ispunct(ch)  ? "  punctuation char\n" : "");
    printf("%s",isspace(ch)  ? "  space char\n" : "");
    printf("%s",isdigit(ch)  ? "  char digit\n" : "");
    printf("%s",isgraph(ch)  ? "  graphics char\n" : "");
    printf("%s",iscntrl(ch)  ? "  control char\n" : "");
    printf("%s",isxdigit(ch) ? "  hexadecimal char\n" : "");
    printf("\n");
  }
  return (0);
}
```

A portion of the information sent to the screen is shown here:

```
The ASCII digit 0 is a(n):
  control char

The ASCII digit 1 is a(n):
  control char

          .
          .
          .
```

```
The ASCII digit 32 is a(n):
  printable char
  space char

The ASCII digit 33 is a(n):
  printable char
  punctuation char
  graphics char

The ASCII digit 34 is a(n):
  printable char
  punctuation char
  graphics char

              .
              .
              .

The ASCII digit 65 is a(n):
  printable char
  uppercase char
  graphics char
  hexadecimal char

The ASCII digit 66 is a(n):
  printable char
  uppercase char
  graphics char
  hexadecimal char
```

Conversions to ASCII, Lowercase, and Uppercase

The following macros and functions allow ASCII-coded integer values to be translated:

Macro	Description
int toascii(ch)	Translates to ASCII character
int tolower(ch)	Translates *ch* to lowercase if uppercase
int _tolower(ch)	Translates *ch* to lowercase
int toupper(ch)	Translates *ch* to uppercase if lowercase
int _toupper(ch)	Translates *ch* to uppercase

The macro **toascii()** converts *ch* to ASCII by retaining only the lower 7 bits. The functions **tolower()** and **toupper()** convert the character value to the format specified. The macros **_tolower()** and **_toupper()** return identical results when supplied proper ASCII values. A valid ASCII character set is assumed. The value *ch* is an integer.

The next example shows how the macro **toascii()** converts integer information to correct ASCII values:

```
/*
 *    20ASCII.C
 *    Demonstrating the use of the toascii function.

 *    Copyright (c) William H. Murray and Chris H. Pappas, 1992
 */

#include <ctype.h>

int ch;

main()
{
  for(ch=0;ch<=512;ch++) {
    printf("The ASCII value for %d is %d\n",
           ch,toascii(ch));
  }
  return (0);
}
```

Here is a partial list of the information sent to the screen:

```
The ASCII value for 0 is 0
The ASCII value for 1 is 1
The ASCII value for 2 is 2
            .
            .
            .
The ASCII value for 128 is 0
The ASCII value for 129 is 1
The ASCII value for 130 is 2
            .
            .
            .
The ASCII value for 256 is 0
The ASCII value for 257 is 1
The ASCII value for 258 is 2
            .
            .
            .
```

```
The ASCII value for 384 is 0
The ASCII value for 385 is 1
The ASCII value for 386 is 2
```

The String Functions (string.h)

Strings in C and C++ are usually considered one-dimensional character arrays terminated with a null character. The string functions, prototyped in string.h, typically use pointer arguments and return pointer or integer values. You can study the syntax of each command in the next section or, in more detail, in your *Microsoft C/C++ Run-Time Library Reference*. Additional, buffer-manipulation functions such as **memccpy()** and **memset()** are also prototyped in string.h. The functions shown in Table 20-4 are the most popular functions in this group. The memory and string functions provide flexible programming power to C and C++ programmers.

Working with Memory Functions

The memory functions, discussed in the previous section, are accessed with the following syntaxes:

void *memccpy(void *dest,void *source,int ch,unsigned count)

void *memchr(void *buf,int ch,unsigned count)

int memcmp(void *buf1,void *buf2,unsigned count)

void *memcpy(void *dest,void *source,unsigned count)

int memicmp(void *buf1,void *buf2,unsigned count)

void *memmove(void *dest,void *source,unsigned count)

void *memset(void *dest,int ch,unsigned count)

Here, *buf, *buf1, *buf2, *dest,* and *source* are pointers to the appropriate string buffer. The integer *ch* points to a character value. The unsigned *count* holds the character count for the function.

The next section includes a number of examples that show the use of many of these functions.

Function	Description
memccpy()	Copies from source to destination
memchr()	Searches buffer for first *ch*
memcmp()	Compares *n* characters in buf1 and buf2
memcpy()	Copies *n* characters from source to destination
memicmp()	Same as memcmp, except case insensitive
memmove()	Moves one buffer to another
memset()	Copies *ch* into *n* character positions in *buf*
strcat()	Appends a string to another string
strchr()	Locates first occurrence of a character in a string
strcmp()	Compares two strings
strcmpi()	Compares two strings (case insensitive)
strcoll()	Compares two strings (locale specific)
strcpy()	Copies string to another string
strcspn()	Locates first occurrence of a character in string from given character set
strdup()	Replicates the string
strerror()	System-error message saved
stricmp()	Same as strcmpi()
strlen()	Length of string
strlwr()	String converted to lowercase
strncat()	Characters of string appended
strncmp()	Characters of separate strings compared
strncpy()	Characters of one string copied to another
strnicmp()	Characters of two strings compared (case insensitive)
strnset()	String characters set to given character
strpbrk()	First occurrence of character from one string in another string
strrchr()	Last occurrence of character in string
strrev()	Reverses characters in a string
strset()	All characters in string set to given character
strspn()	Locates first substring from given character set in string
strstr()	Locates one string in another string
strtok()	Locates tokens within a string
strupr()	Converts string to uppercase
strxfrm()	Transforms locale-specific string

Table 20-4.   *The Most Popular String Functions*

Find a Character in a String

In this example, the buffer is searched for the occurrence of the lowercase character "f," using the **memchr()** function:

```
/*
 *   20MEMCHR.C
 *   Demonstrating the use of the memchr function.
 *   Finding a character in a buffer.
 *   Copyright (c) William H. Murray and Chris H. Pappas, 1992
 */

#include <string.h>
#include <stdio.h>

char buf[35];
char *ptr;

main()
{
  strcpy(buf,"This is a fine day for a search." );
  ptr=(char *)memchr(buf,'f',35);
  if (ptr != NULL)
    printf("character found at location: %d\n",
           ptr-buf+1);
  else
    printf("character not found.\n");
  return (0);
}
```

For this example, if a lowercase "f" is in the string, the **memchr()** function will report the "character found at location: 11."

Compare Characters in Strings

This example highlights the **memicmp()** function. This function compares two strings contained in *buf1* and *buf2*. This function is insensitive to the case of the string characters.

```
/*
 *   20MEMCMP.C
 *   Demonstrating the use of the memicmp function
 *   to compare two string buffers.
 *   Copyright (c) William H. Murray and Chris H. Pappas, 1992
```

```
*/

#include <string.h>

char buf1[40],
     buf2[40];

main()
{
  strcpy(buf1,"Well, are they identical or not?");
  strcpy(buf2,"Well, are they identicle or not?");
  /* 0 - identical strings except for case */
  /* x - any integer, means not identical */

  printf("%d\n",memicmp(buf1,buf2,40));
  /* returns a non-zero value */
  return (0);
}
```

If it weren't for the fact that identical (or is it identicle?) was spelled incorrectly in the second string, both strings would have been the same. A nonzero value, −1, is returned by **memicmp**() for this example.

Loading the Buffer with memset()

Often it is necessary to load or clear a buffer with a predefined character. In those cases you might consider using the **memset()** function, shown here:

```
/*
 *   20MEMSET.C
 *   Demonstrating the use of the memset function
 *   to set the contents of a string buffer.
 *   Copyright (c) William H. Murray and Chris H. Pappas, 1992
 */

#include <string.h>

char buf[20];

main()
{
  printf("The contents of buf: %s",memset(buf,'+',15));
  buf[15] = '\0';
```

```
    return (0);
}
```

In this example, the buffer is loaded with 15 + characters and a null character. The program will print 15 + characters to the screen.

Working with String Functions

The prototypes for using several string manipulating functions contained in string.h are shown here:

int strcmp(const char *s1, const char *s2)	Compares two strings
size_t strcspn(const char *s1, const char *s2)	Finds a substring in a string
char *strcpy(char *s1,const char *s2)	Copies a string
char *strerror(int errnum)	ANSI-supplied number
char *_strerror(char *s)	User-supplied message
size_t strlen(const char *s)	Null-terminated string
char *strlwr(char *s)	String to lowercase
char *strncat(char *s1,const char *s2,size_t n)	Appends *n* char *s2* to *s1*
int strncmp(const char *s1, const char *s2,size_t n)	Compares first *n* characters of two strings
int strnicmp(const char *s1, const char *s2,size_t n)	Compares first *n* characters of two strings (case insensitive)
char *strncpy(char *s1,const char *s2,size_t n)	Copies *n* characters of *s2* to *s1*
char *strnset(char *s,int ch,size_t n)	Sets first *n* characters of string to char setting
char *strpbrk(const char *s1, const char *s2)	Locates character from const *s2* in *s1*
char *strrchr(const char *s,int ch)	Locates last occurrence of *ch* in string
char *strrev(char *s)	Converts string to reverse
char *strset(char *s,int ch)	String to be set with *ch*
size_t strspn(const char *s1, const char *s2)	Searches *s1* with char set in *s2*
char *strstr(const char *s1, const char *s2)	Searches *s1* with *s2*

char *strtok(char *s1,const char *s2)	Finds token in s1. s1 contains token(s), s2 contains the delimiters
char *strupr(char *s)	Converts string to uppercase

Here, *s is a pointer to a string. *s1 and *s2 are pointers to two strings. Usually *s1 points to the string to be manipulated and *s2 points to the string doing the manipulation. ch is a character value.

Comparing the Contents of Two Strings

The following program uses the **strcmp()** function and reports how one string compares to another.

```
/*
 *    20STRCMP.C
 *    Demonstrating the use of the strcmp function
 *    to compare two strings.
 *    Copyright (c) William H. Murray and Chris H. Pappas, 1992
 */

#include <string.h>

char s1[45] = "A group of characters makes a good string.";
char s2[45] = "A group of characters makes a good string?";
int answer;

main()
{
  answer = strcmp(s1,s2);
  if (answer>0) printf("s1 is greater than s2");
    else if (answer==0) printf("s1 is equal to s2");
      else printf("s1 is less than s2");
  return (0);
}
```

Can you predict which of the preceding strings would be greater? Can you do it without running the program? The answer is that s1 is less than s2.

Searching for Several Characters in a String

The next program searches a string for the first occurrence of one or more characters:

```
/*
 *    20STRSPN.C
 *    Demonstrating the use of the strcspn function to find
 *    the, occurrence of one of a group of characters.
 *    Copyright (c) William H. Murray and Chris H. Pappas, 1992
 */

#include <string.h>

char s1[35];
int answer;

main()
{
  strcpy(s1,"We are looking for great strings." );
  answer=strcspn(s1,"abc");
  printf("The first a,b,c appeared at position %d\n",
         answer+1);
  return (0);
}
```

This program will report the position of the first occurrence of an "a", a "b", or a "c". A 1 is added to the answer since the first character is at index position zero. This program reports an "a" at position 4.

The First Occurrence of a Single Character in a String

Have you ever wanted to check a sentence for the occurrence of a particular character? You might consider using the **strchr()** function. The following application looks for the first blank or space character in the string.

```
/*
 *    20STRCHR.C
 *    Demonstrating the use of the strchr function to
 *    locate the first occurrence of a character in a string.
 *    Copyright (c) William H. Murray and Chris H. Pappas, 1992
 */

#include <string.h>

char s1[20] = "What is a friend?";
char *answer;

main()
```

```
{
  answer=strchr(s1,' ');
  printf("After the first blank: %s\n",answer);
  return (0);
}
```

What is your prediction on the outcome after execution? Run the program and see.

Finding the Length of a String

The **strlen()** function reports the length of any given string. Here is a simple example:

```
/*
 *    20STRLEN.C
 *    Demonstrating the use of the strlen function to
 *    determine the length of a string.
 *    Copyright (c) William H. Murray and Chris H. Pappas, 1992
 */

#include <string.h>

char *s1="String length is measured in characters!";

main()
{
  printf("The string length is %d",strlen(s1));
  return (0);
}
```

In this example, the **strlen()** function reports on the total number of characters contained in the string. In this example, there are 40 characters.

Locating One String in Another String

The **strstr()** function searches a given string within a group (a string) of characters, as shown here:

```
/*
 *    20STRSTR.C
 *    Demonstrating the use of the strstr function to
 *    locate a string within a string.
 *    Copyright (c) William H. Murray and Chris H. Pappas, 1992
```

```
*/

#include <string.h>

main()
{
  char *s1="There is always something you miss.";
  char *s2="way";

  printf("%s\n",strstr(s1,s2));
  return (0);
}
```

This program sends the remainder of the string to the **printf()** function after the first occurrence of "way". The string printed to the screen is "ways something you miss".

Converting Characters to Uppercase

A handy function to have in a case-sensitive language is one that can convert the characters in a string to another case. **strupr()** is a function that converts lowercase characters to uppercase, as shown here:

```
/*
 *    20STRUPR.C
 *    Demonstrating the use of the strupr function to
 *    convert lowercase letters to uppercase.
 *    Copyright (c) William H. Murray and Chris H. Pappas, 1992
 */

#include <string.h>

char *s1="Uppercase characters are easier to read.";
char *s2;

main()
{
  s2=strupr(s1);
  printf("The results: %s",s2);
  return (0);
}
```

This program converts each lowercase character to uppercase. Note that only lowercase letters will be changed.

The Math Functions (math.h)

The functions prototyped in the math.h header file permit a great variety of mathematical, algebraic, and trigonometric operations.

The math functions are relatively easy to use and understand for those familiar with algebraic and trigonometric concepts. Many of these functions were demonstrated in earlier chapters. When using trigonometric functions, remember that angle arguments are always specified in radians. The math functions are shown in Table 20-5.

Programmers desiring complex number arithmetic must resort to using **struct** complex and the **_cabs()** function described in math.h. Following is the only structure available for complex arithmetic in Microsoft C/C++:

struct complex {double *x*,double *y*}

This structure is used by the **_cabs()** function. The **_cabs()** function returns the absolute value of a complex number.

Building a Table of Trigonometric Values

Since math functions have already been used extensively in this book, the only example for this section involves an application that will generate a table of sine, cosine, and tangent values for the angles from zero to 45 degrees.

This application also takes advantage of the special C++ formatting abilities. Study the following listing to determine how the output will be sent to the screen:

```
//
//  20MATH.CPP
//  A program that demonstrates the use of several
//  math functions.
//  Copyright (c) William H. Murray and Chris H. Pappas, 1992
//

#include <iostream.h>
#include <iomanip.h>
#include <math.h>

#define PI 3.14159265359

main()
{
  int i;
  double x,y,z,ang;
```

Math Function	Description
int abs(int *x*)	Absolute value
double acos(double *x*)	Arc cosine
double asin(double *x*)	Arc sine
double atan(double *x*)	Arc tangent
double atan2(double *y*,double *x*)	Arc tan of 2 nums
double ceil(double *x*)	Greatest integer
double cos(double *x*)	Cosine
double cosh(double *x*)	Hyperbolic cosine
int _dieeetomsbin(double *,double *)	IEEE to MS conversion
int _dmsbintoieee(double *,double *)	MS to IEEE conversion
double exp(double *x*)	Exponential value
double fabs(double *x*)	Absolute value
int _fieeetomsbin(float*,float *)	IEEE to MS conversion
double floor(double *x*)	Smallest integer
double fmod(double *x*,double *y*)	Modulus operator
int _fmsbintoieee(float *,float *)	MS to IEEE conversion
double fre*x*p(double *x*,int *exponent)	Split to mantissa and exponent
double hypot(double *x*,double *y*)	Hypotenuse
double _j0(double *x*)	Bessel routine
double _j1(double *x*)	Bessel routine
double _jn(int n,double *x*)	Bessel routine
long labs(long *x*)	Absolute value
double lde*x*p(double *x*,int exponent)	*x* times 2 to exp power
double log(double *x*)	Natural log
double log10(double *x*)	Common log
double modf(double *x*,double *ipart)	Mantissa and exponent
double pow(double *x*,double *y*)	*x* to *y* power
double sin(double *x*)	Sine
double sinh(double *x*)	Hyperbolic sine
double sqrt(double *x*)	Square root
double tan(double *x*)	Tangent
double tanh(double *x*)	Hyperbolic tangent
double _y0(double *x*)	Bessel routine
double _y1(double *x*)	Bessel routine
double _yn(int n,double *x*)	Bessel routine

Note: There are additional prototypes that pass and return long double values. Their function names end with an extra "l." For example: **asinl()**, **cosl()**, **powl()**, **sqrtl()**, **_y0l()**, and so on.

Table 20-5.   Math Functions

```
for (i=0;i<=45;i++) {
  ang=PI*i/180;  // convert degrees to radians
  x=sin(ang);
  y=cos(ang);
  z=tan(ang);
  // formatting output columns
  cout << setiosflags(ios::left) << setw(8)
       << setiosflags(ios::fixed) << setprecision(6);
  // data to print
  cout << i << "\t" << x << "\t" <<
          y << "\t" << z << "\n";
}
  return (0);
}
```

This application uses the **sin()**, **cos()**, and **tan()** functions to produce a formatted trigonometric table. The angles are stepped from zero to 45 degrees and are converted to radians before being sent to each function. If you are unsure about how the formatting is achieved, you might want to review Chapter 17.

Following is a partial output from this application:

```
0 0.000000 1.000000 0.000000
1 0.017452 0.999848 0.017455
2 0.034899 0.999391 0.034921
.    .       .        .
.    .       .        .
.    .       .        .
28 0.469472 0.882948 0.531709
29 0.484810 0.874620 0.554309
30 0.500000 0.866025 0.577350
31 0.515038 0.857167 0.600861
32 0.529919 0.848048 0.624869
.    .       .        .
.    .       .        .
.    .       .        .
43 0.681998 0.731354 0.932515
44 0.694658 0.719340 0.965689
45 0.707107 0.707107 1.000000
```

The Time Functions (time.h)

The following table shows some of the time and date function names in time.h:

Names	Description
asctime()	Converts date and time to an ASCII string and uses *tm* structure
ctime()	Converts date and time to a string
difftime()	Calculates the difference between two times
gmtime()	Converts date and time to GMT using *tm* structure
localtime()	Converts date and time to *tm* structure
strftime()	Allows formatting of date and time data for output
time()	Obtains current time (system)
_tzset()	Sets time variables for environment variable *TZ*

These functions offer a variety of ways to obtain time and/or date formats for programs. A discussion of the syntax for each function is included in the next section.

Time and Date Structures and Syntax

Many of the date and time functions described in the previous section use the *tm* structure defined in time.h. This structure is shown here:

```
struct tm  {
   int  tm_sec;
   int  tm_min;
   int  tm_hour;
   int  tm_mday;
   int  tm_mon;
   int  tm_year;
   int  tm_wday;
   int  tm_yday;
   int  tm_isdst;
};
```

The syntax for calling each date and time function differs according to the function's ability. The syntax for each function is shown here:

char *asctime(const struct *tm* *tblock)	Converts the structure into a 26-character string. For example: Wed Oct 14 10:18:20 1992\n\0
char *ctime(const time_t *time)	Converts a time value, pointed to by *time into a 26-char string (see **asctime()**)
double difftime(time_t *time2,* time_t *time1)*	Calculates the difference between *time2* and *time1* and returns a double

struct tm *gmtime(const time_t *timer)	Accepts address of a value returned by the function **time()** and returns a pointer to the structure with GMT information
struct tm *localtime (const time_t *timer)	Accepts address of a value returned by the function **time()** and returns a pointer to the structure with local time information
size_t strftime (char *s, size_t *maxsize*, const char *fmt*, const struct tm *t*)	Formats date and time information for output. *s* points to the string information, *maxsize* is maximum string length, *fmt* represents the format, and *t* points to a structure of type *tm*. The formatting options include

%a	Abbreviate weekday name
%A	Full weekday name
%b	Abbreviate month name
%B	Full month name
%c	Date and time information
%d	Day of month (01 to 31)
%H	Hour (00 to 23)
%I	Hour (00 to 12)
%j	Day of year (001 to 366)
%m	Month (01 to 12)
%M	Minutes (00 to 59)
%p	AM or PM
%S	Seconds (0 to 59)
%U	Week number (00 to 51), Sunday is first day
%w	Weekday (0 to 6)
%W	Week number (00 to 51), Monday is first day
%x	Date
%X	Time
%y	Year, without century (00 to 99)
%Y	Year, with century
%Z	Time zone name
%%	Character %

time_t time(time_t *timer)	Returns the time in seconds since 00:00:00 GMT, January 1, 1970
void _tzset(void)	Sets the global variables *daylight, timezone,* and *tzname* based on the environment string. The *TZ* environment string uses the following syntax:

$$TZ = zzz[+/-]d[d]\{lll\}$$

Here, *zzz* represents a three-character string with the local time zone—for example, "EST" for Eastern Standard Time. The [+/]*d*[*d*] argument contains an adjustment for the local time zone's difference from GMT. Positive numbers are a westward adjustment, while negative numbers are an eastward adjustment. For example, a five (5) would be used for EST. The last argument, {*lll*}, represents the local time zone's daylight savings time—for example, EDT for Eastern Daylight Savings Time

Several of these functions are used in example programs in the next section.

Working with the localtime() and asctime() Functions

Many times it is necessary to obtain the time and date in a programming application. The next program returns these values by using the **localtime()** and **asctime()** functions:

```
/*
 *    20ASCTIM.C
 *    Demonstrating the use of the localtime and asctime
 *    functions.
 *    Copyright (c) William H. Murray and Chris H. Pappas, 1992
 */

#include <time.h>
#include <stdio.h>

struct tm *date_time;
time_t timer;
```

```
main()
{
  time(&timer);
  date_time=localtime(&timer);

  printf("The present date and time is: %s\n",
  asctime(date_time));
  return (0);
}
```

This program formats the time and date information in the manner shown here:

```
The present date and time is: Wed Oct 14 13:16:20 1992
```

Working with the gmtime() and asctime() Functions

There are other functions that you can also use to return time and date information. The next program is similar to the last example, except that the **gmtime()** function is used.

```
/*
 *    20GMTIME.C
 *    Demonstrating the use of the gmtime and asctime
 *    functions.
 *    Copyright (c) William H. Murray and Chris H. Pappas, 1992
 */

#include <time.h>
#include <stdio.h>

main()
{
  struct tm *date_time;
  time_t timer;

  time(&timer);
  date_time=gmtime(&timer);

  printf("%.19s\n",asctime(date_time));
  return (0);
}
```

The following date and time information was returned by this program:

```
Mon May 18 14:13:25
```

Working with the strftime Function

The **strftime()** function provides the greatest formatting flexibility of all the date and time functions. The following program illustrates several formatting options.

```
/*
 *   20STRTM.C
 *   Demonstrating the use of the strftime function.
 *   Copyright (c) William H. Murray and Chris H. Pappas, 1992
 */

#include <time.h>
#include <stdio.h>

main()
{
  struct tm *date_time;
  time_t timer;
  char str[80];

  time(&timer);
  date_time=localtime(&timer);
  strftime(str,80,"It is %X on %A, %x",
           date_time);
  printf("%s\n",str);
  return (0);
}
```

Here is a sample of the output for this program:

```
It is 17:18:45 on Wednesday, 04/10/92
```

You may find that the **strftime()** function is not portable from one system to another. Use it with caution if portability is a consideration.

Working with the ctime() Function

The following C++ program illustrates how to make a call to the **ctime()** function. This program shows how easy it is to obtain date and time information from the system.

```
//
//  20CTIME.CPP
//  Demonstrating the use of the ctime function.
//  Copyright (c) William H. Murray and Chris H. Pappas, 1992
//

#include <time.h>
#include <iostream.h>

time_t longtime;

main()
{
  time(&longtime);
  cout << "The time and date are " <<
          ctime(&longtime) << "\n";
  return (0);
}
```

The output, sent to the screen, would appear in the following format:

```
The time and date are Sat Feb 22 14:23:27 1992
```

Building a Delay Routine

Usually it is desirable for programs to execute as quickly as possible. However, there are times when slowing down information makes it easier for the user to view and understand. The **time_delay()** function in the following application delays program execution. The delay variable is in seconds. For this example, there is a two-second delay between each line of output to the screen.

```
/*
 *    20TDELAY.C
 *    A C program that demonstrates how to create a delay
 *    function for slowing program output.
 *    Copyright (c) William H. Murray and Chris H. Pappas, 1992
 */

#include <stdio.h>
#include <time.h>

void time_delay(int);

main()
```

```
{
  int i;

  for (i=0;i<25;i++) {
    time_delay(2);
    printf("The count is %d\n",i);
  }
  return (0);
}

void time_delay(int t)
{
  long initial,final;
  long ltime;

  initial=time(&ltime);
  final=initial+t;

  while (time(&ltime) < final);
  return;
}
```

What other uses might the **time_delay()** function have? One case might be where the computer is connected to an external data sensing device, such as a thermocouple or strain gauge. The function could be used to take readings every minute, hour, or day.

System-dependent Functions

Microsoft C/C++ libraries provide functions that allow you to tap into various software and hardware features. These system features usually make programs nonportable from one system to another (for example, IBM-compatible to Apple) and from one compiler to another (for example, Microsoft and Borland). They are obviously not part of the ANSI standard. However, given that many programmers and users work on IBM-compatible computers under DOS with Microsoft C/C++, the compatibility problem might not be a significant issue. Why use functions that are system or hardware dependent at all? The answer is simple: these are the functions that provide the bells and whistles in programming. They are the functions that allow you to tap the power of the computer hardware and provide control of printers, plotters, CD ROM drives, mice, modems, and so on. You'll certainly want to make use of these functions, but learning how to use them with the proper respect is very important.

Without the BIOS and DOS capabilities provided with C and C++, hardware control would be exclusively in the realm of assembly language programmers. With these built-in C and C++ functions, it is now possible to write many programs without the need of assembly language patches. You will see in Chapter 21 how assembly language can provide many of the same features for controlling system hardware. In Chapter 21 you will learn how to splice C/C++ code and assembly code together to help solve programming problems that cannot be handled with the simple functions described in this chapter.

The bios.h Header File

The seven functions shown in the following table allow immediate access to powerful BIOS (basic input and output) services built into IBM compatible computers:

Function	Description
_bios_disk()	Issues disk operations through BIOS
_bios_equiplist()	Checks hardware of system
_bios_keybrd()	Keyboard interface
_bios_memsize()	Returns RAM (640K maximum) memory size
_bios_printer()	Perform printer I/O with BIOS
_bios_serialcom()	Serial communication services
_bios_timeofday()	Time and date services

Again, these functions are very hardware dependent and may not operate on systems that are not 100 percent compatible. The BIOS functions include disk control, RS-232 communications, memory size, timer control, and more.

You saw in the last section that there are other standard C and C++ functions that also permit many of these same operations. This book recommends that you use ANSI functions when possible and avoid the problem of incompatibility with systems that do not permit the use of the Microsoft BIOS functions. At other times, the use of Microsoft's BIOS functions will be your only solution to the programming problem.

BIOS Function Call Syntax

The syntax for using each BIOS function is relatively simple, as you can see from the function prototypes included here. You can find more information for the various arguments in the *Microsoft C/C++ Run-Time Library Reference*.

```
unsigned _bios_disk(unsigned, struct _diskinfo_t *)
unsigned _bios_equiplist(void)
```

```
unsigned _bios_keybrd(unsigned)
unsigned _bios_memsize(void)
unsigned _bios_printer(unsigned,unsigned,unsigned)
unsigned _bios_serialcom(unsigned,unsigned,unsigned)
unsigned _bios_timeofday(unsigned,long *)
```

The next two applications illustrate a use for several of these BIOS functions. Use the preceding list in conjunction with your reference manual as a quick reference.

Checking the Computer's Base Memory   This program uses a BIOS function to check for the total base memory in a computer system. The range of memory can be between zero and 640K. Making the function call is straightforward. Examine the following C++ program:

```
//
//  20MEMORY.CPP
//  A demonstration of how to use the _bios_memsize
//  function for obtaining the amount of installed RAM memory.
//  This value can vary from 0 to 640K and does not
//  include extended or expanded memory.
//  Copyright (c) William H. Murray and Chris H. Pappas, 1992
//

#include <iostream.h>
#include <bios.h>

main()
{
  unsigned base_memory;

  base_memory=_bios_memsize();

  cout << "There is " << base_memory
       << "K of base memory installed.";
  return (0);
}
```

This function is limited to reporting memory in the range zero to 640K and will not report extended or expanded memory amounts. At this time, there is no simple function that will allow you to determine this extra memory.

Checking for an Internal Modem   The following program allows a software program to check for the presence of an internal modem. If a modem is present, bit 13 of the value returned by the function will be high or logic 1. Otherwise, the bit is a zero, or logic 0. Binary bit 13, alone, produces a binary number of 10000000000000_2. This binary number is equivalent to the hexadecimal value 4000_{16}. An *and* mask is created with this same value. The purpose of the mask is to isolate that single bit, examine it, and determine if it is a 1 or zero, TRUE or FALSE.

Other bit values can provide additional information, as the following table shows:

Bit	Meaning
0	Disk drive present
1	Coprocessor present
2-3	RAM in 16K blocks
4-5	Initial video mode
6-7	Number of floppy drives
8	False if DMA chip installed
9-11	Number of serial ports
12	Game adapter present
13	Internal modem present
14-15	Number of printers

Examine the program listing and make sure you understand how the mask is being applied:

```
//
//  20EQUIP.CPP
//  A demonstration of how to use the _bios_equiplist
//  function for obtaining current hardware information.
//  Copyright (c) William H. Murray and Chris H. Pappas, 1992
//

#include <iostream.h>
#include <bios.h>

#define MODEM 0x4000

main()
{
  unsigned online_equip;

  online_equip=_bios_equiplist();

  if (online_equip & MODEM)
    cout << "There is an internal modem installed.\n";
```

```
  else
    cout << "There is no internal modem installed.\n";
  return (0);
}
```

If the value returned by the BIOS function and the mask produce a TRUE condition, an internal modem is present. Programs such as this are useful for determining which hardware items the program can take advantage of in a given system.

The dos.h Header File

The DOS functions listed in Table 20-6 allow immediate access to powerful DOS interrupt capabilities built into IBM and 100-percent-compatible computers. These functions are very hardware dependent and may not function properly on non-compatible machines. As you can see, the DOS functions permit a broader range of operations than the previous BIOS functions.

Many of the DOS functions permit operations similar to the BIOS routines. For example, notice that there are several time and date functions, disk I/O functions, and so on. DOS functions tend to be more robust in their abilities. This book continues to recommend, however, that the functions that are included in the ANSI standard be used where possible if they achieve the same results for your program.

DOS Functions	Description
_bdos()	DOS system call using DX and AL registers
_chain_intr()	Chain interrupt handlers together
_disable()	Interrupt disable
_dos_allocmem()	Allocates a block of memory
_dos_close()	Closes a file
_dos_commit()	Flushs a file to disk
_dos_creat()	Creates a new file (erases one of same name)
_dos_creatnew()	Creates new file (error if one exists)
_dos_findfirst()	Finds first file of given name
_dos_findnext()	Finds next file of same name as _dos_findfirst()

Table 20-6.   *DOS Functions that Allow Immediate Access to DOS Interrupt Capabilities*

DOS Functions	Description
_dos_freemem()	Frees a block of memory
_dos_getdate()	Gets system date
_dos_getdiskfree()	Disk volume information
_dos_getdrive()	Gets default drive
_dos_getfileattr()	Current file or directory attributes
_dos_getftime()	Date/time of last input to file
_dos_gettime()	Current system time
_dos_getvect()	Value of interrupt vector
_dos_keep()	Installs TSR program
_dos_open()	Opens a file
_dos_read()	Reads a file
_dos_setblock()	Changes block size
_dos_setdate()	Sets system date
_dos_setdrive()	Sets default drive
_dos_setfileattr()	Sets file attribute
_dos_setftime()	Sets date/time of last input to file
_dos_settime()	Sets system time
_dos_setvect()	Sets a value for the interrupt vector
_dos_write()	Sends output to a file
_dosexterr()	Opens error information
_harderr()	Establishs hard error handler
_hardresume()	Returns to DOS after hardware error
_hardretn()	Returns to application after hardware error
_int86()	Provides a DOS interrupt
_int86x()	Provides a DOS interrupt with segment registers
_intdos()	DOS interrupt with additional registers
_intdosx()	Same as _intdos() with segment registers
_enable()	Enables interrupts
_segread()	Reads segment registers

Table 20-7. *DOS Functions that Allow Immediate Access to DOS Interrupt Capabilities* (continued)

DOS Function Call Syntax

The syntax for using each DOS function is as easy as it is for the BIOS function calls. Examine the DOS function prototypes and notice the wide range of services they provide. You can find detailed information for the various DOS function arguments in the *Microsoft C/C++ Run-Time Library Reference*.

```
int _bdos(int,unsigned int,unsigned int);
void _chain_intr(void (_ _interrupt _ _far *)());
void _disable(void);
unsigned _dos_allocmem(unsigned,unsigned *);
unsigned _dos_close(int);
unsigned _dos_commit(int);
unsigned _dos_creat(const char *,unsigned,int *);
unsigned _dos_creatnew(const char *,unsigned,int *);
unsigned _dos_findfirst(const char *,unsigned,struct _find_t *);
unsigned _dos_findnext(struct _find_t *);
unsigned _dos_freemem(unsigned);
void _dos_getdate(struct _dosdate_t *);
void _dos_getdrive(unsigned *);
unsigned _dos_getdiskfree(unsigned,struct _diskfree_t *);
unsigned _dos_getfileattr(const char *,unsigned *);
unsigned _dos_getftime(int,unsigned *,unsigned *);
void _dos_gettime(struct _dostime_t *);
void (_ _interrupt _ _far * _dos_getvect(unsigned))();
void _dos_keep(unsigned,unsigned);
unsigned _dos_open(const char *,unsigned,int *);
unsigned _dos_read(int,void _ _far *,unsigned,unsigned *);
unsigned _dos_setblock(unsigned,unsigned,unsigned *);
unsigned _dos_setdate(struct _dosdate_t *);
void _dos_setdrive(unsigned,unsigned *);
unsigned _dos_setfileattr(const char *,unsigned);
unsigned _dos_setftime(int,unsigned,unsigned);
unsigned _dos_settime(struct _dostime_t *);
void _dos_setvect(unsigned,void (_ _interrupt _ _far *)());
unsigned _dos_write(int,const void _ _far *,unsigned,unsigned *);
int _dosexterr(struct _DOSERROR *);
void _enable(void);
void _harderr(void (_ _far *)());
void _hardresume(int);
void _hardretn(int);
int _intdos(union _REGS *,union _REGS *);
int _intdosx(union _REGS *,union _REGS *,struct _SREGS *);
int _int86(int,union _REGS *,union _REGS *);
int _int86x(int,union _REGS *,union _REGS *,struct _SREGS
```

```
int bdos(int,unsigned int,unsigned int);
int intdos(union REGS *,union REGS *);
int intdosx(union REGS *,union REGS *,struct SREGS *);
int int86(int,union REGS *,union REGS *);
int int86x(int,union REGS *,union REGS *,struct SREGS *);
int dosexterr(struct DOSERROR *);
void segread(struct SREGS *);
```

In the next section, two functions are used to illustrate DOS function capabilities. For situations where a particular function call is not available, a general DOS interrupt can be used.

Examining Free Memory on a Disk   You learned how to read and write to the disk drive in Chapters 11, 12, and 17. It is often a good idea to know how much free disk space is available before a write attempt is made. The **_dos_getdiskfree()** function provides that information. In the following example, available space on the C drive will be reported to the user:

```
/*
 *   20FREESP.C
 *   A program that demonstrates how to use the
 *   _dos_getdiskfree function for obtaining free
 *   disk space on drive C.
 *   Copyright (c) William H. Murray and Chris H. Pappas, 1992
 */

#include <dos.h>
#include <stdio.h>

main()
{
  struct _diskfree_t df;
  unsigned f_disk;

  _dos_getdiskfree(3,&df);

  f_disk=df.total_clusters*df.sectors_per_cluster*
         df.bytes_per_sector;
  printf("Drive C has %lu bytes of memory for use.\n",f_disk);
  return (0);
}
```

The C drive is identified with the number 3 (A is 1 and B is 2). Data concerning memory is returned to the **_diskfree_t** structure. This structure holds information on the available clusters, total clusters, bytes per sector, and sectors per cluster. You can see how that information is spliced together, in the preceding program, to provide the total free disk space.

Using DOS Interrupt Functions   The DOS and BIOS functions provide a "hook" to many of the interrupts provided on the computer. When a particular function has not been created for your specific needs, it is possible to call a general interrupt function and supply the necessary parameters. The next application does just that. It will issue an interrupt 33h and make the mouse pointer (if a mouse is installed) visible for 45 seconds.

```
/*
 *    20INT86.C
 *    A program that demonstrates the use of the int86
 *    function to show the mouse pointer for 45 seconds!
 *    (Appendix B lists all possible mouse interrupts.)
 *    Copyright (c) William H. Murray and Chris H. Pappas, 1992
 */

#include <dos.h>
#include <time.h>

void time_delay(int);

main()
{
  union REGS regs;

  regs.x.ax=1;
  int86(0x33,&regs,&regs);

  time_delay(45);

  regs.x.ax=0;
  int86(0x33,&regs,&regs);

  return (0);
}

void time_delay(int t)
{
  long initial,final;
  long ltime;
```

```
    initial=time(&ltime);
    final=initial+t;

    while (time(&ltime) < final);
    return;
}
```

As you examine the mouse interrupts given in Appendix B, notice that it is also possible to detect mouse button clicks and coordinate positions using these functions. This program simply switches the default mouse pointer on and off. While the pointer is on, it is possible to move the mouse about on the screen.

This application makes use of the union REGS described in the dos.h header file. Using this union, the user has access to the **ax**, **bx**, **cx**, **dx**, **bp**, **si**, **di**, **ds**, **es**, and **flag** registers of the microprocessor. As you examine the function prototype shown earlier, observe that register information can be set and passed into the microprocessor registers with *inregs*. Likewise, the function can return the contents of the system registers through the union *outregs*. For 16-bit registers use *reg.x*, and for 8-bit registers use *reg.h*. The syntax is simply

regs.x.ax = *desired value*, for 16-bit registers
regs.h.bl = *desired value*, for 8-bit registers

In the next chapter, you will learn how to combine C, C++, and assembly language code into a single executable program. Many of the DOS and BIOS features discussed in this chapter can be incorporated into these programs.

Chapter 21

Binding Microsoft C/C++ and Assembly Language

There are times when the built-in C and C++ functions, described in Chapter 20, are not sufficient for the needs of the application being developed. Under these circumstances, C and C++ programmers typically turn to assembly language patches. Assembly language offers you two major advantages: superior execution speed and the ability to write functions that are not part of the included C/C++ libraries.

Microsoft C/C++ offers two options for adding assembly in C and C++ projects: inline code and stand-alone assembly modules. In the former case, the Microsoft C/C++ compiler is fully capable of compiling assembly language code that is inserted within the C and C++ host program. In the latter case, a macro assembler such as Microsoft's MASM is needed in addition to the C/C++ compiler to produce an object file. The object file is then combined with the host C or C++ module at link time.

The focus of this chapter is on calling assembly language code from C or C++ host applications. Thus, the C or C++ code will appear as the main program and the assembly language code as an external function. It is also possible, although not as common, to call C and C++ programs from assembly language source code, where the assembly code acts as the main program.

This chapter assumes you have a working knowledge of fundamental assembly language programming. The assembly language code is kept very simple since the focus of the chapter is on binding C, C++, and assembly language modules.

Inline Assembly Language

Using inline code is a quick and efficient solution when adding short assembly language routines to your C and C++ code. Inline coding permits the placement of assembly language code within the C or C++ source file. This technique is ideal for simple assembly language routines like DOS and BIOS interrupt calls.

To write an inline assembly language routine, you use the **_asm** keyword. The inline code is then contained between two braces. For example:

```
_asm {
    push    ax              ;save general registers
    push    bx
    push    cx
    push    dx
    mov     cx,0            ;upper corner of window
    mov     dx,2479H        ;lower corner of window
    mov     bh,7            ;normal screen attribute
    mov     ax,0600H        ;BIOS interrupt value
    int     10H     /       ;call interrupt
    pop     dx
    pop     cx
    pop     bx
    pop     ax              ;restore general registers
}
```

This assembly language routine clears the text screen by calling the BIOS interrupt function. Additional BIOS and DOS interrupt values are listed in Appendix B. You can include many of these interrupts in your C or C++ code in inline assembly language routines.

Producing Sound

A useful assembly language routine that is easy to construct inline is one that produces a tone from the computer's internal speaker. You create a tone by addressing port 61H. As you can see from observing the program listing, there is more assembly language here than C++ code:

```
//
//  21SOUND.CPP
//  Demonstrates how to use inline assembly language to
```

```
//  produce a sound from the computer's internal speaker.
//  Copyright (c) William H. Murray and Chris H. Pappas, 1992
//

main()
{
  int freq;

  //sound from speaker port
  _asm {
    mov    dx,0             ;initialize sound count to 0
    in     al,61h           ;obtain speaker port info
    and    al,0FCh          ;discard lower two bits
  noise:
    mov    freq,50          ;initialize starting frequency
    inc    dx               ;increment counter
    cmp    dx,20            ;do same sound 20 times
    je     theend           ;done yet?
  more:
    xor    al,02h           ;toggle bit in al
    mov    cx,freq          ;current frequency
    cmp    cx,2000          ;2000 hertz yet?
    je     noise            ;if yes, do it again
    inc    freq             ;if not, increment frequency
    out    61h,al           ;send to speaker port
  here: loop here           ;short time delay
    jmp    more             ;repeat again
  theend:                   ;done with routine
  }

  return (0);
}
```

The assembly language routine produces a sound from the speaker by toggling the speaker port on and off. With the correct combination of loops, a gradual tone from 50 hertz to 2000 hertz can be produced. In this application, that frequency is repeated 20 times. This sound generator is highly dependent upon the speed of the CPU clock. On a 50MHz 80486 system, it will produce a sound similar to a canary chirping, while on a slower 80286 the sound will be closer to laser guns. Notice that a variable declared in C++ is shared with, or passed to, the assembly language module. The C++ integer data type corresponds to the assembly language word data type.

Experiment with some DOS or BIOS interrupts that interest you. Perhaps you'd like a routine to change the background color, alter the cursor's shape, or control the mouse. They're all available to you as inline assembly code.

The Parallel Port as a General-purpose I/O Port

The next application using inline code allows interaction with the computer's parallel port. This project could be accomplished with the use of C or C++ functions, but the use of inline assembly language serves as a simple example of useful coding.

First, here is some background information on the parallel port. The parallel port on most IBM-compatible computers is a general-purpose 8-bit communications port used to drive a wide range of devices. These devices can include printers, plotters, and other external circuits. Information can be sent to the parallel port with an **out** assembly language mnemonic. Data from parallel port lines can be used to control hardware circuits of your own choosing.

The IBM family of PS/2 computers and recent compatibles have parallel ports that can be programmed to read 8 bits of data and respond to another assembly language instruction: **in***.*

The parallel port is an 8-bit data port. This means that 8 bits of data can be sent to the port. The 8-bit assembly language data type is the **byte**, and the corresponding C or C++ data type is the **char**. The 16-bit assembly language data type is the **word**, and the corresponding C or C++ type is the **int**. Data can be written to the output pins when a write (**out**) assembly language instruction occurs. The output signals from the parallel port have sink currents of approximately 20 mA. and can source 0.55 mA. The high-level output voltage is 5.0 Vdc, and the low-level output voltage is 0.5 Vdc. Data is present at pins 2 through 9 and represents the data lines D0 to D7. The following illustration shows the pin arrangement on the D-shell connector:

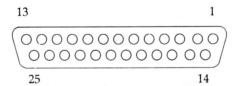

Table 21-1 describes the pin assignment for the parallel port connector. This is standard for all compatible computers.

Using the parallel port is straightforward. The application described in the next section is a complete program that makes two calls to inline assembly language routines. The first assembly language routine clears the screen, and the second sends a data value to the parallel port.

Controlling LED Lights

In the previous section, the parallel port was described as being capable of having sink currents of 20 mA. and source currents of 0.55 mA. The output voltage from the

Pin	Description
1	-STROBE
2	Data bit 0
3	Data bit 1
4	Data bit 2
5	Data bit 3
6	Data bit 4
7	Data bit 5
8	Data bit 6
9	Data bit 7
10	-ACK
11	BUSY
12	PE
13	SELECT
14	-AUTO FEED XT
15	ERROR
16	-INIT
17	-SELECT IN
18-25	GROUND

Table 21-1.   *The Pin Assignments for the 8-bit Parallel Port Connector*

parallel port is TTL compatible; that is, logic 1 is 5.0 Vdc, while logic 0 is 0.5 Vdc. With these capabilities, the parallel port can directly drive small LED lights.

If you are interested in wiring eight LED lights to your parallel port, you will need only a few parts. First obtain or build a cable that will connect the parallel port to a prototyping board. Purchase some hookup wire and eight LED lights. (The authors used a 25-pin D-shell connector to connect to the parallel port with a ribbon cable terminating in a 24-pin male dip header. Pin 13 from the D-shell connector is not connected. The prototyping board was simply the type that allows DIP chips to be easily inserted and removed. These parts can be found at electronics supply stores, such as Radio Shack, throughout the United States. If you purchase connectors that clamp over the ribbon cable, no soldering will be necessary.)

The voltages present at the parallel port are lower than those of a car battery and do not present a shock hazard. It is also just about impossible to do any damage to the computer, even if wrong connections are made.

You must remember that you are making "live" connections to the computer. Be very careful not to connect the parallel port to any external device or outlet where unsafe voltages are present. Figure 21-1 shows a wiring schematic for the LED lamp assembly.

The following C++ code contains a screen-clearing routine similar to the one shown earlier in this chapter and a routine that permits access to the parallel port.

```
//
//   21INLINE.CPP
//   Demonstrates how to use inline assembly language to
//   clear the screen and access the parallel port. This
//   program will sequence 8 LED lamps connected to data
//   lines D0 - D7 of port 956 (LPT1). Note: Your computer
//   might use port 888.
//   Copyright (c) William H. Murray and Chris H. Pappas, 1992
//

#include <dos.h>
#include <iostream.h>
#include <math.h>
```

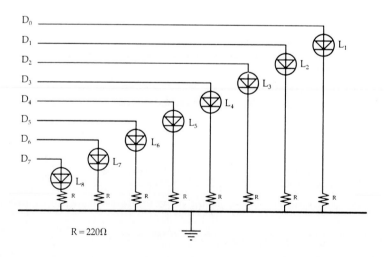

Figure 21-1.   *A schematic of the LED lamp hookup*

```c
#include <time.h>

void time_delay(unsigned long);

main()
{
  int i,temp;
  int port=956;

  /*clear the text screen*/
  _asm {
    mov     cx,0              ;upper corner of window
    mov     dx,2479H          ;lower corner of window
    mov     bh,7              ;normal screen attribute
    mov     ax,0600H          ;BIOS interrupt value
    int     10H               ;call interrupt
  }

  for (i=0;i<9;i++) {
    temp=(int) pow(2.0,(double) i);

    //gain access to the parallel port
    _asm {
      mov     dx,port         ;the parallel port number
      mov     ax,temp         ;value to be sent to port
      out     dx,al           ;send only lower 8-bits
    }

    cout << temp << "\n" << flush;
    time_delay(2); //slow down light sequence
  }

  return (0);
}

void time_delay(unsigned long t)
{
  unsigned long initial,final;
  unsigned long ltime;

  initial=time(&ltime);
  final=initial+t;
  while (time(&ltime) < final);
  return;
}
```

The first inline code routine clears the text screen by calling a BIOS interrupt, described in Appendix B. In this case, registers are loaded with data values that will clear the entire screen. BIOS routines form an integral part of the computer's operating system. The second assembly language routine sends data values to the parallel port. These data values are generated with the **pow()** function. The data values are also printed to the screen. The output stream requires the use of *flush* to flush the stream buffer.

Because the **pow()** function is used, data values can be generated that will sequence each of the port lines (D0-D7). If lights are connected to the port, it is possible to create a set of miniature chaser lights. This is possible since each data bit, at the parallel port, corresponds to an integer power of 2; the numbers 1, 2, 4, 8, 16, 32, 64, 128 are generated with the C/C++ **pow()** function and sent to the parallel port. (Actually, 256 is also generated and has the effect of turning the sequence off at the completion of the program.)

Why not wire this circuit and experiment with what you can achieve? Can you alter the program so that successive pairs of LED lights are sequenced?

Creating C/C++ and Assembly Language Modules

Inline assembly language code becomes unmanageable and hard to understand as the code size increases. When more complicated assembly language routines are required, a separate assembly language procedure is often the best solution.

When separate assembly language modules are used, they are treated as external functions and called from the C or C++ host program. The assembly language routine must, therefore, be prototyped as a function in the host program, along with a list of arguments that are to be passed. The technique for performing this operation is described in the remaining sections of this chapter.

When developing separate C, C++, and assembly modules, it is important that your path information be complete. Your path information should include the location for both the C/C++ compiler and the macro assembler. You can do this by setting the location in your path statement given in the AUTOEXEC.BAT file.

Passing Function Arguments

The first important step in combining C, C++, and assembly language code is determining how arguments (parameters) are passed from the host program to the assembly language routine.

There are two methods frequently used for passing parameters in C and C++. One method is older and more complicated; the newer method is more streamlined and easier to understand. The old method demands a comprehensive understanding of the computer's stack frame and an assembly language programming skill that allows receiving and dealing with the values from the C or C++ calling program. The new method is much more civilized and puts much less demand on you to understand the computer's architecture. The Microsoft C/C++ compiler allows the use of both methods. The strongest argument for learning the old technique is that some people are still writing code in that form. If you need more information on the older technique, refer to the _Microsoft C/C++ Programming Techniques_ manual for information on using the stack frame for passing arguments. The following examples utilize the new method of passing arguments.

An assembly language function that is external to the host C or C++ code might be prototyped in the host program something like this:

```
extern int write_port(int,int);      /*in C*/
extern "C" int write_port(int,int); //in C++
```

This prototype is similar to those used for regular C and C++ functions contained within the host program. The assembly language program can intercept these passed arguments with the following line of code:

```
write_port  PROC   C   n1:SWORD,n2:SWORD
```

The capital **C**, a keyword, tells the program to expect the arguments to be passed from right to left via the stack. The alternate form is to use **pascal** instead of **C**. If **pascal** is used in a C program, the arguments are passed from left to right. The **C** form of passing arguments is the preferred technique and the one used in all of the examples in this chapter. The **pascal** form is an alternate form employed by Microsoft for calling Windows C functions. (Additional information on these techniques can be found in your Microsoft C/C++ manuals.)

The other new feature is the way arguments are listed in the assembly module. In assembly language, the most frequently used data types include the **byte**, **word**, and **dword**. This is because these data types can be placed directly in microprocessor registers. This new method of argument passing is a major improvement over the older method and eliminates keeping track of the C or C++ stack values.

Passing Arguments of Differing Data Types

The application in this section uses three separate files. The first is a make file named 21MATH.MAK, the second the C++ program named 21MATH.CPP, and the third the assembly language module named 21ARITH.ASM. Because multiple object files will be produced, the use of make files is recommended. With the use of make files, programs are compiled and assembled from the DOS command line. An alternative technique is to use a project file from within PWB.

This application shows how to pass an 8-bit character, a 16-bit integer, and a 32-bit long value to the assembly language program. The assembly language program performs several operations on these values and returns a 16-bit integer. The value is returned to the C or C++ host program via the **ax** register of the assembly language module. In other words, the contents of the **ax** register are automatically returned to the host application at the end of the assembly language module's execution. This return type corresponds to a C or C++ integer data type. The returned value can also be a 16-bit pointer.

The following listing contains all three files, which must be broken apart and entered separately before compiling and assembling. Again, make sure your system's path correctly points to the location of your C/C++ compiler and assembler.

```
THE MAKE FILE (21MATH.MAK):

all : 21math.exe

21math.obj: 21math.cpp
  cl -c 21math.cpp

21arith.obj: 21arith.asm
  masm 21arith.asm

21math.exe: 21math.obj 21arith.obj
  link 21math 21arith;



THE C++ PROGRAM (21MATH.CPP):

//
//  21MATH.CPP
//  A program that demonstrates how to pass several
//  data types to an external assembly language routine.
//  The program uses the new argument-passing technique.
//  Copyright (c) William H. Murray and Chris H. Pappas, 1992
//

#include <iostream.h>

extern "C" int task(char,int,long);

main()
{
  char num1=243;
  int  num2=2277;
  long num3=55664488;
  int answer;
```

```
    answer=task(num1,num2,num3);

    cout << answer;

    return (0);
}
```

THE ASSEMBLY MODULE (21ARITH.ASM):

```
;21ARITH.ASM
;Assembly Language Programming Application
;Copyright (c) William H. Murray and Chris H. Pappas, 1992

;Program accepts several arguments from a C++ calling program
;and performs mathematical & logical operations with them.
;This is an 80386 program.

        DOSSEG                  ;use Intel segment-ordering
        .MODEL small, c         ;set model size
        .386                    ;80386 instructions

        .DATA
little  db      5

task    PROTO C num1:SBYTE,num2:SWORD,num3:SWORD

        .CODE
        PUBLIC C task
task    PROC    C num1:SBYTE,num2:SWORD,num3:SDWORD
        mov     ax,DGROUP
        mov     ds,ax

        mov     edx,0
        mov     eax,num3        ;get 32-bit (long) in eax
        div     WORD PTR num2   ;divide & discard remainder
        and     eax,DWORD PTR num1 ;mask and keep 16-bits
        sub     al,little        ;subtract a small number

        ret                     ;return to calling program
task    ENDP                    ;end main procedure
        END
```

    The files can be compiled, assembled and linked by typing the following on the DOS command line:

NMAKE 21MATH.MAK

The assembly language module makes use of the **PROTO** keyword for prototyping the function or procedure. Any external assembly module that is shared with a C or C++ host program must be declared public.

Of particular interest in this application is the use of the make file. The following section of the make file is responsible for compiling the C++ code:

```
21math.obj: 21math.cpp
 cl -c 21math.cpp
```

The statement requests that the C++ code be compiled but not linked. The C++ code is compiled into an object file.

The next section of the make file's code requests that the macro assembler create an object file from the assembly code module:

```
21arith.obj: 21arith.asm
 masm 21arith.asm
```

The final statement in the make file controls the linker. Here, the object modules of the C++ and assembly language code are linked together to produce one executable file:

```
21math.exe: 21math.obj 21arith.obj
 link 21math 21arith;
```

In this application, two object files are linked together. The first was produced by the C++ host program, and the second was created by the assembler. By default, the resulting executable file will take on the name of the first object file. Make files are an ideal way of communicating the compilation and assembly language process to book and magazine readers.

The program code itself is straightforward and was used primarily to illustrate how values are passed. Incidentally, the *answer* printed to the screen is 253.

A Simple C and Assembly Language Connection

Earlier in this chapter you used inline assembly language code to clear the screen and send information to the parallel port. Following is a program that operates identically to that earlier program but is built with separate assembly language modules. This program uses one external routine to clear the screen and another to send information to the parallel port.

More Sequencing LED Lights

Four separate files are needed to compile and assemble the following application. The first file is a make file named 21SEQUE.MAK. The second is a C program named 21SEQUE.C. The last two files are assembly language routines. The first is named 21CLEAR.ASM and the second 21PORT.ASM.

The following listing contains all four files. They must be entered as separate programs before compiling and assembling.

```
THE MAKE FILE (21SEQUE.MAK):

all : 21seque.exe

21seque.obj: 21seque.c
  cl -c 21seque.c

21clear.obj: 21clear.asm
  masm 21clear.asm

21port.obj: 21port.asm
  masm 21port.asm

21seque.exe: 21seque.obj 21clear.obj 21port.obj
  link 21seque 21clear 21port;



THE C PROGRAM (21SEQUE.C):

/*
 *   21SEQUE.C
 *   A program that demonstrates how to call an external
 *   assembly language program to access the parallel port.
 *   Program will sequence 8 LED lamps connected to data
 *   lines D0 - D7 of port 956 (LPT1). Your port may be
 *   port 888.
 *   Copyright (c) William H. Murray and Chris H. Pappas, 1992
 */

#include <dos.h>
#include <stdio.h>
#include <math.h>
#include <time.h>
```

```c
void time_delay(unsigned long);
extern void clsscr(void);
extern void outport(int,int);

main()
{
  int i,temp;
  int port=956;

  clsscr();

  for (i=0;i<9;i++) {
    temp=(int) pow(2.0,(double) i);
    outport(temp,port);
    printf("%d\n",temp);
    time_delay(2);
  }

  return (0);
}

void time_delay(unsigned long t)
{
  unsigned long initial,final;
  unsigned long ltime;

  initial=time(&ltime);
  final=initial+t;
  while (time(&ltime) < final);
  return;
}
```

THE ASSEMBLY MODULE (21CLEAR.ASM):

```asm
;21CLEAR.ASM
;Assembly Language Programming Application
;Copyright (c) William H. Murray and Chris H. Pappas, 1992

;Program will clear the screen by calling a BIOS interrupt.

        DOSSEG                  ;use Intel segment-ordering
        .MODEL small, c         ;set model size
        .8086                   ;8086 instructions
```

```
clsscr PROTO   C

       .CODE
       PUBLIC C clsscr
clsscr PROC    C

       mov     cx,0            ;upper corner of window
       mov     dx,2479H        ;lower corner of window
       mov     bh,7            ;normal screen attribute
       mov     ax,0600H        ;BIOS interrupt value
       int     10H             ;call interrupt
       ret                     ;return to calling program

clsscr ENDP                    ;end main procedure
       END
```

THE OUTPORT ASSEMBLY MODULE (21PORT.ASM):

```
;21PORT.ASM
;Assembly Language Programming Application
;Copyright (c) William H. Murray and Chris H. Pappas, 1992

;Program accepts two arguments from C calling program and
;makes access to the specified port.

       DOSSEG                  ;use Intel segment-ordering
       .MODEL small, c         ;set model size
       .8086                   ;8086 instructions

outport PROTO C temp:SWORD,port:SWORD

       .CODE
       PUBLIC C outport
outport PROC  C temp:SWORD,port:SWORD

       mov     dx,port         ;port id in dx register
       mov     ax,temp         ;value to be sent
       out     dx,al           ;send lower 8 bits to port
       ret                     ;return to calling program

outport ENDP                   ;end main procedure
       END
```

Study the C host program and notice that it is very similar to the earlier inline example. The main differences are the inclusion of the function prototypes and actual function calls. As you examine the two assembly language modules, you will also observe that the code itself is identical to the inline assembly language code of the earlier example.

Wiring a Hardware Interface Using C and Assembly Language

In the next example, you will again see the 21CLEAR.ASM and 21PORT.ASM modules developed in the previous examples. However, this time the interface will be made with C in an example that simulates the roll of a die. The C program will generate pseudorandom numbers between 1 and 6 and send the number to the parallel port's data lines D0 to D2. The binary representation of the decimal numbers is 001, 010, 011, 100, 101, 110, and 111.

You can create a die by arranging 7 LED lights in the pattern shown in Figure 21-2. You can wire the LED lights in a manner similar to the earlier example.

A decoding scheme is also necessary to convert the binary numbers to the correct LED lighting sequence. Decoding can be accomplished with software or hardware. The authors chose hardware for decoding. Figure 21-3 shows the logic circuit required to decode the binary information.

If you choose to interface this circuit with a computer's parallel port, you will need a cable to connect the parallel port to a prototyping board, hookup wire, seven LED lights, a 5-volt power supply, a 7408 (AND gates) chip, and a 7432 (OR gates) chip. The authors used a 25-pin D-shell connector to connect to the parallel port with a

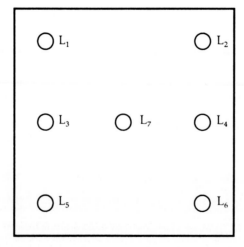

Figure 21-2.   *Arranging LED lights to simulate a die*

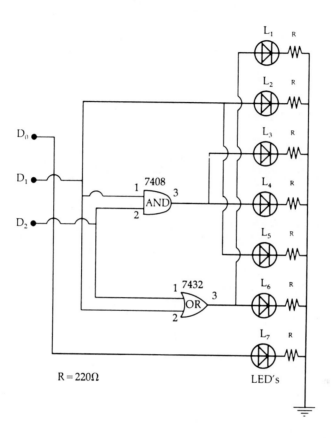

Figure 21-3. *A TTL hardware logic circuit for decoding binary numbers to light LED lamps in a simulated die*

ribbon cable terminating in a 24-pin male dip header. Pin 13 was discarded from the D-shell connector. The prototyping board is the type that allows TTL DIP chips to be easily inserted and removed. All of these parts can be found at electronics supply stores, as mentioned earlier.

Simulating the Roll of a Die

Examine the following listing and notice that it contains four files that must be entered and saved separately. The first file is the make file, 21DIE.MAK. The next file is the C program, 21DIE.C. The last two files are the familiar assembly language routines 21CLEAR.ASM and 21PORT.ASM.

```
THE MAKE FILE (21DIE.MAK):

all : 21die.exe

21die.obj: 21die.c
  cl -c 21die.c

21clear.obj: 21clear.asm
  masm 21clear.asm

21port.obj: 21port.asm
  masm 21port.asm

21die.exe: 21die.obj 21clear.obj 21port.obj
  link 21die 21clear 21port;


THE C PROGRAM (21DIE.C):

/*
 *   21DIE.C
 *   A program that demonstrates how to call an external
 *   assembly language program to access the parallel port.
 *   Program will simulate the roll of a die and light the
 *   appropriate LED lamps connected to the parallel port.
 *   Port 956 (LPT1) and data lines D0 - D2 are used.
 *   Your computer might use port 888.
 *   Copyright (c) William H. Murray and Chris H. Pappas, 1992
/*

#include <dos.h>
#include <stdio.h>
#include <stdlib.h>
#include <time.h>

extern void clsscr(void);
extern void outport(int,int);
void time_delay(unsigned long);

main()
{
  char ch;
  int i,temp;
  int port=956;
```

```
  void clsscr();

  for (;;) {
    printf("(Q) to quit, (Enter) to roll the die: ");
    ch=getchar();
    if (ch =='Q' || ch=='q') break;

    for (i=0;i<50;i++) {
      temp=1 + (rand()/3 % 6);
      outport(temp,port);
    }

    time_delay(2); /*simulate time to roll*/
    printf("%d\n",temp);
  }

  return (0);
}

void time_delay(unsigned long t)
{
  unsigned long initial,final;
  unsigned long ltime;

  initial=time(&ltime);
  final=initial+t;
  while (time(&ltime) < final);
  return;
}



THE ASSEMBLY MODULE (21CLEAR.ASM):

;21CLEAR.ASM
;Assembly Language Programming Application
;Copyright (c) William H. Murray and Chris H. Pappas, 1992
;Program will clear the screen by calling a BIOS interrupt.

        DOSSEG                  ;use Intel segment-ordering
        .MODEL small, c         ;set model size
        .8086                   ;8086 instructions

        .CODE
        PUBLIC C clsscr
clsscr PROC     C
```

```
        mov     cx,0            ;upper corner of window
        mov     dx,2479H        ;lower corner of window
        mov     bh,7            ;normal screen attribute
        mov     ax,0600H        ;BIOS interrupt value
        int     10H             ;call interrupt
        ret                     ;return to calling program

clsscr ENDP                     ;end main procedure
       END
```

THE ASSEMBLY MODULE (21PORT.ASM):

```
;21PORT.ASM
;Assembly Language Programming Application
;Copyright (c) William H. Murray and Chris H. Pappas, 1992

;Program accepts two arguments from C calling program and
;makes access to the specified port.

        DOSSEG                  ;use Intel segment-ordering
        .MODEL small, c         ;set model size
        .8086                   ;8086 instructions

        .CODE
        PUBLIC C outport
outport PROC  C temp,port:WORD

        mov     dx,port         ;port id in dx register
        mov     ax,temp         ;value to be sent
        out     dx,al           ;send lower 8 bits to port
        ret                     ;return to calling program

outport ENDP                    ;end main procedure
        END
```

In earlier examples you learned how the function arguments are passed from the source code to the assembly language routines. This program generates pseudo-random numbers by calling the **rand()** function:

```
temp=1 + (rand()/3 % 6);
```

The random number generator returns values in the range zero to RAND_MAX. RAND_MAX is defined in stdlib.h and is approximately 32,768. The random number generator can also be initialized, or *seeded,* with a call to the **srand**() function. True random number generators are difficult to create, and a pseudo-random generator is a close approximation to the real thing.

Limiting the random numbers generated to a range of 1 to 6 is done with the modulus operator. Actually, the random numbers are in the range of zero to 5 after applying the modulus operator. A 1 is added as an offset to these values.

If you have a little technical experience, a whole world of hardware interfacing has been opened to you. Instead of LED lamps, the parallel port's data lines can be wired to speech chips or digital-to-analog converters. These circuits will allow you to control a wide range of electronic devices.

Passing Arrays from C to Assembly Language

The final application in this chapter will show you how to pass two arrays (call-by-reference) to an assembly language routine. The assembly language routine will add each element of each array together and produce a final sum that will be returned to the C host program. The three files include the make file, 21ARRAY.MAK; the C program, 21ARRAY.C; and the assembly language module, 21ADDARY.ASM. Each of these files must be created separately with your editor.

```
THE MAKE FILE (21ARRAY.MAK):

all : 21array.exe

21array.obj: 21array.c
  cl -c 21array.c

21addary.obj: 21addary.asm
  masm 21addary.asm

21array.exe: 21array.obj 21addary.obj
  link 21array 21addary;


THE C PROGRAM (21ARRAY.C):

/*
 *    21ARRAY.C
 *    A demonstration of how to pass two arrays to an
```

```
*     external assembly language program. The assembly
*     language program will add the elements of both
*     arrays together and return the sum to the C program.
*     Copyright (c) William H. Murray and Chris H. Pappas, 1992
*/

#include <stdio.h>

extern int myasm(int array1[],int array2[]);

main()
{
  int array1[10]={1,3,5,7,9,11,13,15,17,19};
  int array2[10]={2,2,3,3,4,4,5,5,6,6};
  int temp;

  temp=myasm(array1,array2);
  printf("%d\n",temp);

  return (0);
}
```

```
THE ASSEMBLY LANGUAGE MODULE (21ADDARY.ASM):

;21ADDARY.ASM
;Assembly Language Programming Application
;Copyright (c) William H. Murray and Chris H. Pappas, 1992

;The program will accept array information from C host
;program. Arrays are passed by reference. The assembly
;language routine will add the elements of both arrays
;together and return the final sum.

        DOSSEG                    ;use Intel segment-ordering
        .MODEL small, c    ;set model size
        .8086              ;8086 instructions

myasm   PROTO   C array1:SWORD,array2:SWORD

        .CODE
        PUBLIC C myasm
myasm   PROC    C array1:SWORD,array2:SWORD
        mov     ax,0              ;initialize ax to 0
        mov     cx,10             ;array size
```

```
        mov    bx,array1      ;address of array1
        mov    bp,array2      ;address of array2
more:   add    ax,[bx]        ;value at array1 address
        add    ax,[bp]        ;value at array2 address
        add    bx,2           ;point to next array1 number
        add    bp,2           ;point to next array2 number
        loop   more           ;till all elements summed

        ret                   ;return to calling program
myasm   ENDP                  ;end main procedure
        END
```

In all of the previous examples, arguments were passed by value. When array information is passed, it is passed by reference. Thus, the intercepted values are the addresses of the arrays. In assembly language, you can place the addresses in the **bx** and **bp** registers. You can use indirect register addressing to obtain the array elements. Recall that indirect register addressing places square brackets around the register containing the address. This, in turn, returns the value stored at that address. For this example, the answer is 140.

Part *V*

Programming for Windows

Chapter 22

Windows Programming: Concepts and Tools

Microsoft's main development languages for Windows are C and C++. While assembly language plays a major role in time-sensitive areas, all important applications such as Windows itself are written in C or C++. Microsoft has provided all of the necessary tools, with this version of the compiler, for developing Windows programs from within the C/C++ environment.

The Windows applications created in the remaining chapters of this book are all designed with the tools provided with the compiler. When installing your Microsoft C/C++ compiler, you must specifically request that the setup program include the development tools for Windows and DOS.

This chapter is divided into three major sections. The first section deals with the language, definitions, and terms used with Windows. This section also includes a discussion of the graphics-based environment. The second section is devoted to a discussion of those Windows items most frequently used by application developers. Here, Windows components such as borders, icons, bitmaps, and so on are examined. The third section includes a description of Windows resources and many of the C/C++ tools provided for building them. Windows resources include icons, cursors, bitmaps, menus, hot keys, dialog boxes, and fonts. The resource tools provided in Microsoft C/C++ are an Image Editor, Dialog Editor, Font Editor, and HotSpot Editor.

The Language of Windows

Microsoft Windows is the graphics-based operating environment that functions over DOS. This operating environment brings together point-and-shoot control, pop-up menus, and the ability to run applications written specially for Windows, as well as standard applications that are DOS specific. The purpose of this portion of the chapter is to introduce you to Windows concepts and vocabulary. The graphics user interface is the interface of the future, and Windows gives you that ability now.

A Quick Perspective of the Windows Environment

As stated earlier, Windows is a graphics-based multitasking operating environment that runs over DOS. Programs developed for this environment (those written specifically for Windows) all have a consistent look and command structure. To the user, this makes learning each successive Windows application easier.

To help in the development of Windows applications, Windows provides numerous built-in functions that allow for the easy implementation of pop-up menus, scroll bars, dialog boxes, icons, and many other features that represent a user-friendly interface. You can take advantage of the extensive graphics programming language provided with Windows and easily format and output text in a variety of fonts and pitches.

Windows permits the application's treatment of the video display, keyboard, mouse, printer, serial port, and system timers in a hardware-independent manner. Device or hardware independence allows the same application to run identically on a variety of computers with differing hardware configurations.

Advantages of Using Windows

There are numerous advantages under Windows to users and programmers alike over the more conventional DOS text-based environment. Windows provides several major programming capabilities that include a standardized graphics interface, a multitasking capability, an OOP approach in programming, memory control, hardware independence, and the use of dynamic link libraries (DLLs).

A Graphics User Interface

The most noticeable Windows feature is the standardized graphics user interface, which is also the most important one for the user. The consistent interface uses pictures, or *icons,* to represent disk drives, files, subdirectories, and many of the operating system commands and actions. Figure 22-1 shows a typical Windows window.

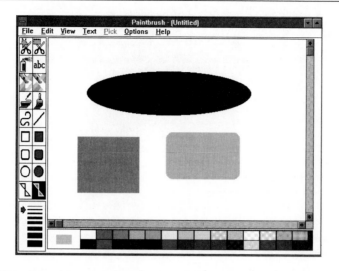

Figure 22-1.   *A typical Windows window*

Here, programs are identified by caption bars, and many of the basic file manipulation functions are accessed through the program's menus by pointing and clicking with the mouse. Most Windows programs provide both a keyboard and a mouse interface. Although you can access most Windows functions with just the keyboard, the mouse is the preferred tool of most users.

A similar look and feel is common to all Windows applications. Once a user learns how to manipulate common Windows commands, each new application becomes easier to master. For example, a Windows Excel screen is shown in Figure 22-2 and a Word for Windows screen is shown in Figure 22-3. These screens illustrate the similarity between applications including common File and Edit options.

The consistent user interface provides advantages for the programmer also. For example, you can tap into built-in Windows functions for constructing menus and dialog boxes. All menus have the same style keyboard and mouse interface because Windows, rather than the programmer, handles the interface.

A Multitasking Environment

The Windows multitasking environment allows the user to have several applications, or several instances of the same application, running at the same time. The screen in Figure 22-4 shows several Windows applications running at the same time. Each application occupies a rectangular window on the screen. At any given time, the user can move the windows on the screen, switch between different applications, change the windows' sizes, and exchange information from window to window.

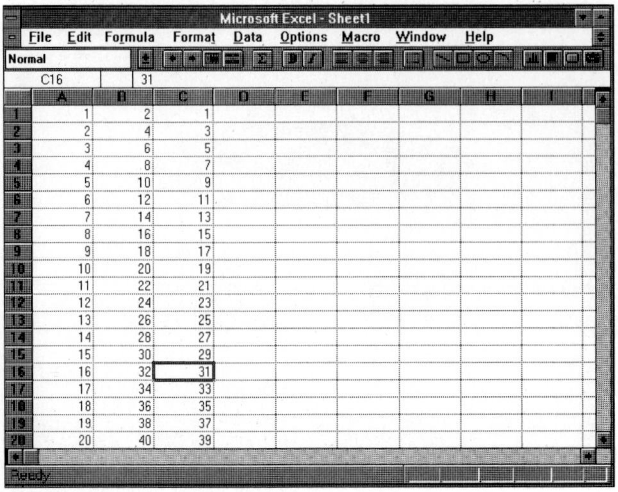

Figure 22-2. *A Microsoft Excel spreadsheet screen*

The example shown in Figure 22-4 is a group of four concurrently running processes—well, not really. In reality, only one application can be using the processor at any one time. The distinction between a task that is processing and one that is merely running is important. There is also a third state to consider. An application

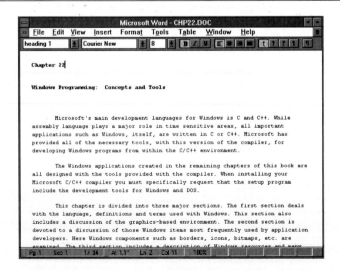

Figure 22-3. *A Microsoft Word for Windows screen*

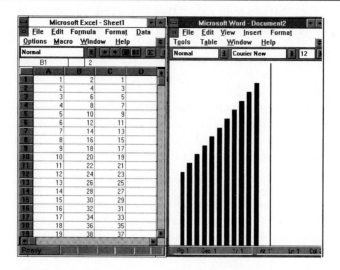

Figure 22-4.   *Several Windows applications showing data linked to more than one program*

may be in the active state. An *active application* is one that is receiving the user's attention. Just as there can be only one application that is processing at any given instant, so too there can be only one active application at a time. However, there can be any number of concurrently running tasks. Partitioning of the microprocessor's processing time, called *time slicing*, is the responsibility of Windows. It is Windows that controls the sharing of the microprocessor by using queued input or messages.

Before multitasking was achieved under Windows, applications assumed they had exclusive control of all the computer's resources, including the input and output devices, memory, the video display, and even the CPU itself. Under Windows, all of these resources must be shared. Memory management, for example, is controlled by Windows instead of by the application.

Advantages of a Queued Input

Under Windows, memory is a shared resource, and so are most input devices such as the keyboard and mouse. Although a Windows program is written in C or C++, it is no longer possible to read directly from the keyboard with a **getchar()** function call or by using the C++ I/O stream. With Windows, an application does not make explicit calls to read from the keyboard or mouse. Rather, Windows receives all input from the keyboard, mouse, and timer in the system queue. It is the queue's responsibility to redirect the input to the appropriate program since more than one application can be running. This is done by copying the message from the system queue into the application's queue. At this point, when the application is ready to process the input, it reads from its queue and dispatches a message to the correct window.

Input is provided in a uniform format called an *input message*. All input messages specify the system time, state of the keyboard, scan code of any depressed key, position of the mouse, and which mouse button has been pressed (if any), as well as information specifying which device generated the message.

Keyboard, mouse, and timer messages all have identical formats and are processed in a similar manner. Further, with each message, Windows provides a device-independent virtual keycode that identifies the key, regardless of which keyboard it is on, and the device-dependent scan code generated by the keyboard, as well as the status of other keys on the keyboard, including NUM LOCK, ALT, SHIFT, and CTRL.

The keyboard and mouse are a shared resource. One keyboard and one mouse must supply all the input information for each program running under Windows. Windows sends all keyboard input messages directly to the currently active window. Mouse messages, on the other hand, are handled differently. Mouse messages are sent to the window that is physically underneath the mouse cursor.

Another shared resource is timer messages. *Timer messages* are similar to keyboard and mouse messages. Windows allows a program to set a system timer so that one of its windows receives a message at periodic intervals. This timer message goes directly into the application's message queue. It is also possible for other messages to be passed into an application's message queue as a result of the program's calling certain Windows functions.

An OOP Approach: Messages

The message system under Windows is the underlying structure used to disseminate information in the multitasking environment. From the application's perspective, a message is a notification that some event of interest has occurred that may or may not need a specific action. The user may initiate these events by clicking or moving the mouse, changing the size of a window, or making a menu selection. The events can also be initiated by the application itself. For example, a graphics-based spreadsheet could finish a recalculation that results in the need to update a graphics pie chart. In this situation, the application would send an "update window" message to itself.

Windows itself can also generate messages, as in the case of the "close session" message. In this example, Windows informs each application of the intent to shut down.

When considering the role of messages in Windows, consider the following points. It is the message system that allows Windows to achieve its multitasking capabilities. The message system makes it possible for Windows to share the processor among different applications. Each time Windows sends a message to the application program, it also grants processor time to the application. In reality, the only way an application can get access to the microprocessor is when it receives a message. Second, messages enable an application to respond to events in the environment.

These events can be generated by the application itself, by other concurrently running applications, by the user, or by Windows. Each time an event occurs, Windows makes a note and distributes an appropriate message to the interested applications.

Memory Management

One of the most important shared resources under Windows is system memory—at least when multitasking applications are involved. When more than one application is running at the same time, each application must cooperate to share memory in order not to exhaust the total resources of the system. Also, as new programs are started and old ones are terminated, memory can become fragmented. Windows is capable of consolidating free memory space by moving blocks of code and data in memory.

It is also possible to overcommit memory under Windows. For example, an application can contain more code than can actually fit into memory at one time. Windows can discard currently unused code from memory and later reload the code from the program's executable file.

Windows applications can share routines located in other executable files. The files that contain shareable routines are called *dynamic link libraries (DLLs)*. Windows includes the mechanism to link the program with the DLL routines at run time. Windows itself is a set of dynamic link libraries. To facilitate all of this, Windows programs use a new format of executable file, called the *New Executable format*. These files include the information Windows needs to manage the code and data segments and to perform the dynamic linking.

Hardware Independence

Windows also provides hardware or device independence. Windows frees you from having to build programs that take into consideration every possible monitor, printer, and input device available for computers. As you know from the DOS graphics examples in Chapter 19, a non-Windowed application must be written to include drivers for every possible device. Likewise, to make a non-Windowed application capable of printing on any printer, you must furnish a different driver for each printer. This requires many software companies to write essentially the same device driver over and over again—an HP LaserJet driver for Microsoft Word for DOS, one for Microsoft Works, and so on.

Under Windows, a device driver for each hardware device is written once. This device driver can be supplied by Microsoft, the application vendor, or the user. Microsoft includes many drivers with Windows.

It is hardware independence that makes programming a snap for the application developer. The application interacts with Windows rather than with any specific device. It doesn't need to know what printer is hooked up. The application instructs Windows to draw a filled rectangle, and Windows worries about how to accomplish it on the installed hardware. Likewise, each device driver works with every Windows application. Developers save time, and users do not have to worry about whether each new Windows application will support their hardware configuration.

You achieve hardware independence by specifying the minimum capabilities the hardware must have. These capabilities are the minimum specifications required to ensure that the appropriate routines will function correctly. Every routine, regardless of its complexity, is capable of breaking itself down into the minimal set of operations required for a given device. This is a very impressive feature. For example, not every plotter is capable of drawing a circle by itself. As an application developer, however, you can still use the routines for drawing a circle, even if the plotter has no specific circle capabilities. Since every plotter connected to Windows must be capable of drawing a line, Windows is capable of breaking down the circle routine into a series of small lines.

Windows can specify a set of minimum capabilities to ensure that your application will receive only valid, predefined input. Windows has predefined the set of legal keystrokes allowed by applications. The valid keystrokes are very similar to those produced by the IBM PC keyboard. Should a manufacturer produce a keyboard that contains additional keys that do not exist in the Windows list of acceptable keys, the manufacturer would also have to supply additional software that would translate these illegal keystrokes into Windows' legal keystrokes. This predefined Windows legal input covers all the input devices, including the mouse. Therefore, even if someone should develop a four-button mouse, you don't have to worry. The manufacturer would supply the software necessary to convert all mouse input to the Windows predefined possibilities of mouse-button clicks.

Dynamic Link Libraries

Dynamic link libraries provide much of Windows' functionality; they enhance the base operating system by providing a powerful and flexible graphics user interface. Dynamic link libraries contain predefined functions that are linked with an application program when it is loaded (dynamically), instead of when the executable file is generated (statically). Dynamic link libraries use the .DLL file extension.

Storing frequently used routines in libraries was not an invention of the Windows product. For example, the Microsoft C/C++ language depends heavily on libraries to implement standard functions for different systems. The linker makes copies of run-time library functions, such as **getchar()** and **printf()**, into a program's executable file. Libraries of functions save each programmer from having to re-create a new procedure for a common operation such as reading in a character or formatting output. Programmers can easily build their own libraries to include additional capabilities, such as changing a character font or justifying text. Making the function available as a general tool eliminates redundant design—a key feature in OOP.

Windows libraries are dynamically linked. In other words, the linker does not copy the library functions into the program's executable file. Instead, while the program is executing, it makes calls to the function in the library. Naturally, this conserves memory. No matter how many applications are running, there is only one copy of the library in RAM at a given time, and this library can be shared.

When a call is made to a Windows function, the C/C++ compiler must generate machine code for a far intersegment call to the function located in a code segment in one of the Windows libraries. This presents a problem since, until the program is actually running inside Windows, the address of the Windows function is unknown. Doesn't this sound suspiciously similar to the concept of late binding, discussed in the OOP section of this book? The solution to this problem in Windows is called *delayed binding* or *dynamic linking*. Starting with Windows 3.0 and Microsoft C 6.0, the linker allows a program to have calls to functions that cannot be fully resolved at link time. Only when the program is loaded into memory to be run are the far function calls resolved.

Special Windows *import libraries* are included with the C/C++ compiler; they are used to properly prepare a Windows program for dynamic linking. The import library SLIBCEW.LIB is the import library that will be used for small-model Windows programs. SLIBCEW.LIB contains a record for each Windows function that your program can call. This record defines the Windows module that contains this function and, in many cases, an ordinal value that corresponds to the function in the module.

Windows applications typically make a call to the Windows **PostMessage( )** function. When your application is linked at compile time, the linker finds the **PostMessage( )** function listed in SLIBCEW.LIB. The linker obtains the ordinal number for the function and embeds this information in the application's executable file. When the application is run, Windows connects the call your application makes with the actual **PostMessage( )** function.

The New Windows Executable Format

An executable file format has been developed for Windows called the New Executable format. This new format includes a *new-style header* capable of holding information about dynamic link library functions.

For example, DLL functions are included for the KERNEL, USER, and GDI modules. These libraries contain routines that help programs carry out various chores, such as sending and receiving messages. The library modules provide functions that can be called from the application program or from other library modules. To the module that contains the functions, the functions are known as *exports*. The New Executable format identifies these exported functions with a name and an ordinal number. Included in the New Executable format is an *Entry Table* section that indicates the address of each of these exported functions within the module.

From the perspective of the application program, the library functions that an application uses are known as *imports*. These imports use the various relocation tables and can identify the far calls that the application makes to an imported function. Almost all Windows programs contain at least one exported function. This window function is usually located in one of the library modules and is the one that receives window messages. It is important that the application indicate that this function is exported so Windows can properly allow the function to be called from an external module.

This new format also provides the additional information on each of the code and data segments in a program or library. Typically, code segments are flagged as moveable and discardable, while data segments are flagged as moveable. This allows Windows to move code and data segments in memory and even discard code segments if additional memory is needed. If Windows later decides it needs a discarded code segment, it can reload the code segment from the original executable file. Windows has another category called *load on call.* This defines a program or library code segment that will not be loaded into memory at all unless a function in the code segment is called from another code segment. Through this sophisticated memory-management scheme, Windows can simultaneously run several programs in a memory space that would normally be sufficient for only one program.

Windows Programming: Concepts and Vocabulary

Windows programming is unique to even seasoned programmers. This is because Windows includes new programming concepts and its own vocabulary. These concepts and vocabulary can be broken down into two major categories: the features of Windows that are visible to the user, such as menus, dialog boxes, icons, and so on; and the invisible features such as messages, function access, and so on. There is a standard vocabulary associated with Windows programming development designed to give application developers the ability to communicate effectively with one another. Thus, all Windows features have been given a name and an associated usage. In this section you will learn a variety of Windows terms that will give you the ability to confidently discuss and develop many Windows applications.

The Windows Window

A Windows window appears to the user as a rectangular portion of the display device; its appearance is independent of the particular application at hand. To an application, however, the window is a rectangular area of the screen that is under the direct control of the application. The application has the ability to create and control everything about the main window, including its size and shape. When the user starts a program, a window is created. Each time the user clicks a window option, the application responds. Closing a window causes the application to terminate. Multiple windows convey to the user the multitasking capabilities of Windows. By partitioning the screen into different windows, the user can direct input to a specific application within the multitasking environment by using the keyboard or a mouse to select one of the concurrently running applications. Windows then intercepts the user's input and allocates any necessary resources (such as the microprocessor) as needed.

The Windows Layout

Features such as borders, control boxes, About boxes, and so on, are common to all Windows applications. It is this common interface that gives Windows a comforting predictability from one application to another. Figure 22-5 illustrates the fundamental components of a Windows window.

The Windows Border

A Windows window has a *border* surrounding it. The border is made up of lines that frame a window. To the novice, the border may appear only to delineate one application's screen viewport from another. Upon closer examination of the border, however, a different conclusion will be drawn. The border not only serves as a screen boundary but also indicates which window is active. By positioning the mouse pointer over a border and clicking, the user can change the size of the application's window.

The Windows Title Bar

The name of the application program is displayed at the top of the window in the *title bar*. Title bars are located and centered at the top of each associated window. Title

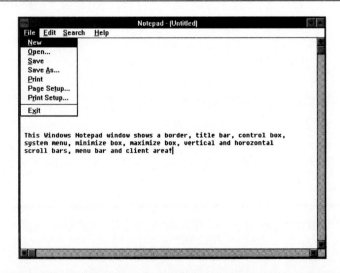

Figure 22-5.   *The components making up a Windows window*

bars can be very useful in helping to remember which applications are currently running.

The Windows Control Box

A *control box* is used by each Windows application. The control box is a small square box with a line through it in each window's upper-left corner. Clicking the mouse pointer on the control box (referred to as clicking the control box) causes Windows to display the system menu.

The Windows System Menu

You activate the *system menu* by clicking the mouse pointer on the control box. The system menu provides standard application options such as Restore, Move, Size, Minimize, Maximize, and Close.

The Windows Minimize Box

Each Windows application displays two vertical arrows in the upper right-hand corner of the screen. One arrow represents the *minimize box*. The minimize box contains a downward-pointing arrow that causes the window to be shrunk to a small picture called an icon.

The Windows Maximize Box

The *maximize box* is in the upper-right corner of each window. This box displays an upward-pointing arrow. You use the maximize box to make an application's window fill the entire screen. If this box is selected, all other application windows will be covered.

The Windows Vertical Scroll Bar

An application can show a *vertical scroll bar* if desired. The vertical scroll bar is located directly below each window's maximize box. The vertical scroll bar has opposite-pointing arrows at its extremes, a colored band, and a transparent window block. The transparent window block is used to visually represent the orientation between the currently displayed contents and the overall document (the colored band). You use the vertical scroll bar to select which of multiple pages of output you would like displayed. Clicking the mouse on either arrow shifts the display one line at a time. Clicking the mouse on the transparent window block, below the up arrow, and dragging it causes screen output to be quickly updated to any portion of the application's screen output. One of the best uses of the vertical scroll bar is for quickly moving through a multipage word processing document. Word processors such as Microsoft Word for Windows and WordPerfect take advantage of this feature.

The Windows Horizontal Scroll Bar

It is also possible to display a *horizontal scroll bar.* If displayed, it is at the bottom of each window. The horizontal scroll bar is similar in function to the vertical scroll bar. You use the horizontal scroll bar to select which of multiple columns of information you would like displayed. Clicking the mouse on either arrow causes the screen image to be shifted one column at a time. Clicking the mouse on the transparent window block, to the right of the left-pointing arrow, and dragging it causes the screen output to be quickly updated to any horizontally shifted portion of the application's screen output. One of the best uses for the horizontal scroll bar is for quickly moving through the multiple columns of a spreadsheet application, where the number of columns of information cannot fit into one screen width. Microsoft's Excel spreadsheet program uses this feature.

The Windows Menu Bar

A *menu bar* can also be produced below the title bar, if desired. You use the menu bar for making menu and submenu selections. You can make these selections by pointing and clicking the menu command or, alternately, by using a hot-key combination. Hot-key combinations often use the ALT key in conjunction with the underlined letter in a command, as the "F" is in the command File.

The Windows Client Area

The *client area* actually occupies the largest portion of each window. The client area is the primary output area for the application. Managing the client area is the responsibility of the application program. Additionally, only the application can output to the client area.

A Windows Class in C/C++

The basic components of a window help define the standard appearance of an application. There are also occasions when an application program will create two windows with a similar appearance and behavior. Windows Paintbrush is one such example. The fashion in which Paintbrush allows the user to clip or copy a portion of a graphics image is achieved by running two instances (or copies) of Paintbrush. Information is then copied from one instance to the other. Each instance of Paintbrush looks and behaves like its counterpart. This requires each instance to create its own window with an identical appearance and functionality.

Windows created in this manner that look alike and behave in a similar fashion are said to be of the same *window class.* However, windows that you create can take on different characteristics. They may be different sizes, placed in different areas of the display, have different text in the caption bars, have different display colors, or use different mouse cursors.

Each window created must be based on a window class. With applications developed in C using traditional function calls, five window classes are registered by the Windows application during its initialization phase. Your application may register additional classes of its own. In order to allow several windows to be created and based on the same window class, Windows specifies some of a window's characteristics as parameters to the **CreateWindow()** function, while others are specified in a window class structure. Also, when you register a window class, the class becomes available to all programs running under Windows. For C++ Windows applications utilizing Microsoft's foundation classes, much of this registration work is already done through the use of predefined objects. In Chapter 23 you learn how to write Windows applications in C using traditional function calls. Chapters 24 and 25 are designed to teach you how to write similar applications with Microsoft's C++ foundation classes.

Windows of similar appearance and behavior can be grouped together into classes, thereby reducing the amount of information that needs to be maintained. Since each window class has its own shareable window class structure, there is no needless replication of the window class' parameters. Also, two windows of the same class use the same function and any of its associated subroutines. This feature saves time and storage because there is no code duplication.

OOPs and Windows

Even traditional C Windows programs take on the characteristics of object-oriented programs. Recall that in object-oriented programming, an *object* is an abstract data type that consists of a data structure and various functions that act on the data structure. Likewise, objects receive messages that can cause them to change.

For example, a Windows *graphics object* is a collection of data that can be manipulated as a whole entity and that is presented to the user as part of the visual interface. In particular, a graphics object implies both the data and the presentation of data. Menus, title bars, control boxes, and scroll bars are examples of graphics objects. The next sections describe several new graphics objects that affect the user's view of an application.

Windows Icons

An icon is a small graphics object used to remind the user of a particular operation, idea, or product. For example, whenever a spreadsheet application is minimized, it could display a very small histogram icon to remind the user that the application is running. Clicking the mouse on the histogram would then cause Windows to bring the application to active status. Icons can be very powerful tools. They are good for gaining the user's attention, as in the case of an error warning, and also when presenting choices to the user. Windows provides several stock icons including a question mark, an exclamation point, an asterisk, and an upturned palm icon. It is also possible to design your own device-independent color icons with the Image Editor provided with the Microsoft C/C++ compiler and described in the section "The Microsoft C/C++ Windows Tools" later in this chapter.

Windows Cursors

Cursors are also Windows graphics symbols and thus are different from the standard DOS blinking underscore. The graphics cursor follows the movement of the pointing device. The graphics symbol is capable of changing shapes to indicate particular Windows actions. For example, the standard Windows arrow cursor changes to the small hourglass cursor to indicate a pause while a selected command is being executed. Windows provides several stock cursors: a diagonal arrow, a vertical arrow, an hourglass, a cross hair, an I-beam, and several others. You can also use the Image Editor to create your own cursors.

Windows Carets

Carets are symbols your application places in a window to show the user where input will be received. Carets are distinguished from other screen markers because they blink. Most of the time, mouse input is associated with a cursor and keyboard input with a caret. However, the mouse can move or change the input emphasis of a caret. To help clarify the difference between a cursor and a caret, Windows carets behave most similarly to the standard DOS cursor. One of the carets provided for you automatically, when entering a dialog box, is the I-beam caret. Unlike in the cases of icons and cursors, an application must create its own carets using special functions. There are no stock carets.

Windows Message Boxes

The *message box* is another common Windows graphics object. Message boxes are pop-up windows that contain a title, an icon, and a message. Here is the standard message box presented when terminating a Windows session:

The application needs to supply the message title, the message itself, and instructions on which stock icon to use (if any) and indicate if a stock response is allowed (such as OK). Additional stock user responses include Yes/No, Yes/No/Cancel, OK/Cancel, and Retry/Cancel. Stock icons include IconHand, IconQuestion, IconExclamation, and IconAsterisk.

Windows Dialog Boxes

A *dialog box* is similar to a message box in that it too is a pop-up window. Dialog boxes, however, are primarily used to receive input from the user rather than to just present output. A dialog box allows an application to receive information, one field at a time or one box's worth of information at a time, rather than a character at a time. Figure 22-6 shows a typical Windows dialog box. The graphic design of a dialog box is done automatically for you by Windows. The layout of a dialog box is normally done with the Dialog Editor provided with the C/C++ compiler and is also explained in the section "The Microsoft C/C++ Windows Tools" later in this chapter.

Windows Fonts

A *font* is a graphics object or resource that defines a complete set of characters from one typeface. These characters are all of a certain size and style that can be manipulated to give text a variety of appearances. A *typeface* is a basic character design,

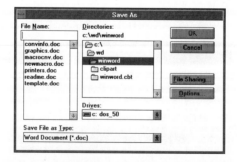

Figure 22-6.   *A Windows dialog box*

defined by certain serifs and stroke widths. For instance, your application can use any of the different fonts provided with Windows including System, Courier, and Times Roman, or custom fonts that you define and include in the application program's executable file. By using built-in routines, Windows allows for the dynamic modification of a font, including boldface, italics, underline, and changing the size of the font. Windows provides all of the necessary functions for displaying text anywhere within the client area. Additionally, because of Windows device independence, an application's output will have a consistent appearance from one output device to the next. TrueType font technology, first supplied with Windows 3.1, provides improved fonts for the screen and printer. You can create and alter fonts with the Font Editor supplied with the C/C++ compiler.

Windows Bitmaps

Bitmaps serve as a photographic image of the display (in pixels) and are stored in memory. Bitmaps are used whenever an application must display a graphics image quickly. Since bitmapped images are transferred directly from memory, they can be displayed more quickly than by executing the code necessary to re-create the image. There are two basic uses for bitmaps. First, bitmaps are used to draw pictures on the display. For example, Windows uses many small bitmaps for drawing arrows in scroll bars; displaying the check marks when selecting pop-up menu options; and drawing the system menu box, the size box, and many others. Bitmaps are also used for creating brushes. Brushes allow you to paint and fill objects on the screen.

There are two disadvantages to using bitmaps. First, depending on their size, bitmaps can occupy an unpredictably large portion of memory. For each pixel that is being displayed, there needs to be an equivalent representation in memory. Displaying the same bitmap on a color monitor versus a monochrome monitor would also require more memory. On a monochrome monitor, one bit can be used to define a pixel's being on or off. However, on a color monitor that can display 16 colors, each pixel would require 4 bits, or a nibble, to represent its characteristics. Also, as the resolution of the display device increases, so too does the memory requirement for the bitmap. Another disadvantage of bitmaps is that they contain only a picture. For example, if an automobile is represented by a bitmap, there is no way to access the picture's various components, such as tires, hood, window, and so on. However, if the automobile had been constructed from a series of primitive drawing routines, an application would be able to change the data sent to these routines and modify individual items in the picture. For example, an application could modify the roof line and convert the sedan to a convertible. You can create or modify bitmaps with the Image Editor.

Windows Pens

When Windows draws a shape on the screen, it uses information on the current pen and brush. You use *pens* to draw lines and to outline shapes. They have three basic characteristics: line width, style (dotted, dashed, solid), and color. Windows always has a pen for drawing black lines and one for drawing white lines available to each application. It is also possible to create your own pens. For example, you might want to create a thick light-gray line to outline a portion of the screen or a dot-dash-dot line for spreadsheet data analysis.

Windows Brushes

Windows uses *brushes* to paint colors and fill areas with predefined patterns. Brushes have a minimum size of 8x8 pixels and, like pens, have three basic characteristics: size, pattern, and color. With their 8x8-pixel minimum, brushes are said to have a pattern, not a style as pens do. The pattern may be a solid color, hatched, diagonal, or any other user-definable combination.

Sending and Receiving Windows Messages

With Windows, an application does not write directly to the screen, process any hardware interrupts, or output directly to the printer. Instead, the application uses the appropriate Windows functions or waits for an appropriate message to be delivered. Applications development under Windows must now incorporate the processing of the application and the user's view of the application through Windows.

The Windows message system is the underlying structure used to disseminate information in a multitasking environment. From your application's viewpoint, a message is seen as a notification that some event of interest has occurred that may or may not need a specific response. These events may have been initiated on the part of the user, such as clicking or moving the mouse, changing the size of a window, or making a menu selection. However, the signaled event could also have been generated by the application itself.

The overall effect of this process is that your application must now be totally oriented toward the processing of messages. It must be capable of awakening, determining the appropriate action based on the type of message received, taking that action to completion, and returning to sleep.

Windows applications are significantly different from their DOS counterparts. Windows provides an application program with access to hundreds of function calls directly or, through foundation classes, indirectly. These function calls are handled by three main modules called the KERNEL, GDI (graphics device interface), and USER modules. The KERNEL is responsible for memory management, loading and running an application, and scheduling. The GDI contains all of the routines to create and display graphics. The USER module takes care of all other application requirements.

The next section takes a closer look at the message system by examining the format and sources of messages and looking at several common message types and the ways in which both Windows and your application process messages.

The Format of a Windows Message

Messages notify a program that an event of interest has occurred. Technically, a message is not just of interest to the application, but also to a specific window within that application. Therefore, every message is addressed to a window.

Only one message system exists under Windows—the system message queue. However, each program currently running under Windows also has its own program message queue. Each message in the system message queue must eventually be transferred by the USER module to a program's message queue. The program's message queue stores all messages for all windows in that program.

Four parameters are associated with all messages, regardless of their type, if they were developed for 16-bit Windows applications: a window handle (16-bit word), a message type (16-bit word), one WORD parameter (16-bit word), and one LONG parameter (32-bit word). The first parameter specified in a window message is the handle of the window to which the message is addressed. These parameters are different for 32-bit Windows applications, such as those being developed for Windows NT. In an object-oriented programming environment, a *handle* is just the identifier of an object, which for the current syntax is the identifier of the particular window to which the message is addressed.

A handle is a 16-bit unsigned number. This handle will reference an object that is located in a moveable portion of memory. Even though the portion of memory can be moved, the handle remains the same. This fact allows Windows to manage memory efficiently while leaving the relocation invisible to the application.

Since multiple windows can be created based on the same window class, a single window function can process messages for more than one window within a single program. Here, the application can use the handle to determine which window is receiving the message.

The second parameter in a message is its message type. This is one of the identifiers specified in windows.h. With Windows, each message type begins with a two-character mnemonic, followed by the underscore character and finally a descriptor. The most frequently encountered type of message in traditional C Windows applications is the window message. Windows messages include WM_CREATE, WM_PAINT, WM_CLOSE, WM_COPY, and WM_PASTE. Other message types include control window messages (BM_), edit control messages (EM_), and list box messages (LB_). An application can also create and register its own message type. This permits the use of private message types.

The last two parameters provide additional information necessary to interpret the message. The contents of these last two parameters will therefore vary depending on the message type. Examples of the types of information that would be passed include which key was just struck, the position of the mouse, the position of the vertical or horizontal scroll bar elevators, and the selected pop-up menu item.

How Windows Messages Are Created

It is the message-passing concept that allows Windows to be multitasking. Thus, all messages must be processed by Windows. There are four basic sources for a message.

An application can receive a message from the user, from Windows itself, from the application program itself, or from other applications.

User messages include keystroke information, mouse movements, point-and-click coordinates, any menu selections, the location of scroll bar elevators, and so on. The application program will devote a great deal of time to processing user messages. User-originated messages indicate that the person running the program wishes to change the way the application is viewed.

A message is sent to an application whenever a state change is to take effect. An example of this would be when the user clicks an application's icon indicating that he or she wants to make that application the active application. Here, Windows tells the application that its main window is being opened, that its size and location are being modified, and so on. Depending on the current state of an application, Windows-originated messages can be processed or ignored.

In Chapter 23, you learn how to write simple Windows applications in C. What you will see is that your program is broken down into specific procedures, with each procedure processing a particular message type for a particular window. One procedure, for example, will deal with resizing the application's window. It is quite possible that the application may want to resize itself. In other words, the source of the message is the application itself.

Currently, most applications written for Windows do not take full advantage of the fourth type of message source, inter-task communication. However, this category will become increasingly important as more and more applications take advantage of this Windows integration capability. To facilitate this type of message, Microsoft has developed the dynamic data exchange protocol (DDE).

Responding to a Windows Message

Traditional C Windows applications have a procedure for processing each type of message it may encounter. Different windows can respond differently to messages of the same type. For example, one application may have created two windows that respond to a mouse-button click in two different ways. The first window could respond to a mouse-button click by changing the background color, while the second window may respond to the mouse-button click by placing a crosshatch on a spreadsheet. It is because the same message can be interpreted differently by different windows that Windows addresses each message to a specific window within an application. Not only will the application have a different procedure to handle each message type, it will also need a procedure to handle each message type for each window. The window procedure groups together all the message type procedures for an application.

The Message Loop

A basic component of all Windows applications is the message-processing loop. The message loop is processed in the CWinAPP foundation class for C++ applications.

Each C application performs the operation internally. C applications contain procedures to create and initialize windows, followed by the message-processing loop and finally some code required to close the application. The message loop is responsible for processing a message delivered by Windows to the main body of the program. Here, the program acknowledges the message and then requests Windows to send it to the appropriate window procedure for processing. When the message is received, the window procedure executes the desired action.

Two factors that can influence the sequence in which a message is processed are the message queue and the dispatching priority. Messages can be sent from one of two queues—either the system queue or the application's message queue. Messages, regardless of the source, are first placed in the system queue. When a given message reaches the front of the queue, it is sent to the appropriate application's message queue. This dual-mode action allows Windows to keep track of all messages and permits each application to concern itself with only those messages that pertain to it.

Messages are placed in the queues as you would expect: FIFO (first-in-first-out) order. These are called *synchronous messages*. Most Windows applications use this type of dispatching method. However, there are occasions when Windows will push a message to the end of the queue, thereby preventing it from being dispatched. Messages of this type are called *asynchronous messages*. Care must be taken when sending an asynchronous message that overrides the application's normal sequence of processing.

Three types of asynchronous messages exist: paint, timer, and quit. A timer message, for example, causes a certain action to take effect at a specified time, regardless of the messages to be processed at that moment. A timer message has priority and will cause all other messages in the queue to be pushed farther from the queue front.

A few asynchronous messages can be sent to other applications. What is unique is that the receiving application doesn't put the message into its queue. Rather, the received message directly calls the application's appropriate window procedure, where it is immediately executed.

How does Windows dispatch messages that are pending for several applications at the same time? Windows handles this problem in one of two ways. One method of message processing is called *dispatching priority*. Whenever Windows loads an application, it sets the application's priority to zero. Once the application is running, however, the application can change its priority from a –15 to a +15. With everything else being equal, Windows will settle any message-dispatching contention by sending messages to the highest priority application.

One example of a high-priority program would be a data communications application. Tampering with an application's priority level is very uncommon. Windows has another method for dispatching messages to concurrent applications of the same priority level. Whenever Windows sees that a particular application has a backlog of unprocessed messages, it hangs onto the new message while continuing to dispatch other new messages to the other applications.

Gaining Access to Windows Functions

As mentioned earlier, Windows provides the application developer with hundreds of functions. Examples of these functions include **DispatchMessage()**, **PostMessage()**, **RegisterWindowMessage()**, and **SetActiveWindow()**. For C++ programmers using foundation classes, many of these functions are dispatched automatically. The interface to these functions is through a far intersegment call. An intersegment call is necessary because Windows treats the function as if it were located in a code segment other than the code segment that the program occupies. In the call-based API (application program interface), parameters are passed to the various modules that make up Windows, using the system stack. Since all Windows modules have code and data segments separate from an application's code, the Windows functions must be accessed by using 32-bit far addresses. This address can be broken down into two components: the 16-bit segment address and the 16-bit offset address.

Using a Pascal Calling Convention

Function declarations in Windows include the **pascal** modifier. As just discussed, parameters to all Windows functions are passed via the system stack. In a C program, for example, function parameters are first pushed onto the stack and then the function is called. Normally, the parameters are pushed from the rightmost parameter to the leftmost parameter. Upon return from the function, the calling procedure must adjust the stack pointer to a value equal to the number of bytes originally pushed onto the stack.

The Pascal parameter-passing sequence makes things look slightly different. Function parameters are pushed from left to right. It is the called function's responsibility to adjust the stack before the return; it is no longer the job of the calling procedure to adjust the stack. Windows uses this calling convention because it turns out to be more space efficient. Therefore, the compiler understands that any function declared with the reserved word **pascal** is to use the more efficient calling convention. The efficiency of using the Pascal calling convention doesn't come without its own set of problems. The Pascal calling sequence makes coding functions with a variable number of parameters more difficult. For example, whenever the wrong number of parameters is passed, the application program tends to crash.

The Windows Header File: windows.h

The windows.h header file contains over a thousand constant declarations, **typedef** declarations, and hundreds of function prototypes. One of the main reasons a Windows application takes longer to compile than a typical C or C++ program is the size of this file. windows.h is an integral part of all C and C++ programs. Traditionally, it is an include file specified in C applications. When you are using the foundation class library in C++, windows.h is included via afxwin.h. Because of the importance of windows.h, it is suggested that you print a hard copy to keep as a convenient reference.

Usually, the **#define** statements found in windows.h associate a numeric constant with a text identifier. For example:

```
#define WM_CREATE 0x0001
```

The C/C++ compiler will use the hexadecimal constant 0x0001 as a replacement for WM_CREATE during preprocessing.

Other **#define** statements may appear a bit unusual. For example:

```
#define NEAR near
#define VOID void
```

In Microsoft C, both **near** and **void** are reserved words. Your applications should use the uppercase **NEAR** and **VOID** for one very good reason: if you port your application to another C/C++ compiler, it will be much easier to change the **#define** statements within the header file than to change all of the occurrences of a particular identifier in your application.

The Components of a Windows Application

There are several important steps that are common in developing all Windows applications:

1. Create the **WinMain()** and associated windows functions in C or utilize foundation classes, such as CWinAPP, in C++.

2. Create the menu, dialog box, and any additional resource descriptions and put them into a resource script file.

3. (Optional) Use the Image Editor supplied with the C/C++ compiler to create unique cursors, icons, and bitmaps.

4. (Optional) Use the Dialog Editor supplied with the C/C++ compiler to create dialog boxes.

5. Create any module definitions and place them in the module definition file.

6. Compile and link all C/C++ language sources.

7. Compile the resource script file and add it to the executable file.

The actual creation of a Windows application requires the use of several new development tools. Before developing applications in C or C++, an understanding of these tools is needed. The next section briefly discusses the tools supplied with the C/C++ compiler as they relate to creating a Windows application.

The Microsoft C/C++ Windows Tools

The Microsoft C/C++ compiler contains several resource editors: the Image Editor, Dialog Editor, Font Editor, and HotSpot Editor. The Image Editor allows for the quick definition of icons, cursors, and bitmaps. The Font Editor provides a convenient method for creating your own unique fonts. The Dialog Editor makes it easy to create dialog-box descriptions for data entry. The HotSpot Editor allows the developer to specify hotspot locations and formats.

Resources have the capability of turning ordinary Windows applications into truly exciting graphical presentations. When you develop application icons, cursors, menus, bitmaps, and more, graphical flare can make your programs presentation quality. Resource files also let you add user-interactive components to your program such as menus, keyboard accelerators, and dialog boxes.

Graphics objects such as icons, cursors, carets, message boxes, dialog boxes, fonts, bitmaps, pens, and brushes are all examples of resources. A *resource* represents data that is included in an application's executable file. Technically speaking, however, it does not reside in a program's normal data segment. When Windows loads a program into memory for execution, it usually leaves all of the resources on the disk. Consider, as an example, when the user first requests to see an application's About box. Before Windows can display the About box it must first access the disk to copy this information from the program's executable file into memory.

Applications typically define their resources as read only and discardable. The attributes allow Windows to discard the resource whenever additional memory is required. If the resource is requested again, Windows will simply read the disk and reload the data back into system memory. Finally, if the user chooses to have multiple instances of the same application running concurrently (such as Windows Paintbrush), Windows will share not only the application's program code, but its resource definitions too.

The resource compiler, RC.EXE, is a compiler for Windows resources. Many times a Windows application will use its own resources, such as dialog boxes, menus, and icons. Each one of these resources must be predefined in a file called a *resource script file*. These files are created with the editors mentioned previously. The files are then compiled by the resource compiler and the additional information is added to the application's final executable file. This allows Windows to load and use the resources from the executable file.

The use of resources and additional compilers adds an extra layer of complexity to application development. The NMAKE utility is of great help here.

The Need for a Make File

The NMAKE.EXE program provides an efficient means of overseeing the compilation of resources and program code as well as keeping the executable version of an application up to date. It accomplishes its incremental operation by keeping track of the dates of its source files. Because Windows applications can require the incorporation of so many source files, NMAKE is very important. NMAKE requires a make file that contains a description of the job it is to perform. Make files typically have the same name as the application. Make files for the DOS command line usually don't have a file extension. A make file contains a combination of commands and filenames. NMAKE will execute a command only if the file referenced in the command has changed.

For example, say you have created a Windows application that simulates the flight of an arrow. All of a sudden, you decide to create your own unique cursor. Instead of pointing with the standard arrow provided by Windows, you decide to create a cursor that looks like an apple with an arrow through it. When the application is recompiled, the program only really needs to accommodate the changes in the cursor resource file, APPLE.CUR. Thus, NMAKE will ensure that only the information about the new cursor is updated during recompilation.

Creating Resources

Customizing a Windows application with your own icons, pointers, and bitmaps is easy when you use the Microsoft Image Editor. The Image Editor, in conjunction with the C/C++ compiler, gives you a complete environment in which to develop graphical resources. The C/C++ Dialog Editor will help you create menus and dialog boxes— the basic means of data entry in Windows. In this section you learn how to use these editors to create icons, cursors, menus, and dialog boxes. The editors can also help you manipulate individual bitmaps, keyboard accelerators, and strings. The cursor, menu, and dialog box created separately in this chapter will be assembled into a presentation-quality pie chart program in Chapter 23.

Using the Image and Dialog Editors

Each resource editor is included with the Microsoft C/C++ compiler for developing Windows applications. Each editor is a completely integrated environment designed to run under Windows. You can start each editor by clicking the proper icon in the C/C++ Windows group box.

Creating Icons, Cursors, and Bitmaps

This section describes the operation of the Image Editor and then creates a custom icon and cursor for an application that will be created in the next chapter. Icons and cursors are both really small bitmaps. The Image Editor allows you to design device-independent color bitmap images. The icons and cursors created with this editor are functionally device independent in respect to resolution.

This image-file format allows for the tailoring of a bitmap that has a consistent look on each particular display resolution. For example, one icon might consist of four definitions (called DIBs): one designed for monochrome displays, one for CGAs, one for EGAs, and one for VGAs. Whenever the application displays the icon, it simply refers to it by name; Windows then automatically selects the icon image best suited to the current display.

Table 22-1 is a list of the Image Editor's main menu items and the associated drop-down options for the menu selection. Figure 22-7 shows the editor window during the construction of an icon.

Initially, a color palette appears at the bottom of the editor for selecting the drawing color. Associated with this palette is a color box that shows the currently selected value. You can also create custom colors. A group of editing tools is also visible at the extreme right of the window.

A large editing area is provided for drawing the icons, cursors, or bitmaps. For VGA mode, a 32x32 grid is available for icon design. You can add grid lines to the main drawing canvas to aid in figure alignment. The editor also provides a small View window to allow you to view the graphics in true size.

A Custom Icon and Cursor

Creating your first icon or cursor is simple. You first choose the File option, followed by New. Then select the proper resource type (Bitmap, Icon, Cursor) from the

File	Edit	Options	Help
New...	Undo	Grid	Contents
Open...	Restore	Brush Size	Search
Save	Copy	Show Color Palette	About...
Save As...	Paste	Show View Window	
Load Colors...	Clear	Show Toolbox	
Save Colors...	New Image...		
Restore Default Colors	Select Image...		
Exit	Delete Image		

Table 22-1.   *Items Available from the Image Editor's Main Menu*

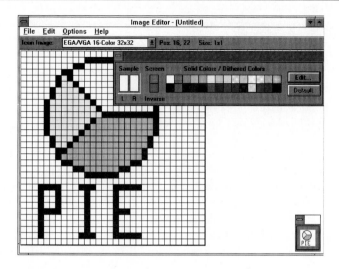

Figure 22-7. *Constructing an icon in the Image Editor*

options listed. This clears the editing area if any previous design is present and gives you a clean canvas.

After selecting the icon or cursor screen mode and size in pixels, you need to pick a drawing tool from the toolbox or use the default drawing pen. You can select brush widths from the Options menu.

The Image Editor can provide a broad spectrum of painting colors for icons and a selection of dithered colors for cursors. Click the color choice from the palette of colors shown. Now it is possible to draw the icon, cursor, or bitmap to your program's specification. You can also select Edit from the palette and create custom colors. Be sure to save your final results by selecting the File menu and either the Save or Save As option.

Figure 22-8 shows a cursor editor window with a completed cursor design. This cursor will be used in the pie chart application created in Chapter 23. When looking at the completed designs, you will note that there are actually two renditions of the design. The larger one, within the editing area, allows your eyes to easily create an image. The smaller version, to the right, represents the actual size of the design as it will appear in the application's window.

It takes a great deal of patience and practice to create a meaningful icon, cursor, or bitmap. This process often requires several trial-and-error attempts. Whenever you come up with a design that looks good, stop and save a copy of it. It is too easy to get your design to a point where you really like it and make one additional change, only to ruin hours of work.

The first time you select the Save option from the File menu, the editor prompts you for a filename. If you are creating an icon, the file system will automatically

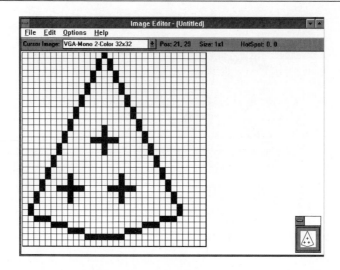

Figure 22-8.   *A cursor created in the Image Editor*

append an .ICO file extension. The .CUR file extension is used for cursors. (Note that the file extension *must* be .ICO or .CUR, respectively.) If you are creating several possible designs, make certain you choose the Save As... option, *not* Save. Save overwrites your original file, but Save As allows you to create multiple copies.

When you are creating cursors, you can select an optional hotspot from the toolbox. The *hotspot* on cursors is a point that will be used to return the current screen coordinates during the application's use. The hotspot on the pie wedge cursor is located at the point of the pie wedge.

Once you have selected the HotSpot option, a very small set of cross hairs appears in the drawing box. Simply place the cross hairs on the pixel you want to select as the hotspot and click the mouse. The coordinates of the selected hotspot will be added to the display box's list of statistics. Only one hotspot per cursor is allowed.

How to Design Menus

Menus are one of Windows' most important tools for creating interactive programs. Menus form the gateway for easy, consistent interfacing across applications. In their simplest form, menus allow the user to point and click selections that have been predefined. These selections include screen color choices, sizing options, and file operations. More advanced menu options allow the user to select dialog boxes from the menu list.

Dialog boxes permit data entry from the keyboard. They allow the user to enter string, integer, and even real number information in applications. However, before you can get to a dialog box, you typically must pass through a menu.

The menu created in this section is also used in the pie chart application developed in the next chapter.

Menu Mechanics

The following sections describe what a menu is, what it looks like, how it is created, and the various menu options available to the programmer. Menus are very easy to create and implement in a program.

What Is a Menu?   A *menu* is a list of items or names that represent options that an application can take. In some cases, the items in a menu can even be bitmaps. The user can select an option by using the mouse, the keyboard, or a hot key. Windows, in turn, responds by sending a message to the application stating which command was selected.

Designing a Menu   The Programmer's WorkBench (PWB) lets you use the editor to design and edit menu resources. The PWB is capable of creating or reading menu descriptions contained in resource script files (.RC). Resource script files are simply uncompiled text files. If a header file is available describing constants used in a menu's description, these can be added at the start of the menu's description. For example, the constant IDM_ABOUT might be identified with 40 in a header file. Figure 22-9 shows a menu (PieMenu) being developed in the PWB editor.

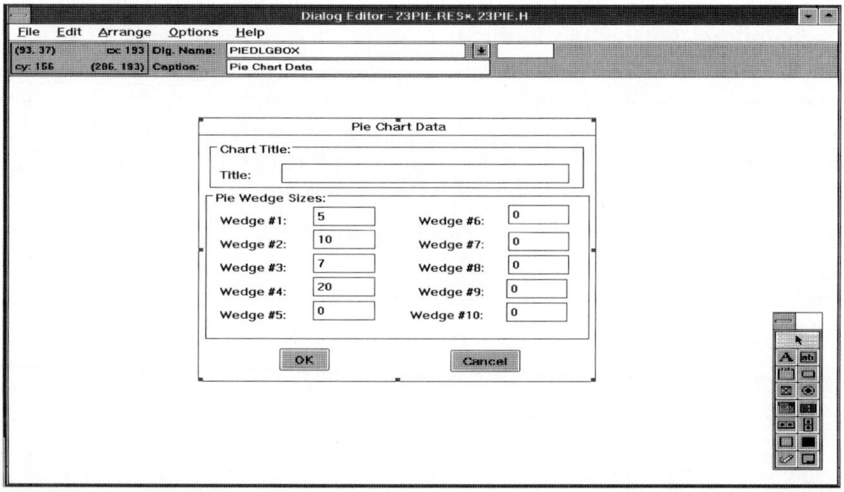

Figure 22-9.   *The components of a simple menu*

Different styles and attributes for application menus can be included in this file. These styles and attributes include checkmarks to indicate the status of an item or define styles for an item's text (normal or grayed) and separator lines to divide menus (menu bar breaks), align menu items in column format, and assign a help attribute to a menu item.

Menus and the Resource Compiler   By following a set of simple rules, Windows will draw and manage menus for you. In so doing, Windows will produce consistent menus from one application to another. Menu resource information will be compiled by the resource compiler. The compiled file (.RES) will be combined with your program application at link time, forming the final executable file (.EXE).

The structure of a simple menu is quite easy to understand. Here is a resource script file created in the PWB:

```
PIEMENU MENU LOADONCALL MOVEABLE PURE DISCARDABLE
BEGIN
  POPUP "Pie_Chart_Data"
  BEGIN
    MenuItem "About Box...",    IDM_ABOUT
    MenuItem "Data Entry...",   IDM_INPUT
    MenuItem "Exit",            IDM_EXIT
  END
END
```

By studying this listing, you can identify a number of additional menu keywords such as **MENU**, **POPUP**, and **MENUITEM**. You can use brackets ({}) instead of the keywords **BEGIN** and **END**. It is also easy to identify the menu items that will appear in this menu: About Box..., Data Entry..., and Exit. The three dots following a menu selection indicate a dialog box to the user.

Menu Keywords and Options   The name of this program's menu definition is PIEMENU. The menu definition name is followed by the keyword **MENU**. This particular example describes the pop-up menu Pie_Chart_Data, which will appear on the menu bar. Pop-up menus are arranged from left to right on the menu bar. If a large number of pop-up items is used, an additional bar is provided automatically. Only one pop-up menu can be displayed at a time.

You can use an ampersand to produce an underscore under the character that follows the ampersand in the selection list. The ampersand allows the menu item to be selected from the keyboard. The simple menu in the example does not take advantage of this feature, but if the "A" in the About Box... choice had been preceded with an ampersand, that selection could have been made with a key combination of ALT-A. With the example menu, the item can be selected by positioning the mouse pointer on the item and clicking the left button. When a pop-up menu is selected, Windows pops the menu to the screen immediately under the selected item on the menu bar. Each **MENUITEM** describes one menu item or name, for example, "Data Entry...."

Identification numbers or constants from a header file appear to the right of the menu items. If numbers are present, they can be replaced with values identified in header files—for example, IDM_ABOUT 40, IDM_INPUT 50 and IDM_EXIT 70. IDM stands for the identification number of a menu item. This form of ID has become very popular but is not required. What is important, however, is that each menu item have a unique identification associated with it.

Keyboard Accelerators   Keyboard accelerators are most often used by menu designers as a sort of "fast-key" combination for selecting menu items. For example, a menu may have 12 color items for selecting a background color. The user could point and click the menu for each color or could use keyboard accelerators. If a keyboard accelerator is used, the function keys, for example, could be used for color selection without the menu popping up at all.

How to Enter Data with Dialog Boxes

In the previous section, menus were considered as a means of simple data entry by the user. This section investigates a more significant means of data entry—the dialog box. While data can be entered directly into the application program's window, dialog boxes are the preferred entry form for maintaining consistency across Windows programs.

Dialog boxes allow the user to check items in a window list, set push buttons for various choices, directly enter strings and integers from the keyboard, and indirectly enter real numbers (floats). Starting with Windows 3.0, dialog boxes can also contain combo boxes. *Combo boxes* allow a combination of a single-line edit field and list boxes. The dialog box is the programmer's key to serious data entry in Windows programs. The dialog box is also the programmer's secret for ease of programming since Windows handles all necessary overhead.

Dialog boxes can be called when selected as a choice from a menu and appear as a pop-up window to the user. To distinguish a dialog box choice from ordinary selections in a menu, three dots (an ellipsis) follow the dialog option name. In the previous section, the About Box... and Data Entry... menu items referred to dialog box selections. Figure 22-10 shows a completed dialog box taken from an example that is developed in the next chapter.

Here is the resource script file for this dialog box:

```
PieDlgBox DIALOG LOADONCALL MOVEABLE DISCARDABLE
          93,37,193,156
          CAPTION "Pie Chart Data"
          STYLE WS_BORDER|WS_CAPTION|WS_DLGFRAME|WS_POPUP
BEGIN
  CONTROL "Chart Title:",100,"Button",BS_GROUPBOX|WS_TABSTOP,
```

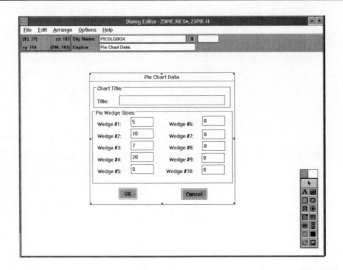

Figure 22-10.   *A data entry dialog box for a pie chart application*

```
        5,3,182,30
CONTROL "Pie Wedge Sizes:",101,"Button",BS_GROUPBOX|
        WS_TABSTOP,3,34,187,95
CONTROL "Title: ",-1,"Static",0x0000,10,21,30,8
CONTROL "",DM_TITLE,"Edit",WS_BORDER|WS_TABSTOP,40,18,
        140,12
CONTROL "Wedge #1: ",-1,"Static",0x0000,10,50,40,8
CONTROL "Wedge #2: ",-1,"Static",0x0000,10,65,40,8
CONTROL "Wedge #3: ",-1,"Static",0x0000,10,80,40,8
CONTROL "Wedge #4: ",-1,"Static",0x0000,10,95,40,8
CONTROL "Wedge #5: ",-1,"Static",0x0000,10,110,40,8
CONTROL "Wedge #6: ",-1,"Static",0x0000,106,50,40,8
CONTROL "Wedge #7: ",-1,"Static",0x0000,106,65,40,8
CONTROL "Wedge #8: ",-1,"Static",0x0000,106,80,40,8
CONTROL "Wedge #9: ",-1,"Static",0x0000,106,95,40,8
CONTROL "Wedge #10:",-1,"Static",0x0000,102,110,45,8
CONTROL "10",DM_P1,"Edit",WS_BORDER|WS_TABSTOP,55,45,30,12
CONTROL "20",DM_P2,"Edit",WS_BORDER|WS_TABSTOP,55,60,30,12
CONTROL "30",DM_P3,"Edit",WS_BORDER|WS_TABSTOP,55,75,30,12
CONTROL "40",DM_P4,"Edit",WS_BORDER|WS_TABSTOP,55,90,30,12
CONTROL "0",DM_P5,"Edit",WS_BORDER|WS_TABSTOP,55,105,30,12
```

```
    CONTROL "0",DM_P6,"Edit",WS_BORDER|WS_TABSTOP,150,44,30,12
    CONTROL "0",DM_P7,"Edit",WS_BORDER|WS_TABSTOP,150,61,30,12
    CONTROL "0",DM_P8,"Edit",WS_BORDER|WS_TABSTOP,150,76,30,12
    CONTROL "0",DM_P9,"Edit",WS_BORDER|WS_TABSTOP,149,91,30,12
    CONTROL "0",DM_P10,"Edit",WS_BORDER|WS_TABSTOP,149,106,30,12
    CONTROL "OK",IDOK,"Button",WS_TABSTOP,39,135,24,14
    CONTROL "Cancel",IDCANCEL,"Button",WS_TABSTOP,122,136,34,14
END
```

The specifications that make up a dialog box are typically produced with the Dialog Editor. The Dialog Editor is designed to read and save resource files in the compiled format (.RES). A text version of the dialog box specifications is also saved simultaneously in a file with a .DLG extension. Text files make it easy to combine several menu and dialog box specifications in one file.

Dialog Box Concepts   Dialog boxes are actually "child" windows that pop up when selected from the user's menu. When various dialog box buttons, check boxes, and so on are selected, Windows provides the means necessary for processing the message information.

Dialog boxes can be produced in two basic styles—modal and modeless. Modal dialog boxes are the most popular and are used for the example developed in the next chapter. When a modal dialog box is created, no other options within the current program will be available until the user ends the dialog box by clicking an OK or Cancel button. The OK button will process any new information selected by the user, while the Cancel button will return the user to the original window without processing new information. Windows expects the ID values for these push buttons to be 1 and 2, respectively.

Modeless dialog boxes are more closely related to ordinary windows. A pop-up window can be created from a parent window, and the user can switch back and forth between the two. The same thing is permitted with a modeless dialog box. Modeless dialog boxes are preferred when a certain option must remain on the screen, such as a color select dialog box.

The Dialog Editor

There are two ways to enter dialog box information into a resource file (.RES). If you are entering information from a magazine or book listing, it will be easiest for you to use the PWB Editor and simply copy the given menu and dialog box specifications into a resource script file with an .RC extension. When the resource script file is compiled, you will also have a file with an .RES extension. If you are creating a new dialog box from scratch for your project, you should use the Dialog Editor directly. The next few sections discuss the fundamentals of using the editor and help you get started creating simple dialog boxes. Microsoft's on-line help utility will provide additional information for more advanced features and editing.

One look at the resource script file containing dialog box information shown earlier in this chapter will convince you of the need for a special editor. The editor allows you to design the dialog box graphically.

Where do all those terms come from? What do all those numbers mean? Without the Dialog Editor, it would be up to you to create, size, and place dialog boxes and their associated controls on the screen experimentally. The Dialog Editor, on the other hand, will do all this for you automatically. Except for being able to claim that you created a dialog box without the editor at least once in your life, there is no reason for you not to design dialog boxes with the graphical environment of the editor.

Using the Dialog Editor

If your dialog box information is entered in ASCII form from a book or magazine article, it must be compiled before editing is permitted. This involves the use of the resource compiler, described shortly. On the other hand, if you are creating a new dialog box for a project from scratch, simply enter the Dialog Editor. You do this by clicking the Dialog Editor icon in the C/C++ group box. A screen similar to the one in Figure 22-11 should appear.

The New option should be selected for the dialog box from the File menu. The screen now contains the initial outline for the new dialog box. This initial dialog box can be moved about the screen and sized to fit your needs. The screen in Figure 22-12 shows the initial dialog box moved and sized.

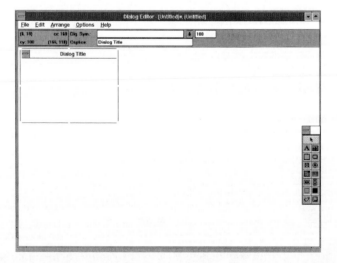

Figure 22-11.   *The entry level window for the Dialog Editor*

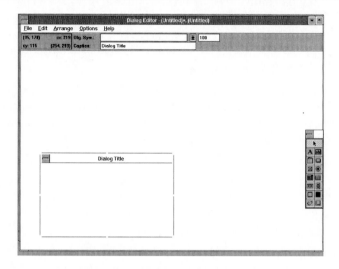

Figure 22-12.   *A moved and resized dialog box outline*

Dialog Editor Features   The main dialog box menu contains five menu items that you can select when working with a new dialog box. If you have gotten to this point, you have already used the File menu to open a new dialog box for construction. The remaining menu items include Edit, Arrange, Options, and Help. Many of the individual menu items are self-explanatory, and only the most important are discussed here.

- The Edit menu, in addition to other options, allows for a quick restore if a mistake is made during the dialog box creation process. You can also cut, copy, paste, and delete items as you do with most Windows applications.

- The Arrange menu permits alignment, spacing, sizing, push buttons, groups, and optional settings.

- The Options menu allows the toolbox's visibility to be set, along with various design modes, such as, Test, Hex, and Translate. Dialog box features can be tested during design with the Test Mode option.

- Help is another menu option that can provide additional details on any of the previously mentioned features.

Placing Controls with the Toolbox   By far the most important aspect of using the Dialog Editor is an understanding of the various controls that are provided for the user in the toolbox. Here is an explanation of the most important controls.

- The check box control creates a small square box, called a check box, with a label to its right. Check boxes are usually marked or checked by clicking with the mouse, but they can also be selected with the keyboard. Several check boxes usually appear together in a dialog box; they allow the user to check one or more features at the same time.

- The radio button control creates a small circle, called a radio button, with a label to its right. Radio buttons, like check boxes, typically appear in groups. However, unlike check boxes, only one radio button can be selected at a time in any particular group.

- The push button control, sometimes called simply a button, is a small, rounded, rectangular button that can be sized. The push button contains a label within it. Push buttons are used for an immediate choice such as accepting or canceling the dialog box selections made by the user.

- The group box control creates a rectangular outline within a dialog box to enclose a group of controls that are to be used together. The group box contains a label on its upper-left edge.

The horizontal scroll bar and vertical scroll bar controls allow horizontal and vertical scroll bars to be created for the dialog box. These are usually used in conjunction with another window or control that contains text or graphics information.

- The list box control creates a rectangular outline with a vertical scroll bar. List boxes are useful when scrolling is needed to allow the user to select a file from a long directory listing.

- The edit text control creates a small interactive rectangle on the screen in which the user can enter string information. The Edit box can be sized to accept short or long strings. This string information can be processed directly as character or numeric integer data and indirectly as real-number data in the program. The Edit box is the most important control for data entry.

- The static text control allows the insertion of labels and strings within the dialog box. These can be used, for example, to label an Edit box.

- The icon control is used for the placement of a dialog box icon. The icon control creates the rectangular space for the icon.

- The combo box is made up of two elements. It is a combination of a single-line edit field (which is also called "static text") and a list box. With a combo box, the user has the ability to enter something into the Edit box or scroll through the List box looking for an appropriate selection. Windows 3.1 provides several styles of combo boxes.

You can place controls in the current dialog box by selecting the appropriate control from the toolbox, positioning the mouse pointer in the dialog box, and clicking the mouse button. If the placement is not where you desired, you can use the mouse for repositioning.

Creating a Dialog Box

In this section, a simple About dialog box is created. You use About dialog boxes to identify the project, identify the developers, give a copyright date, and so on. They usually contain only one push button—OK. They are the easiest dialog boxes to design. Figure 22-13 shows a sized and positioned dialog box outline awaiting the placement of text and button controls.

In this dialog box example, only two types of controls will be used—the text and push button controls. To enter text, decide on the type of text alignment and click that control option in the toolbox. You can then use the mouse to position the text box in the dialog window. Clicking the mouse within the box after positioning it will allow editing of the actual text string. The screen in Figure 22-14 illustrates this concept.

The string to be printed is entered in the Text window, where the word "Text" now appears. The ID value is automatically supplied. To place an OK push button in the About box, select the Push Button option from the toolbox. Place the OK button on the screen. Then click the mouse to set the position of the button in the window. Clicking the mouse within the set button allows you to enter the text for the button. In this case, it will be "OK". Figure 22-15 shows the placement of the push button and the final dialog box.

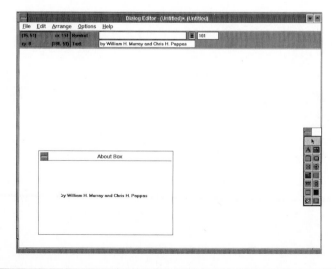

Figure 22-13. *A partially completed About dialog box*

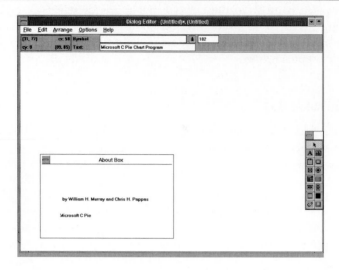

Figure 22-14. *Editing a text string in a dialog box*

You can then save the dialog box information by selecting the Save option from the File menu. Remember that the Dialog Editor will save this file in the compiled resource form (.RES). Using the Dialog Editor efficiently is a skill learned with practice. Large dialog boxes, utilizing many controls, will initially take hours to design. Again, use the detailed information contained in the Help menu and your

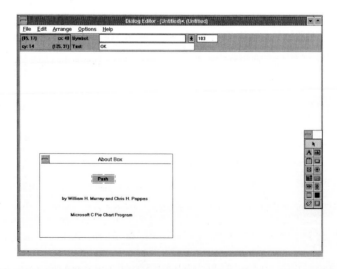

Figure 22-15. *Placing push buttons in a dialog box*

Microsoft user's manuals. Start with simple dialog boxes and work toward more complicated designs.

Examining the Resource Script   You can examine the script file information before saving the dialog box. You do this by selecting the Resource menu option and selecting the Edit As Text item. The previous About box would appear like this:

```
AboutDlgBox DIALOG LOADONCALL MOVEABLE DISCARDABLE
           50,300,180,80
           STYLE WS_DLGFRAME|WS_POPUP
BEGIN
   CONTROL "Microsoft C Pie Chart Program",-1,"static",
           SS_CENTER|WS_CHILD,2,60,176,10
   CONTROL "by William H. Murray and Chris H. Pappas",-1,
           "static",SS_CENTER|WS_CHILD,2,45,176,10
   CONTROL "OK",IDOK,"button",
           BS_PUSHBUTTON|WS_TABSTOP|WS_CHILD,75,10,32,14
END
```

The name of this dialog box is ABOUTDLGBOX. The editor has affixed various segment values along with size specifications for the box. The various style options further identify the dialog box as one that has a frame and is a pop-up type. Three controls are listed.

The first and second control specifications are for static text. The word "static" identifies the control as a static text box. The remaining specifications establish the text position and type.

The third control specifies an OK push button. The text within the first set of double quotes specifies what will appear within the push button. The labels for the ID values for the push button are a system default.

Remember that it is not necessary to view this information at all. The Dialog Editor will convert the graphics dialog box you see on the screen directly into a resource file (.RES). The only time you will need this information is when you are entering dialog box specifications from a book or magazine.

The About box, shown earlier, is used in the next chapter.

Using the Resource Compiler (RC) from the Command Line

You can use the resource compiler directly without the use of the Dialog Editor or PWB. This direct use is usually limited to applications taken from books or magazine articles. These are cases where the menu or dialog box resource information is entered in the form of a text file rather than being created directly within the Dialog Editor.

The resource file created by the Dialog Editor for dialog boxes contains resource information stored in binary format (.RES). The Dialog Editor allows you to edit this binary information directly and save the results back into the original file. Another type of optional file is called a resource script file and contains resource information in text format (ASCII). As previously mentioned, this file has an .RC file extension.

Recall that a dialog box resource script file, with a .DLG file extension, is created along with the .RC file. Usually, resource script files are not needed because the Dialog Editor allows you to edit resource files directly. The only real, but very important, use for resource script files is for reproducing resource information for use in book and magazine article listings or for creating your own resources from such articles.

A Look at Resource Statements

You can also use resource script files for combining menu and dialog resources in one file. If you opt for resource script files when creating dialog boxes or if you enter resource script files from book and magazine listings, you can use the resource statements shown in Table 22-2.

Defining additional resources for an application is as simple as naming the resource ID followed by a resource compiler keyword and then the actual filename. Suppose you've created a resource script file called MYRES.RC:

```
myicon   ICON   myicon.ico
mycursor CURSOR mycursor.cur
mybitmap BITMAP mybitmap.bmp
```

Directive	Single-line	Multiple-line	User-defined
#include	BITMAP	ACCELERATORS	Supplied by
#define	CURSOR	DIALOG	user
#undef	FONT	MENU	
#ifdef	ICON	RCDATA	
#ifndef		STRINGTABLE	
#if			
#elif			
#else			
#endif			

Table 22-2.   Resource Compiler Statements

MYRES.RC is a text file that defines three new resources. The names of the three resources are MYICON, MYCURSOR, and MYBITMAP. **ICON**, **CURSOR**, and **BITMAP** are reserved keywords defining the type of the resource. These are followed by the actual filenames containing the resource information; for example: MYICON.ICO, MYCURSOR.CUR, and MYBITMAP.BMP.

There are five additional options that can be included with each single-line statement. These options follow the resource-type keyword and include PRELOAD, LOADONCALL, FIXED, MOVEABLE, and DISCARDABLE. The first two options define load options; the latter define memory options. For example:

```
resourceID resource-type [[load-option]] [[memory-option]]
         filename
```

The PRELOAD option automatically loads the resource whenever the application is run. LOADONCALL loads the resource only when it is called.

If a FIXED memory option is selected, the resource remains at a fixed memory address. Selecting MOVEABLE allows Windows to move the resource to compact and conserve memory. The last choice, DISCARDABLE, allows Windows to discard the resource if it is no longer needed. However, it can be reloaded should a call be made requesting the particular resource. For example, making *mybitmap* LOADONCALL and DISCARDABLE is as simple as entering the following modified single-line statement into the resource script:

```
myicon   ICON   myicon.ico
mycursor CURSOR mycursor.cur
mybitmap BITMAP LOADONCALL DISCARDABLE mybitmap.bmp
```

Compiling Resources

Resource script files must be compiled. You can do this directly from the DOS command line. The command to run the resource compiler includes the name of the resource script file, the name of the executable file that will receive the compiler's binary format output, and any optional instructions from the list in Table 22-3.

Resource Compiler Syntax   The syntax for using the resource compiler is simple. From the command line, type

```
rc [[compiler options]] filename.rc [[executable filename]]
```

For example, invoking the resource compiler with the example resource script described earlier would look like one of the following three lines:

Resource Compiler Option	Description
-r	Instructs the resource compiler to put its output into a file with an .RES file extension instead of putting it into the executable file
-d	Defines a symbol for the preprocessor that you can test with the #ifdef directive
-fo	Renames the .RES file
-fe	Renames the .EXE file
-i	Searches the specified directory before searching the directories specified by the INCLUDE environment variable
-v	Displays messages that report on the progress of the compiler
-x	Prevents the resource compiler from checking the INCLUDE environment variable when searching for include files or resource files
-l	Causes the resource compiler to compile an application that will be using the expanded memory supported by the Lotus Intel Microsoft Expanded Memory Specification, Version 3.2
-m*	Causes the resource compiler to compile an application using EMS so that multiple instances of the application will use different EMS memory banks
-e*	For a dynamic link library, changes the default location of global memory from below the EMS bank line to above the EMS bank line
-p*	Creates a private dynamic link library that can be called by only one application. This lets Windows load the library above the EMS bank line
-? or -h	Displays a list of the resource compiler's command-line options
-t*	Creates a protected-mode-only application
-k*	Keeps segments in .def order
-31	Marks as 3.1 or greater
-30	Marks as 3.0 or greater
-z	Tells the compiler to not check the RCINCLUDE statement

*Not valid when -r is also specified

Table 22-3.   *Resource Compiler Options*

```
rc myres
rc myres.rc
rc -r myres.rc
```

The first two examples read the MYRES.RC resource script file, create the compiled resource file MYRES.RES, and copy the resources into the executable file MYRES.EXE. The third command performs the same actions except that it does *not* put the resource into MYRES.EXE. If the third command were executed, the MYRES.RES binary file could be added to the MYRES.EXE file at a later date by using the following command structure:

```
rc myres.res
```

This causes the resource compiler to search for the compiled resource file (.RES) and places it into the executable file (.EXE) of the same filename.

Additional Resource Information

In addition to the information contained in this chapter, the Microsoft user's guides provide a wealth of information on each of these topics. While using the various resource editors, avail yourself of the extensive built-in help engine that is available. Details on the creation of actual Windows resources can be found in the books mentioned in this and earlier chapters and in various magazine articles. Developing serious Windows code is a major undertaking, but don't forget to have fun while learning.

The next chapter will put these programming concepts into practice as you learn how to develop traditional C Windows applications.

Chapter *23*

Writing Windows
Applications in C

Chapter 22 concentrated on Windows terms, definitions, and tools in order to prepare you for the applications you'll develop in this chapter. The most attractive features of Windows applications are the common visual interface, device independence, and concurrent execution. It is now time to put theory to practice and develop applications with these exciting features.

This chapter teaches you how to write Windows applications in C. In Chapters 24 and 25, you will learn how to write Windows applications in C++ and incorporate Microsoft's Foundation Class library into your code. Even if you plan to do all of your development work in C++, this is still an important chapter for you to study. By studying the C applications developed here, you'll have a much better understanding of how the Foundation Class library aids in C++ code development.

A Framework for All Applications

In this section you learn about the various components that make up a program called 23SWA.C (Simple Windows Application). The 23SWA.C program incorporates all of the Windows components minimally necessary to create and display a window (a main window with a border, a title bar, a system menu, and maximize/minimize boxes), draw a diagonal line, print a text message, and gracefully quit. You also learn that the 23SWA.C program and all of its related files can serve as templates for future C Windows applications you develop. Understanding code that is used over and over will save you time and help foster an understanding of how Windows applications are put together and why they work. Before getting started, take a moment to look over the Windows data types and structures listed in Tables 23-1 and 23-2. These tables will help you understand what each Windows function call is passing in terms of parameter values.

Using Handles Effectively

Windows functions use handles to identify many different types of objects, such as menus, icons, controls, memory allocations, output devices, pens and brushes, windows, and even instances. This allows Windows to run more than one copy of the same application at a time. Windows can keep track of these various instances by providing each with its own unique handle.

A handle is usually used as an index into an internal table. By using a handle to reference a table element, rather than actually containing a memory address, Windows can dynamically continue to rearrange all resources by simply inserting a resource's new address into the identical position within the table. For example, if Windows assigns a particular application's icon resource with table lookup position 22, then regardless of where Windows moves the icon in memory, table position 22 still contains the current location.

Windows is very efficient in its management of multiple instances. Windows saves system resources by using the same code for all instances of an application. In these cases, only the data segment for each instance is uniquely managed. Usually, the first instance of an application has a very important job. The first instance of an application creates all of the objects necessary for the functioning of the application. This usually includes dialog boxes, menus, and so on, and also window classes. These resources then become available to all other instances of the application.

Data Type	Meaning
HANDLE	Defines a 16-bit unsigned integer used as a handle
HWND	Specifies a 16-bit unsigned integer used as the handle to a window
LONG	Defines a 32-bit signed integer
LPSTR	Identifies a 32-bit pointer to a character data type
FARPROC	Identifies a 32-bit pointer to a function
WORD	Defines a 16-bit unsigned integer

Table 23-1.   Frequently Used Windows Data Types

Structure	Usage
MSG	Specifies the fields of an input message
PAINTSTRUCT	Specifies the paint structure to be used when drawing within a window
RECT	Specifies a rectangle
WNDCLASS	Specifies a window class

Table 23-2.   Frequently Used Windows Structures

Examining the Components in a Windows Application

At the highest level, a Windows application can be broken down into two major components: the **WinMain**() function and the window function. Microsoft Windows requires that the main body of your C program be named **WinMain**(). This function acts as the entry point for the application and behaves in a similar manner to the **main**() function in a standard C program. The window function, however, has a unique role. Your Windows applications never actually access any Windows functions directly. Instead, the application makes a request to Windows to carry out the specified operation. In order to facilitate this communication, Windows requires a function called a call back function. A *call back* function is registered with Windows, and it is called back whenever Windows wants to execute an operation on a window.

The WinMain() Function

All Windows applications must have a **WinMain**() function. **WinMain**() is responsible for

- Registering the application's window classes
- Performing necessary initializations
- Creating and starting the application's message-processing loop
- Accessing the application's message queue
- Upon receiving a WM_QUIT message, terminating the application

WinMain() receives four parameters from Windows. For the 23SWA.C application developed in this chapter, the function call looks like this:

```
int PASCAL WinMain(hInst,hPreInst,lpszCmdLine,nCmdShow)
HINSTANCE hInst,hPreInst;
LPSTR   lpszCmdLine;
int     nCmdShow;
```

Notice, first, the use of the PASCAL calling convention discussed in the preceding chapter. The first parameter, *hInst,* is passed the instance handle of the application. *hPreInst* contains a null if no previous instance exists; otherwise it returns the handle to the previous instance of the program. *lpszCmdLine* is a long pointer to a null-terminated string that points to the application's parameter line. (It contains null if the application was started using the Windows Executive.) *nCmdShow* defines whether or not the application is to be displayed as a window (SW_SHOWNORMAL) or as an icon (SW_SHOWMINNOACTIVE).

Registration of the Window Class

Each window created for a Windows application must be based on a window class. The windows you create for Windows can have a variety of styles, colors, text fonts, placement, caption bars, icons, and so on. The *window class* serves as a resource that defines these attributes. Once an application registers a window class, the class becomes available to all programs running under Windows. Since this is possible, take care to avoid any conflicting names between window class applications.

The window class is essentially a data structure. The windows.h header file contains the **typedef** statement that defines the structure WNDCLASS:

```
typedef struct tagWNDCLASS {
    WORD    style;
    long    (FAR PASCAL *lpfnWndProc)();
    int     cbClsExtra;
    int     cbWndExtra;
    HANDLE  hInstance;
    HICON   hIcon;
    HCURSOR hCursor;
    HBRUSH  hbrBackground;
    LPSTR   lpszMenuName;
    LPSTR   lpszClassName;
} WNDCLASS;
```

Windows provides several predefined window classes, but most applications define their own window classes. To define a window class, your application must define a structure variable of the following type:

```
WNDCLASS wc23SWA;
```

The *wc23SWA* structure is then filled with information about the window class. The following sections describe the various fields within the WNDCLASS structure. Some of the fields may be assigned a null, directing Windows to use predefined values, while others must be given specific values.

style   The *style* field names the class style. The styles can be combined with the bitwise OR operator. The style field is made up of a combination of the following:

Value	Meaning
CS_BYTEALIGNCLIENT	Aligns a client area on a byte boundary
CS_BYTEALIGNWINDOW	Aligns a window on the byte boundary
CS_CLASSDC	Provides the window class a display context
CS_DBLCLKS	Sends a double-click message to the window
CS_GLOBALCLASS	States that the window class is an application global class
CS_HREDRAW	Redraws the window when horizontal size changes
CS_NOCLOSE	Inhibits the close option from the system menu
CS_OWNDC	Each window receives an instance for its own display context (DC)
CS_PARENTDC	Sends the parent window's display context (DC) to the window class
CS_SAVEBITS	Saves that part of a screen that is covered by another window
CS_VREDRAW	Redraws the window when the vertical size changes

lpfnWndProc   *lpfnWndProc* receives a pointer to the window function that will carry out all of the tasks for the window.

cbClsExtra   *cbClsExtra* gives the number of bytes that must be allocated after the window class structure. It can be null.

cbWndExtra   *cbWndExtra* gives the number of bytes that must be allocated after the window instance. It can be null.

hInstance   *hInstance* defines the instance of the application registering the window class. This must be an instance handle and cannot be null.

hIcon   *hIcon* defines the icon to be used when the window is minimized. This can be null.

hCursor   *hCursor* defines the cursor to be used with the application. This handle can be null. The cursor is valid only within the application's client area.

hbrBackground   *hbrBackground* provides the identification for the background brush. This can be a handle to the physical brush or it can be a color value. Color values must be selected from one of the standard colors in the following list. A value of 1 must be added to the selected color.

> COLOR_ACTIVEBORDER
> COLOR_ACTIVECAPTION
> COLOR_APPWORKSPACE
> COLOR_BACKGROUND
> COLOR_BTNFACE
> COLOR_BTNSHADOW
> COLOR_BTNTEXT
> COLOR_CAPTIONTEXT
> COLOR_GRAYTEXT
> COLOR_HIGHLIGHT
> COLOR_HIGHLIGHTTEXT
> COLOR_INACTIVEBORDER
> COLOR_INACTIVECAPTION
> COLOR_MENU
> COLOR_MENUTEXT
> COLOR_SCROLLBAR
> COLOR_WINDOW
> COLOR_WINDOWFRAME
> COLOR_WINDOWTEXT

If *hbrBackground* is null, the application paints its own background.

lpszMenuName   *lpszMenuName* is a pointer to a null-terminated character string. The string is the resource name of the menu. This item can be null.

lpszClassName   *lpszClassName* is a pointer to a null-terminated character string. The string is the name of the window class.

The following code section shows how the WNDCLASS structure has been defined and initialized for 23SWA.C:

```
char    szProgName[]="ProgName";
     .
     .
     .
  WNDCLASS wc23SWA;
```

```
               .
               .
               .
   if (!hPreInst) {
     wc23SWA.lpszClassName=szProgName;
     wc23SWA.hInstance    =hInst;
     wc23SWA.lpfnWndProc  =WindowProc;
     wc23SWA.hCursor      =LoadCursor(NULL,IDC_ARROW);
     wc23SWA.hIcon        =NULL;
     wc23SWA.lpszMenuName =NULL;
     wc23SWA.hbrBackground=GetStockObject(WHITE_BRUSH);
     wc23SWA.style        =CS_HREDRAW|CS_VREDRAW;
     wc23SWA.cbClsExtra   =0;
     wc23SWA.cbWndExtra   =0;
     if (!RegisterClass (&wc23SWA))
       return FALSE;
   }
```

For the Simple Windows Application example being developed, *wc23SWA.lpszClassName* is assigned the generic "ProgName." This should be changed for each new window class created. When the **WinMain()** function is called, it will return a value for *wc23SWA.hInstance* indicating the current instance of the application. The *wc23SWA.lpfnWndProc* field is supplied a pointer to the window function that will accomplish all of the tasks for the window. For this example, the function is called **WindowProc()** and must be declared in the program code before the assignment statement.

The next field, *wc23SWA.hCursor,* is assigned the handle to the application instance's cursor (IDC_ARROW, the standard arrow cursor). In this example, no user-defined icon is being supplied, so *wc23SWA.hIcon* is assigned null. You can load cursors and icons by using the **LoadCursor()** and **LoadIcon()** Windows functions. A null assigned to *wc23SWA.lpszMenuName* also indicates that the current application does not have a menu. If it did, the menu would have a name and it would appear between quotation marks at this spot.

The **GetStockObject()** function returns a handle to a brush used to paint the background color of the client area of a window created in this class. In this example, the function returns a handle to one of Windows predefined brushes (WHITE_BRUSH).

The window class style has been set to CS_HREDRAW or CS_VREDRAW. All window class styles have identifiers in windows.h that begin with CS_. Each identifier represents a bit value. The logical OR operation is used to combine these bit flags. The two parameters used in this case instruct Windows to redraw the entire client area whenever the horizontal or vertical size of the window is changed.

The last two fields, *wc23SWA.cbClsExtra* and *wc23SWA.cbWndExtra,* are frequently assigned zero. These fields indicate the count of extra bytes that have been reserved at the end of the window class structure and the window data structure used for each window class.

What do you think the next piece of code might accomplish?

```
if (!hPreInst) {
  .
  .
  .
  if (!RegisterClass (&wc23SWA))
    return FALSE;
}
```

From an earlier discussion concerning instances, you learned that an application needs to register a window class only if it is the first instance. Windows can check the number of instances by examining the *hPreInst* parameter. If this value is null, then this is the application's first instance. Thus, the first **if** statement fills the WNDCLASS structure only for the first instance. The last **if** statement takes care of registering a new window class. It does this by sending a far pointer to the address of the window class structure. The actual parameter's near pointer (&ws23SWA) is converted to a far pointer by the compiler since the function **RegisterClass()** is expecting a far pointer. If Windows cannot register the window class, the **RegisterClass()** function returns a zero and terminates the application.

Establishing a Window

Whether this is the first instance of an application or subsequent instances, a window must be created. All windows are of a predefined class type. The previous section illustrated how and when to initialize and register a window class. This section describes the steps necessary for creating the actual window.

You create a window by calling the Windows **CreateWindow()** function. While the window class defines the general characteristics of a window, allowing the same window class to be used for many different windows, the parameters to **CreateWindow()** specify more detailed information about the window. This additional information falls under the following categories: the class, title, style, screen position, window's parent handle, menu handle, instance handle, and 32 bits of additional information. For the 23SWA.C application, this function would take on the following appearance:

```
hWnd=CreateWindow(szProgName,"Simple Windows Application",
                  WS_OVERLAPPEDWINDOW,CW_USEDEFAULT,
                  CW_USEDEFAULT,CW_USEDEFAULT,
                  CW_USEDEFAULT,(HWND)NULL,(HMENU)NULL,
                  (HANDLE)hInst,(LPSTR)NULL);
```

The first field, *szProgName* (assigned earlier), defines the window's class, followed by the title to be used for the window's title bar (Simple Windows Application). The style of the window is the third parameter (WS_OVERLAPPEDWINDOW). This standard Windows style represents a normal overlapped window with a caption bar, a system menu box, minimize and maximize icons, and a thick window frame.

The next six parameters (either CS_USEDEFAULT or null) represent the initial *x* and *y* positions and *x* and *y* size of the window, along with the parent window handle and window menu handle. Each of these fields has been assigned a default value. The *hInst* field contains the instance of the program, followed by no additional parameters (null).

Displaying and Updating a Window

To display a window, you must do more than simply register a window class and create a window from that class. Displaying an actual window requires a call to the **ShowWindow()** function:

```
ShowWindow(hWnd,nCmdShow);
```

The second parameter to **ShowWindow()**, *nCmdShow,* determines how the window is initially displayed. The value of *nCmdShow* can specify that the window be displayed as a normal window (SW_SHOWNORMAL), and there are several other possibilities. For example, substituting *nCmdShow* with the windows.h constant SW_SHOWMINNOACTIVE causes the window to be drawn as an icon:

```
ShowWindow(hWnd,SW_SHOWMINNOACTIVE);
```

Other possibilities include SW_SHOWMAXIMIZED, which causes the window to be active and fills the entire display, and its counterpart, SW_SHOWMINIMIZED.

The last step in displaying a window requires a call to the **UpdateWindow()** function:

```
UpdateWindow(hWnd);
```

When **ShowWindow()** is called with a SW_SHOWNORMAL parameter, the function erases the window's client area with the background brush specified in the window's class. (Recall that in this application, a WHITE_BRUSH is being used.) It is the call to **UpdateWindow()** that causes the client area to be painted by generating a WM_PAINT message.

Examining the Message Loop

With the application's window created and displayed, the application is ready to perform its main task—processing messages. Recall that Windows does not send input from the mouse or keyboard directly to an application. Rather, Windows places all input into the application's queue. This queue can contain messages generated by Windows or other applications. Once the **WinMain()** function has established and displayed the window, it needs to create a program message loop. This message loop is frequently formed by using a **while** loop:

```
while (GetMessage(&msg,NULL,NULL,NULL)) {
  TranslateMessage(&msg);
  DispatchMessage(&msg);
}
```

The GetMessage() Function   The **GetMessage()** function is responsible for retrieving the next message from the application's message queue, coping it into the *msg* structure, and sending it to the main body of the program. The three null parameters instruct the function to retrieve all of the messages.

Windows is a *nonpreemptive multitasking system,* which means it cannot take control from an application. The application must yield control before Windows can reassign control to another application. In this type of system, the **GetMessage()** function can automatically release control of the processor to another application if the current application has no messages waiting. The current application will pick up execution following the **GetMessage()** statement whenever a message finally does arrive in the application's message queue.

Applications can normally return control to Windows any time before starting the message loop. For example, an application will normally make certain that all steps leading up to the message loop have executed properly. Usually, this involves making sure each window class is registered and has been created. Once the message loop has been entered, however, only one message can terminate the loop. Whenever the message to be processed is WM_QUIT, the value returned is FALSE. This message causes the processing to advance to the main loop's closing routine. The WM_QUIT message is the only way for an application to exit the message loop.

The TranslateMessage() Function   The **TranslateMessage()** function is required only for applications that need to process character input from the keyboard. The ability to process this type of information is useful because it allows the user to make menu selections without using the mouse. Specifically, the **TranslateMessage()** function creates an ASCII character message (WM_CHAR) from a WM_KEYDOWN and WM_KEYUP message. When this function is included in the message loop, the keyboard interface will be in effect.

The DispatchMessage() Function   The **DispatchMessage()** function is responsible for routing the message to the correct window procedure. By using this function, it is easy to add additional windows and dialog boxes to your application, allowing **DispatchMessage( )** to automatically route each message to the appropriate window procedure.

The Window Function

Every Windows application must have a **WinMain( )** function and a window function, as mentioned earlier. Recall that Windows applications never directly access any window functions. Rather, each application makes a request to Windows to carry out any specified operations. This process is accomplished with the use of a call back function. A call back function is registered with Windows, and it is called back whenever Windows wants to execute an operation on a window. The window function itself may be very small, processing only one or two messages, or it may be very complex. Advanced windows functions will not only process many types of messages, but they will also deal with a variety of application windows.

Initially, this concept of an operating system making a call to the application program can be quite a surprise. For the 23SWA.C application, the call back function takes on the following appearance:

```
LONG FAR PASCAL WindowProc(hWnd,messg,wParam,lParam)
HWND    hWnd;
UINT messg;
WPARAM    wParam;
LPARAM    lParam;
{
  PAINTSTRUCT ps;
  HDC   hdc;
  HPEN hPen;

  switch (messg)
  {
    case WM_PAINT:
      hdc=BeginPaint(hWnd,&ps);

/*--------- your routines below ---------*/

      MoveTo(hdc,0,0);
      LineTo(hdc,639,429);
      TextOut(hdc,55,20,"<- a diagonal line",18);

/*--------- your routines above ---------*/

      ValidateRect(hWnd,NULL);
      EndPaint(hWnd,&ps);
      break;
```

```
    case WM_DESTROY:
      PostQuitMessage(0);
      break;
    default:
      return(DefWindowProc(hWnd,messg,wParam,lParam));
      break;
  }
  return(0L);
}
```

It is important to note that the name of this Windows function, for this example **WindowProc()**, must be referenced by name in the *wc23SWA.lpfnWndProc* field of the window class structure. **WindowProc()** will be the window function for all windows that are created from this window class. The following listing reviews this initialization:

```
            .
            .
            .


if (!hPreInst)  {
  wc23SWA.lpszClassName=szProgName;
  wc23SWA.hInstance     =hInst;
  wc23SWA.lpfnWndProc   =WindowProc;
    .
    .
    .
```

Windows has hundreds of different messages that it can send to the window function. These messages are identified with names that begin with WM_. The messages are defined in windows.h and are actually constants that refer to numbered codes. Windows can call the window function for various reasons, including window creation, resizing, moving, being turned into an icon, when a menu item has been selected, when a scroll bar is being moved or changed by a mouse click, when repainting a client area, and when the window is being destroyed.

The **WindowProc()** function also uses the PASCAL calling convention. The first parameter of the function, *hWnd,* contains the handle to the window that Windows will send the message to. Remember that one window function can process messages for several windows created from the same window class. By using the window handle, **WindowProc()** can determine which window is receiving the message.

The second function parameter, *messg,* specifies the actual message as defined in windows.h. The last two parameters, *wParam* and *lParam,* contain additional information related to each specific message. Sometimes the values returned are null and can be ignored; other times, they can contain two byte values and a far pointer or two word values.

The WM_PAINT Message

The window function must first examine the type of the message it is about to process and then select the appropriate action to be taken. This selection is performed by the **switch** statement. The first message the window function will process is WM_PAINT. The paint procedure prepares the application's client area for updating and obtains a display context for the window. The display context comes equipped with a default pen, brush, and font. This is very important because all of the display functions a Windows application uses require a handle to the display context.

Since Windows is a multitasking environment, it is possible for one application to display its dialog box over another application's client area. This could create a display problem whenever the dialog box is closed—that is, a hole in the client area of the other application. Windows handles this possible "back-hole" problem by sending the application a WM_PAINT message, requesting that the application's client area be updated or repainted.

Except for the first WM_PAINT message, which is sent by the call to **UpdateWindow()** in **WinMain()**, additional WM_PAINT messages are sent under the following conditions:

- When resizing a window

- Whenever a portion of a client area has been hidden by a menu or dialog box that has just been closed

- When using the **ScrollWindow()** function

- When forcing a WM_PAINT message with a call to the **InvalidateRect()** or **InvalidateRgn()** function

Here is how the process works. Any portion of an application's client area that has been corrupted by the overlay of a dialog box, for example, has that area of the client area marked as invalid. Windows makes the redrawing of a client area efficient by keeping track of the diagonal coordinates of this invalid rectangle. It is the presence of an invalid rectangle that prompts Windows to send the WM_PAINT message.

If several portions of the client area are invalidated, Windows will adjust the invalid rectangle coordinates to encapsulate all invalid regions. In other words, Windows does not send a WM_PAINT message for each invalid rectangle.

The call to **InvalidateRect()** allows Windows to mark the client area as invalid, thereby forcing a WM_PAINT message. An application can obtain the coordinates of the invalid rectangle by calling the **GetUpdateRect()** function. A call to the

ValidateRect() function validates any rectangular region in the client area and deletes any pending WM_PAINT messages.

The processing of the WM_PAINT message ends with a call to the **EndPaint()** function. The **EndPaint()** function is called whenever the application is finished sending information to the client area. This function tells Windows that the application has finished processing all paint messages. It also tells Windows that it is now OK to remove the display context.

An application can be terminated by selecting the Close option from the system menu. This selection initiates a WM_DESTROY message that causes the **PostQuitMessage()** function to place a WM_QUIT message in the message queue. The application ends after retrieving this message. **DefWindowProc()** (the default window function) is used to process any WM_PAINT messages not processed by the window function.

Writing a Module Definition File

In the Simple Windows Application that is being developed, two files are needed: the C source code and a module definition file. A *module definition file* contains definitions and descriptive information that tells the linker how to organize the application's executable file. This information becomes part of the header section of the New Executable file format.

For this example, the module definition file takes on the following appearance:

```
NAME        23SWA
DESCRIPTION 'Simple Windows Application'
EXETYPE     WINDOWS
STUB        'WINSTUB.EXE'
CODE        PRELOAD MOVEABLE DISCARDABLE
DATA        PRELOAD MOVEABLE MULTIPLE
HEAPSIZE    4096
STACKSIZE   9216
EXPORTS     WindowProc      @1
```

The NAME statement defines 23SWA as a Windows program (not a dynamic link library) and gives the module a name. This name should be the same name as the program's executable (.EXE) file.

The DESCRIPTION line copies the text into the executable file. Often this is used to embed added information such as a release date, version number, or copyright notice.

The EXETYPE refers to the type of executable file to create.

The STUB statement specifies the name of a program segment that is to be inserted into the executable file. If the application is run from the DOS command line, it will warn the user that it is a Windows program. WINSTUB.EXE is a file supplied with the Microsoft C/C++ compiler.

Both the CODE and DATA segments have been marked as preloadable and moveable, allowing Windows to relocate them for any dynamic memory allocation requests. The MULTIPLE statement also instructs Windows to create unique data segments for each instance of the application. The use of DISCARDABLE allows Windows to discard unused program code. This code can be automatically reloaded if necessary.

The HEAPSIZE statement specifies an amount of extra, expandable, local memory from within the application's data segment. The STACKSIZE has been set to 9216. You can experiment with various sizes. Larger values may be necessary for applications with large nonstatic variables or those applications using recursion.

Finally, the EXPORTS statement identifies the application's dynamic link entry point and specifies the name of the procedure, in this case, WindowProc.

Writing a Make File

Microsoft provides a program maintenance utility named NMAKE.EXE. This utility was briefly discussed in Chapter 22. The NMAKE utility is particularly important with multiple source and data files. It affords an efficient means to bring everything together. The use of the NMAKE utility requires the creation of another file. This file contains the information necessary to create the final executable version of an application. In this example, it will be called 23SWA, without an extension. The .MAK extension is usually used by Microsoft as a project make file for applications created from within the PWB. These files are included on the optional disk should you desire to work from within the integrated environment.

From the command line, call the NMAKE utility by typing

NMAKE 23SWA

The utility operates by comparing dates and times. For example, if the date of 23SWA.C is 6/18/92 and that of 23SWA.OBJ is 5/18/92, the utility will recompile and link the C program in order to update the .OBJ and .EXE files. If a program contains five separate C source code files and only one of them has changed, the utility will recompile only that particular file and then link all of the .OBJ files together to produce a final .EXE file. All of this is accomplished quickly and automatically from within the NMAKE utility.

For the template program, 23SWA.C, the make file looks like this:

```
all : 23SWA.exe

23SWA.obj: 23SWA.c
    cl -c -AS -Gsw -Oas 23SWA.c
```

```
23SWA.exe: 23SWA.obj 23SWA.def
    link /NOD 23SWA,,,libw slibcew, 23SWA.def
```

In a make file, the file named to the left of each colon is the file the NMAKE utility will update if any of the files to the right of the colon have a later date. The action taken by the utility is specified on the second and third lines.

The first line of the make file compares the dates of the 23SWA.OBJ file with 23SWA.C. If the C source code has a more recent date, the C/C++ compiler will be invoked (using the compiler directives specified on the second line) to update the 23SWA.OBJ file.

The second set of statements compares the final 23SWA.EXE date with all of those files necessary to create it, in this case 23SWA.OBJ and 23SWA.DEF. If there were any discrepancies, the linker would then be invoked (using the directives specified in the fourth line). Notice that if the 23SWA.OBJ file had been updated by the compiler, this would necessarily force a new linking.

A Simple Application and Template

For your convenience, the following is a complete listing of all the code necessary to create the Simple Windows Application. Enter the three separate files shown in the following composite listing: 23SWA (the make file), 23SWA.DEF (the module definition file), and 23SWA.C (the C source code file).

```
THE 23SWA MAKE FILE:

all : 23SWA.exe

23SWA.obj: 23SWA.c
  cl -c -AS -Gsw -Oas 23SWA.c

23SWA.exe: 23SWA.obj 23SWA.def
  link /NOD 23SWA,,,libw slibcew, 23SWA.def


THE 23SWA.DEF MODULE DEFINITION FILE:

NAME        23SWA
DESCRIPTION 'Simple Windows Application'
EXETYPE     WINDOWS
CODE        PRELOAD MOVEABLE DISCARDABLE
DATA        PRELOAD MOVEABLE MULTIPLE
```

```
HEAPSIZE     4096
STACKSIZE    9216
EXPORTS      WindowProc      @1



THE 23SWA.C APPLICATION FILE:
/*
 *   23SWA.C
 *   Simple Windows Application
 *   Copyright (c) William H. Murray and Chris H. Pappas, 1992
 */


#include <windows.h>

LONG FAR PASCAL WindowProc(HWND,UINT,WPARAM,LPARAM);


char szProgName[]="ProgName";


int PASCAL WinMain(hInst,hPreInst,lpszCmdLine,nCmdShow)
HINSTANCE hInst,hPreInst;
LPSTR  lpszCmdLine;
int    nCmdShow;
{
  HWND hWnd;
  MSG  msg;
  WNDCLASS wc23SWA;
  if (!hPreInst) {
    wc23SWA.lpszClassName=szProgName;
    wc23SWA.hInstance    =hInst;
    wc23SWA.lpfnWndProc  =WindowProc;
    wc23SWA.hCursor       =LoadCursor(NULL,IDC_ARROW);
    wc23SWA.hIcon         =NULL;
    wc23SWA.lpszMenuName =NULL;
    wc23SWA.hbrBackground=GetStockObject(WHITE_BRUSH);
    wc23SWA.style         =CS_HREDRAW|CS_VREDRAW;
    wc23SWA.cbClsExtra    =0;
    wc23SWA.cbWndExtra    =0;
    if (!RegisterClass (&wc23SWA))
      return FALSE;
  }
  hWnd=CreateWindow(szProgName,"Simple Windows Application",
               WS_OVERLAPPEDWINDOW,CW_USEDEFAULT,
                 CW_USEDEFAULT,CW_USEDEFAULT,
```

```
                        CW_USEDEFAULT,(HWND)NULL,(HMENU)NULL,
                        (HANDLE)hInst,(LPSTR)NULL);
  ShowWindow(hWnd,nCmdShow);
  UpdateWindow(hWnd);
  while (GetMessage(&msg,NULL,NULL,NULL)) {
    TranslateMessage(&msg);
    DispatchMessage(&msg);
  }
  return(msg.wParam);
}

LONG FAR PASCAL WindowProc(hWnd,messg,wParam,lParam)
HWND    hWnd;
UINT messg;
WPARAM    wParam;
LPARAM    lParam;
{
  PAINTSTRUCT ps;
  HDC   hdc;

  switch (messg)
  {
    case WM_PAINT:
      hdc=BeginPaint(hWnd,&ps);
/*--------- your routines below ---------*/


      MoveTo(hdc,0,0);
      LineTo(hdc,639,429);
      TextOut(hdc,55,20,"<- a diagonal line",18);

/*--------- your routines above ---------*/
    ValidateRect(hWnd,NULL);
      EndPaint(hWnd,&ps);
      break;
    case WM_DESTROY:
      PostQuitMessage(0);
      break;
    default:
      return(DefWindowProc(hWnd,messg,wParam,lParam));
      break;
  }
  return(0L);
}
```

Notice that within the body of the WindowProc procedure, there are two comments:

```
/*--------- your routines below ---------*/

     MoveTo(hdc,0,0);
     LineTo(hdc,639,429);
     TextOut(hdc,55,20,"<- a diagonal line",18);

/*--------- your routines above ---------*/
```

It is between these comments that you can experiment with a wide variety of Windows GDI graphics drawing functions, which are called drawing primitives.

If you haven't done so yet, execute the NMAKE utility. If everything goes OK, you'll end up with two additional files in your 23SWA collection: 23SWA.OBJ and 23SWA.EXE. The executable file can be run under Windows. Give it a try.

As shown in Figure 23-1, the application draws a diagonal line on the screen and prints the text message.

Take the time to experiment with the various Windows drawing primitives discussed in the following sections.

If you are slightly dazed by all of the new vocabulary and concepts necessary for understanding and writing Windows applications, here is some good news: the template code just developed serves as a foundation upon which many applications can be developed. It is your foundation for developing many Windows applications in C.

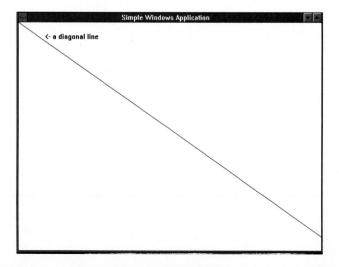

Figure 23-1.   *A very simple Windows application*

Drawing an Ellipse

You use the **Ellipse()** function for drawing an ellipse or a circle. The center of the ellipse is also the center of an imaginary rectangle described by the points $x1,y1$ and $x2,y2$, as shown in Figure 23-2.

An ellipse is filled because it is a closed figure. The handle for the device context is given by *hdc*. All other parameters are of type **int**. This function returns a type **BOOL**.

The syntax for the command is

Ellipse(hdc,*x1,y1,x2,y2*)

For example, the following code draws a small ellipse in the user's window:

```
/*--------- your routines below ---------*/

    Ellipse(hdc,200,200,275,250);
    TextOut(hdc,210,215,"<- an ellipse",13);

/*--------- your routines above ---------*/
```

Figure 23-3 shows how the ellipse will appear on the screen.

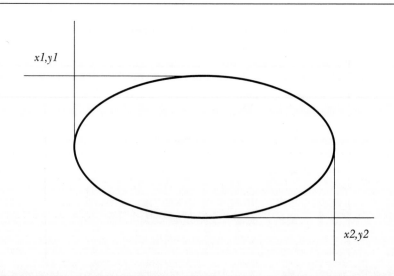

Figure 23-2.   *The components of an ellipse*

Figure 23-3.   *An ellipse drawn in the window*

Drawing a Chord

The **Chord()** function is a closed figure with a line between two arc points, *x3,y3* and *x4,y4*. Figure 23-4 shows these points. A chord is filled with the current brush because it is a closed figure.

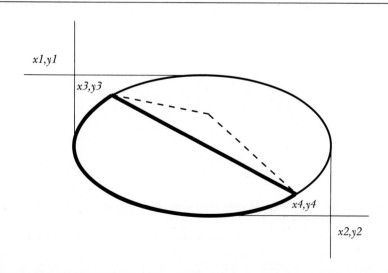

Figure 23-4.   *The components of a chord*

The handle for the device context is given by *hdc*. All other parameters are of type **int**. This function returns a type **BOOL**.

The syntax for the command is

Chord(hdc,*x1,y1,x2,y2,x3,y3,x4,y4*)

For example, the following code draws a small chord in the user's window:

```
/*--------- your routines below ---------*/

        Chord(hdc,550,20,630,80,555,25,625,70);
        TextOut(hdc,470,30," A Chord ->",11);

/*--------- your routines above ---------*/
```

Figure 23-5 shows the chord section and its location on the user's screen.

Drawing a Pie Wedge

You use the **Pie()** function for drawing pie-shaped wedges. The center of the elliptical arc is also the center of an imaginary rectangle described by the points *x1,y1* and *x2,y2*, as shown in Figure 23-6.

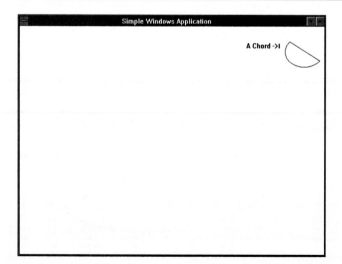

Figure 23-5.   *Drawing a chord in a window*

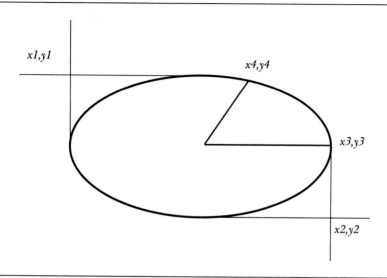

Figure 23-6. *The components of a pie wedge*

The starting and ending points of the arc are points *x3,y3* and *x4,y4*. Two lines are drawn from each end point to the center of the rectangle. Drawing is done in a counterclockwise direction. The pie wedge is filled because it is a closed figure. The handle for the device context is given by *hdc*. All other parameters are of type **int**. This function returns a type **BOOL**.

The syntax for the command is

Pie(hdc,*x1,y1,x2,y2,x3,y3,x4,y4*)

For example, the following code draws a small pie-shaped wedge in the window:

```
/*--------- your routines below ---------*/

        Pie(hdc,300,50,400,150,300,50,300,100);
        TextOut(hdc,350,80,"<- A Pie Wedge",14);

/*--------- your routines above ---------*/
```

Figure 23-7 shows the pie wedge on the screen.

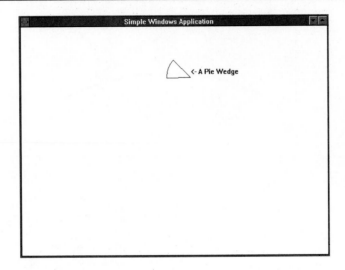

Figure 23-7. *Drawing a pie wedge in a window*

Drawing a Rectangle

The **Rectangle()** function draws a rectangle or box described by *x1,y1* and *x2,y2*. Again, the rectangle is filled because it is a closed figure. The values for the parameters cannot exceed 32,767 (7FFFH). The handle for the device context is given by *hdc*. All other parameters are of type **int**. This function returns a type **BOOL**.

The syntax for the command is

Rectangle(hdc,*x1,y1,x2,y2*)

As an example, the following code draws a rectangular figure in the user's window:

```
/*--------- your routines below ---------*/

     Rectangle(hdc,50,300,150,400);
     TextOut(hdc,160,350,"<- A Rectangle",14);

/*--------- your routines above ---------*/
```

Figure 23-8 shows the rectangle produced on the screen.

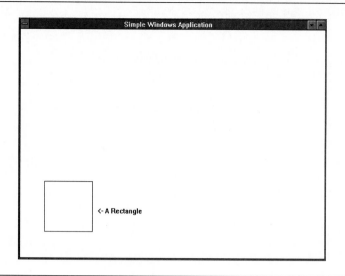

Figure 23-8. *A small rectangle drawn to the window*

Using the SWA to Develop a Sine Wave Application

The previous section described the development of a template that would allow you to experiment with various Windows functions. This template serves as the basis of many simple applications requiring only minor changes in coding. The next example illustrates how you can use the template to design a simple application. This particular program will draw a sine wave in the window.

The following composite listing contains the three files needed to create the application. They are 23SINE, 23SINE.DEF, and 23SINE.C. Examine and compare this code with that of the template application, SWA.C.

```
THE 23SINE MAKE FILE:

all: 23sine.exe

23sine.obj: 23sine.c
    cl -c -AS -FPi -Gsw -Oas 23sine.c

23sine.exe: 23sine.obj 23sine.def
    link /NOD 23sine,,,libw slibcew,23sine.def
```

THE 23SINE.DEF MODULE DEFINITION FILE:

```
NAME        23SINE
DESCRIPTION 'Simplified Windows Platform'
EXETYPE     WINDOWS
STUB        'WINSTUB.EXE'
CODE        PRELOAD MOVEABLE DISCARDABLE
DATA        PRELOAD MOVEABLE MULTIPLE
HEAPSIZE    4096
STACKSIZE   9216
EXPORTS     WindowProc      @1
```

THE 23SINE.C APPLICATION FILE:

```c
/*
 *   23SINE.C
 *   An Application Which Draws A Sine Wave In A
 *   Window. Developed From The SWA Template.
 *   Copyright (c) William H. Murray and Chris H. Pappas, 1992
 */
#include <windows.h>
#include <math.h>

#define pi 3.14159265359


LONG FAR PASCAL WindowProc(HWND,UINT,WPARAM,LPARAM);

char    szProgName[]="ProgName";

int PASCAL WinMain(hInst,hPreInst,lpszCmdLine,nCmdShow)
HINSTANCE hInst,hPreInst;
LPSTR   lpszCmdLine;
int     nCmdShow;
{
  HWND hWnd;
  MSG  msg;
  WNDCLASS wcSwp;
  if (!hPreInst) {
    wcSwp.lpszClassName=szProgName;
    wcSwp.hInstance     =hInst;
    wcSwp.lpfnWndProc   =WindowProc;
```

```
      wcSwp.hCursor      =LoadCursor(NULL,IDC_ARROW);
      wcSwp.hIcon        =NULL;
      wcSwp.lpszMenuName =NULL;
      wcSwp.hbrBackground=GetStockObject(WHITE_BRUSH);
      wcSwp.style        =CS_HREDRAW|CS_VREDRAW;
      wcSwp.cbClsExtra   =0;
      wcSwp.cbWndExtra   =0;
      if (!RegisterClass (&wcSwp))
        return FALSE;
    }
  hWnd=CreateWindow(szProgName,"A Sine Wave",
                    WS_OVERLAPPEDWINDOW,CW_USEDEFAULT,
                    CW_USEDEFAULT,CW_USEDEFAULT,
                    CW_USEDEFAULT,(HWND)NULL,(HMENU)NULL,
                    (HANDLE)hInst,(LPSTR)NULL);
  ShowWindow(hWnd,nCmdShow);
  UpdateWindow(hWnd);
  while (GetMessage(&msg,NULL,NULL,NULL)) {
    TranslateMessage(&msg);
    DispatchMessage(&msg);
  }
  return(msg.wParam);
}


LONG FAR PASCAL WindowProc(hWnd,messg,wParam,lParam)
HWND    hWnd;
UINT    messg;
WPARAM  wParam;
LPARAM  lParam;
{
  PAINTSTRUCT ps;
  HDC hdc;
  double y;
  int i;

  switch (messg)
  {
    case WM_PAINT:
      hdc=BeginPaint(hWnd,&ps);
/*--------- your routines below ---------*/

      /* draw the x & y coordinate axes */
      MoveTo(hdc,100,50);
      LineTo(hdc,100,350);
      MoveTo(hdc,100,200);
```

```
        LineTo(hdc,500,200);
        MoveTo(hdc,100,200);

        /* draw the sine wave */
        for (i=0;i<400;i++) {
          y=120.0*sin(pi*i*(360.0/400.0)/180.0);
          LineTo(hdc,i+100,(int) (200.0-y));
        }

/*--------- your routines above ---------*/
        ValidateRect(hWnd,NULL);
        EndPaint(hWnd,&ps);
        break;
      case WM_DESTROY:
        PostQuitMessage(0);
        break;
      default:
        return(DefWindowProc(hWnd,messg,wParam,lParam));
        break;
    }
  return(0L);
}
```

As you can see, this application makes only minor changes to the 23SWA template of the previous section. Notice that new variables are declared in **WindowProc()**:

```
double y;
int i;
```

The actual sine wave plotting takes place under WM_PAINT. The coordinate axes are drawn with several calls to the **MoveTo()** and **LineTo()** functions:

```
/* draw the x & y coordinate axes */
MoveTo(hdc,100,50);
LineTo(hdc,100,350);
MoveTo(hdc,100,200);
LineTo(hdc,500,200);
MoveTo(hdc,100,200);
```

The sine wave is drawn and scaled in one operation. In this application, the waveform will extend 120 pixels above and below the horizontal axis. The **sin()** function from math.h is used to generate the sine values. The use of the constant *PI* is needed to convert angles from degrees to radians.

```
/* draw the sine wave */
for (i=0;i<400;i++) {
  y=120.0*sin(pi*i*(360.0/400.0)/180.0);
  LineTo(hdc,i+100,(int)(200.0-y));
}
```

Since this application was designed to work in the default drawing mode, the program draws directly in screen pixels. On a VGA monitor, the figure will fill the entire screen. Figure 23-9 shows the output of the program on a VGA screen. If a high-resolution monitor operating in 1024x768 graphics mode is used, the figure will be drawn in the upper-left corner of the monitor. Changes in figure size such as this are usually considered undesirable, and you'll see a technique for avoiding these variations in the 23PIE.C example.

Creating a Windows Pie Chart Application

A pie chart is a useful business application that also allows you to incorporate many of the resources studied in the last chapter into a presentation-quality program. This particular pie chart will use a menu, an about dialog box, and a data entry dialog box for user input. All three items were designed in the previous chapter. The data entry dialog box will prompt the user to enter up to ten numbers that define the size of each pie wedge. These integer numbers are then scaled in order to make each pie

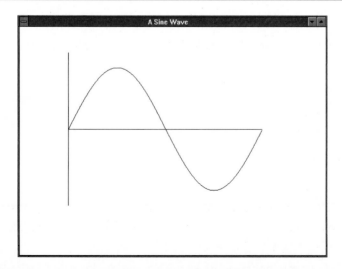

Figure 23-9. *A sine wave drawing application developed with the SWA template*

slice proportional in the 360-degree pie chart. Slices are colored in a sequential manner. The sequence is defined by the programmer and contained in the global array *lColor[]*. The program also allows the user to enter a title for the pie chart that is centered below the pie figure. You may wish to continue the development of this example by adding a legend, label, or value for each pie slice, as was done in the DOS graphics section of this book (Chapter 19).

When you complete the project development cycle, you will have nine files on your disk when the MAKE utility is finished: 23PIE, 23PIE.DEF, 23PIE.H, 23PIE.RC, 23PIE.C, 23PIE.CUR, 23PIE.RES, 23PIE.OBJ and 23PIE.EXE. Before a discussion of the individual file components, let's look at the complete code listing. Remember, this is a composite listing. Five separate programs must be extracted in order to compile the application.

```
THE 23PIE MAKE FILE:

all: 23pie.exe

23pie.obj: 23pie.c 23pie.h
    cl -c -AS -FPi -Oas 23pie.c

23pie.res: 23pie.rc 23pie.cur
    RC -r 23pie.rc

23pie.exe: 23pie.obj 23pie.def 23pie.res
    link /NOD 23pie,,,libw slibcew,23pie
    rc 23pie.res
```

```
THE 23PIE.DEF MODULE DEFINITION FILE:

;23PIE.DEF for C Compiling

NAME            23pie
DESCRIPTION     'Pie Chart Program'
EXETYPE         WINDOWS
STUB            'WINSTUB.EXE'
CODE            PRELOAD MOVABLE
DATA            PRELOAD MOVEABLE MULTIPLE
HEAPSIZE        4096
STACKSIZE       9216
EXPORTS         AboutDlgProc    @1
                PieDlgProc      @2
                WindowProc      @3
```

THE 23PIE.H HEADER FILE:

```
#define IDM_ABOUT     10
#define IDM_INPUT     20
#define IDM_EXIT      30

#define DM_TITLE     150
#define DM_P1        151
#define DM_P2        152
#define DM_P3        153
#define DM_P4        154
#define DM_P5        155
#define DM_P6        156
#define DM_P7        157
#define DM_P8        158
#define DM_P9        159
#define DM_P10       160
```

THE 23PIE.RC RESOURCE SCRIPT FILE:

```
#include "windows.h"
#include "23pie.h"

PieCursor CURSOR 23pie.cur

PieMenu   MENU
BEGIN
  POPUP "Pie_Chart_Data"
  BEGIN
    MENUITEM "About...",  IDM_ABOUT
    MENUITEM "Input...",  IDM_INPUT
    MENUITEM "Exit",      IDM_EXIT
  END
END

AboutDlgBox DIALOG LOADONCALL MOVEABLE DISCARDABLE
        50,300,180,80
          STYLE WS_DLGFRAME|WS_POPUP
BEGIN
  CONTROL "Microsoft C Pie Chart Program",-1,"static",
          SS_CENTER|WS_CHILD,2,60,176,10
```

```
    CONTROL "by William H. Murray and Chris H. Pappas",-1,
            "static",SS_CENTER|WS_CHILD,2,45,176,10
    CONTROL "OK",IDOK,"button",
            BS_PUSHBUTTON|WS_TABSTOP|WS_CHILD,75,10,32,14
END


PieDlgBox DIALOG LOADONCALL MOVEABLE DISCARDABLE
            93,37,193,156
            CAPTION "Pie Chart Data"
            STYLE WS_BORDER|WS_CAPTION|WS_DLGFRAME|WS_POPUP
BEGIN
    CONTROL "Chart Title:",100,"Button",BS_GROUPBOX|WS_TABSTOP,
            5,3,182,30
    CONTROL "Pie Wedge Sizes:",101,"Button",BS_GROUPBOX|
            WS_TABSTOP,3,34,187,95
    CONTROL "Title: ",-1,"Static",0x0000,10,21,30,8
    CONTROL "",DM_TITLE,"Edit",WS_BORDER|WS_TABSTOP,40,18,
            140,12
    CONTROL "Wedge #1: ",-1,"Static",0x0000,10,50,40,8
    CONTROL "Wedge #2: ",-1,"Static",0x0000,10,65,40,8
    CONTROL "Wedge #3: ",-1,"Static",0x0000,10,80,40,8
    CONTROL "Wedge #4: ",-1,"Static",0x0000,10,95,40,8
    CONTROL "Wedge #5: ",-1,"Static",0x0000,10,110,40,8
    CONTROL "Wedge #6: ",-1,"Static",0x0000,106,50,40,8
    CONTROL "Wedge #7: ",-1,"Static",0x0000,106,65,40,8
    CONTROL "Wedge #8: ",-1,"Static",0x0000,106,80,40,8
    CONTROL "Wedge #9: ",-1,"Static",0x0000,106,95,40,8
    CONTROL "Wedge #10:",-1,"Static",0x0000,102,110,45,8
    CONTROL "5",DM_P1,"Edit",WS_BORDER|WS_TABSTOP,55,45,30,12
    CONTROL "10",DM_P2,"Edit",WS_BORDER|WS_TABSTOP,55,60,30,12
    CONTROL "7",DM_P3,"Edit",WS_BORDER|WS_TABSTOP,55,75,30,12
    CONTROL "20",DM_P4,"Edit",WS_BORDER|WS_TABSTOP,55,90,30,12
    CONTROL "0",DM_P5,"Edit",WS_BORDER|WS_TABSTOP,55,105,30,12
    CONTROL "0",DM_P6,"Edit",WS_BORDER|WS_TABSTOP,150,44,30,12
    CONTROL "0",DM_P7,"Edit",WS_BORDER|WS_TABSTOP,150,61,30,12
    CONTROL "0",DM_P8,"Edit",WS_BORDER|WS_TABSTOP,150,76,30,12
    CONTROL "0",DM_P9,"Edit",WS_BORDER|WS_TABSTOP,149,91,30,12
    CONTROL "0",DM_P10,"Edit",WS_BORDER|WS_TABSTOP,149,106,30,12
    CONTROL "OK",IDOK,"Button",WS_TABSTOP,39,135,24,14
    CONTROL "Cancel",IDCANCEL,"Button",WS_TABSTOP,122,136,34,14
END
```

```
THE 23PIE.C APPLICATION FILE:

/*
 *   23PIE.C
 *   A Pie Chart Application in C, with Resources
 *   Copyright (c) William H. Murray and Chris H. Pappas, 1992
 */

#include <windows.h>
#include <string.h>
#include <math.h>
#include "23pie.h"

#define radius      180
#define maxnumwedge 10
#define pi          3.14159265359

LONG FAR PASCAL WindowProc(HWND,UINT,WPARAM,LPARAM);
BOOL FAR PASCAL AboutDlgProc(HWND,UINT,WPARAM,LPARAM);
BOOL FAR PASCAL PieDlgProc(HWND,UINT,WPARAM,LPARAM);

char szProgName[]="ProgName";
char szApplName[]="PieMenu";
char szCursorName[]="PieCursor";
char szTString[80]="(bar chart title area)";
unsigned int iWedgesize[maxnumwedge]={5,10,7,20};
long lColor[maxnumwedge]={0x0L,0xFFL,0xFF00L,0xFFFFL,0xFF0000L,
                          0xFF00FFL,0xFFFF00L,0xFFFFFFL,
                          0x8080L,0x808080L};

int PASCAL WinMain(hInst,hPreInst,lpszCmdLine,nCmdShow)
HINSTANCE hInst,hPreInst;
LPSTR  lpszCmdLine;
int    nCmdShow;
{
  HWND hWnd;
  MSG  msg;
  WNDCLASS wcSwp;
  if (!hPreInst) {
    wcSwp.lpszClassName=szProgName;
    wcSwp.hInstance    =hInst;
    wcSwp.lpfnWndProc  =WindowProc;
    wcSwp.hCursor      =LoadCursor(hInst,szCursorName);
    wcSwp.hIcon        =LoadIcon(hInst,szProgName);
    wcSwp.lpszMenuName =szApplName;
```

```
      wcSwp.hbrBackground=GetStockObject(WHITE_BRUSH);
      wcSwp.style       =CS_HREDRAW|CS_VREDRAW;
      wcSwp.cbClsExtra   =0;
      wcSwp.cbWndExtra   =0;
      if (!RegisterClass (&wcSwp))
        return FALSE;
  }
  hWnd=CreateWindow(szProgName,"C Pie Chart Program",
                    WS_OVERLAPPEDWINDOW,CW_USEDEFAULT,
                    CW_USEDEFAULT,CW_USEDEFAULT,
                    CW_USEDEFAULT,NULL,NULL,
                    hInst,NULL);
  ShowWindow(hWnd,nCmdShow);
  UpdateWindow(hWnd);
  while (GetMessage(&msg,NULL,NULL,NULL))
  {
    TranslateMessage(&msg);
    DispatchMessage(&msg);
  }
  return(msg.wParam);
}


BOOL FAR PASCAL AboutDlgProc(hdlg,messg,wParam,lParam)
HWND hdlg;
UINT messg;
WPARAM wParam;
LPARAM lParam;
{
  switch (messg)
  {
    case WM_INITDIALOG:
      break;
    case WM_COMMAND:
      switch (wParam)
      {
        case IDOK:
          EndDialog(hdlg,TRUE);
          break;
        default:
          return FALSE;
      }
      break;
    default:
      return FALSE;
  }
```

```
      return TRUE;
}


BOOL FAR PASCAL PieDlgProc(hdlg,messg,wParam,lParam)
HWND hdlg;
UINT messg;
WPARAM wParam;
LPARAM lParam;
{
  switch (messg)
  {
    case WM_INITDIALOG:
      return FALSE;
    case
WM_COMMAND:
      switch (wParam)
      {
        case IDOK:
          GetDlgItemText(hdlg,DM_TITLE,szTString,80);
          iWedgesize[0]=GetDlgItemInt(hdlg,DM_P1,NULL,0);
          iWedgesize[1]=GetDlgItemInt(hdlg,DM_P2,NULL,0);
          iWedgesize[2]=GetDlgItemInt(hdlg,DM_P3,NULL,0);
          iWedgesize[3]=GetDlgItemInt(hdlg,DM_P4,NULL,0);
          iWedgesize[4]=GetDlgItemInt(hdlg,DM_P5,NULL,0);
          iWedgesize[5]=GetDlgItemInt(hdlg,DM_P6,NULL,0);
          iWedgesize[6]=GetDlgItemInt(hdlg,DM_P7,NULL,0);
          iWedgesize[7]=GetDlgItemInt(hdlg,DM_P8,NULL,0);
          iWedgesize[8]=GetDlgItemInt(hdlg,DM_P9,NULL,0);
          iWedgesize[9]=GetDlgItemInt(hdlg,DM_P10,NULL,0);
          EndDialog(hdlg,TRUE);
          break;
        case IDCANCEL:
          EndDialog(hdlg,FALSE);
          break;
        default:
          return FALSE;
      }
      break;
    default:
      return FALSE;
  }
  return TRUE;
}


LONG FAR PASCAL WindowProc(hWnd,messg,wParam,lParam)
```

```
HWND hWnd;
UINT messg;
WPARAM wParam;
LPARAM lParam;
{
  HDC           hdc;
  PAINTSTRUCT ps;
  HBRUSH        hBrush;
  static FARPROC lpfnAboutDlgProc;
  static FARPROC lpfnPieDlgProc;
  static HWND hInst1,hInst2;
  static short xClientView,yClientView;

  unsigned int iTotalWedge[maxnumwedge+1];
  int           i,iNWedges;

  iNWedges=0;
  for (i=0;i<maxnumwedge;i++) {
    if(iWedgesize[i]!=0) iNWedges++;
  }

  iTotalWedge[0]=0;

  for (i=0;i<iNWedges;i++)
    iTotalWedge[i+1]=iTotalWedge[i]+iWedgesize[i];

  switch (messg)
  {
    case WM_SIZE:
      xClientView=LOWORD(lParam);
      yClientView=HIWORD(lParam);
      break;
    case WM_CREATE:
      hInst1=((LPCREATESTRUCT) lParam)->hInstance;
      hInst2=((LPCREATESTRUCT) lParam)->hInstance;
      lpfnAboutDlgProc=MakeProcInstance(AboutDlgProc,hInst1);
      lpfnPieDlgProc=MakeProcInstance(PieDlgProc,hInst2);
      break;
    case WM_COMMAND:
      switch (wParam)
      {
        case IDM_ABOUT:
          DialogBox(hInst1,"AboutDlgBox",hWnd,lpfnAboutDlgProc);
          break;
        case IDM_INPUT:
```

```
              DialogBox(hInst2,"PieDlgBox",
                        hWnd,lpfnPieDlgProc);
              InvalidateRect(hWnd,NULL,TRUE);
              UpdateWindow(hWnd);
              break;
            case IDM_EXIT:
              SendMessage(hWnd,WM_CLOSE,0,0L);
              break;
            default:
              break;
        }
    break;
    case WM_PAINT:
       hdc=BeginPaint(hWnd,&ps);
/*--------- your routines below ---------*/

       SetMapMode(hdc,MM_ISOTROPIC);
       SetWindowExt(hdc,500,500);
       SetViewportExt(hdc,xClientView,-yClientView);
       SetViewportOrg(hdc,xClientView/2,yClientView/2);

       if (xClientView > 200) {
          TextOut(hdc,strlen(szTString)*(-8/2),
                  240,szTString,strlen(szTString));
       }

       for(i=0;i<iNWedges;i++) {
          hBrush=CreateSolidBrush(lColor[i]);
          SelectObject(hdc,hBrush);
          Pie(hdc,-200,200,200,-200,
              (int)(radius*cos(2*pi*iTotalWedge[i]/
                    iTotalWedge[iNWedges])),
              (int)(radius*sin(2*pi*iTotalWedge[i]/
                    iTotalWedge[iNWedges])),
              (in)(radius*cos(2*pi*iTotalWedge[i+1]/
                    iTotalWedge[iNWedges])),
              (int)(radius*sin(2*pi*iTotalWedge[i+1]/
                    iTotalWedge[iNWedges])));
       }

/*--------- your routines above ---------*/
       ValidateRect(hWnd,NULL);
       EndPaint(hWnd,&ps);
       break;
    case WM_DESTROY:
```

```
        PostQuitMessage(0);
        break;
    default:
        return(DefWindowProc(hWnd,messg,wParam,lParam));
  }
  return(0L);
}
```

The 23PIE and 23PIE.DEF Files

This program uses a pointer, specified in 23PIE.CUR, as seen in the 23PIE make file listing. This pointer was designed in the Image Editor and illustrated in the previous chapter. You can design your own unique pointer or use the image provided on the optional disk. This program also uses trigonometric functions requiring the math.h header file. These functions require that the program be compiled with the floating-point option, /FPi. The 23PIE.DEF file varies only a little from the 23SWA.DEF file discussed earlier. This .DEF file contains three EXPORTS: AboutDlgProc, PieDlgProc, and WindowProc. You'll see how those procedures are used in the discussion of the main program in "The 23PIE.C Program," later in this chapter.

The 23pie.h Header File

The header file 23pie.h contains identification information for various menu and dialog items. Additionally, note the ten unique identification numbers, which represent the ten values for wedge sizes. These are input from the dialog box by the user.

The 23PIE.RC Resource File

The resource file 23PIE.RC contains information in script form for the pointer (PieCursor), menu (PieMenu), and two dialog boxes (AboutDlgBox and PieDlgBox). Figure 23-10 shows the about box and Figure 23-11 shows the data entry box.

Both of these dialog boxes were designed in the previous chapter. This composite resource script file was created within the PWB, using the .DLG files for each dialog box. When using the Dialog Editor, you must have a fairly clear idea of how you want to represent various data fields and so on before starting the design. The CONTROL values, which determine position, size, and so on, of dialog box items, are calculated by the editor. If you are entering this program, it will be easiest for you just to type this resource file as it appears in the listing. Scan the listing and notice that some CONTROL statements begin with either text or a number in quotes. The numbers in quotes will appear in the data entry fields of the final dialog box and serve as default values for the application program.

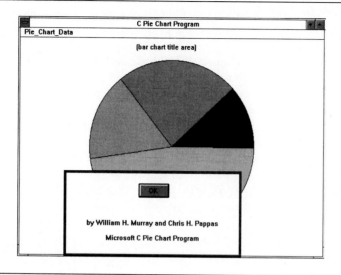

Figure 23-10.   *A simple about box*

The 23PIE.C Program

The C application code 23PIE.C allows the user to develop a pie chart with as many as ten slices. As application will allow the user to input the data on pie-slice sizes

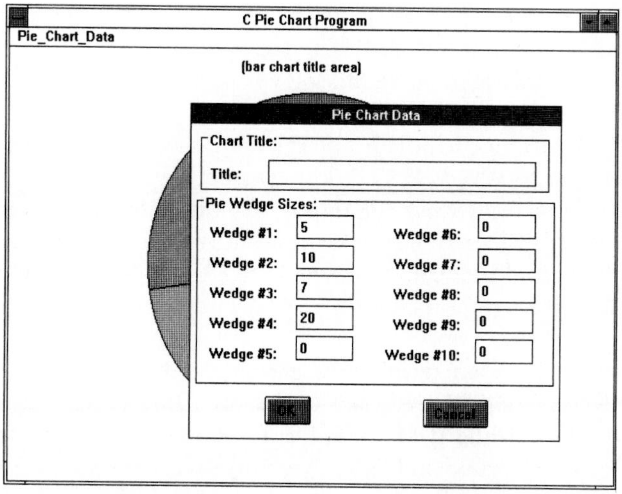

Figure 23-11.   *A data entry dialog box*

directly to a dialog box. In addition to data on pie sizes, the user may enter the title of the pie chart. Don't let the size of this C code listing scare you; much of the code you see is the template code developed in the previous example. It would be a good idea to compare the 23SWA.C and 23PIE.C code at this time and discover the exact differences in the listings. This example concentrates on the new concepts for the application by extracting each important feature from the listing. Many of the Windows functions used in this application are listed in Appendix C.

Dialog box information is processed with the **case IDOK** statement under the PieDlgProc. When the user selects the data entry item (a dialog box) from the program's menu, he or she is allowed to enter a pie chart title and the data for up to ten pie slices. This data is accepted when the user selects the OK push button. The title is returned as a text string with the **GetDlgItemText()** function. Numeric information is returned with the **GetDlgItemInt()** function. This function translates the "numeric" string information entered by the user into an integer that can be a signed or unsigned number. The **GetDlgItemInt()** function requires four parameters. The handle and ID number are self-explanatory. The third parameter, which is null in this case, is used to flag a successful conversion. The fourth parameter is used to indicate signed and unsigned numbers. In this case, a zero states that the dialog box is returning unsigned numbers. These numbers are saved in the global array *iWedgesize[]* for future use.

The major work in this application is done in the **WindowProc()** function. Various pieces of information and data are sent as messages and examined by the five case statements. Study the code and make sure you can find these "message" case statements: WM_SIZE, WM_CREATE, WM_COMMAND, WM_PAINT, and WM_DE-STROY.

Determining the size of the client or application window is achieved with the help of WM_SIZE. Windows sends a message to WM_SIZE any time the window is resized. In this case, the size will be returned in two variables, *xClientView* and *yClientView*. This information will be used by WM_PAINT to scale the pie chart to the window. It will also produce a miniature icon of the window when the "minimum" option is selected from the main menu.

The program's instance handle is obtained and saved as *hInst1* and *hInst2* when processing messages to WM_CREATE. These values are used by the **MakeProcInstance()** function to create an *instance thunk* for each dialog box procedure or function. This is necessary because each dialog box procedure is a far procedure. The address returned by **MakeProcInstance()** points to a fixed portion of memory called the instance thunk. Two are required in this case because two dialog box procedures are being used.

Dialog boxes can be opened with messages sent to WM_COMMAND. Notice that WM_COMMAND contains three case statements. IDM_ABOUT is the ID for the about box procedure, while IDM_INPUT is the ID for the data entry dialog box. IDM_EXIT allows a graceful exit from the application.

The routines for actually drawing the pie wedges are processed under WM_PAINT.

The mapping mode is changed to MM_ISOTROPIC from MM_TEXT. The default drawing mode is MM_TEXT. When in MM_TEXT, drawings are made in "pixel" coordinates with point 0,0 in the upper-left corner of the window. This is why the previous example changed in size as the number of pixels changed on the monitor.

```
SetMapMode(hdc,MM_ISOTROPIC);
SetWindowExt(hdc,500,500);
SetViewportExt(hdc,xClientView,-yClientView);
SetViewportOrg(hdc,xClientView/2,yClientView/2);
```

Table 23-3 shows additional mapping modes available under Windows.

MM_ISOTROPIC allows you to select the extent of both the x and y axes. The mapping mode is changed by calling the function **SetMapMode()**. When the function **SetWindowExt()** is called, with both parameters set to 500, the height and width of the client or application area are equal. These are logical sizes, which Windows adjusts (scales) to fit the physical display device. The display size values are used by the **SetViewportExt()** function. The negative sign for the *y* coordinate specifies increasing *y* values from the bottom of the screen. It should be no surprise that these are the values previously obtained under WM_SIZE.

For this example, the pie chart will be placed on a traditional *x,y* coordinate system, with the center of the chart at 0,0. The **SetViewportOrg()** function is used for this purpose.

Value	Meaning
MM_ANISOTROPIC	Maps one logical unit to an arbitrary physical unit. The x and y axes are scaled
MM_HIENGLISH	Maps one logical unit to 0.001 inch. Positive y is up
MM_HIMETRIC	Maps one logical unit to 0.01 millimeter. Positive y is up
MM_ISOTROPIC	Maps one logical unit to an arbitrary physical unit. X and Y unit lengths are equal
MM_LOENGLISH	Maps one logical unit to 0.01 inch. Positive y points up
MM_LOMETRIC	Maps one logical unit to 0.1 millimeter. Positive y points up
MM_TEXT	Maps one logical unit to one pixel. Positive y points down. This is the default mode
MM_TWIPS	Maps one logical unit to 1/20 of a printer's point. Positive y points up

Table 23-3.   *Windows Mapping Modes*

The pie chart title is printed to the screen using the coordinates for the current mapping mode. The program centers the title on the screen by estimating the size of the character font and knowing the string length. For really small windows, the title is not printed. Information on font characteristics is covered in Chapter 19.

```
if (xClientView > 200) {
  TextOut(hdc,strlen(szTString)*(-8/2),
          240,szTString,strlen(szTString));
}
```

Before actually discussing how the pie wedges are plotted, let's return to the beginning of the WindowProc procedure in order to gain an understanding of how the wedges are scaled to fit a complete circle. There are several pieces of code that are very important.

This code determines how many wedges have been requested by the user:

```
iNWedges=0;
for (i=0;i<maxnumwedge;i++) {
  if(iWedgesize[i]!=0) iNWedges++;
}
```

It is assumed that there is at least one wedge of some physical size, so the array *iWedgesize[]* can be scanned for the first zero value. For each nonzero value returned, *iNWedges* will be incremented. Thus, when leaving this routine, *iNWedges* will contain the total number of wedges for this plot.

A progressive total on wedge size values will be returned to the *iTotalWedge[]* array. These values will help determine where one pie slice ends and the next begins. For example, if the user entered 5, 10, 7, and 20 for wedge sizes, *iTotalWedge[]* would contain the values 0, 5, 15, 22, and 42. Study the following code to make sure you understand how these results are achieved:

```
iTotalWedge[0]=0;
for (i=0;i<iNWedges;i++)
  iTotalWedge[i+1]=iTotalWedge[i]+iWedgesize[i];
```

The values contained in *iTotalWedge[]* are needed in order to calculate the beginning and ending angles for each pie wedge. You might recall that the **Pie()** function accepts nine parameters. The first parameter is the handle, and the next four specify the coordinates of the bounding rectangle. In this case, for the mapping mode chosen, they are –200, 200, 200, and –200. The remaining four parameters are used to designate the starting *x,y* pair and the ending *x,y* pair for the pie arc. To calculate *x* values, the cosine function is used, and to calculate *y* values, the sine function is used. For example, the first *x* position is determined by multiplying the radius of the pie by the cosine of *2*pi*iTotalWedge[0]*. The *2*pi* value is needed in the conversion of degrees to radians. The *y* value is found with the sine function in an identical way. Those two values serve as the *x,y* starting coordinates for the first slice. The ending coordinates are found with the same equations, but using the next value in *iTotalWedge[]*. In order to scale each of these points to make all slices proportional and fit a 360-degree pie, each coordinate point is divided by the grand total of all individual slices. This total is the last number contained in *iTotalWedge[]*. Observe how this calculation is achieved in the next piece of code:

```
for(i=0;i<iNWedges;i++) {
  hBrush=CreateSolidBrush(lColor[i]);
  SelectObject(hdc,hBrush);
  Pie(hdc,-200,200,200,-200,
      (int)(radius*cos(2*pi*iTotalWedge[i]/
            iTotalWedge[iNWedges])),
      (int)(radius*sin(2*pi*iTotalWedge[i]/
            iTotalWedge[iNWedges])),
      (int)(radius*cos(2*pi*iTotalWedge[i+1]/
            iTotalWedge[iNWedges])),
      (int)(radius*sin(2*pi*iTotalWedge[i+1]/
            iTotalWedge[iNWedges])));
}
```

In order to draw and fill all slices, a loop is used. This loop will index through all *iNWedge* values.

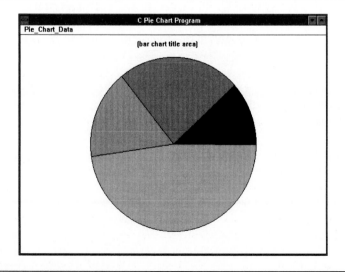

Figure 23-12.   *A default pie chart produced by 23PIE.C*

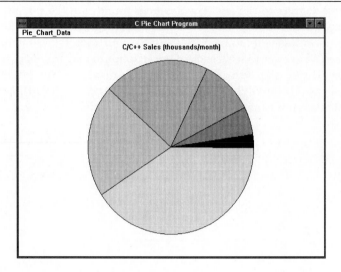

Figure 23-13.   *A unique pie chart*

Figure 23-12 shows the default pie chart plot, and Figure 23-13 shows a unique pie chart application.

More on Traditional C Windows Programming

The techniques presented in this chapter have been used by almost all C programmers developing Windows code. Many books and magazine articles show applications developed in the C language. Applications developed in C++ can also have a similar structure and appearance, but they can also include the advantages of Microsoft's Foundation Classes. Foundation Classes provide you with access to reusable code—a chief advantage of C++. The remaining chapters of this book concentrate on the use of Microsoft's Foundation Class library when writing C++ Windows applications. You'll find the use of the library classes intuitive and your application code easier to construct and read.

Chapter 24

Windows Programming: The Foundation Class Library

Microsoft has provided a Foundation Class library containing a new set of tools for the development of C++ and C++ Windows applications. The Foundation Class library holds two groups of important classes; one group contains more than two dozen class definitions for Windows, while the other group contains more than three dozen OLE (object linking and embedding) classes. The first group is designed specifically for Windows applications, while the second group can be used in both C++ and Windows development. This chapter focuses on the Windows library classes. When you use these classes in conjunction with the Windows concepts and tools discussed in earlier chapters, the result will be simplified code development and program maintenance.

In Chapter 23, you learned that even the simplest Windows applications, when created with the standard API function calls, are difficult and time consuming to develop. For example, the bare bones 23SWA.C template from Chapter 23 contains over two pages of C code and Windows function calls. Most of that code is used repeatedly from application to application and is required just to establish a window on the screen. While Windows applications have been easy to use, they have certainly not been a joy to write.

This chapter examines the advantages of using the Microsoft Foundation Class library for Windows code development. It discusses terms, definitions, and techniques that can then be applied to C++ application code developed in Chapter 25.

The Foundation Class library is a new and powerful toolkit for the programmer. If conventional Windows developers have a hammer and crosscut saw in their toolkit, the C++ Windows developer, using the Foundation Class library, is equipped with a pneumatic hammer and circular power saw.

The Need for a Foundation Class Library

The Foundation Class library provides you with easy-to-use objects. Windows, from its very inception, has followed many principles of object-oriented programming design, within the framework of a non-object-oriented language like C. These features were discussed in the previous two chapters. The marriage of C++ and Windows was a natural that can take full advantage of object-oriented features. The Foundation Class library development team designed a comprehensive implementation of the Windows Application Program Interface (API). This C++ library encapsulates the most important data structures and API function calls within a group of approximately 60 reusable classes.

Class libraries such as the Foundation Class library offer many advantages over the traditional function libraries used by C programmers and discussed in Chapters 22 and 23.

This list includes many of the usual advantages of C++ classes, such as

- Encapsulation of code and data within the class

- Inheritance

- Elimination of function and variable name collisions

- Resulting classes appearing to be natural extensions of the language

- Often, reduced code size resulting from well-designed class libraries

With the use of the Foundation Class library, the code required to establish a window has been reduced to approximately one-third the length of a conventional application. This allows you, the developer, to spend less time communicating with Windows and more time developing your application's code.

Foundation Class Library Design Considerations

The Foundation Class library design team set rigorous design principles that had to be followed in the implementation of the Foundation Class library. These principles and guidelines include the following:

- Utilize the power of C++ without overwhelming the programmer

- Make the transition from standard API function calls to the use of class libraries as simple as possible

- Allow the mixing of traditional functions calls with the use of new class libraries

- Balance power and efficiency in the design of class libraries

- Produce a class library that can migrate easily to new platforms, such as Windows NT

The design team felt that good code design had to start with the Foundation Class library itself. The C++ foundation classes are designed to be small in size and fast in execution time. Their simplicity makes them very easy to use, and their execution speed is close to the bulkier function libraries of C. When all the Foundation Class library classes are compiled, with the use of the small memory model, they consume under 40K of total object code.

These classes were designed in a fashion that requires minimal relearning of function names for seasoned Windows programmers. This feature was achieved by carefully naming and designing class features. The Foundation Class library team also designed the Foundation Class library to allow a "mixed-mode" operation. That is, classes and traditional function calls can be intermixed in the same source code.

Microsoft was also aware that class libraries should be usable. Some class libraries are designed with too high a level of abstraction. These "heavy classes," as Microsoft calls them, tend to produce applications that are large in size and slow in execution. The Foundation Class library provides a reasonable level of abstraction while keeping code sizes small. Microsoft claims only a 5 percent speed penalty when using Foundation Class library classes over traditional C function calls.

With Windows NT on the horizon, the development team designed the class library to be dynamic rather than static. The dynamic architecture will allow classes to be scaled to a growing Windows environment in the future.

Key Foundation Class Library Features

Class libraries for Windows are available from other C++ compiler manufacturers, but Microsoft claims several real advantages for its Foundation Class library.

- Complete support for all Windows functions, controls, messages, GDI graphics primitives, menus, and dialog boxes

- Use of the same naming convention as the conventional Windows API. Thus, the action of a class is immediately recognized by its name

- Elimination of switch/case statements that are a source of error. All messages are mapped to member functions, within a class. This direct message-to-method mapping is available for all messages

- Better diagnostics support through the ability to send information about objects to a file. Also included is the ability to validate member variables

- An extensive exception-handling design that makes application code less subject to failure. Support for "out of memory," and so on, is provided

- Determination of the type of a data object at run time. This allows for a dynamic manipulation of a field when classes are instantized

- Small code with a fast implementation. As mentioned earlier, the Foundation Class library adds less than 40K of object code overhead and executes only 5 percent more slowly than conventional C Windows applications

The experienced Windows programmer will immediately appreciate two of these features: the familiar naming convention and the message-to-method mapping. If you reexamine the source code for the applications developed in Chapter 23, you will see extensive use of the error-prone switch/case statements. Also notice that these applications make extensive use of API function calls. Both groups of problems are eliminated when you use the Foundation Class library.

Professional developers will certainty appreciate Microsoft's dedication to better diagnostics and the small code overhead imposed by the Foundation Class library. Now programmers can take advantage of the Foundation Class library without gaining a size penalty on their application's code.

It All Begins with CObject

Libraries such as the Foundation Class library often start with a few parent classes. Additional classes are then derived from the parent classes. **CObject** is one parent class used extensively in developing Windows applications. The Foundation Class library header files located in the MFC/INCLUDE subdirectory provide a wealth of information on defined classes.

Let's take a brief look at **CObject**, which is defined in the afx.h header file. This code is a slightly edited version of the actual code.

```
class CObject
{
public:
  virtual CRuntimeClass* GetRuntimeClass() const;
  virtual ~CObject();
```

```
    void* operator new(size_t, void* p);
    void* operator new(size_t nSize);
    void operator delete(void* p);

    void* operator new(size_t nSize, const char FAR*
                       lpszFileName, int nLine);

protected:
    CObject();

private:
    CObject(const CObject& objectSrc);
    void operator=(const CObject& objectSrc);

public:
    BOOL IsSerializable() const;

    virtual void Serialize(CArchive& ar);
    virtual void AssertValid() const;
    virtual void Dump(CDumpContext& dc) const;

public:
    BOOL IsKindOf(const CRuntimeClass* pClass) const;
    static void PASCAL Construct(void* pMemory);
    static CRuntimeClass classCObject;
};
```

Upon inspection of the **CObject** listing, notice the components that make up this class definition. First, **CObject** is divided into public, protected, and private parts. **CObject** also provides normal and dynamic type checking and serialization. Recall that dynamic type checking allows the type of object to be determined at run time. The state of the object can be saved to a storage medium, such as a disk, through a concept called *persistence*. Object persistence allows object member functions to also be persistent, permitting retrieval of object data.

CGdiObject is an example of a class derived from **CObject**. Here is the **CGdiObject** definition as found in afxwin.h. Again, this listing has been edited for clarity.

```
class CGdiObject : public CObject
{
  DECLARE_DYNAMIC(CGdiObject)
public:
  HANDLE m_hObject;
  HANDLE GetSafeHandle() const;
```

```
static CGdiObject* FromHandle(HANDLE hObject);
static void DeleteTempMap();
BOOL Attach(HANDLE hObject);
HANDLE Detach();

CGdiObject();
virtual ~CGdiObject();
void DeleteObject();

int GetObject(int nCount, LPSTR lpObject) const;
BOOL CreateStockObject(int nIndex);
BOOL UnrealizeObject();

};
```

CGdiObject and its member functions allow drawing items such as stock and custom pens, brushes, and fonts to be created and used in a Windows application.

Microsoft has provided complete source code for the Foundation Class library in order to allow the utmost in programming flexibility and customization. However, for the beginner, it is not even necessary to know how the various classes are defined in order to use them efficiently.

For example, in traditional C Windows applications, the **DeleteObject**() function is called with the following syntax:

```
DeleteObject(hBRUSH);   /*hBRUSH is the brush handle*/
```

In C++, with the Foundation Class library, the same results will be achieved by accessing the member function with the following syntax:

```
newbrush.DeleteObject(); //newbrush is current brush
```

As you can see, switching between C Windows function calls and class library objects can be intuitive. Microsoft has used this approach in developing all Windows classes, making the transition from traditional function calls to Foundation Class library objects very easy.

Important Foundation Library Classes

Table 24-1 lists all of the important Windows Foundation library classes. All of these classes are derived from **CObject**, except where noted.

Class	Base Class Purpose
CWinApp	Holds the initialization, running, and exiting code for the application
CWnd	The parent class for all windows
CFrameWnd	The preferred base class for Windows based upon the Single Document Interface
CMDIFrameWnd	The preferred base class for Windows based upon the Multiple Document Interface
CMDIChildWnd	For child windows based upon the Multiple Document Interface
CDialog	For creating modeless dialog boxes
CModalDialog	For creating modal dialog boxes
CButton	For button controls
CComboBox	For combo boxes
CEdit	For edit controls
CListBox	For list boxes
CScrollBar	For scroll bars
CStatic	For static controls
CDC	For display contexts
CClientDC	For client area display contexts
CMetaFileDC	For metafile device contexts
CPaintDC	For display contexts used by **OnPaint** member functions such as **LineTo()**, **Ellipse()**, and so on
CWindowDC	For display contexts for entire windows
CGdiObject	For all GDI drawing tools
CBitmap	For GDI physical bitmaps
CBrush	For GDI physical brushes
CFont	For GDI physical fonts
CPalette	For GDI physical palettes
CPen	For GDI physical pens
CRgn	For GDI physical regions
CMenu	For creating menu structures
CPoint	For coordinate points (x,y) in a device context. Not derived from the **CObject** class
CRect	For rectangular regions in a device context. Not derived from the **CObject** class

Table 24-1. *Foundation Class Library Windows Classes*

A Simplified Application

Before writing complicated application code, let's see what is required to just establish a window on the screen. As mentioned, that process in C requires a program length of two pages. When you use the power of the Foundation Class library, the initial program code can be reduced to one-third this size.

This section examines the *simplest* possible Windows application, 24SIMPLE. The 24SIMPLE application will establish a window on the screen and place a title in its title bar area.

Establishing a Window with 24SIMPLE.CPP

In order to compile this application, you need to enter the following files, which are part of the composite listing: 24SIMPLE, 24SIMPLE.DEF, and 24SIMPLE.CPP.

```
THE 24SIMPLE MAKE FILE:

all : 24SIMPLE.exe

24SIMPLE.obj: 24SIMPLE.cpp
  cl /Oxs /c 24SIMPLE.cpp

24SIMPLE.exe: 24SIMPLE.obj 24SIMPLE.def
  link /NOD /FAR 24SIMPLE,,,safxcw libw slibcew,24SIMPLE.def;



THE 24SIMPLE.DEF MODULE DEFINITION FILE:

NAME        24SIMPLE
DESCRIPTION 'Establishing A Window with MFCL'
EXETYPE     WINDOWS
STUB        'WINSTUB.EXE'
CODE        PRELOAD MOVEABLE DISCARDABLE
DATA        PRELOAD MOVEABLE MULTIPLE
HEAPSIZE    2048
STACKSIZE   8192



THE 24SIMPLE.CPP APPLICATION FILE:

//
```

```
//  24SIMPLE.CPP
//  The minimum code needed to establish a window with
//  the Microsoft Foundation Class library
//  Copyright (c) William H. Murray and Chris H. Pappas, 1992
//

#include <afxwin.h>

class CTheApp : public CWinApp
{
public:
  virtual BOOL InitInstance();
};

class CMainWnd : public CFrameWnd
{
public:
  CMainWnd()
  {
    Create(NULL,"Hello MFC World",
           WS_OVERLAPPEDWINDOW,rectDefault,NULL,NULL);
  }
};

BOOL CTheApp::InitInstance()
{
  m_pMainWnd=new CMainWnd();
  m_pMainWnd->ShowWindow(m_nCmdShow);
  m_pMainWnd->UpdateWindow();

  return TRUE;
}

CTheApp TheApp;
```

Once these files are entered, you can compile this application from the command line by typing

nmake 24SIMPLE

The following sections examine how each piece of code works in establishing the window on the screen.

Using afxwin.h

The afxwin.h header file is the gateway to Windows programming with the Foundation Class library. afxwin.h calls all subsequent header files, including windows.h, as they are needed. Using one header file also aids in creating precompiled header files. Precompiled header files save time when repeated compilation is being done during application development.

It is a good idea to print a copy of afxwin.h for your reference as you develop your own applications using the Foundation Class library. This header file is approximately 40 pages long.

Deriving a Class from CWinApp

This application starts by deriving a class, **CTheApp**, from the Foundation Class Library class, **CWinApp**. This object is defined by the programmer.

```
class CTheApp : public CWinApp
{
public:
  virtual BOOL InitInstance();
};
```

The class **CTheApp** overrides the member function, **InitInstance()**, of **CWinApp**. You will find that overriding member functions occurs frequently. By overriding **InitInstance()**, you can customize the initialization and execution of the application. In **CWinApp**, it is also possible to override **InitApplication()**, **ExitInstance()**, and **OnIdle()**, but for most applications this will not be necessary.

Here is an edited portion of the **CWinApp** class description, as found in the afxwin.h header file:

```
class CWinApp : public CObject
{
  DECLARE_DYNAMIC(CWinApp)
public:
  CWinApp(const char* pszAppName=NULL);
  void SetCurrentHandles();

  const char* m_pszAppName;
  HANDLE m_hInstance;
  HANDLE m_hPrevInstance;
  LPSTR m_lpCmdLine;
  int m_nCmdShow;

  CWnd* m_pMainWnd;
```

```
HCURSOR LoadCursor(LPSTR lpCursorName);
HCURSOR LoadCursor(WORD nIDCursor);
HCURSOR LoadStandardCursor(LPSTR lpCursorName);
HCURSOR LoadOEMCursor(WORD nIDCursor);

HICON LoadIcon(LPSTR lpIconName);
HICON LoadIcon(WORD nIDIcon);
HICON LoadStandardIcon(LPSTR lpIconName);
HICON LoadOEMIcon(WORD nIDIcon);

BOOL PumpMessage();

virtual BOOL InitApplication();
virtual BOOL InitInstance();

virtual int Run();

virtual BOOL PreTranslateMessage(MSG* pMsg);
virtual BOOL OnIdle(LONG lCount);
virtual int ExitInstance();

protected:
  MSG m_msgCur;
};
```

The **CWinApp** class is responsible for establishing and implementing the Windows message loop. The message loop was discussed in Chapter 23. This action, alone, eliminates many lines of repetitive code.

CFrameWnd

The application window, established by the **CMainWnd** class, is defined from the base class, **CFrameWnd**, as shown in the following segment of code:

```
class CMainWnd : public CFrameWnd
{
public:
  CMainWnd()
  {
    Create(NULL,"Hello MFC World",
           WS_OVERLAPPEDWINDOW,rectDefault,NULL,NULL);
  }
};
```

The constructor for the class, **CMainWnd()**, calls the **Create()** member function to establish initial window parameters. In this application, the window's style and caption are provided as parameters. You'll see in Chapter 25 that it is also possible to specify a menu name and an accelerator table when this member function is used.

Here is an edited portion of **CFrameWnd**, also found in the afxwin.h header file:

```
class CFrameWnd : public CWnd
{
  DECLARE_DYNAMIC(CFrameWnd)

protected:
  HANDLE m_hAccelTable;

public:
  static const CRect rectDefault;

  CFrameWnd();

  BOOL LoadAccelTable(const char FAR* lpAccelTableName);
  BOOL Create(const char FAR* lpClassName,
              const char FAR* lpWindowName,
              DWORD dwStyle = WS_OVERLAPPEDWINDOW,
              const RECT& rect = rectDefault,
              const CWnd* pParentWnd = NULL,
              const char FAR* lpMenuName = NULL);

public:
  virtual ~CFrameWnd();
  virtual CFrameWnd* GetParentFrame();
  virtual CFrameWnd* GetChildFrame();

protected:
  virtual BOOL PreTranslateMessage(MSG* pMsg);
};
```

The first parameter in **Create()** allows a class name to be specified in compliance with the traditional Windows API **RegisterClass()** function. Normally, this will be set to null in the applications you develop and a class name will not be required.

Implementing the InitInstance() Member Function

Recall that the derived **CTheApp** class object overrode the **InitInstance()** member function. Here is how this application implements **InitInstance()**:

```
BOOL CTheApp::InitInstance()
{
  m_pMainWnd=new CMainWnd();
  m_pMainWnd->ShowWindow(m_nCmdShow);
  m_pMainWnd->UpdateWindow();

  return TRUE;
}
```

The **new** operator invokes the constructor **CMainWnd**, discussed in the previous section. The *m_pMainWnd* member variable (m_ indicates a member variable) holds the location for the application's main window. **ShowWindow()**, also a member function, is required to display the window on the screen. The parameter, *m_nCmd-Show,* is initialized by the application's constructor. **UpdateWindow()** displays and paints the window being sent to the screen.

The Constructor

The last piece of code invokes the application's constructor at startup:

```
CTheApp TheApp;
```

The application code for this example is very simple and straightforward. The application merely establishes a window; it does not permit you to draw anything in the window.

In the next chapter, you will create a more generalized template, as you did in Chapter 23, that will allow you to use basically the same code from one application to another. This code will allow you to draw in the client area of the window.

Running 24SIMPLE.CPP

Figure 24-1 shows a window similar to the one that will appear on your screen. While the application didn't draw anything in the client area of the window, it did give the application a new title!

This code forms the foundation for all Windows Foundation Class library applications developed in this book. You might want to review the important details one more time, before going on to the applications created in Chapter 25.

Figure 24-1. *Establishing a window with the use of Microsoft's Foundation Class library*

A Simplified Design Ensures Easy Maintenance

Reusable classes are one of C++'s main drawing cards for simplified design and application maintenance. The Foundation Class library for Windows allows C++ to be extended in a natural way, making these classes appear to be part of the language itself. In the next chapter you'll explore many additional features of the Foundation Class library as you develop applications that range from a simple program template to a robust bar chart program using menus and dialog boxes.

Chapter **25**

Windows Programming: Using the Foundation Class Library

Now is the time to put your accumulated Windows theory to practical use. In Chapter 22 through Chapter 24, you learned about various Windows components such as menus, dialog boxes, keyboard accelerators, and so on. Chapter 24 described the theory and specifications of Microsoft's Foundation Class library. This chapter contains four complete Foundation Class library Windows applications that will aid in your understanding of this class library.

Each example in this chapter builds on the knowledge gained from the previous program. Various Windows and Foundation Class library components are added to each successive example. It is imperative, therefore, to study each application in the order in which it appears. By the fourth application, you will be working with a complex Windows application that uses several Windows resources, depends heavily on the Foundation Class library, and produces a presentation-quality bar chart.

The program listings for each application are quite long, so enter them carefully. Remember as you type that these listings are still far shorter than their function-library counterparts in Chapter 23.

A Simple Application and Template

In Chapter 24, you learned how to establish a window on the screen with the use of the Foundation Class library. That example serves as a gateway to all such Windows applications, which utilize the client area for printing and drawing.

The first application in this chapter, 25SFCWA, simply prints a message in the window's client area. The name of this program is derived from "Simple Foundation Class Windows Application."

Before a discussion of the important aspects of the application, examine a complete program listing. The listing that follows is a composite of the four separate files needed to compile this application:

- The command-line make file, 25SFCWA

- The module definition file, 25SFCWA.DEF

- The header file, 25Sfcwa.h

- The application file, 25SFCWA.CPP

Enter each file carefully and save it with the filename and extension shown. When all four files are entered and saved, the application can be compiled from the command line with the following statement:

```
nmake 25SFCWA
```

Here is the complete listing:

```
THE 25SFCWA MAKE FILE:

CPPFLAGS= /AS /W3 /GA /GEs /G2
LINKFLAGS=/NOD
CPPFLAGS=$(CPPFLAGS) /Oselg /Gs
LINKFLAGS=$(LINKFLAGS) /FAR /PACKC
LIBS=safxcw libw slibcew


all : 25SFCWA.exe


25SFCWA.obj:  25SFCWA.h


25SFCWA.exe:  25SFCWA.obj 25SFCWA.def
   link $(LINKFLAGS) 25SFCWA,25SFCWA,NUL,$(LIBS),25SFCWA.def;



THE 25SFCWA.DEF MODULE DEFINITION FILE:
```

```
NAME         25SFCWA
DESCRIPTION  'A Simple Foundation Class Windows Application'
EXETYPE      WINDOWS
STUB         'WINSTUB.EXE'
CODE         PRELOAD MOVEABLE DISCARDABLE
DATA         PRELOAD MOVEABLE MULTIPLE
HEAPSIZE     4096
STACKSIZE    9216
```

THE 25SFCWA.H HEADER FILE:

```cpp
class CMainWnd : public CFrameWnd
{
public:
  CMainWnd();
  afx_msg void OnPaint();
  DECLARE_MESSAGE_MAP();
};

class C25SFCWAApp : public CWinApp
{
public:
  BOOL InitInstance();
};
```

THE 25SFCWA.CPP APPLICATION FILE:

```cpp
//
//  25SFCWA.CPP
//  A Simple Foundation Class Windows Application.
//  This code can serve as a template for the development
//  of other simple foundation class applications.
//  Copyright (c) William H. Murray and Chris H. Pappas, 1992
//

#include <afxwin.h>
#include "25SFCWA.h"

C25SFCWAApp theApp;

CMainWnd::CMainWnd()
{
```

```
    Create(NULL,"A Simple Foundation Class Windows Application",
         WS_OVERLAPPEDWINDOW,rectDefault,NULL,NULL);
}


void CMainWnd::OnPaint()
{
  CPaintDC dc(this);
//---------- your routines below ----------------------//

  dc.TextOut(200,200,"The Foundation Class Library",28);

//---------- your routines above ----------------------//
}

BEGIN_MESSAGE_MAP(CMainWnd,CFrameWnd)
  ON_WM_PAINT()
END_MESSAGE_MAP()

BOOL C25SFCWAApp::InitInstance()
{
  m_pMainWnd=new CMainWnd();
  m_pMainWnd->ShowWindow(m_nCmdShow);
  m_pMainWnd->UpdateWindow();

  return TRUE;
}
```

This composite listing gives you a chance to examine all of the code necessary to produce a working application. The next sections examine those details that are unique to this application. Recall that the purposes of make, definition, and header files have been covered in earlier Windows chapters.

Understanding the 25SFCWA Make File

The make file is responsible for directing the compiler, linker, and optional resource compiler on how to compile and link your application from the command line. You use command-line make filenames, without extensions, to separate them from project make files with the .MAK extension. Chapter 3 discussed various compiler and linker switches that are used in this chapter. If you have questions concerning these switches, you might want to review this material.

This chapter uses a make file style similar to that used by Microsoft in its Foundation Class examples. Notice that the basic style of the make file is identical to those used in Chapter 23, with the addition of several special terms. Groups of switch values can be collected under one of several terms, as shown next:

```
CPPFLAGS= /AS /W3 /GA /GEs /G2
LINKFLAGS=/NOD
CPPFLAGS=$(CPPFLAGS) /Oselg /Gs
LINKFLAGS=$(LINKFLAGS) /FAR /PACKC
LIBS=safxcw libw slibcew
```

These terms are then substituted into a standard make file format. This technique allows you to change switches in a whole make file by changing them in just one location. It also shortens individual make file lines, as you can see:

```
all : 25SFCWA.exe

25SFCWA.obj:  25SFCWA.h

25SFCWA.exe:  25SFCWA.obj 25SFCWA.def
   link $(LINKFLAGS) 25SFCWA,25SFCWA,NUL,$(LIBS),25SFCWA.def;
```

Take a minute and compare the contents of this make file with one in Chapter 23.

Understanding the 25SFCWA.DEF Module Definition File

The module definition files developed for Foundation Class library applications remain the same as those for standard C applications.

```
NAME          25SFCWA
DESCRIPTION   'A Simple Foundation Class Windows Application'
EXETYPE       WINDOWS
STUB          'WINSTUB.EXE'
CODE          PRELOAD MOVEABLE DISCARDABLE
DATA          PRELOAD MOVEABLE MULTIPLE
HEAPSIZE      4096
STACKSIZE     9216
```

The main exception is that the use of EXPORTS is not required since the Foundation Class library handles this communication automatically.

Understanding the 25Sfcwa.h Header File

This chapter uses two types of header files. The first type, shown in the example in this section, is used to contain class definitions that are unique to the application. This header file type will always be identified by the filename and the (.h) extension—for example, 25Sfcwa.h. The second header file type, which you already used in Chapter 23, contains menu and dialog box resource identification values. When these header files are used, they are identified with an additional "r," which represents resource, at the end of the filename. For example, if this application had used a resource ID header file, it would have been named 25sfcwar.h. You'll see this second type used in the final two examples in this chapter.

The definitions for two classes are contained here; **CMainWnd** is derived from **CWinApp** and **C25SFCWAApp** from **CFrameWnd**.

```
class CMainWnd : public CFrameWnd
{
public:
  CMainWnd();
  afx_msg void OnPaint();
  DECLARE_MESSAGE_MAP();
};

class C25SFCWAApp : public CWinApp
{
public:
  BOOL InitInstance();
};
```

These classes were part of the body of the 24SIMPLE.CPP application and were explained in the last chapter. Putting them in a separate header file is just a matter of style—one encouraged by Microsoft.

Notice, in particular, that **CMainWnd** contains a function declaration, **OnPaint()**, and the addition of a message map. For member functions such as **OnPaint()**, the **afx_msg** keyword is used instead of **virtual**. **OnPaint()** is a member function of the **CWnd** class that the **CMainWnd** class overrides. This allows the client area of the window to be altered. The **OnPaint()** function is automatically called when a WM_PAINT message is sent to a CMainWnd object.

DECLARE_MESSAGE_MAP is used in virtually all Windows applications. This line states that the class overrides the handling of certain messages. (See the body of the application.) Microsoft uses this technique, rather than virtual functions, because it is more space efficient.

The 25SFCWA.CPP Application

The majority of this application's code is the same as 24SIMPLE.CPP, with the addition of the **OnPaint()** message handler function. Examine the piece of code shown next:

```
void CMainWnd::OnPaint()
{
  CPaintDC dc(this);
//---------- your routines below ----------------------//

  dc.TextOut(200,200,"The Foundation Class Library",28);

//---------- your routines above ----------------------//
}
```

A device context is created for handling the WM_PAINT message. Now, any Windows GDI functions that are encapsulated in the device context can be used between the comments "your routines below" and "your routines above." This is similar in concept to the template created in Chapter 23. When the **OnPaint()** function is complete, the destructor for CPaintDC is called automatically.

This application uses a fairly short message map, as the following code indicates:

```
BEGIN_MESSAGE_MAP(CMainWnd,CFrameWnd)
  ON_WM_PAINT()
END_MESSAGE_MAP()
```

Two classes are specified by BEGIN_MESSAGE_MAP: **CMainWnd** and **CFrameWnd**. **CMainWnd** is the target class and **CFrameWnd** is a class based on **CWnd**. The **ON_WM_PAINT()** function handles all WM_PAINT messages and directs them to the **OnPaint()** member function just discussed. In upcoming applications, you'll see many additional functions added to the message map.

The use of message maps has eliminated the need for the case/switch statements that are so typical of C Windows applications.

Running 25SFCWA

If you have entered the application code and received an error-free compilation, now is the time to run the program. If you are still in the PWB, you can launch the application there. If you're in Windows, select File from the main menu and then select the Run option. The screen should be similar to the one shown in Figure 25-1.

If you want to experiment with other GDI primitives, just remove the **TextOut()** function call and insert the function of your choice into the template code. Appendix C lists numerous Windows functions. The next example in this chapter uses the template, almost without alteration, to illustrate the use of several graphics functions that will draw a line, a chord, an arc, and so on.

Figure 25-1. *The window created by the 25SFCWA application*

Drawing Graphics Primitives in a Window

The second application in this chapter, 25GDI, will draw several graphics shapes in the window's client area. These are the same GDI drawing primitives discussed (and used separately) in Chapter 23.

The listing that follows is a composite of the four separate files needed to compile this application:

- The command-line make file, 25GDI

- The module definition file, 25GDI.DEF

- The header file, 25gdi.h

- The application file, 25GDI.CPP

Enter each of the four files carefully. When all four files are entered, the application can be compiled from the command line with the following statement:

```
nmake 25GDI
```

```
THE 25GDI MAKE FILE:

CPPFLAGS= /AS /W3 /GA /GEs /G2
LINKFLAGS=/NOD
CPPFLAGS=$(CPPFLAGS) /Oselg /Gs
LINKFLAGS=$(LINKFLAGS) /FAR /PACKC
LIBS=safxcw libw slibcew


all : 25GDI.exe

25GDI.obj:  25GDI.h

25GDI.exe:  25GDI.obj 25GDI.def
  link $(LINKFLAGS) 25GDI,25GDI,NUL,$(LIBS),25GDI.def;


THE 25GDI.DEF MODULE DEFINITION FILE:

NAME        25GDI
DESCRIPTION 'Experimenting with graphics drawing primitives'
EXETYPE     WINDOWS
STUB        'WINSTUB.EXE'
CODE        PRELOAD MOVEABLE DISCARDABLE
DATA        PRELOAD MOVEABLE MULTIPLE
HEAPSIZE    4096
STACKSIZE   9216


THE 25GDI.H HEADER FILE:

class CMainWnd : public CFrameWnd
{
public:
  CMainWnd();
  afx_msg void OnPaint();
  DECLARE_MESSAGE_MAP();
};

class C25GDIAApp : public CWinApp
{
public:
  BOOL InitInstance();
};
```

THE 25GDI.CPP APPLICATION FILE:

```
//
//   25GDI.CPP
//   An extension of the Simple Foundation Class Windows
//   Application that allows experimenting with graphics
//   drawing primitives.
//   Copyright (c) William H. Murray and Chris H. Pappas, 1992
//

#include <afxwin.h>
#include "25GDI.h"

C25GDIAApp theApp;

CMainWnd::CMainWnd()
{
  Create(NULL,"Experimenting With Graphics Drawing Primitives",
        WS_OVERLAPPEDWINDOW,rectDefault,NULL,NULL);
}

void CMainWnd::OnPaint()
{
  static DWORD dwColor[9]={RGB(0,0,0),          //black
                           RGB(255,0,0),        //red
                           RGB(0,255,0),        //green
                           RGB(0,0,255),        //blue
                           RGB(255,255,0),      //yellow
                           RGB(255,0,255),      //magenta
                           RGB(0,255,255),      //cyan
                           RGB(127,127,127),    //gray
                           RGB(255,255,255)};   //white
  short xcoord;
  POINT polylpts[4],polygpts[5];

  CBrush newbrush;
  CBrush* oldbrush;
  CPen   newpen;
  CPen* oldpen;

  CPaintDC dc(this);
//---------- your routines below ---------------------//
```

```
// draws a wide black diagonal line
newpen.CreatePen(PS_SOLID,6,dwColor[0]);
oldpen=dc.SelectObject(&newpen);
dc.MoveTo(0,0);
dc.LineTo(640,430);
dc.TextOut(70,20,"<-diagonal line",15);

// draws a blue arc
newpen.CreatePen(PS_DASH,1,dwColor[3]);
oldpen=dc.SelectObject(&newpen);
dc.Arc(100,100,200,200,150,175,175,150);
dc.TextOut(80,180,"small arc->",11);

// draws a wide green chord
newpen.CreatePen(PS_SOLID,8,dwColor[2]);
oldpen=dc.SelectObject(&newpen);
dc.Chord(550,20,630,80,555,25,625,70);
dc.TextOut(485,30,"chord->",7);

// draws and fills a red ellipse
newpen.CreatePen(PS_SOLID,1,dwColor[1]);
oldpen=dc.SelectObject(&newpen);
newbrush.CreateSolidBrush(dwColor[1]);
oldbrush=dc.SelectObject(&newbrush);
dc.Ellipse(180,180,285,260);
dc.TextOut(210,215,"ellipse",7);

// draws and fills a blue circle with ellipse function
newpen.CreatePen(PS_SOLID,1,dwColor[3]);
oldpen=dc.SelectObject(&newpen);
newbrush.CreateSolidBrush(dwColor[3]);
oldbrush=dc.SelectObject(&newbrush);
dc.Ellipse(380,180,570,370);
dc.TextOut(450,265,"circle",6);

// draws a black pie wedge and fills with green
newpen.CreatePen(PS_SOLID,1,dwColor[0]);
oldpen=dc.SelectObject(&newpen);
newbrush.CreateSolidBrush(dwColor[2]);
oldbrush=dc.SelectObject(&newbrush);
dc.Pie(300,50,400,150,300,50,300,100);
dc.TextOut(350,80,"<-pie wedge",11);

// draws a black rectangle and fills with gray
newbrush.CreateSolidBrush(dwColor[7]);
```

```
oldbrush=dc.SelectObject(&newbrush);
dc.Rectangle(50,300,150,400);
dc.TextOut(160,350,"<-rectangle",11);

// draws a black rounded rectangle and fills with blue
newbrush.CreateHatchBrush(HS_CROSS,dwColor[3]);
oldbrush=dc.SelectObject(&newbrush);
dc.RoundRect(60,310,110,350,20,20);
dc.TextOut (120,310,"<------rounded rectangle",24);

// draws several green pixels
for(xcoord=400;xcoord<450;xcoord+=3)
  dc.SetPixel(xcoord,150,0L);
dc.TextOut(455,145,"<-pixels",8);

// draws several wide magenta lines with polyline
newpen.CreatePen(PS_SOLID,3,dwColor[5]);
oldpen=dc.SelectObject(&newpen);
polylpts[0].x=10;
polylpts[0].y=30;
polylpts[1].x=10;
polylpts[1].y=100;
polylpts[2].x=50;
polylpts[2].y=100;
polylpts[3].x=10;
polylpts[3].y=30;
dc.Polyline(polylpts,4);
dc.TextOut(10,110,"polyline",8);

// draws a wide cyan polygon and
// fills with diagonal yellow
newpen.CreatePen(PS_SOLID,4,dwColor[6]);
oldpen=dc.SelectObject(&newpen);
newbrush.CreateHatchBrush(HS_FDIAGONAL,dwColor[4]);
oldbrush=dc.SelectObject(&newbrush);
polygpts[0].x=40;
polygpts[0].y=200;
polygpts[1].x=100;
polygpts[1].y=270;
polygpts[2].x=80;
polygpts[2].y=290;
polygpts[3].x=20;
polygpts[3].y=220;
polygpts[4].x=40;
polygpts[4].y=200;
```

```
dc.Polygon(polygpts,5);
dc.TextOut(70,210,"<-polygon",9);

// delete brush objects
dc.SelectObject(oldbrush);
newbrush.DeleteObject();

// delete pen objects
dc.SelectObject(oldpen);
newpen.DeleteObject();

//---------- your routines above ---------------------//
}

BEGIN_MESSAGE_MAP(CMainWnd,CFrameWnd)
  ON_WM_PAINT()
END_MESSAGE_MAP()

BOOL C25GDIAApp::InitInstance()
{
  m_pMainWnd=new CMainWnd();
  m_pMainWnd->ShowWindow(m_nCmdShow);
  m_pMainWnd->UpdateWindow();

  return TRUE;
}
```

The 25GDI Make, 25GDI.DEF Module Definition, and 25gdi.h Header Files

Only the application file, 25GDI.CPP, is altered in this example. This means that except for the application's name change, the make, module definition, and header files are identical to those of the last example.

The 25GDI.CPP Application

In addition to showing the use of several GDI drawing primitives, this application will also teach you how to incorporate new brushes and pens into your application. Examine the code at the start of the **OnPaint()** message handler function. An array is established to hold the RGB values for nine unique brush and pen colors. You'll see shortly how colors are picked from this array.

```
static DWORD dwColor[9]={RGB(0,0,0),        //black
                         RGB(255,0,0),      //red
```

```
RGB(0,255,0),        //green
RGB(0,0,255),        //blue
RGB(255,255,0),      //yellow
RGB(255,0,255),      //magenta
RGB(0,255,255),      //cyan
RGB(127,127,127),    //gray
RGB(255,255,255)};   //white
```

The **CBrush** and **CPen** classes permit the brush or pen object to be passed to any CDC (base class for display context) member function. Brushes can be solid, hatched, or patterned, while pens can draw solid, dashed, or dotted lines. For additional combinations, refer to your Microsoft *Class Libraries Reference* manual. Here is the syntax that was used used to create a new brush and pen object:

```
CBrush newbrush;
CBrush* oldbrush;
CPen  newpen;
CPen* oldpen;
```

Since each GDI primitive's code is somewhat similar to the others, you'll now examine two typical sections. The first piece of code is used to draw a wide black diagonal line in the window:

```
// draws a wide black diagonal line
newpen.CreatePen(PS_SOLID,6,dwColor[0]);
oldpen=dc.SelectObject(&newpen);
dc.MoveTo(0,0);
dc.LineTo(640,430);
dc.TextOut(70,20,"<-diagonal line",15);
```

The pen object is initialized by **CreatePen()** to draw black solid lines six logical units wide. Once the pen is initialized, the **SelectObject()** member function is overloaded for the pen object class and attaches the pen object to the device context. The previously attached object is returned. The **MoveTo()** and **LineTo()** functions set the range for the diagonal line that is drawn by the selected pen. Finally, a label is attached to the figure with the use of the **TextOut()** function.

Brushes can be handled in a similar way. This brush is initialized to be a hatched brush filled with blue crosses (HS_CROSS). The brush object is selected in the same way the pen object was selected:

```
// draws a black rounded rectangle and fills with blue
  newbrush.CreateHatchBrush(HS_CROSS,dwColor[3]);
  oldbrush=dc.SelectObject(&newbrush);
```

```
dc.RoundRect(60,310,110,350,20,20);
dc.TextOut (120,310,"<------rounded rectangle",24);
```

The **RoundRect()** function draws a rounded rectangle in black at the given screen coordinates. A label is also printed for this figure.

The remaining shapes are drawn to the screen using a similar technique.

Running the 25GDI Application

This application has a minor drawback, which you might have observed. All coordinate points for GDI functions are set to pixel values valid for VGA monitors. What happens if you are using an EGA or a Super-VGA display? If you are using a monitor with a lower resolution, such as an EGA, you will get a partial image that seems magnified. If you are using a higher resolution display, such as a Super-VGA, the image will fill in only the upper left part of your screen.

To eliminate this problem, your application must determine your display's characteristics and adjust accordingly. This adds an extra layer of complexity to the application code, which has been kept as simple as possible to this point. However, the final two examples in this chapter will teach you how to scale your figures to fit the current display type.

If you haven't done so by this point, run the 25GDI application. Your screen should look something like the one in Figure 25-2 if you are using a VGA monitor. The various GDI objects are displayed in very vivid colors.

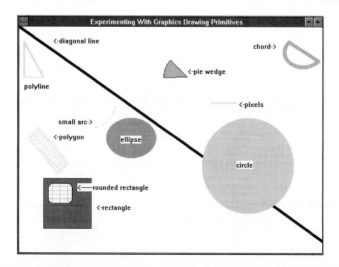

Figure 25-2. *Drawing several colorful GDI graphics objects with 25GDI*

A Scientific Waveform with Menu and Dialog Boxes

The third application in this chapter, 25FOUR, will draw a Fourier series waveform in the window's client area. (Fourier waves were also discussed in Chapter 19.) This application utilizes two Windows resources: a menu and dialog box. You may want to refer to Chapter 22 for details on the techniques for creating each of these.

The listing that follows is a composite of the seven separate files needed to compile this application:

- The command-line make file, 25FOUR

- The module definition file, 25FOUR.DEF

- The header file, 25four.h

- The resource header file, 25fourr.h

- The resource script file, 25FOUR.RC

- The dialog script file, 25FOUR.DLG

- The application file, 25SFCWA.CPP

Enter each file carefully. When all seven files are complete, the application can be compiled from the command line with the following statement:

```
nmake 25FOUR
```

Here is the complete listing:

```
THE 25FOUR MAKE FILE:

CPPFLAGS= /AS /W3 /GA /GEs /G2
LINKFLAGS=/NOD
CPPFLAGS=$(CPPFLAGS) /Oselg /Gs
LINKFLAGS=$(LINKFLAGS) /FAR /PACKC
LIBS=safxcw libw slibcew

all : 25FOUR.exe

25four.obj: 25four.h 25fourr.h

25four.res: 25fourr.h 25four.ico 25four.dlg

25four.exe: 25four.obj 25four.def 25four.res
   link $(LINKFLAGS) 25four,25four,NUL,$(LIBS),25four.def;
```

```
rc /t 25four.res
```

THE 25FOUR.DEF MODULE DEFINITION FILE:

```
NAME          25FOUR
DESCRIPTION   'Drawing A Fourier Series Wave Form'
EXETYPE       WINDOWS
STUB          'WINSTUB.EXE'
CODE          PRELOAD MOVEABLE DISCARDABLE
DATA          PRELOAD MOVEABLE MULTIPLE
HEAPSIZE      4096
STACKSIZE     9216
```

THE 25FOUR.H HEADER FILE:

```
class CMainWnd : public CFrameWnd
{
public:
  CMainWnd();

  afx_msg void OnPaint();
  afx_msg void OnSize(UINT,int,int);
  afx_msg int  OnCreate(LPCREATESTRUCT cs);
  afx_msg void OnAbout();
  afx_msg void OnFourierData();
  afx_msg void OnExit();

  DECLARE_MESSAGE_MAP()
};

class CTheApp : public CWinApp
{
public:
  virtual BOOL InitInstance();
};

class CFourierDataDialog : public CModalDialog
{
public:
  CFourierDataDialog(CWnd* pParentWnd=NULL)
                    : CModalDialog("FourierData",pParentWnd)
                    {  }
  virtual void OnOK();
```

```
};


THE 25FOURR.H RESOURCE HEADER FILE:

#define IDM_FOUR     100
#define IDM_ABOUT    110
#define IDM_EXIT     120

#define IDD_TERMS    200
#define IDD_TITLE    201



THE 25FOUR.RC RESOURCE SCRIPT FILE:

#include <windows.h>
#include <afxres.h>
#include "25FOURR.h"

AFX_IDI_STD_FRAME ICON 25FOUR.ico

FourierMenu MENU
BEGIN
  POPUP "Fourier Data"
  BEGIN
    MENUITEM "Fourier Data...",  IDM_FOUR
    MENUITEM "Fourier About...", IDM_ABOUT
    MENUITEM "Exit",             IDM_EXIT
  END
END


rcinclude 25FOUR.dlg



THE 25FOUR.DLG DIALOG SCRIPT FILE:

DLGINCLUDE RCDATA DISCARDABLE
BEGIN
  "25FOURR.H\0"
END

AboutBox DIALOG LOADONCALL MOVEABLE DISCARDABLE
         14,22,200,75
         STYLE WS_BORDER|WS_CAPTION|WS_DLGFRAME|WS_POPUP
```

```
        CAPTION "About Box"
BEGIN
  CONTROL "A Fourier Series Waveform",-1,"Static",
        SS_CENTER|WS_GROUP,30,5,144,8
  CONTROL "A Simple Foundation Class For Windows Application",
        -1,"Static",SS_CENTER|WS_GROUP,30,17,144,8
  CONTROL "By William H. Murray and Chris H. Pappas",-1,
        "Static",SS_CENTER|WS_GROUP,28,28,144,8
  CONTROL "OK",IDOK,"Button",BS_DEFPUSHBUTTON|WS_GROUP|
        WS_TABSTOP,84,55,32,14
  CONTROL "(c) Copyright, 1992",201,"Static",WS_GROUP,
        68,38,83,8
END


FourierData DIALOG LOADONCALL MOVEABLE DISCARDABLE
        74,21,142,70
        STYLE WS_BORDER|WS_CAPTION|
        WS_DLGFRAME|WS_POPUP
        CAPTION "Fourier Data"
BEGIN
  CONTROL "Title: ",-1, "static",SS_LEFT|WS_CHILD,
        6,5,28,8
  CONTROL "Title ",IDD_TITLE,"edit",ES_LEFT|WS_BORDER|
        WS_TABSTOP|WS_CHILD,33,1,106,12
  CONTROL "Number of terms: ",-1,"static",SS_LEFT|
        WS_CHILD,6,23,70,8
  CONTROL "1",IDD_TERMS,"edit",ES_LEFT|WS_BORDER|
        WS_TABSTOP|WS_CHILD,76,18,32,12
  CONTROL "OK",IDOK,"button",BS_PUSHBUTTON|WS_TABSTOP|
        WS_CHILD,25,52,24,14
  CONTROL "Cancel",IDCANCEL,"button",BS_PUSHBUTTON|
        WS_TABSTOP|WS_CHILD,89,53,28,14
END



THE 25FOUR.CPP APPLICATION FILE:


//
//  25FOUR.CPP
//  Drawing A Fourier Series with the use of
//  Microsoft C++ Foundation Classes
//  Copyright (c) William H. Murray and Chris H. Pappas, 1992
//


#include <afxwin.h>
```

```
#include <string.h>
#include <math.h>
#include "25FOURR.h"    // resource ids
#include "25FOUR.h"

int m_cxClient,m_cyClient;
char mytitle[80]="Title";
int nterms=1;

CTheApp theApp;

CMainWnd::CMainWnd()
{
  Create((AfxRegisterWndClass(CS_HREDRAW|CS_VREDRAW,
        LoadCursor(NULL,IDC_CROSS),
        GetStockObject(WHITE_BRUSH),NULL)),
        "Fourier Series Foundation Class Application",
        WS_OVERLAPPEDWINDOW,rectDefault,NULL,"FourierMenu");
}


void CMainWnd::OnSize(UINT,int x,int y)
{
  m_cxClient=x;
  m_cyClient=y;
}


void CMainWnd::OnPaint()
{
  CPaintDC dc(this);
  static DWORD dwColor[9]={RGB(0,0,0),         //black
                           RGB(255,0,0),       //red
                           RGB(0,255,0),       //green
                           RGB(0,0,255),       //blue
                           RGB(255,255,0),     //yellow
                           RGB(255,0,255),     //magenta
                           RGB(0,255,255),     //cyan
                           RGB(127,127,127),   //gray
                           RGB(255,255,255)};  //white

  int i,j,ltitle,ang;
  double y,yp;

  CBrush newbrush;
  CBrush* oldbrush;
```

```
//---------- your routines below ---------------------//

  // create a custom drawing surface
  dc.SetMapMode(MM_ISOTROPIC);
  dc.SetWindowExt(500,500);
  dc.SetViewportExt(m_cxClient,-m_cyClient);
  dc.SetViewportOrg(m_cxClient/20,m_cyClient/2);

  ang=0;
  yp=0.0;

  // draw x & y coordinate axes
  dc.MoveTo(0,240);
  dc.LineTo(0,-240);
  dc.MoveTo(0,0);
  dc.LineTo(400,0);
  dc.MoveTo(0,0);

  // draw actual Fourier waveform
  for (i=0; i<=400; i++)
  {
    for (j=1; j<=nterms; j++)
    {
      y=(150.0/((2.0*j)-1.0))*sin(((j*2.0)-1.0)*0.015708*ang);
      yp=yp+y;
    }
    dc.LineTo(i,(int) yp);
    yp-=yp;
    ang++;
  }

  // prepare to fill interior of waveform
  newbrush.CreateSolidBrush(dwColor[7]);
  oldbrush=dc.SelectObject(&newbrush);
  dc.FloodFill(150,10,dwColor[0]);
  dc.FloodFill(300,-10,dwColor[0]);

  // print waveform title
  ltitle=strlen(mytitle);
  dc.TextOut(200-(ltitle*8/2),185,mytitle,ltitle);

  // delete brush objects
  dc.SelectObject(oldbrush);
  newbrush.DeleteObject();
```

```
//---------- your routines above ---------------------//
}

int CMainWnd::OnCreate(LPCREATESTRUCT)
{
  UpdateWindow();
  return (0);
}

void CMainWnd::OnAbout()
{
  CModalDialog about("AboutBox",this);
  about.DoModal();
}

void CFourierDataDialog::OnOK()
{
  GetDlgItemText(IDD_TITLE,mytitle,80);
  nterms=GetDlgItemInt(IDD_TERMS,NULL,0);
  CModalDialog::OnOK();
}

void CMainWnd::OnFourierData()
{
  CFourierDataDialog dlgFourierData(this);
  if (dlgFourierData.DoModal()==IDOK)
  {
    InvalidateRect(NULL,TRUE);
    UpdateWindow();
  }
};

void CMainWnd::OnExit()
{
  DestroyWindow();
}

BEGIN_MESSAGE_MAP(CMainWnd,CFrameWnd)
  ON_WM_PAINT()
  ON_WM_SIZE()
  ON_WM_CREATE()
  ON_COMMAND(IDM_ABOUT,OnAbout)
  ON_COMMAND(IDM_FOUR,OnFourierData)
  ON_COMMAND(IDM_EXIT,OnExit)
END_MESSAGE_MAP()
```

```
BOOL CTheApp::InitInstance()
{
  m_pMainWnd=new CMainWnd();
  m_pMainWnd->ShowWindow(m_nCmdShow);
  m_pMainWnd->UpdateWindow();

  return TRUE;
}
```

The 25FOUR Make and 25FOUR.DEF Module Definition Files

The command-line make file, 25FOUR, includes information for compiling resources with the Microsoft resource compiler.

Recall from Chapter 22 that the resource compiler compiles Windows resources such as icons, cursors, bitmaps, and dialog boxes. Here is a portion of that file:

```
25four.res: 25fourr.h 25four.ico 25four.dlg
```

The resulting compiled resource file is then combined with the application code at link time, in order to produce a single executable program:

```
25four.exe: 25four.obj 25four.def 25four.res
  link $(LINKFLAGS) 25four,25four,NUL,$(LIBS),25four.def;
  rc /t 25four.res
```

Also note that the module definition file, 25FOUR.DEF, is added at link time. The module definition file remains unchanged to this point.

The 25four.h Header File

CMainWnd now contains several function declarations and a message map. The member functions include **OnPaint()**, **OnSize()**, **OnCreate()**, **OnAbout()**, **OnFourierData()** and **OnExit()**. The **afx_msg** keyword is used instead of **virtual**. **OnPaint()** is a member function of the **CWnd** class that the **CMainWnd** class overrides. This allows the client area of the window to be altered.

```
afx_msg void OnPaint();
afx_msg void OnSize(UINT,int,int);
afx_msg int  OnCreate(LPCREATESTRUCT cs);
afx_msg void OnAbout();
afx_msg void OnFourierData();
afx_msg void OnExit();
```

The **OnPaint()** function is automatically called when a WM_PAINT message is sent to a **CMainWnd** object by Windows or the application. **OnSize()** is called whenever a WM_SIZE message is generated by changing the size of the window. This information will be useful in scaling graphics to the window size. **OnCreate()** points to a structure containing information about the window being created. This structure contains information on the size, style, and so on, of the window. **OnAbout()**, **OnFourierData()**, and **OnExit()** are user-defined functions that respond to WM_COMMAND messages. WM_COMMAND messages are generated when the user selects an option from a menu or dialog box.

DECLARE_MESSAGE_MAP is used again to state that the class overrides the handling of certain messages. (See the body of the application.) Recall that this technique is more space efficient than the use of virtual functions.

The Foundation Class library supports regular and modal dialog boxes with the **CDialog** and **CModalDialog** classes. For very simple dialog boxes, such as about boxes, the Foundation Class can be used directly. For data entry dialog boxes, however, the class will have to be derived. The dialog box for this example will permit the user to enter an integer for the number of harmonics to be drawn in the window and an optional graph title. The **CFourierDataDialog** class is derived from the **CModalDialog** Foundation Class. Modal dialog boxes must be dismissed before other action can be taken in an application.

```
class CFourierDataDialog : public CModalDialog
{
public:
  CFourierDataDialog(CWnd* pParentWnd=NULL)
                    : CModalDialog("FourierData",pParentWnd)
                    {   }
  virtual void OnOK();
};
```

In a derived modal dialog class, member variables and functions can be added to specify the behavior of the dialog box. Member variables can also be used to save data entered by the user or to save data for display. Classes derived from **CModalDialog** require their own message maps, with the exception of the **OnInitDialog()**, **OnOK()**, and **OnCancel()** functions.

In this simple example, the **CFourierDataDialog** constructor supplies the name of the dialog box, "FourierData," and the name of the parent window that owns the dialog box. There is no owner for this modal dialog.

The dialog box will actually return data to the application when the user clicks the OK dialog push button. If either the OK or Cancel push button is clicked, the dialog box closes and is removed from the screen. When the dialog box closes, its member variables are accessed through the member functions in order to retrieve information entered by the user. Dialog boxes requiring initialization can override the **OnInitDialog()** member function for this purpose.

Additional information on dialog box classes and their use can be found in the Microsoft *Class Libraries User's Guide*. Help is also available on line from the QUICKHELP utility.

The 25fourr.h Resource Header, 25FOUR.RC Resource Script, and 25FOUR.DLG Dialog Script Files

All three files are used by the resource compiler to produce a single compiled Windows resource.

The 25fourr.h resource header file contains five identification values. IDM_FOUR, IDM_ABOUT, and IDM_EXIT are used for menu selection choices, while IDD_TERMS and IDD_TITLE are for the data entry dialog box.

The 25FOUR.RC resource script file names a unique icon, created with the Image Editor, that will be used by the application. Figure 25-3 shows this icon being created in the editor.

The resource script file also contains a description of the application's menu, which is shown in Figure 25-4. Compare the menu title and features to the text used in creating the menu in the resource file.

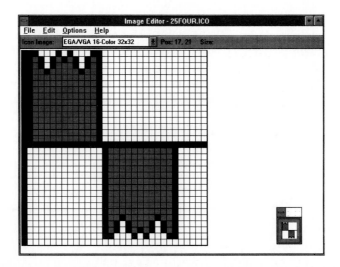

Figure 25-3. *Creating a unique icon for the 25FOUR application*

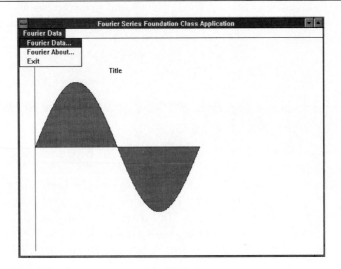

Figure 25-4.   *Menu items for the 25FOUR application*

It would also be possible to merge dialog box script information with the resource script file, as was done in Chapter 23, since they are both script files. In large applications, it is often desirable to leave the dialog script file as a separate entity and combine it with other resources when it is compiled by the resource compiler. In this application, 25FOUR.DLG contains the script information for the AboutBox and FourierData dialog boxes. Here is the about dialog box:

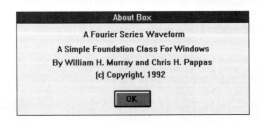

The data entry dialog box looks like this:

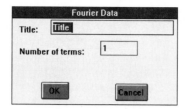

Take a minute to compare the contents of the 25FOUR.DLG file with the figures. Remember that the Dialog Editor, described in Chapter 22, was used to construct both dialog boxes. The Dialog Editor automatically creates the dialog resource script file.

The 25FOUR.CPP Application File

The complexity of the application file for this example has increased greatly because of the inclusion of menus and dialog boxes. Other features have also been added, which you might want to include in your own programs. In the following sections, you'll see how to select a new cursor, set the background color, determine the size of the current window, set a new viewport and origin for drawing, and draw and fill an object in the window. Let's examine these features as they appear in the program.

Creating a Custom CMainWnd Class

The **CMainWnd** class can be customized with the use of **AfxRegisterWndClass** in creating a registration class. A registration class has many fields, but four are easily altered: style, cursor, background, and the minimize icon.

This small piece of code shows the syntax for changing the cursor to a stock cross shape (IDC_CROSS) and setting the brush, which paints the background, to a WHITE_BRUSH:

```
CMainWnd::CMainWnd()
{
  Create((AfxRegisterWndClass(CS_HREDRAW|CS_VREDRAW,
        LoadCursor(NULL,IDC_CROSS),
        GetStockObject(WHITE_BRUSH),NULL)),
        "Fourier Series Foundation Class Application",
        WS_OVERLAPPEDWINDOW,rectDefault,NULL,"FourierMenu");
}
```

Also note that the menu name is identified in the **Create()** member function.

Determining the Window's Current Size

The **OnSize()** member function returns the size of the current client window. A WM_SIZE message is generated whenever the window is resized.

The current window size is saved in two variables, *m_cxClient* and *m_cyClient*.

```
void CMainWnd::OnSize(UINT,int x,int y)
{
  m_cxClient=x;
  m_cyClient=y;
}
```

These values will be used to scale the graphics to fit the current window's dimensions.

Drawing the Waveform

In order to prevent the scaling problems you saw in the last example, a scalable drawing surface is created. You may wish to review the purpose of these functions in Chapter 22 and Appendix C.

The mapping mode is changed to MM_ISOTROPIC with **SetMapMode()**. The MM_ISOTROPIC mapping mode uses arbitrary drawing units:

```
dc.SetMapMode(MM_ISOTROPIC);
```

The window's extent is set to 500 units in both the x and y directions:

```
dc.SetWindowExt(500,500);
```

This simply means that the x and y axes will always have 500 units, regardless of the size of the window. The viewport extent is set to the currently reported window size:

```
dc.SetViewportExt(m_cxClient,-m_cyClient);
```

In this case, you will see all 500 units in the window.

 Using a negative when specifying the y viewport extent forces y to increase in the upward direction.

The viewport origin is set midway on the y axis and a small distance (a fifth of the length) from the left edge for the x axis:

```
dc.SetViewportOrg(m_cxClient/20,m_cyClient/2);
```

Next, x and y coordinate axes are drawn in the window. Compare these values to the axes shown in later screen shots:

```
// draw x & y coordinate axes
dc.MoveTo(0,240);
dc.LineTo(0,-240);
dc.MoveTo(0,0);
dc.LineTo(400,0);
dc.MoveTo(0,0);
```

The technique for drawing this Fourier wave is the same as that for the example discussed in Chapter 19. Two **for** loops are used. The *i* variable controls the angle used by the sine function, while the *j* variable holds the value for the current Fourier harmonic. Each point plotted on the screen is a summation of all the Fourier harmonics for a given angle. Thus, if you request that the application draw 1000 harmonics, $400 \times 1000 = 400,000$ separate calculations will be made.

```
// draw actual Fourier wave form
for (i=0; i<=400; i++)
{
  for (j=1; j<=nterms; j++)
  {
    y=(150.0/((2.0*j)-1.0))*sin(((j*2.0)-1.0)*0.015708*ang);
    yp=yp+y;
  }
  dc.LineTo(i,(int) yp);
  yp-=yp;
  ang++;
}
```

The **LineTo()** function is used to connect each calculated point, forming a waveform drawn with a solid line. This waveform will have its interior region filled with a gray color by using the **FloodFill()** function. The **FloodFill()** function requires the coordinates of a point within the fill region and the bounding color that the figure was drawn with. You can determine these values from the following code:

```
// prepare to fill interior of wave form
newbrush.CreateSolidBrush(dwColor[7]);
oldbrush=dc.SelectObject(&newbrush);
dc.FloodFill(150,10,dwColor[0]);
dc.FloodFill(300,-10,dwColor[0]);
```

Before completing the figure, a title is printed in the window and the brush object deleted:

```
// print waveform title
ltitle=strlen(mytitle);
dc.TextOut(200-(ltitle*8/2),185,mytitle,ltitle);

// delete brush objects
dc.SelectObject(oldbrush);
newbrush.DeleteObject();
```

Remember that all objects drawn within the client area will be scaled to the viewport. This program eliminates the sizing problem of earlier examples and requires only a little additional coding.

The About Dialog Box

About dialog boxes are very easy to create and implement. About dialog boxes are used to communicate information about the program, the program's designers, the copyright date, and so on.

A modal dialog box is created by selecting the Fourier About... option from the application's menu. The OnAbout command handler requires only a few lines of code:

```
void CMainWnd::OnAbout()
{
  CModalDialog about("AboutBox",this);
  about.DoModal();
}
```

The constructor for **CModalDialog** utilizes the current window as the parent window for the object. The **this** pointer is typically used here and refers to the currently used object. The **DoModal()** member function is responsible for drawing the about box in the client area. When the OK button is pushed in the about box, the box is removed and the client area is repainted.

The Data Entry Dialog Box

Dialog boxes that allow user input require a bit more programming than do simple about dialog boxes. A data input dialog box can be selected from the application's menu by selecting Fourier Data....

An illustration of this dialog box was shown earlier. The user is permitted to enter a chart title and an integer representing the number of Fourier harmonics to draw. If the user selects the OK push button, the data entry dialog box is removed from the window and the client area is updated.

```
void CMainWnd::OnFourierData()
{
  CFourierDataDialog dlgFourierData(this);
  if (dlgFourierData.DoModal()==IDOK)
  {
    InvalidateRect(NULL,TRUE);
    UpdateWindow();
  }
};
```

CFourierDataDialog was derived from **CModalDialog** in the header file, 25four.h, as discussed earlier. Notice, however, that it is at this point in the application that data is retrieved. This data was entered in the dialog box by the user.

```
void CFourierDataDialog::OnOK()
{
  GetDlgItemText(IDD_TITLE,mytitle,80);
  nterms=GetDlgItemInt(IDD_TERMS,NULL,0);
  CModalDialog::OnOK();
}
```

The **GetDlgItemText()** function returns chart title information to *mytitle,* in the form of a string. The dialog box location for this information is identified by IDD_TITLE. Integer information can be processed in a similar manner with the **GetDlgItemInt()** function. Its dialog box identification value is IDD_TERMS, and the integer retrieved by the function is returned to *nterms.* The second parameter is used to report translation errors but is not used in this application. If the third parameter is nonzero, a check will be made for a signed number. In this application, only positive numbers are possible.

Responding to OnExit()

The final application menu option is Exit. Exit will destroy the client window by calling the **DestroyWindow()** function:

```
void CMainWnd::OnExit()
{
  DestroyWindow();
}
```

This application menu option gives the user a method of exiting the application without the need to use the system menu.

The Message Map

Again, two classes are specified in BEGIN_MESSAGE_MAP: **CMainWnd** and **CFrameWnd**. **CMainWnd** is the target class and **CFrameWnd** is a class based on **CWnd**. The **ON_WM_PAINT()** function handles all WM_PAINT messages and directs them to the **OnPaint()** member function. ON_WM_SIZE handles WM_SIZE messages and directs them to the **OnSize()** member function. The **ON_WM_CREATE()** function handles WM_CREATE messages and directs them to the **OnCreate()** member function. There is an **ON_COMMAND()** function for each application menu item. Message information is processed on menu items and then returned to the appropriate member function for processing.

```
BEGIN_MESSAGE_MAP(CMainWnd,CFrameWnd)
  ON_WM_PAINT()
  ON_WM_SIZE()
  ON_WM_CREATE()
  ON_COMMAND(IDM_ABOUT,OnAbout)
  ON_COMMAND(IDM_FOUR,OnFourierData)
  ON_COMMAND(IDM_EXIT,OnExit)
END_MESSAGE_MAP()
```

As mentioned in an earlier example, the use of message maps has eliminated the need for the case/switch statements. These statements are typically a source of errors in Windows applications.

Running 25FOUR

Compile the application using the command-line make file. When the application is executed, a default waveform is drawn in the client area. A default value of 1 harmonic produces a sine wave, as shown in Figure 25-5. Figure 25-6 shows three harmonics, while Figure 25-7 shows 20 harmonics.

As the number of harmonics increases, the figure drawn in the client area will approach a perfect square wave. Experiment with various values, but be aware that the drawing time for very large numbers of harmonics is significant.

A Bar Chart with Menu and Dialog Boxes

The final application in this chapter, 25BAR, will draw a presentation-quality bar chart in the window's client area. This application also makes use of several Windows resources, including a menu, an about dialog box, and a data entry dialog box.

The listing that follows is a composite of the eight separate files needed to compile this application:

- The command-line make file, 25BAR

- The project make file, 25BAR.MAK

- The module definition file, 25BAR.DEF

- The header file, 25bar.h

- The resource header file, 25barr.h

- The resource script file, 25BAR.RC

- The dialog script file, 25BAR.DLG

- The application file, 25BAR.CPP

Enter each file carefully. When all eight files are complete, the application can be compiled from the command line with the following statement:

```
nmake 25BAR
```

Alternately, this application can be compiled within the PWB integrated environment by opening the project file, 25BAR.MAK, and selecting the compile option. The 25BAR.MAK file includes debug compile and link options.

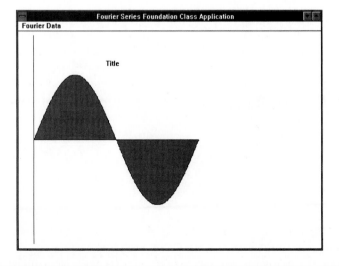

Figure 25-5.   *The default waveform for 25FOUR*

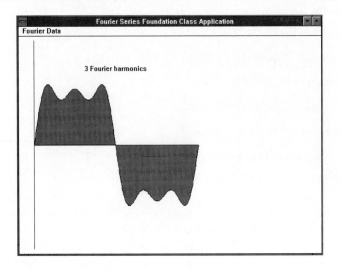

Figure 25-6.   *Creating a wave with three Fourier harmonics*

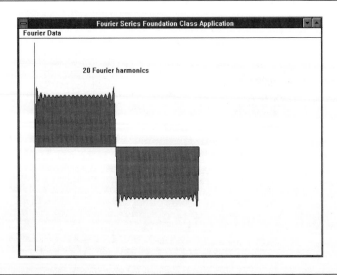

Figure 25-7.   *Creating a wave with 20 Fourier harmonics*

```
THE 25BAR MAKE FILE:

CPPFLAGS= /AS /W3 /GA /GEs /G2
LINKFLAGS=/NOD
CPPFLAGS=$(CPPFLAGS) /Oselg /Gs
LINKFLAGS=$(LINKFLAGS) /FAR /PACKC
LIBS=safxcw libw slibcew

all : 25BAR.exe

25BAR.obj: 25BAR.h 25BARr.h

25BAR.res: 25BARr.h 25BAR.dlg

25BAR.exe: 25BAR.obj 25BAR.def 25BAR.res
  link $(LINKFLAGS) 25BAR,25BAR,NUL,$(LIBS),25BAR.def;
  rc /t 25BAR.res


THE 25BAR.MAK PROJECT MAKE FILE (PWB):

ORIGIN = PWB
PROJ = 25BAR
PROJFILE = 25BAR.mak
DEBUG = 0

CC=cl
CFLAGS_G=/W2 /GA /GEf /Zp /BATCH
CFLAGS_D=/Zi /Od /Gs
CFLAGS_R=/Oe /Og /Os /Gs
CXX=cl
CXXFLAGS_G=/W3 /G2 /GA /GEs /BATCH
CXXFLAGS_D=/f /Od /Zi /D_DEBUG
CXXFLAGS_R=/Os /Ol /Og /Oe /Gs
MAPFILE_D=NUL
MAPFILE_R=NUL
LFLAGS_G=/NOD /BATCH /ONERROR:NOEXE
LFLAGS_D=/CO /NOF /NOPACKC
LFLAGS_R=/FAR /PACKC
LLIBS_G=LIBW.LIB
LINKER=link
ILINK=ilink
LRF=echo > NUL
ILFLAGS=/a /e
RC=rc
```

```
LLIBS_R=SAFXCW /NOD:SLIBCE SLIBCEW
LLIBS_D=SAFXCWD /NOD:SLIBCE SLIBCEW

FILES=25BAR.CPP 25BAR.DEF 25BAR.RC
DEF_FILE=25BAR.DEF
OBJS=25BAR.obj
RESS=25BAR.res

all: $(PROJ).exe

.SUFFIXES:
.SUFFIXES:
.SUFFIXES: .obj .res .cpp .rc

25BAR.obj : 25BAR.CPP 25BARR.h 25BAR.h
!IF $(DEBUG)
  $(CXX) /c $(CXXFLAGS_G) $(CXXFLAGS_D) /Fo25BAR.obj 25BAR.CPP
!ELSE
  $(CXX) /c $(CXXFLAGS_G) $(CXXFLAGS_R) /Fo25BAR.obj 25BAR.CPP
!ENDIF

25BAR.res : 25BAR.RC 25BARR.h 25BAR.dlg
  $(RC) $(RCFLAGS) /r /fo 25BAR.res 25BAR.RC

$(PROJ).exe : $(DEF_FILE) $(OBJS) $(RESS)
!IF $(DEBUG)
  $(LRF) @<<$(PROJ).lrf
$(RT_OBJS: = +^
) $(OBJS: = +^
)
$@
$(MAPFILE_D)
$(LIBS: = +^
) +
$(LLIBS_G: = +^
) +
$(LLIBS_D: = +^
)
$(DEF_FILE) $(LFLAGS_G) $(LFLAGS_D);
<<
!ELSE
  $(LRF) @<<$(PROJ).lrf
$(RT_OBJS: = +^
) $(OBJS: = +^
)
```

```
$@
$(MAPFILE_R)
$(LIBS: = +^
) +
$(LLIBS_G: = +^
) +
$(LLIBS_R: = +^
)
$(DEF_FILE) $(LFLAGS_G) $(LFLAGS_R);
<<
!ENDIF
  $(LINKER) @$(PROJ).lrf
  $(RC) $(RESS) $@

.cpp.obj :
!IF $(DEBUG)
  $(CXX) /c $(CXXFLAGS_G) $(CXXFLAGS_D) /Fo$@ $<
!ELSE
  $(CXX) /c $(CXXFLAGS_G) $(CXXFLAGS_R) /Fo$@ $<
!ENDIF

.rc.res :
  $(RC) $(RCFLAGS) /r /fo $@ $<

run: $(PROJ).exe
  WX $(WXFLAGS) $(PROJ).exe $(RUNFLAGS)

debug: $(PROJ).exe
  WX $(WXFLAGS) CVW $(CVFLAGS) $(PROJ).exe $(RUNFLAGS)
```

THE 25BAR.DEF MODULE DEFINITION FILE:

```
;25BAR.DEF for Microsoft C/C++

NAME            25BAR
DESCRIPTION     'Microsoft Foundation Class Bar Chart Program'
EXETYPE         WINDOWS
STUB            'WINSTUB.EXE'
CODE            PRELOAD MOVABLE
DATA            PRELOAD MOVEABLE MULTIPLE
HEAPSIZE        4096
STACKSIZE       9216
```

```
THE 25BAR.H HEADER FILE:

class CMainWnd : public CFrameWnd
{
public:
  CMainWnd();

  afx_msg void OnPaint();
  afx_msg void OnSize(UINT,int,int);
  afx_msg int  OnCreate(LPCREATESTRUCT cs);
  afx_msg void OnAbout();
  afx_msg void OnBarData();
  afx_msg void OnExit();

  DECLARE_MESSAGE_MAP()
};

class CTheApp : public CWinApp
{
public:
  virtual BOOL InitInstance();
};

class CBarDataDialog : public CModalDialog
{
public:
  CBarDataDialog(CWnd* pParentWnd=NULL)
                 : CModalDialog("BarDlgBox",pParentWnd)
                 {   }
  virtual void OnOK();
};


THE 25BARR.H RESOURCE HEADER FILE:

#define IDM_ABOUT    10
#define IDM_INPUT    20
#define IDM_EXIT     30

#define DM_TITLE     300
#define DM_XLABEL    301
#define DM_YLABEL    302
#define DM_P1        303
#define DM_P2        304
#define DM_P3        305
```

```
#define DM_P4        306
#define DM_P5        307
#define DM_P6        308
#define DM_P7        309
#define DM_P8        310
#define DM_P9        311
#define DM_P10       312


THE 25BAR.RC RESOURCE SCRIPT FILE:

#include <windows.h>
#include <afxres.h>
#include "25BARR.h"

BarMenu   MENU
BEGIN
  POPUP "Bar_Chart"
  BEGIN
    MENUITEM "About Box...",   IDM_ABOUT
    MENUITEM "Bar Values...",  IDM_INPUT
    MENUITEM "Exit",           IDM_EXIT
  END
END


rcinclude 25BAR.dlg


THE 25BAR.DLG DIALOG SCRIPT FILE:

DLGINCLUDE RCDATA DISCARDABLE
BEGIN
  "25BARR.H\0"
END

AboutDlgBox DIALOG LOADONCALL MOVEABLE DISCARDABLE
            14,22,200,75
            STYLE WS_BORDER|WS_CAPTION|
            WS_DLGFRAME|WS_POPUP
            CAPTION "About Box"
BEGIN
  CONTROL "A Bar Chart Application",-1,"Static",
          SS_CENTER|WS_GROUP,30,5,144,8
  CONTROL "A Simple Foundation Class For Windows Application",
          -1,"Static",SS_CENTER|WS_GROUP,30,17,144,8
```

```
    CONTROL "By William H. Murray and Chris H. Pappas",-1,
            "Static",SS_CENTER|WS_GROUP,28,28,144,8
    CONTROL "OK",IDOK,"Button",BS_DEFPUSHBUTTON|WS_GROUP|
            WS_TABSTOP,84,55,32,14
    CONTROL "(c) Copyright, 1992",201,"Static",WS_GROUP,
            68,38,83,8
END

BarDlgBox DIALOG LOADONCALL MOVEABLE DISCARDABLE
          42,-10,223,209
          CAPTION "Bar Chart Data"
          STYLE WS_BORDER|WS_CAPTION|
          WS_DLGFRAME|WS_POPUP
BEGIN
  CONTROL "Bar Chart Title:",100,"button",
          BS_GROUPBOX|WS_TABSTOP|WS_CHILD,5,11,212,89
  CONTROL "Bar Chart Heights",101,"button",
          BS_GROUPBOX|WS_TABSTOP|WS_CHILD,5,105,212,90
  CONTROL "Title: ",-1,"static",SS_LEFT|WS_CHILD,
          43,35,28,8
  CONTROL "",DM_TITLE,"edit",ES_LEFT|WS_BORDER|WS_TABSTOP|
          WS_CHILD,75,30,137,12
  CONTROL "x-axis label:",-1,"static",SS_LEFT|
          WS_CHILD,15,55,55,8
  CONTROL "",DM_XLABEL,"edit",ES_LEFT|WS_BORDER|WS_TABSTOP|
          WS_CHILD,75,50,135,12
  CONTROL "y-axis label:",-1,"static",SS_LEFT|
          WS_CHILD,15,75,60,8
  CONTROL "",DM_YLABEL,"edit",ES_LEFT|WS_BORDER|WS_TABSTOP|
          WS_CHILD,75,70,135,12
  CONTROL "Bar #1: ",-1,"static",SS_LEFT|
          WS_CHILD,45,125,40,8
  CONTROL "Bar #2: ",-1,"static",SS_LEFT|
          WS_CHILD,45,140,40,8
  CONTROL "Bar #3: ",-1,"static",SS_LEFT|
          WS_CHILD,45,155,40,8
  CONTROL "Bar #4: ",-1,"static",SS_LEFT|
          WS_CHILD,45,170,40,8
  CONTROL "Bar #5: ",-1,"static",SS_LEFT|
          WS_CHILD,45,185,40,8
  CONTROL "Bar #6: ",-1,"static",SS_LEFT|
          WS_CHILD,130,125,40,8
  CONTROL "Bar #7: ",-1,"static",SS_LEFT|
          WS_CHILD,130,140,40,8
  CONTROL "Bar #8: ",-1,"static",SS_LEFT|
```

```
            WS_CHILD,130,155,40,8
  CONTROL "Bar #9: ",-1,"static",SS_LEFT|
          WS_CHILD,130,170,40,8
  CONTROL "Bar #10:",-1,"static",SS_LEFT|
          WS_CHILD,130,185,45,8
  CONTROL "10",DM_P1,"edit",ES_LEFT|WS_BORDER|WS_TABSTOP|
          WS_CHILD,90,120,30,12
  CONTROL "20",DM_P2,"edit",ES_LEFT|WS_BORDER|WS_TABSTOP|
          WS_CHILD,90,135,30,12
  CONTROL "50",DM_P3,"edit",ES_LEFT|WS_BORDER|WS_TABSTOP|
          WS_CHILD,90,150,30,12
  CONTROL "40",DM_P4,"edit",ES_LEFT|WS_BORDER|WS_TABSTOP|
          WS_CHILD,90,165,30,12
  CONTROL "0",DM_P5,"edit",ES_LEFT|WS_BORDER|WS_TABSTOP|
          WS_CHILD,90,180,30,12
  CONTROL "0",DM_P6,"edit",ES_LEFT|WS_BORDER|WS_TABSTOP|
          WS_CHILD,180,120,30,12
  CONTROL "0",DM_P7,"edit",ES_LEFT|WS_BORDER|WS_TABSTOP|
          WS_CHILD,180,135,30,12
  CONTROL "0",DM_P8,"edit",ES_LEFT|WS_BORDER|WS_TABSTOP|
          WS_CHILD,180,150,30,12
  CONTROL "0",DM_P9,"edit",ES_LEFT|WS_BORDER|WS_TABSTOP|
          WS_CHILD,180,165,30,12
  CONTROL "0",DM_P10,"edit",ES_LEFT|WS_BORDER|WS_TABSTOP|
          WS_CHILD,180,180,30,12
  CONTROL "OK",IDOK,"button",BS_PUSHBUTTON|WS_TABSTOP|
          WS_CHILD,54,195,24,14
  CONTROL "Cancel",IDCANCEL,"button",BS_PUSHBUTTON|
          WS_TABSTOP|WS_CHILD,124,195,34,14
END


THE 25BAR.CPP APPLICATION FILE:


//
//  25BAR.CPP
//  A Presentation Quality Bar Chart Application
//  Using Microsoft C++ Foundation Classes
//  Copyright (c) William H. Murray and Chris H. Pappas, 1992
//

#include <afxwin.h>
#include <string.h>
#include <math.h>
#include <stdlib.h>
```

```
#include "25BARR.h"    // resource ids
#include "25BAR.h"

#define maxnumbar 10

char szTString[80]="(bar chart title area)";
char szXString[80]="x-axis label";
char szYString[80]="y-axis label";
int iBarSize[maxnumbar]={20,10,40,50};
int m_cxClient,m_cyClient;

CTheApp theApp;

CMainWnd::CMainWnd()
{
  Create((AfxRegisterWndClass(CS_HREDRAW|CS_VREDRAW,
        LoadCursor(NULL,IDC_CROSS),
        GetStockObject(WHITE_BRUSH),NULL)),
        "Bar Chart Foundation Class Application",
        WS_OVERLAPPEDWINDOW,rectDefault,NULL,"BarMenu");
}

void CMainWnd::OnSize(UINT,int x,int y)
{
  m_cxClient=x;
  m_cyClient=y;
}

void CMainWnd::OnPaint()
{
  CPaintDC dc(this);
  static DWORD dwColor[10]={RGB(0,0,0),        //black
                            RGB(255,0,0),      //red
                            RGB(0,255,0),      //green
                            RGB(0,0,255),      //blue
                            RGB(255,255,0),    //yellow
                            RGB(255,0,255),    //magenta
                            RGB(0,255,255),    //cyan
                            RGB(0,80,80),      //blend 1
                            RGB(80,80,80),     //blend 2
                            RGB(255,255,255)}; //white
  CFont newfont;
  CFont* oldfont;
  CBrush newbrush;
  CBrush* oldbrush;
```

```
int i,iNBars,iBarWidth,iBarMax;
int ilenMaxLabel;
int x1,x2,y1,y2;
int iBarSizeScaled[maxnumbar];
char sbuffer[10],*strptr;

//---------- your routines below ----------------------//

iNBars=0;
for (i=0;i<maxnumbar;i++)
{
  if(iBarSize[i]!=0) iNBars++;
}

iBarWidth=400/iNBars;

// Find bar with maximum height and scale
iBarMax=iBarSize[0];
for(i=0;i<iNBars;i++)
  if (iBarMax<iBarSize[i]) iBarMax=iBarSize[i];

// Convert maximum y value to a string
strptr=_itoa(iBarMax,sbuffer,10);
ilenMaxLabel=strlen(sbuffer);

// Scale bars in array. Highest bar = 270
for (i=0;i<iNBars;i++)
  iBarSizeScaled[i]=iBarSize[i]*(270/iBarMax);

// Create custom view port and map mode
dc.SetMapMode(MM_ISOTROPIC);
dc.SetWindowExt(640,400);
dc.SetViewportExt(m_cxClient,m_cyClient);
dc.SetViewportOrg(0,0);

// Print text to window if large enough
if (m_cxClient > 200) {
  newfont.CreateFont(12,12,0,0,FW_BOLD,
                     FALSE,FALSE,FALSE,OEM_CHARSET,
                     OUT_DEFAULT_PRECIS,
                     CLIP_DEFAULT_PRECIS,
                     DEFAULT_QUALITY,
                     VARIABLE_PITCH|FF_ROMAN,
                     "Roman");
    oldfont=dc.SelectObject(&newfont);
```

```
      dc.TextOut((300-(strlen(szTString)*10/2)),
               15,szTString,strlen(szTString));
      dc.TextOut((300-(strlen(szXString)*10/2)),
               365,szXString,strlen(szXString));
      dc.TextOut((90-ilenMaxLabel*12),
               70,strptr,ilenMaxLabel);
      newfont.CreateFont(12,12,900,900,FW_BOLD,
                         FALSE,FALSE,FALSE,
                         OEM_CHARSET,
                         OUT_DEFAULT_PRECIS,
                         CLIP_DEFAULT_PRECIS,
                         DEFAULT_QUALITY,
                         VARIABLE_PITCH|FF_ROMAN,
                         "Roman");
      oldfont=dc.SelectObject(&newfont);
      dc.TextOut(50,200+(strlen(szXString)*10/2),
               szYString,strlen(szYString));

      // delete font objects
      dc.SelectObject(oldfont);
      newfont.DeleteObject();
    }

  // Draw coordinate axis
  dc.MoveTo(99,49);
  dc.LineTo(99,350);
  dc.LineTo(500,350);
  dc.MoveTo(99,350);

  // Initial values
  x1=100;
  y1=350;
  x2=x1+iBarWidth;

  // Draw Each Bar
  for(i=0;i<iNBars;i++)
  {
    newbrush.CreateSolidBrush(dwColor[i]);
    oldbrush=dc.SelectObject(&newbrush);
    y2=350-iBarSizeScaled[i];
    dc.Rectangle(x1,y1,x2,y2);
    x1=x2;
    x2+=iBarWidth;
  }
```

```
  // delete brush objects
  dc.SelectObject(oldbrush);
  newbrush.DeleteObject();

//---------- your routines above ----------------------//
}

int CMainWnd::OnCreate(LPCREATESTRUCT)
{
  UpdateWindow();
  return (0);
}

void CMainWnd::OnAbout()
{
  CModalDialog about("AboutDlgBox",this);
  about.DoModal();
}

void CBarDataDialog::OnOK()
{
  GetDlgItemText(DM_TITLE,szTString,80);
  GetDlgItemText(DM_XLABEL,szXString,80);
  GetDlgItemText(DM_YLABEL,szYString,80);
  iBarSize[0]=GetDlgItemInt(DM_P1,NULL,0);
  iBarSize[1]=GetDlgItemInt(DM_P2,NULL,0);
  iBarSize[2]=GetDlgItemInt(DM_P3,NULL,0);
  iBarSize[3]=GetDlgItemInt(DM_P4,NULL,0);
  iBarSize[4]=GetDlgItemInt(DM_P5,NULL,0);
  iBarSize[5]=GetDlgItemInt(DM_P6,NULL,0);
  iBarSize[6]=GetDlgItemInt(DM_P7,NULL,0);
  iBarSize[7]=GetDlgItemInt(DM_P8,NULL,0);
  iBarSize[8]=GetDlgItemInt(DM_P9,NULL,0);
  iBarSize[9]=GetDlgItemInt(DM_P10,NULL,0);

  CModalDialog::OnOK();
}

void CMainWnd::OnBarData()
{
  CBarDataDialog dlgBarData(this);
  if (dlgBarData.DoModal()==IDOK)
  {
    InvalidateRect(NULL,TRUE);
    UpdateWindow();
```

```
  }
};

void CMainWnd::OnExit()
{
  DestroyWindow();
}

BEGIN_MESSAGE_MAP(CMainWnd,CFrameWnd)
  ON_WM_PAINT()
  ON_WM_SIZE()
  ON_WM_CREATE()
  ON_COMMAND(IDM_ABOUT,OnAbout)
  ON_COMMAND(IDM_INPUT,OnBarData)
  ON_COMMAND(IDM_EXIT,OnExit)
END_MESSAGE_MAP()

BOOL CTheApp::InitInstance()
{
  m_pMainWnd=new CMainWnd();
  m_pMainWnd->ShowWindow(m_nCmdShow);
  m_pMainWnd->UpdateWindow();

  return TRUE;
}
```

The 25BAR Command-line Make, 25BAR.MAK Project Make, and 25BAR.DEF Module Definition Files

The make files, 25BAR and 25BAR.MAK, allow the user to compile from the DOS command line or from within the PWB integrated environment. Both files include Windows resources that are compiled with the Microsoft resource compiler and added to a final executable file by the linker. The previous example discussed how these features are added and compiled with the use of the command-line make file.

A style of project file is adopted here that is used by Microsoft in building its Foundation Class library examples. This project file allows the inclusion of debug information for use during the early development of an application. Refer to Chapter 2 and your Microsoft documentation for additional details on the use of the PWB integrated environment.

The module definition file, 25BAR.DEF, is also added at link time. The module definition file remains unchanged, except for the application name.

The 25bar.h Header File

This application will use many of the features of the previous application. For example, note the similar function declarations in **CMainWnd** and the message map.

```
afx_msg void On Paint();
afx_msg void OnSize(UINT,int,int);
afx_msg int  OnCreate(LPCREATESTRUCT cs);
afx_msg void OnAbout();
afx_msg void OnBarData();
afx_msg void OnExit();
```

The creation of the about and data entry dialog boxes parallels the last example. In this application, however, the data entry dialog box will process more user input than the previous example. You may want to review the information dealing with dialog boxes in the previous example at this time.

The 25bar.h Resource Header, 25BAR.RC Resource Script, and 25BAR.DLG Dialog Script Files

The 25barr.h, 25BAR.RC, and 25BAR.DLG files are combined by the Microsoft resource compiler into a single compiled Windows resource, 25BAR.RES.

The 25bar.h resource header file contains three menu identification values: IDM_ABOUT, IDM_INPUT, and IDM_EXIT.

Thirteen identification values are also included for use by the modal dialog box. Three are for titles and labels: DM_TITLE, DM_XLABEL, and DM_YLABEL. The remaining ten values, DM_P1 to DM_P10, are for retrieving the height of the individual bars. They will be integer values.

The resource script file, 25BAR.RC, contains a description of the application's menu, which is shown in Figure 25-8. Compare the menu title and features to the text used in creating the menu in the resource file.

The dialog script file, 25BAR.DLG, contains a description of the application's about and data entry dialog boxes. The data entry dialog box is shown in Figure 25-9. The about dialog box is shown here:

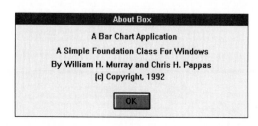

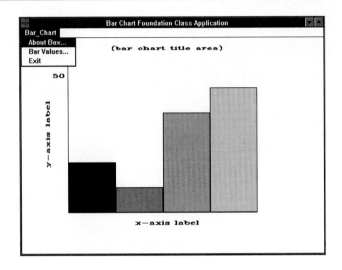

Figure 25-8.   *A menu for the 25BAR application*

The Dialog Editor, provided with the Microsoft C/C++ compiler, was used to construct both dialog boxes. The Dialog Editor automatically creates the dialog resource script file with the .DLG extension.

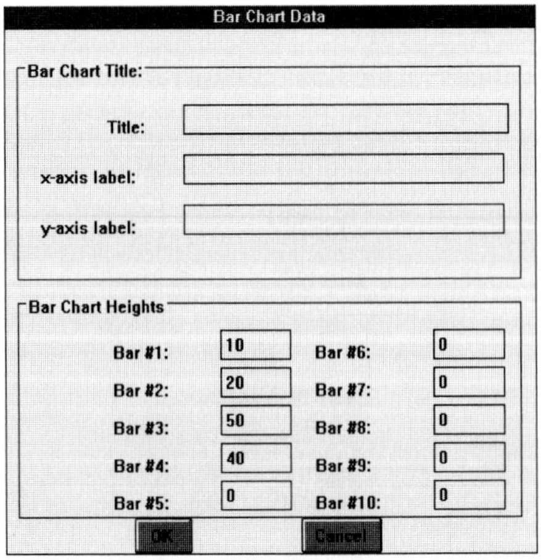

Figure 25-9.   *The data entry dialog box for the 25BAR application*

The 25BAR.CPP Application File

This section concentrates on those features that are new to the applications developed in this chapter. The 25BAR.CPP application will allow the user to draw a presentation-quality bar chart in the client area of a window. With the use of a modal dialog box, the user can specify a chart title, axis labels, and the height of up to ten bars. The chart will then be correctly scaled to the window, with each bar's color selected from an array of predefined values.

The maximum number of bars, *maxnumbar*, is set to ten at the start of the application.

```
#define maxnumbar 10
```

This value can be changed slightly, but remember that a good bar chart doesn't crowd too many bars on a single chart.

Global data types hold initial bar chart values for titles, axes labels, and bar heights:

```
char szTString[80]="(bar chart title area)";
char szXString[80]="x-axis label";
char szYString[80]="y-axis label";
int iBarSize[maxnumbar]={20,10,40,50};
```

The size of the client area will also be saved as a global value. These are the same variable names used in the previous example:

```
int m_cxClient,m_cyClient;
```

By keeping track of the client area size, this bar chart can be scaled to fit the current window size.

Bar colors are selected from the *dwColor* array, in a sequential manner. If the bar chart has three bars, they will be black, red, and green. Colors can be exchanged if you so desire.

The **CFont** and **CBrush** classes permit the font or brush object to be passed to any CDC (base class for display context) member function. New fonts will be needed for drawing the chart title and axes. Brushes were discussed earlier in this chapter. Additional information for these classes is available in your Microsoft *Class Libraries Reference* manual. Here is the syntax used to create a new font and brush object:

```
CFont newfont;
CFont* oldfont;
CBrush newbrush;
CBrush* oldbrush;
```

Manipulating Bar Data

It is first necessary to determine how many bar values are being held in the global array, *iBarSize*. This can be determined by counting values until the first zero value is encountered:

```
iNBars=0;
for (i=0;i<maxnumbar;i++)
{
  if(iBarSize[i]!=0) iNBars++;
}
```

Data values are returned to this array whenever the data entry dialog box is closed.

The width of each bar drawn in the chart is dependent upon the total number of bars. The chart will always be drawn to the same width. Bar width is determined with

```
iBarWidth=400/iNBars;
```

The height of each bar is determined relative to the largest bar value entered by the user. The largest bar value is always drawn to the same chart height. The size of the largest bar value is easy to determine:

```
// Find bar with maximum height and scale
iBarMax=iBarSize[0];
for(i=0;i<iNBars;i++)
  if (iBarMax<iBarSize[i]) iBarMax=iBarSize[i];
```

This chart will also print the height of the largest bar value on the vertical axis. The **_itoa()** function is used to convert this value to a string.

```
// Convert maximum y value to a string
strptr=_itoa(iBarMax,sbuffer,10);
ilenMaxLabel=strlen(sbuffer);
```

The remaining bars in the array are then scaled to the largest bar's value:

```
// Scale bars in array. Highest bar = 270
for (i=0;i<iNBars;i++)
  iBarSizeScaled[i]=iBarSize[i]*(270/iBarMax);
```

Preparing the Window

Before it is time to begin drawing in the window's client area, the mapping mode, window extent, viewport extent, and origin are set:

```
// Create custom view port and map mode
dc.SetMapMode(MM_ISOTROPIC);
dc.SetWindowExt(640,400);
dc.SetViewportExt(m_cxClient,m_cyClient);
dc.SetViewportOrg(0,0);
```

This same action was taken for the previous example to ensure that as the window is sized, the chart will remain proportionally the same size. As a matter of fact, in this application the chart can be reduced to an icon, with all of the bars still clearly visible. See the last application for additional details on these function calls.

Drawing Text to the Window

This application needs several font sizes and orientations. Before continuing, let's look at how these can be created. There are actually two ways to create and manipulate fonts in Windows. This example uses the **CreateFont()** function.

What Is a Font?   A *font* can be defined as a complete set of characters of the same typeface and size. Fonts include letters, punctuation marks, and additional symbols. The size of a font is measured in points. For example, 12-point Arial is a different font from 12-point Times New Roman, 14-point Times New Roman, or 12-point Lucida Bright. A *point* is the smallest unit of measure used in typography. There are 12 points in a pica and 72 points in an inch.

A *typeface* is a basic character design that is defined by a stroke width and a serif (a smaller line used to finish off a main stroke of a letter, as at the top and bottom of the uppercase letter "M"). A font represents a complete set of characters from one specific typeface, all with a certain size and style, such as italics or bold. Usually the system owns all of the font resources and shares them with the application program. Fonts are not usually compiled into the final executable version of a program.

Applications such as 25BAR.CPP treat fonts like other drawing objects. Windows supplies several fonts: System, Terminal, Courier, Helvetica, Modern, Roman, Script, and Times Roman, as well as several new TrueType fonts. These are called *GDI-supplied fonts*.

The CreateFont() Function Syntax   The **CreateFont()** function is defined in the windows.h header file. This function selects a logical font from the GDI's pool of physical fonts that most closely matches the characteristics specified by the developer in the function call. Once created, this logical font can be selected by any device. The syntax for **CreateFont()** is

```
CreateFont(Height,Width,Escapement,Orientation,Weight
          Italic,Underline,StrikeOut,CharSet,
          OutputPrecision,ClipPrecision,Quality,
          PitchAndFamily,Facename)
```

With 14 parameters, **CreateFont** requires quite a bit of skill when used. Table 25-1 gives a brief description of the **CreateFont()** parameters.

The first time **CreateFont()** is called, the parameters are set to the following values:

```
Height = 12
Width  = 12
Escapement = 0
```

CreateFont() Parameters	Description
(int) Height	Desired font height in logical units
(int) Width	Average font width in logical units
(int) Escapement	Angle (tenths of a degree) for each line written in the font
(int) Orientation	Angle (tenths of a degree) for each character's baseline
(int) Weight	Weight of font (0 to 1000). 400 is normal, 700 is bold
(byte) Italic	Italic font
(byte) Underline	Underline font
(byte) StrikeOut	Struck out fonts (redline)
(byte) CharSet	Character set (ANSI_CHARSET, OEM_CHARSET)
(byte) OutputPrecision	How closely must output match the requested specifications? (OUT_CHARACTER_PRECIS, OUT_DEFAULT_PRECIS, OUT_STRING_PRECIS, OUT_STROKE_PRECIS)
(byte) ClipPrecision	How to clip characters outside of clipping range. (CLIP_CHARACTER_PRECIS, CLIP_DEFAULT_PRECIS, CLIP_STROKE_PRECIS)
(byte) Quality	How carefully the logical attributes are mapped to the physical font. (DEFAULT_QUALITY, DRAFT_QUALITY, PROOF_QUALITY)
(byte) PitchAndFamily	Pitch and family of font. (DEFAULT_PITCH, FIXED_PITCH, PROOF_QUALITY, FF_DECORATIVE, FF_DONTCARE, FF_MODERN, FF_ROMAN, FF_SCRIPT, FF_SWISS)
(lpstr) Facename	A string pointing to the typeface name of the desired font

Table 25-1.   *CreateFont() Parameters*

```
Orientation = 0
Weight = FW_BOLD
Italic = FALSE
Underline = FALSE
StrikeOut = FALSE
CharSet = OEM_CHARSET
OutputPrecision = OUT_DEFAULT_PRECIS
ClipPrecision = CLIP_DEFAULT_PRECIS
Quality = DEFAULT_QUALITY
PitchAndFamily = VARIABLE_PITCH | FF_ROMAN
Facename = "Roman"
```

An attempt will be made to find a font to match the preceding specifications. This font will be used to print a horizontal string of text in the window. The next time **CreateFont()** is called, the parameters are set to the following values:

```
Height = 12
Width  = 12
Escapement = 900
Orientation = 900
Weight = FW_BOLD
Italic = FALSE
Underline = FALSE
StrikeOut = FALSE
CharSet = OEM_CHARSET
OutputPrecision = OUT_DEFAULT_PRECIS
ClipPrecision = CLIP_DEFAULT_PRECIS
Quality = DEFAULT_QUALITY
PitchAndFamily = VARIABLE_PITCH | FF_ROMAN
Facename = "Roman"
```

Again, an attempt will be made to find a match to the preceding specifications. Examine the listing and notice that only *Escapement* and *Orientation* are changed. Both of these parameters use angle values specified in tenths of a degree. Thus, 900 represents an angle of 90.0 degrees. The *Escapement* parameter rotates the line of text from horizontal to vertical. Orientation rotates each character, in this application, by 90.0 degrees. This font will be used to print a vertical axis label in the application.

Here is how the vertical axis label was printed in this application:

```
newfont.CreateFont(12,12,900,900,FW_BOLD,
                   FALSE,FALSE,FALSE,
                   OEM_CHARSET,
                   OUT_DEFAULT_PRECIS,
                   CLIP_DEFAULT_PRECIS,
```

```
                            DEFAULT_QUALITY,
                            VARIABLE_PITCH|FF_ROMAN,
                            "Roman");
oldfont=dc.SelectObject(&newfont);
dc.TextOut(50,200+(strlen(szXString)*10/2),
           szYString,strlen(szYString));
```

When developing your own applications, be sure to examine the documentation on the **CreateFont**() function and additional typefaces available for your use.

Drawing the Axes and Bars

Simple x and y coordinate axes are drawn with the use of the **MoveTo**() and **LineTo**() functions:

```
// Draw coordinate axis
dc.MoveTo(99,49);
dc.LineTo(99,350);
dc.LineTo(500,350);
dc.MoveTo(99,350);
```

Preparation is then made for drawing each bar. The first bar always starts at position 100,350 on the chart, as defined by *x1* and *y1*. The width of the first bar and all subsequent bars is calculated from the last drawing position and the width of each bar. The second x value is defined by *x2*.

```
// Initial values
x1=100;
y1=350;
x2=x1+iBarWidth;
```

Bars are drawn by retrieving the scaled bar height value from **iBarSizeScaled**. This scaled value, saved in *y2*, is used in the **Rectangle**() function. Since the **Rectangle**() function draws a closed figure, the figure will be filled with the current brush color. The color selected from the array is incremented during each pass through the loop.

```
// Draw Each Bar
for(i=0;i<iNBars;i++)
{
  newbrush.CreateSolidBrush(dwColor[i]);
  oldbrush=dc.SelectObject(&newbrush);
  y2=350-iBarSizeScaled[i];
  dc.Rectangle(x1,y1,x2,y2);
```

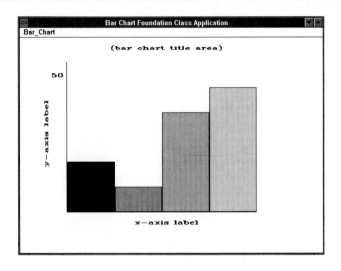

Figure 25-10.   *The default bar chart for the 25BAR application*

```
  x1=x2;
  x2+=iBarWidth;
}
```

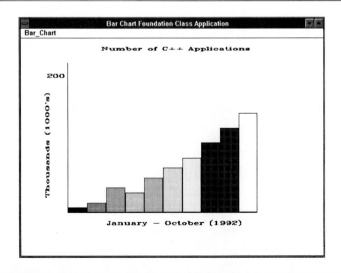

Figure 25-11.   *A custom bar chart with chart title and labels*

After each bar is drawn, the values in *x1* and *x2* are updated to point to the next bar's position. This process is repeated in the **for** loop until all bars are drawn.

Running 25BAR

Compile the 25BAR application either from the DOS command line or from within the PWB integrated environment. When you execute the application, a default bar chart, similar to the one in Figure 25-10, will be drawn in the window. A custom bar chart, as shown in Figure 25-11, can be created by entering a chart title, axis labels, and unique bar values.

You can continue the development of this application by adding axis tick marks, a legend, and so on. Customization is limited only by your imagination.

Part VI

Appendixes

Appendix *A*

Extended ASCII Table

Decimal	Hexadecimal	Symbol		Decimal	Hexadecimal	Symbol
0	0			16	10	►
1	1	☺		17	11	◄
2	2	☻		18	12	↕
3	3	♥		19	13	‼
4	4	♦		20	14	¶
5	5	♣		21	15	§
6	6	♠		22	16	▬
7	7	✚		23	17	↨
8	8	◘		24	18	↑
9	9	○		25	19	↓
10	A	◙		26	1A	→
11	B	♂		27	1B	←
12	C	♀		28	1C	∟
13	D	♪		29	1D	↔
14	E	♫		30	1E	▲
15	F	☼		31	1F	▼

Decimal	Hexadecimal	Symbol	Decimal	Hexadecimal	Symbol
32	20		66	42	B
33	21	!	67	43	C
34	22	"	68	44	D
35	23	#	69	45	E
36	24	$	70	46	F
37	25	%	71	47	G
38	26	&	72	48	H
39	27	'	73	49	I
40	28	(	74	4A	J
41	29	)	75	4B	K
42	2A	*	76	4C	L
43	2B	+	77	4D	M
44	2C	,	78	4E	N
45	2D	-	79	4F	O
46	2E	.	80	50	P
47	2F	/	81	51	Q
48	30	0	82	52	R
49	31	1	83	53	S
50	32	2	84	54	T
51	33	3	85	55	U
52	34	4	86	56	V
53	35	5	87	57	W
54	36	6	88	58	X
55	37	7	89	59	Y
56	38	8	90	5A	Z
57	39	9	91	5B	[
58	3A	:	92	5C	\
59	3B	;	93	5D	]
60	3C	<	94	5E	^
61	3D	=	95	5F	_
62	3E	>	96	60	`
63	3F	?	97	61	a
64	40	@	98	62	b
65	41	A	99	63	c

Decimal	Hexadecimal	Symbol		Decimal	Hexadecimal	Symbol
100	64	d		134	86	å
101	65	e		135	87	ç
102	66	f		136	88	ê
103	67	g		137	89	ë
104	68	h		138	8A	è
105	69	i		139	8B	ï
106	6A	j		140	8C	î
107	6B	k		141	8D	ì
108	6C	l		142	8E	Ä
109	6D	m		143	8F	Å
110	6E	n		144	90	É
111	6F	o		145	91	æ
112	70	p		146	92	Æ
113	71	q		147	93	ô
114	72	r		148	94	ö
115	73	s		149	95	ò
116	74	t		150	96	û
117	75	u		151	97	ù
118	76	v		152	98	ÿ
119	77	w		153	99	Ö
120	78	x		154	9A	Ü
121	79	y		155	9B	¢
122	7A	z		156	9C	£
123	7B	{		157	9D	¥
124	7C	¦		158	9E	Pt
125	7D	}		159	9F	ƒ
126	7E	~		160	A0	á
127	7F			161	A1	í
128	80	Ç		162	A2	ó
129	81	ü		163	A3	ú
130	82	é		164	A4	ñ
131	83	â		165	A5	Ñ
132	84	ä		166	A6	ª
133	85	à		167	A7	º

Decimal	Hexadecimal	Symbol	Decimal	Hexadecimal	Symbol
168	A8	¿	202	CA	╩
169	A9	⌐	203	CB	╦
170	AA	¬	204	CC	╠
171	AB	½	205	CD	=
172	AC	¼	206	CE	╬
173	AD	¡	207	CF	╧
174	AE	«	208	D0	╨
175	AF	»	209	D1	╤
176	B0	░	210	D2	╥
177	B1	▒	211	D3	╙
178	B2	▓	212	D4	╘
179	B3	│	213	D5	╒
180	B4	┤	214	D6	╓
181	B5	╡	215	D7	╫
182	B6	╢	216	D8	╪
183	B7	╖	217	D9	┘
184	B8	╕	218	DA	┌
185	B9	╣	219	DB	█
186	BA	║	220	DC	▄
187	BB	╗	221	DD	▌
188	BC	╝	222	DE	▐
189	BD	╜	223	DF	▀
190	BE	╛	224	E0	α
191	BF	┐	225	E1	β
192	C0	└	226	E2	Γ
193	C1	┴	227	E3	π
194	C2	┬	228	E4	Σ
195	C3	├	229	E5	σ
196	C4	─	230	E6	μ
197	C5	┼	231	E7	τ
198	C6	╞	232	E8	φ
199	C7	╟	233	E9	θ
200	C8	╚	234	EA	Ω
201	C9	╔	235	EB	δ

Decimal	Hexadecimal	Symbol	Decimal	Hexadecimal	Symbol
236	EC	∞	246	F6	÷
237	ED	∅	247	F7	≈
238	EE	∈	248	F8	°
239	EF	∩	249	F9	•
240	F0	≡	250	FA	·
241	F1	±	251	FB	√
242	F2	≥	252	FC	n
243	F3	≤	253	FD	2
244	F4	⌠	9254	FE	∎
245	F5	⌡	255	FF	(blank)

Appendix *B*

DOS 10H, 21H, and 33H Interrupt Parameters

This appendix contains the most popular DOS, BIOS, and MOUSE interrupts and parameters.

Screen Control with Bios-type 10H Interrupts

Syntax: INT 10H (when the following parameters are set to the required values)

Interface Control of the CRT

AH Value	Function	Input	Output
AH = 0	Set the mode of display	AL = 0	40 x 25 color text
		AL = 1	40 x 25 color text
		AL = 2	80 x 25 color text
		AL = 3	80 x 25 color text
		AL = 4	320 x 200 4-color graphics
		AL = 5	320 x 200 4-color graphics

AH Value	Function	Input	Output
		AL = 6	640 x 200 2-color graphics
		AL = 7	80 x 25 monochrome text
		AL = 13	320 x 200 16-color graphics
		AL = 14	640 x 200 16-color graphics
		AL = 15	640 x 350 monochrome graphics
		AL = 16	640 x 350 16-color graphics
		AL = 17	640 x 480 2-color graphics
		AL = 18	640 x 480 16-color graphics
		AL = 19	320 x 200 256-color graphics
AH = 1	Set cursor type	CH =	Bits 4-0 start of line for cursor
		CL =	Bits 4-0 end of line for cursor
AH = 2	Set cursor position	DH =	Row
		DL =	Column
		BH =	Page number of display (zero for graphics)
AH = 3	Read cursor position		DH = row
			DL = column
			CH = cursor mode
			CL = cursor mode
			BH = page number of display
AH = 4	Get light pen position		AH = 0, switch not down/ triggered
			AH = 1, valid answers as follows:
			DH = row
			DL = column
			CH = graph line (0-199)
			BX = graph column (0-319/639)
AH = 5	Set active display page	AL =	New page value
			(0-7) modes 0 and 1
			(0-3) modes 2 and 3
AH = 6	Scroll active page up	AL =	Number of lines, 0 for entire screen
		CH =	Row, upper-left corner
		CL =	Column, upper-left corner
		DH =	Row, lower-right corner
		DL =	Column, lower-right corner
		BH =	Attribute to be used

AH Value	Function	Input	Output
AH = 7	Scroll active page down	AL =	Number of lines, 0 for entire screen
		CH =	Row, upper-left corner
		CL =	Column, upper-left corner
		DH =	Row, lower-right corner
		DL =	Column, lower-right corner
		BH =	Attribute to be used

Handling Characters

AH Value	Function	Input	Output
AH = 8	Read attribute/ character at cursor position	BH =	Display page
		AL =	Character read
		AH =	Attribute of character
AH = 9	Write attribute/ character at cursor position	BH =	Display page
		CX =	Count of characters to write
		AL =	Character to write
		BL =	Attribute of character
AH = 10	Write character at cursor position	BH =	Display page
		CX =	Count of characters to write
		AL =	Character to write

Graphics Interface

AH Value	Function	Input	Output
AH = 11	Select color palette	BH =	Palette ID (0-127)
		BL =	Color for above ID
			0—background (0-15)
			1—palette
			0—green(1), red(2), yellow(3)
			1—cyan(1), magenta(2),
			white (3)
AH = 12	Draw dot on screen	DX =	Row (0-199)
		CX =	Column (0-319/639)
		AL =	Color of dot

AH Value	Function	Input	Output
AH = 13	Read dot information	DX =	Row (0-199)
		CX =	Column (0-319/639)
		AL =	Value of dot

ASCII Teletype Output

AH Value	Function	Input	Output
AH = 14	Write to active page	AL =	Character to write
		BL =	Foreground color
AH = 15	Get video state	AL =	Current mode
		AH =	Number of screen columns
		BH =	Current display page
AH = 16	(Reserved)		
AH = 17	(Reserved)		
AH = 18	(Reserved)		
AH = 19	Write string	ES:BP =	Point to string
		CX =	Length of string
		DX =	Cursor position for start
		BH =	Page number
		AL = 0	BL = attribute (char,char, char...char) cursor not moved
		AL = 1	BL = attribute (char,char, char...char) cursor is moved
		AL = 2	(char,attr,char,attr...) cursor not moved
		AL = 3	(char,attr,char,attr...) cursor is moved
AH = 1A	R/W display combination code		
AH = 1B	Return functionality state information		
AH = 1C	Save/restore video state		

Specifications and Requirements for the DOS 21H Interrupt

Syntax: INT 21H (when the following parameters are set to the required values)

AH Value	Function	Input	Output
AH = 0	End of program		(similar to INT 20H)
AH = 1	Wait and display keyboard character with CTRL-BREAK check		AL = character entered
AH = 2	Display character with CTRL-BREAK check	DL =	Character to display
AH = 3	Asynchronous character input		AL = character entered
AH = 4	Asynchronous character output	DL =	Character to send
AH = 5	Character to write	DL =	Character to write
AH = 6	Input keyboard character	DL =	0FFH if character entered, 0 if none
AH = 7	Wait for keyboard character (no display)		AL = character entered
AH = 8	Wait for keyboard character (no display— CTRL-BREAK check)		AL = character entered
AH = 9	String display	DS:DX =	Address of string; must end with $ sentinel
AH = A	Keyboard string to buffer	DS:DX =	Address of buffer. First byte = size, second = number of characters read
AH = B	Input keyboard status		AL—no character = 0FFH character = 0
AH = C	Clear keyboard buffer and call function	AL =	1,6,7,8,0A (function #)
AH = D	Reset default disk drive	None	None

AH Value	Function	Input	Output

AH = E	Select default disk drive		AL = number of drives
			DL—0 = A drive
			    1 = B drive,
			    and so forth

AH = F	Open file with unopened FCB	DS:DX =	Location AL = 0FFH if not found AL = 0H if found
AH = 10	Close file with FCB	DS:DX =	Location (same as AH = 0FH)
AH = 11	Search directory for match of unopened FCB. DTA contains directory entry	DS:DX =	AL = OFFH if not found AL = 0H if found Location
AH = 12	Search (after AH = 11) for other files that match wildcard specifications		(same as AH = 11H)
AH = 13	Delete file named by FCB	DS:DX =	Location (same as AH = 11H)
AH = 14	Sequential read of open file. Number of bytes in FCB (record size)	DS:DX =	Location AL = 0 transfer OK AL = 1 end of file AL = 2 overrun DTA segment AL = 3 EOF/partial read
AH = 15	Sequential write of open file. Transfer from DTA to file, with FCB update of current record	DS:DX =	Location AL = 0 transfer OK AL = 1 disk full/ROF AL = 2 overrun DTA segment
AH = 16	Create file (length set to zero)	DS:DX =	Location (same as AH = 11H)
AH = 17	Rename file	DS:DX =	Location AL = 0 rename OK AL = 0FFH no match found
AH = 18	(DOS internal use)		

AH = 19	Drive code (default)		AL—0 = A drive
			    1 = B drive,
			    and so forth

AH = 1A	Set Data Transfer Add	DS:DX =	Points to location

AH Value	Function	Input	Output
AH = 1B	File Allocation Table	DS:DX =	Address of FAT DX = number of units AL = record/alloc. unit CX = sector size (same as AH = 1B)
AH = 1C	Disk drive FAT information	DL =	Drive number: 0 = default 1 = A 2 = B
AH = 1D	(DOS internal use)		
AH = 1E	(DOS internal use)		
AH = 1F	(DOS internal use)		
AH = 20	(DOS internal use)		
AH = 21	Random read file	DS:DX =	Location of FCB (same as AH = 14H)
AH = 22	Random write file	DS:DX =	(same as AH = 21H)
AH = 23	Set file size	DS:DX =	Location of FCB AL = 0 if set AL = 0FFH if not set
AH = 24	Random record size	DS:DX =	Location of FCB
AH = 25	Set interrupt vector (change address)	DS:DX = AL =	Address of vector table Interrupt number
AH = 26	Create program segment	DX =	Segment number
AH = 27	Random block read	DS:DX =	Address of FCB AL—0 read OK 1 EOF 2 wrap around 3 partial record
AH = 28	Random block write	DS:DX =	Address of FCB AL—0 write OK 1 lack of space
AH = 29	Parse file name	DS:SI = DS:DI =	Point to command line Memory location for FCB AL = bits to set options
AH = 2A	Read date		CX = year (80 to 99) DH = month (1 to 12) DL = day (1 to 31)

AH Value	Function	Input	Output
AH = 2B	Set date		CX & DX (same as above) AL—0 if valid 0FF if not valid
AH = 2C	Read time		CH = hours (0-23) CL = minutes (0-59)
AH = 2D	Set time		CX & DX (same as above) AL—0 if valid 0FF if not valid
AH = 2E	Set verify state	DL = AL =	0 0 = verify off 1 = verify on
AH = 2F	Get DTA	ES:BX =	Get DTA into ES
AH = 30	Get DOS version		AL = version number AH = sub number
AH = 31	Terminate and remain resident		AL = exit code DX = memory size in paragraphs
AH = 32	(DOS internal use)		
AH = 33	CTRL-BREAK check	AL = AL =	0, request state 1, set the state DL = 0 for off DL = 1 for on
AH = 34	(DOS internal use)		
AH = 35	Read interrupt address	AL =	Interrupt number ES:BX point to vector address
AH = 36	Disk space available	DL =	Drive (0 = default, 1 = A, 2 = B, and so forth) AX = sectors/cluster (FFFF if invalid) BX = number of free clusters CX = bytes per sector DX = total number of clusters
AH = 37	(DOS internal use)		
AH = 38	Country- dependent information (32-byte block)	DS:DX	Location of memory Date/time Currency symbol Thousands separator Decimal separator
AH = 39	Make directory	DS:DX =	Address of string for directory
AH = 3A	Remove directory	DS:DX =	Address of string for directory
AH = 3B	Change directory	DS:DX =	Address of string for new directory

AH Value	Function	Input	Output
AH = 3C	Create a file	DS:DX =	Address of string for file
			AX = file handle
		CX =	File attribute
AH = 3D	Open a file	DS:DX =	Address of string for file
		AL =	0 = open for reading
			1 = open for writing
			2 = open for both
			AX returns file handle
AH = 3E	Close a file handle	BX =	File handle
AH = 3F	Read a file or device	BX =	File handle
		CX =	Number of bytes to read
		DS:DX =	Address of buffer
			AX = number of bytes read
AH = 40	Write a file or device	BX =	File handle
		CX =	Number of bytes to write
		DS:DX =	Address of buffer
			AX = number of bytes written
AH = 41	Delete a file	DS:DX =	Address of file string
AH = 42	Move file pointer	BX =	File handle
		AL =	Pointer's starting location
		CX:DX	Number of bytes
		DX:AX	Current file pointer
AH = 43	Set file attribute	AL = 1	
		CX =	Attribute
		DS:DX =	Address of file string
AH = 45	Duplicate file handle	BX	File handle
			AX = returned file handle
AH = 46	Force duplicate file handle	BX	File handle
			CX = second file handle
AH = 47	Current directory	DL =	Drive number (0 = default, 1 = A drive, 2 = B drive)
		DS:SI =	Buffer address
			DS:SI returns address of string
AH = 48	Allocate memory	BX	Number of paragraphs
			AX = allocated block
AH = 49	Free allocated memory	ES	Segment of returned block
AH = 4A	Set block	ES	Segment block
		BX	New block size

AH Value	Function	Input	Output
AH = 4B	Load/execute program	DS:DX	Location of ASCIIZ string (drive/path/filename) AL—0 =load and execute 3 = load/no execute
AH = 4C	Terminate (exit)	AL	Binary return code (all files closed)
AH = 4D	Retrieve return code		AX returns exit code of another program
AH = 4E	Find first matching file	DS:DX	Location of ASCIIZ string (drive/path/filename) CX = search attribute DTA completed
AH = 4F	Next matching file		(AH = 4EH called first)
AH = 50	(DOS internal use)		
AH = 51	(DOS internal use)		
AH = 52	(DOS internal use)		
AH = 53	(DOS internal use)		
AH = 54	Verify state	none	AL—0 if verify off 1 if verify on
AH = 55	(DOS internal use)		
AH = 56	Rename file	DS:DX =	Address of string for old information
		ES:DI =	Address of string for new information
AH = 57	Get/set file date/time	AL	00 (return) 01 (set)
		BX	File handle
		DX and CX	Date and time information
AH = 59	Extended error code	BX =	DOS version (3.0 = 0) AX = error code BH = class of error BL = suggested action CH = where error occurred
AH = 5A	Create temporary file		CX = file attribute CF = Set on error AX = error code
		DS:DX =	Points to string
AH = 5B	Create a new file		(same as above)

Note: For DOS versions above 2.0, use AH = 36H + for file management.

Mouse Control Functions Accessed Through Interrupt 33H

Syntax: INT 33H (when the following parameters are set to the required values)

AH Value	Function	Input	Output
AX = 0	Install flag and reset	BX = CX = DX =	If AX = 0 and BX = –1 Mouse support not available AX = –1, then BX = number of supported mouse buttons
AX = 1	Show pointer	BX = CX = DX =	Does nothing if already visible, otherwise increments the pointer-draw flag by 1 Shows pointer image when pointer-draw flag = 0
AX = 2	Hide pointer	BX = CX = DX =	Does nothing if already hidden, otherwise decrements the pointer-draw flag. Value of –1 hides image
AX = 3	Get position and button status	BX = CX = DX =	For 2- or 3-button mice, BX returns which button pressed: 0 leftmost, 1 rightmost, 2 center button. Buttons 3-15 reserved. CX = x coordinate; DX = y coordinate of pointer in pixels
AX = 4	Set pointer position	CX = DX =	New horizontal position in pixels New vertical position in pixels For values that exceed screen boundaries, screen maximum and minimum are used
AX = 5	Get button press information	BX =	Button status requested, where 0 = leftmost, 1 = rightmost, 2 = center button. AX—bit 0 (leftmost) = 0 or 1 bit 1 (rightmost) = 0 or 1 bit 2 (center) = 0 or 1 If 0 button up, and if 1 button down. BX = number of times button pressed since last call CX = horizontal coordinate of mouse DX = vertical coordinate of mouse

AH Value	Function	Input	Output
AX = 6	Get button release information	BX =	Button status requested, same format as for AX = 5 above. AX, BX, CX, and DX as above. If 0, button up; if 1, button down
AX = 7	Set minimum and maximum horizontal position	CX = DX =	Minimum virtual-screen horizontal coordinate in pixels Maximum virtual-screen horizontal coordinate in pixels
AX = 8	Set minimum and maximum vertical position	CX = DX =	Minimum virtual-screen vertical coordinate in pixels Maximum virtual-screen vertical coordinate in pixels
AX = 9	Set graphics pointer block	BX = CX = DX = ES =	Pointer hot-spot horizontal coordinate in pixels Pointer hot-spot vertical coordinate in pixels Address of screen/pointer masks Segment of screen/pointer masks
AX = 10	Set text pointer	BX = CX = DX =	Pointer select value Screen mask value/ hardware cursor start scan line Pointer mask value/ hardware cursor stop scan line BX = 0 select software text pointer BX = 1 select hardware cursor CX and DX bits map to: 0-7 character 8-10 foreground color 11 intensity 12-14 background color 15 blinking
AX = 11	Read mouse motion counters	BX = CX = DX =	CX = horizontal count DX = vertical count Range –32,768 to +32,768 read in mickeys

AH Value	Function	Input	Output
AX = 12	Set user-defined subroutine	CX = DX = ES =	Call mask Offset of subroutine Segment of subroutine CX word bit map: 0 pointer position changed 1 leftmost button pressed 2 leftmost button released 3 rightmost button pressed 4 rightmost button released 5 center button pressed 6 center button released 7-15 reserved = 0 Following values loaded when subroutine is called: AX = condition of mask BX = button status CX = pointer horizontal coordinate DX = pointer vertical coordinate SI = last vertical mickey count read DI = last horizontal mickey count read
AX = 13	Light pen emulation on	BX = CX = DX =	Instructs mouse driver to emulate a light pen Vertical mickey/pixel ratio Ratios specify number of mickeys per 8 pixels
AX = 14	Light pen emulation off	BX = CX = DX =	Disables mouse driver light pen emulation (Same as AX = 13)
AX = 15	Set mickey/pixel ratio	CX = DX =	Horizontal mickey/pixel ratio (Same as AX = 13)
AX = 16	Conditional off	CX = DX = SI = DI =	Left column coordinate in pixels Upper row coordinate in pixels Right column coordinate in pixels Lower row coordinate in pixels Defines an area of the screen for updating
AX = 19	Set double speed threshold	BX = DX =	Doubles pointer motion Threshold speed in mickeys/second

AH Value	Function	Input	Output
AX = 20	Swap user-defined subroutine	CX = DX = ES =	Call mask Offset of subroutine Segment of subroutine Sets hardware interrupts for call mask and subroutine address, returns previous values CX word call mask: 0 pointer position changed 1 leftmost button pressed 2 leftmost button released 3 rightmost button pressed 4 rightmost button released 5 center button pressed 6 center button released 7-12 reserved = 0 Following values loaded when subroutine is called: AX = condition of mask BX = button status CX = pointer horizontal coordinate DX = pointer vertical coordinate SI = last vertical mickey count read DI = last horizontal mickey count read
AX = 21	Get mouse state storage requirements	BX = CX = DX =	Gets size of buffer in bytes needed to store state of the mouse driver BX = size of buffer in bytes
AX = 22	Save mouse driver state	BX = CX = DX = ES =	Saves the mouse driver state Offset of buffer Segment of buffer
AX = 23	Restore mouse driver state	BX = CX = DX = ES =	Restores the mouse driver state from a user buffer Offset of buffer Segment of buffer

Appendix C

Windows API Functions and Foundation Class Library Items

This appendix contains the frequently used API functions and various Foundation Class library classes, objects, and functions discussed in Chapters 22 to 25. You can find additional information in your Microsoft C/C++ compiler documentation and through the Microsoft QuickHelp on-line help utility.

API: int AddFontResource(lpFilename)

Function

This function adds the fonts specified by lpFilename to the list of available fonts. This makes the fonts available for applications to use.

Parameter

lpFilename (LPSTR) contains a character string that names the font resource file.

Value Returned

The return value contains the number of fonts added; otherwise, the function returns a zero.

Notes

To save memory, applications should remove any unused font resources as soon as possible.

API: BOOL Arc(hDC,X1,Y1,X2,Y2,X3,Y3,X4,Y4)
MFC: BOOL Arc(X1,Y1,X2,Y2,X3,Y3,X4,Y4)
BOOL Arc(lpRect,ptStart,ptEnd)

Function

This function draws an elliptical arc with the center of the arc bounded by the rectangle defined by X1, Y1 and X2, Y2. The arc begins at X3, Y3 and ends at X4, Y4.

Parameters

hDC (HDC) identifies the device context.

X1 and Y1 (int) define the logical x and y coordinates of the upper-left corner of the bounding rectangle.

X2 and Y2 (int) define the logical x and y coordinates of the lower-right corner of the bounding rectangle.

X3 and Y3 (int) define the logical x and y coordinates of the arc's starting point.

X4 and Y4 (int) define the logical x and y coordinates of the arc's ending point.

lpRect specifies the bounding rectangle in logical units. You can pass an LPRECT or a CRect object for this parameter.

ptStart and ptEnd are the arc's starting and ending points. A POINT structure or CPoint object can be used.

Value Returned

TRUE if the function is successful; otherwise, FALSE.

Notes

The width and height of the rectangle must not exceed 32,767 units.

MFC: BEGIN_MESSAGE_MAP(derived_win_class,base_win_class)

Function

This macro is used to start the definition of an application's message map. This map contains entries for each message handler function. The macro is ended with the END_MESSAGE_MAP macro.

Parameters

derived_win_class is the window class name that the message map belongs to.

base_win_class is the window class name of the base class of derived_win_class.

Value Returned

None.

API: HDC BeginPaint(hWnd,lpPaint)
MFC: CDC* BeginPaint(lpPaint)

Function

This function gets the window ready for painting and using the lpPaint parameter, which points to a paint structure and fills the structure with information about the painting to be performed.

Parameters

hWnd indicates the window to be repainted.

lpPaint (LPPAINTSTRUCT) points to a PAINTSTRUCT structure that will receive the painting parameters.

Value Returned

Returns the device context for the specified window.

Notes

BeginPaint must be called in response to a WM_PAINT message.

MFC: CFrameWnd

Function

This class provides the ability to construct a Windows overlapped or pop-up frame window. Frame windows are derived from CFrameWnd and can contain member variables. Message-handler functions and a message map are used to define the outcome of messages directed to the window.

Members

rectDefault is used to choose size and position.

CFrameWnd constructs CFrameWnd object.

~CFrameWnd destroys CFrameWnd object.

Create creates and initializes the frame window.

LoadAccelTable loads the accelerator table.
Operations can include those from the following list:

GetChildFrame
GetParentFrame
Protected Members: m_hAccelTable

API: void CheckDlgButton(hDlg,nIDButton,wCheck)
MFC: void CheckDlgButton(nIDButton,nCheck)

Function

This function places or removes a check mark from a button control or changes the state of a three-state button.

Parameters

hDlg (HWND) specifies the dialog box containing the button.

nIDButton (int) defines the button control to be modified.

wCheck (WORD) or nCheck (UINT) defines the action to be performed. A nonzero value causes a check mark to be placed next to the button. A zero value removes the check mark. With a three-state button: 2 grays the button; 1 checks the button; a zero value removes a checkmark.

Value Returned

None.

Notes

The function sends a BM_SETCHECK message to the button control of the specified dialog box.

API: BOOL CheckMenuItem(hMenu,wIDCheckItem,wCheck)
MFC: UINT CheckMenuItem(nIDCheckItem,nCheck)

Function

Using the pop-up menu pointed to by the hMenu parameter, this function either positions a check mark next to a menu item or removes the check mark from a previously selected menu item.

Parameters

hMenu (HMENU) identifies the pop-up menu.

    wIDCheckItem (WORD) or nIDCheckItem (UINT) indicates which menu item is to be checked or unchecked.

    wCheck (WORD) or nCheck (UINT)—the check parameter—can be any combination of options combined using the logical OR operation. These include MF_CHECKED, MF_UNCHECKED, MF_BYPOSITION, and MF_BYCOMMAND. The wCheck parameter defines how to check the menu item, along with a specification of how to locate the item.

Check Option	Description
MF_CHECKED	Causes a check mark to be placed next to the selected menu item
MF_UNCHECKED	Removes the check mark from a previously selected menu item
MF_BYPOSITION	Uses the IDCheckItem parameter and indicates that the position of the menu item has been given. The first menu item begins at position 0
MF_BYCOMMAND	With this option the IDCheckItem parameter contains the menu item ID. MF_BYCOMMAND is the default option

Value Returned

The return value indicates the previous state of the selected menu item (MF_UNCHECKED, MF_CHECKED) or –1 if the menu item does not exist.

Notes

Top-level menu items cannot be checked. The IDCheckItem parameter can specify a menu or submenu item.

API: void CheckRadioButton(HDlg,nIDFirstButton,nIDLastButton, nIDCheckButton)
MFC: void CheckRadioButton(nIDFirstButton,nIDLastButton, nIDCheckButton)

Function

This function checks the radio button identified by the nIDCheckButton parameter while simultaneously removing any previous check marks from all radio buttons referenced by the nIDFirstButton to the last radio button defined by nIDLastButton.

Parameters

hDlg (HWND) specifies the dialog box.

    nIDFirstButton (int) is an integer value indicating the first radio button in the selected group.

    nIDLastButton (int) is an integer value indicating the last radio button in the selected group.

    nIDCheckButton (int) is an integer value indicating the radio button that is to be checked.

Value Returned

None.

Notes

The function sends a BM_SETCHECK message to the radio button control referenced by the ID in the given dialog box.

API: BOOL Chord(hDC,X1,Y1,X2,Y2,X3,Y3,X4,Y4)
MFC: BOOL Chord(x1,y1,x2,y2,x3,y3,x4,y4)
BOOL Chord(lpRect,ptStart,ptEnd)

Function

This function draws a chord using the selected pen, with a fill pattern based on the selected brush. A chord is defined as an area bounded by the intersection of an ellipse and a line segment.

Parameters

hDC (HDC) specifies the device context on which the chord will be drawn.

    X1 (int) defines the upper-left corner *x* coordinate of the bounding rectangle.

    Y1 (int) defines the upper-left corner *y* coordinate of the bounding rectangle.

    X2 (int) defines the lower-right corner *x* coordinate of the bounding rectangle.

    Y2 (int) defines the lower-right corner *y* coordinate of the bounding rectangle.

    X3 (int) defines the *x* coordinate of one end of the line segment.

    Y3 (int) defines the *y* coordinate of one end of the line segment.

    X4 (int) defines the *x* coordinate of the opposite end of the line segment.

    Y4 (int) defines the *y* coordinate of the opposite end of the line segment.

lpRect specifies the bounding rectangle in logical units. You can pass an LPRECT or CRect object for this parameter. ptStart and ptEnd are the the arc's starting and ending points. A POINT structure or CPoint object can be used.

Value Returned

TRUE if successful; otherwise, FALSE.

Notes

X1, Y1, X2, and Y2 define the rectangle bounding the ellipse that is part of the chord. X3, Y3, X4, and Y4 define the line that intercepts the ellipse.

MFC: CModalDialog

Function

This class provides modal dialog boxes. Modal dialog boxes require the user to respond before any further action is possible. Except for simple about boxes, an application should derive its modal dialog class from CModalDialog. Derived classes can add member variables and member functions to define the behavior of the dialog box. These classes require their own message maps. For the three most commonly used functions—OnOK, OnCancel, and CDialog::OnInitDialog—no message-map entry is required.

Parameters

CreateIndirect initializes an object in the second step of the creation of an indirect dialog box.
    DoModal calls the dialog box and returns when finished.

Members That Can Be Overridden

OnOK and OnCancelcan.

MFC: BOOL Create(const char FAR* lpClassName,
const char FAR* lpWindowName,
DWORD dwStyle=WS_OVERLAPPEDWINDOW,
const RECT& rect=rectDefault,
const CWnd* pParentWnd=NULL,
const char FAR* lpMenuName=NULL)

Function

This function constructs a CFrameWnd object.

Parameters

lpClassName points to a null-terminated string. The string identifies the class (WNDCLASS struct). The name can be any registered with the afxRegisterWndClass function. Control class names can be used. NULL forces use of the predefined default CFrameWnd attributes.

lpWindowName points to a null-terminated string for the window's name. This is the title bar text.

dwStyle defines the style attributes for the window.

rect gives the size and position of the window.

rectDefault specifies the size and position of the CFrameWnd object.

pParentWnd names the parent window of the frame window (NULL for top level).

lpMenuName gives the name of the menu for the window. MAKEINTRESOURCE is used when the menu has an ID number.

Value Returned

TRUE if initialization is successful; otherwise, FALSE.

Notes

Create initializes the window's class name and window name and registers default values for its style, parent, and associated menu.

API: HBRUSH CreateBrushIndirect(lpLogBrush)
MFC: BOOL CreateBrushIndirect(lpLogBrush)

Function

This function uses the data structure pointed to by lpLogBrush to create a logical brush. The LOGBRUSH data structure defines the intended brush's style, color, and pattern.

Parameter

lpLogBrush (LOGBRUSH FAR *) points to a LOGBRUSH data structure.

Value Returned

If successful, a logical brush is created. Otherwise, a NULL is returned. MFC: TRUE if successful; otherwise, FALSE.

Notes

A BS_INDEXED style will guarantee that the first eight indexed brushes will be unique for any selected device.

API: HWND CreateDialog(hInstance,lpTemplateName,hWndParent, lpDialogFunc)

Function

This function creates a modeless dialog box. The lpTemplateName defines the size, style, and any controls associated with the modeless dialog box the function will create. The hWndParent parameter specifies the owner window of the dialog box, with lpDialogFunc pointing to a message-processing function that will handle any messages received by the dialog box.

Parameters

hInstance (HANDLE) specifies the instance of the module whose executable file owns the resource.

lpTemplateName (LPSTR) points to a null-terminated character string naming the dialog box template.

hWndParent (HWND) is a handle to the window that owns the dialog box.

lpDialogFunc (FARPROC) is a procedure-instance address for the dialog function. The dialog function address must have been created by using the MakeProcInstance function. The callback function must use the Pascal calling convention and be declared FAR, using the following form:

```
HWND FAR PASCAL DialogFunc(hWnd,wMsg,wParam,
                          lParam)
HWND hwnd;      /* identifies message receiving
                   dialog box                  */
unsigned wMsg;  /* indicates the message number */
WORD wParam;    /* specifies 16-bits of additional
                   message-dependent information */
DWORD lParam;   /* specifies 32-bits of additional
                   message-dependent information */
```

Value Returned

A successful return contains a valid handle for the dialog box. A –1 is returned if the function call was unsuccessful.

Notes

This function is used only if the dialog class is used for the dialog box. This is the default class that is used whenever no explicit class is given in the dialog box template. The function must not call DefWindowProc but must process all unwanted messages internally by the dialog-class window function.

You should use the WS_VISIBLE style for the dialog box template if the dialog box should appear in the parent window during creation. You should use the DestroyWindow function to delete a dialog box created by the CreateDialog function.

API: HWND CreateDialogIndirect(hInstance,lpDialogTemplate, hWndParent,lpDialogFunc)

Function

This function creates a modeless dialog box. The lpDialogTemplate data structure defines the size, style, and any controls associated with the modeless dialog box the function will create. The hWndParent parameter specifies the owner window of the dialog box, with lpDialogFunc pointing to a message-processing function that will handle any messages received by the dialog box.

Parameters

hInstance (HANDLE) specifies the instance of the module whose executable file owns the resource.

lpDialogTemplate (LPSTR) points to a dialog box template structure.

hWndParent (HWND) is the handle to the window that owns the dialog box.

lpDialogFunc (FARPROC) is a procedure-instance address for the dialog function. The dialog function address must have been created by using the MakeProcInstance function. The callback function must use the Pascal calling convention and be declared FAR, using the following form:

```
HWND FAR PASCALDialogFunc(hWnd,wMsg,wParam,
                          lParam)
HWND hwnd;       /* identifies message receiving
                    dialog box                    */
unsigned wMsg;  /* indicates the message number   */
WORD wParam;     /* specifies 16-bits of additional
                    message-dependent information */
DWORD lParam;    /* specifies 32-bits of additional
                    message-dependent information */
```

Value Returned

A successful return contains a valid handle for the dialog box. A –1 is returned if the function call was unsuccessful.

Notes

CreateDialogIndirect sends a WM_INITDIALOG message to the dialog function before displaying the dialog box, allowing the dialog function to initialize the dialog box controls. This function is used only if the dialog class is used for the dialog box. This is the default class that is used whenever no explicit class is given in the dialog box template. The function must not call DefWindowProc but must process all unwanted messages internally by using the dialog class window function. Use the WS_VISIBLE style for the dialog box template if the dialog box should appear in the parent window during creation. Use the DestroyWindow function to delete a dialog box created by the CreateDialog function.

API: HFONT CreateFont(nHeight,nWidth,nEscapement,nOrientation,
nWeight,cItalic,cUnderline,cStrikeOut,
cCharSet,cOutputPrecision,cClipPrecision,
cQuality,cPitchAndFamily,lpFacename)
MFC: BOOL CreateFont(nHeight,nWidth,nEscapement,nOrientation,
nWeight,cItalic,cUnderline,cStrikeOut,
cCharSet,cOutputPrecision,cClipPrecision,
cQuality,cPitchAndFamily,lpFacename)

Function

This function creates a logical font that can be selected as the font for any device. The logical font that is created is based on the following options.

Parameters

nHeight (int), the logical font's height, can be defined in one of three ways:

- nHeight > 0 transforms the height into device units and matches it with the cell height of the available fonts.

- nHeight = 0 Selects a reasonable default size.

- nHeight < 0 Transforms the height into device units and the absolute value is matched against the character height of the available fonts.

The font mapper uses the following rule precedents for all height comparisons: The font mapper first looks for the largest font that does not exceed the requested font size. If there is no such font available, the font mapper then looks for the smallest font available.

nWidth (int), using logical units, defines the average width of the characters in the font. When nWidth contains a zero value, the aspect ratio of the device will be matched with the digitization aspect ratio of the available fonts to select the best match.

nEscapement (int), using tenths-of-a-degree increments, defines the angle of each line of text output in the specified font relative to the bottom of the page.

nOrientation (int), using tenths-of-a-degree increments, specifies the angle of each character's baseline relative to the bottom of the page.

nWeight (int) indicates the preferred weight of the font in the range of zero to 1000. A value of zero selects the default weight, with a value of roughly 450 defining a normal weight and 750 representing bold.

cItalic (BYTE) indicates if the font is italic or not.

cUnderline (BYTE) indicates if the font is underlined or not.

cStrikeOUT_(BYTE) indicates if the characters in the font are struck out.

cCharSet (BYTE) indicates which character set is desired. Two values (ANSI_CHARSET and OEM_CHARSET) are predefined. Others can be purchased through specific font manufacturers.

cOutputPrecision (BYTE) indicates the preferred output precision. This specifies just how closely the output must match the requested font's characteristics. There are four choices:

OUT_CHARACTER_PRECIS
OUT_DEFAULT_PRECIS

OUT_STRING_PRECIS
OUT_STROKE_PRECIS

cClipPrecision (BYTE) indicates the preferred clipping precision. Clipping precision references just how each character that extends beyond the clipping region is to be "clipped." There are three choices:

CLIP_CHARACTER_PRECIS
CLIP_DEFAULT_PRECIS
CLIP_STROKE_PRECIS

cQuality (BYTE) selects the preferred output quality. This parameter selects just how carefully the Graphics Device Interface (GDI) must attempt to match the logical font with the actual physical fonts provided for the requested output device. There are three possible match conditions:

DEFAULT_QUALITY
DRAFT_QUALITY
PROOF_QUALITY

cPitchAndFamily (BYTE) selects the pitch and family of the font. There are three pitch choices:

DEFAULT_PITCH
FIXED_PITCH
VARIABLE_PITCH

There are six possible font families:

FF_DECORATIVE
FF_DONTCARE
FF_MODERN
FF_ROMAN
FF_SCRIPT
FF_SWISS

lpFacename (LPSTR) is a (30-character maximum) null-terminated string that identifies the typeface name of the font. If there is a question as to the typefaces that are available, the EnumFonts function can be invoked to list the fonts.

Value Returned

A successful return contains a value identifying the created logical font. A NULL value indicates an unsuccessful creation. MFC: TRUE if successful; otherwise, FALSE.

Notes

It is important to understand that the CreateFont function does not create a new font. All it does is to match, as closely as possible, based on the matching parameters specified, your preference with the actual physical fonts available.

API: HFONT CreateFontIndirect(lpLogFont)
MFC: BOOL CreateFontIndirect(lpLogFont)

Function

This function creates a logical font based on the parameters specified in the lpLogFont data structure.

Parameter

lpLogFont (LOGFONT FAR *) points to a LOGFONT data structure defining the logical font's characteristics.

Value Returned

NULL if the function was unsuccessful; otherwise, the value returned identifies the created logical font. MFC: TRUE if successful; otherwise, FALSE.

Notes

CreateFontIndirect is identical in purpose to CreateFont with the exception that the "matching" parameters are stored in a data structure pointed to by lpLogFont rather than being explicitly declared. For a complete analysis of the various font matching options, see the "Parameters" section for the CreateFont function earlier in this appendix.

API: HBRUSH CreateHatchBrush(nIndex,rgbColor)
MFC: BOOL CreateHatchBrush(nIndex,crColor)

Function

This function creates a logical brush with the defined color and hatched pattern. Once created, the brush can then be selected as the current brush for any device.

Parameters

nIndex (int) selects one of the following hatch styles for the brush:

Hatch Style	Description
HS_BDIAGONAL	45-degree left-to-right hatch (upward)
HS_CROSS	Horizontal and vertical crosshatching
HS_DIAGCROSS	45-degree crosshatch
HS_FDIAGONAL	45-degree left-to-right hatch (downward)
HS_HORIZONTAL	Horizontal hatch
HS_VERTICAL	Vertical hatch

rgbColor (DWORD) or crColor (DWORD) selects an RGB color for the color of the hatch lines to be drawn.

Value Returned

The value returned identifies the logical brush that has been created. An unsuccessful attempt will return a NULL. MFC: TRUE or FALSE.

API: HMENU CreateMenu()
MFC: BOOL CreateMenu()

Function

This function creates a menu. While the created menu is initially empty, it can be filled by using the ChangeMenu function. MFC creates a menu and attaches it to the CMenu object.

Parameters

None.

Value Returned

Identifies the newly created menu. A NULL value indicates an unsuccessful attempt. MFC: TRUE if successful; otherwise, FALSE.

API: HPALETTE CreatePalette(lpLogPalette)
MFC: BOOL CreatePalette(lpLogPalette)

Function

This function creates a logical color palette.

Parameter

lpLogPalette (PALETTE FAR*) points to a LOGPALETTE data structure.

Value Returned

Specifies a logical palette if the function was successful. Otherwise, it is NULL. MFC: TRUE if successful; otherwise, FALSE.

API: HBRUSH CreatePatternBrush(hBitmap)
MFC: BOOL CreatePatternBrush(pBitmap)

Function

Using the hBitmap parameter, this function creates a logical brush with the selected pattern.

Parameters

hBitmap (HBITMAP) is supposed to point to a previously created bitmap, with a minimum size pattern fill bitmap of 8x8. MFC: Bitmap identified by pBitmap. Initialized using the CBitmap::CreateBitmap, CBitmap::CreateBitmapIndirect, CBitmap::LoadBitmap, or CBitmap::CreateCompatibleBitmap function.

Value Returned

Either identifies the created logical brush or a NULL for an unsuccessful attempt. MFC: TRUE if successful; otherwise, FALSE.

Notes

Once created, the brush pattern can be selected for any device that supports raster operations. Logical pattern brushes can be deleted with a call to DeleteObject without affecting the bitmap used to create the brush, thereby allowing the bitmap to be used to create other pattern brushes.

API: HPEN CreatePen(nPenStyle,nWidth,rgbColor)
MFC: BOOL CreatePen(nPenStyle,nWidth,crColor)

Function

This function creates a logical pen based on the style, width, and color selected.

Parameters

nPenStyle (int) selects the pen style from the list of six possibilities:

Constant	Pen Style
0	Solid
1	Dash
2	Dot
3	Dash-dot
4	Dash-dot-dot
5	NULL

nWidth (int) defines the pen's width in logical units.
rgbColor (DWORD) or crColor (DWORD) selects an RGBcolor for the pen.

Value Returned

Identifies the logical pen if successful, or returns a NULL. MFC: TRUE if successful; otherwise, FALSE.

Notes

Any pen created with a physical width greater than one pixel will always have either a solid or null style.

API: HPEN CreatePenIndirect(lpLogPen)
MFC: BOOL CreatePenIndirect(lpLogPen)

Function

This function creates a logical pen based on the parameters stored in the data structure pointed to by lpLogPen.

Parameter

lpLogPen (LOGPEN FAR *) points to a LOGPEN data structure.

Value Returned

Either a valid logical pen identifier or NULL for an unsuccessful attempt. MFC: TRUE if successful; otherwise, FALSE.

Notes

See the CreatePen function description earlier in this appendix for an explanation of the pen's possible appearances.

API: HRGN CreatePolygonRgn(lpPoints,nCount,nPolyFillMode)
MFC: BOOL CreatePolygonRgn(lpPoints,nCount,nMode)

Function

This function creates a polygon region.

Parameters

lpPoints (LPPOINT) points to a POINT data structure that identifies the x and y coordinates of one angle of the polygon.

nCount (int) identifies the number of elements in the array.

nPolyFillMode (int) or nMode (int) selects either an ALTERNATE or WINDING polygon-filling mode.

Value Returned

Identifies the new region if successful; otherwise, returns NULL. MFC: TRUE if successful;, otherwise, FALSE.

API: HMENU CreatePopupMenu()
MFC: BOOL CreatePopupMenu()

Function

This function creates and returns a handle to an empty pop-up menu. Using the InsertMenu and AppendMenu functions, an application can add items to the pop-up menu.

Parameters

None.

Value Returned

Specifies the newly created menu if successful; otherwise, NULL. MFC: TRUE if successful; otherwise, FALSE.

API: HRGN CreateRectRgn(X1,Y1,X2,Y2)
MFC: BOOL CreateRectRgn(X1,Y1,X2,Y2)

Function

This function creates a rectangle.

Parameters

X1 (int) indicates the upper-left corner x coordinate.
    Y1 (int) indicates the upper-left corner y coordinate.
    X2 (int) indicates the lower-right corner x coordinate.
    Y2 (int) indicates the lower-right corner y coordinate.

Value Returned

The returned value either identifies the newly created rectangular region, or, otherwise, an unsuccessful attempt returns a NULL. MFC: TRUE if successful; otherwise, FALSE.

Notes

The width and height of the rectangle, defined by the absolute value of X2–X1 and Y2–Y1, must not exceed 32,767.

API: HRGN CreateRectRgnIndirect(lpRect)
MFC: BOOL CreateRectRgnIndirect(lpRect)

Function

This function creates a rectangle. It is identical to the CreateRectRgn function defined earlier, except that its parameters are passed in a RECT data structure rather than being explicitly defined.

Parameter

lpRect (LPRECT) points to a RECT data structure containing the upper-left and lower-right limits for the rectangular region to be created.

Value Returned

If successful, the returned value identifies the newly created region; otherwise, a NULL is returned. MFC: TRUE if successful; otherwise, FALSE.

Notes

The width and height of the rectangle must not exceed 32,767.

API: HRGN CreateRoundRectRgn(X1,Y1,X2,Y2,X3,Y3)
MFC: BOOL CreateRoundRectRgn(X1,Y1,X2,Y2,X3,Y3)

Function

This function creates a rounded rectangular region.

Parameters

X1 (int) identifies the logical *x* coordinate of the upper-left corner of the region.

Y1 (int) identifies the logical *y* coordinate of the upper-left corner of the region.

X2 (int) identifies the logical *x* coordinate of the lower-right corner of the region.

X2 (int) identifies the logical *y* coordinate of the lower-right corner of the region.

X3 (int) identifies the width of the ellipse that will be used to draw the rounded corners.

Y3 (int) identifies the height of the ellipse that will be used to draw the rounded corners.

Value Returned

If successful, the returned value identifies the newly created region; otherwise, a NULL is returned. MFC: TRUE if successful; otherwise, FALSE.

API: HBRUSH CreateSolidBrush(rgbColor)
MFC: BOOL CreateSolidBrush(crColor)

Function

This function creates a logical brush using the selected color.

Parameters

rgbColor (DWORD) and crColor (DWORD) select an RGB color for the brush.

Value Returned

If successful, the return value identifies the newly created solid brush; otherwise, a NULL return indicates an unsuccessful creation attempt. MFC: TRUE if successful; otherwise, FALSE.

API: HWND
CreateWindow(lpClassName,lpWindowName,dwStyle,X,Y,
nWidth,nHeight,hWndParent,hMenu,
hInstance,lpParam)

Function

This frequently invoked Windows function creates an overlapped, pop-up, or child window. The function specifies the window's class, title, and style and can even set the window's initial position and size. If the window to be created has an owning parent or menu, this also is defined. The function also sends the necessary WM_CRE-ATE, WM_GETMINMAXINFO, and WM_NCCREATE messages to the window. If the WS_VISIBLE style option has been selected, all necessary window messages are sent to activate and visually display the window.

Parameters

lpClassName (LPSTR) points to a null-terminated character string naming the window's class.

lpWindowName (LPSTR) points to a null-terminated character string identifying the window by name.

dwStyle specifies the window's style.

X (int) defines the initial *x* coordinate position for the window. For overlapped/pop-up windows, this is the *x* coordinate of the window's upper-left corner in screen coordinates. If the value is CW_USEDEFAULT, Windows selects the default upper-left *x* coordinate. For child windows, this is the *x* coordinate of the upper-left corner of the window in the client area of its parent window.

Y (int) defines the initial *y* coordinate position for the window. For overlapped/pop-up windows, this is the *y* coordinate of the window's upper-left corner in screen coordinates. If the value is CW_USEDEFAULT, Windows selects the default upper-left *y* coordinate. For child windows, this is the *y* coordinate of the upper-left corner of the window in the client area of its parent window.

nWidth (int), using device units, defines the width of the window. For overlapped windows, this is either the window's width in screen coordinates or CW_USEDEFAULT. If the latter, Windows selects the width and height for the window.

nHeight (int), using device units, defines the height of the window. For overlapped windows, this is either the window's height in screen coordinates or CW_USEDEFAULT. If the latter, Windows ignores nHeight.

hWndParent (HWND) specifies the parent window for the window that is about to be created. Overlapped windows must not have a parent (hWndParent must be NULL). A valid parent handle must be passed when creating a child window.

hMenu (HMENU), dependent on the window's style, specifies a menu or a child window identifier. For overlapped/pop-up menus, this identifies the menu to be used with the window. A NULL value specifies the use of the class's menu. For a child menu, this contains a child window identifier. This is determined by the application and is to be unique for all child windows of the same parent.

hInstance (HANDLE) specifies the instance of the module to be identified with the window.

lpParam (LPSTR) points to the value passed to the window through the lParam parameter of the WM_CREATE message.

Value Returned

A valid new window identifier if successful; otherwise, returns a NULL.

Window Control Classes

Following is an alphabetical listing of window control classes.

BUTTON   The BUTTON control identifies a small rectangular child window displaying a button the user can turn on or off with a mouse click. Buttons usually

change display appearance when selected/deselected. The BUTTON control styles
are

    BS_AUTOCHECKBOX
    BS_AUTORADIOBUTTON
    BS_AUTO3STATE
    BS_CHECKBOX
    BS_DEFPUSHBUTTON
    BS_GROUPBOX
    BS_LEFTTEXT
    BS_PUSHBUTTON
    BS_RADIOBUTTON
    BS_3STATE
    BS_USERBUTTON

EDIT   The EDIT control identifies a small rectangular child window that the user
can use to enter text from the keyboard. Input focus can be changed by clicking the
mouse button or using the TAB key. EDIT control classes allow the user to repeatedly
select the input focus, make entries, backspace over mistakes, and reenter correct
information. The user inserts text whenever the control display exhibits a flashing
caret. The EDIT control styles are

    ES_AUTOHSCROLL
    ES_AUTOVSCROLL
    ES_CENTER
    ES_LEFT
    ES_MULTILINE
    ES_NOHIDESEL
    ES_RIGHT

LISTBOX   The LISTBOX control identifies a list of character strings. It is most
frequently used whenever an application needs to present a list of names, such as
available filenames, from which the user can select. Options are selected by moving
the mouse and clicking the selected item. This causes the item to be highlighted,
along with a notification of the choice being passed to the parent window. Whenever
the list is long, LISTBOX controls can be used in conjunction with SCROLLBAR
controls. The LISTBOX control styles are

    LBS_MULTIPLESEL
    LBS_NOREDRAW
    LBS_NOTIFY
    LBS_SORT
    LBS_STANDARD

SCROLLBAR   The SCROLLBAR control displays a stretched rectangular box containing a page position reference, sometimes called a thumb, along with direction arrows at both ends. The user selects a position within the list by sliding the thumb up or down the bar. SCROLLBAR controls are identical in appearance to scroll bars used in ordinary windows. However, SCROLLBAR controls can appear anywhere within a window. Automatically associated with the SCROLLBAR controls is a SIZEBOX control. This small rectangle allows the user to change the size of the window. The SCROLLBAR control styles are

SBS_BOTTOMALIGN
SBS_HORZ
SBS_LEFTALIGN
SBS_RIGHTALIGN
SBS_SIZEBOX
SBS_SIZEBOXBOTTOMRIGHTALIGN
SBS_SIZEBOXTOPLEFTALIGN
SBS_TOPALIGN
SBS_VERT

STATIC   The STATIC control class defines a simple text field, box, or rectangle and is most frequently used to identify, box, or separate other controls. These controls therefore output or input information. The STATIC control styles are

SS_BLACKFRAME
SS_BLACKRECT
SS_CENTER
SS_GRAYFRAME
SS_GRAYRECT
SS_ICON
SS_LEFT
SS_RIGHT
SS_SIMPLE
SS_USERITEM
SS_WHITEFRAME
SS_WHITERECT

Window Styles

Following is an alphabetical listing of window styles.

WS_BORDER   Creates a bordered window.

WS_CAPTION   Adds a title bar to the bordered window.

WS_CHILD   Creates a child window. Not to be used with WS_POPUP style windows.

WS_CHILDWINDOW   Creates a child window of the WS_CHILD style.

WS_CLIPCHILDREN   Used when creating the parent window, the WS_CLIPCHILDREN window style prohibits drawing of the parent window within the area occupied by any child windows.

WS_CLIPSIBLINGS   Used with the WS_CHILD style only, this window style clips all other child windows whenever a particular child window receives a paint message. Without this, it would be possible to draw within the client area of another child window.

WS_DISABLED   Creates an initially disabled window.

WS_DLGFRAME   Creates a double bordered window without a title.

WS_GROUP   Used only by dialog boxes, this window style defines the first control of a group of controls. The user can move from one control to another by using the arrow keys.

WS_HSCROLL   Creates a window with a horizontal scroll bar.

WS_ICONIC   Used with the WS_OVERLAPPED style, WS_ICONIC creates a window that is initially displayed in its iconic form.

WS_MAXIMIZE   Creates a window of maximum size.

WS_MAXIMIZEBOX   Creates a window that includes a maximize box.

WS_MINIMIZE   Creates a window of minimum size.

WS_MINIMIZEBOX   Creates a window that includes a minimize box.

WS_OVERLAPPED   Creates an overlapped window.

WS_OVERLAPPEDWINDOW   Uses the WS_CAPTION, WS_OVERLAPPED, WS_THICKFRAME, and WS_SYSMENU styles to create an overlapped window.

WS_POPUP   Not to be used with WS_CHILD style, this window style creates a pop-up window.

WS_POPUPWINDOW   Uses the WS_BORDER, WS_POPUP, and WS_SYSMENU styles to create a pop-up window.

WS_SYSMENU   Used only with windows including title bars, this window style creates a window with a system menu box displayed in its title bar. When used with a child window, this style creates only a close box instead of the standard system menu box.

WS_TABSTOP   Used only by dialog boxes, this window style indicates any number of controls that the user can move by using the TAB key. When the user presses the TAB key, each successive press moves through all possible controls specified by the WS_TABSTOP style.

WS_THICKFRAME   Creates a thick framed window that can be used to size the window.

WS_VISIBLE   Creates a window that is automatically displayed. It can be used with overlapped and pop-up windows.

WS_VSCROLL   Creates a window with a vertical scroll bar.

BUTTON Class Control Styles

Following is an alphabetical listing of BUTTON class control styles.

BS_AUTOCHECKBOX   Identical in usage to BS_CHECKBOX, except for the fact that the button automatically toggles its state when the user selects it by clicking the mouse button.

BS_AUTORADIOBUTTON   Identical in usage to BS_RADIOBUTTON, except that when the button is selected, a BN_CLICKED message is sent to the application, removing check marks from any other radio buttons in the group.

BS_AUTO3STATE   Identical to BS_3STATE, except that the button automatically toggles its state when the user selects it by clicking the mouse button.

BS_CHECKBOX   Defines a small rectangular button that can be checked. Any associated text is printed to the right of the button, with the box's border boldfaced whenever the user clicks the button.

BS_DEFPUSHBUTTON   Defines a small elliptical bold-bordered button. It is usually used to identify a user default response. Any associated text is displayed within the button.

BS_GROUPBOX   Defines a rectangular-region-bounding button group. Text is displayed within the rectangle's upper-left corner.

BS_LEFTTEXT   Forces text to be displayed on the left side of the radio or checkbox button. It can be used with the BS_CHECKBOX, BS_RADIOBUTTON, or BS_3STATE control style.

BS_PUSHBUTTON   Defines a small elliptical button containing the specified text. This control sends a message to the parent window whenever the user clicks the button.

BS_RADIOBUTTON   Defines a small circular button with a border that is bold-faced whenever the user selects it with a mouse button click. The parent window is also notified via a message. A subsequent click produces a normal border, with another message being sent to the parent window indicating the change.

BS_3STATE   Identical to BS_CHECKBOX, but the button can be grayed as well as checked. In the grayed state, the user is given a visual reminder that the current check box has been disabled.

BS_USERBUTTON   Defines a user-designated button. The parent window is notified when the button is clicked, sending a request to paint, invert, and disable the button.

EDIT Class Control Styles

Following is an alphabetical listing of EDIT class control styles.

ES_AUTOHSCROLL   Automatically scrolls text ten characters to the right whenever the user enters data at the end of a line. When the user presses ENTER, the text scrolls back to the left edge border.

ES_AUTOVSCROLL   Automatically scrolls text up one page when the user presses ENTER at the last line.

ES_CENTER   Centers text.

ES_LEFT   Uses flush-left text alignment.

ES_MULTILINE   Provides multiple-line editing control. When used in conjunction with the ES_AUTOVSCROLL style, it scrolls text vertically when the user presses ENTER. If the ES_AUTOVSCROLL style is not specified, this control beeps when the user presses ENTER, and no more lines can be displayed. A similar condition exists with the ES_AUTOHSCROLL style. If ES_AUTOHSCROLL is selected, ES_MULTI-LINE allows the user to remain on the same line, shifting text to the left. When the style is deactivated, text not fitting on the same line within the window causes a new line to be created. ES_MULTILINE styles can include scroll bars.

ES_NOHIDESEL   Overrides the default action, preventing the EDIT control from hiding the selection whenever the control loses the input focus, and does not invert the selection when the control receives the input focus.

ES_RIGHT   Uses flush-right text alignment.

STATIC Class Control Styles

The following provides an alphabetical listing of STATIC class control styles.

SS_BLACKFRAME   Defines a box with a black frame.

SS_BLACKRECT   Defines a black-filled rectangle.

SS_CENTER   Takes the given text and centers it within a simple rectangle. All text is formatted. Any text not fitting on one line is automatically wordwrapped to the next line, with the next line also being automatically centered.

SS_GRAYFRAME   Defines a gray framed box.

SS_GRAYRECT   Defines a gray-filled rectangle.

SS_ICON   Automatically sizes and displays an icon within the dialog box.

SS_LEFT   Similar to SS_CENTER except the text displayed within the rectangle is aligned flush left. This includes auto wordwrap and next line flush-left alignment.

SS_RIGHT   Similar to SS_CENTER, except the text displayed within the rectangle is aligned flush right. This includes auto wordwrap and next line flush-right alignment.

SS_SIMPLE   Defines a rectangle that will display a single line of text aligned flush left.

SS_USERITEM   Defines a user-defined item.

SS_WHITEFRAME   Defines a white framed box.

SS_WHITERECT   Defines a white-filled rectangle.

LISTBOX Class Control Styles

Following is an alphabetical listing of LISTBOX class control styles.

LBS_MULTIPLESEL   Allows for the selection of any number of strings, with the string selection toggling each time the user clicks or double-clicks the string.

LBS_NOREDRAW   LISTBOX display is not updated when changes are made.

LBS_NOTIFY   Whenever the user clicks or double-clicks a string, the parent window receives an input message.

LBS_SORT   Sorts the strings in the LISTBOX alphabetically.

LBS_STANDARD   Sorts the strings in the LISTBOX alphabetically, sending a message to the parent window whenever the user clicks or double-clicks a string. The LISTBOX contains a vertical scroll bar and borders on all sides.

SCROLLBAR Class Control Styles

Following is an alphabetical listing of SCROLLBAR class control styles.

SBS_BOTTOMALIGN   Used in conjunction with the SBS_HORZ style. Scroll bar alignment is along the bottom edge of the rectangle defined by X, Y, nWidth, and nHeight, using the system default scroll bar height.

SBS_HORZ   Defines a horizontal scroll bar. The height, width, and position of the scroll bar will be determined by the CreateWindow function if neither the SBS_BOTTOMALIGN nor the SBS_TOPALIGN style is requested.

SBS_LEFTALIGN   Used in conjunction with SBS_VERT style. Here the left edge of the scroll bar is aligned with the left edge of a rectangle defined by X, Y, nWidth, and nHeight, using the system default scroll bar height.

SBS_RIGHTALIGN   Used in conjunction with SBS_VERT style. Here the right edge of the scroll bar is aligned with the right edge of a rectangle defined by X, Y, nWidth, and nHeight, using the the system default scroll bar height.

SBS_SIZEBOX   Defines a size box. The size box will have the height, width, and position given by the CreateWindow function if neither the SBS_SIZEBOXBOTTOMRIGHTALIGN nor the SBS_SIZEBOXTOPLEFTALIGN style is not selected.

SBS_SIZEBOXBOTTOMRIGHTALIGN   Used in conjunction with the SBS_SIZEBOX style. Here the lower-right corner of the scroll bar is aligned with the lower-right corner of a rectangle defined by X, Y, nWidth, and nHeight, using the system default scroll bar height.

SBS_SIZEBOXTOPLEFTALIGN   Used in conjunction with the SBS_SIZEBOX style. Here the upper-left corner of the scroll bar is aligned with the upper-left corner of a rectangle defined by X, Y, nWidth, and nHeight, using the system default scroll bar height.

SBS_TOPALIGN   Used in conjunction with the SBS_HORZ style. Scroll bar alignment is along the top edge of the rectangle defined by X, Y, nWidth, and nHeight, using the system default scroll bar height.

SBS_VERT   Defines a vertical scroll bar. The height, width, and position of the scroll bar will be determined by the CreateWindow function if neither the SBS_RIGHTALIGN nor the SBS_LEFTALIGN style is requested.

API: HWND
CreateWindowEx(dwExStyle,lpClassName,lpWindowName,
dwStyle,x,y,nWidth,nHeight,
hWndParent,hMenu,hInstance,lpParam)

Function

This function creates an overlapped, pop-up, or child window with an extended style. Otherwise, the function is identical to the CreateWindow function.

Parameters

dwExStyle (DWORD) defines the extended style of the window being created. It can be set to WS_EXDLGMODALFRAME; this causes the window to be drawn with a modal dialog frame.

lpClassName (LPSTR) points to a null-terminated character string naming the window's class.

lpWindowName (LPSTR) points to a null-terminated character string identifying the window by name.

dwStyle (DWORD) specifies the style of window being created.

x (int) defines the initial x coordinate position for the window. For overlapped/pop-up windows, this is the x coordinate of the window's upper-left corner in screen coordinates. If the value is CW_USEDEFAULT, Windows selects the default upper-left x coordinate. For child windows, this is the x coordinate of the upper-left corner of the window in the client area of its parent window.

y (int) defines the initial y coordinate position for the window. For overlapped/pop-up windows, this is the y coordinate of the window's upper-left corner in screen coordinates. If the value is CW_USEDEFAULT, Windows selects the default upper-left y coordinate. For child windows, this is the y coordinate of the upper-left corner of the window in the client area of its parent window.

nWidth (int), using device units, defines the width of the window. For overlapped windows, this is either the window's width in screen coordinates or CW_USEDEFAULT. If the latter, Windows selects the width and height for the window.

nHeight (int), using device units, defines the height of the window. For overlapped windows, this is either the window's height in screen coordinates or CW_USEDEFAULT. If the latter, Windows ignores nHeight.

hWndParent (HWND) specifies the parent window for the window that is about to be created. Overlapped windows must not have a parent (hWndParent must be NULL). A valid parent handle must be passed when creating a child window.

hMenu (HMENU), dependent on the window's style, specifies a menu or a child-window identifier. For overlapped/pop-up windows, this identifies the menu to be used with the window. A NULL value specifies the use of the class's menu. For child windows, this contains a child window identifier. This is determined by the application and is to be unique for all child windows of the same parent.

hInstance (HANDLE) specifies the instance of the module to be identified with the window.

lpParam (LPSTR) points to the value passed to the window through the lParam parameter of the WM_CREATE message.

Value Returned

If successful, a valid new window identifier; otherwise, returns a NULL.

Notes

See the CreateWindow function for window control classes, window styles, and control styles.

MFC: CWnd

Function

This class provides the base for all windows classes in the Foundation Class library. The CWnd class and the associated message map hide the WndProc function so common to C Windows programmers. The Foundation Class library permits the derivation of specific window types. The most commonly used derived classes are CFrameWnd, CMDIFrameWnd, and CMDIChildWnd.

Members

Include the following: caret functions, child window attributes, coordinate mapping functions, window text data members, construction/destruction, dialog box item functions, menu functions, functions, update/painting functions, scrolling functions, clipboard functions, initialization general message handlers, input message handlers, non-client-area message handlers, clipboard message handlers, initialization, window state functions, mdi message handlers, control message handlers, system message handlers, timer functions, alert functions, message window size and position, and window access. Protected members: initialization and operation.

MFC: CWinApp

Function

The CWinApp class is used to create an application object. The application object defines member functions for initializing and running the application. Only one CWinApp object per application is permitted. Usually, an application class is derived from CWinApp and used to override the InitInstance of the member function. You can use global functions to access the CWinApp object:

Function	Description
AfxGetApp	Obtains a pointer to the CWinApp object
AfxGetInstanceHandle	Obtains a handle to an instance of the current application
AfxGetResourceHandle	Obtains a handle to application's resources
AfxGetAppName	Obtains a pointer to a string containing the application's name

Parameters

Here is a list of parameters:

Parameter	Description
m_pszAppName	Application's name
m_hInstance	Similar to hInstance passed to WinMain
m_hPrevInstance	Similar to hPrevInstance passed to WinMain
m_lpCmdLine	Similar to lpCmdLine passed to WinMain
m_nCmdShow	Similar to nCmdShow passed to WinMain
m_pMainWnd	Pointer to the application's main window

Operations can include any of the following:

LoadCursor
LoadStandardCursor
LoadOEMCursor
LoadIcon
LoadStandardIcon
LoadOEMIcon
InitApplication
InitInstance
Run
OnIdle
ExitInstance
PreTranslateMessage
Protected Member: m_msgCur gives the last window message returned by Run

MFC: DECLARE_MESSAGE_MAP( )

Function

Typically, each derived window's class in the application should provide a message map. This macro is used for that purpose. See BEGIN_MESSAGE_MAP and END_MESSAGE_MAP.

Parameters

None.

Value Returned

None.

API: BOOL DeleteDC(hDC)
MFC: BOOL DeleteDC()

Function

This function deletes the designated device context. MFC: Do not call the function; that is the destructor's job.

Parameter

hDC (HDC) identifies the device context.

Value Returned

TRUE if successful; otherwise, FALSE.

Notes

If the device context to be deleted is the last device context for a given device, the device is notified, with all subsequent system storage resources used by the device being released.

API: BOOL DeleteMenu(hMenu,nPosition,wFlags)
MFC: BOOL DeleteMenu(nPosition,nFlags)

Function

This function deletes an item from the menu.

Parameters

hMenu (HMENU) specifies the menu to be changed.

nPosition (WORD) or (UINT) defines the menu item to be deleted.

wFlags (WORD) or nFlags (UINT) defines how the nPosition parameter is to be interpreted.

The default is MF_BYCOMMAND, but it can also be set to MF_BYPOSITION.

Value Returned

TRUE if the function is successful; otherwise, FALSE.

Notes

MF_POSITION specifies the position of the menu item with the first item being numbered zero. However, if MF_BYCOMMAND is specified, nPosition specifies the ID of the existing menu item.

API: BOOL DeleteObject(hObject)
MFC: void DeleteObject()

Function

This function deletes a logical font, pen, brush, bitmap, or region from memory.

Parameter

hObject (HANDLE) represents a handle to the object (font, pen, brush, bitmap, or region).

Value Returned

A successful delete returns TRUE; otherwise, a FALSE is returned, indicating that the handle was not valid.

Notes

To delete an object selected into a device context, the device context must be deleted first, followed by the deletion of the object itself.

API: BOOL DestroyMenu(hMenu)
MFC: BOOL DestroyMenu()

Function

This function destroys and frees any system memory associated with the menu pointed to by hMenu.

Parameter

hMenu (HMENU) defines the menu to be deleted.

Value Returned

TRUE for success; otherwise, FALSE.

API: BOOL DestroyWindow(hWnd)
MFC: virtual BOOL DestroyWindow()

Function

This function destroys the designated window. This complicated process of destroying a window involves possibly hiding or permanently closing the window. Also, messages are sent to the window to deactivate it or remove its input focus. Destroying the window additionally involves sending a message to flush the associated message queue. Messages sent include WM_DESTROY and WM_NCDESTROY.

Parameter

hWnd (HWND) indicates the window to be destroyed.

Value Returned

TRUE if successful; otherwise, FALSE

Notes

Should the parent window have any children, the associated child windows will be destroyed first, followed by the owning parent window.

API: int DialogBox(hInstance,lpTemplateName,hWndParent, lpDialogFunc)

Function

This function creates a modal dialog box.

Parameters

hInstance (HANDLE) specifies the instance of the module whose executable file contains the dialog box template.

lpTemplateName (LPSTR) points to a null-terminated character string naming the dialog box template.

hWndParent (HWND) specifies the window that owns the dialog box.

lpDialogFunc (FARPROC) contains the current procedure-instance address of the dialog function.

The callback function must use the Pascal calling convention and be declared FAR, using the following form:

```
HWND FAR PASCAL DialogFunc(hWnd,wMsg,wParam,
                           lParam)
HWND hwnd;      /* identifies message receiving
                   dialog box                   */
unsigned wMsg; /* indicates the message number  */
WORD wParam;    /* specifies 16 bits of additional
                   message-dependent information */
DWORD lParam;  /* specifies 32 bits of additional
                   message-dependent information */
```

Value Returned

Values returned by an application's dialog box are not processed by the application; instead, they are processed by Windows. The return value is –1 if the function fails.

Notes

The size, style, and controls for the dialog box are referenced by the lpTemplateName parameter. Care should be taken since the DialogBox function first calls GetDC to obtain the display context. If the Windows display context cache has been filled by making calls to GetDC, DialogBox could accidentally access some other display context.

API: int DialogBoxIndirect(hInstance,hDTemplate,hWndParent, lpDialogFunc)

Function

This function is similar to the DialogBox function in that it creates a modal dialog box. However, instead of explicitly defining each parameter, the hDTemplate parameter points to a DLGTEMPLATE data structure containing the equivalent information.

Parameters

hInstance (HANDLE) specifies the instance of the module whose executable file contains the dialog box template.

hDTemplate (HANDLE) identifies a DLGTEMPLATE data structure.

hWndParent (HWND) specifies the window that owns the dialog box.

lpDialogFunc (FARPROC) contains the current procedure-instance address of the dialog function.

The callback function must use the Pascal calling convention and be declared FAR, using the following form:

```
HWND FAR PASCAL DialogFunc(hWnd,wMsg,wParam,
                           lParam)
HWND hwnd;        /* identifies message receiving
                     dialog box                      */
unsigned wMsg;  /* indicates the message number   */
WORD wParam;     /* specifies 16 bits of additional
                     message-dependent information */
DWORD lParam;    /* specifies 32 bits of additional
                     message-dependent information */
```

Value Returned

Values returned by an application's dialog box are not processed by the application; instead, they are processed by Windows. The return value is −1 if the function fails.

Notes

The size, style, and controls for the dialog box are referenced by the lpTemplateName parameter. Care should be taken since the DialogBox function first calls GetDC to obtain the display context. If the Windows display context cache has been filled by making calls to GetDC, DialogBox could accidentally access some other display context.

API: LONG DispatchMessage(lpMsg)

Function

This function sends a message from the MSG data structure pointed to by lpMsg. The message is sent to the window function of the designated window.

Parameter

lpMsg (LPMSG) points to a MSG data structure. This structure contains message information from the Windows application queue.

Value Returned

The return value is determined by the window function. Generally, the returned value is not used; however, its meaning is dependent on the message that is actually being dispatched.

Notes

The MSG data structure must contain only valid message values.

MFC: int DoModal()

Function

This function establishes the dialog box and returns the results when completed. All interaction is done through this function. OnOK and OnCancel member functions end a modal dialog box.

Parameters

None.

Value Returned

The int value gives the value of the parameter passed to CDialog::EndDialog.

API: BOOL DrawIcon(hDC,X,Y,hIcon)
MFC: BOOL DrawIcon(X,Y,hIcon)
BOOL DrawIcon(point,hIcon)

Function

This function draws an icon on the selected device.

Parameters

hDC (HDC) represents the device context for a window.

   X (int) defines the logical upper-left corner x coordinate of the icon.

   Y (int) defines the logical upper-left corner y coordinate of the icon.

   point specifies the upper-left corner of the icon. A POINT structure or CPoint object can be used.

   hIcon (HICON) is the icon to be drawn.

Value Returned

TRUE if successful; otherwise, FALSE.

Notes

Subject to the current mapping mode of the device context, the icon's upper-left corner will be placed at the location represented by the x and y coordinates.

API: int DrawText(hDC,lpString,nCount,lpRect,wFormat)
MFC: int DrawText(lpString,nCount,lpRect,nFormat)

Function

This function draws formatted text within a rectangle. The text's tabs are expanded as needed, and the text is left, right, or center aligned, with each line of text being broken as necessary to make certain all lines fit within the defined area.

Parameters

hDC (HDC) specifies the device context.

lpString (LPSTR) points to the string to be drawn. However, if the nCount value is –1, the string pointed to must be null terminated.

nCount (int) represents the number of bytes the string occupies. When nCount is –1, the DrawText function assumes lpString is null terminated. Under these conditions the function automatically computes the character count.

lpRect (LPRECT) points to a RECT data structure containing the diagonal coordinates (logical units) for the rectangle the text must fit within.

wFormat (WORD) or nFormat (UINT) indicates the type of formatting to use. The values can be combined using the logical OR operation.

Following are the possible DrawText formats:

DT_BOTTOM   Selects single-line, bottom-justified text.

DT_CALCRECT   For single-line text, the right side of the rectangle will be modified to contain the entire string. For multiline texts, the rectangle width remains as defined; however, the height of the rectangle is modified to accommodate the entire text. Both modes return the resulting height of the rectangle.

DT_CENTER   Centers the text.

DT_EXPANDTABS   Expands tabs.

DT_EXTERNALLEADING   Incorporates the font's external leading into the line height. Normally, this is not included.

DT_LEFT   Flush-left text alignment.

DT_NOCLIP   Draws without clipping.

DT_NOPREFIX   Ignores processing of prefix characters. When left on, the DrawText function uses the & character to indicate that the string should be underlined. Two ampersands (&&) signal the printing of a single &.

DT_RIGHT   Flush-right text alignment.

DT_SINGLELINE   Defines a single line, ignoring all carriage returns and linefeeds.

DT_TABSTOP   Defines tab stops with the high byte of the wFormat parameter representing the number of characters for each tab stop.

DT_TOP   Selects single-line top-justified text.

DT_VCENTER   Selects vertically centered single-line text.

DT_WORDBREAK   Activates word breaking. It allows text to be broken between lines to accommodate string length in respect to the rectangular perimeter.

Value Returned

The returned value represents the height of the text.

Notes

DrawText uses the selected device context's font, text color, and background color for drawing the text. All formatting assumes multiple lines unless DT_SINGLELINE is specified.

API: BOOL Ellipse(hDC,X1,Y1,X2,Y2)
MFC: BOOL Ellipse(X1,Y1,X2,Y2)
BOOL Ellipse(lpRect)

Function

This function draws an ellipse.

Parameters

hDC (HDC) specifies the device context.
    X1 (int) defines the upper-left corner *x* coordinate of the bounding rectangle.
    Y1 (int) defines the upper-left corner *y* coordinate of the bounding rectangle.
    X2 (int) defines the lower-right corner *x* coordinate of the bounding rectangle.
    Y2 (int) defines the lower-right corner *y* coordinate of the bounding rectangle.
    lpRect is the bounding rectangle. A CRect object can be used.

Value Returned

TRUE if successful; otherwise, FALSE.

Notes

The width and height of the rectangle must not exceed 32,767 units.

API: BOOL EnableMenuItem(hMenu,wIDEnableItem,wEnable)
MFC: UINT EnableMenuItem(nIDEnableItem,nEnable)

Function

This function enables, disables, or grays a menu item.

Parameters

hMenu (HMENU) identifies the menu.

wIDEnableItem (WORD) or nIDEnableItem (UINT) identifies the menu/pop-up menu item to be checked.

wEnable (WORD) or nEnable (UINT) specifies the action to take. The options can be logically ORed together:

Option	Description
MF_BYCOMMAND	Indicates that the wIDEnableItem parameter contains the menu item ID
MF_BYPOSITION	Indicates that the wIDEnableItem parameter contains the position of the menu item
MF_DISABLED	Disables the menu item
MF_ENABLED	Enables the menu item
MF_GRAYED	Grays the menu item

Value Returned

The returned value represents the previous state of the menu item.

Notes

You can use the WM_SYSCOMMAND message to enable or disable input to a menu bar.

API: void EndDialog(hDlg,nResult)
MFC: void EndDialog(nResult)

Function

This function terminates a modal dialog box, sending the result to the DialogBox function. However, the EndDialog function does not immediately terminate the dialog box. Initially it sets the appropriate flag that in turn directs the dialog box to terminate as soon as the dialog function is completed.

Parameters

hDlg (HWND) specifies the dialog box to be destroyed.

nResult (int) defines the value to be returned from the dialog box to the DialogBox function originally creating it.

Value Returned

None.

Notes

The Dialog function can call the EndDialog function at any time.

MFC: END_MESSAGE_MAP( )

Function

This macro is used to end the definition of an application's message map. This map contains entries for each message handler function. The macro is started with the BEGIN_MESSAGE_MAP macro.

Parameters

None.

Value Returned

None.

API: void EndPaint(hWnd,lpPaint)
MFC: void EndPaint(lpPaint)

Function

This function indicates that the painting for a given window is complete.

Parameters

hWnd (HWND) specifies the window that has been repainted.

lpPaint (LPPAINTSTRUCT) points to a PAINTSTRUCT containing the retrieved information given by the BeginPaint function call.

Value Returned

None.

Notes

A call to EndPaint must be made for each call to the BeginPaint function. While a call to BeginPaint can hide the caret, making a call to EndPaint will display the caret.

API: int FillRect(hDC,lpRect,hBrush)
MFC: void FillRect(lpRect,pBrush)

Function

Using the specified brush, this function fills a rectangle.

Parameters

hDC (HDC) specifies the device context.

lpRect (LPRECT) points to a RECT structure containing the coordinates of the rectangle that will be filled with the specified brush.

hBrush (HBRUSH) selects the brush used to fill the rectangle. MFC: pbrush is the brush used for fill.

Value Returned

The function returns an integer value that has no usage and is therefore ignored. MFC: None.

Notes

The rectangle cannot be filled unless a brush has been previously created by calling CreateSolidBrush, CreatePatternBrush, or CreateHatchBrush. The filled rectangle is brushed up to and including the upper border and left-side border. The bottom border and right-side border are left unpainted.

API: BOOL FillRgn(hDC,hRgn,hBrush)
MFC: BOOL FillRgn(pRgn,pBrush)

Function

This function paints a region using the selected brush pattern.

Parameters

hDC (HDC) specifies the device context.

hRgn (HRGN) or pRgn (CRgn*) marks the region to be filled using physical coordinates.

hBrush (HBRUSH) or pBrush (CBrush*) selects the brush to be used for filling the region.

Value Returned

TRUE if successful; otherwise, FALSE.

API: BOOL FloodFill(hDC,X,Y,rgbColor)
MFC: BOOL FloodFill(X,Y,crColor)

Function

This function fills an area of the display surface bounded in the rgbColor or crColor. Painting begins at the x and y coordinates specified.

Parameters

hDC (HDC) specifies the device context.

X (int) specifies the logical x coordinate of where the painting is to begin.

Y (int) specifies the logical y coordinate of where the painting is to begin.

rgbColor or crColor (DWORD) selects the RGB color value to be used to indicate the color of the border boundary.

Value Returned

TRUE is successful; otherwise, FALSE.

Notes

Not all device contexts support FloodFills.

API: int FrameRect(hDC,lpRect,hBrush)
MFC: void FrameRect(lpRect,pBrush)

Function

Using the specified brush, this function draws a border around the specified rectangle.

Parameters

hDC (HDC) specifies the device context.

lpRect (LPRECT) points to a RECT structure containing the coordinates of the rectangle that will be filled with the specified brush.

hBrush (HBRUSH) or pBrush (CBrush*) selects the brush used to fill the rectangle.

Value Returned

The function returns an integer value that has no usage and is therefore ignored. MFC: None.

Notes

The rectangle cannot be filled unless a brush has been previously created by calling CreateSolidBrush, CreatePatternBrush, or CreateHatchBrush. The frame border is always drawn one logical unit in width and height.

API: BOOL FrameRgn(hDC,hRgn,hBrush,nWidth,nHeight)
MFC: BOOL FrameRgn(pRgn,pBrush,nWidth,nHeight)

Function

This function draws a border around the specified region using the selected brush with the defined width and height.

Parameters

hDC (HDC) specifies the device context.

hRgn (HRGN) or pRgn (CRgn*) specifies the region to be enclosed with a border.

hBrush (HBRUSH) or pBrush (CBrush*) selects the brush used to fill the rectangle.

nWidth (int), using logical units, expresses the width of the border to be drawn in vertical brush strokes.

nHeight (int), using logical units, expresses the height of the border to be drawn in horizontal brush strokes.

Value Returned

TRUE if successful; otherwise, FALSE.

API: void FreeProcInstance(lpProc)

Function

This function frees the specified function from the data segment in which it was bound.

Parameter

lpProc (FARPROC) is the procedure-instance address of the function about to be freed.

Value Returned

None.

Notes

lpProc must point to a function that was previously created using the MakeProcInstance function. An unrecoverable error condition can occur if an attempt is made to call the function after it has been freed.

API: DWORD GetBkColor(hDC)
MFC: DWORD GetBkCOlor()

Function

This function returns the current background color of the specified device.

Parameter

hDC (HDC) specifies the device context.

Value Returned

Indicates the current RGB background color value.

API: int GetBkMode(hDC)
MFC: int GetBkMode( )

Function

This function returns the background mode for the specified device.

Parameter

hDC (HDC) specifies the device context.

Value Returned

Indicates the current background mode (TRANSPARENT or OPAQUE).

Notes

The background mode is important because it is used with text, hatched brushes, and nonsolid pen styles.

API: DWORD GetBrushOrg(hDC)
MFC: CPoint GetBrushOrg( )

Function

This function returns the current brush origin for the specified device context.

Parameter

hDC (HDC) specifies the device context.

Value Returned

Returns the origin of the current brush, with the high-order word indicating the device unit's y coordinate and the low-order word indicating the device unit's x coordinate. MFC: CPoint object, which specifies the x and y coordinates of a point.

Notes

The initial brush origin is always set at (0,0).

API: BOOL GetCharWidth(hDC,wFirstChar,wLastChar,lpBuffer)
MFC: BOOL GetCharWidth(nFirstChar,nLastChar,lpBuffer)

Function

Using the current font, this function returns the width of individual characters in consecutive groups of characters.

Parameters

hDC (HDC) specifies the device context.

wFirstChar (WORD) or nFirstChar (UINT), using the current font, specifies the first character in a consecutive group of characters.

wLastChar (WORD) or nLastChar (UINT) is the last character in a consecutive group of characters.

lpBuffer (LPINT) points to the buffer that will receive the width of each character in a group of characters.

Value Returned

TRUE if successful; otherwise, FALSE.

Notes

Any character not defined for the current font will be given a default character width that is usually based on a blank space character.

API: void GetClientRect(hWnd,lpRect)
MFC: void GetClientRect(lpRect)

Function

This function copies the coordinates of a window's client area into the lpRect data structure.

Parameters

hWnd (HWND) specifies the window associated with the client area.

lpRect (LPRECT) points to a RECT structure.

Value Returned

None.

Notes

The returned coordinates represent the upper-left and lower-right corners of the client area. Client coordinates are relative to the window's upper-left corner (0,0).

API: DWORD GetCurrentPosition(hDC)
MFC: CPoint GetCurrentPosition()

Function

This function retrieves the logical coordinates of the current position.

Parameter

hDC (HDC) specifies the device context.

Value Returned

Represents the current position, with the high-order word containing the y coordinate and the low-order word containing the x coordinate. MFC: CPoint object, which represents the x and y coordinates.

API: void GetCursorPos(lpPoint)
MFC: void GetCursorPos(lpPoint)

Function

This function returns the current cursor position using screen coordinates.

Parameter

lpPoint (LPPOINT) points to a POINT data structure receiving the cursor's screen coordinates.

Value Returned

None.

Notes

The current mapping mode of the window containing the cursor has no effect on the screen coordinates returned.

API: CDC* GetDC()
MFC: HDC GetDC(hWnd)

Function

This function returns a handle to a display context for the client area of the specified window.

Parameter

hWnd (HWND) specifies the window whose display context is to be returned.

Value Returned

Indicates the display context if a nonzero value. An unsuccessful call returns a NULL.

Notes

The returned value can be used for subsequent GDI function calls that draw in the client area.

API: LONG GetDCOrg(hDC)
MFC: CPoint GetDCOrg()

Function

This function returns the translation origin for the specified device context.

Parameter

hDC (HDC) specifies the device context.

Value Returned

Contains the final device coordinate translation origin, with the high-order word containing the *y* coordinate and the low-order word containing the *x* coordinate. MFC: CPoint object, which represents the *x* and *y* coordinates.

Notes

The returned coordinates represent the offset used by Windows to translate device coordinates into client coordinates for any points in an application's window. This is relative to the physical origin of the display screen.

API: HWND GetDlgItem(hDlg,nIDDlgItem)
MFC: CWnd* GetDlgItem(nID)

Function

This function returns the handle of the control contained in the specified dialog box.

Parameters

hDlg (HWND) specifies the dialog box that contains the control.

nIDDlgItem (int) or nID (int) represents the integer ID of the item being retrieved.

Value Returned

Indicates the given control. If no control exists as specified by nIDDlgItem, a NULL is returned. MFC: CWnd* points to the control.

Notes

You can also use this function with any parent-child window pair, not just dialog boxes.

API: UINT GetDlgItemInt(hDlg,nIDDlgItem,lpTranslated,bSigned)
MFC: UINT GetDlgItemInt(nID,lpTrans,bSigned)

Function

This function translates the text of a control of the specified dialog box (or parent-child window pair) into an integer value.

Parameters

hDlg (HWND) specifies the dialog box that contains the control.

nIDDlgItem or nID (int) represents the integer ID for the item being translated.

lpTranslated or lpTrans (BOOL FAR *) points to a Boolean variable receiving the translated flag.

bSigned (BOOL) identifies whether or not the retrieved value is signed.

Value Returned

Represents the translated value of the dialog box item text.

Notes

The function translates numeric characters into their equivalent signed/unsigned value. Translation skips over leading blanks and continues until either the end of the string is reached or a nonnumeric character is encountered. If a minus sign is encountered, the value returned is a signed number; otherwise, it is unsigned. A value greater than 32,767 (signed) is returned as a zero. The same is true for a unsigned value greater than 65,635. The function sends a WM_GETTEXT message to the control.

API: int GetDlgItemText(hDlg,nIDDlgItem,lpString,nMaxCount)
MFC: int GetDlgItemText(nID,lpStr,nMaxCount)

Function

This function retrieves the text associated with the specified control into a string, returning the number of characters copied.

Parameters

hDlg (HWND) specifies the dialog box that contains the control.

nIDDlgItem or nID (int) represents the integer ID of the item being translated.

lpString or lpStr (LPSTR) points to the buffer receiving the copied text.

nMaxCount (int) represents the maximum number of characters (in bytes) to be copied to lpString. A string longer than the value specified will automatically be truncated.

Value Returned

Returns the actual number of characters copied. A zero value indicates no text was copied.

API: int GetMapMode(hDC)
MFC: int GetMapMode()

Function

This function returns the current mapping mode.

Parameters

hDC (HDC) specifies the device context.

Value Returned

Represents the current mapping mode.

API: BOOL GetMessage(lpMsg,hWnd,wMsgFilterMin,wMsgFilterMax)

Function

This function takes a message from the application's message queue and places it in the MSG data structure. Control is yielded if no messages are available.

Parameters

lpMsg (LPMSG) points to a MSG structure containing message information supplied by the Windows application queue.

hWnd (HWND) specifies the window whose messages are to be retrieved. If the parameter is NULL, the function will retrieve any message for the window that belongs to the calling application.

wMsgFilterMin (unsigned) is an integer value indicating the lowest message to be examined.

wMsgFilterMax (unsigned) is an integer value indicating the highest message to be examined.

Value Returned

TRUE indicates that some message other than WM_QUIT was retrieved. FALSE indicates that the message retrieved was WM_QUIT.

Notes

Using the WM_KEYFIRST and WM_KEYLAST constants will retrieve only keyboard-input-related messages. The WM_MOUSEFIRST and WM_MOUSELAST constants can filter out and retrieve only those mouse-related messages.

API: DWORD GetMessagePos()

Function

This function returns the screen coordinate mouse position after the last message was obtained by a call to GetMessage.

Parameters

None.

Value Returned

The low-order word contains the x coordinate; the high-order word contains the y coordinate.

Notes

By making a call to the GetCursorPos function instead of GetMessagePos, an application can obtain the current position of the mouse instead of when the last message occurred.

API: DWORD GetNearestColor(hDC,rgbColor)
MFC: DWORD GetNearestColor(crColor)

Function

This function returns the closest physical color to a specified logical color that the requested device can represent.

Parameters

hDC (HDC) specifies the device context.

rgbColor or crColor (DWORD) identifies an RGB color value specifying the color to be matched.

Value Returned

Represents the solid RGB color closest to the rgbColor or crColor request that the device is capable of producing.

API: DWORD GetNearestPaletteIndex(hPalette,rgbColor)
MFC: UINT GetNearestPaletteIndex(crColor)

Function

This function returns the index specifier of the entry in a logical palette that most closely matches an RGB color value.

Parameters

hPalette (HPALETTE) specifies the logical palette.

rgbColor or crColor (DWORD) identifies an RGB color value that specifies the color to be matched.

Value Returned

The logical palette index that most nearly matches the RGB value.

API: int GetObject(hObject,nCount,lpObject)
MFC: int GetObject(nCount,lpObject)

Function

This function assigns the logical data information defining a logical object to the buffer pointed to by lpObject.

Parameters

hObject (HANDLE) specifies a logical font, pen, brush, or bitmap.

nCount (int) represents the number of bytes to be copied to the buffer.

lpObject (LPSTR) points to a LOGFONT, LOGPEN, LOGBRUSH, or LOGBITMAP data structure that will receive the logical object information.

...eturned

...ies the number of bytes actually retrieved. If NULL, some error condition has ...rred.

Notes

If the logical information being retrieved involves a bitmap, the function will return only the width, height, and color format bitmap information. To retrieve the actual bitmap, a call must be made to GetBitmapBits.

API: WORD GetPaletteEntries(hPalette,wStartIndex, wNumEntries,lpBuffer)
MFC: UINT GetPaletteEntries(nStartIndex,nNumEntries, lpPaletteColors)

Function

This function copies the RGB color values and flags contained in a range of entries in a logical palette to a buffer.

Parameters

hPalette (HPALETTE) specifies the logical palette.

wStartIndex (WORD) or nStartIndex (UINT) defines the first entry in the logical palette to be copied.

wNumEntries (WORD) or nNumEntries (UINT) defines the number of entries in the logical palette to be copied.

lpBuffer (LPSTR) points to a buffer to receive the palette entries.

lpPaletteColors (LPPALETTEENTRY) is a data structure to receive palette entries.

Value Returned

The number of entries copied. It is zero if the function failed.

API: DWORD GetPixel(hDC,X,Y,)
MFC: DWORD GetPixel(X,Y)
DWORD GetPixel(point)

Function

This function returns the RGB color value of the point specified by X and Y, and within the clipping region.

Parameters

hDC (HDC) specifies the device context.

    X (int) defines the logical upper-left corner x coordinate of the point to be inspected.

    Y (int) defines the logical upper-left corner y coordinate of the point to be inspected.

    point contains logical x,y coordinates in a POINT structure or a CPoint object.

Value Returned

Contains the RGB color value of the point referenced. A –1 value indicates that the indicated point was not within the clipping region.

Notes

Not all device contexts support this function.

API: int GetPolyFillMode(hDC)
MFC: int GetPolyFillMode()

Function

This function returns the current polygon filling mode (ALTERNATE or WINDING).

Parameter

hDC (HDC) specifies the device context.

Value Returned

ALTERNATE, for alternate polygon filling mode, or WINDING, for winding polygon filling mode.

API: int GetROP2(hDC)
MFC: int GetROP2()

Function

This function returns the current drawing mode.

Parameter

hDC (HDC) specifies the device context.

Value Returned

The drawing mode (see SetROP2).

Notes

The current drawing mode determines how the selected pen or interior color will be combined with the color already on the display.

API: int GetScrollPos(hWnd,nBar)
MFC: int GetScrollPos(nBar)

Function

This function returns the current position of the specified scroll bar thumb.

Parameters

hWnd (HWND) identifies the window containing the standard scroll bar.
    nBar (int) identifies the scroll bar to examine, using one of the following values:

Value	Description
SB_CTL	Returns the position of a scroll bar control, assuming that hWnd points to a window handle of a scroll bar control
SB_HORZ	Returns the position of a window's horizontal scroll bar
SB_VERT	Returns the position of a window's vertical scroll bar

Notes

The returned value is a relative value depending on the current scrolling range; that is, a range of zero to 50 would yield a mid-position value of 25.

API: void GetScrollRange(hWnd,nBar,lpMinPos,lpMaxPos)
MFC: void GetScrollRange(lpMinPos,lpMaxPos)

Function

This function returns the current minimum and maximum scroll bar positions for the defined scroll bar.

Parameters

hWnd (HWND) specifies the window that has a standard scroll bar or scroll bar control.

nBar (int) identifies the scroll bar to examine, using one of the following values:

Value	Description
SB_CTL	Returns the position of a scroll bar control, assuming that hWnd points to a window handle of a scroll bar control
SB_HORZ	Returns the position of a window's horizontal scroll bar
SB_VERT	Returns the position of a window's vertical scroll bar

lpMinPos (LPINT) points to an integer variable that will receive the scroll bar's minimum position value.

lpMaxPos (LPINT) points to an integer variable that will receive the scroll bar's maximum position value.

Value Returned

None.

Notes

The default range for a standard scroll bar is from zero to 100.

API: HANDLE GetStockObject(nIndex)

Function

This function returns the handle to a predefined stock font, pen, or brush.

Parameter

nIndex (int) identifies the type of stock object to be returned:

Value	Description
BLACK_BRUSH	Black brush
DKGRAY_BRUSH	Dark gray brush
GRAY_BRUSH	Gray brush
HOLLOW_BRUSH	Hollow brush
LTGRAY_BRUSH	Light gray brush
NULL_BRUSH	Null brush
WHITE_BRUSH	White brush
BLACK_PEN	Black pen
NULL_PEN	Null pen
WHITE_PEN	White pen
ANSI_FIXED_FONT	ANSI fixed system font
ANSI_VAR_FONT	ANSI proportional system font
DEVICE_DEFAULT_FONT	Device-dependent font
OEM_FIXED_FONT	OEM-supplied fixed font
SYSTEM_FONT	System-dependent fixed font
SYSTEM_FIXED_FONT	Fixed width system font in earlier versions of Windows
DEFAULT_PALETTE	Default color match

Value Returned

Identifies the selected logical object, or a NULL if the function call was unsuccessful.

Notes

DKGRAY_BRUSH, GRAY_BRUSH, and LTGRAY_BRUSH objects should not be used as background brushes for any window not using CS_HREDRAW and CS_VREDRAW styles. Doing so can lead to misalignment of brush patterns when the window is sized or moved.

API: DWORD GetSysColor(nIndex)
MFC: DWORD GetSysColor(nIndex)

Function

This function returns the color value of the specified display object.

Parameter

nIndex (int) indicates the display object whose color is to be returned.

Value Returned

Represents the RGB color value of the selected object.

Notes

Monochrome displays usually interpret various colors as shades of gray.

API: int GetSystemMetrics(nIndex)
MFC: int GetSystemMetrics(nIndex)

Function

This function returns the system's metrics. The measurements represent the widths and heights of various display elements.

Parameter

nIndex (int) identifies the system measurement that is to be retrieved.

Possible System Metric Indexes

Index	Description
SM_CXSCREEN	Screen width
SM_CYSCREEN	Screen height
SM_CXFRAME	Width of sizeable window frame
SM_CYFRAME	Height of sizeable window frame
SM_CXVSCROLL	Width of arrow bitmap on vertical scroll bar
SM_CYVSCROLL	Height of arrow bitmap on vertical scroll bar
SM_CXHSCROLL	Width of arrow bitmap on horizontal scroll bar
SM_CYHSCROLL	Height of arrow bitmap on vertical scroll bar
SM_CYCAPTION	Height of caption
SM_CXBORDER	Width of nonsizeable window frame
SM_CYBORDER	Height of nonsizeable window frame
SM_CXDLGFRAME	Width of WS_DLGFRAME styled window
SM_CYDLGFRAME	Height of WS_DLGFRAME styled window

Index	Description
SM_CXHTHUMB	Width of horizontal scroll bar thumb
SM_CYVTHUMB	Height of horizontal scroll bar thumb
SM_CXICON	Icon width
SM_CYICON	Icon height
SM_CXCURSOR	Cursor width
SM_CYCURSOR	Cursor height
SM_CYMENU	Single-line menu bar height
SM_CXFULLSCREEN	Full-screen client area window width
SM_CYFULLSCREEN	Full-screen client area window height
SM_CYKANJIWINDOW	Kanji window height
SM_CXMINTRACK	Minimum window tracking width
SM_CYMINTRACK	Minimum window tracking height
SM_CXMIN	Window minimum width
SM_CYMIN	Window minimum height
SM_CXSIZE	Title bar bitmap width
SM_CYSIZE	Title bar bitmap height
SM_MOUSEPRESENT	Nonzero when mouse hardware is installed
SM_DEBUG	Nonzero for a Windows debugging version
SM_SWAPBUTTON	Nonzero when the left and right mouse buttons are swapped

Value Returned

Indicates the specified system metric.

Notes

The function can also indicate whether the Windows version being used is capable of debugging, if a mouse is present, and if so, if the left/right buttons have been swapped.

API: WORD GetTextAlign(hDC)
MFC: UINT GetTextAlign()

Function

This function returns the status of the text-alignment flag.

Parameter

hDC (HDC) specifies the device context.

Value Returned

The returned value can be one or a combination of the following:

Value	Description
TA_BASELINE	Selects alignment along the x axis and the baseline of the selected font within the bounding rectangle
TA_BOTTOM	Selects alignment along the x axis and the bottom of the bounding rectangle
TA_CENTER	Selects alignment along the y axis and the center of the bounding rectangle
TA_LEFT	Selects alignment along the y axis and the left side of the bounding rectangle
TA_NOUPDATECP	Notes that the current position is not updated
TA_RIGHT	Selects alignment along the y axis and the right side of the bounding rectangle
TA_TOP	Selects alignment along the x axis and the top of the bounding rectangle
TA_UPDATECP	Notes that the current position is updated

Notes

By using the logical AND operation, a particular flag's value can be checked. A zero value indicates that the flag was not set.

API: DWORD GetTextColor(hDC)
MFC: DWORD GetTextColor()

Function

This function returns the current text color.

Parameter

hDC (HDC) specifies the device context.

Value Returned

Returns an RGB color value.

Notes

The returned color value indicates the color used for the foreground color of characters output by the call to the TextOut function.

API: DWORD GetTextExtent(hDC,lpString,nCount)
MFC: CSize GetTextExtent(lpString,nCount)

Function

This function calculates the height and width of a line of text.

Parameters

hDC (HDC) specifies the device context.

lpString (LPSTR) points to a text string whose height and width are to be calculated.

nCount (int) indicates the number of characters in the text string.

Value Returned

Represents the height and width of the text string: high-order word for the height, low-order word for the width. MFC: CSize object, which represents the string's dimensions (in logical units).

Notes

For those devices that use kerning for character placement, the sum of the extents of the individual characters may not equal the extent of the entire string.

API: int GetTextFace(hDC,nCount,lpFacename)
MFC: int GetTextFace(nCount,lpFacename)

Function

This function copies the typeface name of the desired font into a buffer.

Parameters

hDC (HDC) specifies the device context.
    nCount (int) indicates the buffer size in bytes.
    lpFacename (LPSTR) points to the buffer to receive the name of the typeface.

Value Returned

Either the number of bytes copied into the buffer or a NULL for an unsuccessful attempt.

API: BOOL GetTextMetrics(hDC,lpMetrics)
MFC: BOOL GetTextMetrics(lpMetrics)

Function

This function places the metrics for the selected font into the TEXTMETRICS data structure pointed to by lpMetrics.

Parameters

hDC (HDC) specifies the device context.
    lpMetrics (LPTEXTMETRIC) points to a TEXTMETRIC structure.

Value Returned

TRUE if successful; otherwise, FALSE.

API: DWORD GetViewportExt(hDC)
MFC: CSize GetViewportExt()

Function

This function retrieves the x-extent and y-extent of the selected device's context viewport.

Parameter

hDC (HDC) specifies the device context.

Value Returned

The x- and y-extents are returned using device units. The high-order byte is used for the y-extent, with the low-order byte indicating the x-extent. MFC: CSize object, which represents the viewport's dimensions.

API: DWORD GetViewportOrg(hDC)
MFC: CPoint GetViewportOrg()

Function

This function returns the x coordinate and y coordinate of the viewport origin associated with the specified context.

Parameter

hDC (HDC) specifies the device context.

Value Returned

Using device coordinates, the returned high-order byte contains the y coordinate, with the low-order byte containing the x coordinate. MFC: CPoint object, which represents the x and y coordinates.

API: HDC GetWindowDC(hWnd)
MFC: CDC* GetWindowDC()

Function

This function returns the window's display context.

Parameter

hWnd (HWND) identifies the window to be used in determining the display context.

Value Returned

Either contains the display context for the specified window or, if unsuccessful, returns a NULL. MFC: CDC* pointer.

Notes

Display contexts are very important because they allow painting anywhere in a window. The painting includes title bars, menus, and scroll bars. The origin of the context is always the upper-left corner of the window, not the client area. Once painting beyond the client area is complete (not recommended), a call to ReleaseDC must be made, releasing the display context.

MFC: virtual BOOL InitInstance( );

Function

This function is needed since Windows allows multiple copies of an application to be run at the same time. A one-time application initialization is done the first time the application runs. Then an instance initialization is run for each copy of the application, including the first.

Parameters

None.

Value Returned

TRUE if successful; otherwise, FALSE.

API: BOOL InsertMenu(hMenu,nPosition,wFlags,wIDNewItem, lpNewItem)
MFC: BOOL InsertMenu(nPosition,nFlags,nIDNewItem,lpNewItem)
   BOOL InsertMenu(nPosition,nFlags,nIDNewItem,pBmp)

Function

This function inserts a new item at the position specified, moving other items down.

Parameters

hMenu (HMENU) specifies the menu to be changed.

nPosition (WORD), if wFlags is set to MB_BYCOMMAND, specifies the menu item ID.

If wFlags (WORD) or nFlags (UINT) is set to MB_BYPOSITION, this parameter identifies the position of the existing menu item.

The first item is numbered zero. A −1 value causes the new item to be inserted at the end of the list.

wFlags or nFlags defines which nPosition is to be interpreted.

wIDNewItem (WORD) or nIDNewItem (UINT) defines either the command ID or the menu handle of the pop-up menu.

lpNewItem (LPSTR) defines the content of the new menu item.

pBmp points to a CBitMap object.

Value Returned

TRUE if the function was successful; otherwise, FALSE.

Notes

Whenever the menu changes, the application should call DrawMenuBar.

API: void InvalidateRect(hWnd,lpRect,bErase)
MFC: void InvalidateRect(lpRect,bErase)

Function

This function invalidates the client area within the specified rectangle by adding the rectangle to the window's update region.

Parameters

hWnd (HWND) specifies the window whose update region is about to be modified by the specified rectangle.

lpRect (LPRECT) points to a RECT structure containing the coordinates of the rectangle to be used for adding to the update region. A NULL value will cause the entire client area to be added to the update region.

bErase (BOOL) indicates whether the background in the update region will be erased.

Value Returned

None.

Notes

If the update region is not empty and there are no other application queue messages for that window, Windows will send a WM_PAINT message.

API: void InvalidateRgn(hWnd,hRgn,bErase)
MFC: void InvalidateRgn(pRgn,bErase)

Function

This function adds the current update region of the specified window to the given region in the client area, thereby invalidating it.

Parameters

hWnd (HWND) specifies the window whose update region is about to be changed.

hRgn (HRGN) or pRgn (CRgn*) specifies the region (in client area coordinates) that is to be added to the update region.

bErase (BOOL) defines whether or not the background within the update region is to be erased. A nonzero value erases the background. When zero, the background remains unchanged.

Value Returned

None.

Notes

When the update region is not empty and there are no application queue messages pending, Windows sends a WM_PAINT message.

API: void InvertRect(hDC,lpRect)
MFC: void InvertRect(lpRect)

Function

This function inverts the contents of the specified rectangle.

Parameters

hDC (HDC) specifies the device context.

lpRect (LPRECT) points to a RECT structure containing the logical coordinates of the rectangle to be inverted.

Value Returned

None.

Notes

On color monitors, the color inversion depends on how colors are generated for the display. Monochrome monitors invert the image by making white pixels black and black pixels white. Two calls to the function will restore the original colors of the rectangle. A nonzero value indicates a successful inversion; otherwise, zero.

API: BOOL InvertRgn(hDC,hRgn)
MFC: BOOL InvertRgn(pRgn)

Function

This function inverts the contents of the specified region.

Parameters

hDC (HDC) specifies the device context.

hRgn (HRGN) or pRgn (CRgn*) contains the logical coordinates of the region to be inverted.

Value Returned

TRUE if successful; otherwise, FALSE.

Notes

On color monitors, the color inversion depends on how colors are generated for the display. Monochrome monitors invert the image by making white pixels black and black pixels white. Two calls to the function will restore the original colors of the region. A nonzero value indicates a successful inversion; otherwise, zero.

API: void LineDDA(X1,Y1,X2,Y2,lpLineFunc,lpData)

Function

This function calculates all of the points in a line defined by the x and y coordinates.

Parameters

X1 (int) identifies the logical x coordinate of the starting point.

Y1 (int) identifies the logical y coordinate of the starting point.

X2 (int) identifies the logical x coordinate of the ending point.

Y2 (int) identifies the logical *y* coordinate of the ending point.

lpLineFunc (FARPROC) is the procedure-instance address of the application-defined function.

lpData (LPSTR) points to the application-defined data.

Value Returned

None.

Notes

The callback function must use the pascal calling convention with the FAR option.

API: BOOL LineTo(hDC,X,Y)
MFC: BOOL LineTo(X,Y)
BOOL LineTo(point)

Function

This function draws a line using the current pen from the current position up to, but not including, the point indicated by X and Y. The current position is then set to (X,Y).

Parameters

hDC (HDC) specifies the device context.

X (int) defines the logical *x* coordinate of the ending point for the line.

Y (int) defines the logical *y* coordinate of the ending point for the line.

point is a POINT structure or a CPoint object.

Value Returned

TRUE if successful; otherwise, FALSE.

Notes

None.

API: HCURSOR LoadCursor(hInstance,lpCursorName)
MFC: HCURSOR LoadCursor(lpCursorName)
HCURSOR LoadCursor(nIDCursor)

Function

This function loads the selected cursor from the executable file associated with the module pointed to by hInstance.

Parameters

hInstance (HANDLE) specifies the instance of the module whose executable file contains the cursor to be loaded. When the parameter is NULL, the function can be used to load a predefined Windows cursor, with the lpCursorName being one of the following:

Option	Description
IDC_ARROW	Standard Windows arrow cursor
IDC_CROSS	Standard Windows cross-hair cursor
IDC_IBEAM	Standard Windows I-beam text cursor
IDC_ICON	Standard Windows empty icon
IDC_SIZE	Standard Windows four-pointed arrow
IDC_SIZENESW	Double-pointed cursor with cursors pointing NE and SW
IDC_SIZENS	Double-pointed cursor with cursors pointing N and S
IDC_SIZEWE	Double-pointed cursor with cursors pointing W and E
IDC_SIZENWSE	Double-pointed cursor with cursors pointing NW and SE
IDC_UPARROW	Standard Windows vertical arrow cursor
IDC_WAIT	Standard Windows hourglass cursor

lpCursorName (LPSTR) is a pointer to a null-terminated character string naming the cursor.

nIDCursor, (UINT) is an ID value assigned to the cursor.

Value Returned

Either specifies the selected cursor or returns a NULL if the specified cursor does not exist.

Notes

Using the low-order word of lpCursorName, the function can be used to load a cursor created by a call to the MakeIntResource function.

MFC: m_nCmdShow

Function

This value parallels the nCmdShow parameter passed to WinMain. When m_nCmd-Show is TRUE, the call to CWnd::ShowWindow makes the main window visible.

Parameters

None.

MFC: m_pMainWnd

Function

This data member is used to store a pointer to the application's main window object. Applications are terminated when the window pointed to by m_pMainWnd is closed.

Paramters

None.

Value Returned

None.

API: POINT MakePoint(lInteger)

Function

This function converts a long value containing the x and y coordinates of a particular point into a POINT structure.

Parameter

lInteger (LONG) is the long integer containing the points to be converted.

Value Returned

Identifies the POINT data structure created.

API: FARPROC MakeProcInstance(lpProc,hInstance)

Function

This function creates the procedure-instance address.

Parameters

lpProc (FARPROC) is a procedure-instance address.

hInstance (HANDLE) specifies the instance associated with the specified data segment.

Value Returned

Either points to the function or contains a NULL if unsuccessful.

Notes

The created address points to prologue code that is actually executed before the function itself. This procedure allows the current instance of the function to access variables and data structures in that particular instance's data segment.

API: int MessageBox(hWndParent,lpText,lpCaption,wType)
MFC: int MessageBox(lpText,lpCaption,nType)

Function

This function creates and displays a window containing application-supplied messages, caption, icons, and push buttons.

Parameters

hWndParent (HWND) specifies the window that owns the message box.

lpText (LPSTR) points to the null-terminated message string that will be displayed.

lpCaption (LPSTR) points to a null-terminated string that will be used for the caption in the dialog box. When NULL, the caption displayed will be "Error!"

wType (WORD) or nType (UINT) identifies the contents of the dialog box and can be any single value or logically ORed combination listed in the following "Notes" section.

Value Returned

A zero return value indicates that there is not enough memory to create the message box. A successful creation will return one of the following menu items returned by the dialog box:

Options	Description
IDABORT	The Abort button was pressed
IDCANCEL	The Escape or Cancel button was pressed. If the message box doesn't have a Cancel button, a keypress of the Escape button will be ignored
IDIGNORE	The Ignore button was pressed
IDNO	The No button was pressed
IDOK	The OK button was pressed
IDRETRY	The Retry button was pressed
IDYES	The Yes button was pressed

Notes

Here is an alphabetical list showing the possible contents of a dialog box:

Identifier	Description
MB_ABORTRETRYIGNORE	The message box has three push buttons: Abort, Retry, and Ignore
MB_APPLMODAL	The user must respond to the message box. This is the default. Note that this does not prevent the user from switching to other applications (see MB_SYSTEMMODAL)
MB_DEFBUTTON1	The first button is the default
MB_DEFBUTTON2	The second button is the default
MB_DEFBUTTON3	The third button is the default
MB_ICONASTERISK	An asterisk icon will be displayed in the message box
MB_ICONEXCLAMATION	An exclamation-point icon will be displayed in the message box

Identifier	Description
MB_ICONHAND	A hand icon will be displayed in the message box
MB_ICONINFORMATION	Icon made of a lowercase "c" in a circle
MB_ICONQUESTION	A question-mark icon will be displayed in the message box
MB_ICONSTOP	A stop sign appears in message box
MB_OK	The message box has one push button labeled OK
MB_OKCANCEL	The message box has two push buttons labeled OK and Cancel
MB_RETRYCANCEL	The message box has two push buttons labeled Retry and Cancel
MB_SYSTEMMODAL	Suspends all applications because of the seriousness of the event that is about to occur. The user must respond to the message box and cannot switch to other tasks
MB_TASKMODAL	Same as MP_APPMODAL except that top-level windows are handled differently, depending on whether the hWndOwner parameter is NULL
MB_YESNO	The message box has two push buttons labeled Yes and No
MB_YESNOCANCEL	The message box has three push buttons labeled Yes, No, and Cancel

API: DWORD MoveTo(hDC,X,Y)
MFC: CPoint MoveTo(X,Y)
CPoint MoveTo(point)

Function

This function moves the current position to the *x,y* coordinate specified.

Parameters

hDC (HDC) specifies the device context.
   X (int) identifies the logical *x* coordinate of the new location.
   Y (int) identifies the logical *y* coordinate of the new location.
   point is a POINT structure or a CPoint object.

Value Returned

Contains the coordinates of the previous position. The high-order word contains the *y* coordinate, with the low-order word containing the *x* coordinate.

Notes

A call to MoveTo affects many other functions that use the current position.

API: void OffsetRect(lpRect,X,Y)
MFC: void OffsetRect(X,Y)
void OffsetRect(point)
void OffsetRect(size)

Function

Using the signed X,Y offset values, this function moves the indicated rectangle.

Parameters

lpRect (LPRECT) points to a RECT structure that contains the rectangle about to be moved.

X (int) indicates just how much to move the rectangle left (negative value) or right.

Y (int) indicates just how much to move the rectangle up (negative value) or down.

point is a POINT or CPoint object.

size is SIZE or CSize object.

Value Returned

None.

Notes

The coordinates of the rectangle must not be greater than 32,767 or less than –32,768 units.

API: int OffsetRgn(hRgn,X,Y)
MFC: int OffsetRgn(X,Y)
int OffsetRgn(point)

Function

Using the signed X,Y offset values, this function moves the indicated region.

Parameters

hRgn (HRGN) identifies the region about to be moved.
 X (int) indicates just how much to move the region left (negative value) or right.
 Y (int) indicates just how much to move the region up (negative value) or down.
 point is a POINT or CPoint object.

Value Returned

Indicates the new region's type:

Type	Description
COMPLEXREGION	Identifies a region with overlapping borders
ERROR	Indicates that the region handle is not valid
NULLREGION	Indicates that the region is empty
SIMPLEREGION	Indicates that the region does not have any overlapping borders

Notes

The coordinates of the region must not be greater than 32,767 or less than −32,768 units.

API: DWORD OffsetViewportOrg(hDC,X,Y)
MFC: CPoint OffsetViewportOrg(nWidth,nHeight)

Function

This function modifies the specified viewport origin relative to the current values.

Parameters

hDC (HDC) specifies the device context.

X (int) or nWidth (UINT) indicates how many device units to add to the current origin's *x* coordinate.

Y (int) or nHeight (UINT) indicates how many device units to add to the current origin's *y* coordinate.

Value Returned

Contains the previous viewport origin expressed in device coordinates. The high-order word contains the *y* coordinate, with the low-order word containing the *x* coordinate. CPoint is a CPoint object representing the *x* and *y* coordinates.

Notes

The new viewport origin is calculated by adding the current origin with the X and Y values.

API: DWORD OffsetWindowOrg(hDC,X,Y)
MFC: CPoint OffsetWindowOrg(nWidth,nHeight)

Function

This function modifies the specified window origin relative to the current values.

Parameters

hDC (HDC) specifies the device context.

X (int) or nWidth (UINT) indicates how many device units to add to current origin's *x* coordinate.

Y (int) or nHeight (UINT) indicates how many device units to add to current origin's *y* coordinate.

Value Returned

Contains the previous window origin expressed in device coordinates. The high-order word contains the *y* coordinate, with the low-order word containing the *x* coordinate. CPoint represents the *x* and *y* coordinates.

Notes

The new window origin is calculated by adding the current origin with the X and Y values.

MFC: virtual void OnCancel()

Function

This function overrides the member function to react to the Cancel push button action. The default action causes DoModal to return IDCANCEL.

Parameters

None.

Value Returned

None.

MFC: afx_msg int OnCreate(LPCREATESTRUCT lpCreateStruct)

Function

This function is typically called when the application requests that a CWnd object be created with a call to either the Create or CreateEx member function.

Parameters

lpCreateStruct points to a CREATESTRUCT structure. This structure holds information on the CWnd object being created. This structure holds a copy of the parameters used to create the window.

Value Returned

Zero to continue creation; –1 to destroy.

MFC: virtual void OnOK()

Function

This function overrides the member function to react to the OK push button action. The default action terminates the dialog box. This causes DoModal to return IDOK.

Parameters

None.

Value Returned

None.

MFC: afx_msg void OnPaint()

Function

This function is typically called by the application or Windows to request a repaint of a portion of CWnd. WM_PAINT is intercepted by the member function when the UpdateWindow member function is called.

Parameters

None.

Value Returned

None.

MFC: afx_msg void OnSize(UINT nType,int cx,int cy)

Function

The OnSize function is called after the size of the window has been changed.

Parameters

nType defines the type of resizing. Here are typical values:

Value	Description
SIZEFULLSCREEN	Maximized window
SIZEICONIC	Minimized window
SIZENORMAL	Window resized, but SIZEICONIC or SIZEFULLSCREEN valid
SIZEZOOMHIDE	Sent to pop-up windows when another window is maximized
SIZEZOOMSHOW	Message sent to pop-up windows when another window has been restored

cx gives the new width.
cy gives the new height.

Value Returned

None.

API: COLORREF PALETTEINDEX(nPaletteIndex)

Function

This function accepts an index to a logical color palette entry and returns a palette-entry specifier.

Parameters

nPaletteIndex (int) defines an index to the palette entry containing the color to be used for a graphics operation.

Value Returned

Returns the value of a logical-palette index specifier.

API: BOOL PaintRgn(hDC,hRgn)
MFC: BOOL PaintRgn(pRgn)

Function

This function paints the specified region with the selected brush.

Parameters

hDC (HDC) specifies the device context.
    hRgn (HRGN) or pRgn (CRgn*) specifies the region to be filled.

Value Returned

Zero value for an unsuccessful paint; nonzero value for a successful paint. MFC: TRUE or FALSE.

API: BOOL Pie(hDC,X1,Y1,X2,Y2,X3,Y3,X4,Y4)
MFC: BOOL Pie(X1,Y1,X2,Y2,X3,Y3,X4,Y4)
BOOL Pie(lpRect,ptStart,ptEnd)

Function

This function draws a pie-shaped wedge using the selected pen and then fills the pie shape with the selected brush. Drawing takes place in a counterclockwise direction.

Parameters

hDC (HDC) specifies the device context.

X1 (int) identifies the logical x coordinate of the upper-left corner of the bounding rectangle.

Y1 (int) identifies the logical y coordinate of the upper-left corner of the bounding rectangle.

X2 (int) identifies the logical x coordinate of the lower-right corner of the bounding rectangle.

Y2 (int) identifies the logical y coordinate of the lower-right corner of the bounding rectangle.

X3 (int) identifies the logical x coordinate of the starting point for the arc.

Y3 (int) identifies the logical y coordinate of the starting point for the arc.

X4 (int) identifies the logical x coordinate of the ending point for the arc.

Y4 (int) identifies the logical y coordinate of the ending point for the arc.

lpRect (LPRECT) structure specifies the bounding rectangle. ptStart and ptEnd use a POINT structure to specify the starting and ending points of the figure.

Value Returned

TRUE if successful; otherwise, FALSE.

Notes

The width and height of the rectangle specified must not exceed 32,767. Pie does not use the current position, nor does it update the current position after the pie wedge is drawn.

API: BOOL Polygon(hDC,lpPoints,nCount)
MFC: BOOL Polygon(lpPoints,nCount)

Function

This function draws a polygon consisting of two or more points connected by lines.

Parameters

hDC (HDC) specifies the device context.

lpPoints (LPPOINT) points to an array of POINT structures containing the vertices for the polygon.

nCount (int) indicates the number of elements in the array.

Value Returned

TRUE indicates a successful draw; otherwise, the result is FALSE.

Notes

Polygon does not use the current position, nor does it update the current position after the polygon is drawn. The polygon is drawn using the current polygon-filling mode. In ALTERNATE mode, the current pen is used to draw lines from the first point through subsequent points, with the interior filled using the current brush. While in WINDING mode, the current pen is used to draw a border that is computed using all of the points. The interior is also filled using the current brush.

API: BOOL Polyline(hDC,lpPoints,nCount)
MFC: BOOL Polyline(lpPoints,nCount)

Function

This function draws a set of connected line segments.

Parameters

hDC (HDC) specifies the device context.

lpPoints (LPPOINT) points to an array of POINT structures containing the points to be connected.

nCount (int) indicates the number of elements in the array.

Value Returned

TRUE indicates a successful draw; otherwise, the result is FALSE.

Notes

Polyline does not use the current position, nor does it update the current position after the polyline is drawn.

API: BOOL PtInRect(lpRect,Point)
MFC: BOOL PtInRect(point)

Function

This function identifies whether or not the referenced point is inside the selected rectangle.

Parameters

lpRect (LPRECT) points to a RECT structure identifying the rectangle.
    Point (POINT) points to a POINT structure indicating the point to be checked.

Value Returned

TRUE indicates that the point does lie within the selected rectangle. A FALSE return value indicates that the point is not within the designated rectangle.

API: BOOL PtInRegion(hRgn,X,Y)
MFC: BOOL PtInRegion(X,Y)
BOOL PtInRegion(point)

Function

Using X and Y as point coordinates, this function indicates whether or not the point lies within the specified region.

Parameters

hRgn (HRGN) specifies the region that is to be examined.
    X (int) indicates the logical x coordinate of the point to be checked.
    Y (int) indicates the logical y coordinate of the point to be checked.
    point uses a POINT structure.

Value Returned

TRUE indicates that the point does lie within the selected region. A FALSE return value indicates that the point is not within the designated region.

API: int RealizePalette(hDC)
MFC: UINT RealizePalette()

Function

This function maps to the system palette entries in the logical palette currently selected for a device context.

Parameters

hDC (HDC) specifies the device context.

Value Returned

The returned value identifies how many entries were changed in the system palette.

Notes

When RealizePalette is called, Windows guarantees that it will display all the colors it requests, up to the maximum number simultaneously available on the display, and it displays additional colors by matching them to available colors.

API: BOOL Rectangle(hDC,X1,Y1,X2,Y2)
MFC: BOOL Rectangle(X1,Y1,X2,Y2)
BOOL Rectangle(lpRect)

Function

Using the selected pen, this function draws a rectangle and then fills the interior with the selected pen.

Parameters

X1 (int) indicates the upper-left corner *x* coordinate.
   Y1 (int) indicates the upper-left corner *y* coordinate.
   X2 (int) indicates the lower-right corner *x* coordinate.
   Y2 (int) indicates the lower-right corner *y* coordinate.
   lpRect uses a LPRECT structure.

Value Returned

TRUE if successful; otherwise, FALSE.

Notes

The width and height of the rectangle, defined by the absolute value of X2–X1 and Y2–Y1, must not exceed 32,767.

API: int ReleaseDC(hWnd,hDC)
MFC: int ReleaseDC(pDC)

Function

This function releases the device context, allowing it to be used by other applications.

Parameters

hWnd (HWND) is a handle to the window whose device context is about to be freed.
    hDC (HDC) specifies the device context.
    pDC (CDC*) points to the device context.

Value Returned

A nonzero value for a successful release; otherwise, a NULL is returned.

Notes

For every call that is made to GetWindowDC or GetDC retrieving a common device context, a call to ReleaseDC must be made.

API: BOOL RemoveMenu(hMenu,nPosition,wFlags)
MFC: BOOL RemoveMenu(nPosition,nFlags)

Function

This function deletes an item with an associated pop-up menu from the menu specified.

Parameters

hMenu (HMENU) specifies the menu to be changed.
    nPosition (WORD) or (UINT) defines the position of the menu item to be removed. The first menu item is at position zero.
    wFlags (WORD) or nFlags (UINT) is set to zero.

Value Returned

TRUE for a successful deletion; otherwise, FALSE.

Notes

Whenever a menu changes, the application should call DrawMenuBar.

API: BOOL RestoreDC(hDC,nSavedDC)
MFC: BOOL RestoreDC(nSavedDC)

Function

This function restores the device context specified.

Parameters

hDC (HDC) specifies the device context.

nSavedDC (int) identifies the device context that is to be restored. When the parameter is assigned a –1, the function will restore the most recently saved device context.

Value Returned

TRUE for a successful restore. FALSE otherwise.

Notes

The device context is restored by copying the information saved on the context stack by previous calls to the SaveDC function. Since the context stack can contain the state information for more than one device context, care must be taken when a call is made to RestoreDC. When the device context referenced by nSavedDC is not the top of the stack, the function permanently deletes the state information stored for all device contexts between the top and the nSavedDC context reference.

API: COLORREF RGB(cRed,cGreen,cBlue)

Function

This function selects an RGB color based on the supplied preferences combined with the color capabilities of the selected output device.

Parameters

cRed (BYTE) identifies the intensity for the red color.
cGreen (BYTE) identifies the intensity for the green color.
cBlue (BYTE) identifies the intensity for the blue color.

Value Returned

Indicates the RGB color that has been selected.

Notes

Each color field's intensity can be a value from zero to 255, inclusive. Three zero parameters select the color black, while all three parameters being assigned 255 select white.

API: BOOL RoundRect(hDC,X1,Y1,X2,Y2,X3,Y3)
MFC: BOOL RoundRect(X1,Y1,X2,Y2,X3,Y3)
BOOL RoundRect(lpRect,point)

Function

Using the current pen, this function draws a rectangle with rounded corners. The interior of the rectangle is then painted using the selected brush.

Parameters

hDC (HDC) specifies the device context.

X1 (int) identifies the logical x coordinate of the upper-left corner of the rectangle.

Y1 (int) identifies the logical y coordinate of the upper-left corner of the rectangle.

X2 (int) identifies the logical x coordinate of the lower-right corner of the rectangle.

Y2 (int) identifies the logical y coordinate of the lower-right corner of the rectangle.

X3 (int) identifies the width of the ellipse that will be used to draw the rounded corners.

Y3 (int) identifies the height of the ellipse that will be used to draw the rounded corners.

lpRect (LPRECT) contains rectangle coordinates.

point (POINT) contains ellipse parameters.

Value Returned

TRUE indicates that the rectangle was successfully drawn. FALSE indicates an unsuccessful draw.

Notes

The width and height of the rectangle, defined by the absolute value of X2–X1 and Y2–Y1, must not exceed 32,767. RoundRect does not use the current position, nor does it update the current position after the rectangle is drawn.

API: int SaveDC(hDC)
MFC: int SaveDC( )

Function

This function saves the state of the current device context.

Parameters

hDC (HDC) specifies the device context.

Value Returned

The returned value identifies the saved device context. A zero value indicates that an error has occurred.

Notes

The saved device context state is pushed onto the device context stack and can be restored by invoking the RestoreDC function.

API: HANDLE SelectObject(hDC,hObject)
MFC: CGdiObject* SelectObject(pObject)

Function

This function selects a logical object for the specified device context.

Parameters

hDC (HDC) specifies the device context.

   hObject (HANDLE) or pObject (CGdiObject*) specifies the logical object to be selected and may be any one of the following functions:

Object	Function Name
Bitmap	CreateBitmap
	CreateBitmapIndirect
	CreateCompatibleBitmap
Brush	CreateBrushIndirect
	CreateHatchBrush
	CreatePatternBrush
	CreateSolidBrush
Font	CreateFont
	CreateFontIndirect
Pen	CreatePen
	CreatePenIndirect
Region	CombineRgn
	CreateEllipticRgn
	CreateEllipticRgnIndirect
	CreatePolyRgn
	CreateRectRgn
	CreateRectRgnIndirect

Value Returned

Identifies the object being replaced by hObject of the same type. Otherwise, if an error has occurred, a NULL is returned.

Notes

Selected objects become defaults used by many GDI functions that write text, draw lines, fill interiors, and clip output to selected devices. Device contexts can have up to five objects selected with only one being used at a time. Each call to SelectObject causes the GDI to allocate space for that object in the data segment. DeleteObject should always be called whenever a selected object (font, pen, or brush) is no longer needed to conserve memory. Also, bitmaps can be selected into only one device context at a time.

API: HPALETTE SelectPalette(hDC,hPalette)
MFC: CPalette* SelectPalette(pPalette,bForceBackground)

Function

This function selects the logical palette specified by the hPalette (HANDLE) or pPalette (CPalette*) parameter as the selected logical palette of the device context. The new palette replaces the previous palette.

Parameters

hDC (HDC) specifies the device context.
  hPalette or pPalette (HPALETTE) specifies the logical palette to be selected.
  bForceBackground (BOOL) forces to background palette when TRUE.

Value Returned

Returns the identifier of the logical palette being replaced by hPalette. Otherwise, a NULL is returned.

Notes

An application can select a logical palette for more than one device context.

API: Long SendDlgItemMessage(hDlg,nIDDlgItem,wMsg, wParam,lParam)
MFC: LONG SendDlgItemMessage(nID,message,wParam,lParam)

Function

This function sends a message to a dialog box's control.

Parameters

hDlg (HWND) specifies the dialog box that contains the control.
  nIDDlgItem or nID (int) identifies the dialog item that is to receive the message.
  wMsg or message (UINT) identifies the message value.
  wParam (WORD or UINT) identifies any additional message information.
  lParam (LONG) can be used for additional message information.

Value Returned

If the controller identified is invalid, the function returns a NULL; otherwise, the return value represents the outcome of the function. A successful return value is generated by the control's window function.

Notes

Using SendDlgItemMessage is the same as obtaining a handle to the specified control and then calling SendMessage.

API: LONG SendMessage(hWnd,wMsg,wParam,lParam)
MFC: LONG SendMessage(message,wParam,lParam)

Function

This function sends a message to a single window or multiple windows.

Parameters

hWnd (HWND) specifies the window that will be sent the message. If the parameter is FFFF (hexadecimal), the specified message will be sent to all pop-up windows currently in the system. The message is not sent to any child windows.

wMsg or message (UINT) identifies the message value.

wParam (WORD or UINT) identifies any additional message information.

lParam (LONG) can be used for additional message information.

Value Returned

The value returned depends on the message sent.

Notes

If the receiving window is part of the same application, the window function is called immediately. When the receiving window is part of some other task, Windows will switch to the task and then call the appropriate window function, sending the message. Note that the message is not placed in the destination task's application queue.

API: DWORD SetBkColor(hDC,rgbColor)
MFC: DWORD SetBkColor(crColor)

Function

This function sets the current background color to the color specified. The function will choose the nearest logical color of the device if no direct match exists.

Parameters

hDC (HDC) specifies the device context.

rgbColor or crColor (DWORD) selects an RGB color for the new background color.

Value Returned

Contains the previous RGB background color. A return value of 80000000 (hexadecimal) indicates an error has occurred.

Notes

When the background mode is OPAQUE, the background color is used to fill the gaps between styled lines, hatched lines in brushes, and character cells. The Graphics Device Interface (GDI) also uses the background color for converting bitmaps from color to monochrome or from monochrome to color.

API: int SetBkMode(hDC,nBkMode)
MFC: int SetBkMode(nBkMode)

Function

This function sets the background mode.

Parameters

hDC (HDC) specifies the device context.
nBkMode (int) selects the background mode:

Mode	Description
OPAQUE	When the background mode is OPAQUE, the background color is used to fill the gaps between styled lines, hatched lines in brushes, and character cells
TRANSPARENT	Leaves the background unchanged

Value Returned

Returns the previous background mode, either OPAQUE or TRANSPARENT.

Notes

The function tells the GDI whether or not to remove existing background colors on the device surface before drawing text, hatched brushes, or any nonsolid pen style.

API: DWORD SetBrushOrg(hDC,X,Y)
MFC: CPoint SetBrushOrg(X,Y)
CPoint SetBrushOrg(point)

Function

This function sets the origin for all selected brushes into the specified device context.

Parameters

hDC (HDC) specifies the device context.
X (int) identifies the logical *x* coordinate of the new origin.
Y (int) identifies the logical *y* coordinate of the new origin.
point uses a POINT structure.

Value Returned

Indicates the previous origin of the brush. The high-order word contains the *y* coordinate, with the low-order word containing the *x* coordinate. Returns a CPoint object.

Notes

The original brush origin is always set to the (0,0) coordinate.

API: HCURSOR SetCursor(hCursor)

Function

This function sets the system cursor shape.

Parameters

hCursor (HCURSOR) specifies a previously loaded (LoadCursor) cursor resource.

Value Returned

Identifies the cursor resource defining the previous cursor shape. A zero value indicates that there was no previous shape.

Notes

The cursor shape should be set only when the cursor is in the client area or when it is capturing all mouse input.

API: void SetCursorPos(X,Y)

Function

This function sets the system cursor to the position specified.

Parameters

X (int) identifies the new screen *x* coordinate of the cursor.
   Y (int) identifies the new screen *y* coordinate of the cursor.

Value Returned

None.

Notes

The cursor should be moved only when it is in the window's client area.

API: void SetDlgItemInt(hDlg,nIDDlgItem,wValue,bSigned)
MFC: void SetDlgItemInt(nID,nValue,bSigned)

Function

This function sets the text of a control in the specified dialog box to the string represented by the integer value given by wValue or nValue.

Parameters

hDlg (HWND) specifies the dialog box containing the control.
   nIDDlgItem or nID (int) defines the control to be modified.
   wValue or nValue (UINT) is the value to be set.
   bSigned (BOOL) indicates whether or not the integer value is signed (TRUE or FALSE).

Value Returned

None.

Notes

The function converts the wValue parameter to a string consisting of decimal digits. It then copies the string to the control. The function also sends a WM_SETTEXT message to the specified control.

API: void SetDlgItemText(hDlg,nIDDlgItem,lpString)
MFC: void SetDlgItemText(nID,lpString)

Function

This function sets the text of a control in the dialog box.

Parameters

hDlg (HWND) specifies the dialog box containing the control.

nIDDlgItem or nID (int) defines the control to be modified.

lpString (LPSTR) points to a null-terminated string that will be copied to the control.

Value Returned

None.

Notes

The function sends a WM_SETTEXT message to the specified control.

API: int SetMapMode(hDC,nMapMode)
MFC: int SetMapMode(nMapMode)

Function

This function sets the mapping mode of the selected device context.

Parameters

hDC (HDC) specifies the device context.

nMapMode (int) selects the new mapping mode from one of the following:

Mode	Description
MM_ANISOTROPIC	Maps logical units to arbitrary units with arbitrarily scaled axes
MM_HIENGLISH	Maps each logical unit to 0.001 inch
MM_HIMETRIC	Maps each logical unit to 0.01 millimeter
MM_ISOTROPIC	Maps logical units to arbitrary units with equally scaled axes
MM_LOMETRIC	Maps each logical unit to 0.1 millimeter
MM_LOENGLISH	Maps each logical unit to 0.01 inch
MM_TEXT	Maps each logical unit to one device pixel
MM_TWIPS	Maps each logical unit to 1/20 of a printer's point or approximately 1/1440 inch

Value Returned

Represents the previous mapping mode.

Notes

MM_HIENGLISH, MM_HIMETRIC, MM_LOENGLISH, MM_LOMETRIC, and MM_TWIPS are used most frequently for applications drawing in physically meaningful units such as millimeters or inches. MM_TEXT mode permits the use of device-specific pixels whose size may vary from one device to another. MM_ISOTROPIC enables a 1:1 aspect ratio, which is most useful in maintaining the exact shape of an image. MM_ANISOTROPIC mode allows for independent adjustment of the x and y coordinates.

API: WORD SetPaletteEntries(hPalette,wStartIndex, wNumEntries,lpColors)
MFC: UINT SetPaletteEntries(nStartIndex,nNumEntries, lpPaletteColors)

Function

This function sets RGB color values and flags in a range of entries in a logical palette.

Parameters

hPalette (HPALETTE) specifies the logical palette.

wStartIndex (WORD) or nStartIndex (UINT) identifies the first entry in the logical palette to be set.

wNumEntries (WORD) or nNumEntries (UINT) identifies the number of entries in the logical palette to be set.

lpColors or lpPaletteColors points to the first number of an array of PALETTE-ENTRY.

Value Returned

Indicates the number of entries set in the logical palette. A zero is returned if the function has failed.

Notes

When the logical palette is selected into a device context whenever the application calls SetPaletteEntries, the changes will not take effect until a call is made to RealizePalette.

API: DWORD SetPixel(hDC,X,Y,rgbColor)
MFC: DWORD SetPixel(X,Y,crColor)
DWORD SetPixel(point,crColor)

Function

This function sets the color of the pixel indicated by X and Y.

Parameters

hDC (HDC) specifies the device context.

X (int) specifies the logical *x* coordinate of the point to be set.

Y (int) specifies the logical *y* coordinate of the point to be set.

rgbColor or crColor (DWORD) indicates the RGB color to be used to paint the pixel.

point uses a POINT structure.

Value Returned

Indicates the actual RGB color the pixel was painted. A −1 return value indicates an error condition. The color could be different than the color specified if no direct match exists.

Notes

The point specified must be in the clipping region.

API: int SetPolyFillMode(hDC,nPolyFillMode)
MFC: int SetPolyFillMode(nPolyFillMode)

Function

This function sets the polygon fill mode.

Parameters

hDC (HDC) specifies the device context.
    nPolyFillMode (int) selects the new filling mode. It can be either ALTERNATE or WINDING.

Value Returned

Indicates the previous filling mode. A NULL value indicates an error has occurred.

Notes

ALTERNATE and WINDING modes differ only for those polygons with overlapping complex forms. ALTERNATE mode fills every other enclosed region within the polygon, while WINDING mode fills all regions.

API: void SetRect(X1,Y1,X2,Y2)
MFC: void SetRect(X1,Y1,X2,Y2)

Function

This function creates a new rectangle by assigning the coordinates specified.

Parameters

X1 (int) indicates the upper-left corner *x* coordinate.
    Y1 (int) indicates the upper-left corner *y* coordinate.
    X2 (int) indicates the lower-right corner *x* coordinate.
    Y2 (int) indicates the lower-right corner *y* coordinate.

Value Returned

None.

Notes

The width and height of the rectangle, defined by the absolute value of X2–X1 and Y2–Y1, must not exceed 32,767.

API: void SetRectRgn(hRgn,X1,Y1,X2,Y2)
MFC: void SetRectRgn(X1,Y1,X2,Y2)
void SetRectRgn(lpRect)

Function

This function creates a rectangular region.

Parameters

hRgn (HANDLE) specifies the region.
    X1 (int) indicates the upper-left corner *x* coordinate of the rectangular region.
    Y1 (int) indicates the upper-left corner *y* coordinate of the rectangular region.
    X2 (int) indicates the lower-right corner *x* coordinate of the rectangular region.
    Y2 (int) indicates the lower-right corner *y* coordinate of the rectangular region.
    lpRect uses a LPRECT structure.

Value Returned

None.

Notes

Unlike CreateRectRgn, the SetRectRgn function does not use the local memory manager. Instead the function uses the space allocated for the region. X1, Y1, X2, and Y2 indicate the minimum size of the allocated space.

API: int SetROP2(hDC,nDrawMode)
MFC: int SetROP2(nDrawMode)

Function

This function sets the current drawing mode.

Parameters

hDC (HDC) specifies the device context.
nDrawMode (int) is selected from one of the following drawing modes:

Drawing Mode	Pixel Color
R2_BLACK	Always black
R2_NOTMERGEPEN	The inverse of the R2_MERGEPEN color
R2_MASKNOTPEN	A combination of the colors of the display and the inverse of the pen
R2_NOTCOPYPEN	The inverse of the pen color
R2_MASKPENNOT	A combination of the colors of the pen and the inverse of the display
R2_NOT	The inverse of the display color
R2_XORPEN	A combination of the colors in the pen exclusively ORed in the display, but not in both
R2_NOTMASKPEN	The inverse of the R2_MASKPEN color
R2_MASKPEN	A combination of the colors in both the pen and the display
R2_NOTXORPEN	The inverse of the R2_XORPEN color
R2_NOP	Remains unchanged
R2_MERGENOTPEN	A combination of the display color and the inverse of the pen color
R2_COPYPEN	The pen color
R2_MERGEPENNOT	A combination of the pen color and the inverse of the display color
R2_MERGEPEN	A combination of the pen color and the display color
R2_ WHITE	Always white

Value Returned

Specifies the previous drawing mode.

Notes

The drawing mode is for raster devices only and is not available on vector devices. The drawing modes represent the binary raster operations, providing all of the possible binary Boolean functions AND, OR, and XOR as applied to two variables, along with the unary NOT operation.

API: int SetScrollPos(hWnd,nBar,nPos,bRedraw)
MFC: int SetScrollPos(nBar,nPos,bRedraw)
int SetScrollPos(nPos,bRedraw)

Function

This function sets the current position of a scroll bar thumb.

Parameters

hWnd (HWND) specifies the window whose scroll bar will be set.
    nBar (int) identifies which scroll bar thumb is to be set:

Value	Description
SB_CTL	Sets the position of a scroll bar control, assuming that hWnd points to a window handle of a scroll bar control
SB_HORZ	Sets the position of a window's horizontal scroll bar
SB_VERT	Sets the position of a window's vertical scroll bar

nPos (int) identifies the new position within the valid scrolling range.
    bRedraw (BOOL) indicates whether or not the scroll bar should be redrawn. A nonzero value indicates the scroll bar should be redrawn. If zero, it is not redrawn.

Value Returned

Indicates the previous position of the scroll bar thumb.

API: void SetScrollRange(hWnd,nBar,nMinPos,nMaxPos, bRedraw)
MFC: void SetScrollRange(nBar,nMinPos,nMaxPos,bRedraw)
void SetScrollRange(nMinPos,NMaxPos,bRedraw)

Function

This function sets the minimum and maximum position values for the selected scroll bar.

Parameters

hWnd (HWND) specifies the window whose scroll bar will be set.
  nBar (int) identifies which scroll bar thumb is to be set:

Value	Description
SB_CTL	Sets the position of a scroll bar control, assuming that hWnd points to a window handle of a scroll bar control
SB_HORZ	Sets the position of a window's horizontal scroll bar
SB_VERT	Sets the position of a window's vertical scroll bar

  nMinPos (int) sets the minimum scrolling position.
  nMaxPos (int) sets the maximum scrolling position.
  bRedraw (BOOL) indicates whether or not the scroll bar should be redrawn. A nonzero value indicates the scroll bar should be redrawn. If zero, it is not redrawn.

Value Returned

None.

Notes

If SetScrollRange is called right after SetScrollPos, bRedraw should be set to zero to prevent the scroll bar from being drawn twice.

API: void SetSysColors(nChanges,lpSysColor,lpColorValues)

Function

This function sets the system colors.

Parameters

nChanges (int) defines the number of system colors to be set.
  lpSysColor (LPINT) points to an array of integers that specify the elements to be changed:

Value	Description
COLOR_ACTIVEBORDER	Active window border index
COLOR_ACTIVECAPTION	Active window caption index

Value	Description
COLOR_APPWORKSPACE	MDI (multiple document interface) application background color index
COLOR_BACKGROUND	Desktop index
COLOR_BTNFACE	Shading on button faces
COLOR_BTNSHADOW	Edge shading on push buttons
COLOR_BTNTEXT	Text on push buttons
COLOR_CAPTIONTEXT	Text in caption, scroll bar arrow box, or size box index
COLOR_INACTIVEBORDER	Inactive window border index
COLOR_INACTIVECAPTION	Inactive window caption index
COLOR_MENU	Menu background index
COLOR_MENUTEXT	Text in menus index
COLOR_SCROLLBAR	Scroll bar gray area index
COLOR_WINDOW	Window background and thumb box index
COLOR_WINDOWFRAME	Window border and caption text background index
COLOR_WINDOWTEXT	Text in window index

lpColorValues points to an array of unsigned long RGB color values.

Value Returned

None.

Notes

The function sends a WM_SYSCOLORCHANGE message to all windows informing them of the color change(s). Windows is instructed to repaint the affected portions of all visible windows.

API: WORD SetTextAlign(hDC,wFlags)
MFC: UINT SetTextAlign(nFlags)

Function

This function sets the text alignment flag for the specified device context.

Parameters

hDC (HDC) specifies the device context.

wFlags (WORD) or nFlags (UINT) selects a mask from the following list, affecting the horizontal and vertical alignment:

Mask	Description
TA_BASELINE	Selects alignment along the x axis and the baseline of the selected font within the bounding rectangle
TA_BOTTOM	Selects alignment along the x axis and the bottom of the bounding rectangle
TA_CENTER	Selects alignment along the y axis and the center of the bounding rectangle
TA_LEFT	Selects alignment along the y axis and the left side of the bounding rectangle
TA_NOUPDATECP	Notes that the current position is not updated
TA_RIGHT	Selects alignment along the y axis and the right side of the bounding rectangle
TA_TOP	Selects alignment along the x axis and the top of the bounding rectangle
TA_UPDATECP	Notes that the current position is updated

Value Returned

Indicates the alignment, with the high-order word containing the vertical alignment and the low-order word containing the horizontal alignment.

Notes

Only one of the two flags that alter the current position can be chosen for the wFlags parameter.

API: DWORD SetTextColor(hDC,rgbColor)
MFC: DWORD SetTextColor(crColor)

Function

This function sets the text color.

Parameters

hDC (HDC) specifies the device context.

    rgbColor or crColor (DWORD) selects an RGB color value to be used for text output.

Value Returned

Indicates the previous RGB color value used for text color.

Notes

SetBkColor is used to set the background color.

API: int SetTextJustification(hDC,nBreakExtra,nBreakCount)
MFC: int SetTextJustification(nBreakExtra,nBreakCount)

Function

This function justifies text using the nBreakExtra and nBreakCount parameters.

Parameters

hDC (HDC) specifies the device context.

    nBreakExtra (int) selects the total amount of extra space to be added to the line of text.

    nBreakCount (int) selects the number of break characters in the line.

Value Returned

Indicates the outcome of the function. A value of 1 indicates a successful call; otherwise, a zero value is returned.

Notes

The break character used to delimit words is the ASCII 32 or blank space character. By calling GetTextMetrics, the current font's break character can be obtained.

API: DWORD SetViewportExt(hDC,X,Y)
MFC: CSize SetViewportExt(X,Y)
CSize SetViewportExt(size)

Function

This function sets the x- and y-extents of the viewport of the selected device context.

Parameters

hDC (HDC) specifies the device context.
    X (int), using device units, identifies the x-extent of the viewport.
    Y (int), using device units, identifies the y-extent of the viewport.
    size uses a SIZE structure.

Value Returned

Contains the previous viewport extents, with the high-order word containing the previous y-extent and the low-order word containing the previous x-extent. A NULL return value indicates an error has occurred. CSize contains the previous viewport extents.

Notes

When the following mapping modes are in effect, subsequent calls to SetWindowExt or SetViewportExt are ignored: MM_HIENGLISH, MM_HIMETRIC, MM_LOENGLISH, MM_LOMETRIC, MM_TEXT, or MM_TWIPS.

API: DWORD SetViewportOrg(hDC,X,Y)
MFC: CPoint SetViewportOrg(X,Y)
CPoint SetViewportOrg(point)

Function

This function sets the viewport origin of the specified device context.

Parameters

hDC (HDC) specifies the device context.
    X (int), using device units, indicates the *x* coordinate of the origin of the viewport.
    Y (int), using device units, indicates the *y* coordinate of the origin of the viewport.
    point uses a POINT structure.

Value Returned

Contains the previous viewport origins, with the high-order word containing the previous y-origin and the low-order word containing the previous x-origin. A NULL return value indicates an error has occurred. MFC: CPoint uses a POINT structure or a CPoint object to represent the previous viewpoint origin.

Notes

The viewport origin identifies the point in the device coordinate system that the GDI will use to map the window origin.

API: DWORD SetWindowExt(hDC,X,Y)
MFC: CSize SetWindowExt(X,Y)
CSize SetWindowExt(size)

Function

This function sets the x- and y-extents of the window of the selected device context.

Parameters

hDC (HDC) specifies the device context.
  X (int), using device units, identifies the x-extent of the window.
  Y (int), using device units, identifies the y-extent of the window.
  size uses a SIZE structure.

Value Returned

Contains the previous window extents, with the high-order word containing the previous y-extent and the low-order word containing the previous x-extent. A NULL return value indicates an error has occurred. CSize contains the previous window extents.

Notes

When the following mapping modes are in effect, subsequent calls to SetWindowExt or SetWindowExt are ignored: MM_HIENGLISH, MM_HIMETRIC, MM_LOENGL-ISH, MM_LOMETRIC, MM_TEXT, or MM_TWIPS.

API: DWORD SetWindowOrg(hDC,X,Y)
MFC: CPoint SetWindowOrg(X,Y)
CPoint SetWindowOrg(point)

Function

This function sets the window origin of the specified device context.

Parameters

hDC (HDC) specifies the device context.
X (int), using device units, indicates the x coordinate of the origin of the window.
Y (int), using device units, indicates the y coordinate of the origin of the window.
point uses a POINT structure.

Value Returned

Contains the previous window origins, with the high-order word containing the previous y-origin and the low-order word containing the previous x-origin. A NULL return value indicates an error has occurred. CPoint represents the previous origins.

Notes

The window origin identifies the point in the device coordinate system that the GDI will use to map the window origin.

API: void SetWindowPos(hWnd,hWndInsertAfter,
x,y,cx,cy,wFlags)
MFC: void SetWindowPos(pWndInsertAfter,x,
y,cx,cy,nFlags)

Function

This function changes the size, position, and ordering of child, pop-up, and top-level windows.

Parameters

hWnd (HWND) specifies the window to be positioned.
hWndInsertAfter (HWND) or pWndInsertAfter (CWnd*) specifies the window from the window manager's list that is to precede the positioned window.
x (int) identifies the x coordinate of the window's upper-left corner.

y (int) identifies the *y* coordinate of the window's upper-left corner.

cx (int) specifies the new window's width.

cy (int) specifies the new window's height.

wFlags (WORD) or nFlags (UINT) can be one of the following values:

Value	Description
SWP_DRAWFRAME	Draws a frame around the window
SWP_HIDEWINDOW	Hides the window
SWP_NOACTIVATE	Doesn't activate the window
SWP_NOMOVE	Ignores the x and y parameter and does not move the window
SWP_NOSIZE	Ignores the current cx and cy values and does not change the window's size
SWP_NOREDRAW	Doesn't redraw
SWP_NOZORDER	Ignores the hWndInsertAfter value, retaining the current ordering
SWP_SHOWWINDOW	Displays the specified window

Value Returned

None.

Notes

When SWP_NOZORDER is not specified, Windows places the window in the position following the window specified by hWndInsertAfter.

API: void ShowScrollBar(hWnd,wBar,fShow)
MFC: void ShowScrollBar(nBar,bShow)

Function

This function hides or displays a scroll bar.

Parameters

hWnd (HWND) specifies the window containing the scroll bar.

wBar (WORD) or nBar (UINT) identifies whether or not the scroll bar is a control or part of a window's nonclient area. It can be one of the following values:

Value	Description
SB_CTL	Sets the position of a scroll bar control, assuming that hWnd points to a window handle of a scroll bar control
SB_HORZ	Sets the position of a window's horizontal scroll bar
SB_VERT	Sets the position of a window's vertical scroll bar

fShow or BShow (BOOL) identifies whether (zero value) or not (nonzero value) Windows hides the scroll bar.

Value Returned

None.

Notes

ShowScrollBar does not destroy a scroll bar's position and range when it hides the scroll bar; a call to SetScrollBar will.

API: BOOL TextOut(hDC,X,Y,lpString,nCount)
MFC: BOOL TextOut(X,Y,lpString,nCount)
BOOL TextOut(X,Y,CString& str)

Function

This function writes a character string to the selected display.

Parameters

hDC (HDC) specifies the device context.
    X (int) identifies the logical x coordinate of the string's starting point.
    Y (int) identifies the logical y coordinate of the string's starting point.
    lpString (LPSTR) points to a null-terminated string that is to be drawn.
    nCount (int) identifies the number of characters in the string to be drawn.
    str is a CString object or null-terminated string.

Value Returned

TRUE indicates the string was successfully drawn; otherwise, FALSE is returned.

Notes

The current position is not used or updated by TextOut. All character origins are defined to be at the upper-left corner of the character position.

API: BOOL TrackPopupMenu(hMenu,wFlags,x,y,cx,hWnd)
MFC: BOOL TrackPopupMenu(nFlags,x,y,pWnd, lpRectReserved)

Function

This function displays a "floating" pop-up menu.

Parameters

hMenu (HMENU) specifies the pop-up menu to be displayed.

if wFlags (WORD) or nFlags (UINT) is not used it must be set to zero.

x (int) defines the horizontal position in screen coordinates of the left side of the menu on the screen.

y (int) defines the vertical position in screen coordinates of the top of the menu on the screen.

cx (int) defines the width in screen coordinates of the pop-up menu. A value of zero causes Windows to calculate the width based on the widest menu item.

hWnd (HWND) or pWnd (CWnd*) identifies the window that owns the pop-up menu.

lpRectReserved points to a RECT structure or CPoint object containing the screen coordinates for an internal rectangle that the user can click without dismissing the pop-up menu. If NULL, the pop-up menu is dismissed. NULL is required for Windows version 3.0.

Value Returned

TRUE for a successful call; otherwise, FALSE.

API: int UpdateColors(hDC)
MFC: void UpdateColors()

Function

This function updates the client area of the device context by matching the current colors in the client area to the system palette on a pixel-by-pixel basis.

Parameters

hDC (HDC) specifies the device context.

Value Returned

Return value is not used. MFC: None.

Notes

This function typically updates a client area faster than redrawing the area. This can result in the loss of some color information.

API: void UpdateWindow(hWnd)
MFC: void UpdateWindow( )

Function

This function updates the client area of the specified window by sending a WM_PAINT message.

Parameters

hWnd (HWND) is a handle to the window to be updated.

Value Returned

None.

Notes

The WM_PAINT message is sent directly to the window function of the selected window, bypassing the application queue.

API: void ValidateRect(hWnd,lpRect)
MFC: void ValidateRect(lpRect)

Function

This function validates the client area within the given rectangle by removing the rectangle from the update region of the selected window.

Parameters

hWnd (HWND) is a handle to the window whose update region is about to be modified.

lpRect (LPRECT) points to a RECT structure containing the client coordinate rectangle to be removed from the update region.

Value Returned

None.

Notes

The function automatically validates the entire client area.

API: void ValidateRgn(hWnd,hRgn)
MFC: void ValidateRgn(pRgn)

Function

This function validates the client area within the given region by removing the region from the update region of the selected window.

Parameters

hWnd (HWND) is a handle to the window whose update region is about to be modified.

hRgn (HRGN) or pRgn (CRgn*) specifies the region that defines the area to be removed from the update region.

Value Returned

None.

Notes

The region coordinates are assumed to be in client coordinates.

API: void WaitMessage()

Function

This function yields control to all other applications when the current application has no other tasks to execute.

Parameters

None.

Value Returned

None.

Index

▷*Expand* Your Skills Even More

with help from our expert authors. Now that you've gained greater skills with **Microsoft C/C++ 7: The Complete Reference***, let us suggest the following related titles that will help you use your computer to full advantage.*

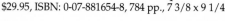

C++: The Complete Reference
by Herbert Schildt
C++ is rapidly winning converts among programmers of all kinds, and Osborne/McGraw-Hill has the book they're looking for: *C++: The Complete Reference* by C expert Herb Schildt. *C++: The Complete Reference* covers C++ in full detail starting with aspects common to the C and C++ languages. This example-filled book thoroughly discusses those features specific to C++ and includes several chapters on effective C++ software development.
$29.95, ISBN: 0-07-881654-8, 784 pp., 7 3/8 x 9 1/4

C++ Inside & Out
by Bruce Eckel
C++ Inside & Out provides a comprehensive, fast-paced guide for all C programmers who want to develop their skills and write full-fledged C++ programs complete with bells and whistles. Eckel covers the latest advancements in C++ and new information on major C++ compilers from Borland and Microsoft.
$27.95, ISBN: 0-07-881809-5, 640 pages, 7 3/8 x 9 1/4

Teach Yourself C++
by Herbert Schildt
Herb Schildt's *Teach Yourself C* has appeared on best-seller lists all over the world! Like its predecessor, *Teach Yourself C++* instructs programmers in the use of the popular C++ programming language through clear descriptions, short chapters, and plenty of exercises and skill checks. This book will prepare you to work with UNIX or DOS programs written in C++, including Borland's Turbo C++.
$24.95, ISBN: 0-07-881760-9, 515 pp., 7 3/8 X 9 1/4

▶ ———— Osborne **McGraw-Hill** ▪ **Available at local book and computer stores**

Borland C++ Handbook, Third Edition
by Chris H. Pappas and William Murray III
Pappas and Murray have now revised and expanded their critically acclaimed book to cover the newest version 3.1 of Borland's powerful compiler. You'll discover how to write and develop applications with the C and C++ compiler, Profiler, Assembler, and Debugger.
$29.95, ISBN: 0-07-881872-9, 937 pages, 7 3/8 x 9 1/4

Turbo C++ for Windows Inside & Out
by Herbert Schildt
Programmer extraordinaire Herb Schildt has written a new guide to Borland's latest hot product, Turbo C++ for Windows. *Turbo C++ for Windows Inside & Out* is written for all C programmers, regardless of skill level, who might be unfamiliar with the Turbo C++ for Windows user interface, with Windows programming, or with C++ and object-oriented programming.
$27.95, ISBN: 0-07-881778-1, 464 pp., 7 3/8 x 9 1/4

Turbo C/C++: The Complete Reference, Second Edition
by Herbert Schildt
The number one reference guide for all Turbo C and Turbo C++ users has now been expanded to include additional coverage of Borland C++. If you're programming or using any of these compilers, you'll definitely want this definitive, single resource that provides you with every Borland C++, Turbo C++ and Turbo C command, feature, and programming technique.
$29.95, ISBN: 0-07-881776-5, 1056 pages, 7 3/8 x 9 1/4

Turbo C++ DiskTutor, Second Edition
(Includes One 5.25-Inch Disk)
by Greg Voss and Paul Chui
Turbo C++ DiskTutor offers an in-depth course in object-oriented programming. This book/disk package will have you writing effective Turbo C++ programs in no time. You get an easy-to-follow comprehensive guide, and a 5.25-inch disk containing programming examples. The book offers an in-depth and effective tutorial on the object-oriented aspects of Turbo C++, Turbo C++ 2nd Edition, and Borland C++.
$39.95, ISBN: 0-07-881737-4, 512 pp., 7 3/8 x 9 1/4

▶ —— Osborne **McGraw-Hill**　■　**Available at local book and computer stores**

Using Turbo C++
by Herbert Schildt
Borland's Turbo C++ with object-oriented programming is thoroughly covered in Herb Schildt's introductory guide for all C programmers. Since Turbo C++ can be used with or without its C++ object-oriented extensions, Schildt has carefully structured the book to cover both environments. Schildt has perfected the way to build programming fundamentals into more sophisticated skills.
$24.95, ISBN: 0-07-881610-6, 755 pp., 7 3/8 x 9 1/4

C: The Complete Reference, Second Edition
by Herbert Schildt
This renowned reference guide, revised to comply with the new ANSI C standard, is the best and most complete reference on ANSI C. C programmers at every level can take advantage of Schildt's expanded sections on the C language and the ANSI libraries. Comprehensive reference sections are conveniently organized by topic for quick fact-finding.
$29.95, ISBN: 0-07-881538-X, 823 pp., 7 3/8 x 9 1/4

The Art of C: Elegant Programming Solutions
(Includes One 5.25-Inch Disk)
by Herbert Schildt
Ace C programmer Herb Schildt has written a book for all programmers who truly appreciate the art of C programming. This sophisticated book provides elegant programming solutions that enable you to write world-class C programs that stand apart from all the rest. A disk of programming examples is included.
$39.95, ISBN: 0-07-881691-2, 459 pp., 7 3/8 x 9 1/4

C DiskTutor
(Includes One 3.5-Inch Disk)
by L. John Ribar
This DiskTutor provides all would-be C programmers with an easy, hassle-free way to learn C programming. A comprehensive yet simple-to-follow book guides you step-by-step along with a disk containing a special version of the Watcom C compiler. With all the examples and screen illustrations, you'll be writing effective ANSI C programs in no time.
$39.95, ISBN: 0-07-881798-6, 464 pages, 7 3/8 x 9 1/4

Teach Yourself C
by Herbert Schildt

Herb Schildt, the widely recognized C expert, is back with another clear, concise volume on the programming language of the 1990s. *Teach Yourself C* uses numerous exercises and skill checks to make sure your programming abilities grow lesson by lesson. By the final chapter, you will possess a solid command of C programming principles.

$24.95, ISBN: 0-07-881596-7, 681 pp., 7 3/8 x 9 1/4

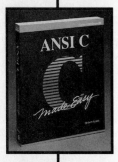

ANSI C Made Easy
by Herbert Schildt

ANSI standards establish new criteria for programming and anyone working in C will want to ensure compliance. This volume is ideal for anyone in the fast-growing C programming field, including students, beginning systems programmers, and career C programmers who need to stay abreast. This "Made Easy" book includes step-by-step exercises that facilitate both quick and lasting comprehension.

$19.95, ISBN: 0-07-881500-2, 450 pp., 7 3/8 x 9 1/4

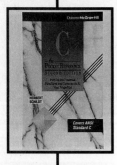
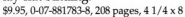

C: The Pocket Reference, Second Edition
by Herbert Schildt

The first edition of this bestseller helped tens of thousands of programmers find valuable C information fast. The second edition has now been revised to cover the ANSI C standard. With this quick reference, you'll find vital C commands, functions, and libraries, arranged alphabetically for easy use along with a state-of-the-art lay-flat binding.

$9.95, 0-07-881783-8, 208 pages, 4 1/4 x 8

Visual Basic for Windows Inside & Out
by Gary Cornell

Here's the best all-round guide for Basic programmers, Windows developers and anyone else who's interested in programming with Visual Basic. Cornell provides comprehensive coverage of structured Basic programming while teaching you how to take full advantage of Visual Basic.

$27.95, 0-07-881764-1, 450 pages, 7 3/8 x 9 1/4

▶——— Osborne **McGraw-Hill** ■ **Available at local book and computer stores**

Windows 3.1 Programming
(Includes One 3.5-Inch)

by William H. Murray and Chris H. Pappas

With this outstanding guide, you'll have the opportunity to learn the powerful programming secrets of Windows 3.1. Murray and Pappas take C programmers into the next generation of Microsoft Windows Release 3.1 with the aid of numerous programming examples that are written in C/C++.

$39.95, ISBN: 0-07-881855-9, 752 pages, 7 3/8 x 9 1/4
Available Winter 1992

Object-Oriented Programming: An Introduction
by Greg Voss

This significant programming advancement and its methodologies are clearly presented as Greg Voss compares and contrasts OOP with traditional structured programming techniques. Object-oriented design is stressed. You'll learn how OOP is used in the real world through examples and exercises that are written in C++ as well as object-oriented Turbo Pascal and QuickPASCAL

$24.95, ISBN: 0-07-881682-3, 584 pp., 7 3/8 x 9 1/4

Turbo Pascal 6: The Complete Reference
by Stephen K. O'Brien

The most complete single resource ever published for all Turbo Pascal programmers is now available in a special edition that covers all the features of Borland's version 6. The revolutionary Turbo Vision application framework is also covered so you can use this tool to write professional-quality applications.

$29.95, ISBN: 0-07-881703-X, 690 pp., 7 3/8 x 9 1/4

Turbo Pascal 6 DiskTutor, Second Edition
(Includes One 5.25-Inch Disk)

by Werner Feibel

A must for beginning and experienced programmers who want to learn Pascal or switch to the leading-edge technology of Turbo Pascal 6.0 with object-oriented programming. This book/disk package features an easy-to-understand text that takes you step-by-step through the practical example programs on disk.

$39.95, ISBN: 0-07-881738-2, 896 pp., 7 3/8 x 9 1/4

► ———— Osborne **McGraw-Hill**   ■   **Available at local book and computer stores**